OUR
WORLDS
AT WAR

**WRITERS**

JEPH LOEB

JOE CASEY

MARK SCHULTZ

JOE KELLY

PETER DAVID

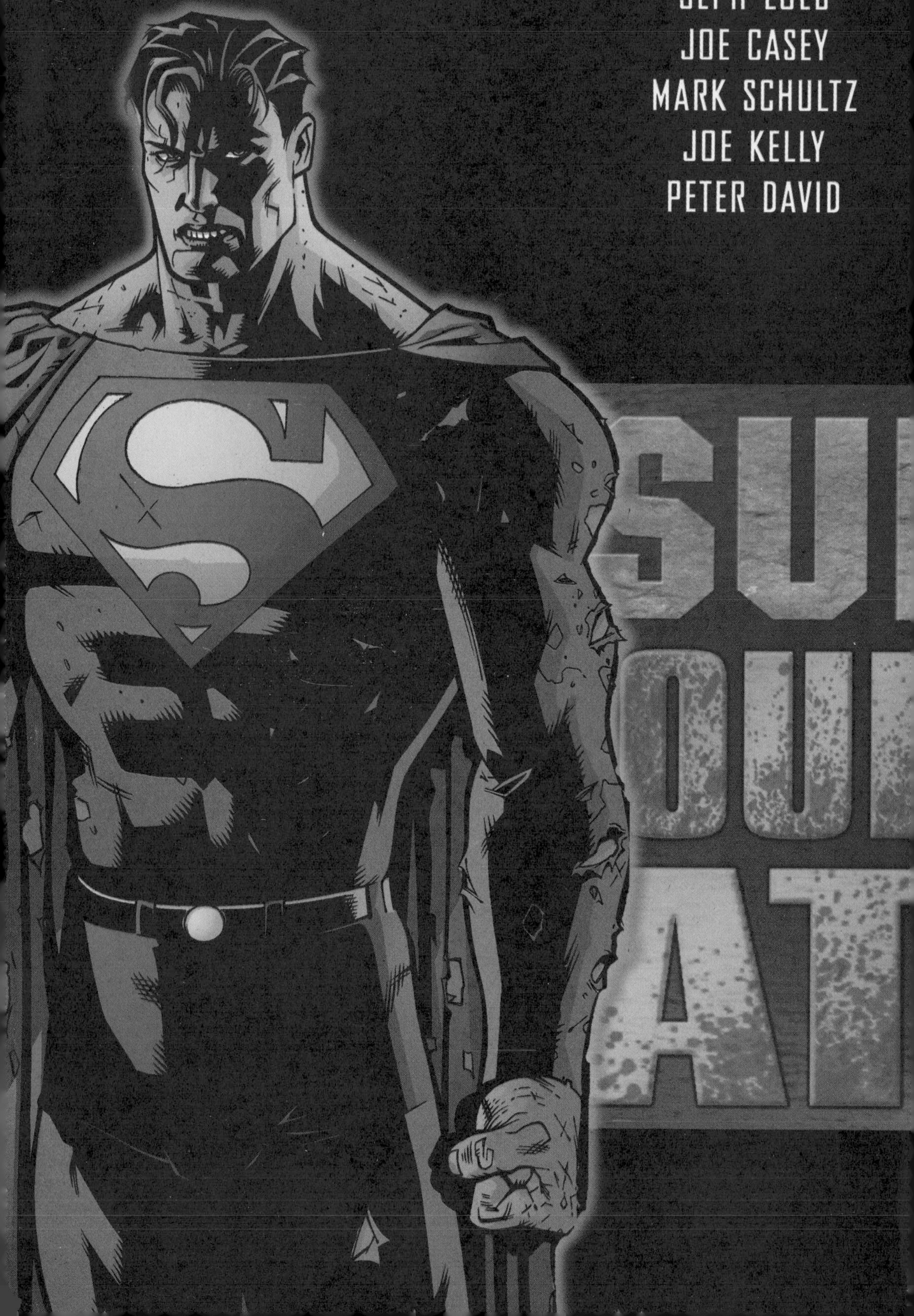

PENCILLERS
MIKE WIERINGO
ED McGUINNESS
DOUG MAHNKE
KANO
RON GARNEY
LEONARD KIRK

INKERS
JOSÉ MARZÁN, JR.
CAM SMITH
MARLO ALQUIZA
MARK MORALES
ROBIN RIGGS
LARY STUCKER
TOM NGUYEN

COLORISTS
WILDSTORM FX
TANYA and RICHARD HORIE
ROB SCHWAGER
GENE D'ANGELO

LETTERERS
RICHARD STARKINGS & COMICRAFT
BILL OAKLEY
KEN LOPEZ

SUPERMAN CREATED BY JERRY SIEGEL and JOE SHUSTER

SUPERMAN:
OUR WORLDS AT WAR

BOOK ONE

SUPERMAN: OUR WORLDS AT WAR BOOK ONE.


DC COMICS, 1700 BROADWAY, NEW YORK, NY 10019 · A DIVISION OF WARNER BROS. – AN AOL TIME WARNER COMPANY
PRINTED IN CANADA. FIRST PRINTING.
ISBN: 1-56389-915-9
COVER ILLUSTRATION BY ED McGUINNESS & CAM SMITH · COVER COLOR BY RICHARD & TANYA HORIE

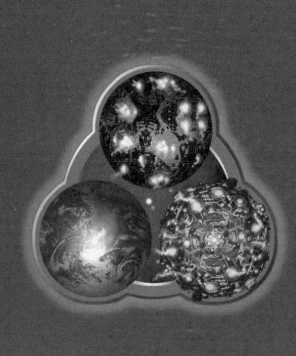

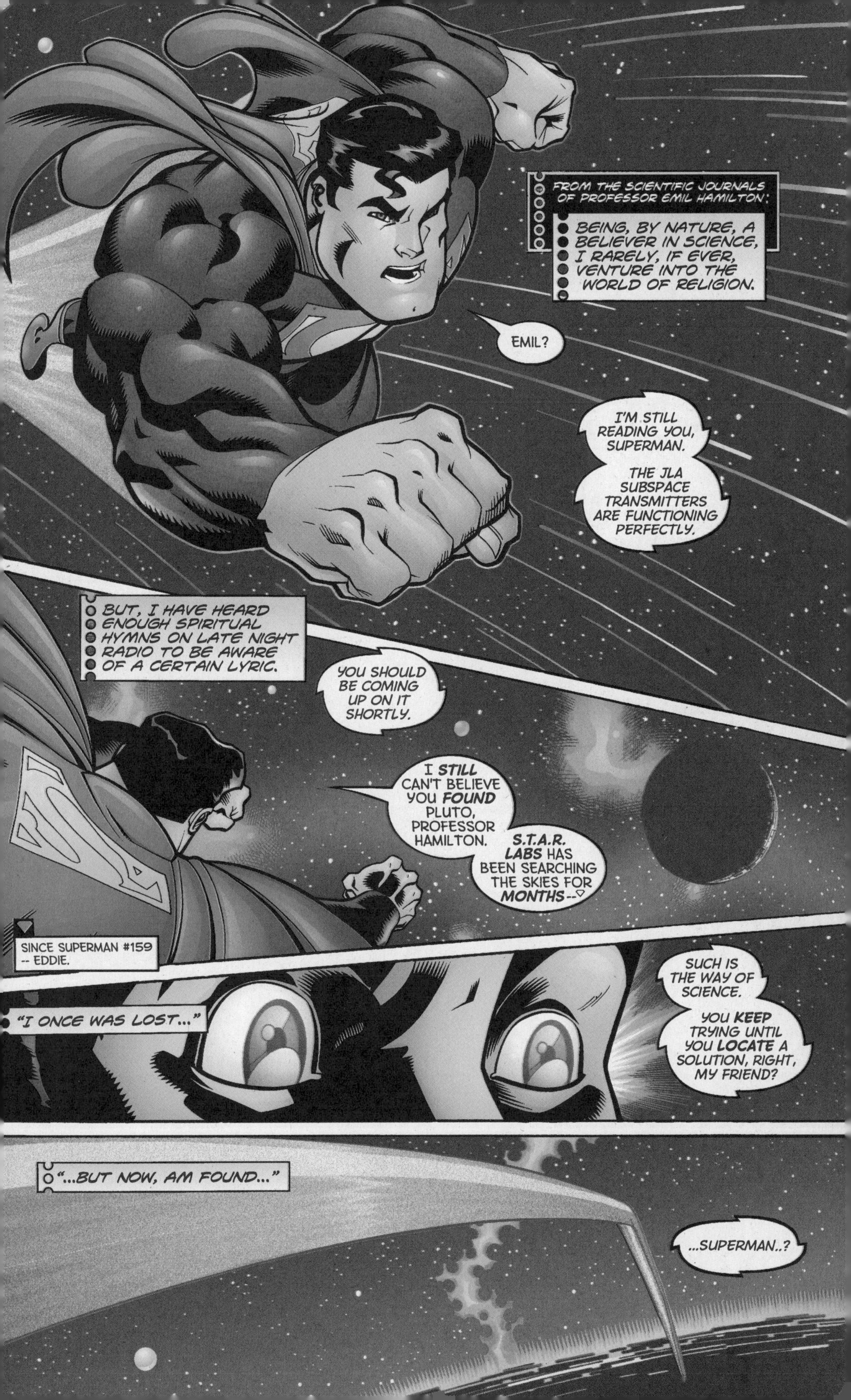

FROM THE SCIENTIFIC JOURNALS OF PROFESSOR EMIL HAMILTON:
BEING, BY NATURE, A BELIEVER IN SCIENCE, I RARELY, IF EVER, VENTURE INTO THE WORLD OF RELIGION.
EMIL?
I'M STILL READING YOU, SUPERMAN.
THE JLA SUBSPACE TRANSMITTERS ARE FUNCTIONING PERFECTLY.
BUT, I HAVE HEARD ENOUGH SPIRITUAL HYMNS ON LATE NIGHT RADIO TO BE AWARE OF A CERTAIN LYRIC.
YOU SHOULD BE COMING UP ON IT SHORTLY.
I STILL CAN'T BELIEVE YOU FOUND PLUTO, PROFESSOR HAMILTON.
S.T.A.R. LABS HAS BEEN SEARCHING THE SKIES FOR MONTHS--
SINCE SUPERMAN #159 -- EDDIE.
"I ONCE WAS LOST..."
SUCH IS THE WAY OF SCIENCE.
YOU KEEP TRYING UNTIL YOU LOCATE A SOLUTION, RIGHT, MY FRIEND?
"...BUT NOW, AM FOUND..."
...SUPERMAN..?

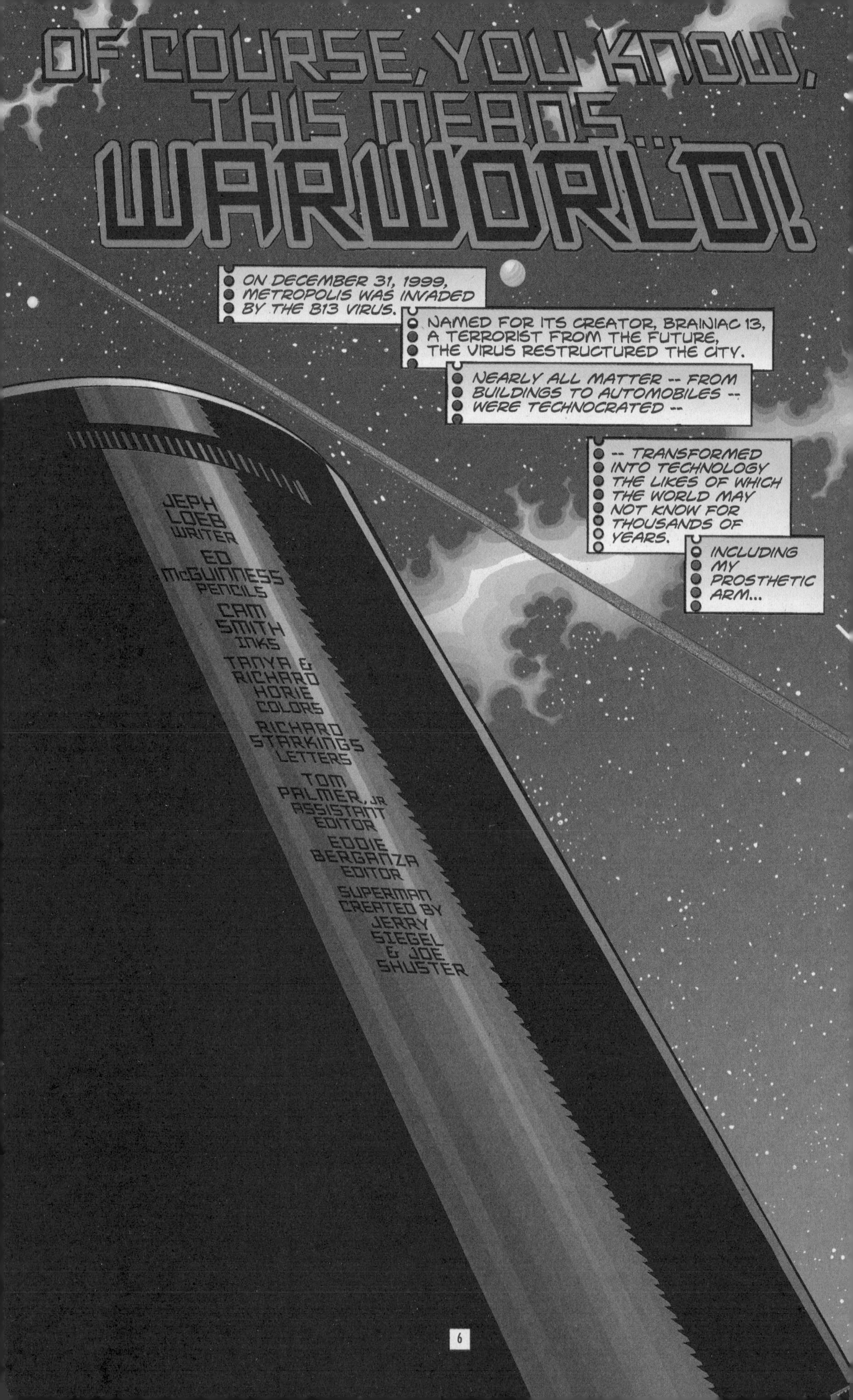
OF COURSE, YOU KNOW, THIS MEANS... WARWORLD!
ON DECEMBER 31, 1999, METROPOLIS WAS INVADED BY THE B13 VIRUS.
NAMED FOR ITS CREATOR, BRAINIAC 13, A TERRORIST FROM THE FUTURE, THE VIRUS RESTRUCTURED THE CITY.
NEARLY ALL MATTER -- FROM BUILDINGS TO AUTOMOBILES -- WERE TECHNOCRATED --
-- TRANSFORMED INTO TECHNOLOGY THE LIKES OF WHICH THE WORLD MAY NOT KNOW FOR THOUSANDS OF YEARS.
INCLUDING MY PROSTHETIC ARM...
JEPH LOEB WRITER
ED McGUINNESS PENCILS
CAM SMITH INKS
TANYA & RICHARD HORIE COLORS
RICHARD STARKINGS LETTERS
TOM PALMER, JR ASSISTANT EDITOR
EDDIE BERGANZA EDITOR
SUPERMAN CREATED BY JERRY SIEGEL & JOE SHUSTER

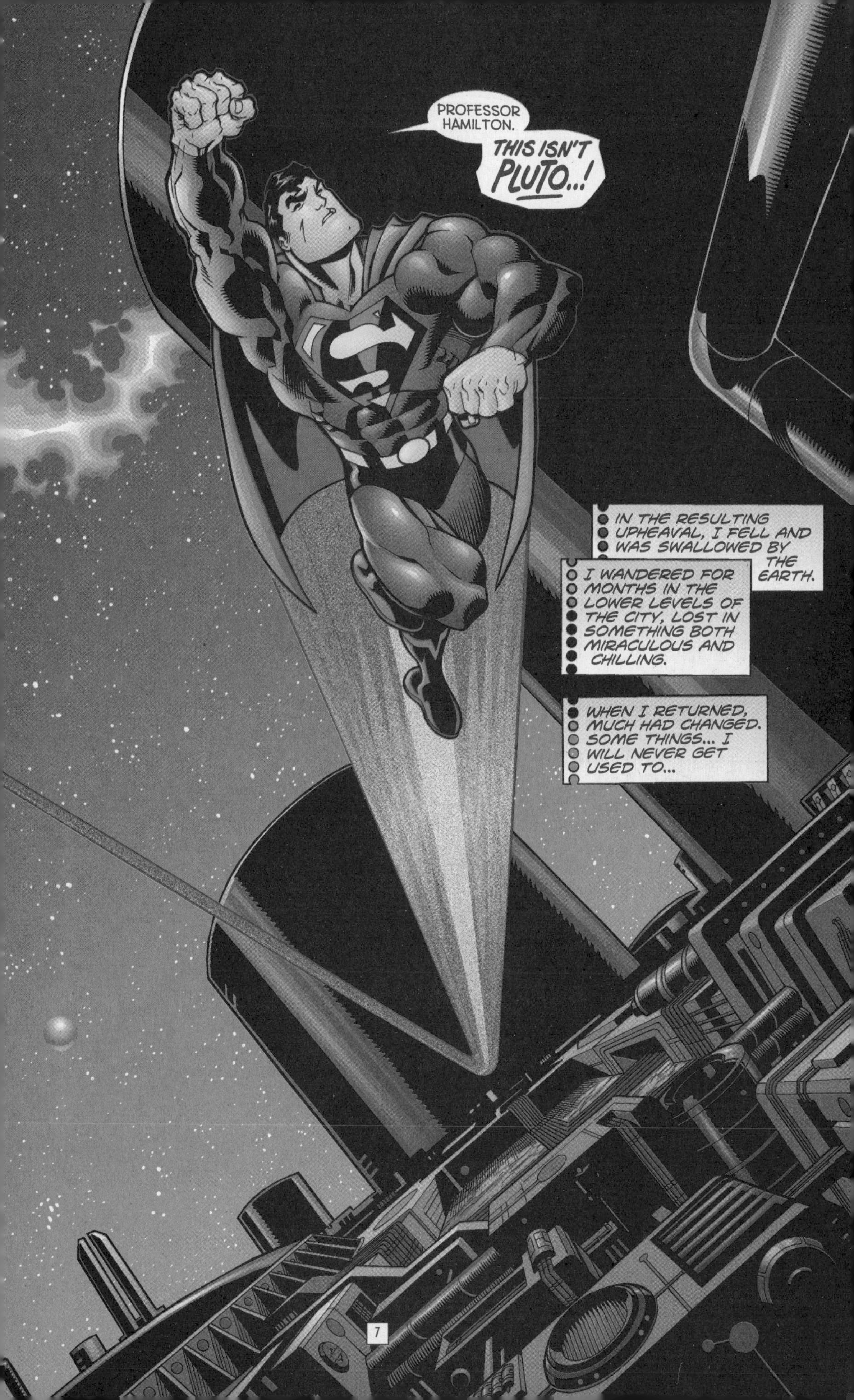
PROFESSOR HAMILTON.
THIS ISN'T PLUTO..!
IN THE RESULTING UPHEAVAL, I FELL AND WAS SWALLOWED BY THE EARTH.
I WANDERED FOR MONTHS IN THE LOWER LEVELS OF THE CITY, LOST IN SOMETHING BOTH MIRACULOUS AND CHILLING.
WHEN I RETURNED, MUCH HAD CHANGED. SOME THINGS... I WILL NEVER GET USED TO...

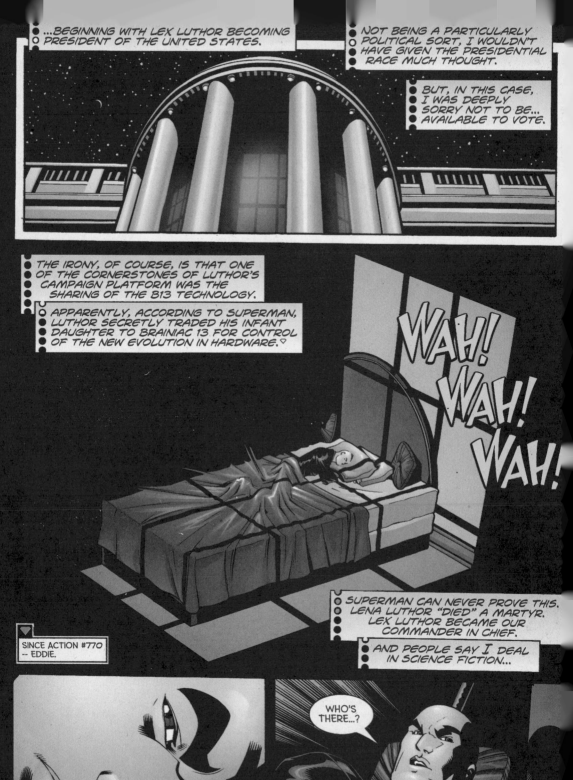

...BEGINNING WITH LEX LUTHOR BECOMING PRESIDENT OF THE UNITED STATES.

NOT BEING A PARTICULARLY POLITICAL SORT, I WOULDN'T HAVE GIVEN THE PRESIDENTIAL RACE MUCH THOUGHT.

BUT, IN THIS CASE, I WAS DEEPLY SORRY NOT TO BE... AVAILABLE TO VOTE.

THE IRONY, OF COURSE, IS THAT ONE OF THE CORNERSTONES OF LUTHOR'S CAMPAIGN PLATFORM WAS THE SHARING OF THE B13 TECHNOLOGY.

APPARENTLY, ACCORDING TO SUPERMAN, LUTHOR SECRETLY TRADED HIS INFANT DAUGHTER TO BRAINIAC 13 FOR CONTROL OF THE NEW EVOLUTION IN HARDWARE.♡

WAH! WAH! WAH!

SUPERMAN CAN NEVER PROVE THIS. LENA LUTHOR "DIED" A MARTYR. LEX LUTHOR BECAME OUR COMMANDER IN CHIEF.

AND PEOPLE SAY I DEAL IN SCIENCE FICTION...

SINCE ACTION #770 -- EDDIE.

WHAT THE -- ?

WHO'S THERE...?

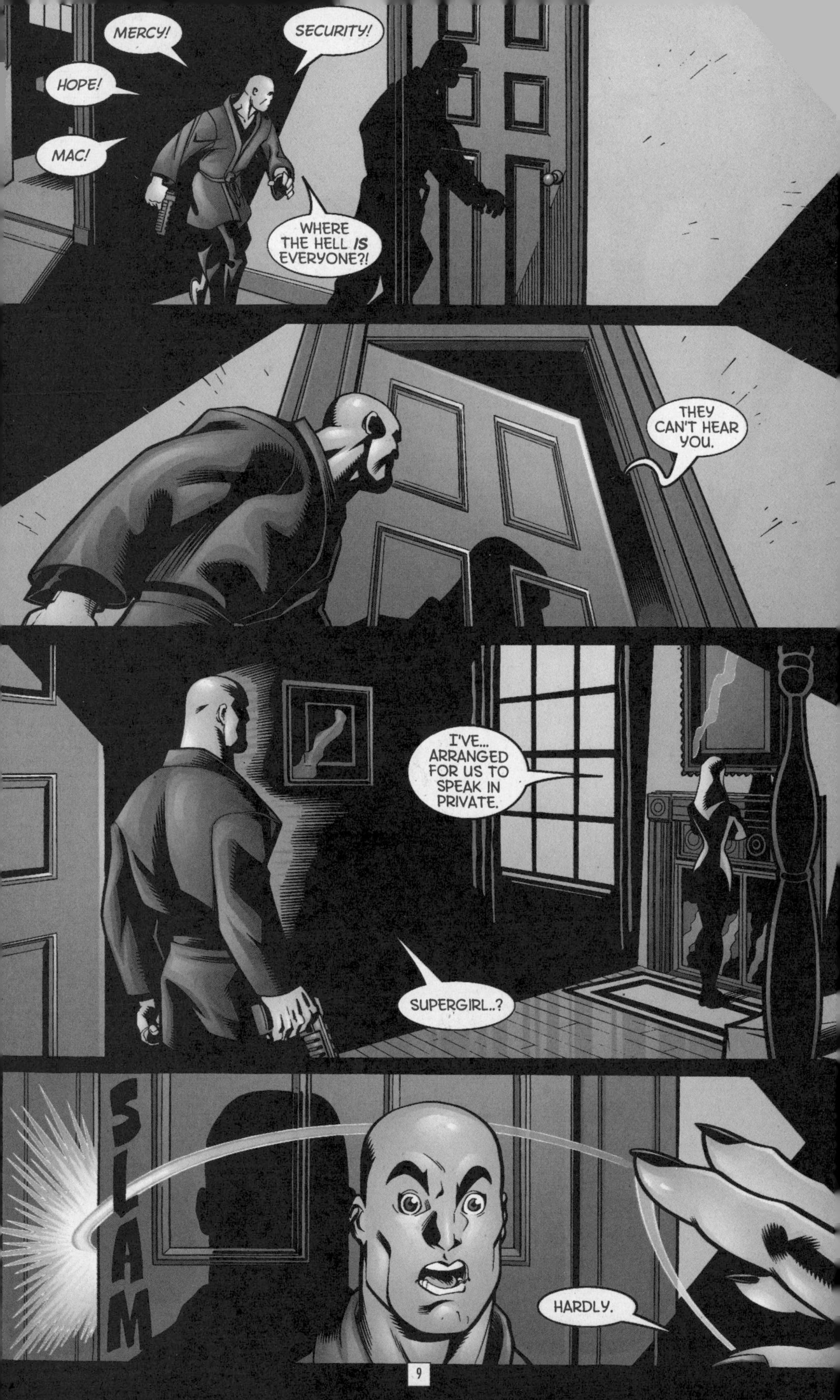
MERCY!
HOPE!
MAC!
SECURITY!
WHERE THE HELL IS EVERYONE?!
THEY CAN'T HEAR YOU.
I'VE... ARRANGED FOR US TO SPEAK IN PRIVATE.
SUPERGIRL..?
SLAM
HARDLY.

HAVE ANY IDEA WHO YOU ARE DEALING WITH?
PRESIDENT OF THE UNITED STATES!
BLAM BLAM BLAM
YES, YOU ARE.
AND WITH MY HELP, YOU MAY BECOME ONE OF THE MOST LEGENDARY AND INFLUENTIAL FIGURES IN HISTORY.
WASHINGTON.
LINCOLN.
ROOSEVELT.
ALL THE GREATEST PRESIDENTS HAD A SINGLE THING IN COMMON.
WHICH IS...?
A WAR.

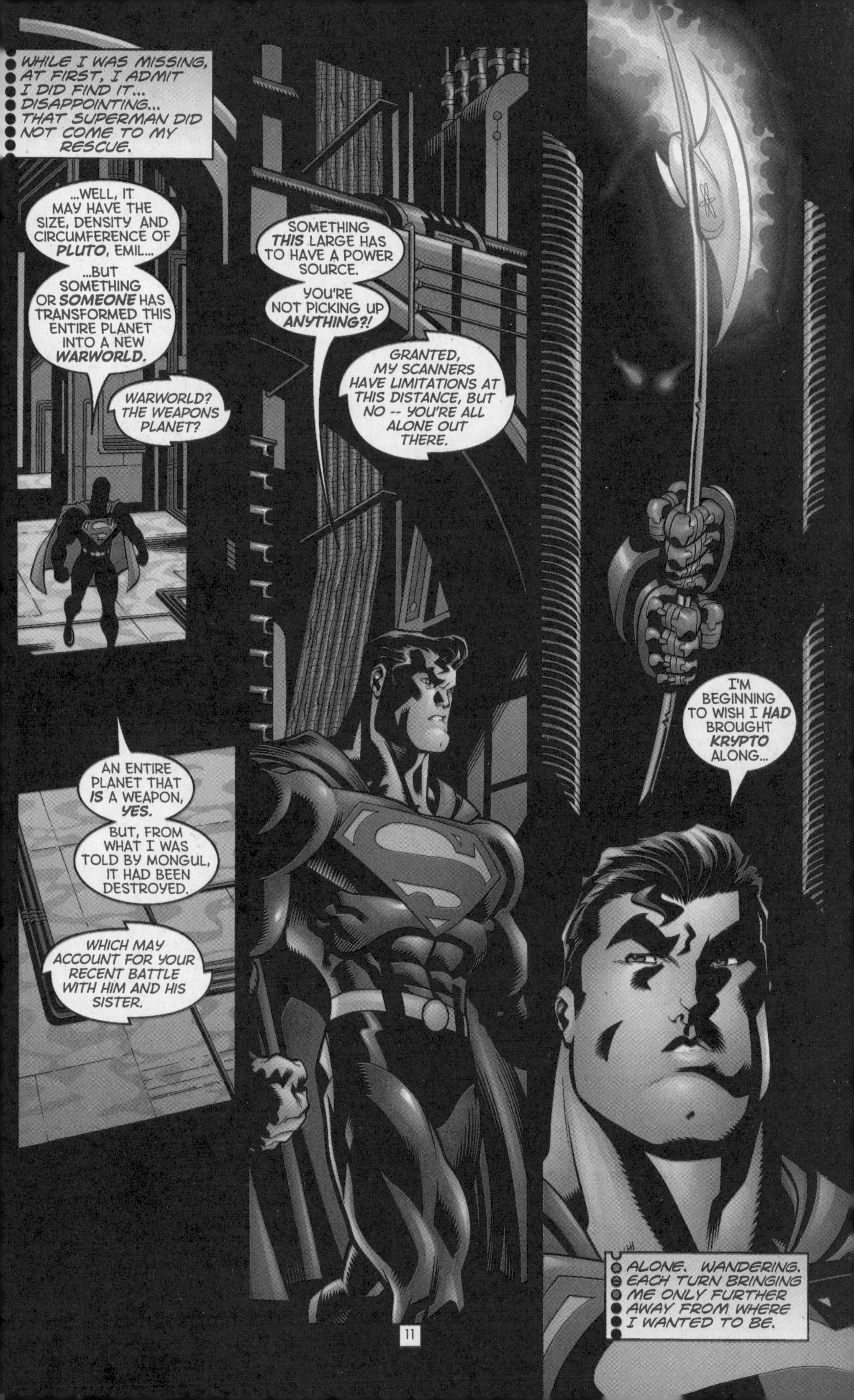
WHILE I WAS MISSING, AT FIRST, I ADMIT I DID FIND IT... DISAPPOINTING... THAT SUPERMAN DID NOT COME TO MY RESCUE.
...WELL, IT MAY HAVE THE SIZE, DENSITY AND CIRCUMFERENCE OF PLUTO, EMIL...
...BUT SOMETHING OR SOMEONE HAS TRANSFORMED THIS ENTIRE PLANET INTO A NEW WARWORLD.
WARWORLD? THE WEAPONS PLANET?
AN ENTIRE PLANET THAT IS A WEAPON, YES.
BUT, FROM WHAT I WAS TOLD BY MONGUL, IT HAD BEEN DESTROYED.
WHICH MAY ACCOUNT FOR YOUR RECENT BATTLE WITH HIM AND HIS SISTER.
SOMETHING THIS LARGE HAS TO HAVE A POWER SOURCE.
YOU'RE NOT PICKING UP ANYTHING?!
GRANTED, MY SCANNERS HAVE LIMITATIONS AT THIS DISTANCE, BUT NO -- YOU'RE ALL ALONE OUT THERE.
I'M BEGINNING TO WISH I HAD BROUGHT KRYPTO ALONG...
ALONE. WANDERING. EACH TURN BRINGING ME ONLY FURTHER AWAY FROM WHERE I WANTED TO BE.

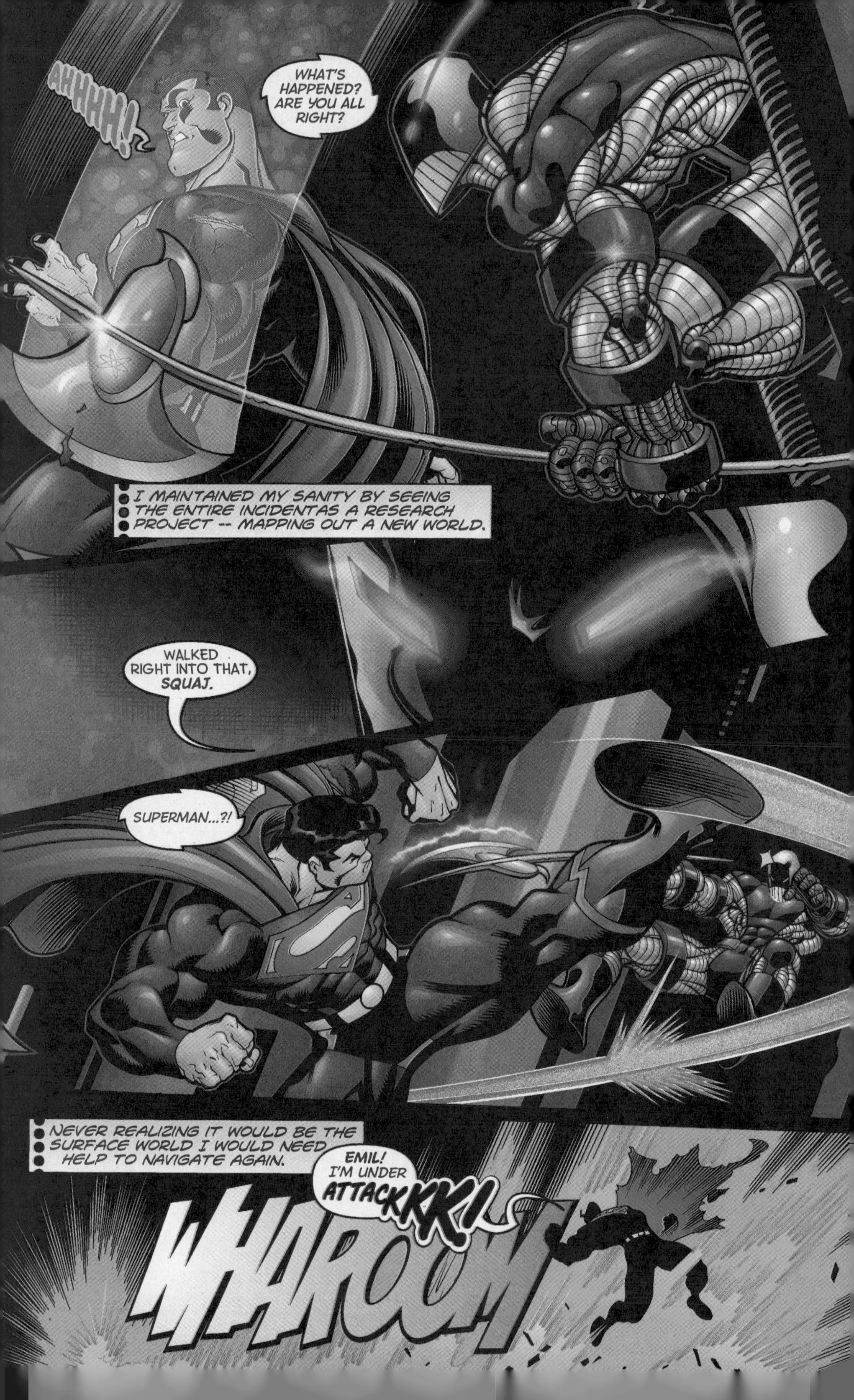
AHHHH!
WHAT'S HAPPENED? ARE YOU ALL RIGHT?
I MAINTAINED MY SANITY BY SEEING THE ENTIRE INCIDENTAS A RESEARCH PROJECT -- MAPPING OUT A NEW WORLD.
WALKED RIGHT INTO THAT, SQUAJ.
SUPERMAN...?!
NEVER REALIZING IT WOULD BE THE SURFACE WORLD I WOULD NEED HELP TO NAVIGATE AGAIN.
EMIL! I'M UNDER ATTACKKK!
WHAROOM

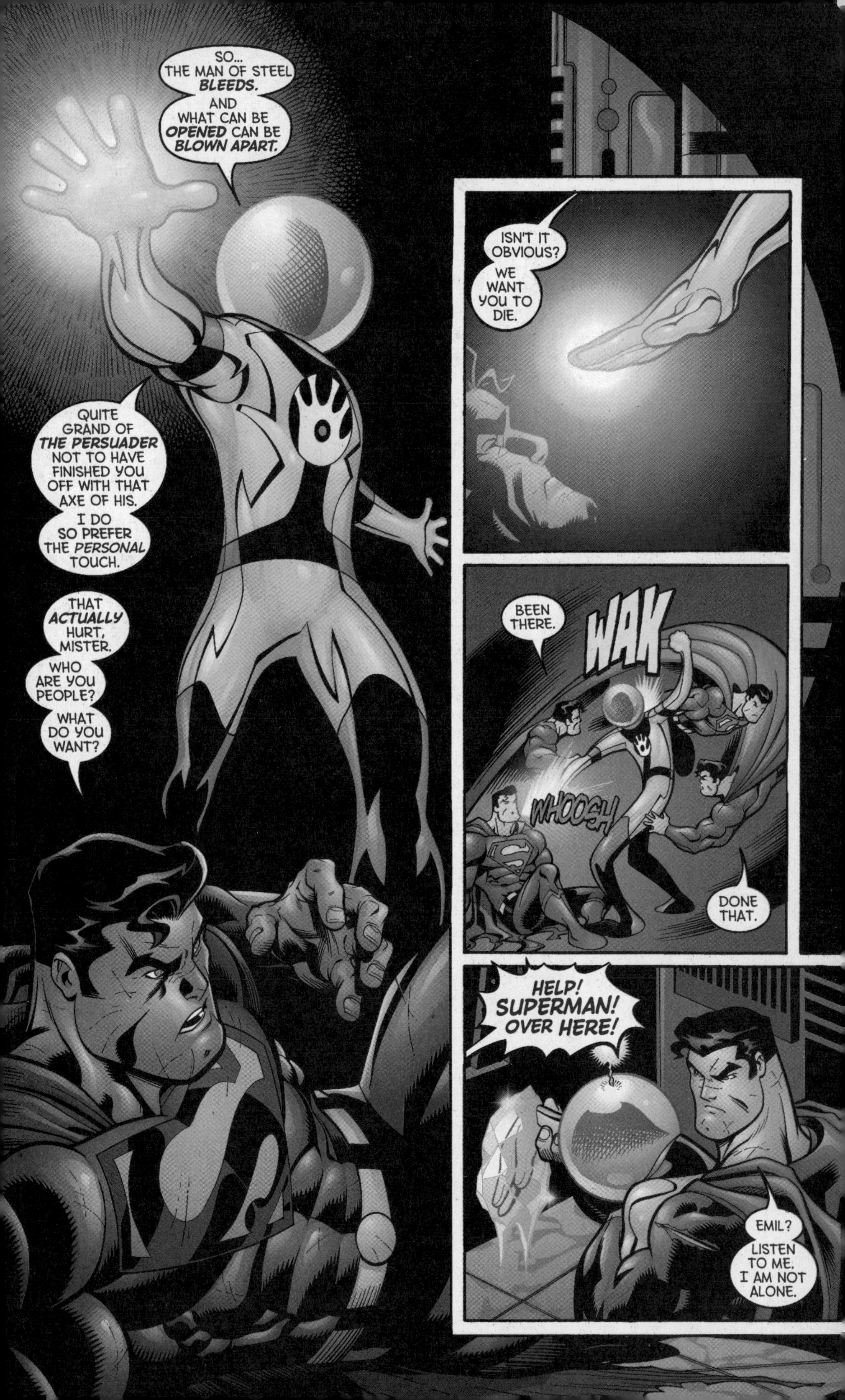
SO... THE MAN OF STEEL BLEEDS.
AND WHAT CAN BE OPENED CAN BE BLOWN APART.
QUITE GRAND OF THE PERSUADER NOT TO HAVE FINISHED YOU OFF WITH THAT AXE OF HIS.
I DO SO PREFER THE PERSONAL TOUCH.
THAT ACTUALLY HURT, MISTER.
WHO ARE YOU PEOPLE?
WHAT DO YOU WANT?
ISN'T IT OBVIOUS?
WE WANT YOU TO DIE.
BEEN THERE.
WAK
WHOOSH
DONE THAT.
HELP! SUPERMAN! OVER HERE!
EMIL?
LISTEN TO ME. I AM NOT ALONE.

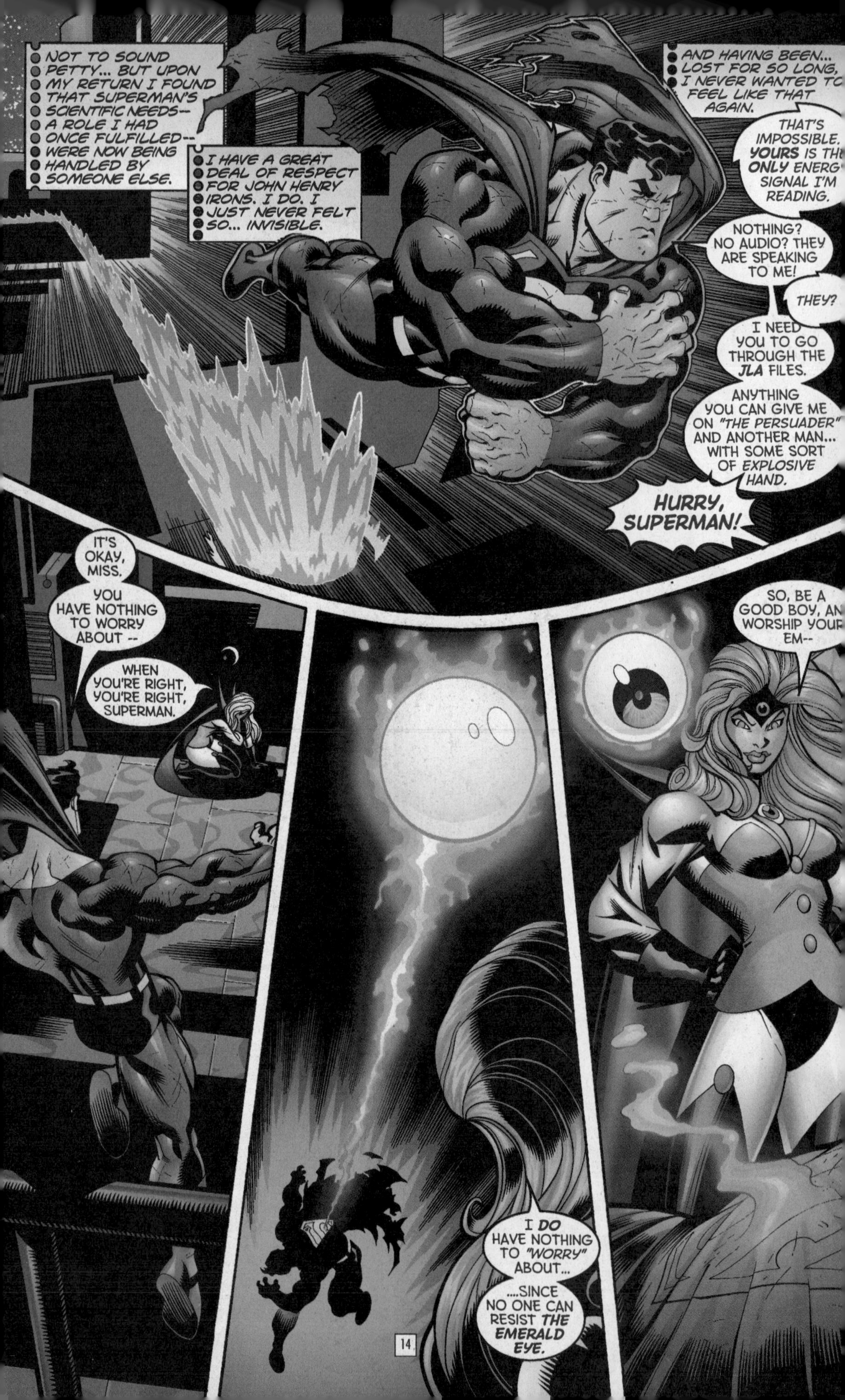
NOT TO SOUND PETTY... BUT UPON MY RETURN I FOUND THAT SUPERMAN'S SCIENTIFIC NEEDS-- A ROLE I HAD ONCE FULFILLED-- WERE NOW BEING HANDLED BY SOMEONE ELSE.
I HAVE A GREAT DEAL OF RESPECT FOR JOHN HENRY IRONS. I DO. I JUST NEVER FELT SO... INVISIBLE.
AND HAVING BEEN... LOST FOR SO LONG, I NEVER WANTED TO FEEL LIKE THAT AGAIN.
THAT'S IMPOSSIBLE. YOURS IS THE ONLY ENERGY SIGNAL I'M READING.
NOTHING? NO AUDIO? THEY ARE SPEAKING TO ME!
THEY?
I NEED YOU TO GO THROUGH THE JLA FILES.
ANYTHING YOU CAN GIVE ME ON "THE PERSUADER" AND ANOTHER MAN... WITH SOME SORT OF EXPLOSIVE HAND.
HURRY, SUPERMAN!
IT'S OKAY, MISS.
YOU HAVE NOTHING TO WORRY ABOUT --
WHEN YOU'RE RIGHT, YOU'RE RIGHT, SUPERMAN.
SO, BE A GOOD BOY, AND WORSHIP YOUR EM--
I DO HAVE NOTHING TO "WORRY" ABOUT...
....SINCE NO ONE CAN RESIST THE EMERALD EYE.

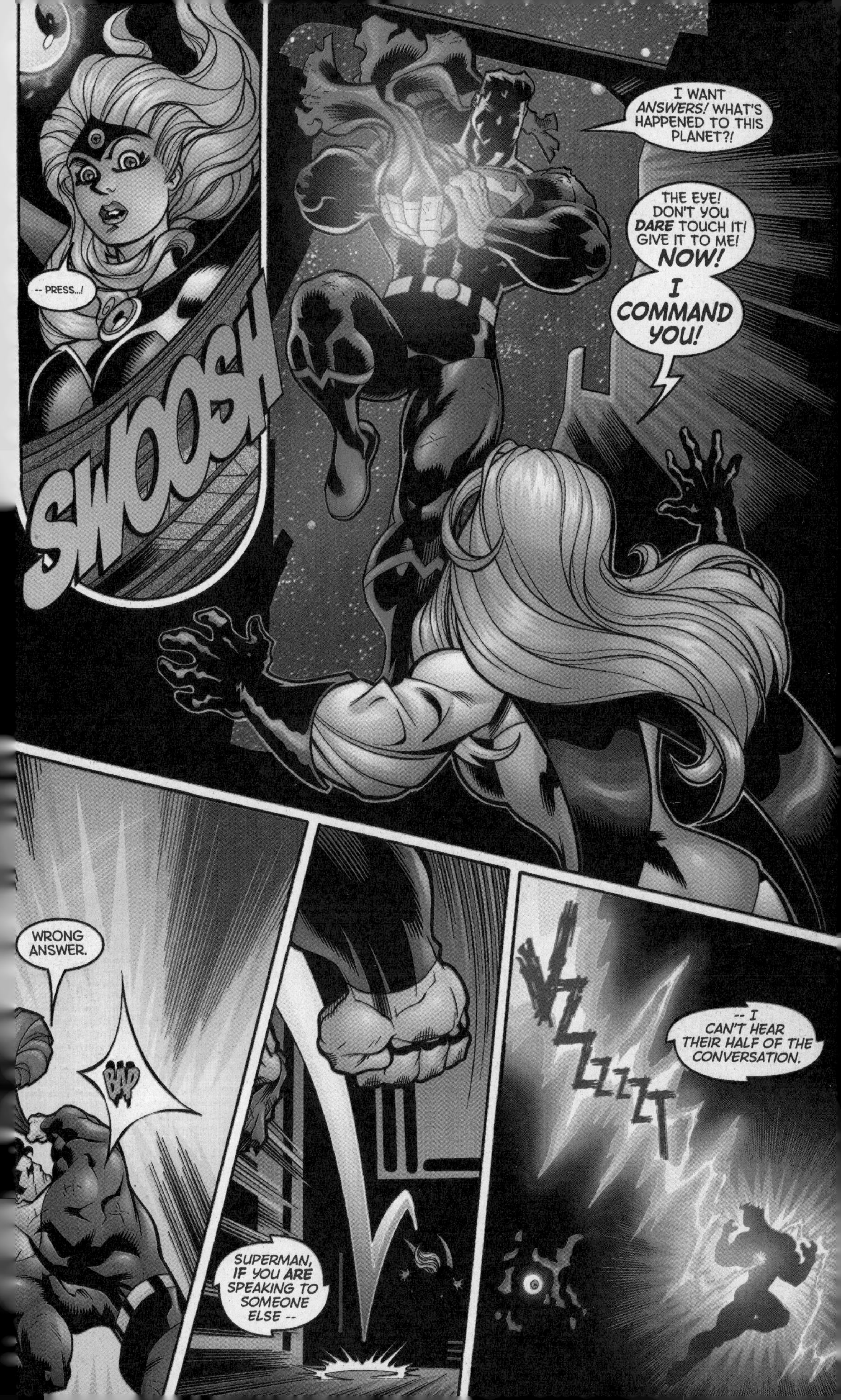
I WANT ANSWERS! WHAT'S HAPPENED TO THIS PLANET?!
THE EYE! DON'T YOU DARE TOUCH IT! GIVE IT TO ME! NOW!
I COMMAND YOU!
-- PRESS...!
SWOOSH
WRONG ANSWER.
BAP
SUPERMAN, IF YOU ARE SPEAKING TO SOMEONE ELSE --
VZZZZZZT
-- I CAN'T HEAR THEIR HALF OF THE CONVERSATION.

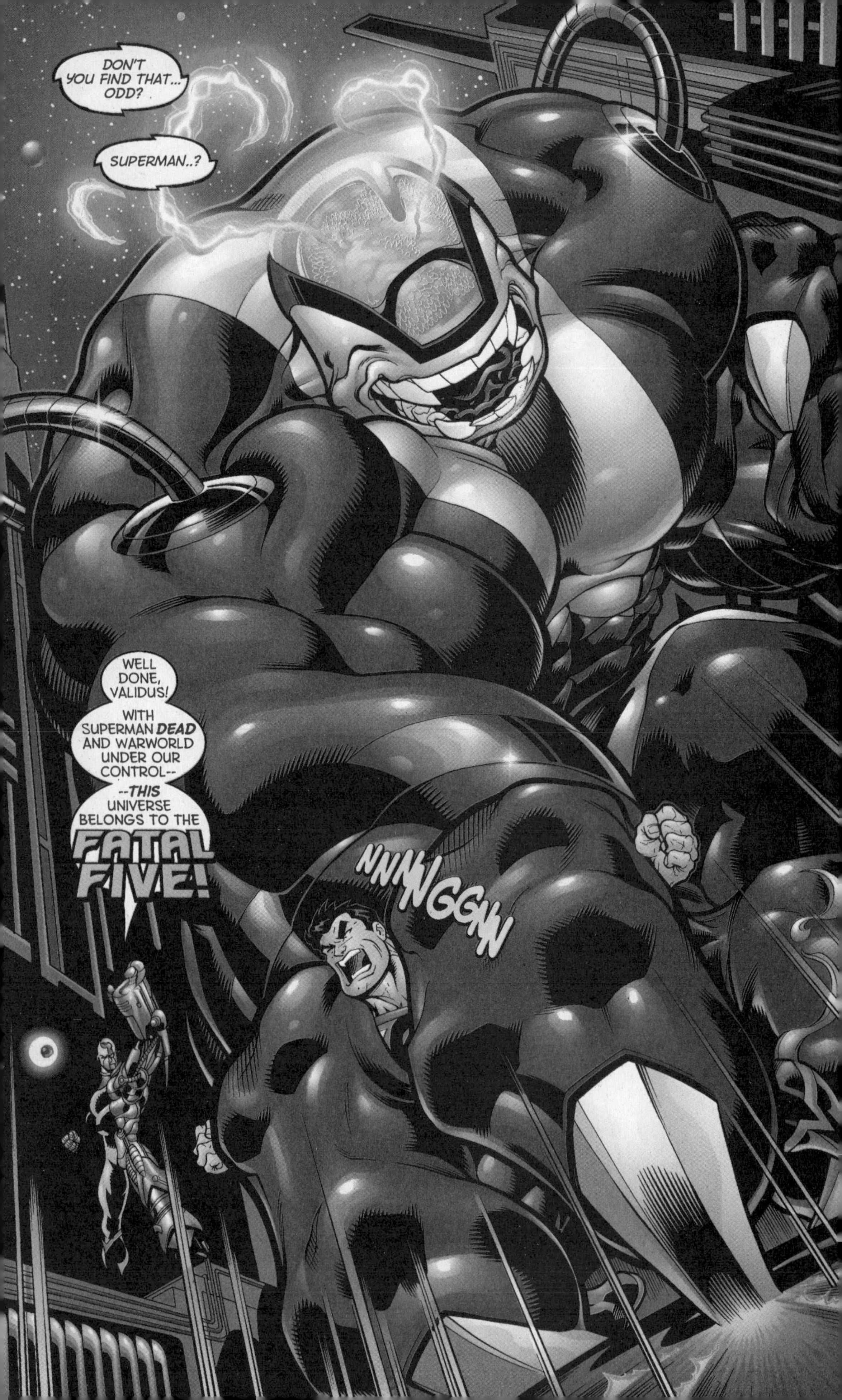
DON'T YOU FIND THAT... ODD?
SUPERMAN..?
WELL DONE, VALIDUS!
WITH SUPERMAN DEAD AND WARWORLD UNDER OUR CONTROL--
--THIS UNIVERSE BELONGS TO THE FATAL FIVE!
NNNNGGNN

IF...
AND IT IS A
VERY LARGE "IF,"
I BELIEVE WHAT
YOU'VE BEEN
SAYING IS
TRUE...

... ALL
THOSE
PEOPLE?

THEY WILL
*HAVE* TO
DIE?

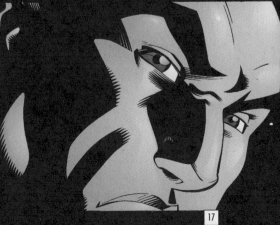

WHAT ARE
A FEW *MILLION*
LIVES WHEN
THE *UNIVERSE* IS
AT STAKE?

YOU -- OF
*ALL* OF THEM --
UNDERSTAND THAT
THE NEEDS OF THE
*MANY* OUTWEIGH THE
NEEDS OF A
FEW.

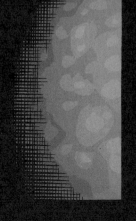

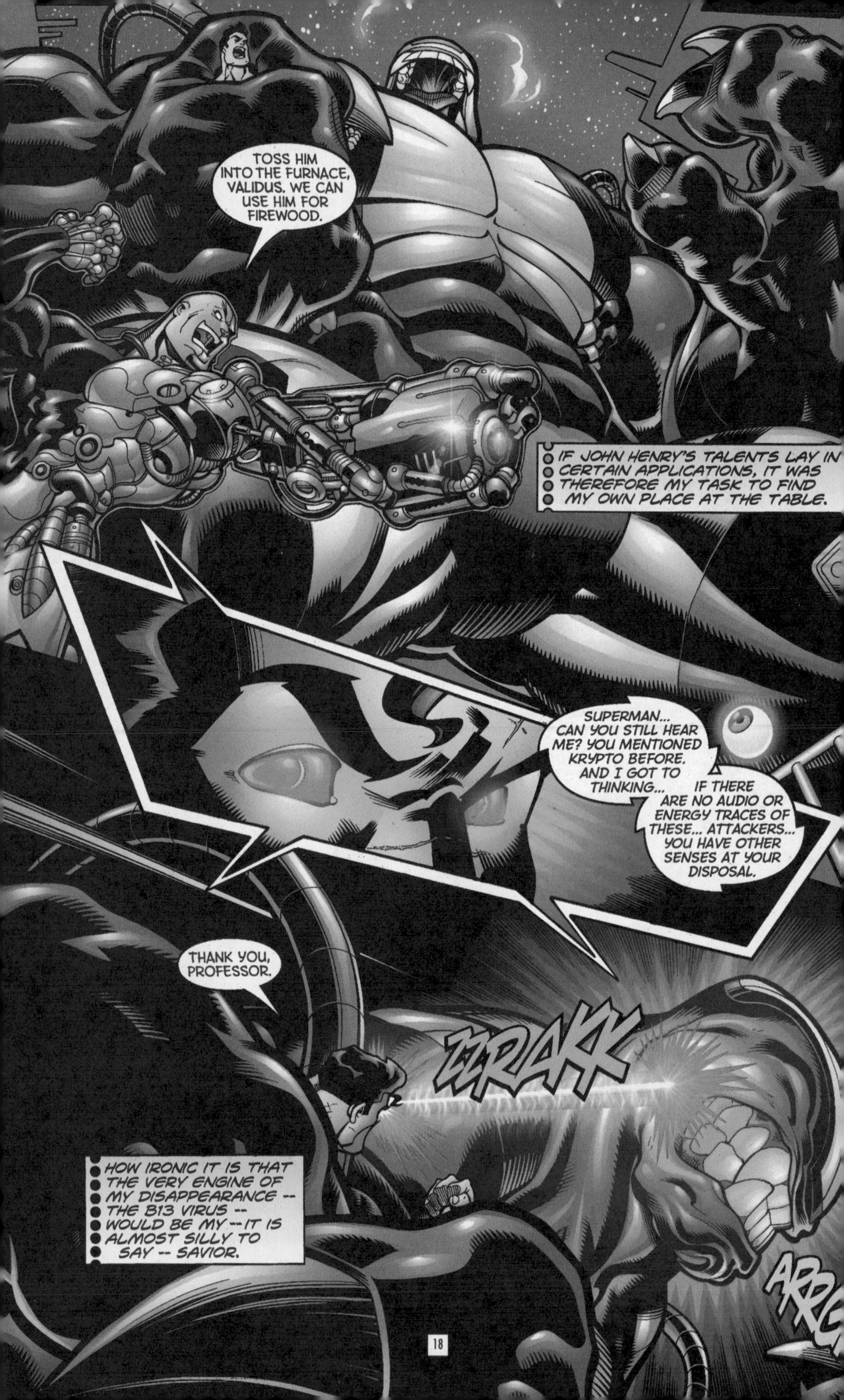
TOSS HIM INTO THE FURNACE, VALIDUS. WE CAN USE HIM FOR FIREWOOD.
IF JOHN HENRY'S TALENTS LAY IN CERTAIN APPLICATIONS, IT WAS THEREFORE MY TASK TO FIND MY OWN PLACE AT THE TABLE.
SUPERMAN... CAN YOU STILL HEAR ME? YOU MENTIONED KRYPTO BEFORE. AND I GOT TO THINKING...
IF THERE ARE NO AUDIO OR ENERGY TRACES OF THESE... ATTACKERS... YOU HAVE OTHER SENSES AT YOUR DISPOSAL.
THANK YOU, PROFESSOR.
ZZRAKK
HOW IRONIC IT IS THAT THE VERY ENGINE OF MY DISAPPEARANCE -- THE B13 VIRUS -- WOULD BE MY -- IT IS ALMOST SILLY TO SAY -- SAVIOR.

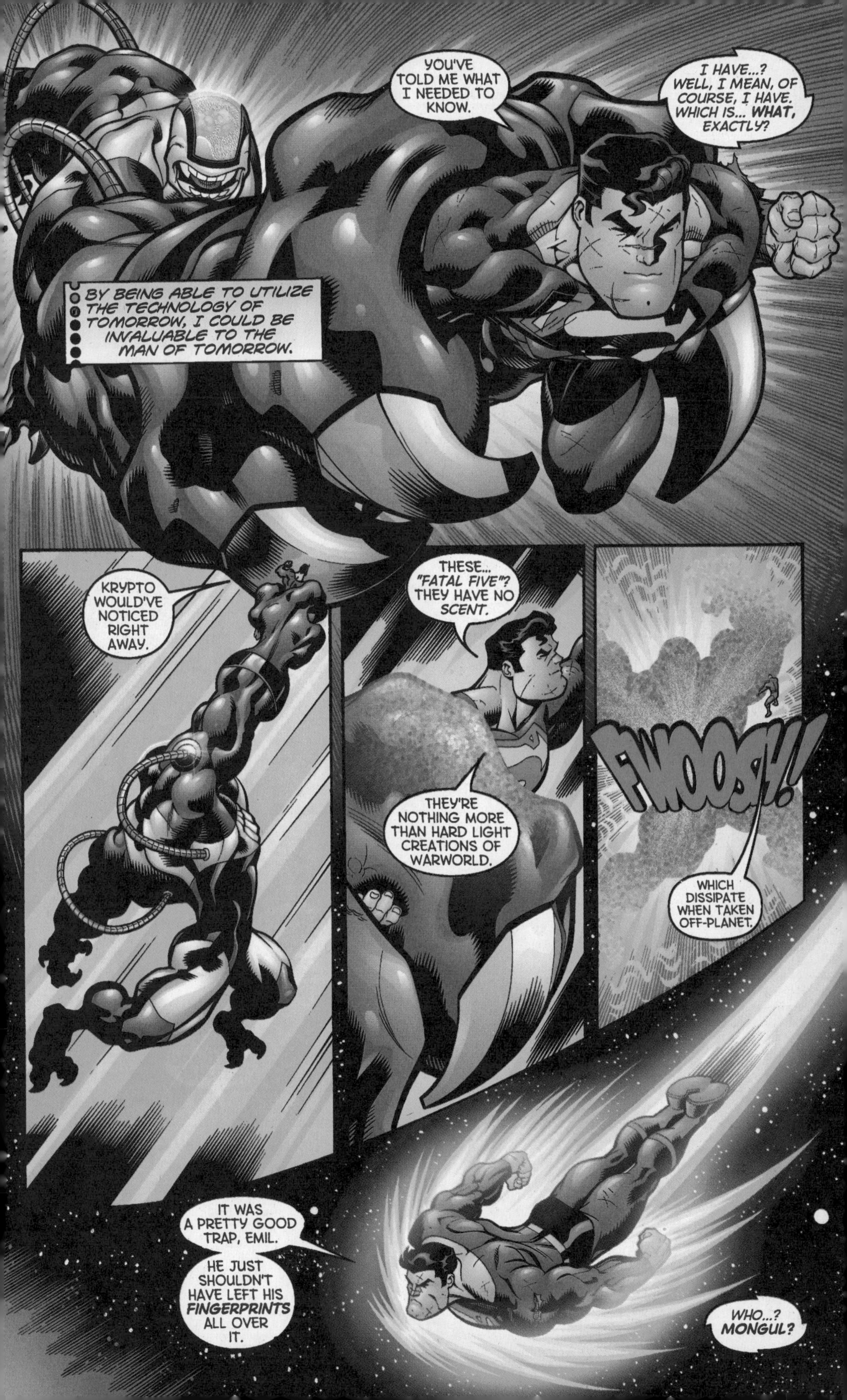
YOU'VE TOLD ME WHAT I NEEDED TO KNOW.
I HAVE...? WELL, I MEAN, OF COURSE, I HAVE. WHICH IS... WHAT, EXACTLY?
BY BEING ABLE TO UTILIZE THE TECHNOLOGY OF TOMORROW, I COULD BE INVALUABLE TO THE MAN OF TOMORROW.
KRYPTO WOULD'VE NOTICED RIGHT AWAY.
THESE... "FATAL FIVE"? THEY HAVE NO SCENT.
THEY'RE NOTHING MORE THAN HARD LIGHT CREATIONS OF WARWORLD.
FWOOSH!!
WHICH DISSIPATE WHEN TAKEN OFF-PLANET.
IT WAS A PRETTY GOOD TRAP, EMIL.
HE JUST SHOULDN'T HAVE LEFT HIS FINGERPRINTS ALL OVER IT.
WHO...? MONGUL?

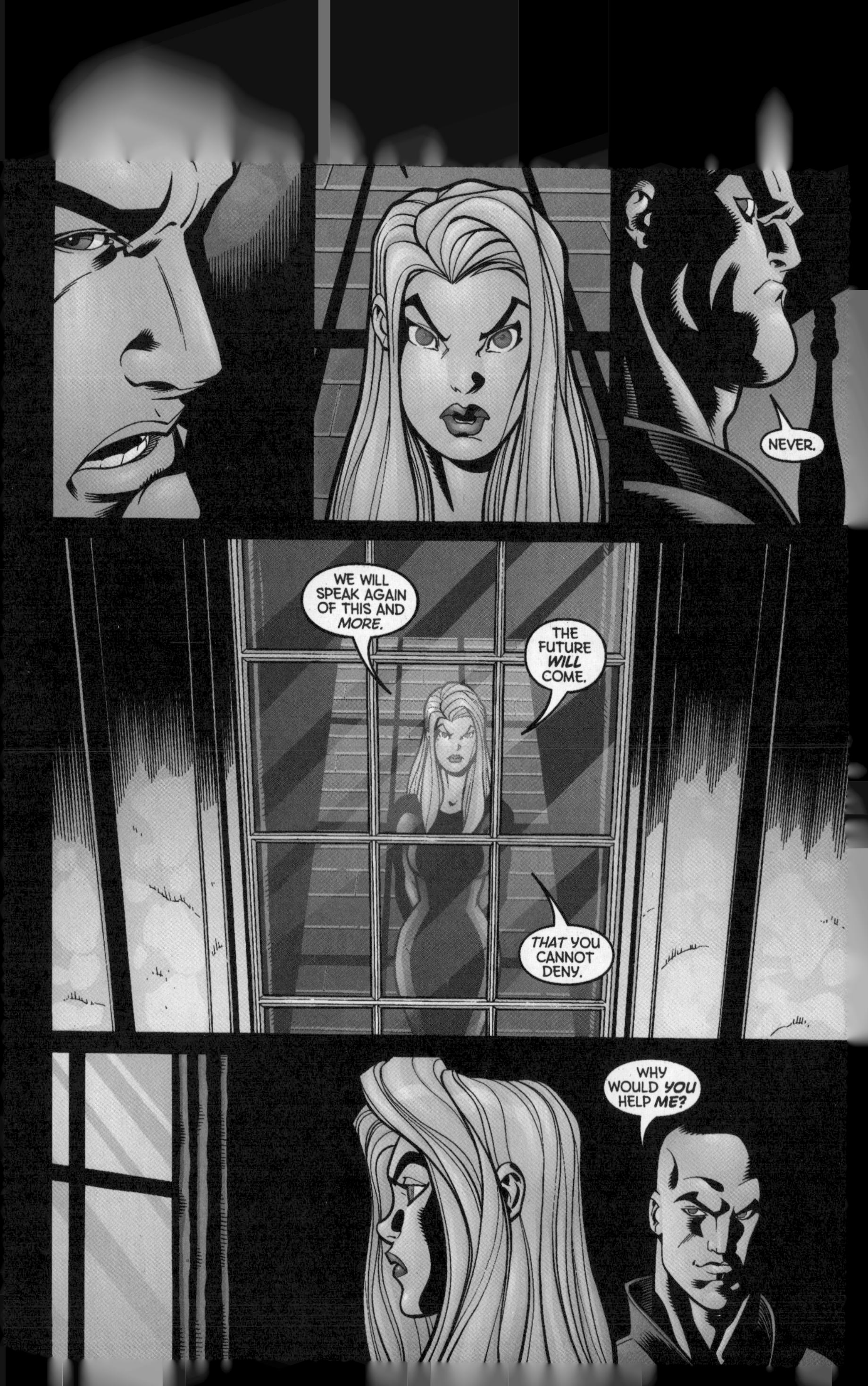
NEVER.
WE WILL SPEAK AGAIN OF THIS AND *MORE*.
THE FUTURE ***WILL*** COME.
*THAT* YOU CANNOT DENY.
WHY WOULD ***YOU*** HELP ***ME***?

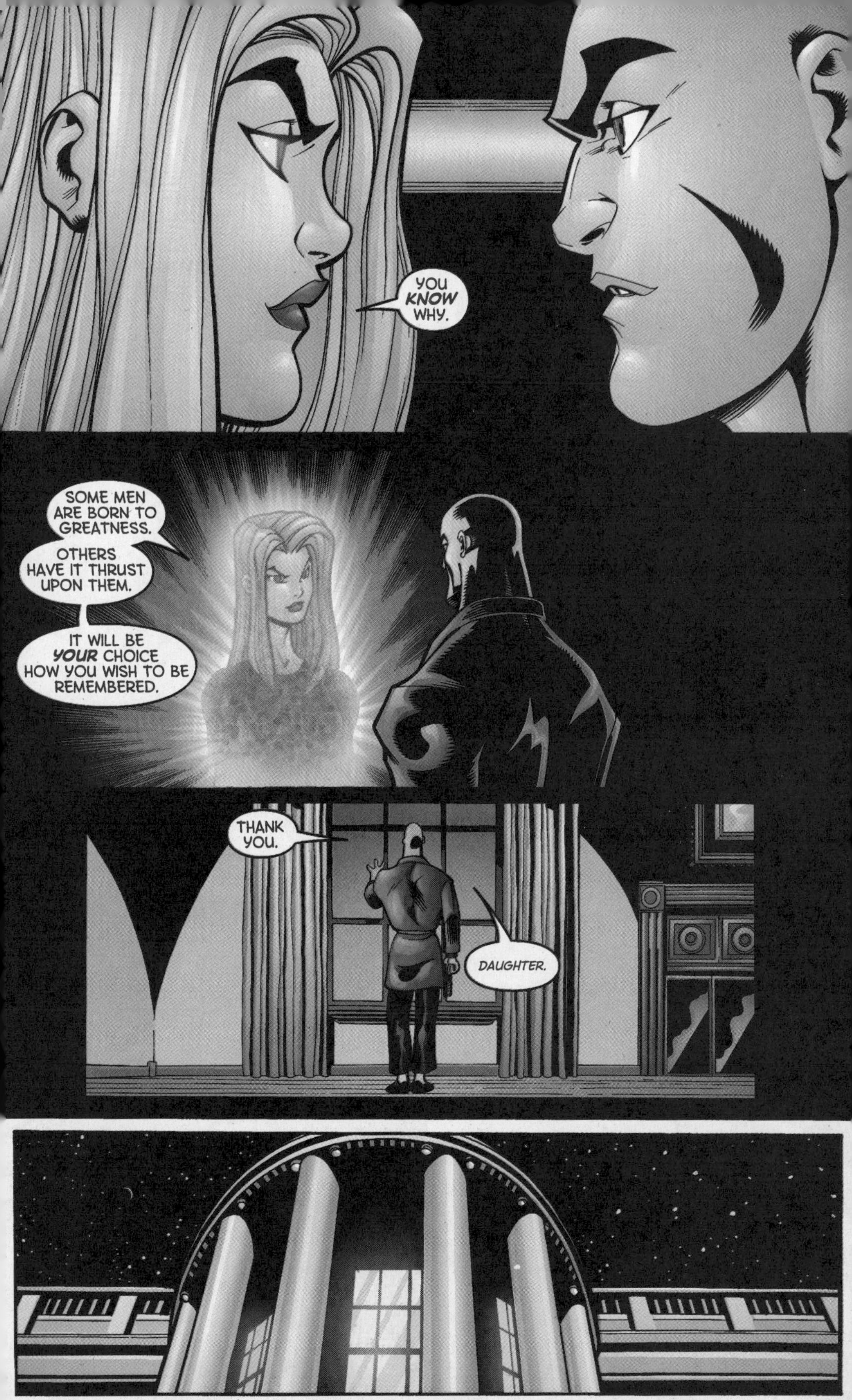
YOU KNOW WHY.
SOME MEN ARE BORN TO GREATNESS.
OTHERS HAVE IT THRUST UPON THEM.
IT WILL BE YOUR CHOICE HOW YOU WISH TO BE REMEMBERED.
THANK YOU.
DAUGHTER.

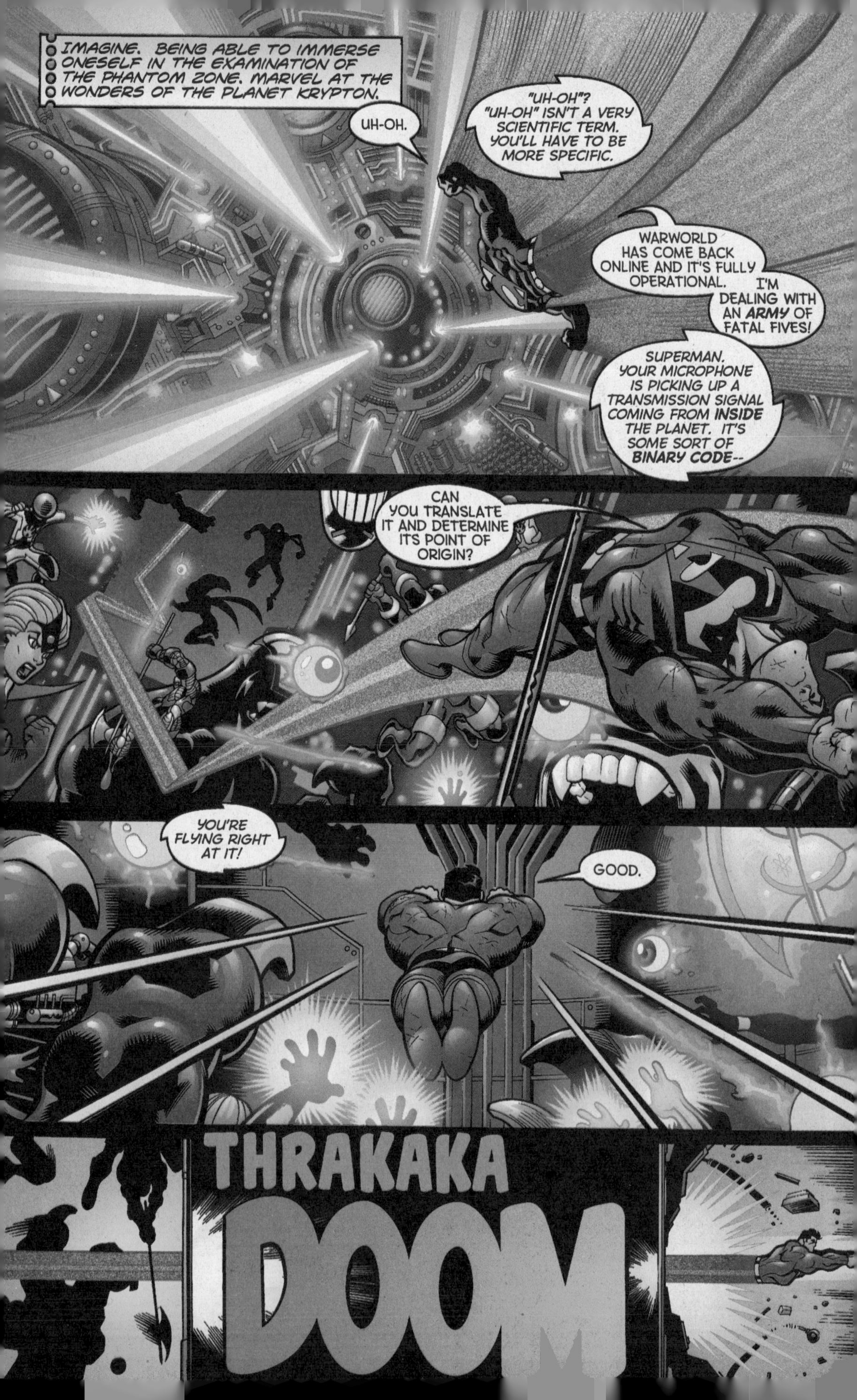
IMAGINE. BEING ABLE TO IMMERSE ONESELF IN THE EXAMINATION OF THE PHANTOM ZONE. MARVEL AT THE WONDERS OF THE PLANET KRYPTON.
UH-OH.
"UH-OH"? "UH-OH" ISN'T A VERY SCIENTIFIC TERM. YOU'LL HAVE TO BE MORE SPECIFIC.
WARWORLD HAS COME BACK ONLINE AND IT'S FULLY OPERATIONAL.
I'M DEALING WITH AN ARMY OF FATAL FIVES!
SUPERMAN. YOUR MICROPHONE IS PICKING UP A TRANSMISSION SIGNAL COMING FROM INSIDE THE PLANET. IT'S SOME SORT OF BINARY CODE--
CAN YOU TRANSLATE IT AND DETERMINE ITS POINT OF ORIGIN?
YOU'RE FLYING RIGHT AT IT!
GOOD.
THRAKAKA
DOOM

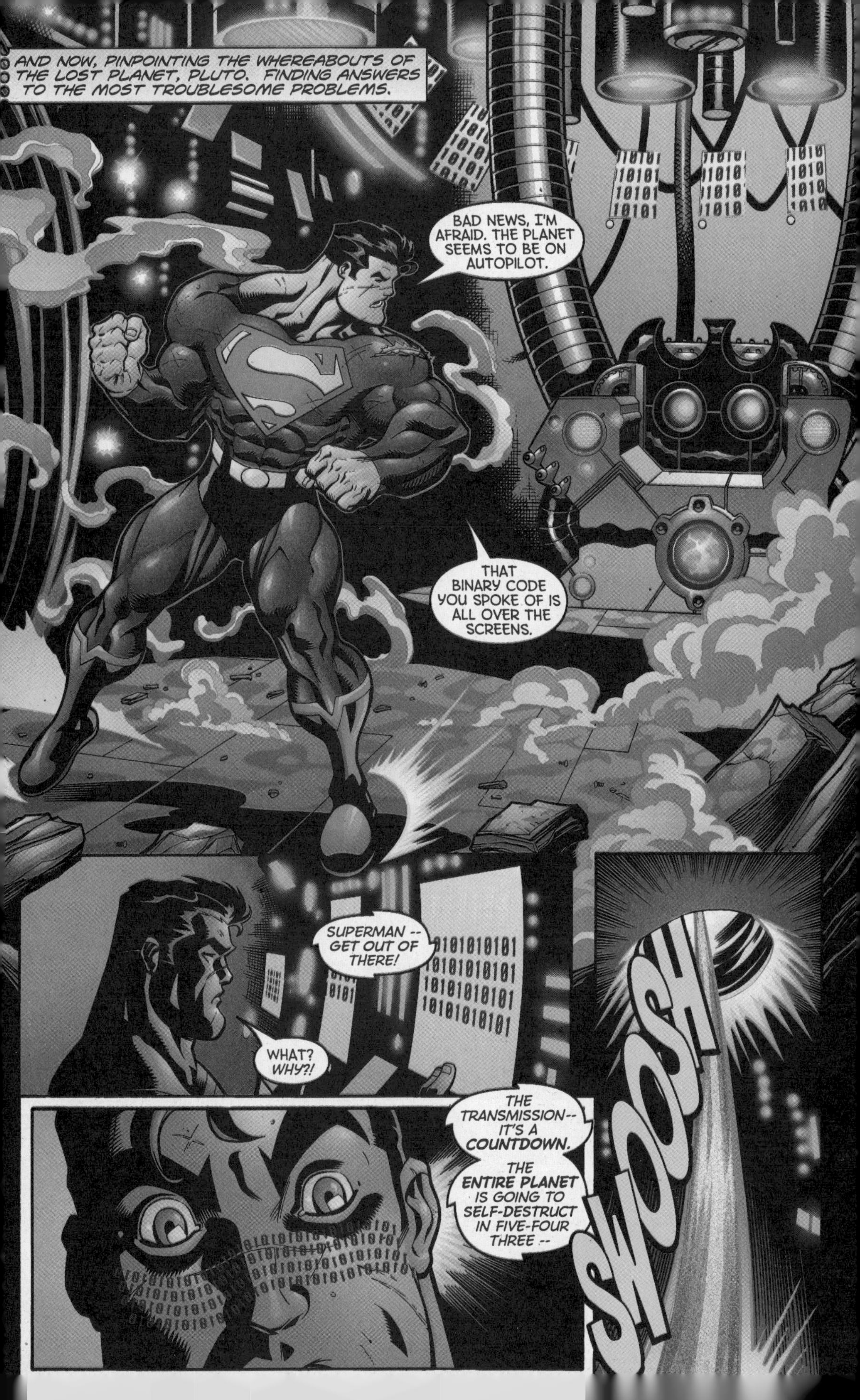
AND NOW, PINPOINTING THE WHEREABOUTS OF THE LOST PLANET, PLUTO. FINDING ANSWERS TO THE MOST TROUBLESOME PROBLEMS.
BAD NEWS, I'M AFRAID. THE PLANET SEEMS TO BE ON AUTOPILOT.
THAT BINARY CODE YOU SPOKE OF IS ALL OVER THE SCREENS.
SUPERMAN -- GET OUT OF THERE!
WHAT? WHY?!
THE TRANSMISSION-- IT'S A COUNTDOWN.
THE ENTIRE PLANET IS GOING TO SELF-DESTRUCT IN FIVE-FOUR THREE --
SWOOSH

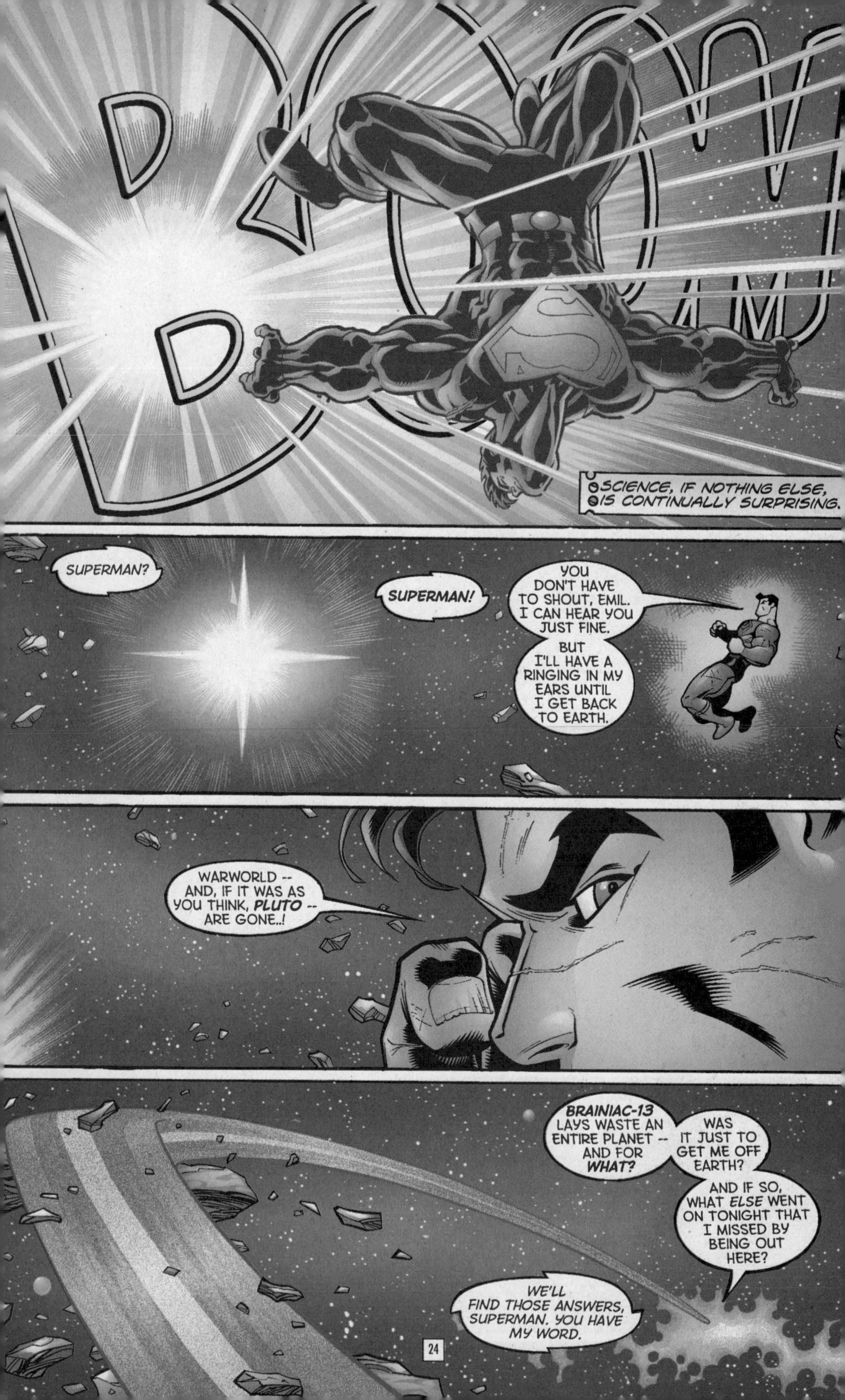
DOOM
SCIENCE, IF NOTHING ELSE, IS CONTINUALLY SURPRISING.
SUPERMAN?
SUPERMAN!
YOU DON'T HAVE TO SHOUT, EMIL. I CAN HEAR YOU JUST FINE.
BUT I'LL HAVE A RINGING IN MY EARS UNTIL I GET BACK TO EARTH.
WARWORLD -- AND, IF IT WAS AS YOU THINK, PLUTO -- ARE GONE..!
BRAINIAC-13 LAYS WASTE AN ENTIRE PLANET -- AND FOR WHAT?
WAS IT JUST TO GET ME OFF EARTH?
AND IF SO, WHAT ELSE WENT ON TONIGHT THAT I MISSED BY BEING OUT HERE?
WE'LL FIND THOSE ANSWERS, SUPERMAN. YOU HAVE MY WORD.

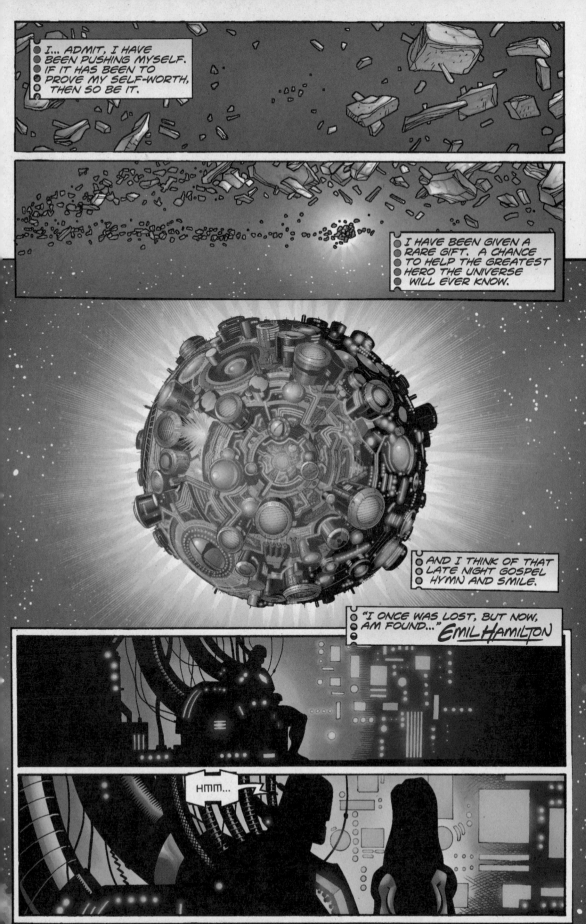

I... ADMIT, I HAVE BEEN PUSHING MYSELF. IF IT HAS BEEN TO PROVE MY SELF-WORTH, THEN SO BE IT.

I HAVE BEEN GIVEN A RARE GIFT. A CHANCE TO HELP THE GREATEST HERO THE UNIVERSE WILL EVER KNOW.

AND I THINK OF THAT LATE NIGHT GOSPEL HYMN AND SMILE.

"I ONCE WAS LOST, BUT NOW, AM FOUND..." *EMIL HAMILTON*

HMM...

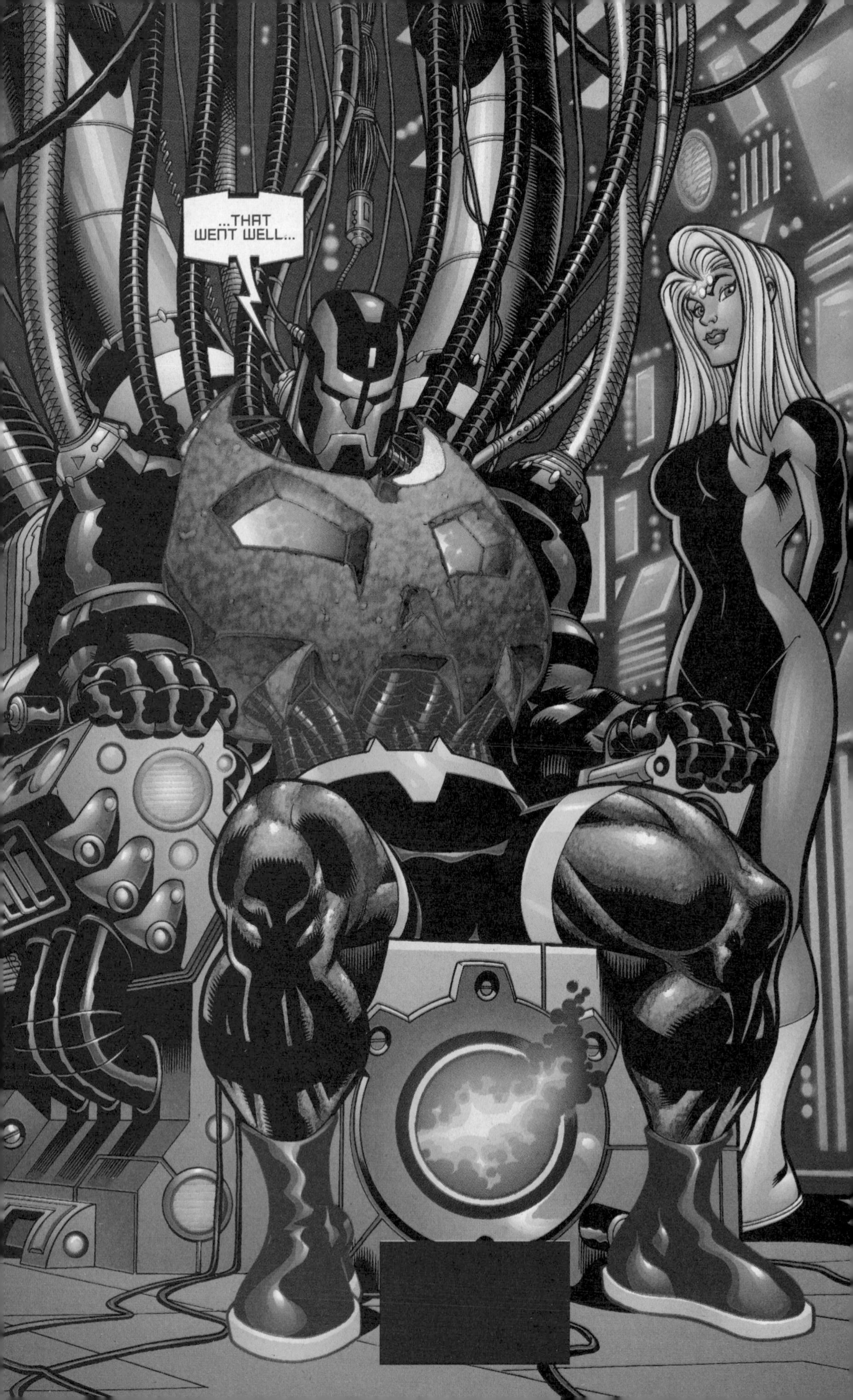
...THAT WENT WELL...
[redacted]

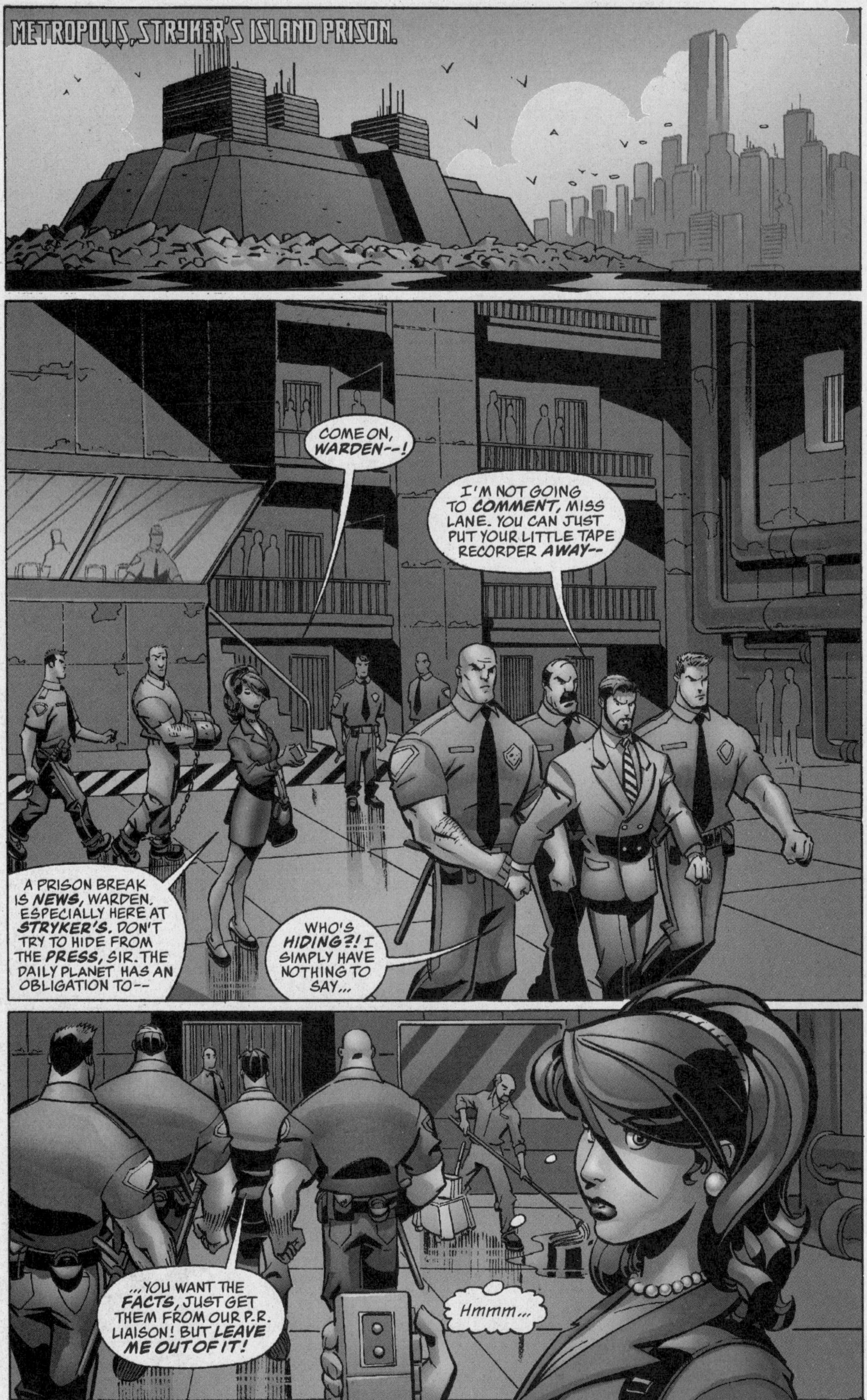
METROPOLIS, STRYKER'S ISLAND PRISON.
COME ON, WARDEN--!
I'M NOT GOING TO COMMENT, MISS LANE. YOU CAN JUST PUT YOUR LITTLE TAPE RECORDER AWAY--
A PRISON BREAK IS NEWS, WARDEN. ESPECIALLY HERE AT STRYKER'S. DON'T TRY TO HIDE FROM THE PRESS, SIR. THE DAILY PLANET HAS AN OBLIGATION TO--
WHO'S HIDING?! I SIMPLY HAVE NOTHING TO SAY...
...YOU WANT THE FACTS, JUST GET THEM FROM OUR P.R. LIAISON! BUT LEAVE ME OUT OF IT!
Hmmm...

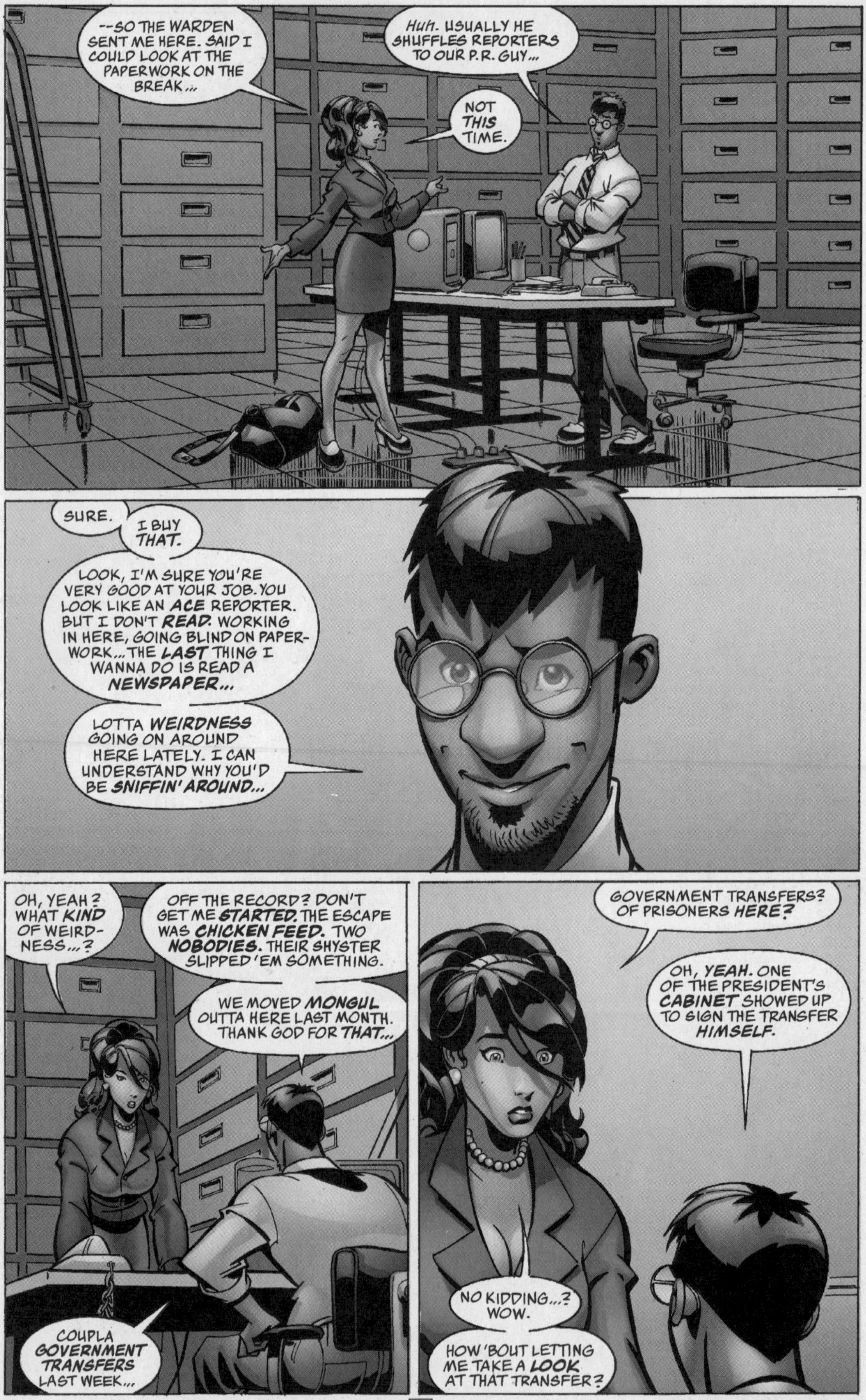
--SO THE WARDEN SENT ME HERE. SAID I COULD LOOK AT THE PAPERWORK ON THE BREAK...
HUH. USUALLY HE SHUFFLES REPORTERS TO OUR P.R. GUY...
NOT THIS TIME.
SURE.
I BUY THAT.
LOOK, I'M SURE YOU'RE VERY GOOD AT YOUR JOB. YOU LOOK LIKE AN ACE REPORTER. BUT I DON'T READ. WORKING IN HERE, GOING BLIND ON PAPERWORK... THE LAST THING I WANNA DO IS READ A NEWSPAPER...
LOTTA WEIRDNESS GOING ON AROUND HERE LATELY. I CAN UNDERSTAND WHY YOU'D BE SNIFFIN' AROUND...
OH, YEAH? WHAT KIND OF WEIRDNESS...?
OFF THE RECORD? DON'T GET ME STARTED. THE ESCAPE WAS CHICKEN FEED. TWO NOBODIES. THEIR SHYSTER SLIPPED 'EM SOMETHING.
WE MOVED MONGUL OUTTA HERE LAST MONTH. THANK GOD FOR THAT...
COUPLA GOVERNMENT TRANSFERS LAST WEEK...
GOVERNMENT TRANSFERS? OF PRISONERS HERE?
OH, YEAH. ONE OF THE PRESIDENT'S CABINET SHOWED UP TO SIGN THE TRANSFER HIMSELF.
NO KIDDING...? WOW.
HOW 'BOUT LETTING ME TAKE A LOOK AT THAT TRANSFER?

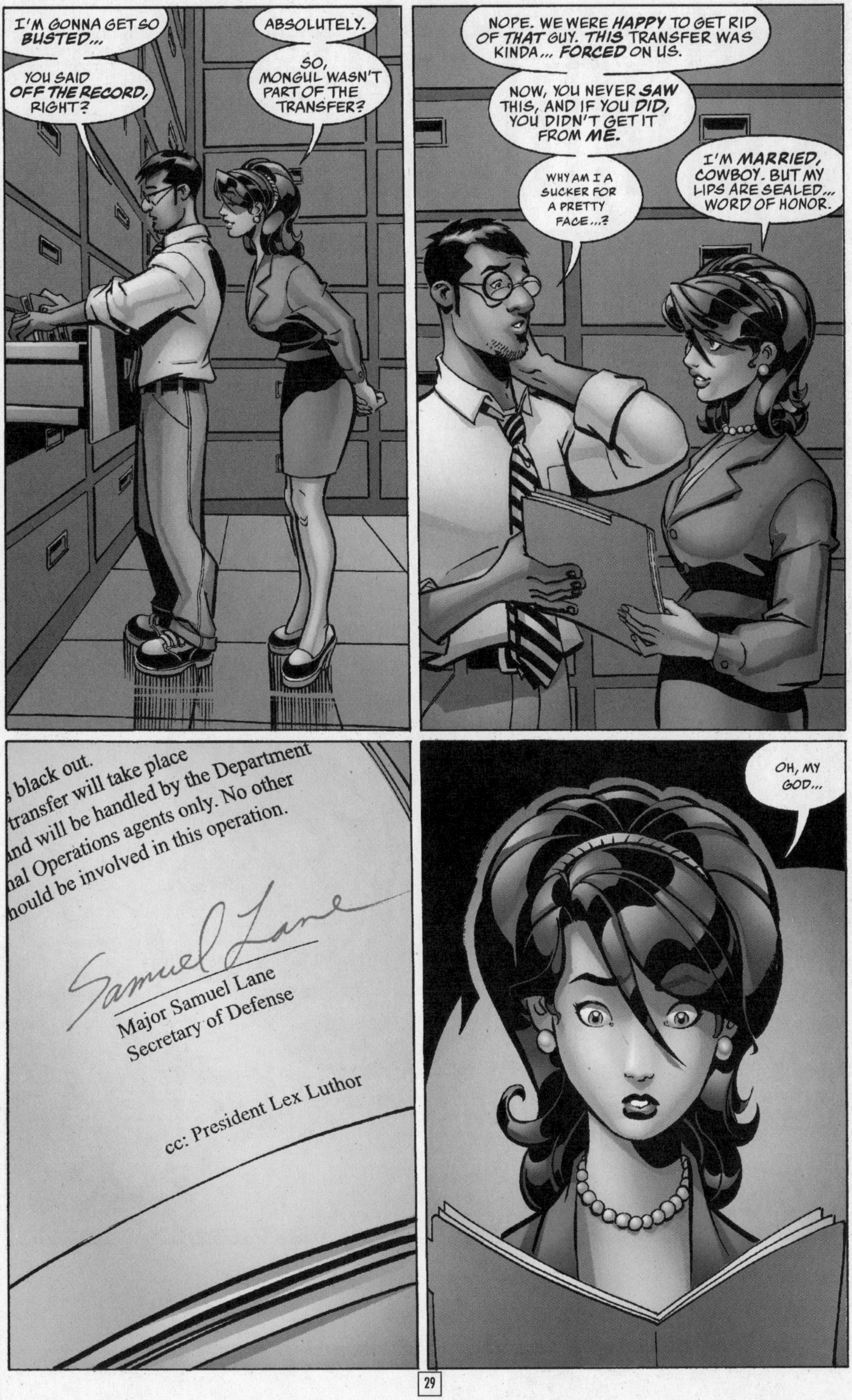
I'M GONNA GET SO BUSTED...
YOU SAID OFF THE RECORD, RIGHT?
ABSOLUTELY.
SO, MONGUL WASN'T PART OF THE TRANSFER?
NOPE. WE WERE HAPPY TO GET RID OF THAT GUY. THIS TRANSFER WAS KINDA... FORCED ON US.
NOW, YOU NEVER SAW THIS, AND IF YOU DID, YOU DIDN'T GET IT FROM ME.
WHY AM I A SUCKER FOR A PRETTY FACE...?
I'M MARRIED, COWBOY. BUT MY LIPS ARE SEALED... WORD OF HONOR.
s black out.
transfer will take place
and will be handled by the Department
nal Operations agents only. No other
hould be involved in this operation.
Samuel Lane
Major Samuel Lane
Secretary of Defense
cc: President Lex Luthor
OH, MY GOD...

# SUICIDE MISSION

**JOE CASEY** writer   **MIKE WIERINGO** pencils   **JOSE MARZAN, JR.** inks   **BILL OAKLEY** letters   **WILDSTORM FX** colors   **TOM PALMER, JR.** asst. ed.   **EDDIE BERGANZA** editor

JERRY SIEGEL & JOE SHUSTER
Superman creators

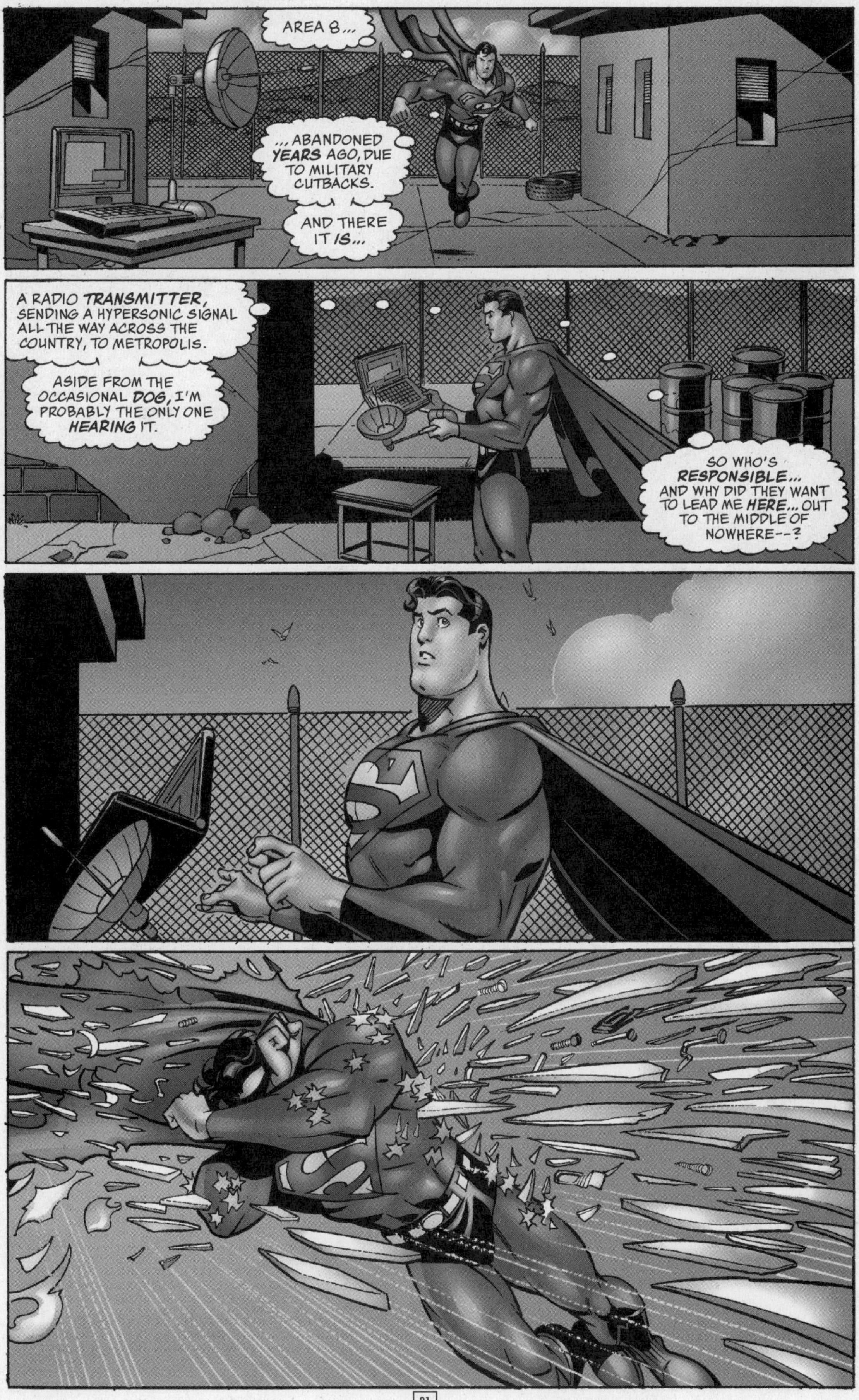
AREA 8...
...ABANDONED YEARS AGO, DUE TO MILITARY CUTBACKS.
AND THERE IT IS...
A RADIO TRANSMITTER, SENDING A HYPERSONIC SIGNAL ALL THE WAY ACROSS THE COUNTRY, TO METROPOLIS.
ASIDE FROM THE OCCASIONAL DOG, I'M PROBABLY THE ONLY ONE HEARING IT.
SO WHO'S RESPONSIBLE... AND WHY DID THEY WANT TO LEAD ME HERE... OUT TO THE MIDDLE OF NOWHERE--?

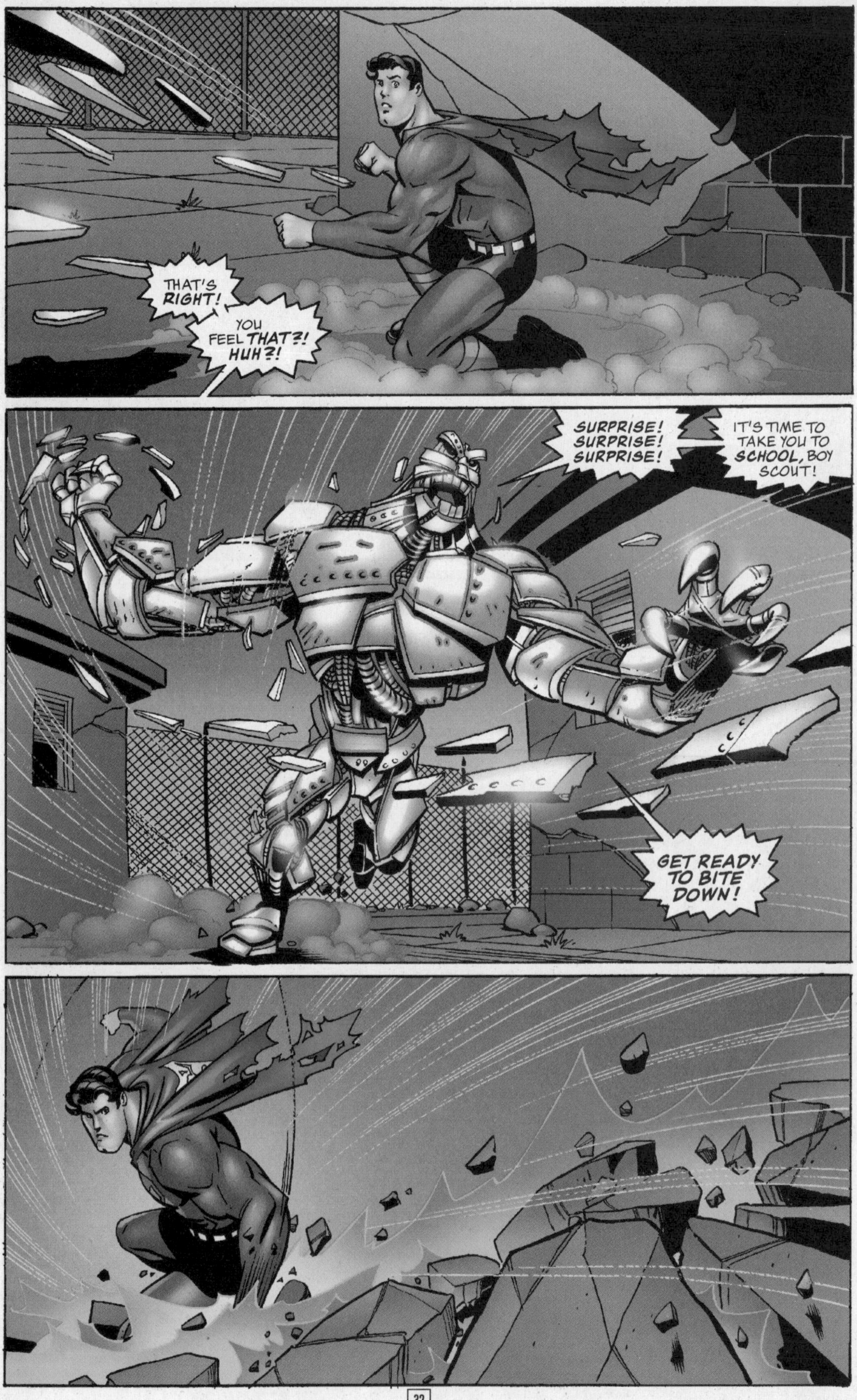
THAT'S RIGHT!
YOU FEEL THAT?! HUH?!
SURPRISE! SURPRISE! SURPRISE!
IT'S TIME TO TAKE YOU TO SCHOOL, BOY SCOUT!
GET READY TO BITE DOWN!

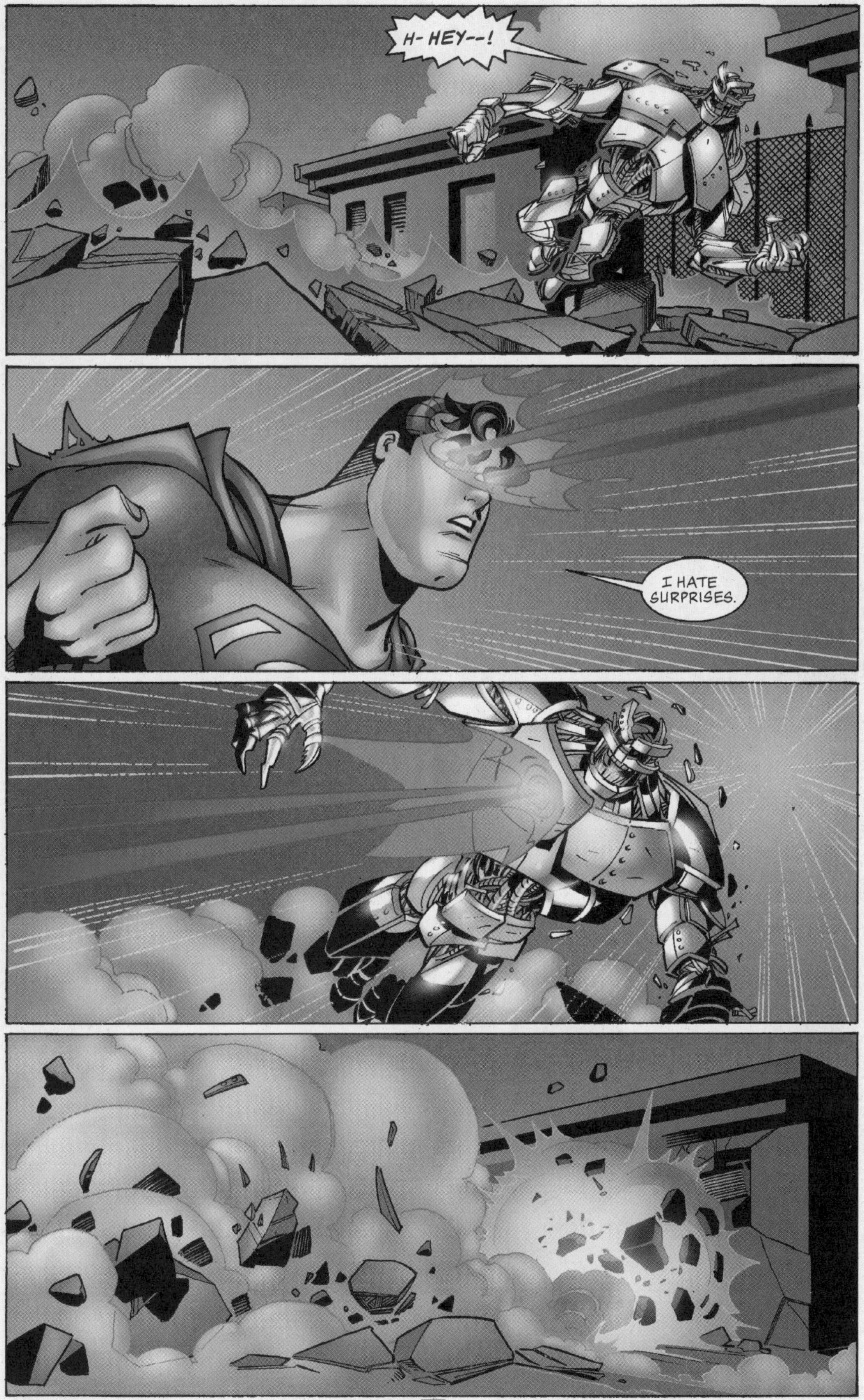
H- HEY--!
I HATE SURPRISES.

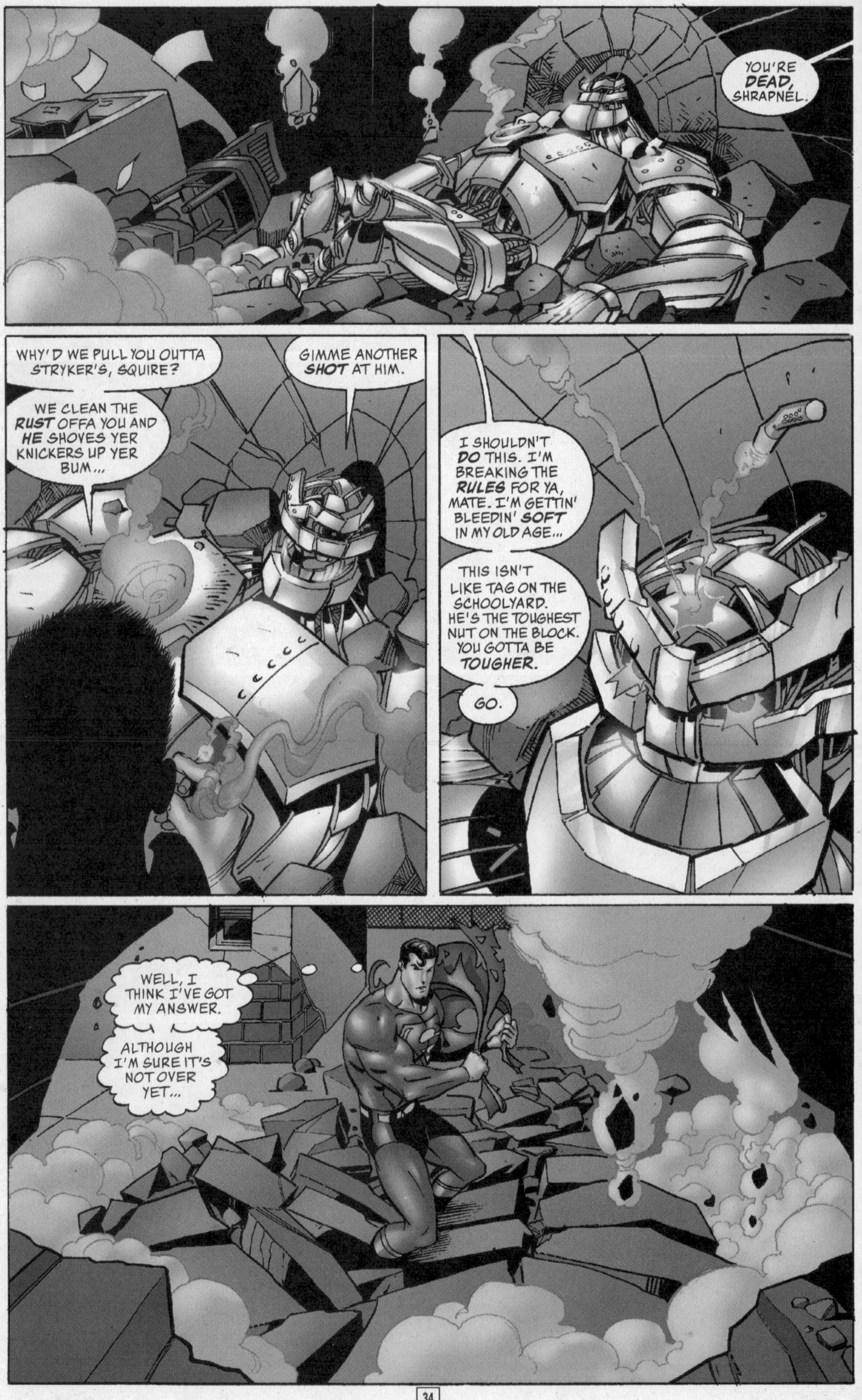
YOU'RE DEAD, SHRAPNEL.
WHY'D WE PULL YOU OUTTA STRYKER'S, SQUIRE?
WE CLEAN THE RUST OFFA YOU AND HE SHOVES YER KNICKERS UP YER BUM...
GIMME ANOTHER SHOT AT HIM.
I SHOULDN'T DO THIS. I'M BREAKING THE RULES FOR YA, MATE. I'M GETTIN' BLEEDIN' SOFT IN MY OLD AGE...
THIS ISN'T LIKE TAG ON THE SCHOOLYARD. HE'S THE TOUGHEST NUT ON THE BLOCK. YOU GOTTA BE TOUGHER.
GO.
WELL, I THINK I'VE GOT MY ANSWER.
ALTHOUGH I'M SURE IT'S NOT OVER YET...

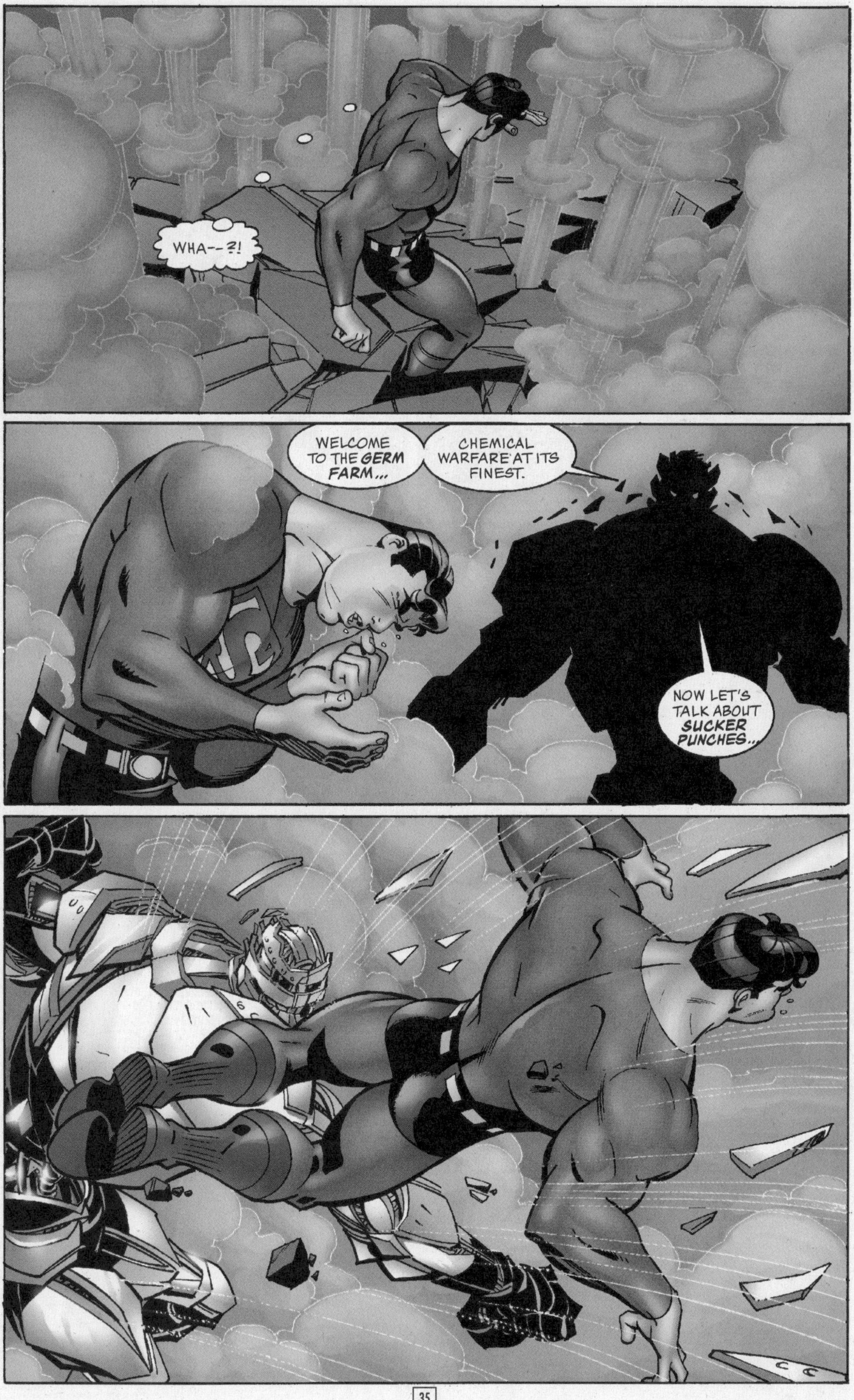
WHA--?!
WELCOME TO THE GERM FARM...
CHEMICAL WARFARE AT ITS FINEST.
NOW LET'S TALK ABOUT SUCKER PUNCHES...

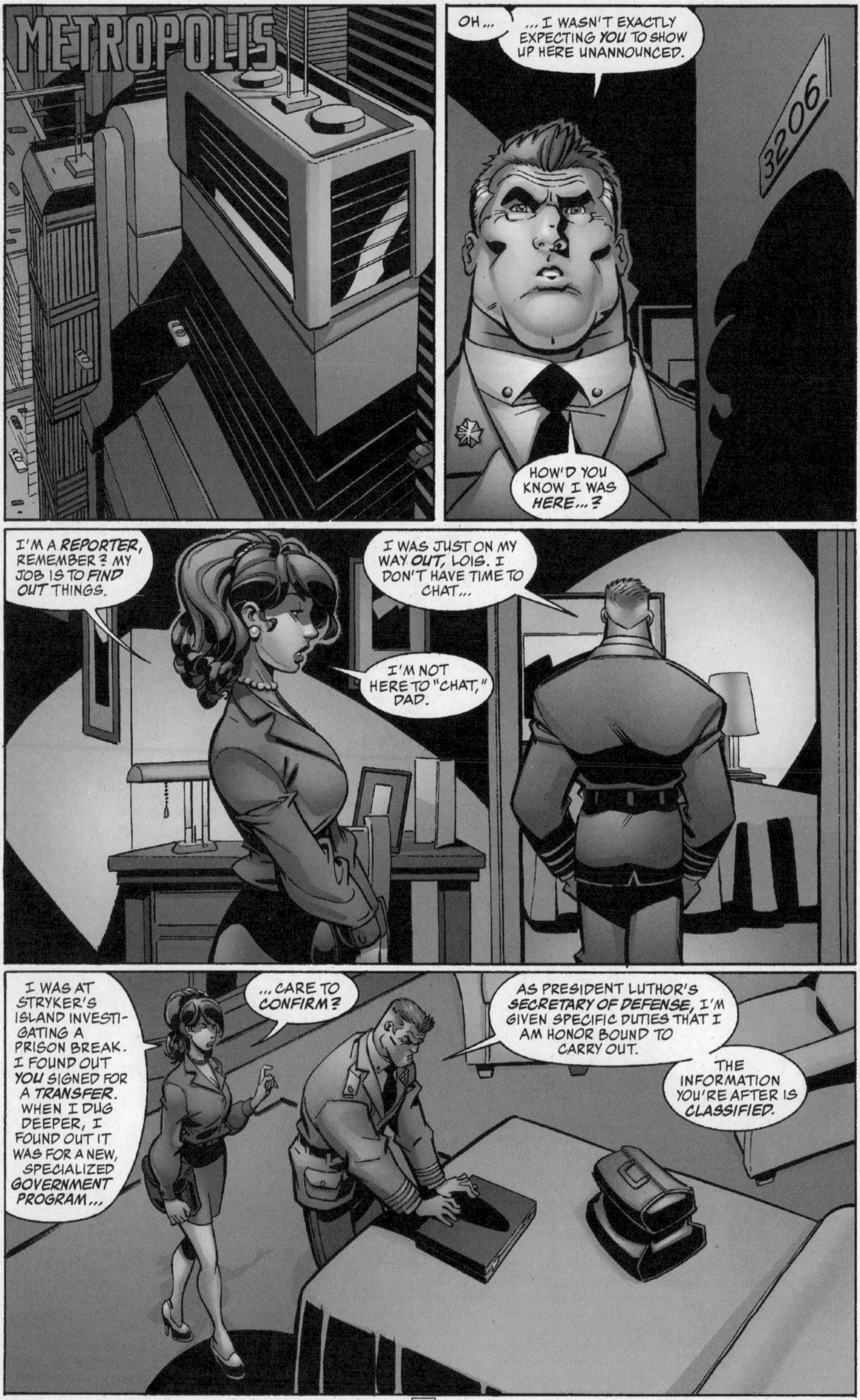
METROPOLIS
OH...
...I WASN'T EXACTLY EXPECTING YOU TO SHOW UP HERE UNANNOUNCED.
3206
HOW'D YOU KNOW I WAS HERE...?
I'M A REPORTER, REMEMBER? MY JOB IS TO FIND OUT THINGS.
I WAS JUST ON MY WAY OUT, LOIS. I DON'T HAVE TIME TO CHAT...
I'M NOT HERE TO "CHAT," DAD.
I WAS AT STRYKER'S ISLAND INVESTI-GATING A PRISON BREAK. I FOUND OUT YOU SIGNED FOR A TRANSFER. WHEN I DUG DEEPER, I FOUND OUT IT WAS FOR A NEW, SPECIALIZED GOVERNMENT PROGRAM...
...CARE TO CONFIRM?
AS PRESIDENT LUTHOR'S SECRETARY OF DEFENSE, I'M GIVEN SPECIFIC DUTIES THAT I AM HONOR BOUND TO CARRY OUT.
THE INFORMATION YOU'RE AFTER IS CLASSIFIED.

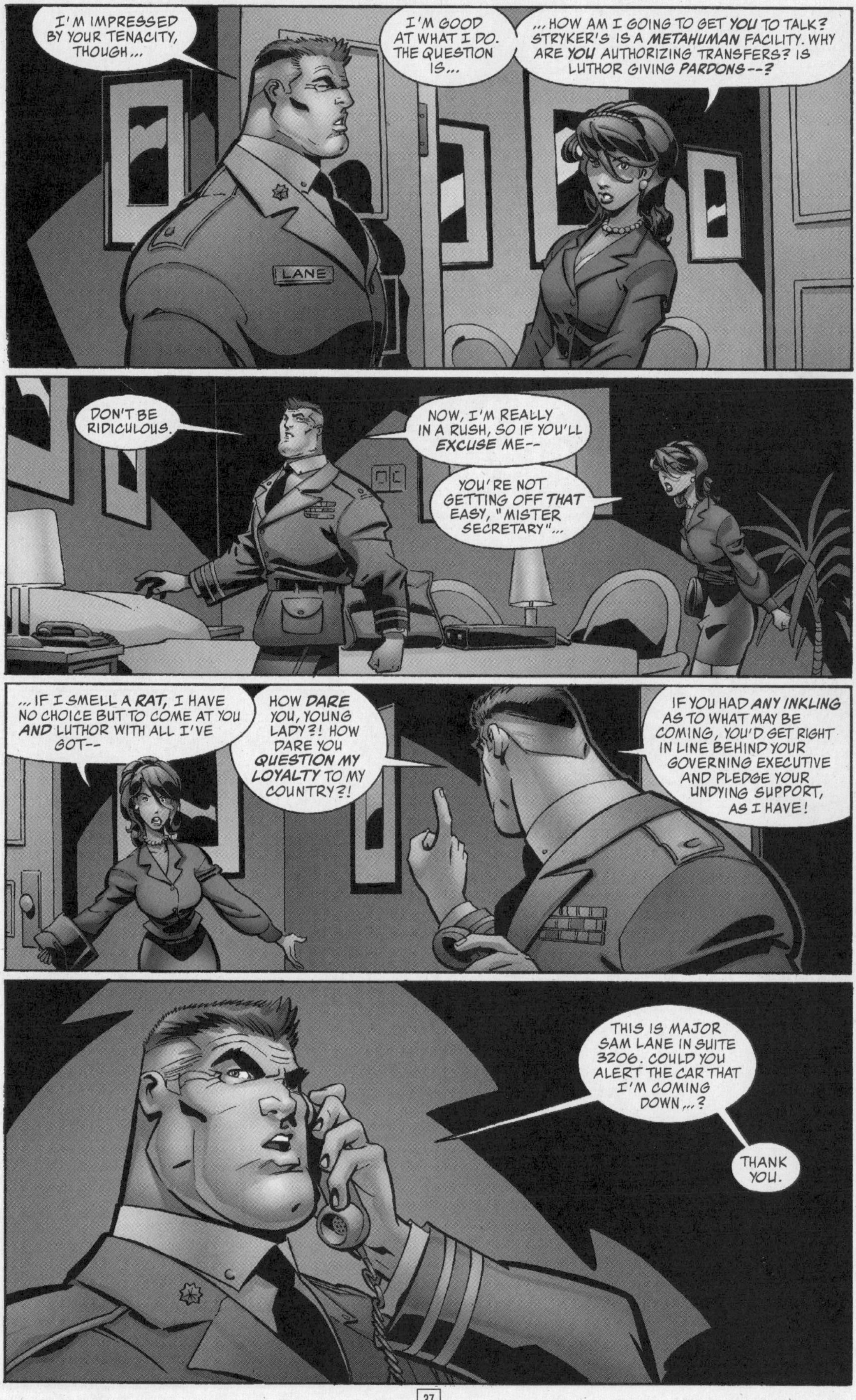
I'M IMPRESSED BY YOUR TENACITY, THOUGH...
I'M GOOD AT WHAT I DO. THE QUESTION IS...
...HOW AM I GOING TO GET YOU TO TALK? STRYKER'S IS A METAHUMAN FACILITY. WHY ARE YOU AUTHORIZING TRANSFERS? IS LUTHOR GIVING PARDONS--?
LANE
DON'T BE RIDICULOUS.
NOW, I'M REALLY IN A RUSH, SO IF YOU'LL EXCUSE ME--
YOU'RE NOT GETTING OFF THAT EASY, "MISTER SECRETARY"...
...IF I SMELL A RAT, I HAVE NO CHOICE BUT TO COME AT YOU AND LUTHOR WITH ALL I'VE GOT--
HOW DARE YOU, YOUNG LADY?! HOW DARE YOU QUESTION MY LOYALTY TO MY COUNTRY?!
IF YOU HAD ANY INKLING AS TO WHAT MAY BE COMING, YOU'D GET RIGHT IN LINE BEHIND YOUR GOVERNING EXECUTIVE AND PLEDGE YOUR UNDYING SUPPORT, AS I HAVE!
THIS IS MAJOR SAM LANE IN SUITE 3206. COULD YOU ALERT THE CAR THAT I'M COMING DOWN...?
THANK YOU.

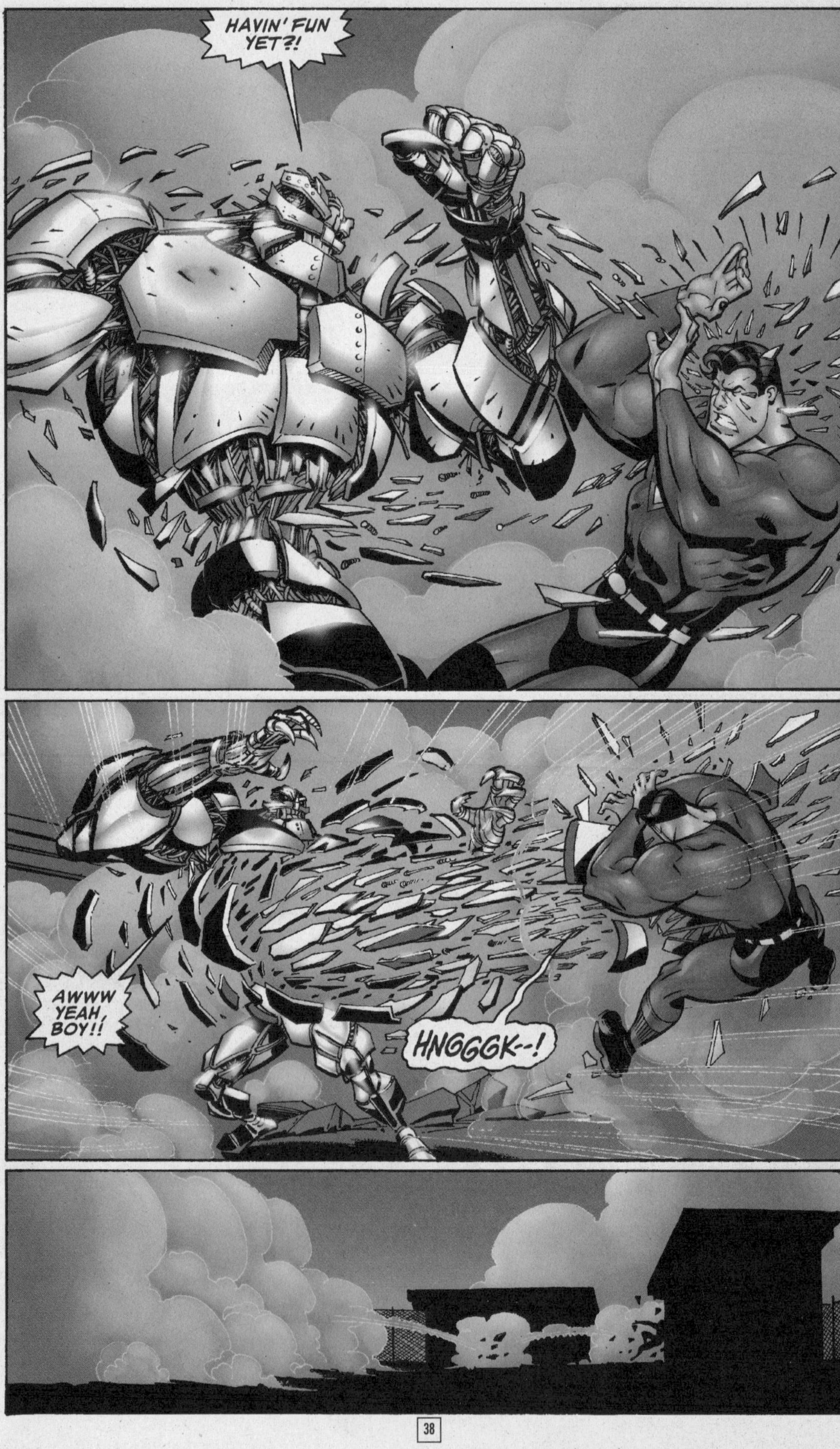
HAVIN' FUN YET?!
AWWW YEAH, BOY!!
HNGGGK--!

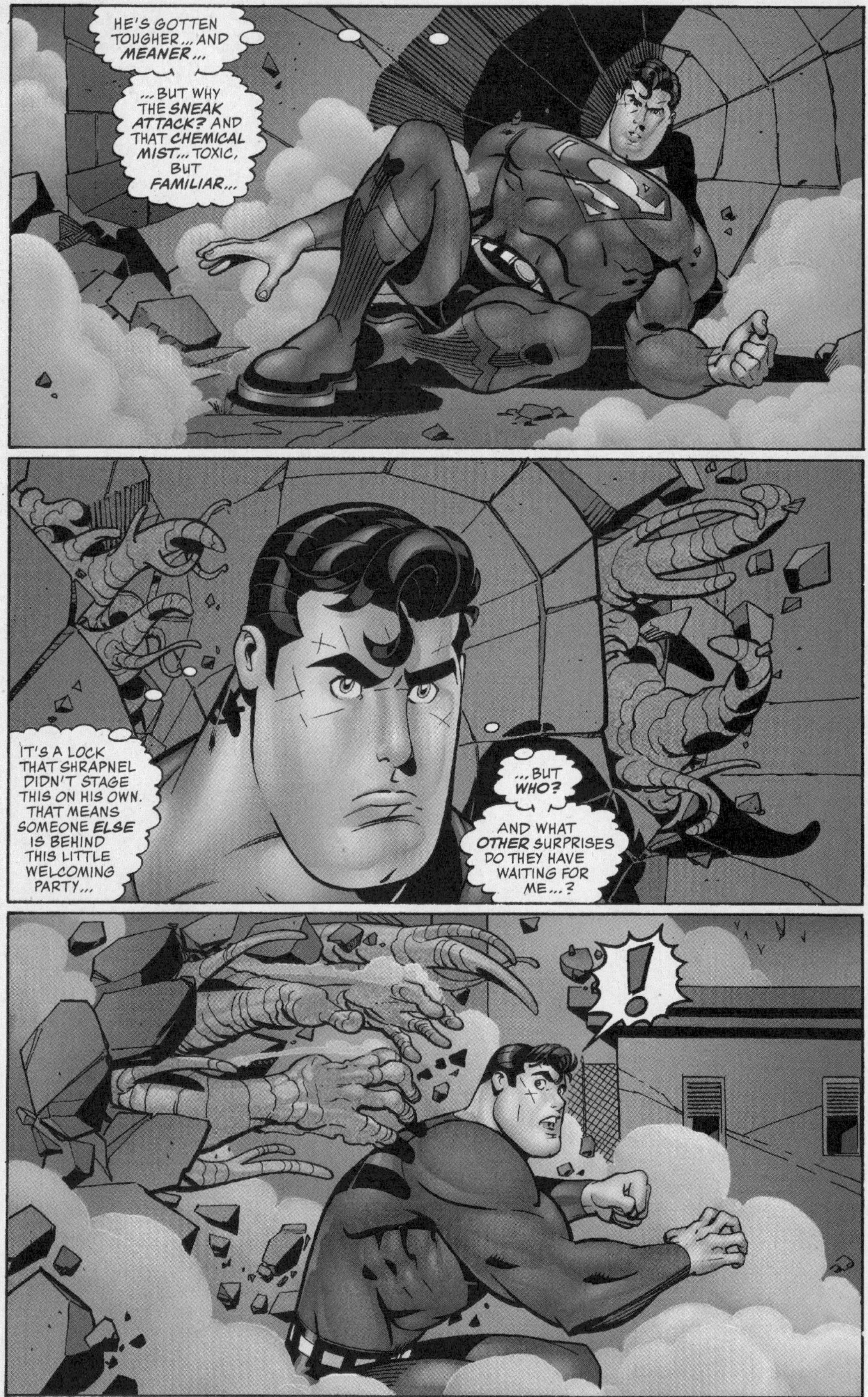
HE'S GOTTEN TOUGHER... AND MEANER...
...BUT WHY THE SNEAK ATTACK? AND THAT CHEMICAL MIST... TOXIC, BUT FAMILIAR...
IT'S A LOCK THAT SHRAPNEL DIDN'T STAGE THIS ON HIS OWN. THAT MEANS SOMEONE ELSE IS BEHIND THIS LITTLE WELCOMING PARTY...
...BUT WHO?
AND WHAT OTHER SURPRISES DO THEY HAVE WAITING FOR ME...?
!

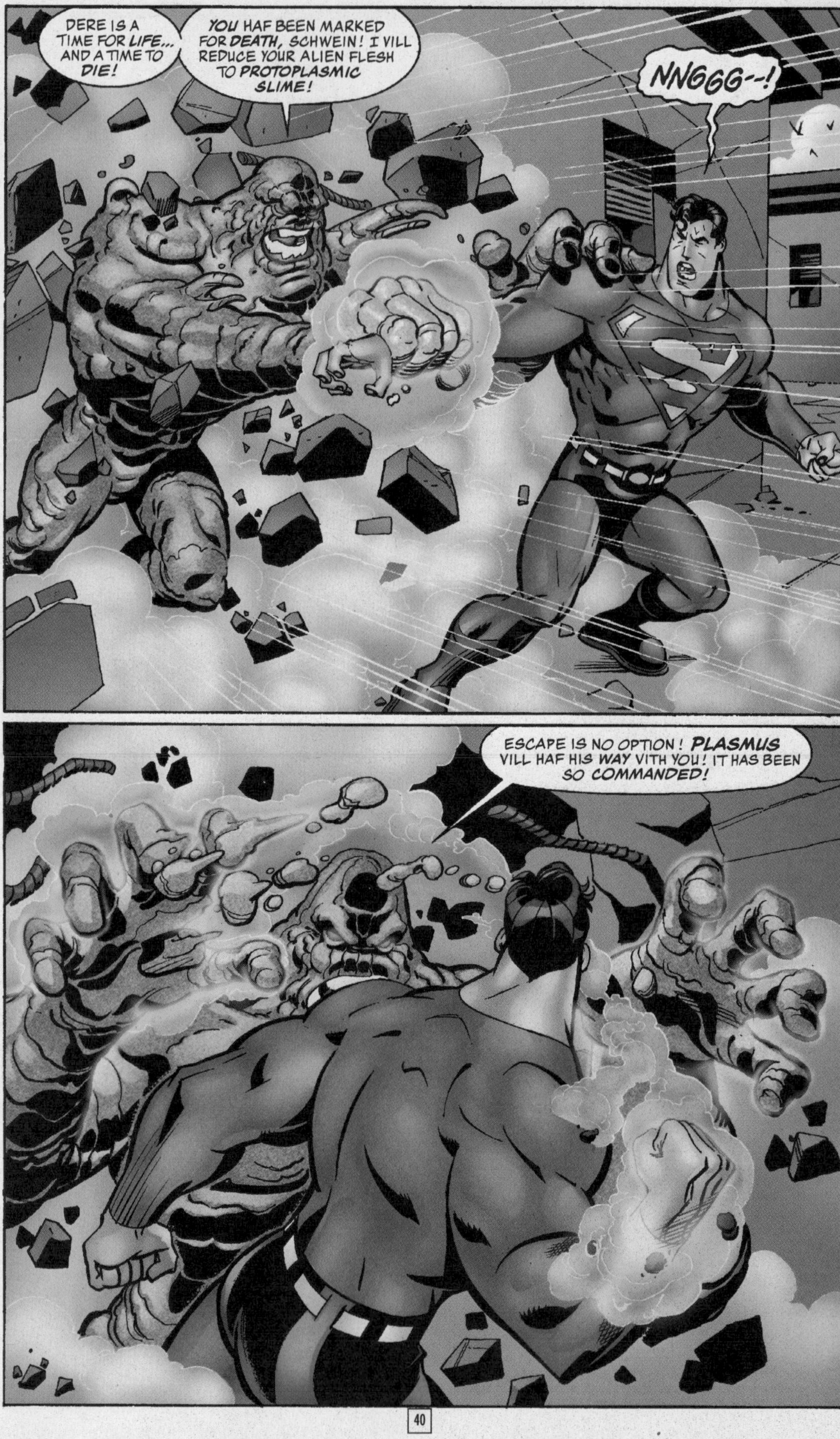
DERE IS A TIME FOR LIFE... AND A TIME TO DIE!
YOU HAF BEEN MARKED FOR DEATH, SCHWEIN! I VILL REDUCE YOUR ALIEN FLESH TO PROTOPLASMIC SLIME!
NNGGG--!
ESCAPE IS NO OPTION! PLASMUS VILL HAF HIS WAY VITH YOU! IT HAS BEEN SO COMMANDED!

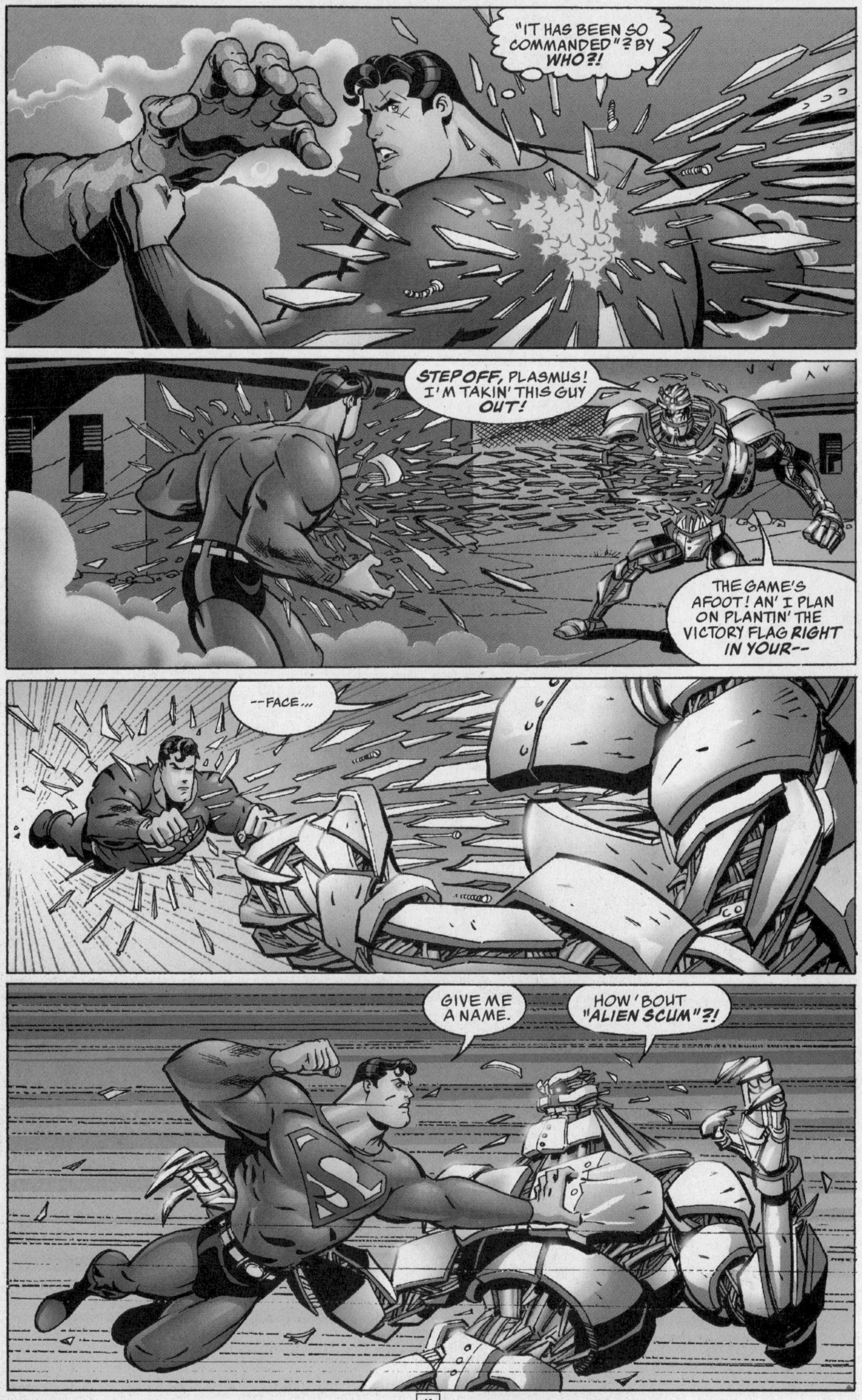
"IT HAS BEEN SO COMMANDED"? BY WHO?!
STEP OFF, PLASMUS! I'M TAKIN' THIS GUY OUT!
THE GAME'S AFOOT! AN' I PLAN ON PLANTIN' THE VICTORY FLAG RIGHT IN YOUR--
--FACE...
GIVE ME A NAME.
HOW 'BOUT "ALIEN SCUM"?!

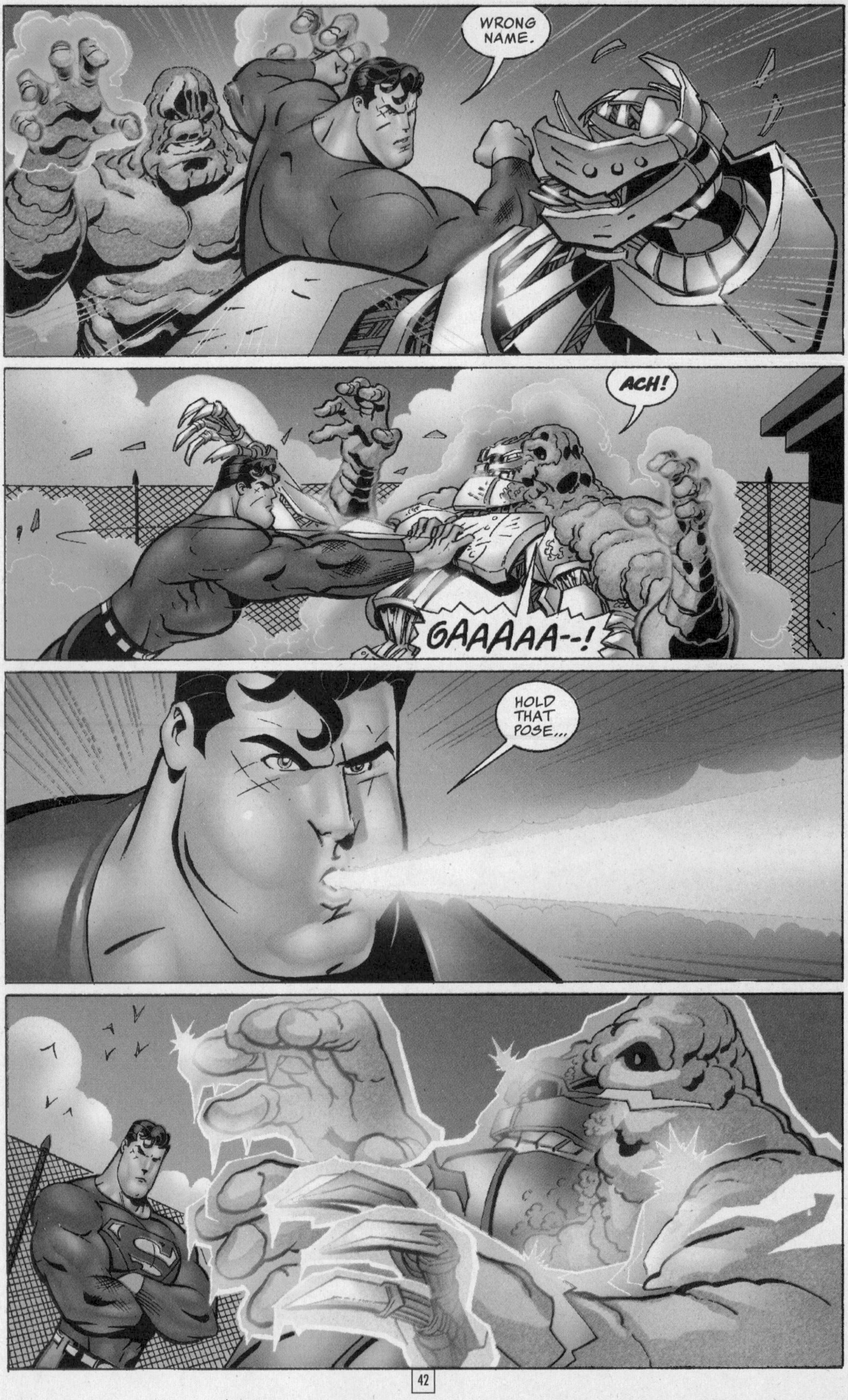
WRONG NAME.
ACH!
GAAAAA--!
HOLD THAT POSE...

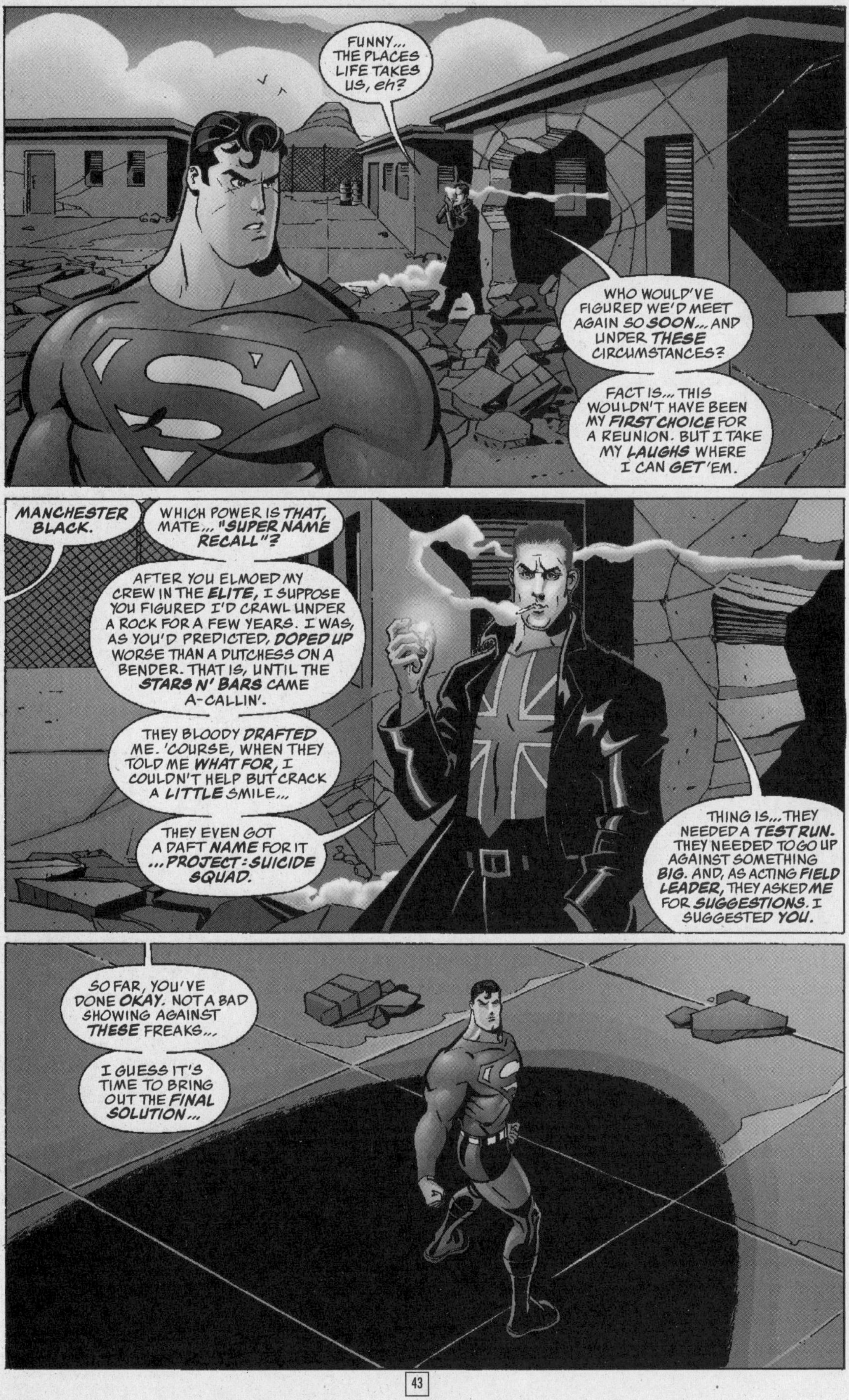
FUNNY... THE PLACES LIFE TAKES US, eh?
WHO WOULD'VE FIGURED WE'D MEET AGAIN SO SOON... AND UNDER THESE CIRCUMSTANCES?
FACT IS... THIS WOULDN'T HAVE BEEN MY FIRST CHOICE FOR A REUNION. BUT I TAKE MY LAUGHS WHERE I CAN GET 'EM.
MANCHESTER BLACK.
WHICH POWER IS THAT, MATE... "SUPER NAME RECALL"?
AFTER YOU ELMOED MY CREW IN THE ELITE, I SUPPOSE YOU FIGURED I'D CRAWL UNDER A ROCK FOR A FEW YEARS. I WAS, AS YOU'D PREDICTED, DOPED UP WORSE THAN A DUTCHESS ON A BENDER. THAT IS, UNTIL THE STARS N' BARS CAME A-CALLIN'.
THEY BLOODY DRAFTED ME. 'COURSE, WHEN THEY TOLD ME WHAT FOR, I COULDN'T HELP BUT CRACK A LITTLE SMILE...
THEY EVEN GOT A DAFT NAME FOR IT ...PROJECT: SUICIDE SQUAD.
THING IS... THEY NEEDED A TEST RUN. THEY NEEDED TO GO UP AGAINST SOMETHING BIG. AND, AS ACTING FIELD LEADER, THEY ASKED ME FOR SUGGESTIONS. I SUGGESTED YOU.
SO FAR, YOU'VE DONE OKAY. NOT A BAD SHOWING AGAINST THESE FREAKS...
I GUESS IT'S TIME TO BRING OUT THE FINAL SOLUTION...

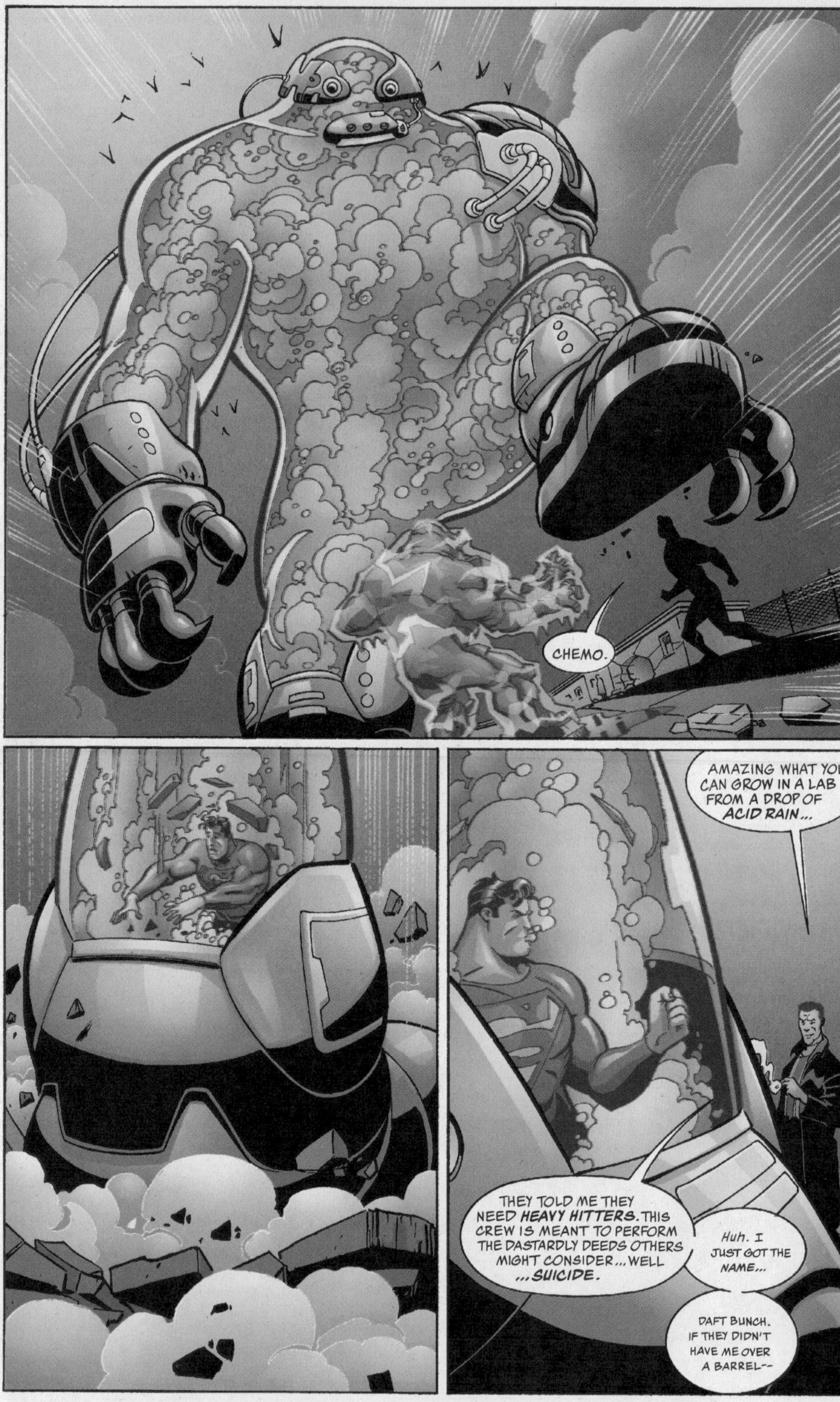
CHEMO.
AMAZING WHAT YOU CAN GROW IN A LAB FROM A DROP OF ACID RAIN...
THEY TOLD ME THEY NEED HEAVY HITTERS. THIS CREW IS MEANT TO PERFORM THE DASTARDLY DEEDS OTHERS MIGHT CONSIDER... WELL ...SUICIDE.
Huh. I JUST GOT THE NAME...
DAFT BUNCH. IF THEY DIDN'T HAVE ME OVER A BARREL--

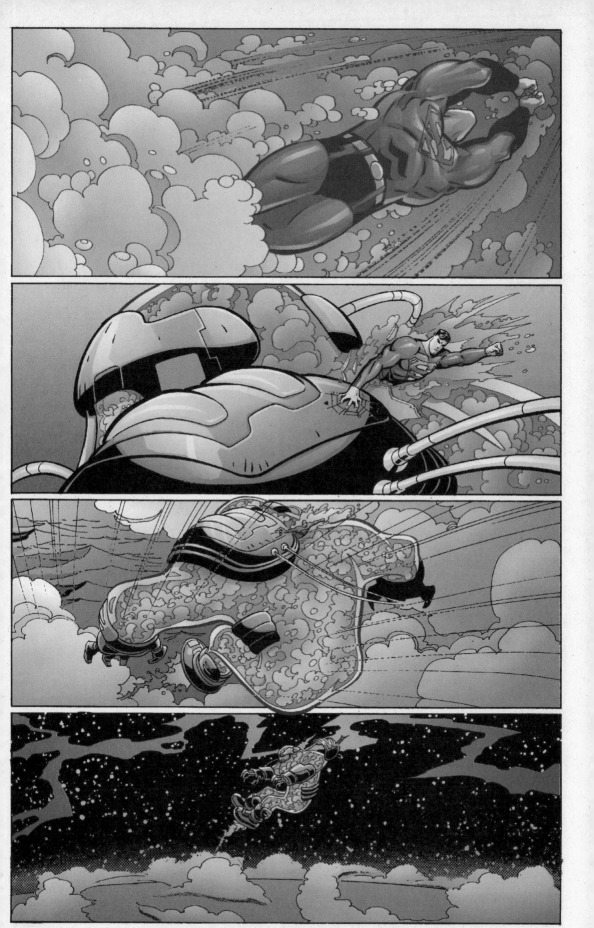

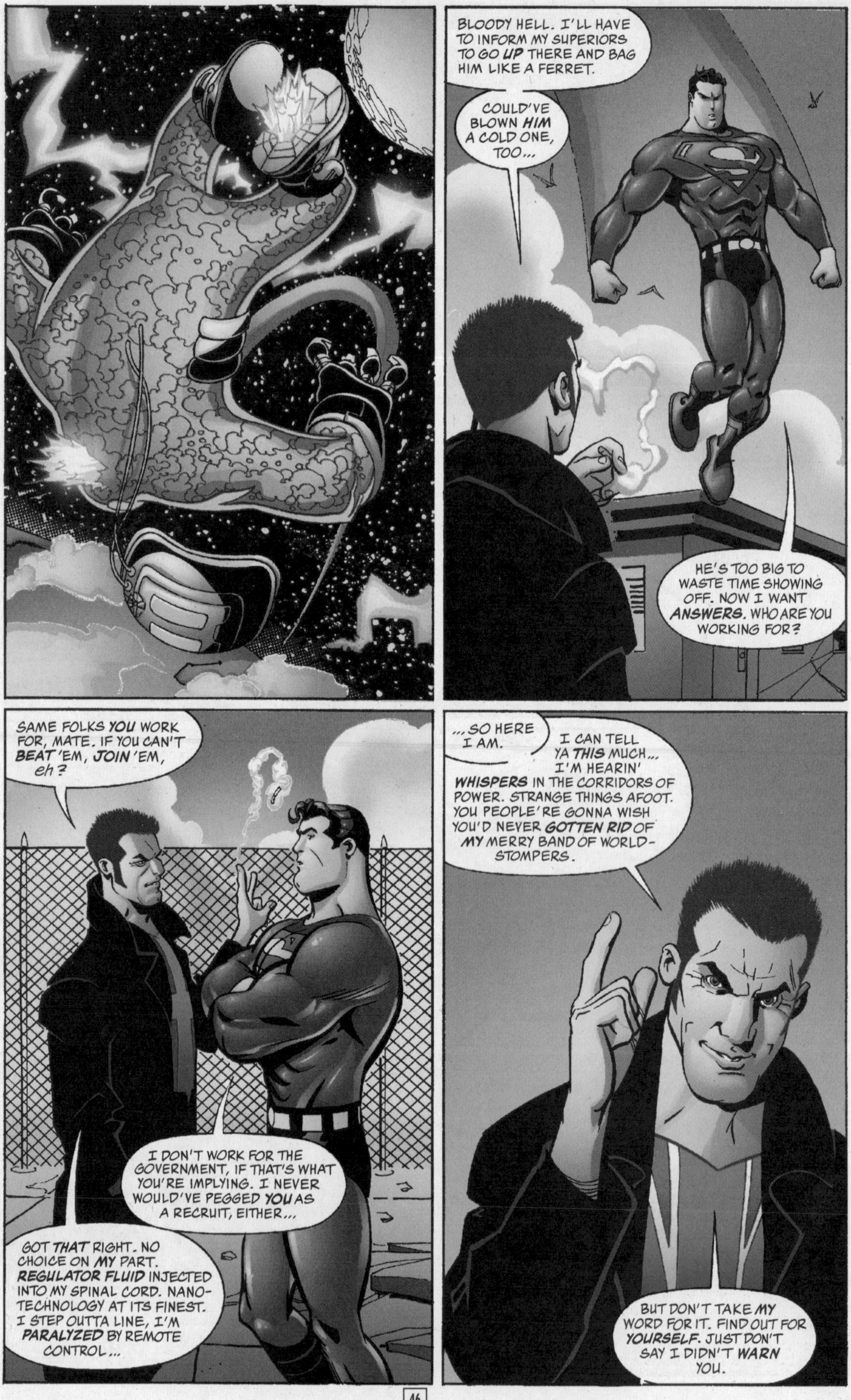
BLOODY HELL. I'LL HAVE TO INFORM MY SUPERIORS TO GO UP THERE AND BAG HIM LIKE A FERRET.
COULD'VE BLOWN HIM A COLD ONE, TOO...
HE'S TOO BIG TO WASTE TIME SHOWING OFF. NOW I WANT ANSWERS. WHO ARE YOU WORKING FOR?
SAME FOLKS YOU WORK FOR, MATE. IF YOU CAN'T BEAT 'EM, JOIN 'EM, eh?
I DON'T WORK FOR THE GOVERNMENT, IF THAT'S WHAT YOU'RE IMPLYING. I NEVER WOULD'VE PEGGED YOU AS A RECRUIT, EITHER...
GOT THAT RIGHT. NO CHOICE ON MY PART. REGULATOR FLUID INJECTED INTO MY SPINAL CORD. NANO-TECHNOLOGY AT ITS FINEST. I STEP OUTTA LINE, I'M PARALYZED BY REMOTE CONTROL...
...SO HERE I AM.
I CAN TELL YA THIS MUCH... I'M HEARIN' WHISPERS IN THE CORRIDORS OF POWER. STRANGE THINGS AFOOT. YOU PEOPLE'RE GONNA WISH YOU'D NEVER GOTTEN RID OF MY MERRY BAND OF WORLD-STOMPERS.
BUT DON'T TAKE MY WORD FOR IT. FIND OUT FOR YOURSELF. JUST DON'T SAY I DIDN'T WARN YOU.

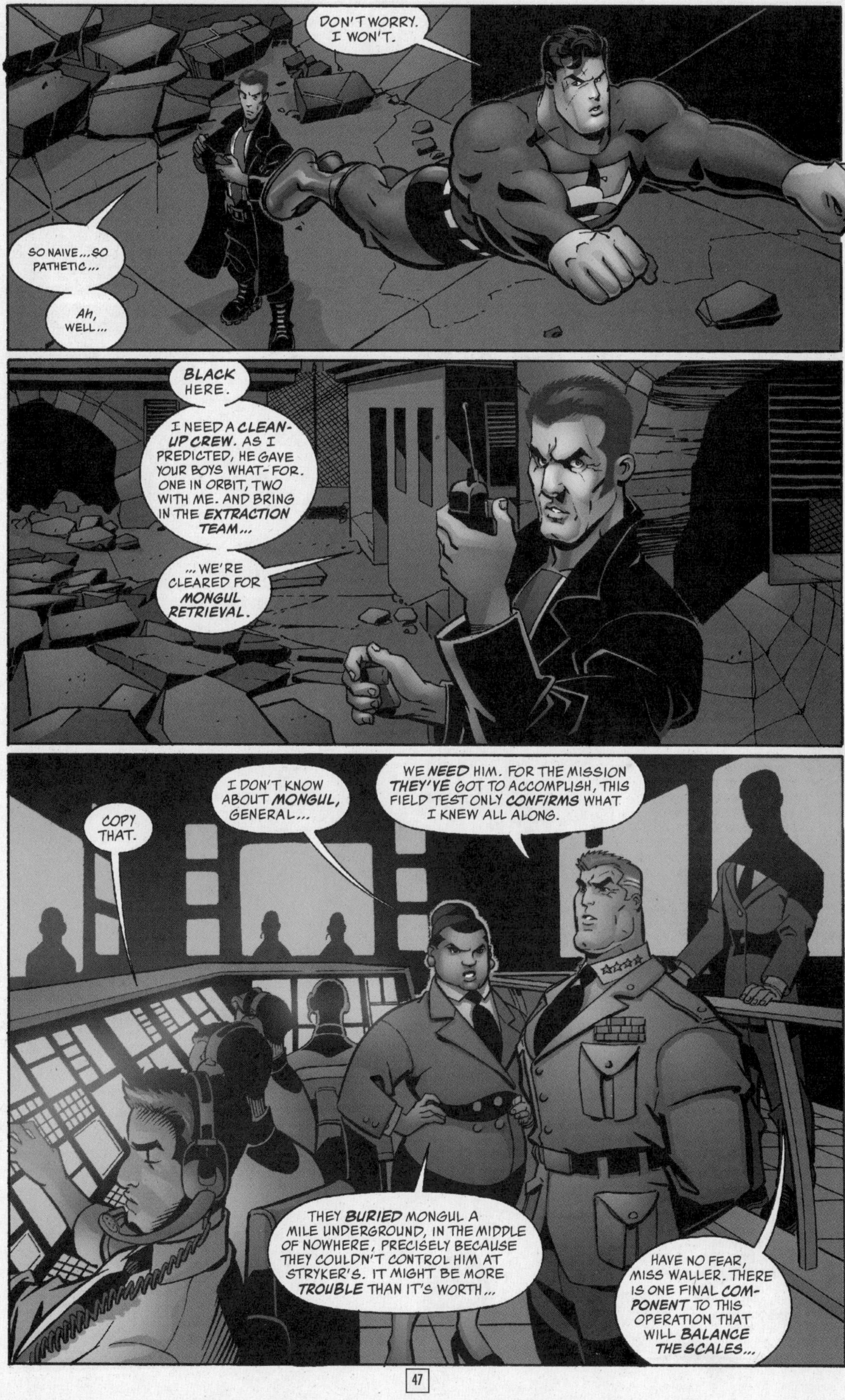
DON'T WORRY. I WON'T.
SO NAIVE...SO PATHETIC...
Ah, WELL...
BLACK HERE.
I NEED A CLEAN-UP CREW. AS I PREDICTED, HE GAVE YOUR BOYS WHAT-FOR. ONE IN ORBIT, TWO WITH ME. AND BRING IN THE EXTRACTION TEAM...
...WE'RE CLEARED FOR MONGUL RETRIEVAL.
COPY THAT.
I DON'T KNOW ABOUT MONGUL, GENERAL...
WE NEED HIM. FOR THE MISSION THEY'VE GOT TO ACCOMPLISH, THIS FIELD TEST ONLY CONFIRMS WHAT I KNEW ALL ALONG.
THEY BURIED MONGUL A MILE UNDERGROUND, IN THE MIDDLE OF NOWHERE, PRECISELY BECAUSE THEY COULDN'T CONTROL HIM AT STRYKER'S. IT MIGHT BE MORE TROUBLE THAN IT'S WORTH...
HAVE NO FEAR, MISS WALLER. THERE IS ONE FINAL COMPONENT TO THIS OPERATION THAT WILL BALANCE THE SCALES...

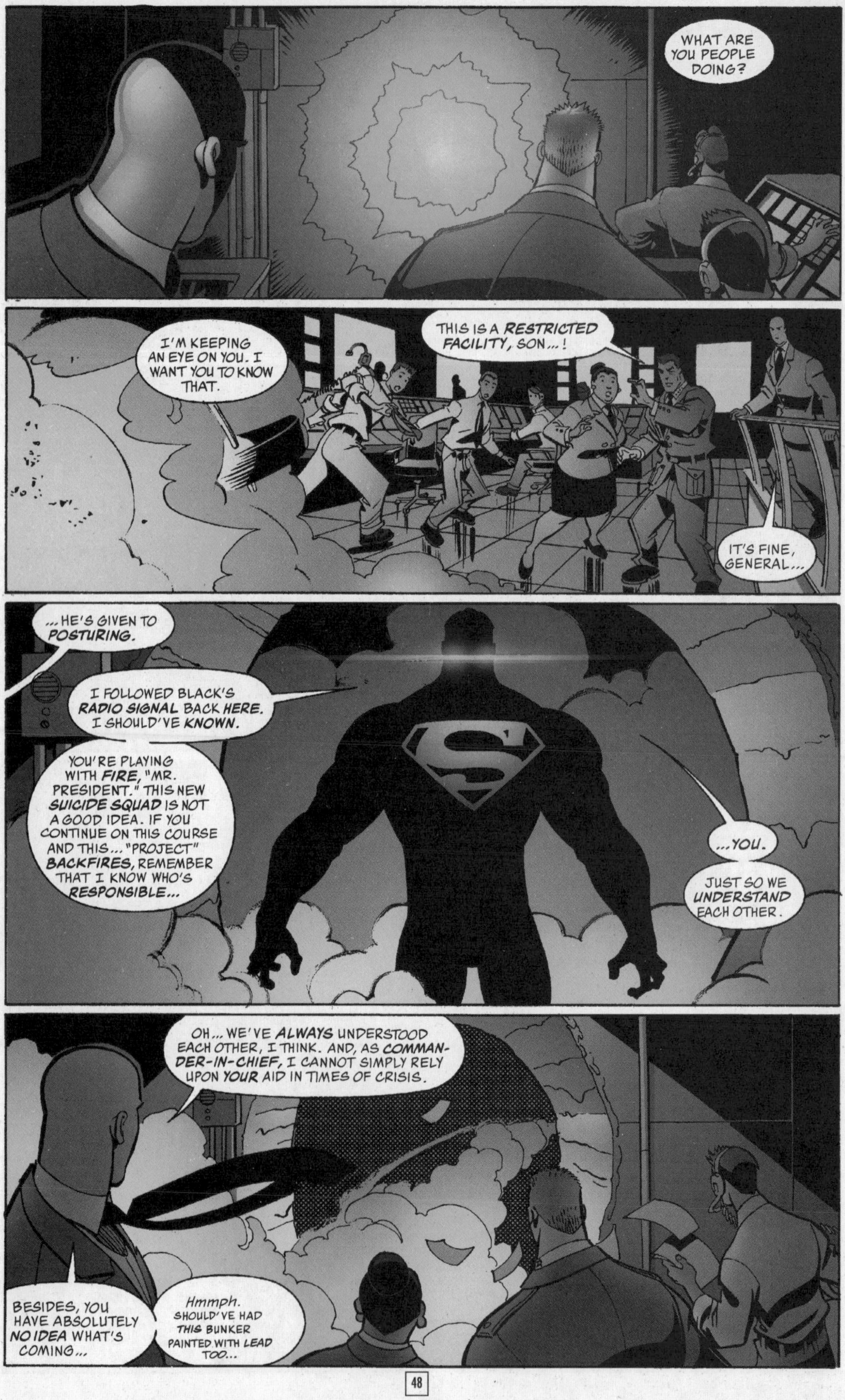
WHAT ARE YOU PEOPLE DOING?
I'M KEEPING AN EYE ON YOU. I WANT YOU TO KNOW THAT.
THIS IS A RESTRICTED FACILITY, SON...!
IT'S FINE, GENERAL...
...HE'S GIVEN TO POSTURING.
I FOLLOWED BLACK'S RADIO SIGNAL BACK HERE. I SHOULD'VE KNOWN.
YOU'RE PLAYING WITH FIRE, "MR. PRESIDENT." THIS NEW SUICIDE SQUAD IS NOT A GOOD IDEA. IF YOU CONTINUE ON THIS COURSE AND THIS... "PROJECT" BACKFIRES, REMEMBER THAT I KNOW WHO'S RESPONSIBLE...
...YOU.
JUST SO WE UNDERSTAND EACH OTHER.
OH... WE'VE ALWAYS UNDERSTOOD EACH OTHER, I THINK. AND, AS COMMANDER-IN-CHIEF, I CANNOT SIMPLY RELY UPON YOUR AID IN TIMES OF CRISIS.
BESIDES, YOU HAVE ABSOLUTELY NO IDEA WHAT'S COMING...
Hmmph. SHOULD'VE HAD THIS BUNKER PAINTED WITH LEAD TOO...

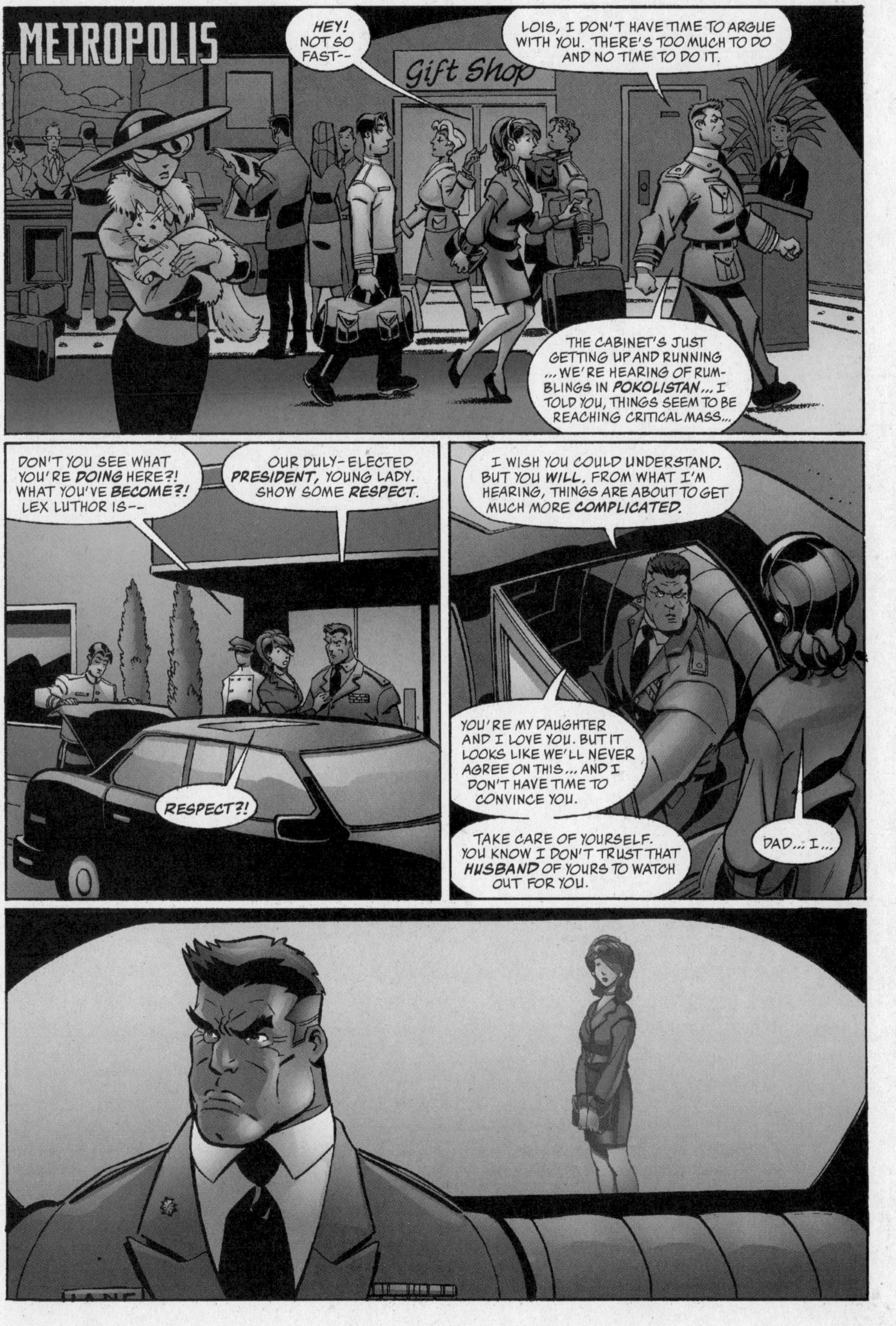
METROPOLIS
HEY! NOT SO FAST--
Gift Shop
LOIS, I DON'T HAVE TIME TO ARGUE WITH YOU. THERE'S TOO MUCH TO DO AND NO TIME TO DO IT.
THE CABINET'S JUST GETTING UP AND RUNNING ... WE'RE HEARING OF RUMBLINGS IN POKOLISTAN... I TOLD YOU, THINGS SEEM TO BE REACHING CRITICAL MASS...
DON'T YOU SEE WHAT YOU'RE DOING HERE?! WHAT YOU'VE BECOME?! LEX LUTHOR IS--
OUR DULY-ELECTED PRESIDENT, YOUNG LADY. SHOW SOME RESPECT.
RESPECT?!
I WISH YOU COULD UNDERSTAND. BUT YOU WILL. FROM WHAT I'M HEARING, THINGS ARE ABOUT TO GET MUCH MORE COMPLICATED.
YOU'RE MY DAUGHTER AND I LOVE YOU. BUT IT LOOKS LIKE WE'LL NEVER AGREE ON THIS ... AND I DON'T HAVE TIME TO CONVINCE YOU.
TAKE CARE OF YOURSELF. YOU KNOW I DON'T TRUST THAT HUSBAND OF YOURS TO WATCH OUT FOR YOU.
DAD... I...

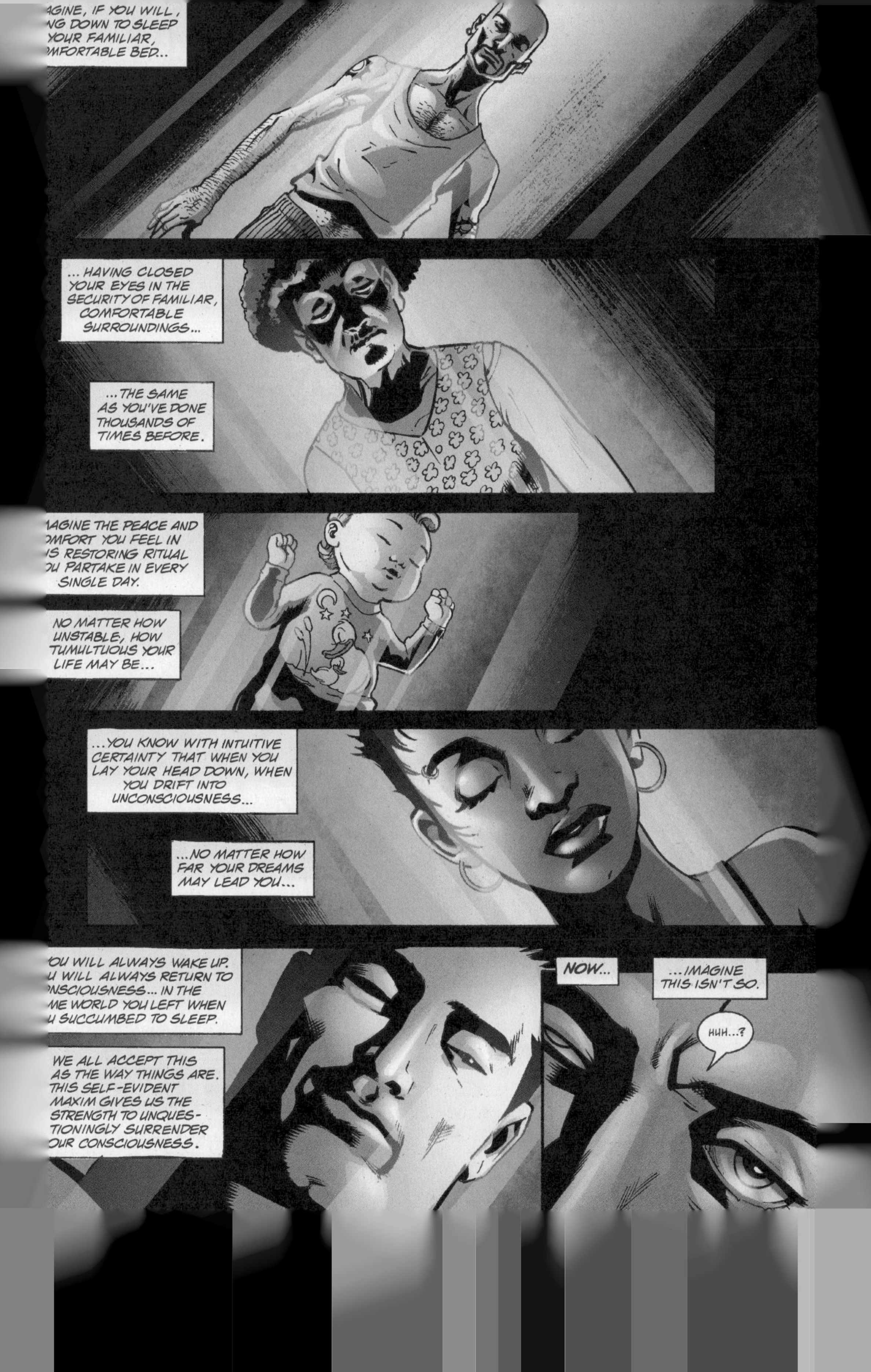
AGINE, IF YOU WILL, NG DOWN TO SLEEP YOUR FAMILIAR, OMFORTABLE BED...
... HAVING CLOSED YOUR EYES IN THE SECURITY OF FAMILIAR, COMFORTABLE SURROUNDINGS...
...THE SAME AS YOU'VE DONE THOUSANDS OF TIMES BEFORE.
AGINE THE PEACE AND OMFORT YOU FEEL IN S RESTORING RITUAL U PARTAKE IN EVERY SINGLE DAY.
NO MATTER HOW UNSTABLE, HOW TUMULTUOUS YOUR LIFE MAY BE...
...YOU KNOW WITH INTUITIVE CERTAINTY THAT WHEN YOU LAY YOUR HEAD DOWN, WHEN YOU DRIFT INTO UNCONSCIOUSNESS...
...NO MATTER HOW FAR YOUR DREAMS MAY LEAD YOU...
OU WILL ALWAYS WAKE UP. U WILL ALWAYS RETURN TO NSCIOUSNESS... IN THE ME WORLD YOU LEFT WHEN U SUCCUMBED TO SLEEP.
WE ALL ACCEPT THIS AS THE WAY THINGS ARE. THIS SELF-EVIDENT MAXIM GIVES US THE STRENGTH TO UNQUES-TIONINGLY SURRENDER OUR CONSCIOUSNESS.
NOW...
...IMAGINE THIS ISN'T SO.
HUH...?

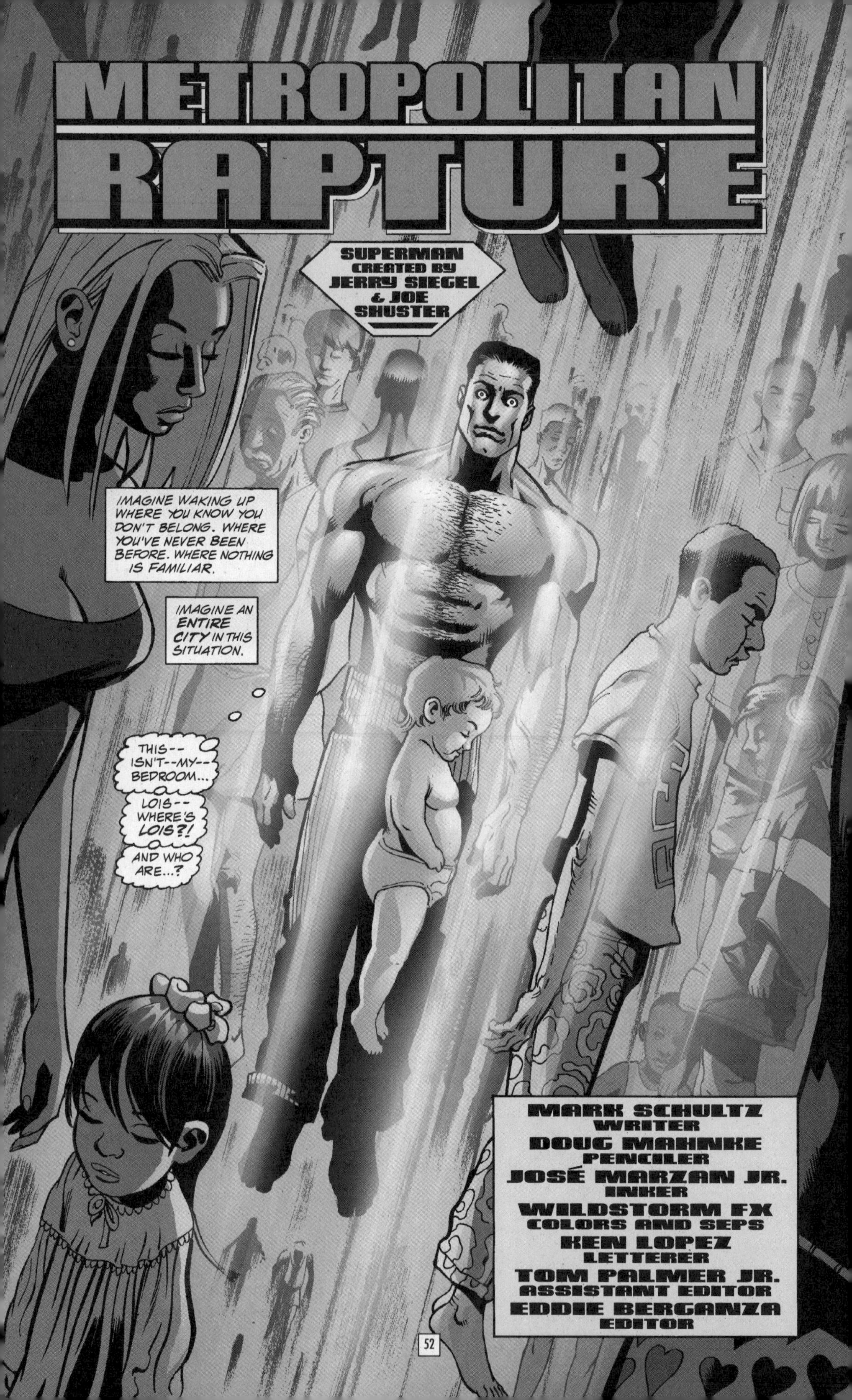

METROPOLITAN RAPTURE
SUPERMAN CREATED BY JERRY SIEGEL & JOE SHUSTER
IMAGINE WAKING UP WHERE YOU KNOW YOU DON'T BELONG. WHERE YOU'VE NEVER BEEN BEFORE. WHERE NOTHING IS FAMILIAR.
IMAGINE AN ENTIRE CITY IN THIS SITUATION.
THIS-- ISN'T--MY-- BEDROOM...
LOIS-- WHERE'S LOIS?!
AND WHO ARE...?
MARK SCHULTZ WRITER
DOUG MAHNKE PENCILER
JOSÉ MARZAN JR. INKER
WILDSTORM FX COLORS AND SEPS
KEN LOPEZ LETTERER
TOM PALMER JR. ASSISTANT EDITOR
EDDIE BERGANZA EDITOR

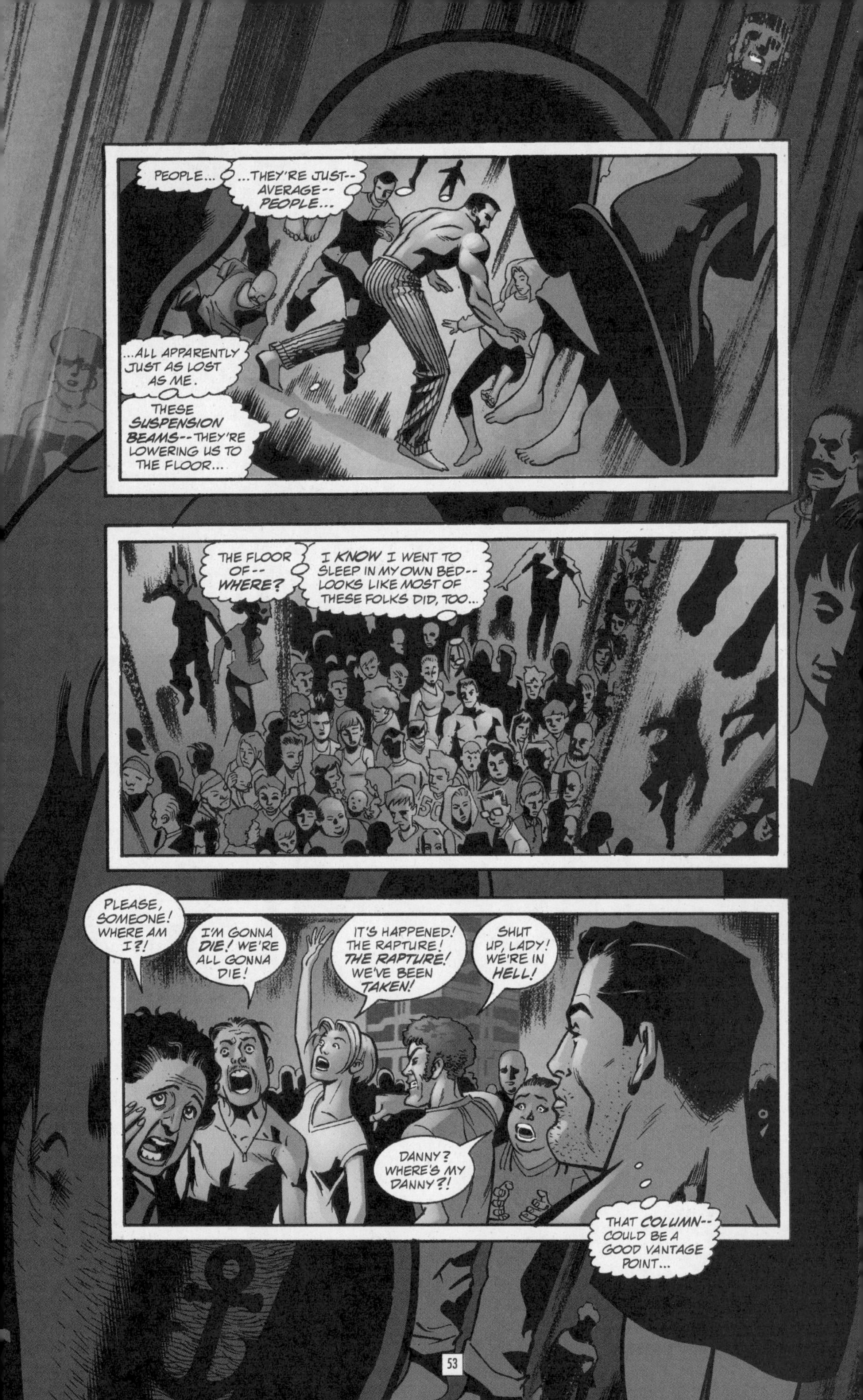
PEOPLE...
...THEY'RE JUST-- AVERAGE-- PEOPLE...
...ALL APPARENTLY JUST AS LOST AS ME.
THESE SUSPENSION BEAMS--THEY'RE LOWERING US TO THE FLOOR...
THE FLOOR OF-- WHERE?
I KNOW I WENT TO SLEEP IN MY OWN BED-- LOOKS LIKE MOST OF THESE FOLKS DID, TOO...
PLEASE, SOMEONE! WHERE AM I?!
I'M GONNA DIE! WE'RE ALL GONNA DIE!
IT'S HAPPENED! THE RAPTURE! THE RAPTURE! WE'VE BEEN TAKEN!
SHUT UP, LADY! WE'RE IN HELL!
DANNY? WHERE'S MY DANNY?!
THAT COLUMN-- COULD BE A GOOD VANTAGE POINT...

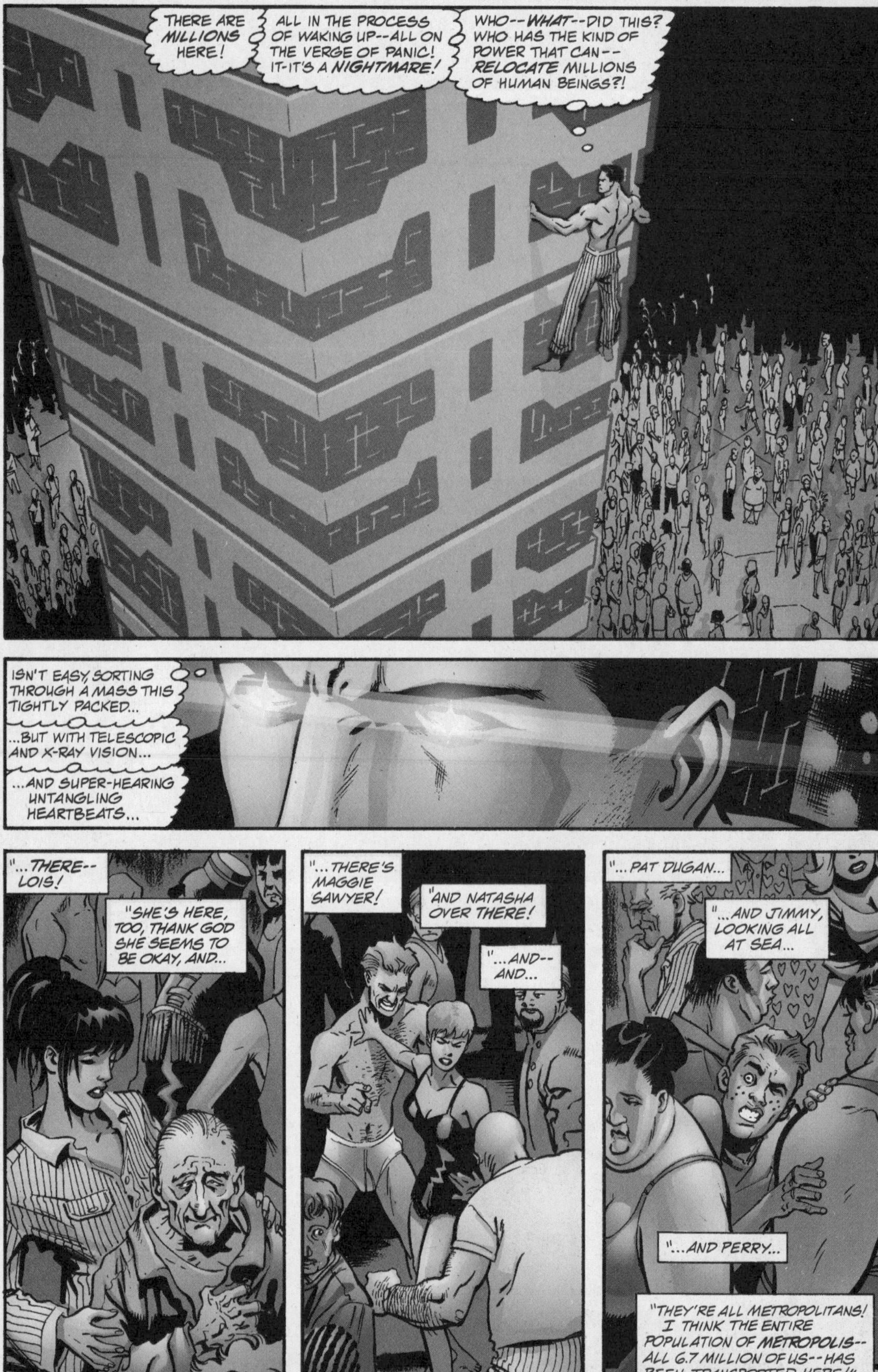
THERE ARE MILLIONS HERE!
ALL IN THE PROCESS OF WAKING UP--ALL ON THE VERGE OF PANIC! IT-IT'S A NIGHTMARE!
WHO--WHAT--DID THIS? WHO HAS THE KIND OF POWER THAT CAN--RELOCATE MILLIONS OF HUMAN BEINGS?!
ISN'T EASY, SORTING THROUGH A MASS THIS TIGHTLY PACKED...
...BUT WITH TELESCOPIC AND X-RAY VISION...
...AND SUPER-HEARING UNTANGLING HEARTBEATS...
"...THERE--LOIS!
"SHE'S HERE, TOO, THANK GOD SHE SEEMS TO BE OKAY, AND...
"...THERE'S MAGGIE SAWYER!
"AND NATASHA OVER THERE!
"...AND--AND...
"...PAT DUGAN...
"...AND JIMMY, LOOKING ALL AT SEA...
"...AND PERRY...
"THEY'RE ALL METROPOLITANS! I THINK THE ENTIRE POPULATION OF METROPOLIS--ALL 6.7 MILLION OF US--HAS BEEN TRANSPORTED HERE!"

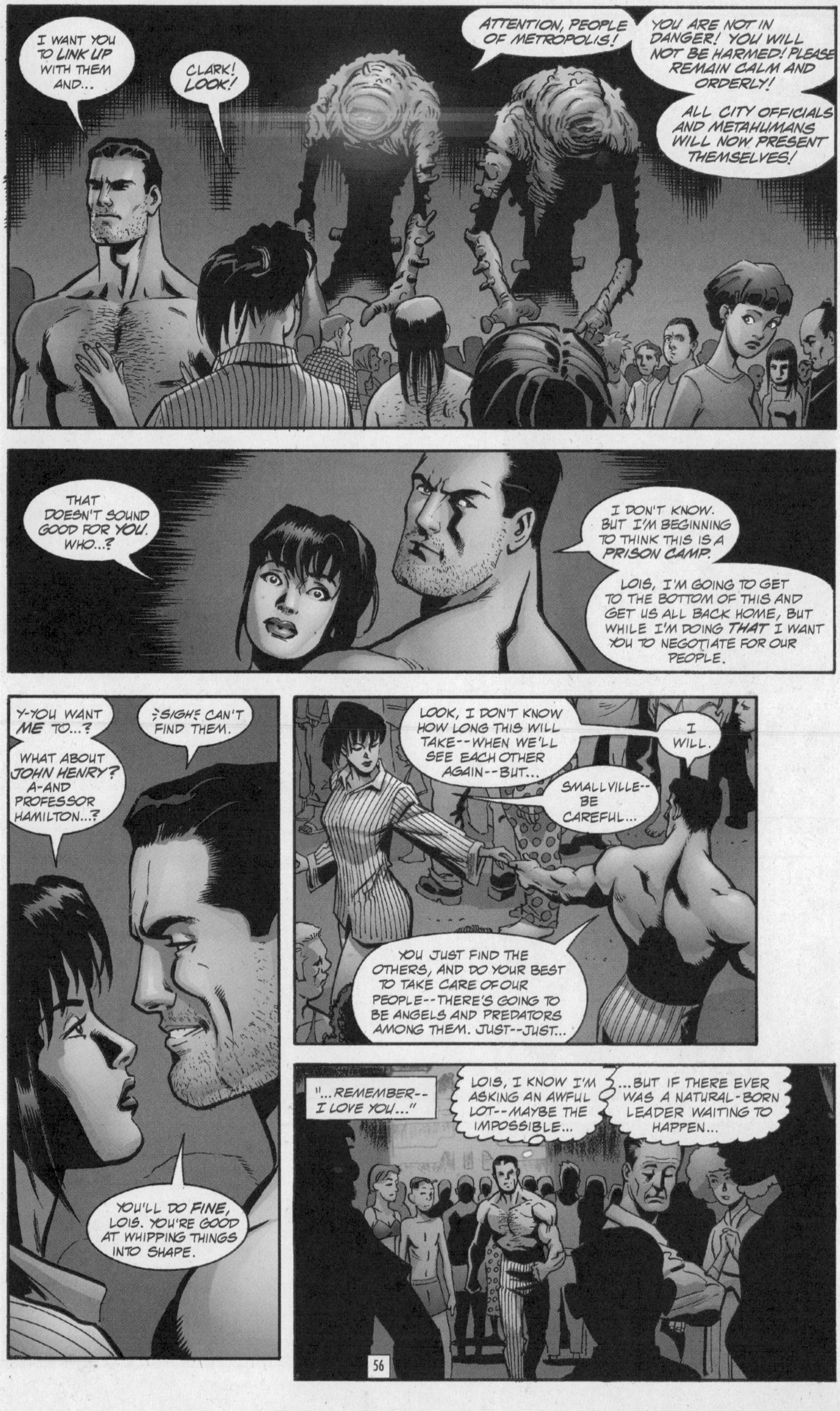

I WANT YOU TO LINK UP WITH THEM AND...
CLARK! LOOK!
ATTENTION, PEOPLE OF METROPOLIS!
YOU ARE NOT IN DANGER! YOU WILL NOT BE HARMED! PLEASE REMAIN CALM AND ORDERLY!
ALL CITY OFFICIALS AND METAHUMANS WILL NOW PRESENT THEMSELVES!
THAT DOESN'T SOUND GOOD FOR YOU. WHO...?
I DON'T KNOW. BUT I'M BEGINNING TO THINK THIS IS A PRISON CAMP.
LOIS, I'M GOING TO GET TO THE BOTTOM OF THIS AND GET US ALL BACK HOME, BUT WHILE I'M DOING THAT I WANT YOU TO NEGOTIATE FOR OUR PEOPLE.
Y-YOU WANT ME TO...?
WHAT ABOUT JOHN HENRY? A-AND PROFESSOR HAMILTON...?
SIGH CAN'T FIND THEM.
YOU'LL DO FINE, LOIS. YOU'RE GOOD AT WHIPPING THINGS INTO SHAPE.
LOOK, I DON'T KNOW HOW LONG THIS WILL TAKE--WHEN WE'LL SEE EACH OTHER AGAIN--BUT...
I WILL.
SMALLVILLE-- BE CAREFUL...
YOU JUST FIND THE OTHERS, AND DO YOUR BEST TO TAKE CARE OF OUR PEOPLE--THERE'S GOING TO BE ANGELS AND PREDATORS AMONG THEM. JUST--JUST...
"...REMEMBER-- I LOVE YOU..."
LOIS, I KNOW I'M ASKING AN AWFUL LOT--MAYBE THE IMPOSSIBLE...
...BUT IF THERE EVER WAS A NATURAL-BORN LEADER WAITING TO HAPPEN...

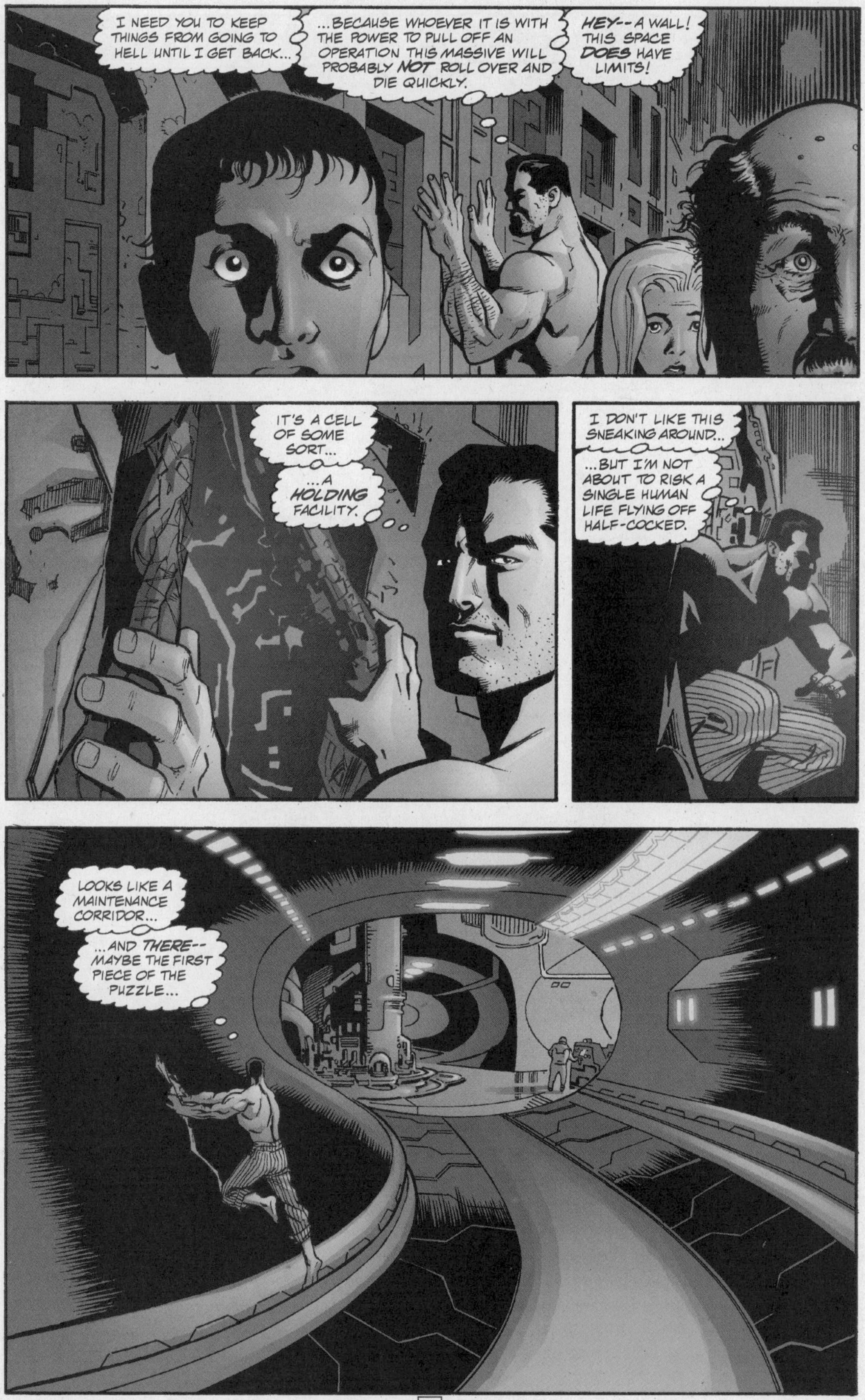
I NEED YOU TO KEEP THINGS FROM GOING TO HELL UNTIL I GET BACK...
...BECAUSE WHOEVER IT IS WITH THE POWER TO PULL OFF AN OPERATION THIS MASSIVE WILL PROBABLY NOT ROLL OVER AND DIE QUICKLY.
HEY--A WALL! THIS SPACE DOES HAVE LIMITS!
IT'S A CELL OF SOME SORT...
...A HOLDING FACILITY.
I DON'T LIKE THIS SNEAKING AROUND...
...BUT I'M NOT ABOUT TO RISK A SINGLE HUMAN LIFE FLYING OFF HALF-COCKED.
LOOKS LIKE A MAINTENANCE CORRIDOR...
...AND THERE--MAYBE THE FIRST PIECE OF THE PUZZLE...

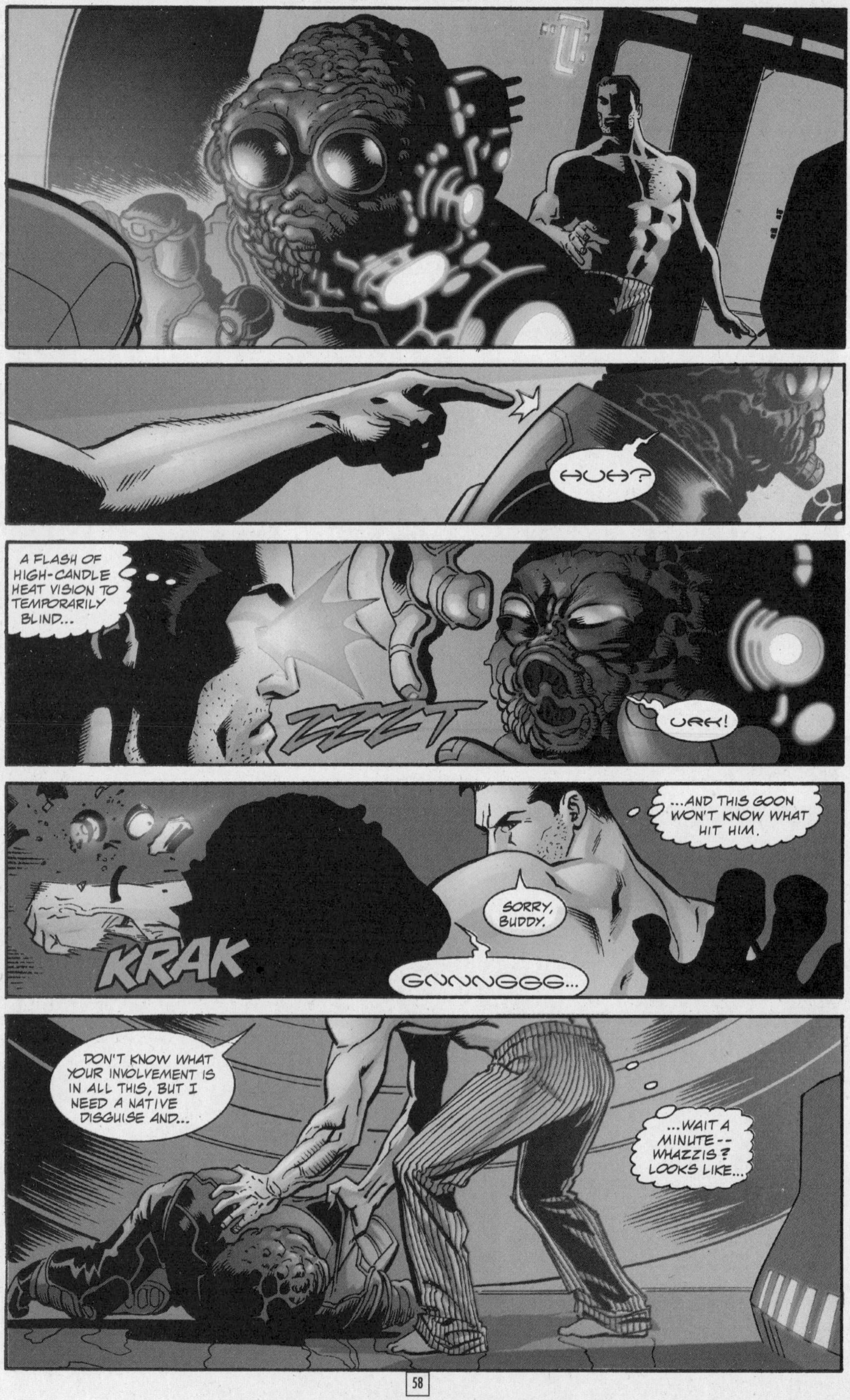

HUH?
A FLASH OF HIGH-CANDLE HEAT VISION TO TEMPORARILY BLIND...
ZZZT
URK!
...AND THIS GOON WON'T KNOW WHAT HIT HIM.
SORRY, BUDDY.
KRAK
GNNNGGG...
DON'T KNOW WHAT YOUR INVOLVEMENT IS IN ALL THIS, BUT I NEED A NATIVE DISGUISE AND...
...WAIT A MINUTE-- WHAZZIS? LOOKS LIKE...

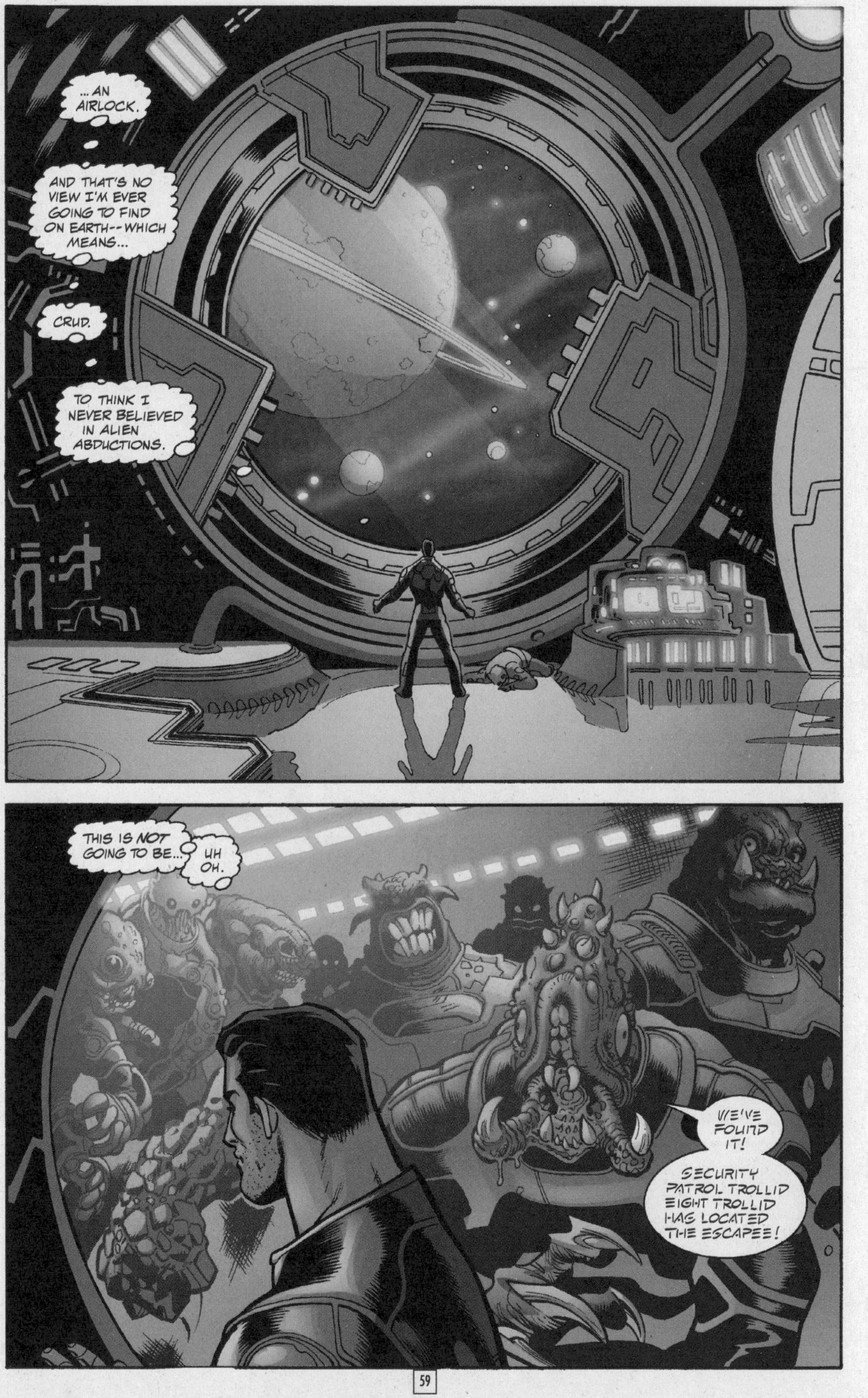
...AN AIRLOCK.
AND THAT'S NO VIEW I'M EVER GOING TO FIND ON EARTH--WHICH MEANS...
CRUD.
TO THINK I NEVER BELIEVED IN ALIEN ABDUCTIONS.
THIS IS NOT GOING TO BE...
UH OH.
WE'VE FOUND IT!
SECURITY PATROL TROLLID EIGHT TROLLID HAS LOCATED THE ESCAPEE!

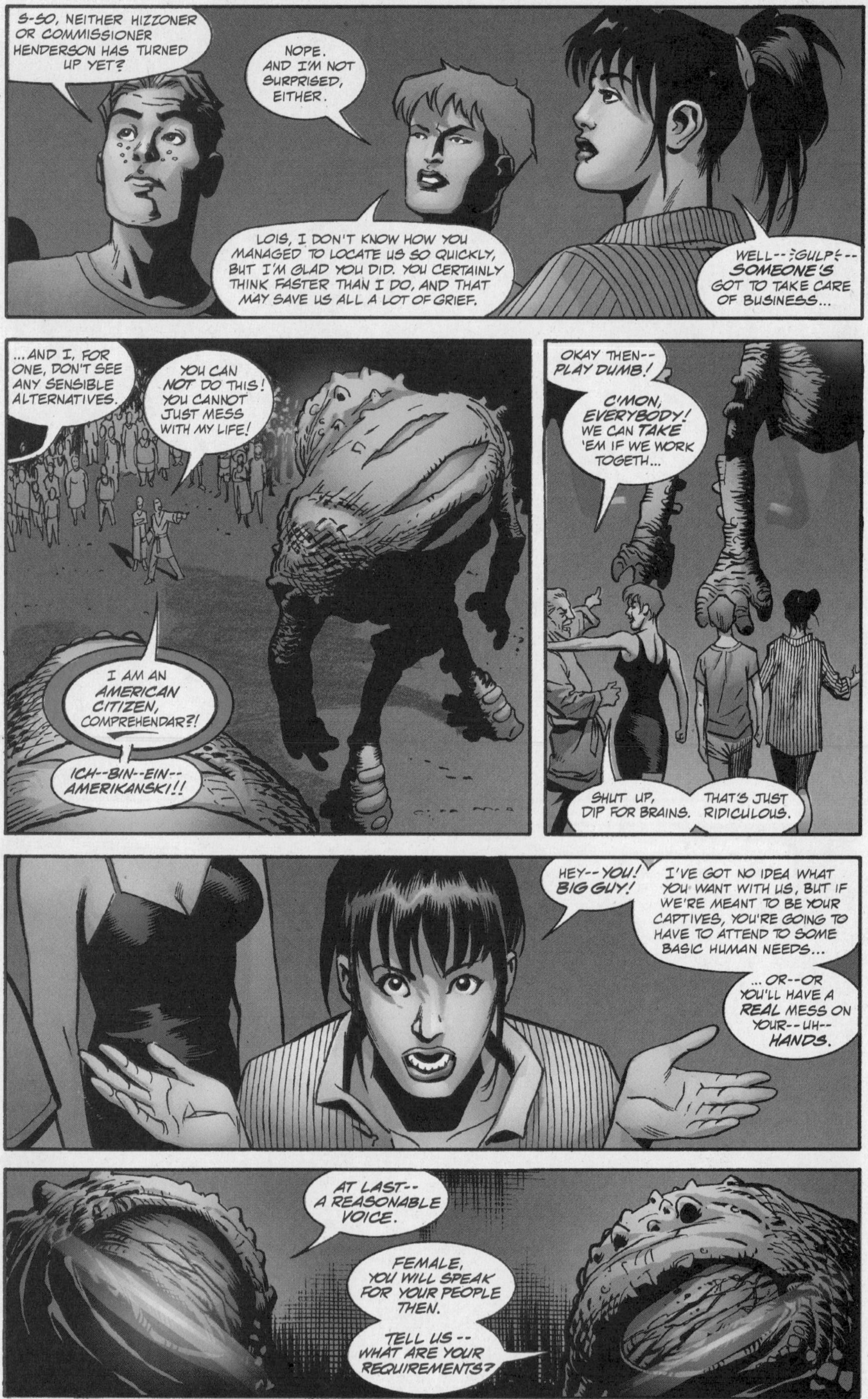
S-SO, NEITHER HIZZONER OR COMMISSIONER HENDERSON HAS TURNED UP YET?
NOPE. AND I'M NOT SURPRISED, EITHER.
LOIS, I DON'T KNOW HOW YOU MANAGED TO LOCATE US SO QUICKLY, BUT I'M GLAD YOU DID. YOU CERTAINLY THINK FASTER THAN I DO, AND THAT MAY SAVE US ALL A LOT OF GRIEF.
WELL-- GULP -- SOMEONE'S GOT TO TAKE CARE OF BUSINESS...
...AND I, FOR ONE, DON'T SEE ANY SENSIBLE ALTERNATIVES.
YOU CAN NOT DO THIS! YOU CANNOT JUST MESS WITH MY LIFE!
I AM AN AMERICAN CITIZEN, COMPREHENDAR?!
ICH--BIN--EIN--AMERIKANSKI!!
OKAY THEN-- PLAY DUMB!
C'MON, EVERYBODY! WE CAN TAKE 'EM IF WE WORK TOGETH...
SHUT UP, DIP FOR BRAINS.
THAT'S JUST RIDICULOUS.
HEY-- YOU! BIG GUY!
I'VE GOT NO IDEA WHAT YOU WANT WITH US, BUT IF WE'RE MEANT TO BE YOUR CAPTIVES, YOU'RE GOING TO HAVE TO ATTEND TO SOME BASIC HUMAN NEEDS...
...OR--OR YOU'LL HAVE A REAL MESS ON YOUR--UH-- HANDS.
AT LAST-- A REASONABLE VOICE.
FEMALE, YOU WILL SPEAK FOR YOUR PEOPLE THEN.
TELL US-- WHAT ARE YOUR REQUIREMENTS?

GGGGGHHH!!

ZZZT

BRONK

VVVP!

GNARRGH...

KRUNCH

THIS IS ABSURD. I'VE LOST THE ELEMENT OF SURPRISE, SO I CAN'T WASTE TIME *FINESSING* THESE DRONES...

...BUT I CAN'T REALLY CUT LOOSE IN HERE WITHOUT RISK TO LIFE-SUPPORT SYSTEMS...

ZZAT

...BUT SINCE WE'RE ALL WEARING OUR *SPACE SUITS* ANYWAY...

ZZZAT

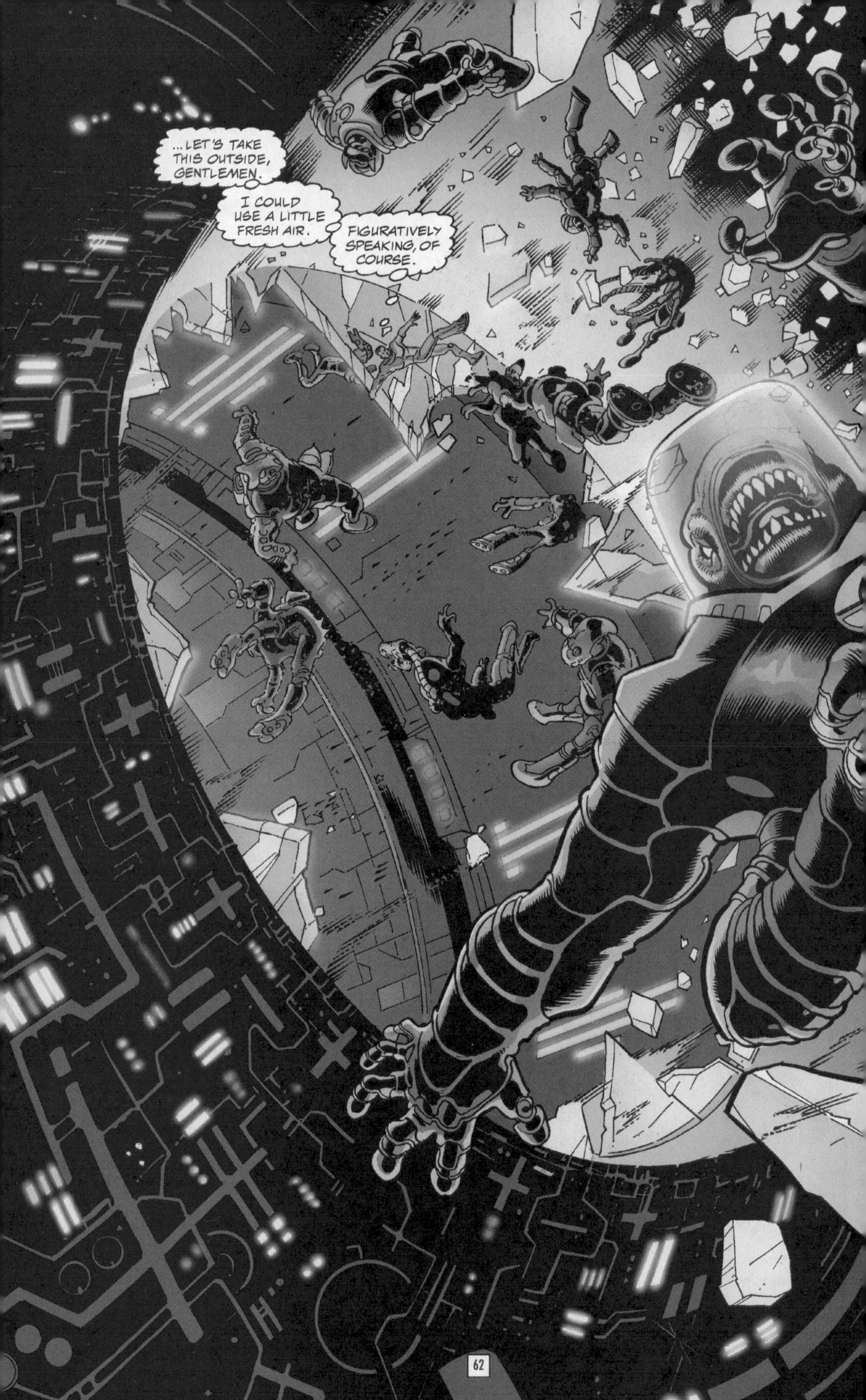
...LET'S TAKE THIS OUTSIDE, GENTLEMEN.
I COULD USE A LITTLE FRESH AIR.
FIGURATIVELY SPEAKING, OF COURSE.

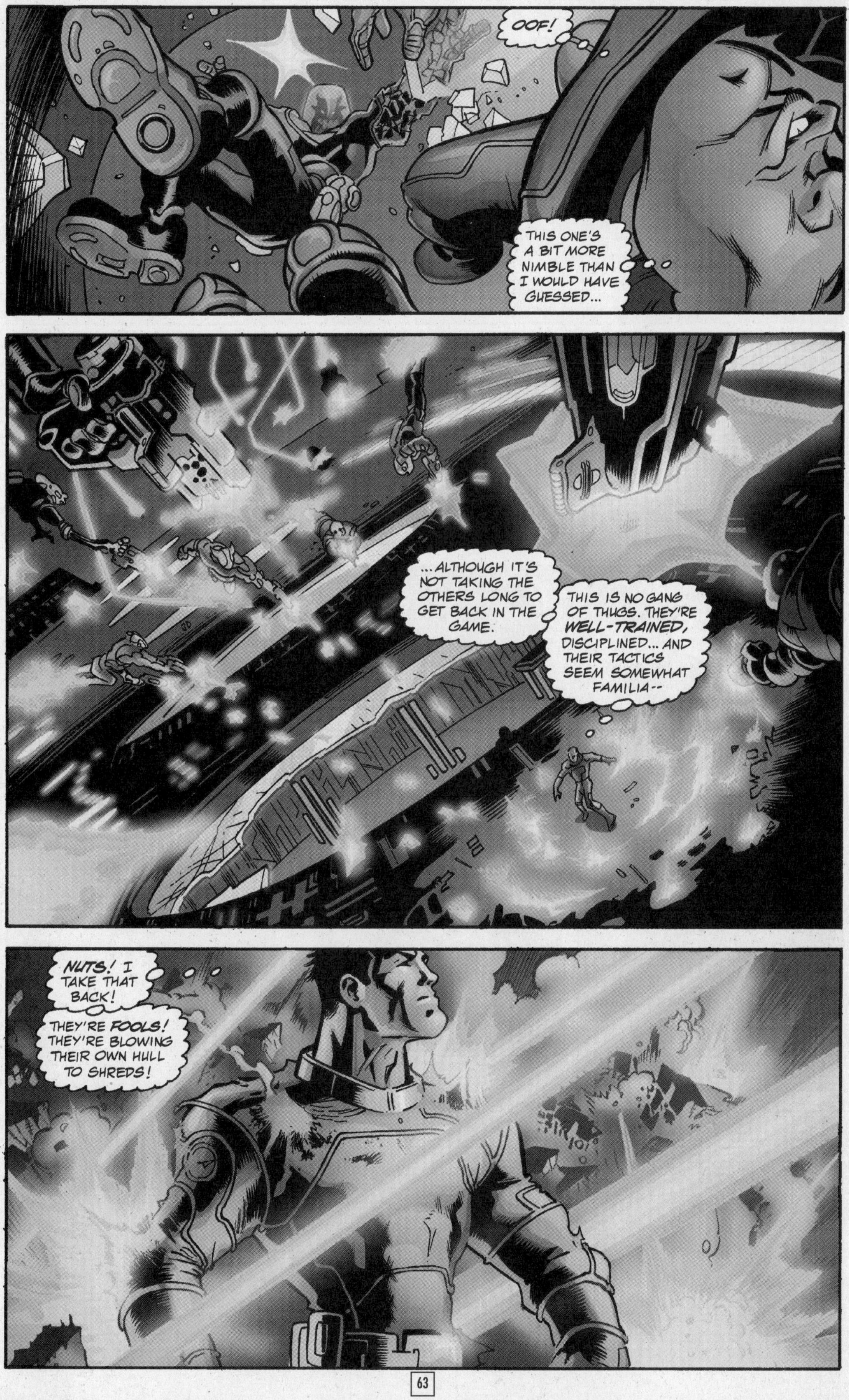
OOF!
THIS ONE'S A BIT MORE NIMBLE THAN I WOULD HAVE GUESSED...
...ALTHOUGH IT'S NOT TAKING THE OTHERS LONG TO GET BACK IN THE GAME.
THIS IS NO GANG OF THUGS. THEY'RE WELL-TRAINED, DISCIPLINED... AND THEIR TACTICS SEEM SOMEWHAT FAMILIA--
NUTS! I TAKE THAT BACK!
THEY'RE FOOLS! THEY'RE BLOWING THEIR OWN HULL TO SHREDS!

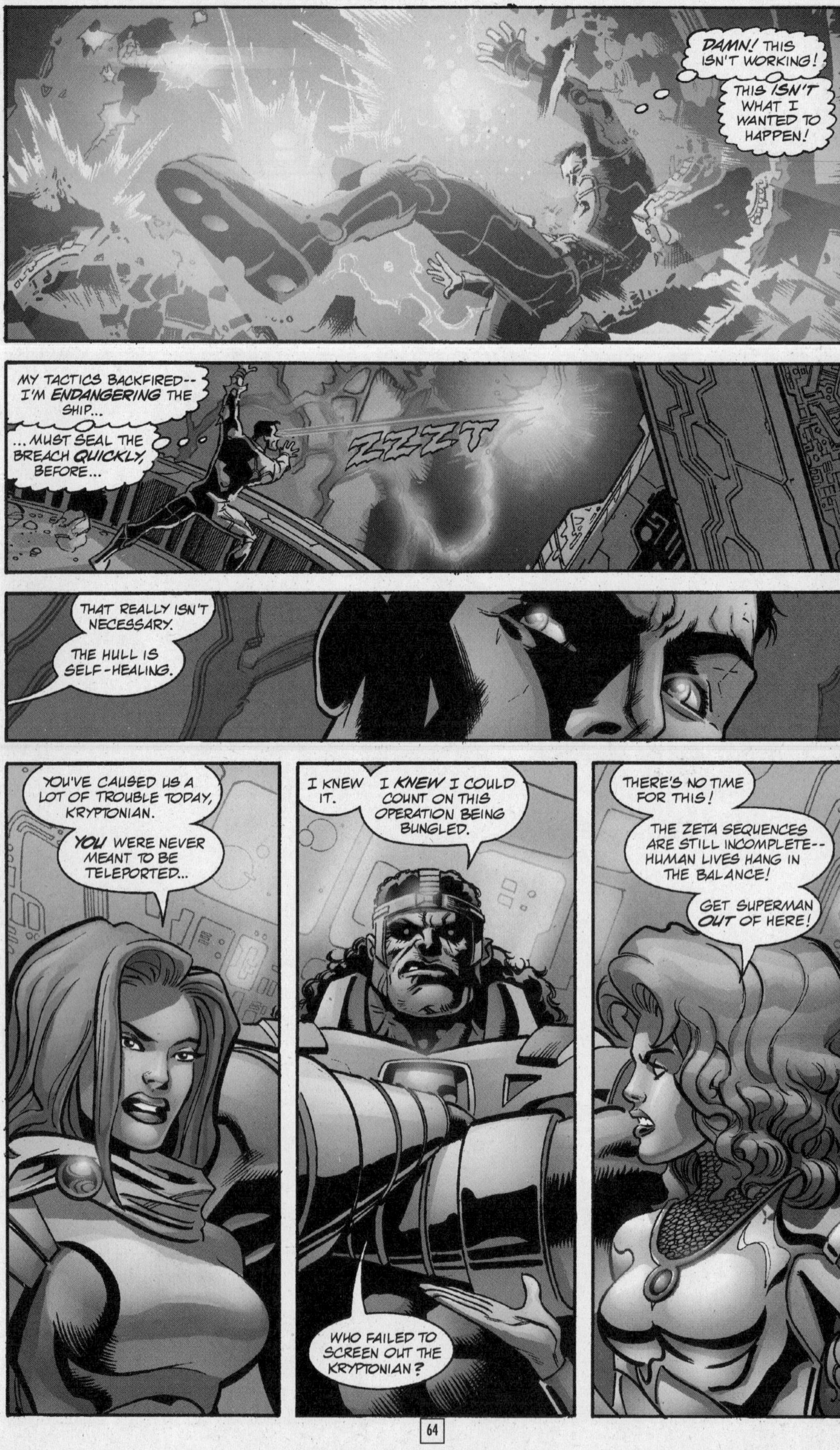
DAMN! THIS ISN'T WORKING!
THIS ISN'T WHAT I WANTED TO HAPPEN!
MY TACTICS BACKFIRED-- I'M ENDANGERING THE SHIP...
...MUST SEAL THE BREACH QUICKLY, BEFORE...
ZZZT
THAT REALLY ISN'T NECESSARY.
THE HULL IS SELF-HEALING.
YOU'VE CAUSED US A LOT OF TROUBLE TODAY, KRYPTONIAN.
YOU WERE NEVER MEANT TO BE TELEPORTED...
I KNEW IT.
I KNEW I COULD COUNT ON THIS OPERATION BEING BUNGLED.
WHO FAILED TO SCREEN OUT THE KRYPTONIAN?
THERE'S NO TIME FOR THIS!
THE ZETA SEQUENCES ARE STILL INCOMPLETE-- HUMAN LIVES HANG IN THE BALANCE!
GET SUPERMAN OUT OF HERE!

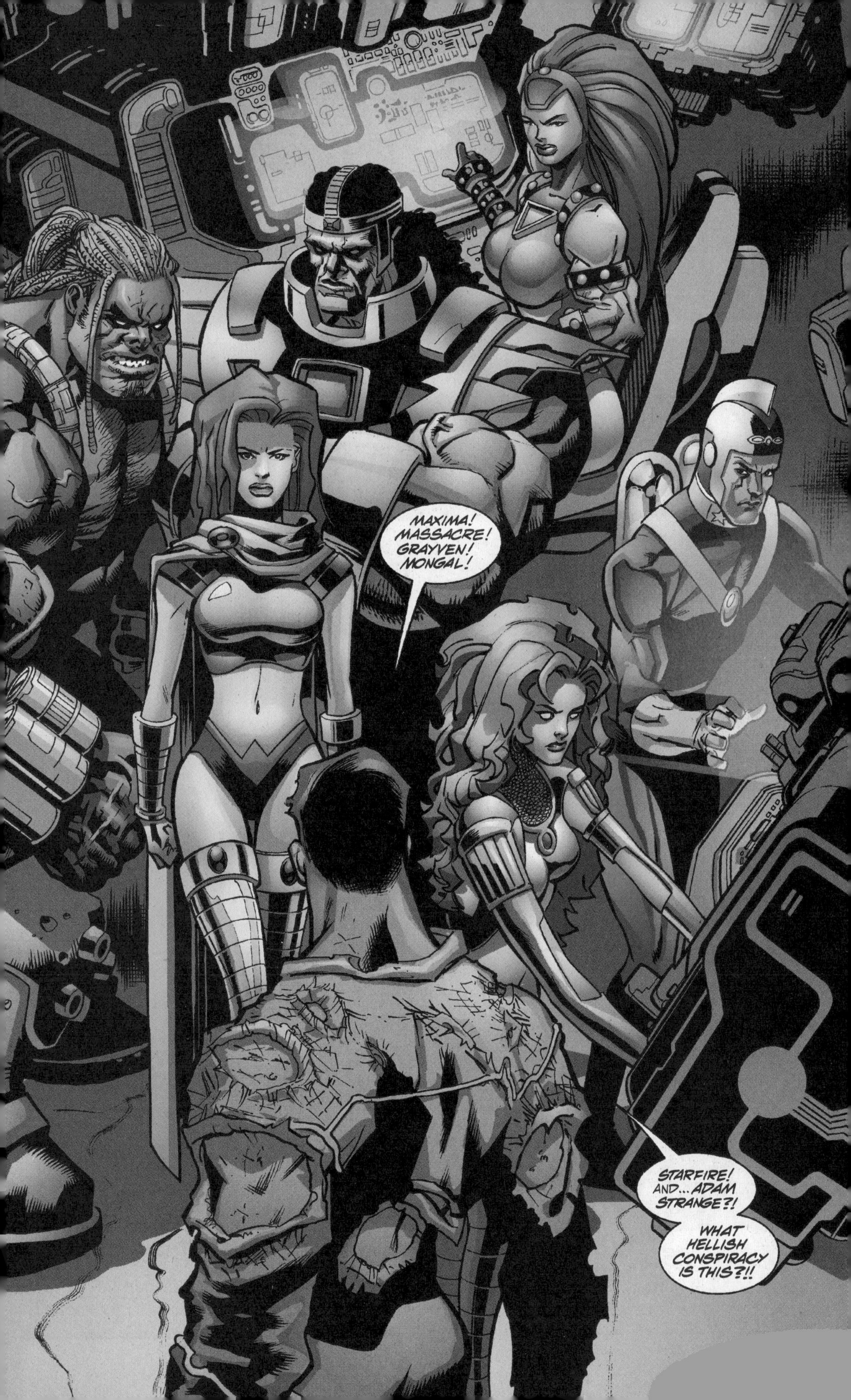
MAXIMA! MASSACRE! GRAYVEN! MONGAL!
STARFIRE! AND... ADAM STRANGE?!
WHAT HELLISH CONSPIRACY IS THIS?!!

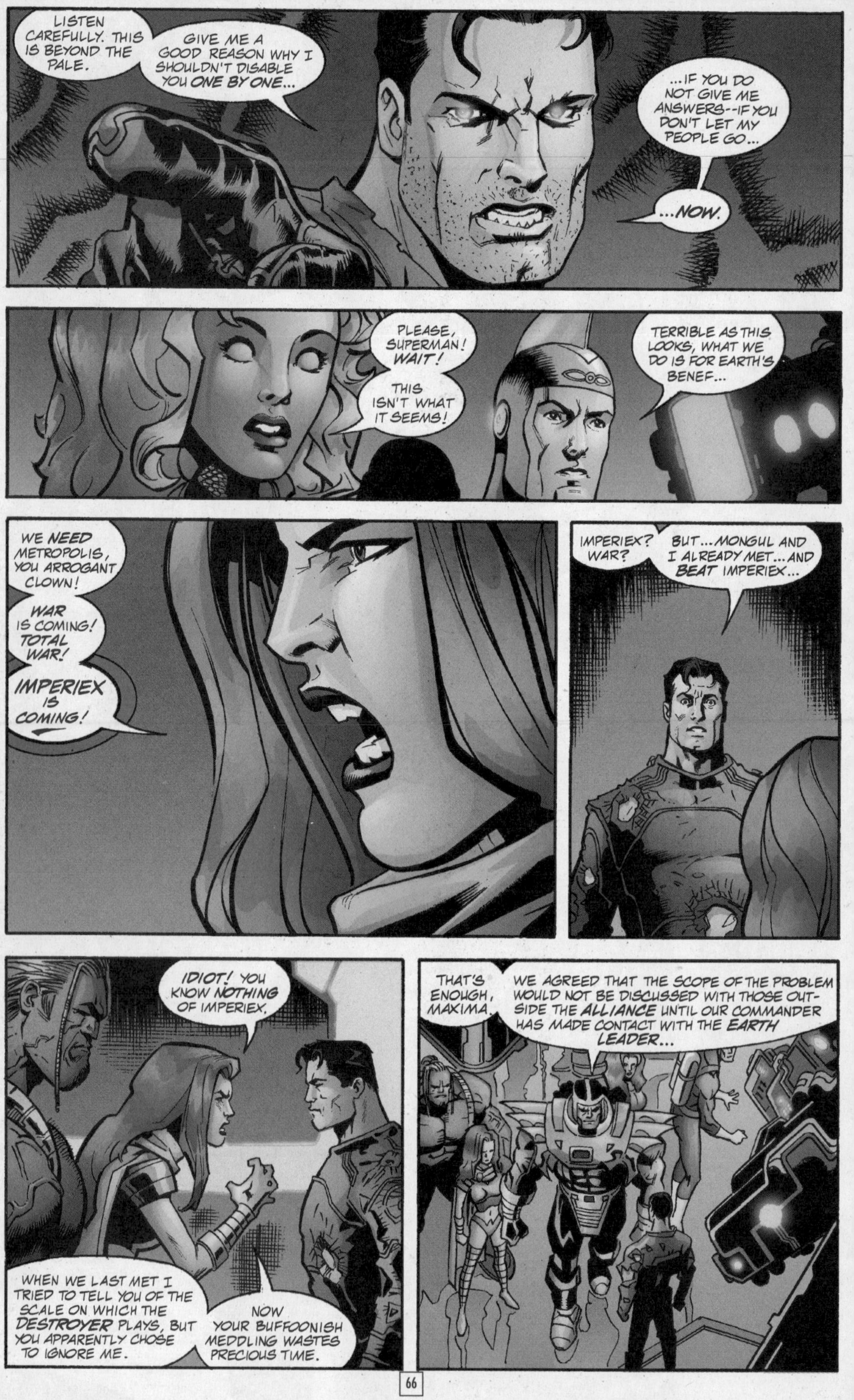
LISTEN CAREFULLY. THIS IS BEYOND THE PALE.
GIVE ME A GOOD REASON WHY I SHOULDN'T DISABLE YOU ONE BY ONE...
...IF YOU DO NOT GIVE ME ANSWERS--IF YOU DON'T LET MY PEOPLE GO...
...NOW.
PLEASE, SUPERMAN! WAIT!
THIS ISN'T WHAT IT SEEMS!
TERRIBLE AS THIS LOOKS, WHAT WE DO IS FOR EARTH'S BENEF...
WE NEED METROPOLIS, YOU ARROGANT CLOWN!
WAR IS COMING! TOTAL WAR!
IMPERIEX IS COMING!
IMPERIEX? WAR?
BUT...MONGUL AND I ALREADY MET...AND BEAT IMPERIEX...
IDIOT! YOU KNOW NOTHING OF IMPERIEX.
WHEN WE LAST MET I TRIED TO TELL YOU OF THE SCALE ON WHICH THE DESTROYER PLAYS, BUT YOU APPARENTLY CHOSE TO IGNORE ME.
NOW YOUR BUFFOONISH MEDDLING WASTES PRECIOUS TIME.
THAT'S ENOUGH, MAXIMA.
WE AGREED THAT THE SCOPE OF THE PROBLEM WOULD NOT BE DISCUSSED WITH THOSE OUTSIDE THE ALLIANCE UNTIL OUR COMMANDER HAS MADE CONTACT WITH THE EARTH LEADER...

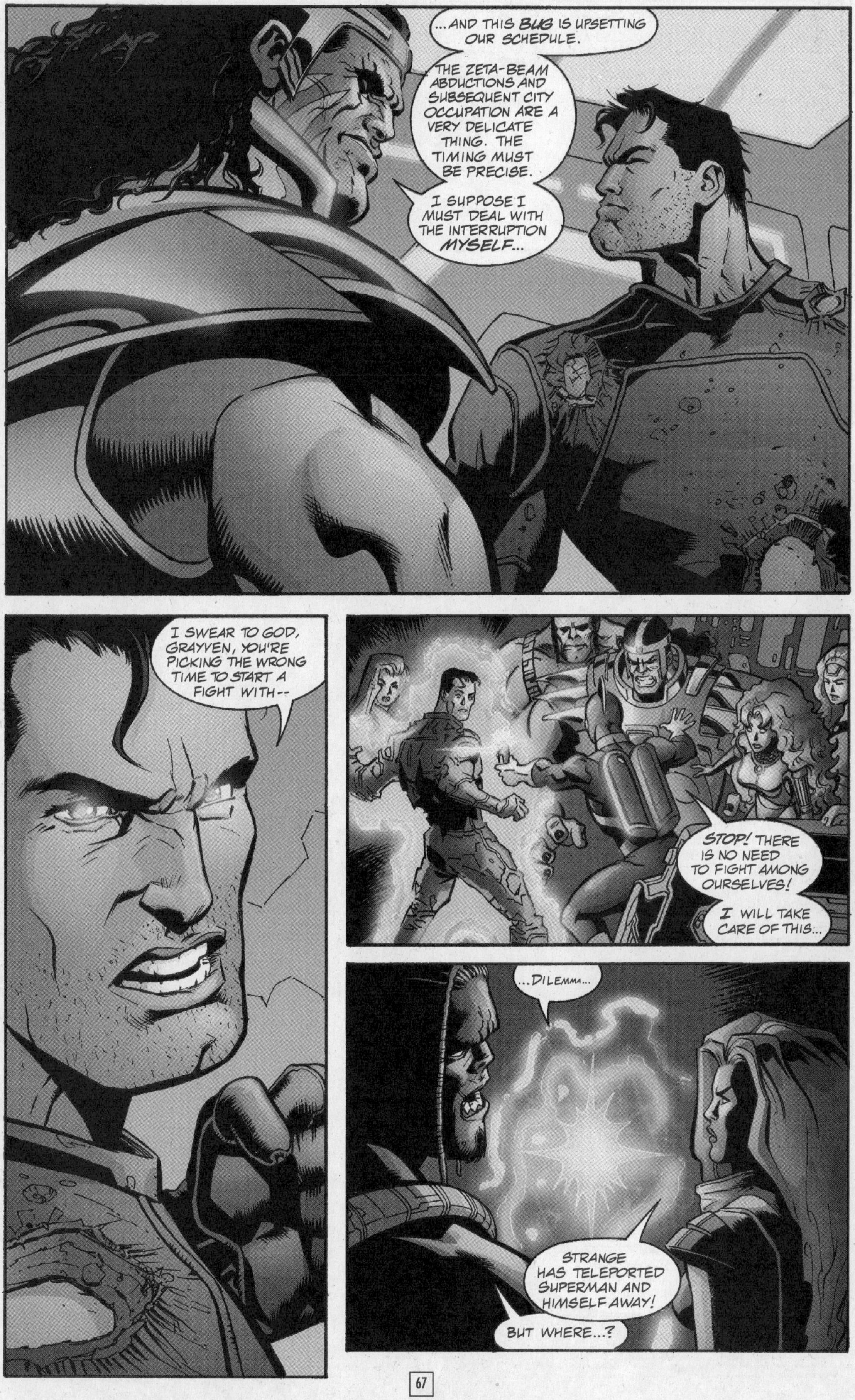
...AND THIS BUG IS UPSETTING OUR SCHEDULE.
THE ZETA-BEAM ABDUCTIONS AND SUBSEQUENT CITY OCCUPATION ARE A VERY DELICATE THING. THE TIMING MUST BE PRECISE.
I SUPPOSE I MUST DEAL WITH THE INTERRUPTION MYSELF...
I SWEAR TO GOD, GRAYVEN, YOU'RE PICKING THE WRONG TIME TO START A FIGHT WITH--
STOP! THERE IS NO NEED TO FIGHT AMONG OURSELVES!
I WILL TAKE CARE OF THIS...
...DILEMMA...
STRANGE HAS TELEPORTED SUPERMAN AND HIMSELF AWAY!
BUT WHERE...?

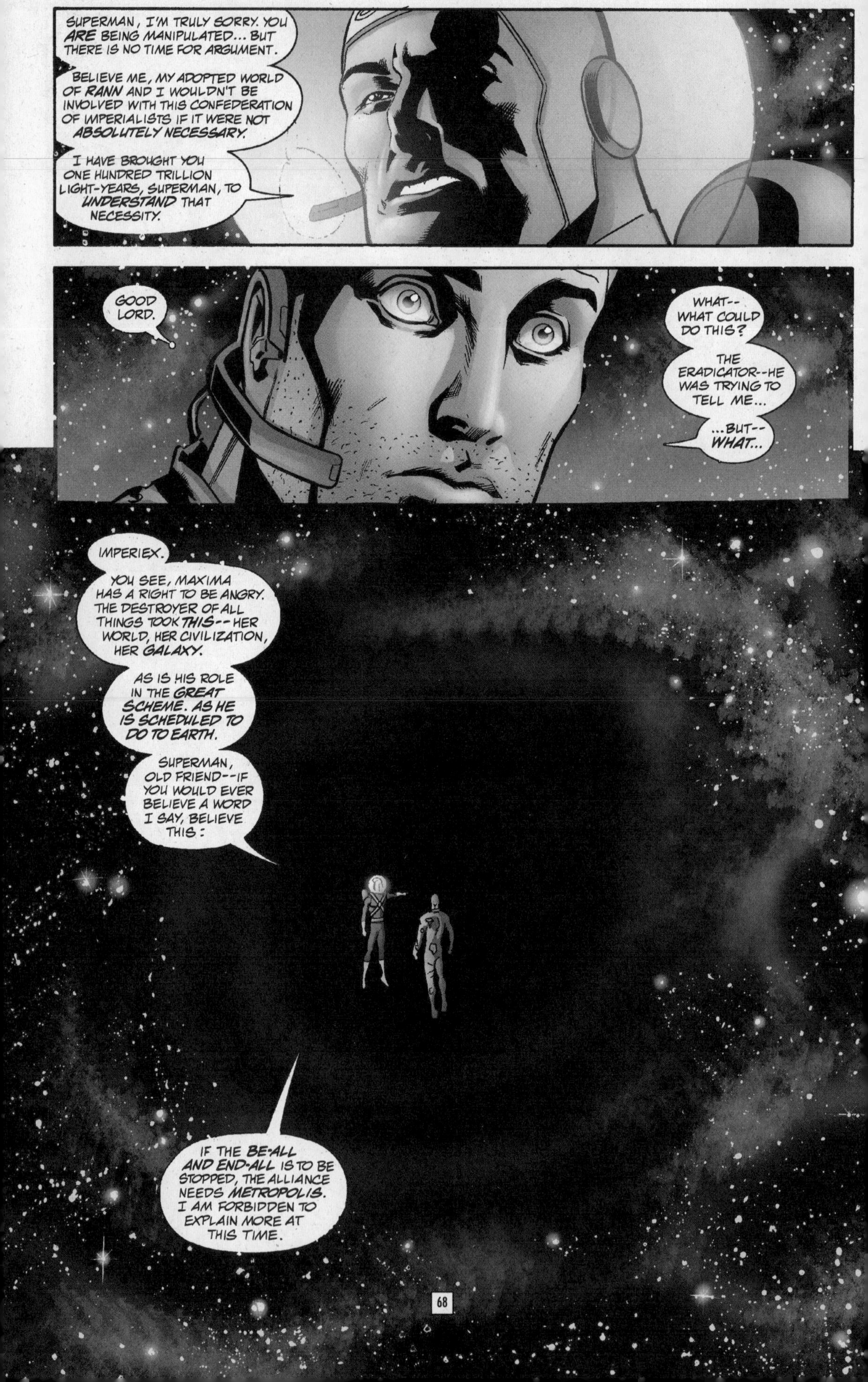

SUPERMAN, I'M TRULY SORRY. YOU ARE BEING MANIPULATED... BUT THERE IS NO TIME FOR ARGUMENT.
BELIEVE ME, MY ADOPTED WORLD OF RANN AND I WOULDN'T BE INVOLVED WITH THIS CONFEDERATION OF IMPERIALISTS IF IT WERE NOT ABSOLUTELY NECESSARY.
I HAVE BROUGHT YOU ONE HUNDRED TRILLION LIGHT-YEARS, SUPERMAN, TO UNDERSTAND THAT NECESSITY.
GOOD LORD.
WHAT-- WHAT COULD DO THIS?
THE ERADICATOR--HE WAS TRYING TO TELL ME...
...BUT-- WHAT...
IMPERIEX.
YOU SEE, MAXIMA HAS A RIGHT TO BE ANGRY. THE DESTROYER OF ALL THINGS TOOK THIS--HER WORLD, HER CIVILIZATION, HER GALAXY.
AS IS HIS ROLE IN THE GREAT SCHEME. AS HE IS SCHEDULED TO DO TO EARTH.
SUPERMAN, OLD FRIEND--IF YOU WOULD EVER BELIEVE A WORD I SAY, BELIEVE THIS:
IF THE BE-ALL AND END-ALL IS TO BE STOPPED, THE ALLIANCE NEEDS METROPOLIS. I AM FORBIDDEN TO EXPLAIN MORE AT THIS TIME.

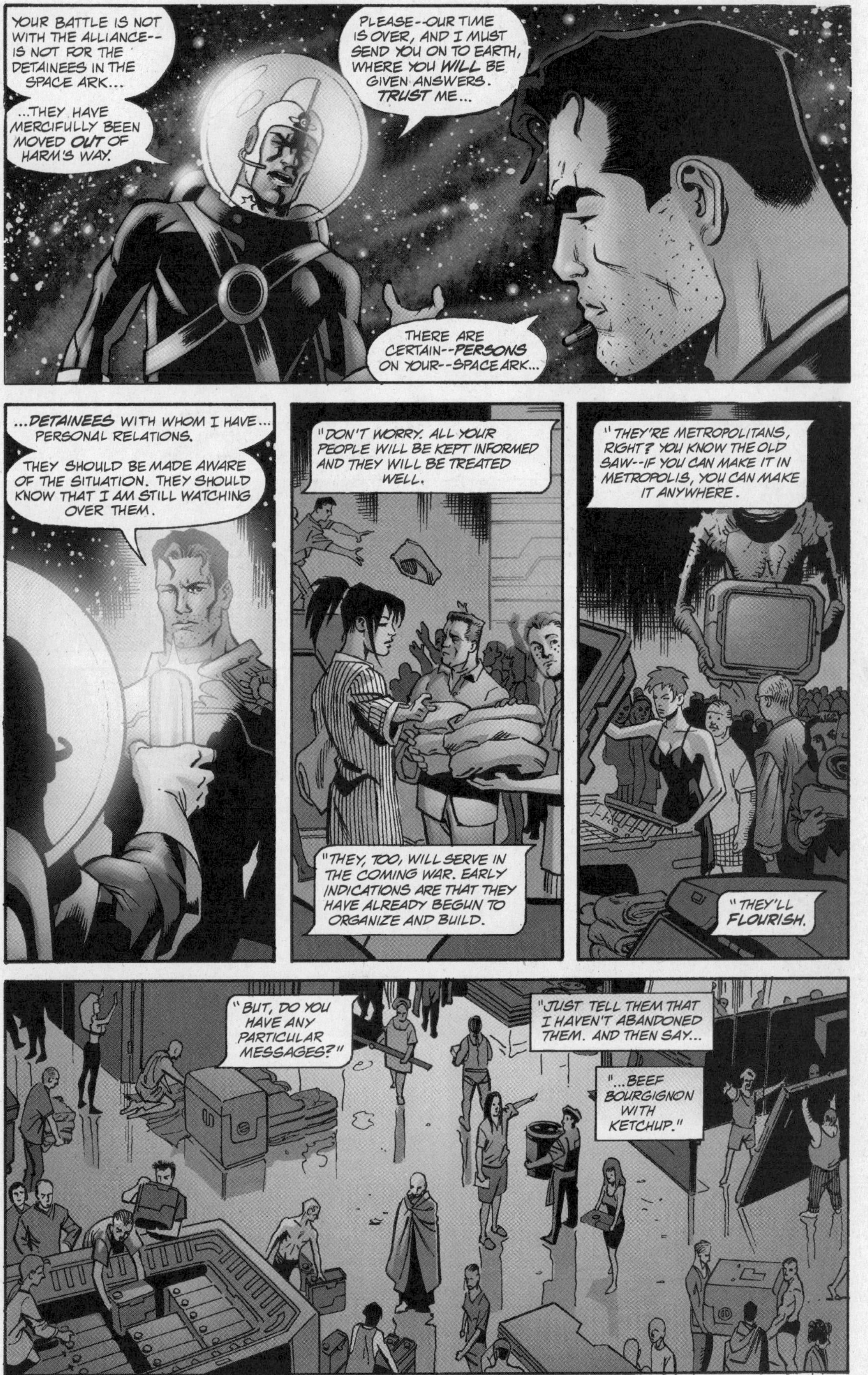
YOUR BATTLE IS NOT WITH THE ALLIANCE-- IS NOT FOR THE DETAINEES IN THE SPACE ARK...
...THEY HAVE MERCIFULLY BEEN MOVED OUT OF HARM'S WAY.
PLEASE--OUR TIME IS OVER, AND I MUST SEND YOU ON TO EARTH, WHERE YOU WILL BE GIVEN ANSWERS. TRUST ME...
THERE ARE CERTAIN--PERSONS ON YOUR--SPACE ARK...
...DETAINEES WITH WHOM I HAVE... PERSONAL RELATIONS.
THEY SHOULD BE MADE AWARE OF THE SITUATION. THEY SHOULD KNOW THAT I AM STILL WATCHING OVER THEM.
"DON'T WORRY. ALL YOUR PEOPLE WILL BE KEPT INFORMED AND THEY WILL BE TREATED WELL.
"THEY, TOO, WILL SERVE IN THE COMING WAR. EARLY INDICATIONS ARE THAT THEY HAVE ALREADY BEGUN TO ORGANIZE AND BUILD.
"THEY'RE METROPOLITANS, RIGHT? YOU KNOW THE OLD SAW--IF YOU CAN MAKE IT IN METROPOLIS, YOU CAN MAKE IT ANYWHERE.
"THEY'LL FLOURISH.
"BUT, DO YOU HAVE ANY PARTICULAR MESSAGES?"
"JUST TELL THEM THAT I HAVEN'T ABANDONED THEM. AND THEN SAY...
"...BEEF BOURGIGNON WITH KETCHUP."

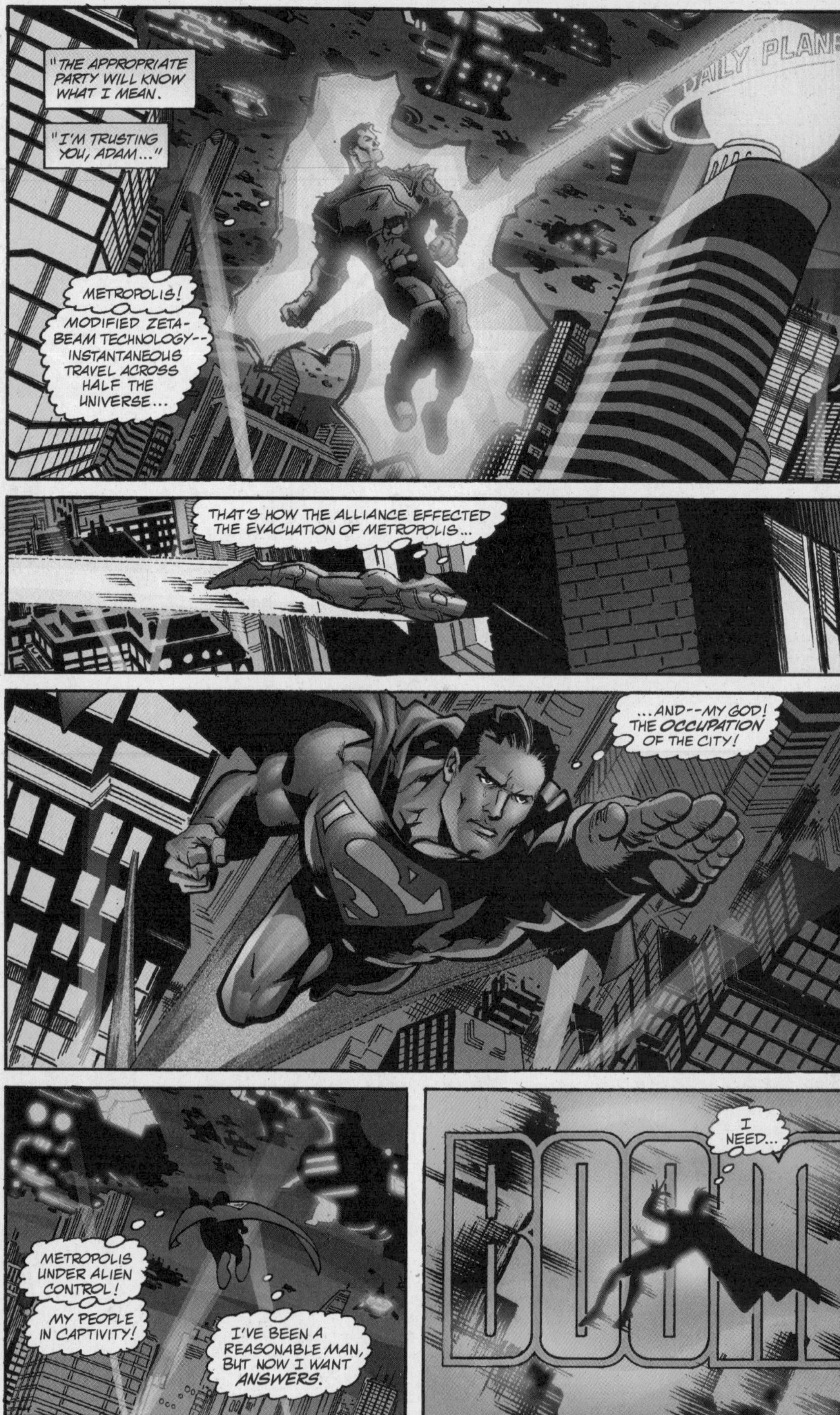

"THE APPROPRIATE PARTY WILL KNOW WHAT I MEAN.
"I'M TRUSTING YOU, ADAM..."
DAILY PLANET
METROPOLIS!
MODIFIED ZETA-BEAM TECHNOLOGY-- INSTANTANEOUS TRAVEL ACROSS HALF THE UNIVERSE...
THAT'S HOW THE ALLIANCE EFFECTED THE EVACUATION OF METROPOLIS...
...AND--MY GOD! THE OCCUPATION OF THE CITY!
METROPOLIS UNDER ALIEN CONTROL!
MY PEOPLE IN CAPTIVITY!
I'VE BEEN A REASONABLE MAN, BUT NOW I WANT ANSWERS.
I NEED...
BOOM

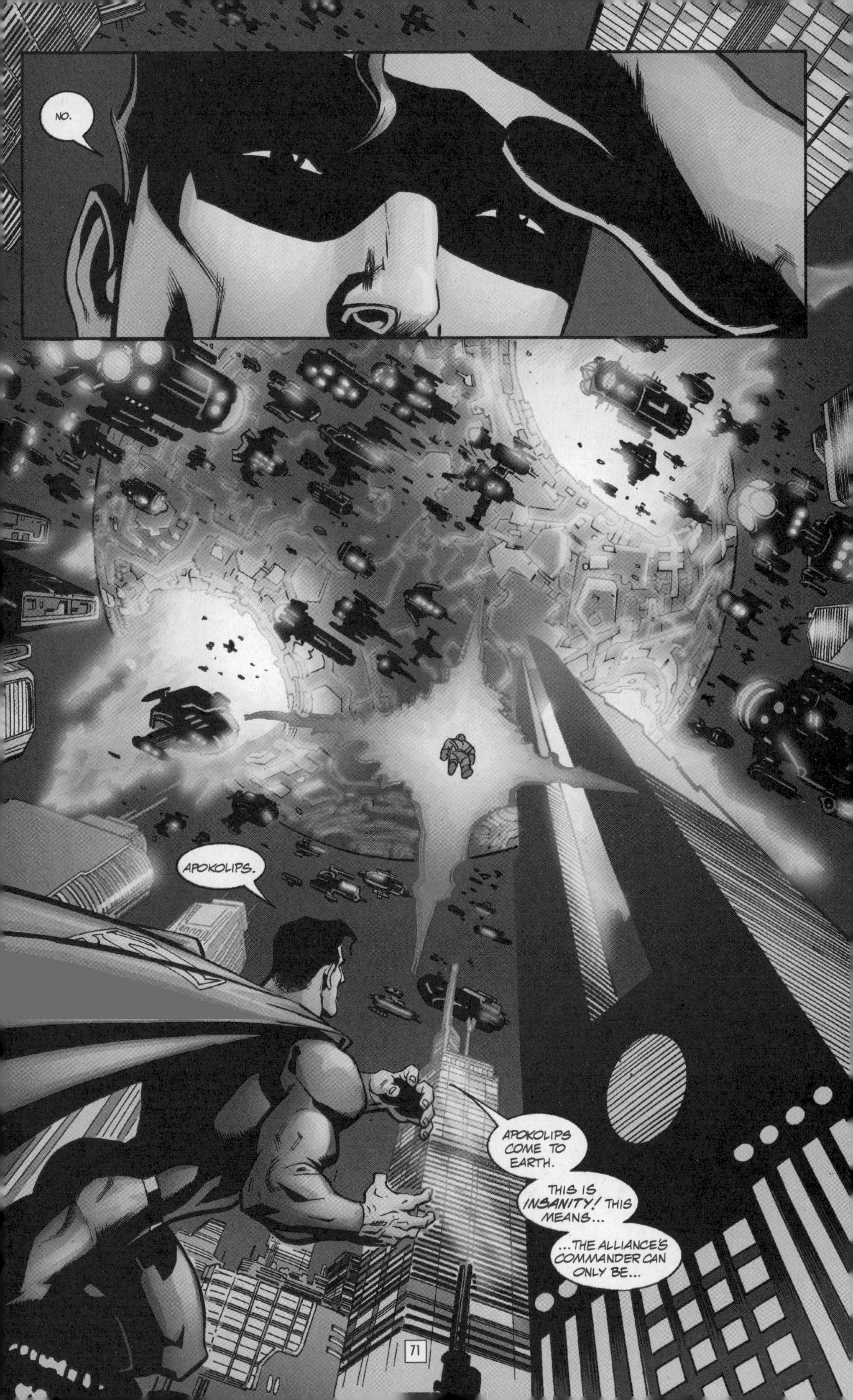
NO.
APOKOLIPS.
APOKOLIPS COME TO EARTH.
THIS IS *INSANITY!* THIS MEANS...
...THE ALLIANCE'S COMMANDER CAN ONLY BE...

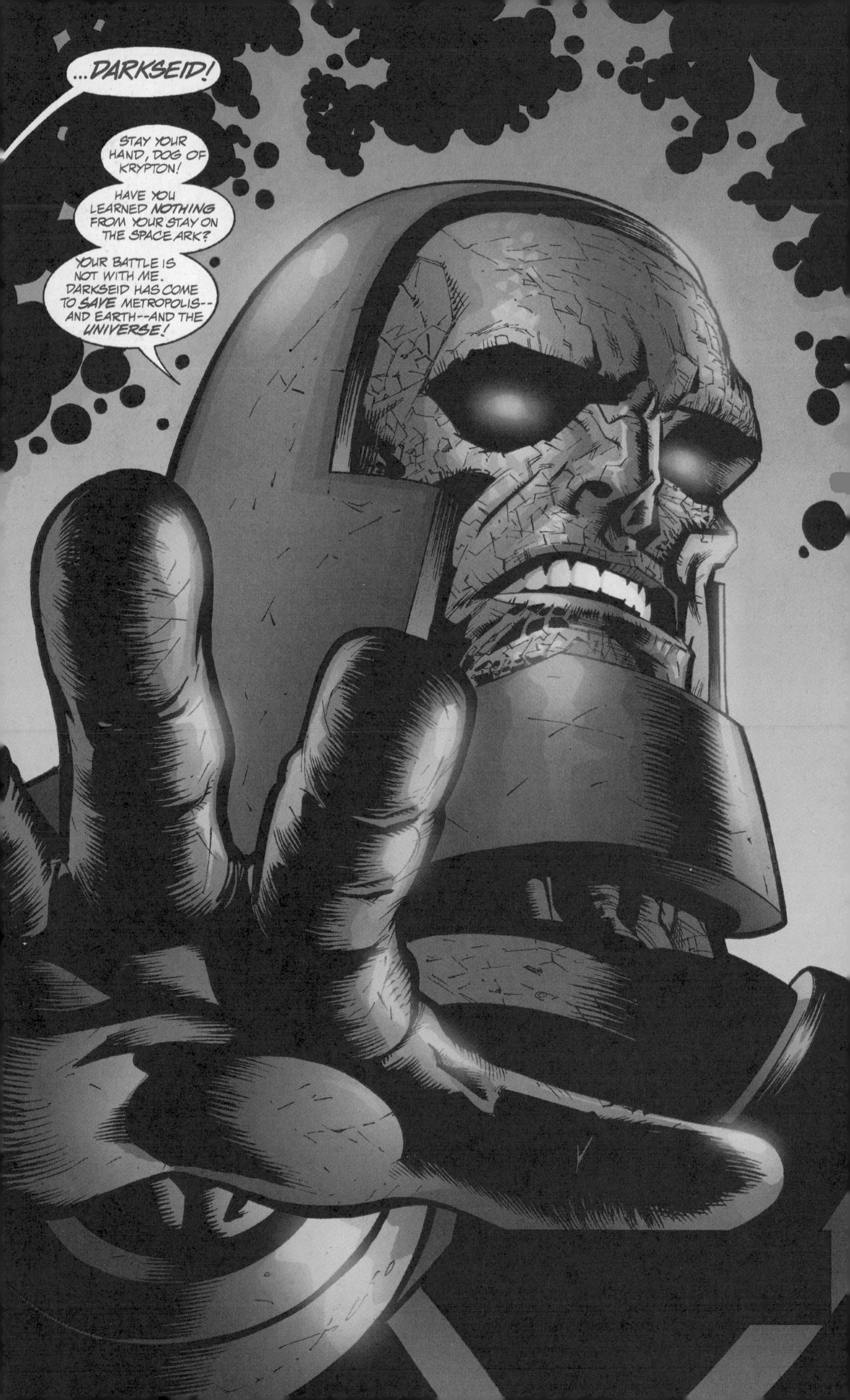
...DARKSEID!
STAY YOUR HAND, DOG OF KRYPTON!
HAVE YOU LEARNED NOTHING FROM YOUR STAY ON THE SPACE ARK?
YOUR BATTLE IS NOT WITH ME. DARKSEID HAS COME TO SAVE METROPOLIS--AND EARTH--AND THE UNIVERSE!

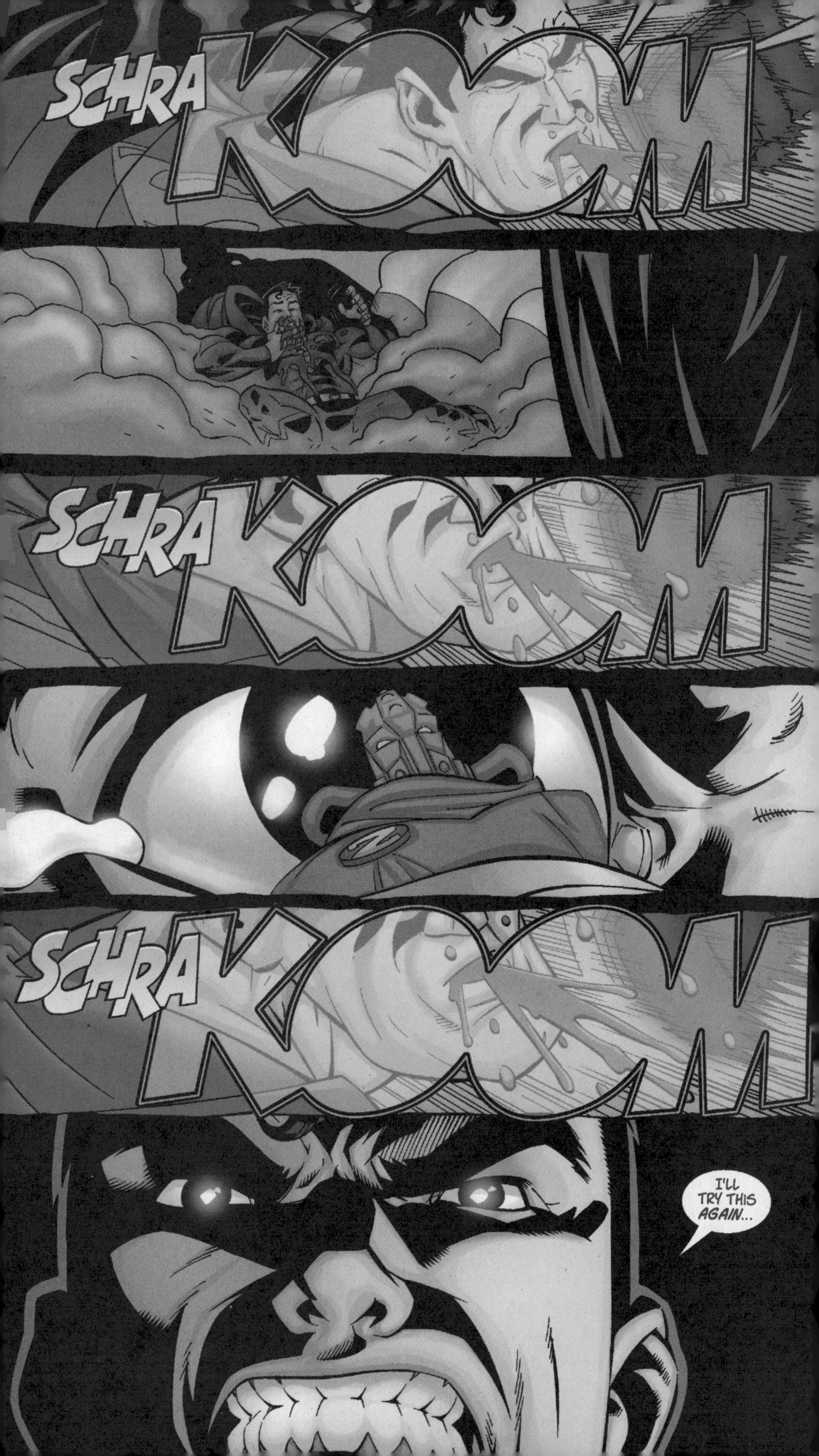
SCHRA
KOOM
SCHRA
KOOM
SCHRA
KOOM
I'LL TRY THIS AGAIN...

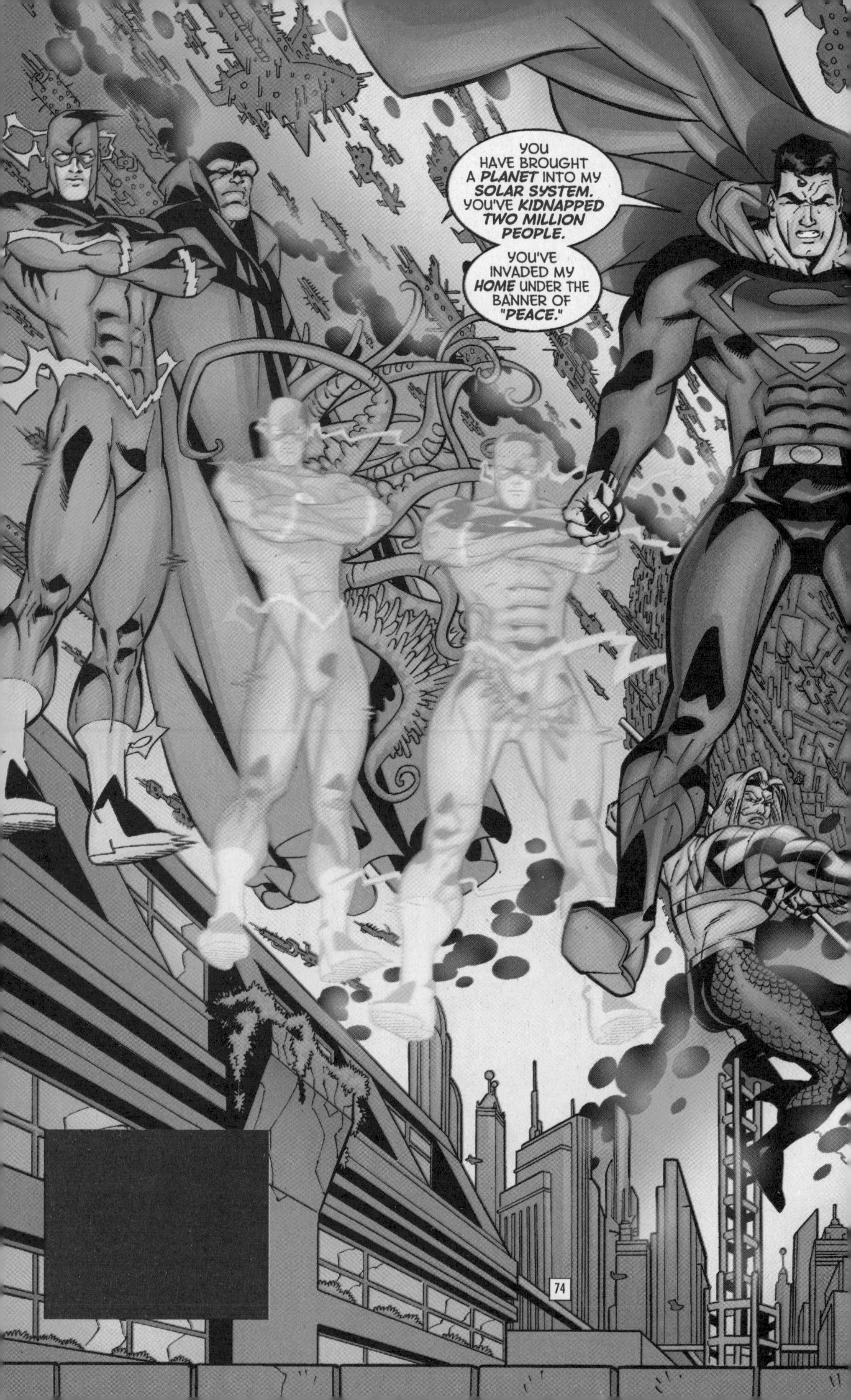
YOU HAVE BROUGHT A *PLANET* INTO MY *SOLAR SYSTEM.* YOU'VE *KIDNAPPED TWO MILLION PEOPLE.*
YOU'VE INVADED MY *HOME* UNDER THE BANNER OF *"PEACE."*
[redacted]

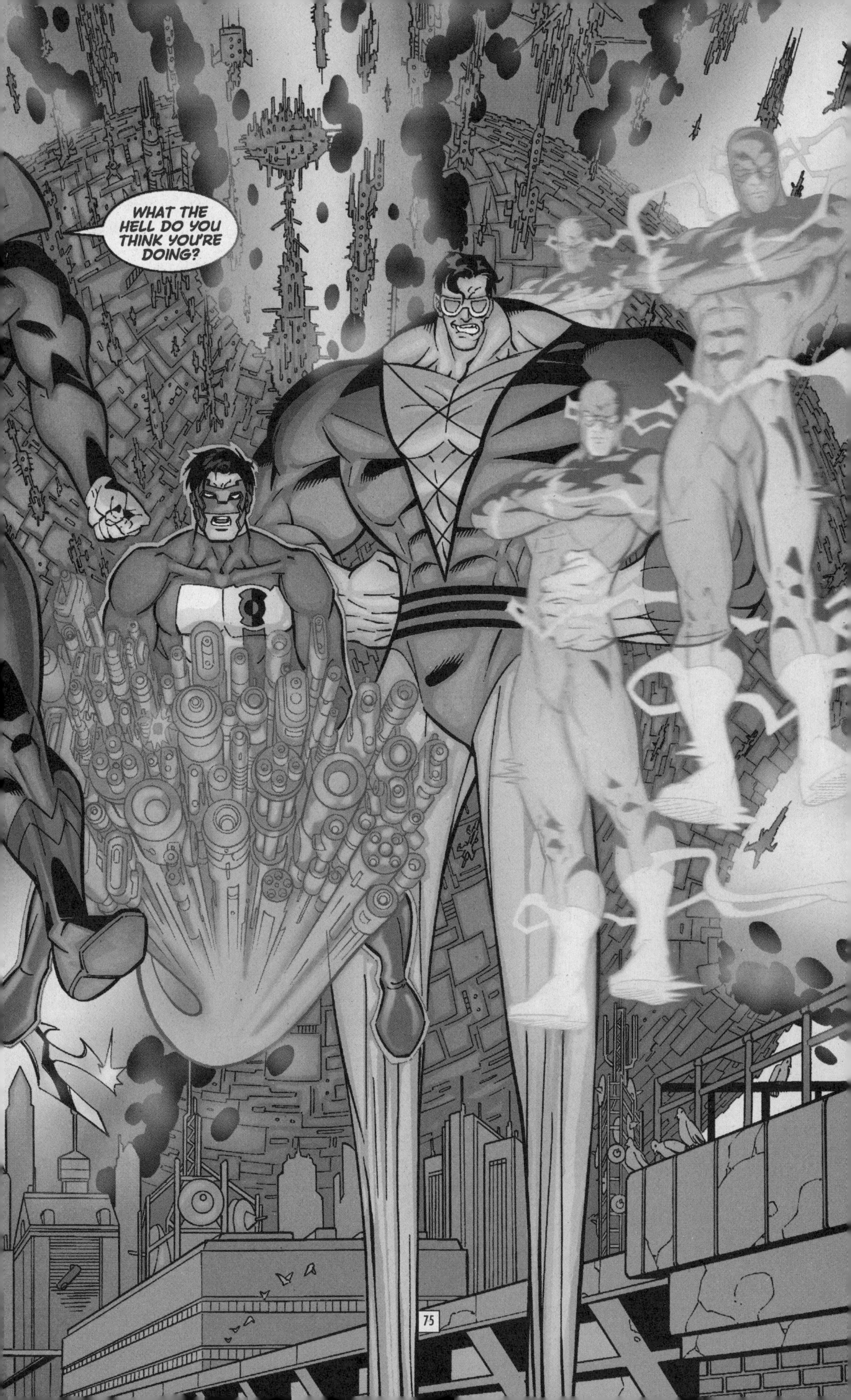
WHAT THE HELL DO YOU THINK YOU'RE DOING?

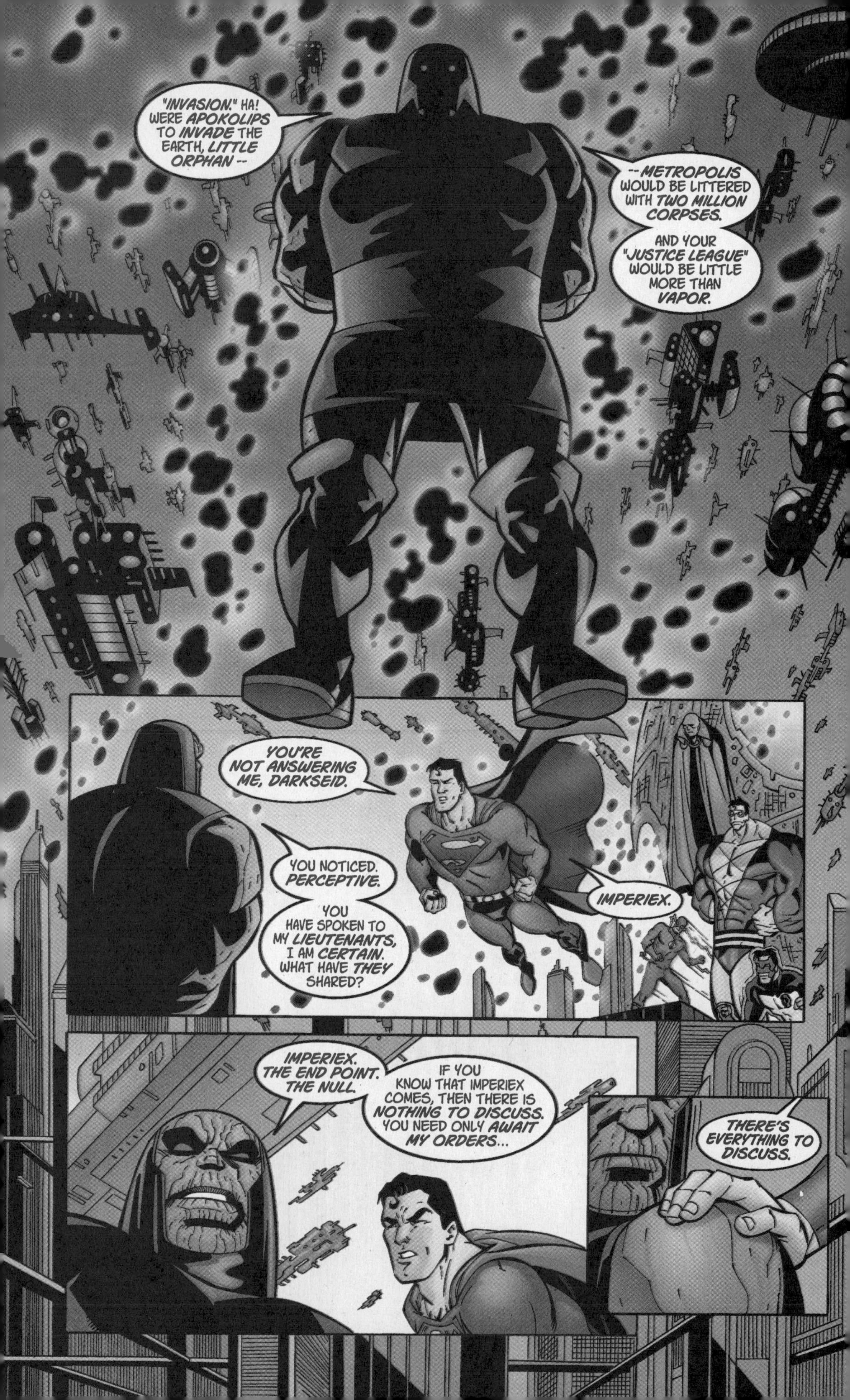
"INVASION." HA! WERE APOKOLIPS TO INVADE THE EARTH, LITTLE ORPHAN --
--METROPOLIS WOULD BE LITTERED WITH TWO MILLION CORPSES.
AND YOUR "JUSTICE LEAGUE" WOULD BE LITTLE MORE THAN VAPOR.
YOU'RE NOT ANSWERING ME, DARKSEID.
YOU NOTICED. PERCEPTIVE.
YOU HAVE SPOKEN TO MY LIEUTENANTS, I AM CERTAIN. WHAT HAVE THEY SHARED?
IMPERIEX.
IMPERIEX. THE END POINT. THE NULL.
IF YOU KNOW THAT IMPERIEX COMES, THEN THERE IS NOTHING TO DISCUSS. YOU NEED ONLY AWAIT MY ORDERS...
THERE'S EVERYTHING TO DISCUSS.

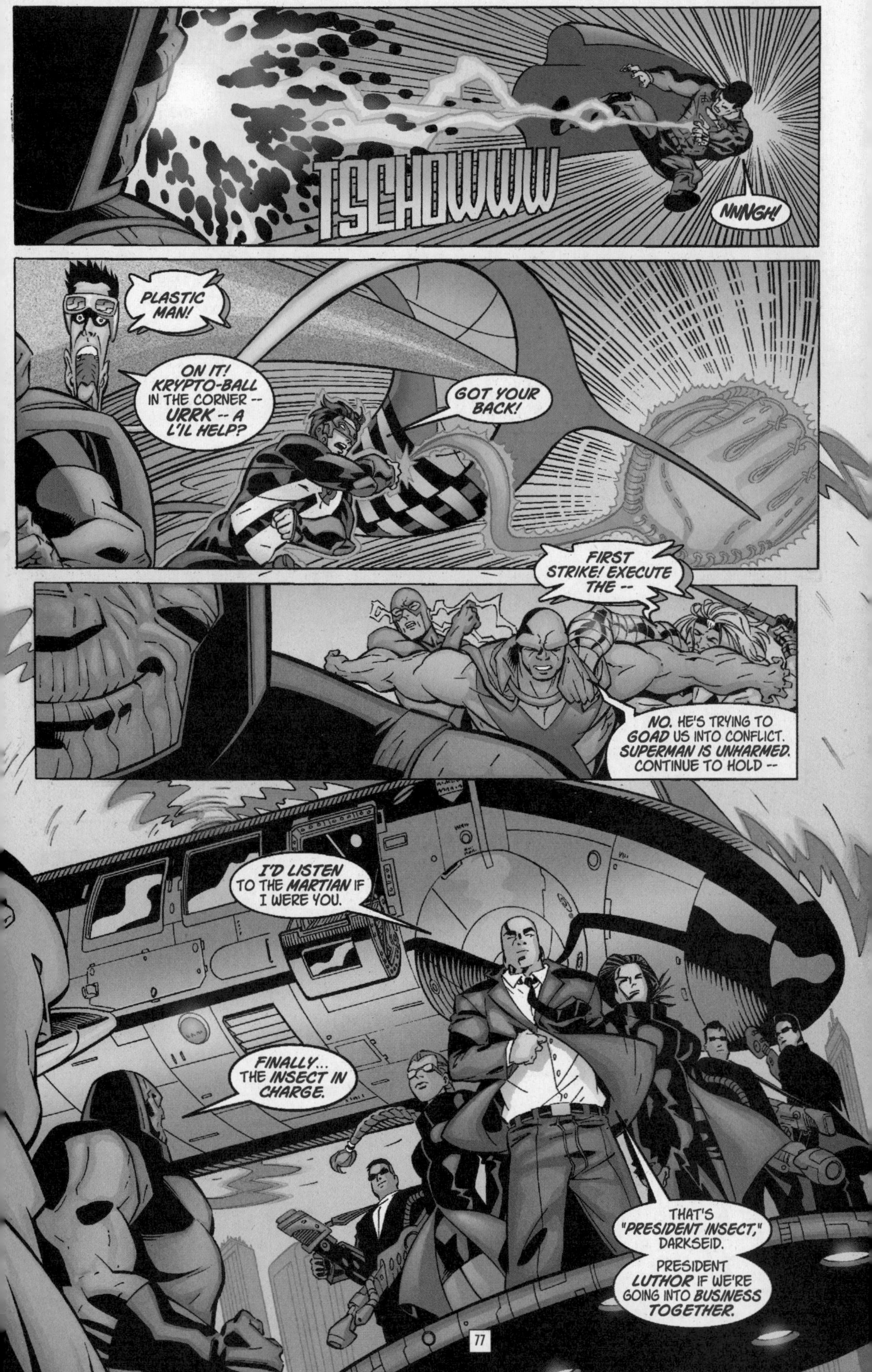
TSCHOWWW
NNNGH!
PLASTIC MAN!
ON IT! KRYPTO-BALL IN THE CORNER -- URRK -- A L'IL HELP?
GOT YOUR BACK!
FIRST STRIKE! EXECUTE THE --
NO. HE'S TRYING TO GOAD US INTO CONFLICT. SUPERMAN IS UNHARMED. CONTINUE TO HOLD --
I'D LISTEN TO THE MARTIAN IF I WERE YOU.
FINALLY... THE INSECT IN CHARGE.
THAT'S "PRESIDENT INSECT," DARKSEID.
PRESIDENT LUTHOR IF WE'RE GOING INTO BUSINESS TOGETHER.

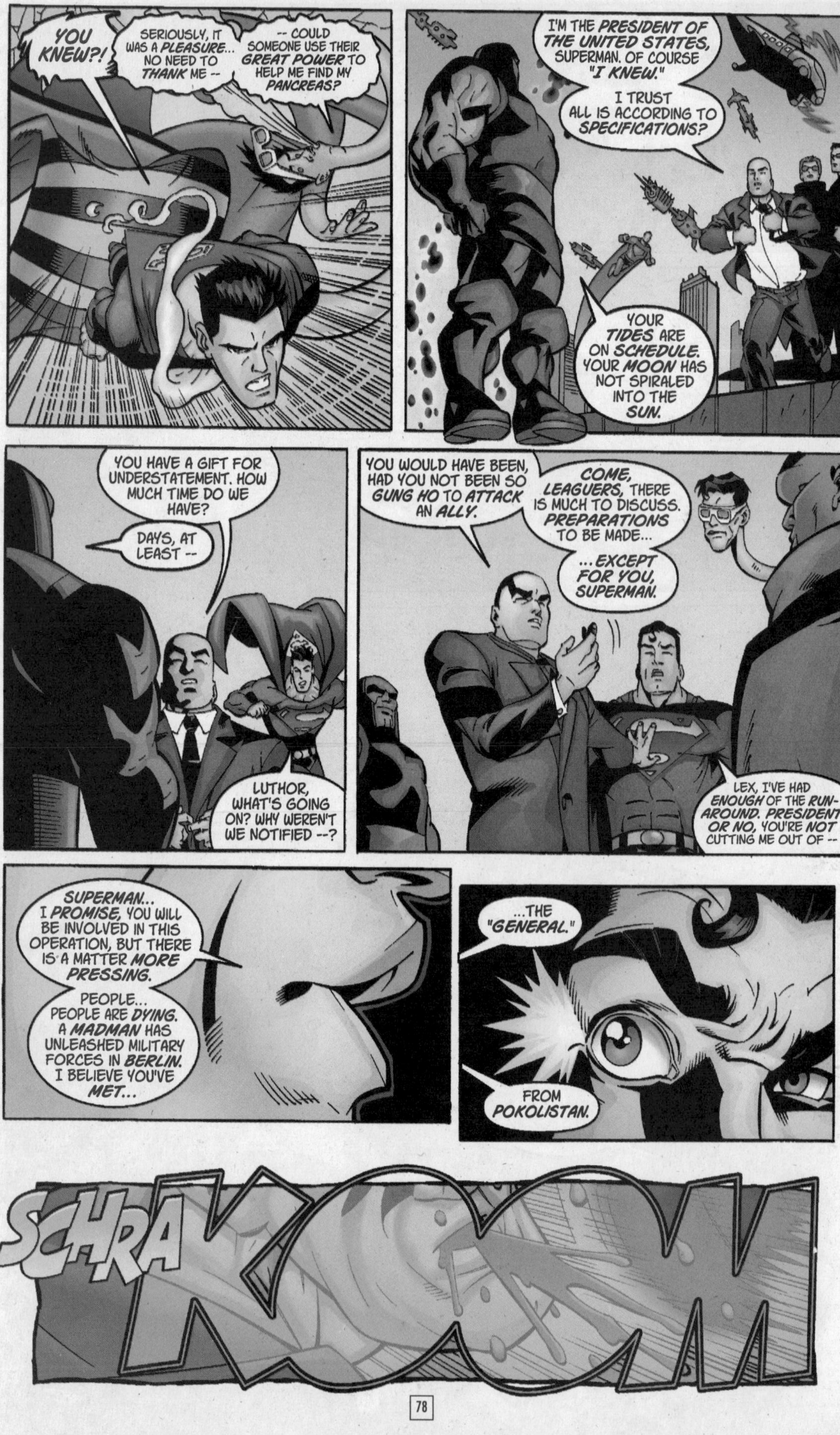

YOU KNEW?!
SERIOUSLY, IT WAS A PLEASURE... NO NEED TO THANK ME --
-- COULD SOMEONE USE THEIR GREAT POWER TO HELP ME FIND MY PANCREAS?
I'M THE PRESIDENT OF THE UNITED STATES, SUPERMAN. OF COURSE "I KNEW."
I TRUST ALL IS ACCORDING TO SPECIFICATIONS?
YOUR TIDES ARE ON SCHEDULE. YOUR MOON HAS NOT SPIRALED INTO THE SUN.
YOU HAVE A GIFT FOR UNDERSTATEMENT. HOW MUCH TIME DO WE HAVE?
DAYS, AT LEAST --
LUTHOR, WHAT'S GOING ON? WHY WEREN'T WE NOTIFIED --?
YOU WOULD HAVE BEEN, HAD YOU NOT BEEN SO GUNG HO TO ATTACK AN ALLY.
COME, LEAGUERS, THERE IS MUCH TO DISCUSS. PREPARATIONS TO BE MADE...
...EXCEPT FOR YOU, SUPERMAN.
LEX, I'VE HAD ENOUGH OF THE RUN-AROUND. PRESIDENT OR NO, YOU'RE NOT CUTTING ME OUT OF --
SUPERMAN... I PROMISE, YOU WILL BE INVOLVED IN THIS OPERATION, BUT THERE IS A MATTER MORE PRESSING.
PEOPLE... PEOPLE ARE DYING. A MADMAN HAS UNLEASHED MILITARY FORCES IN BERLIN. I BELIEVE YOU'VE MET...
...THE "GENERAL."
FROM POKOLISTAN.
SCHRAKOOM

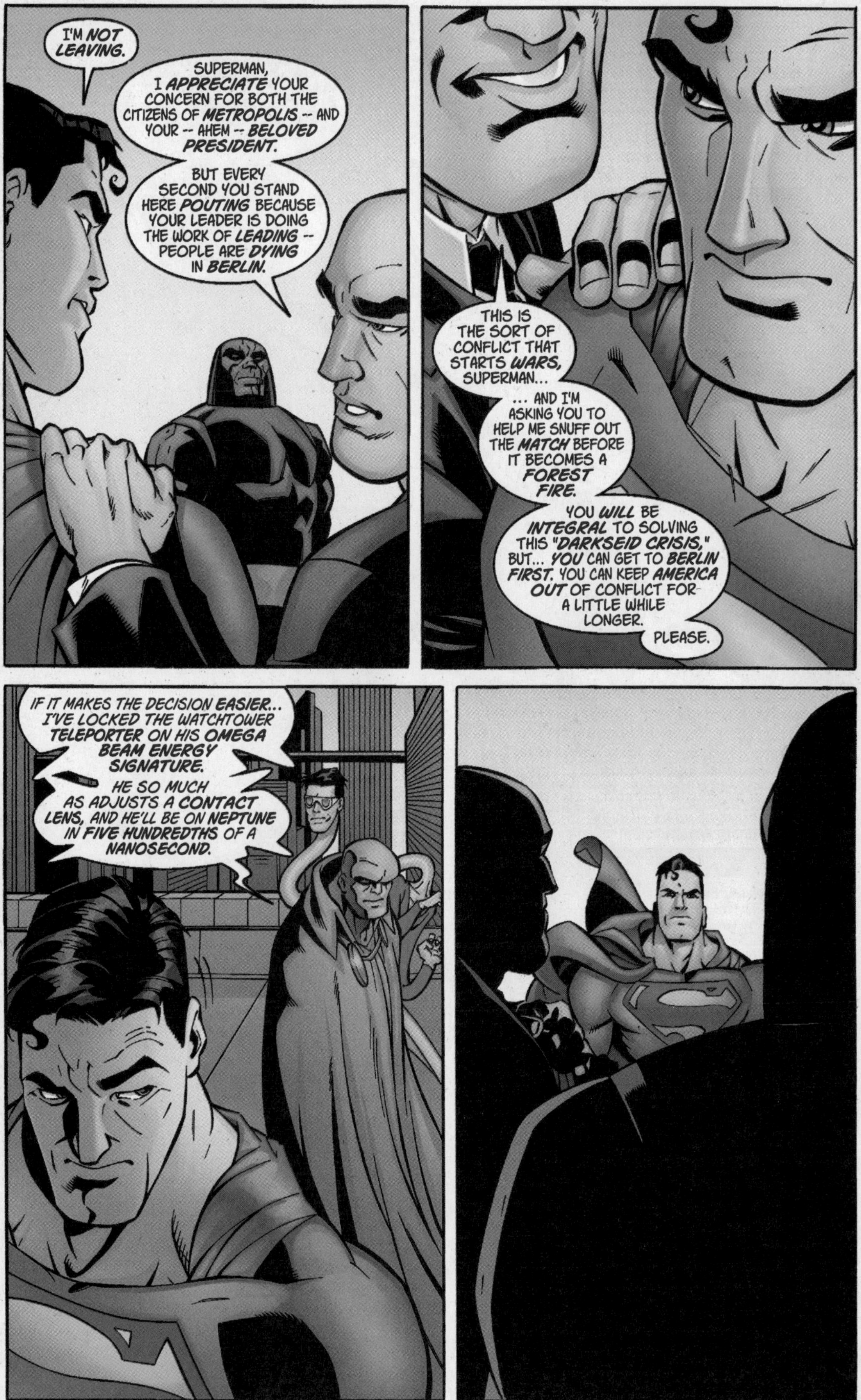
I'M NOT LEAVING.
SUPERMAN, I APPRECIATE YOUR CONCERN FOR BOTH THE CITIZENS OF METROPOLIS -- AND YOUR -- AHEM -- BELOVED PRESIDENT.
BUT EVERY SECOND YOU STAND HERE POUTING BECAUSE YOUR LEADER IS DOING THE WORK OF LEADING -- PEOPLE ARE DYING IN BERLIN.
THIS IS THE SORT OF CONFLICT THAT STARTS WARS, SUPERMAN...
... AND I'M ASKING YOU TO HELP ME SNUFF OUT THE MATCH BEFORE IT BECOMES A FOREST FIRE.
YOU WILL BE INTEGRAL TO SOLVING THIS "DARKSEID CRISIS," BUT... YOU CAN GET TO BERLIN FIRST. YOU CAN KEEP AMERICA OUT OF CONFLICT FOR A LITTLE WHILE LONGER.
PLEASE.
IF IT MAKES THE DECISION EASIER... I'VE LOCKED THE WATCHTOWER TELEPORTER ON HIS OMEGA BEAM ENERGY SIGNATURE.
HE SO MUCH AS ADJUSTS A CONTACT LENS, AND HE'LL BE ON NEPTUNE IN FIVE HUNDREDTHS OF A NANOSECOND.

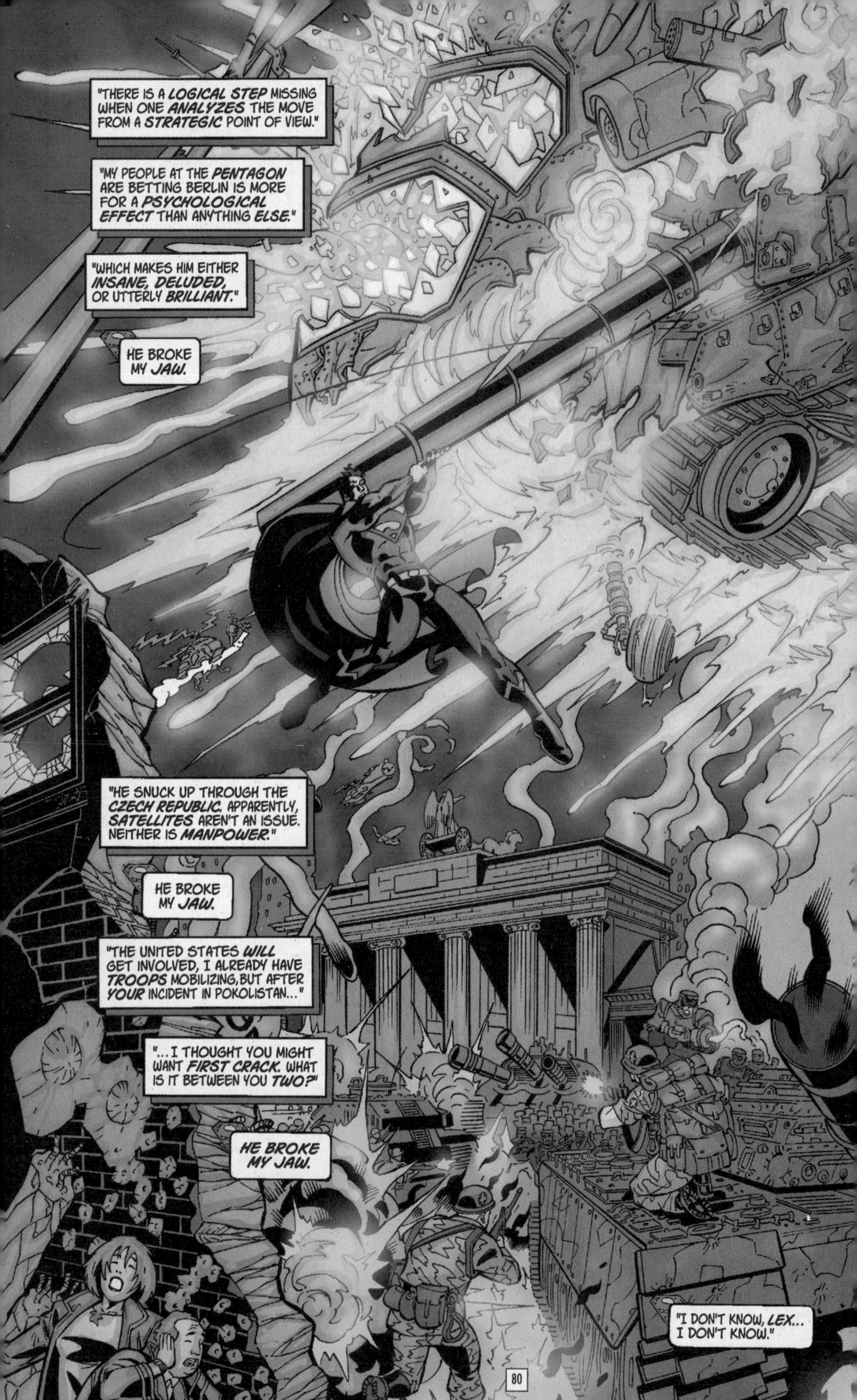
"THERE IS A LOGICAL STEP MISSING WHEN ONE ANALYZES THE MOVE FROM A STRATEGIC POINT OF VIEW."
"MY PEOPLE AT THE PENTAGON ARE BETTING BERLIN IS MORE FOR A PSYCHOLOGICAL EFFECT THAN ANYTHING ELSE."
"WHICH MAKES HIM EITHER INSANE, DELUDED, OR UTTERLY BRILLIANT."
HE BROKE MY JAW.
"HE SNUCK UP THROUGH THE CZECH REPUBLIC. APPARENTLY, SATELLITES AREN'T AN ISSUE. NEITHER IS MANPOWER."
HE BROKE MY JAW.
"THE UNITED STATES WILL GET INVOLVED, I ALREADY HAVE TROOPS MOBILIZING, BUT AFTER YOUR INCIDENT IN POKOLISTAN..."
"...I THOUGHT YOU MIGHT WANT FIRST CRACK. WHAT IS IT BETWEEN YOU TWO?"
HE BROKE MY JAW.
"I DON'T KNOW, LEX... I DON'T KNOW."

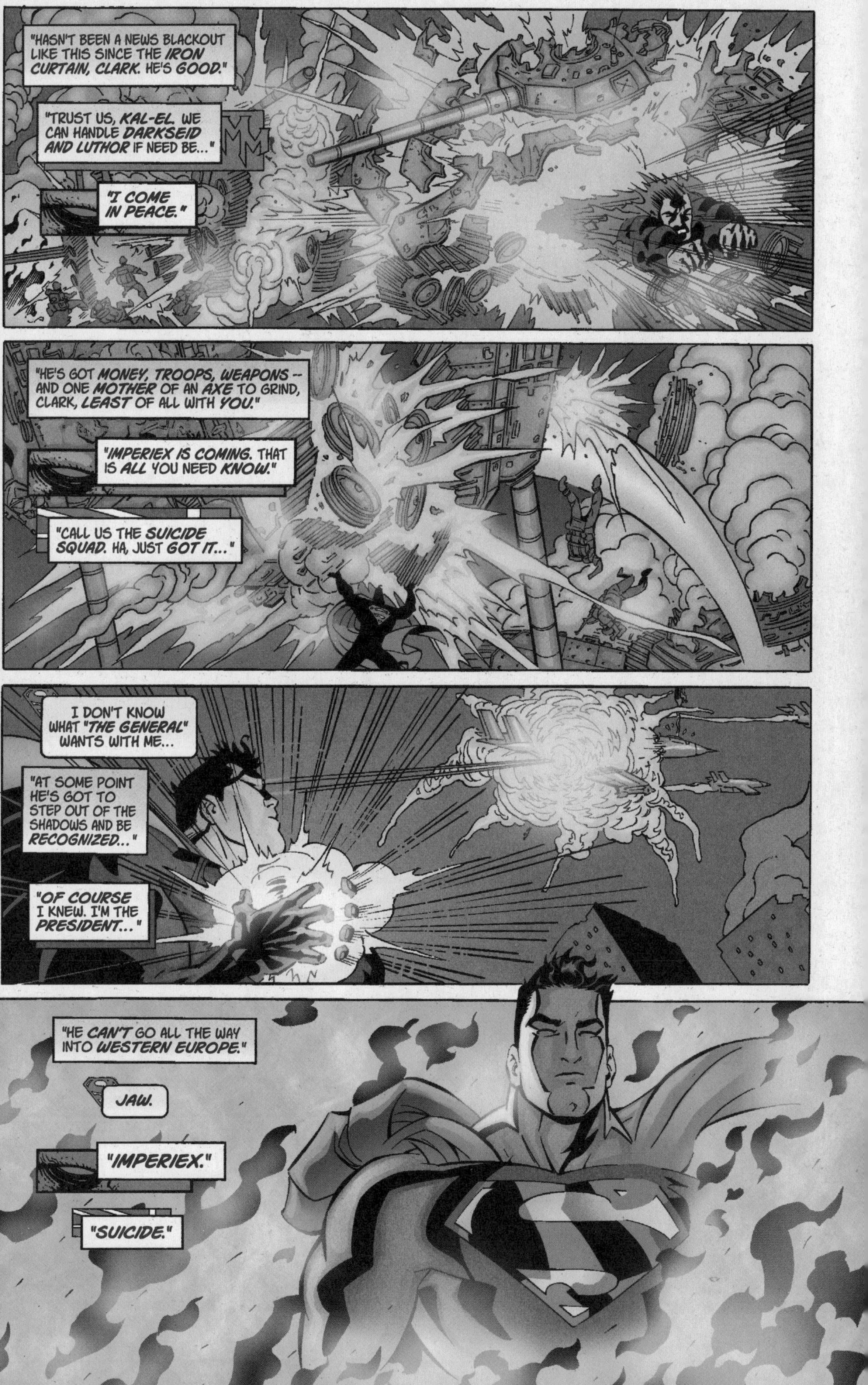
"HASN'T BEEN A NEWS BLACKOUT LIKE THIS SINCE THE IRON CURTAIN, CLARK. HE'S GOOD."
"TRUST US, KAL-EL. WE CAN HANDLE DARKSEID AND LUTHOR IF NEED BE..."
"I COME IN PEACE."
"HE'S GOT MONEY, TROOPS, WEAPONS -- AND ONE MOTHER OF AN AXE TO GRIND, CLARK, LEAST OF ALL WITH YOU."
"IMPERIEX IS COMING. THAT IS ALL YOU NEED KNOW."
"CALL US THE SUICIDE SQUAD. HA, JUST GOT IT..."
I DON'T KNOW WHAT "THE GENERAL" WANTS WITH ME...
"AT SOME POINT HE'S GOT TO STEP OUT OF THE SHADOWS AND BE RECOGNIZED..."
"OF COURSE I KNEW. I'M THE PRESIDENT..."
"HE CAN'T GO ALL THE WAY INTO WESTERN EUROPE."
JAW.
"IMPERIEX."
"SUICIDE."

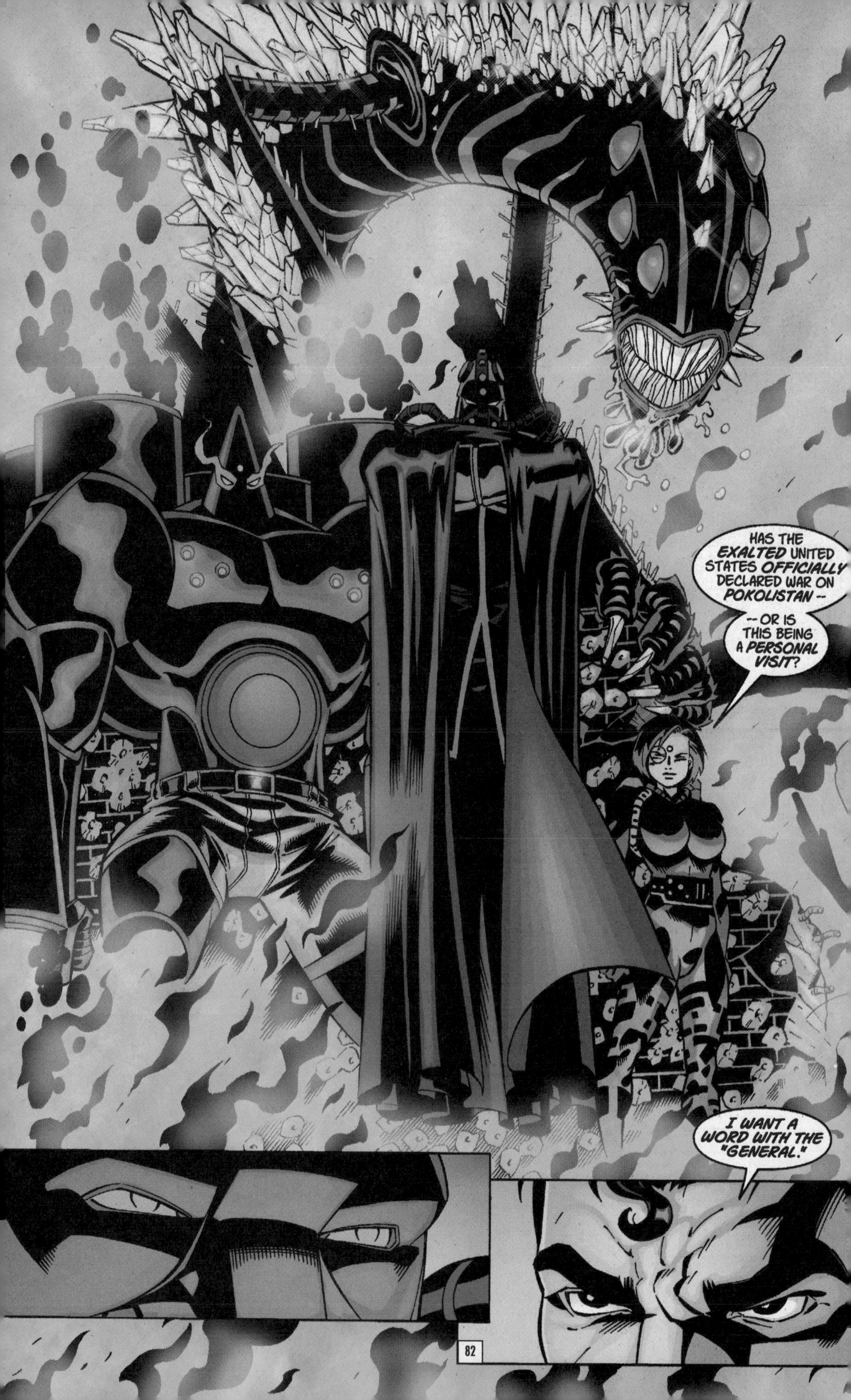
HAS THE EXALTED UNITED STATES OFFICIALLY DECLARED WAR ON POKOLISTAN --
-- OR IS THIS BEING A PERSONAL VISIT?
I WANT A WORD WITH THE "GENERAL."

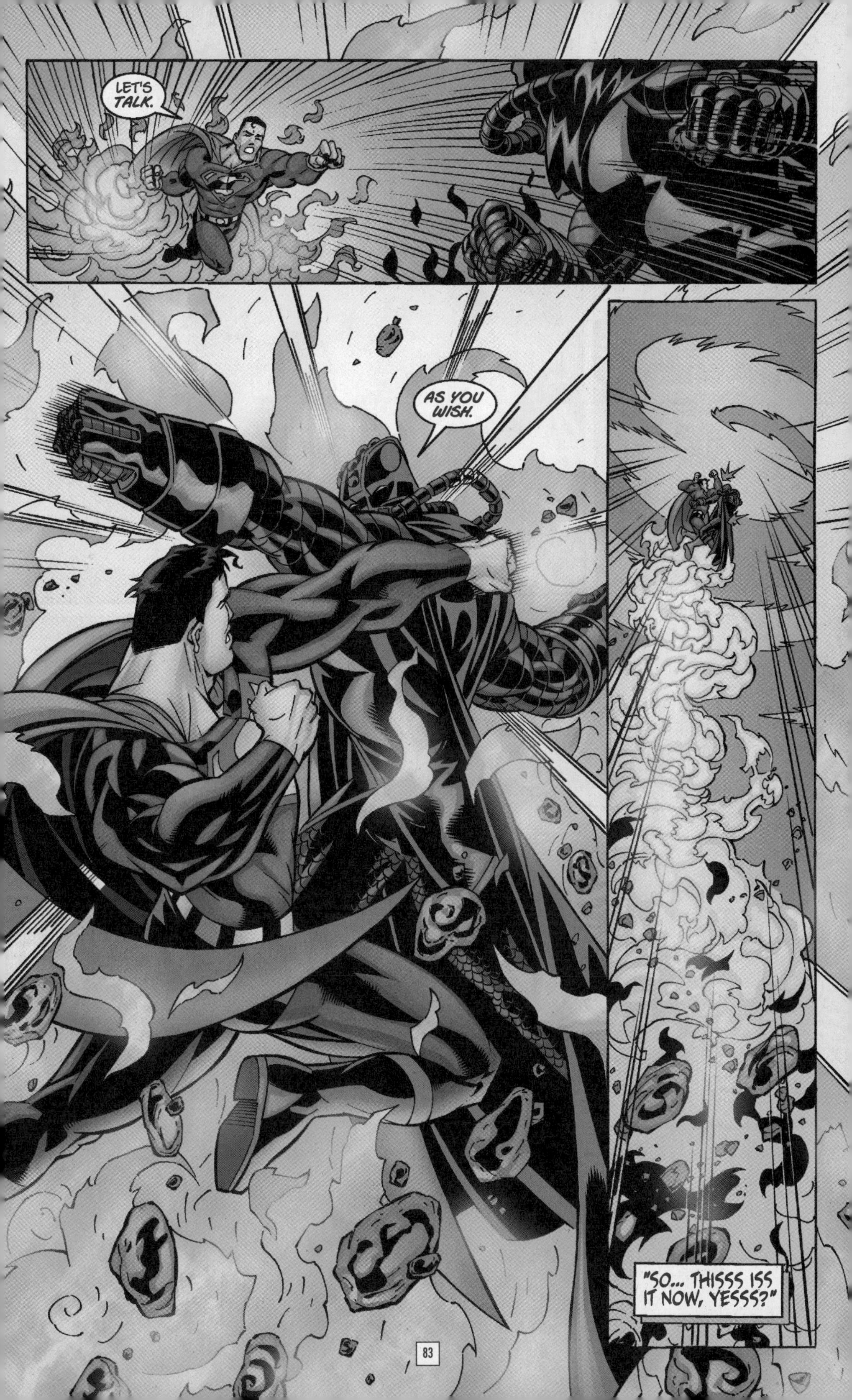
LET'S TALK.
AS YOU WISH.
"SO... THISSS ISS IT NOW, YESSS?"

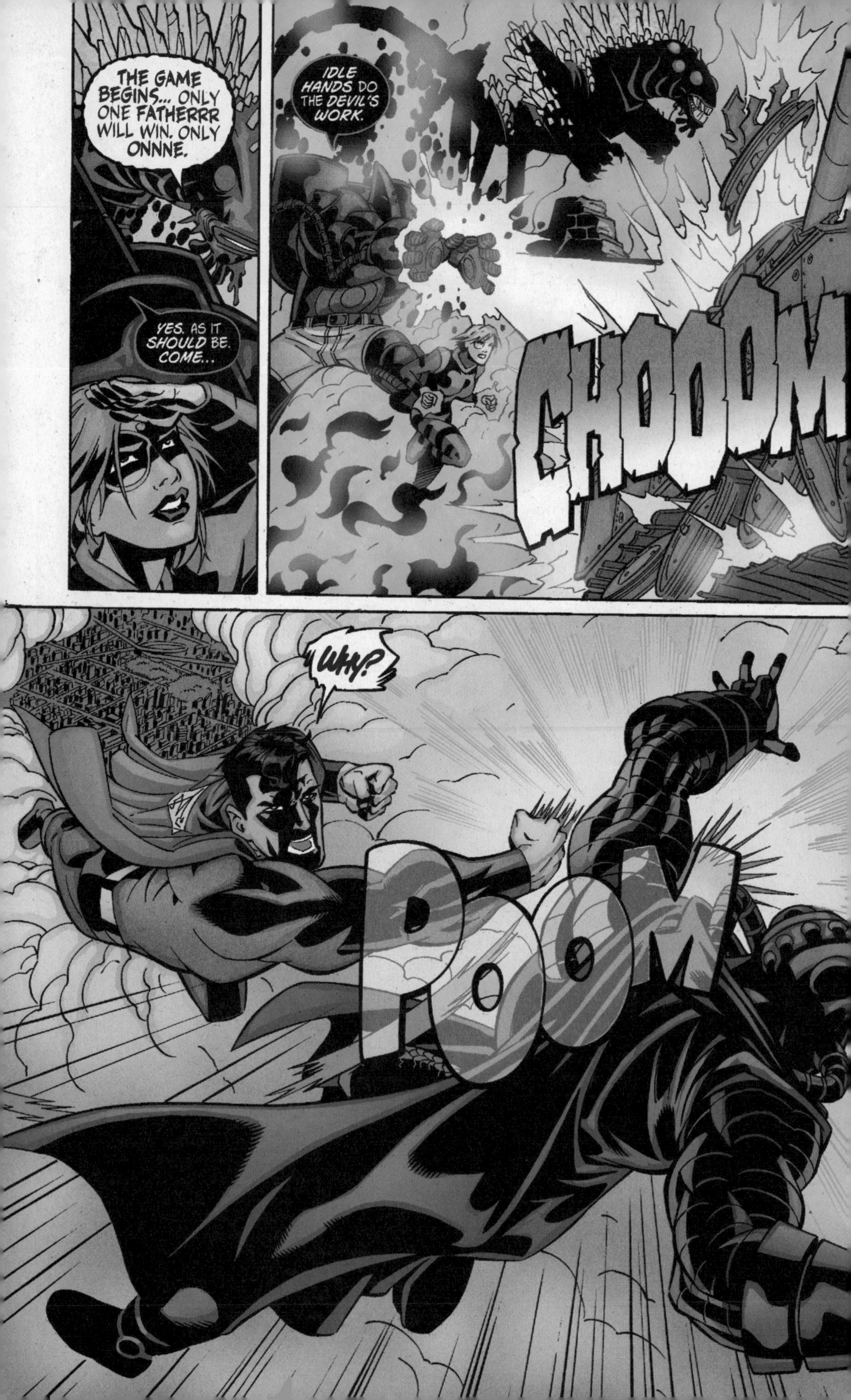
THE GAME BEGINS... ONLY ONE FATHERRR WILL WIN. ONLY ONNNE.
YES. AS IT SHOULD BE. COME...
IDLE HANDS DO THE DEVIL'S WORK.
CHOOOM
WHY?
POOOM

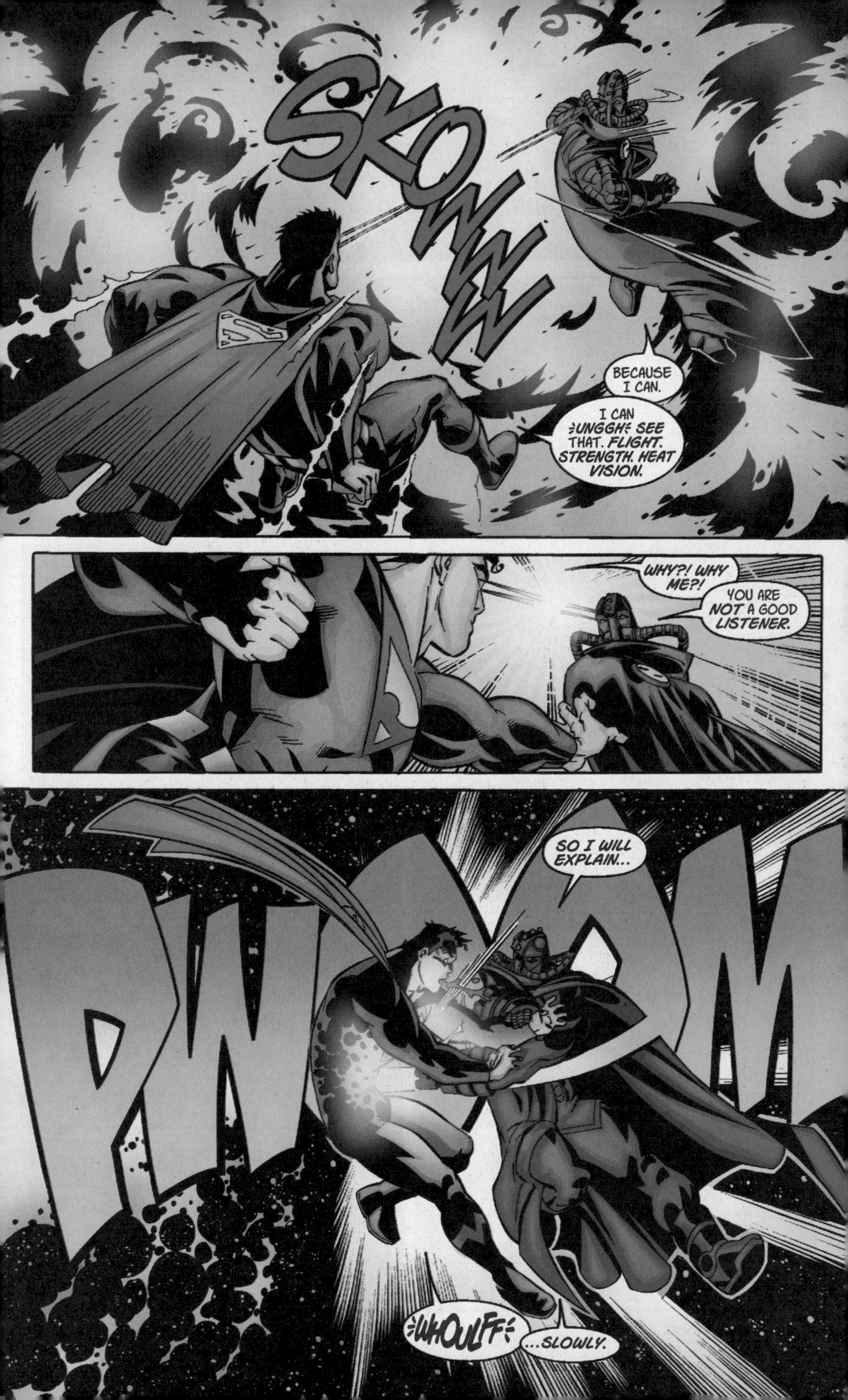
SKOWWW
BECAUSE I CAN.
I CAN UNGGH SEE THAT. FLIGHT. STRENGTH. HEAT VISION.
WHY?! WHY ME?!
YOU ARE NOT A GOOD LISTENER.
SO I WILL EXPLAIN...
WHOULFF
...SLOWLY.

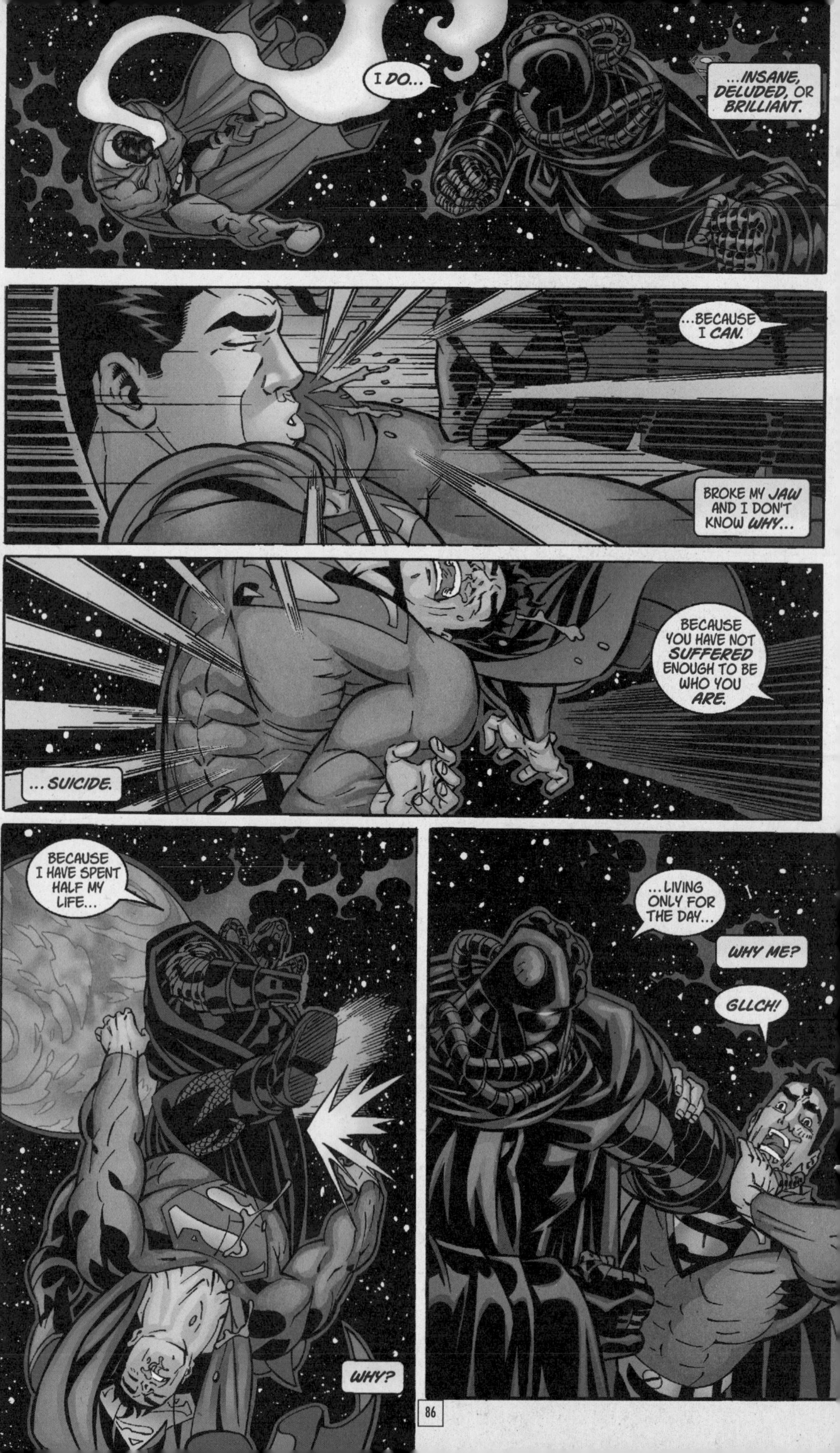
I DO...
...INSANE, DELUDED, OR BRILLIANT.
...BECAUSE I CAN.
BROKE MY JAW AND I DON'T KNOW WHY...
BECAUSE YOU HAVE NOT SUFFERED ENOUGH TO BE WHO YOU ARE.
...SUICIDE.
BECAUSE I HAVE SPENT HALF MY LIFE...
WHY?
...LIVING ONLY FOR THE DAY...
WHY ME?
GLLCH!

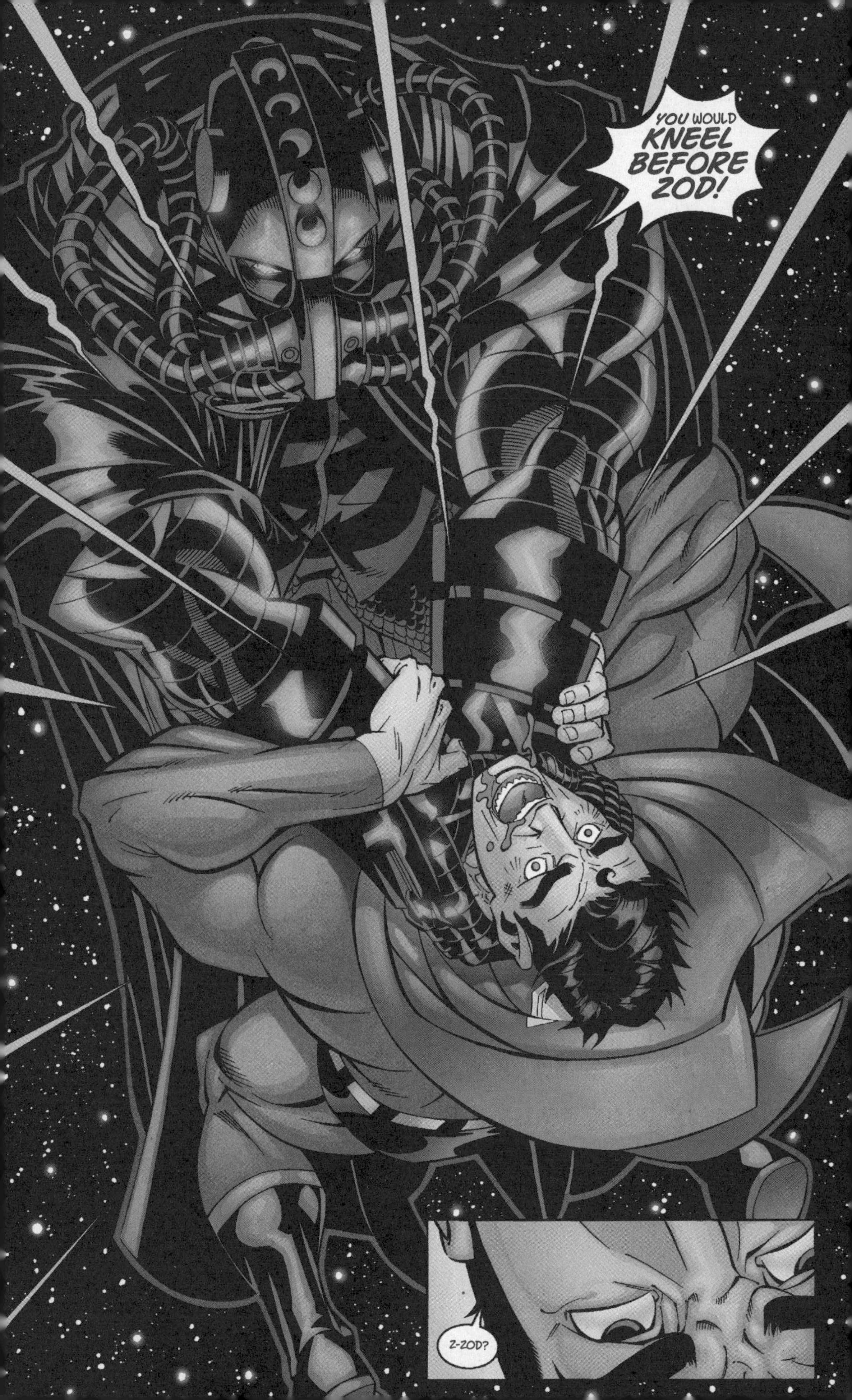
YOU WOULD KNEEL BEFORE ZOD!
Z-ZOD?

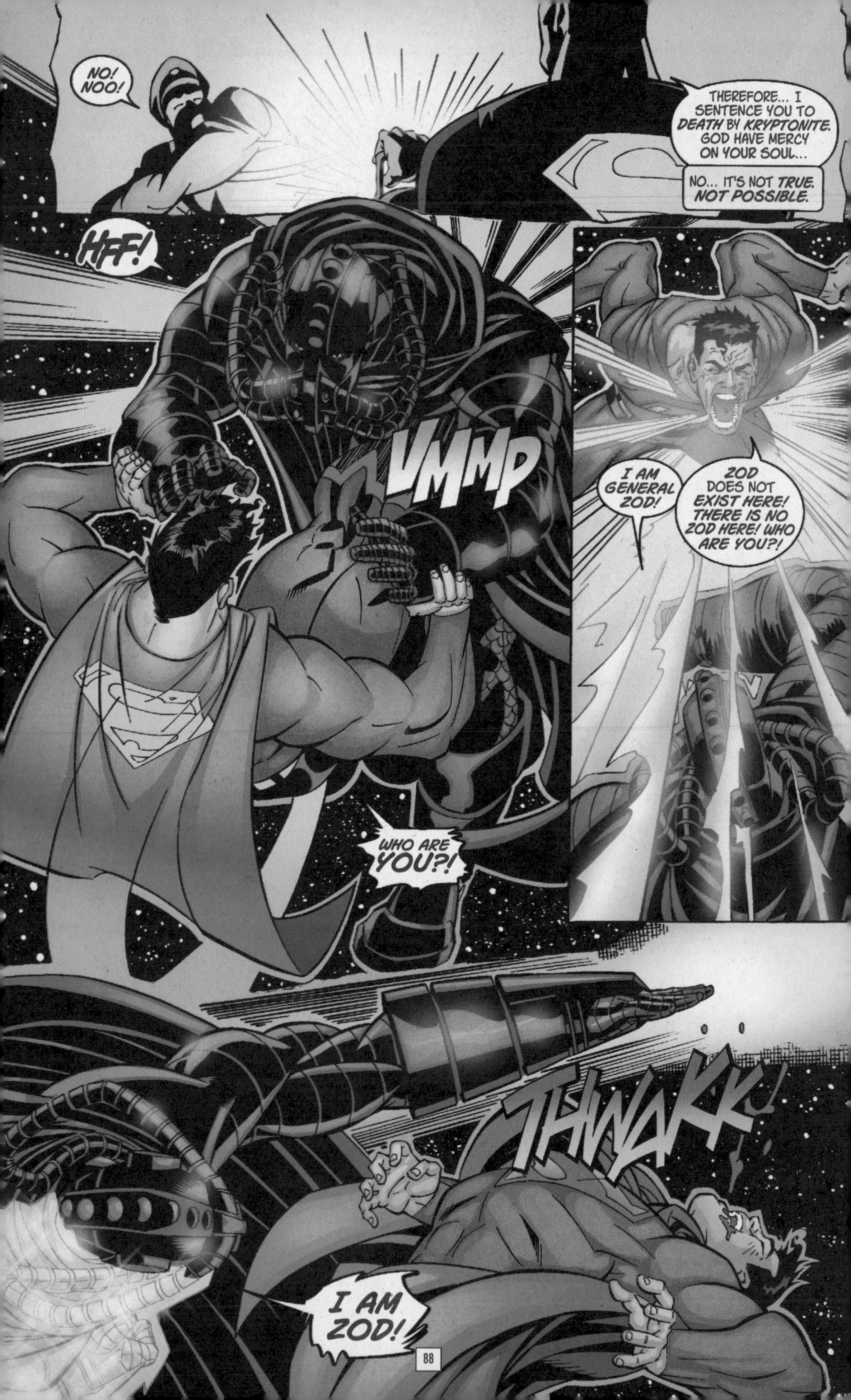
NO! NOO!
THEREFORE... I SENTENCE YOU TO DEATH BY KRYPTONITE. GOD HAVE MERCY ON YOUR SOUL...
NO... IT'S NOT TRUE. NOT POSSIBLE.
HFF!
UMMP
WHO ARE YOU?!
I AM GENERAL ZOD!
ZOD DOES NOT EXIST HERE! THERE IS NO ZOD HERE! WHO ARE YOU?!
THWAKK!
I AM ZOD!

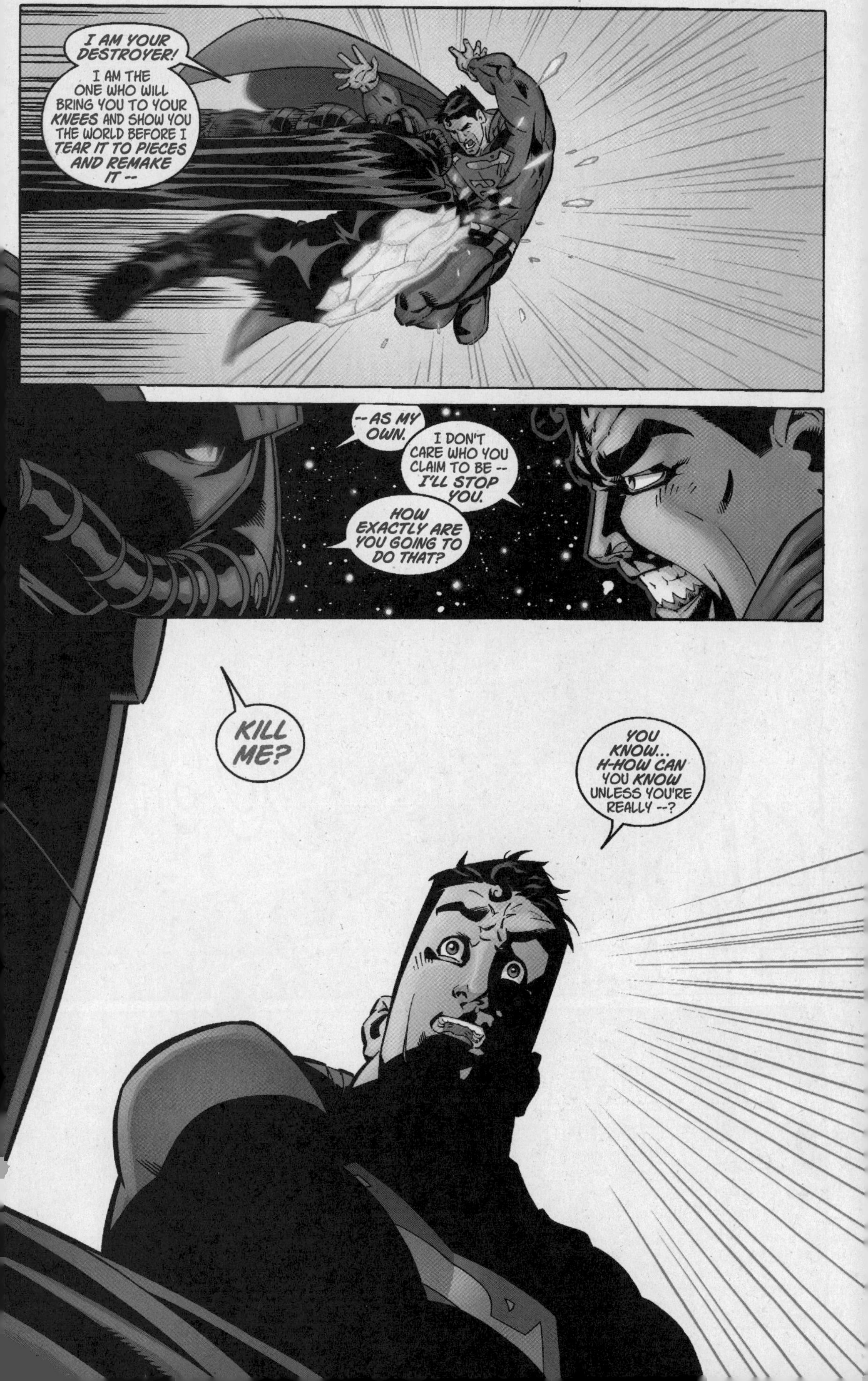
I AM YOUR DESTROYER!
I AM THE ONE WHO WILL BRING YOU TO YOUR KNEES AND SHOW YOU THE WORLD BEFORE I TEAR IT TO PIECES AND REMAKE IT --
--AS MY OWN.
I DON'T CARE WHO YOU CLAIM TO BE -- I'LL STOP YOU.
HOW EXACTLY ARE YOU GOING TO DO THAT?
KILL ME?
YOU KNOW... H-HOW CAN YOU KNOW UNLESS YOU'RE REALLY --?

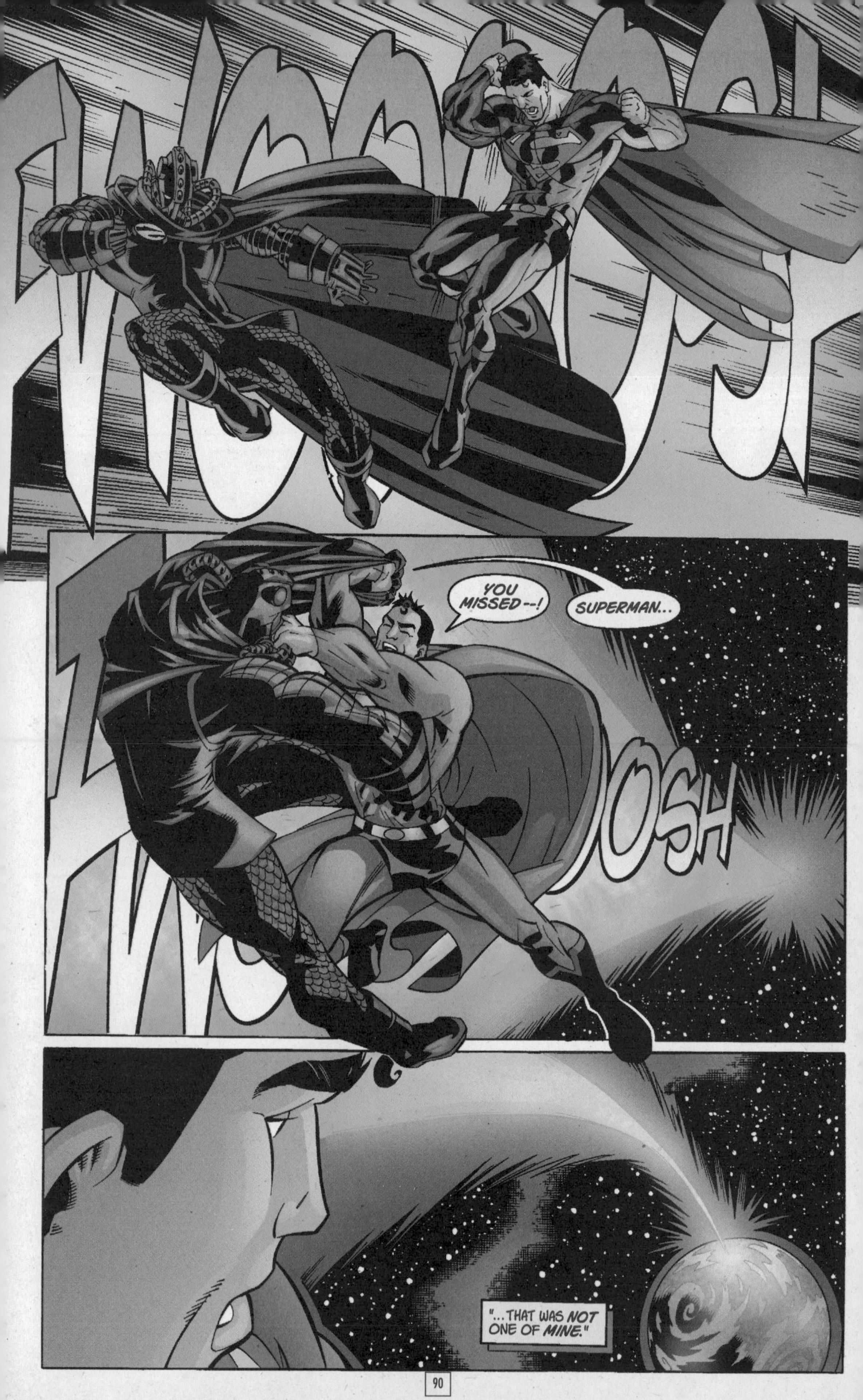
YOU MISSED--!
SUPERMAN...
OSH
"...THAT WAS NOT ONE OF MINE."

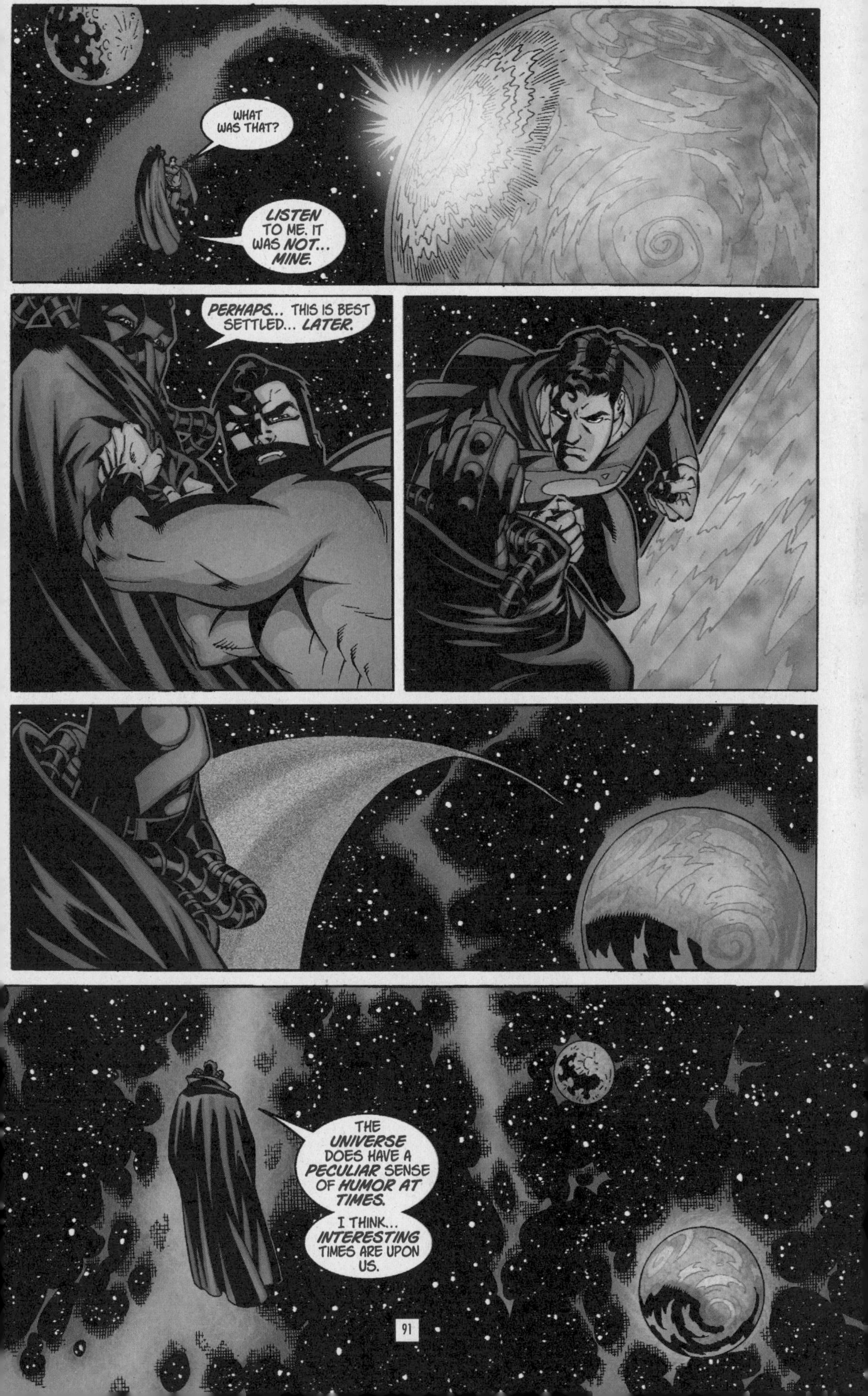
WHAT WAS THAT?
LISTEN TO ME. IT WAS NOT... MINE.
PERHAPS... THIS IS BEST SETTLED... LATER.
THE UNIVERSE DOES HAVE A PECULIAR SENSE OF HUMOR AT TIMES.
I THINK... INTERESTING TIMES ARE UPON US.

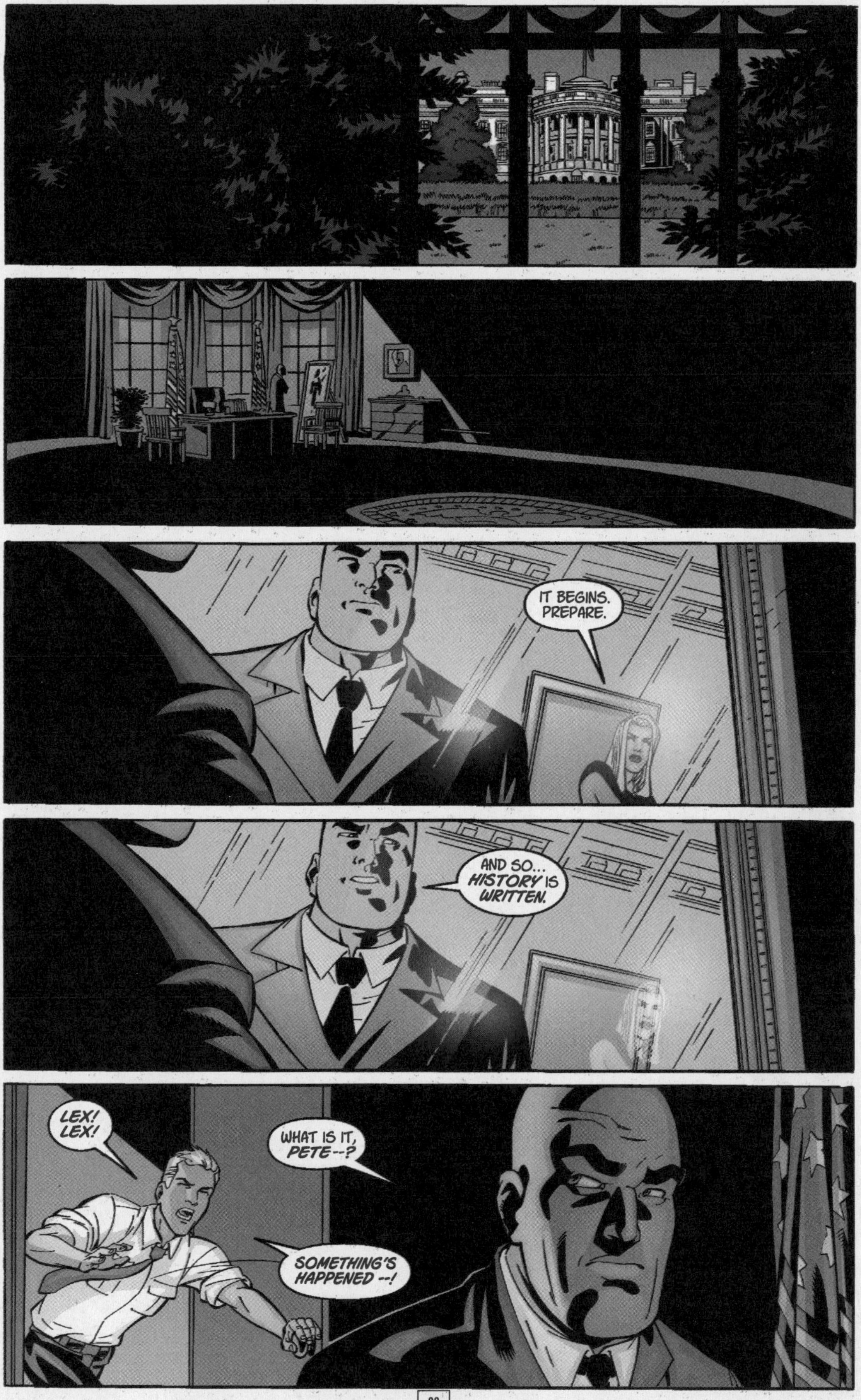
IT BEGINS. PREPARE.
AND SO... HISTORY IS WRITTEN.
LEX! LEX!
WHAT IS IT, PETE--?
SOMETHING'S HAPPENED --!

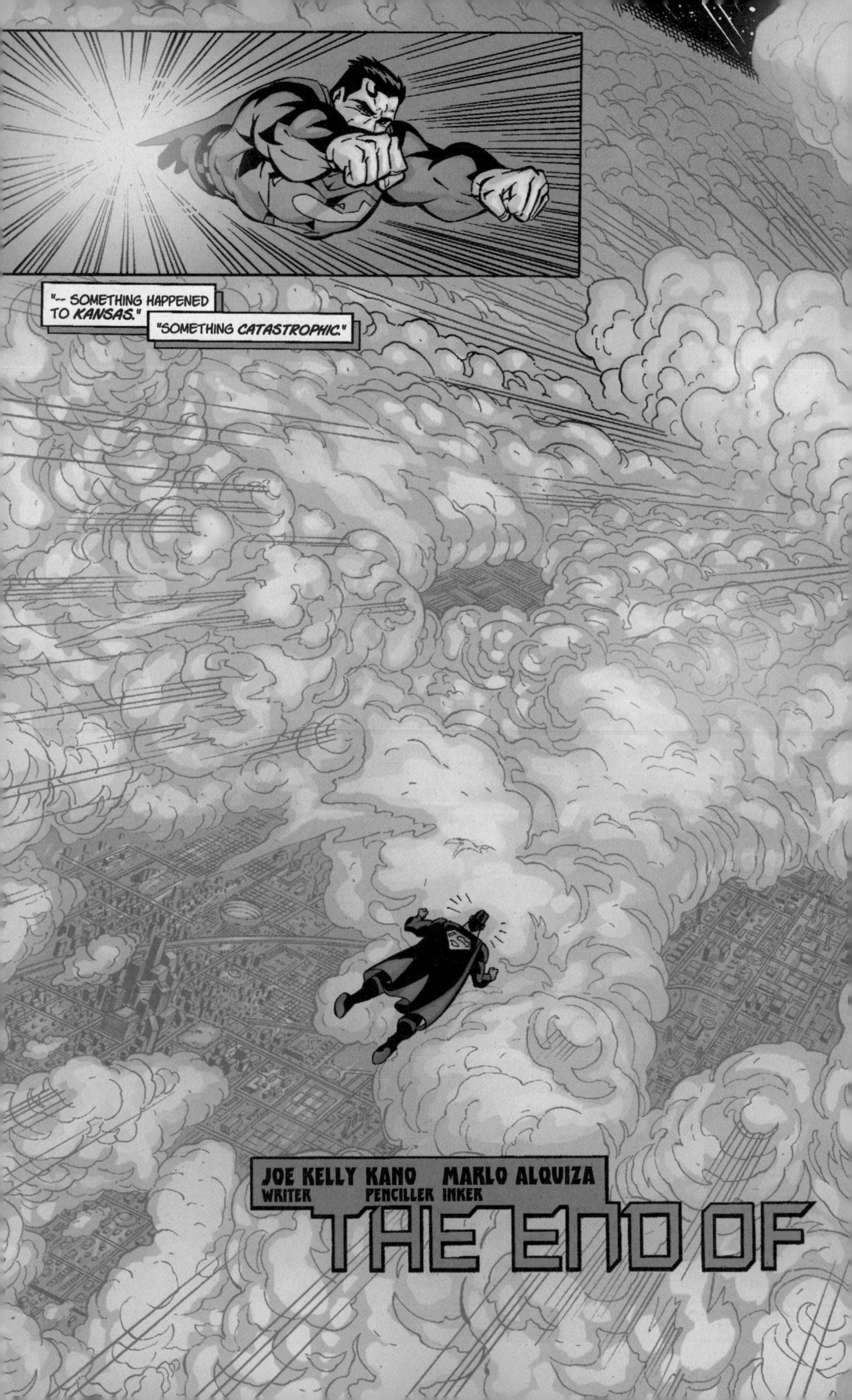
"-- SOMETHING HAPPENED TO KANSAS."
"SOMETHING CATASTROPHIC."
JOE KELLY WRITER
KANO PENCILLER
MARLO ALQUIZA INKER
THE END OF

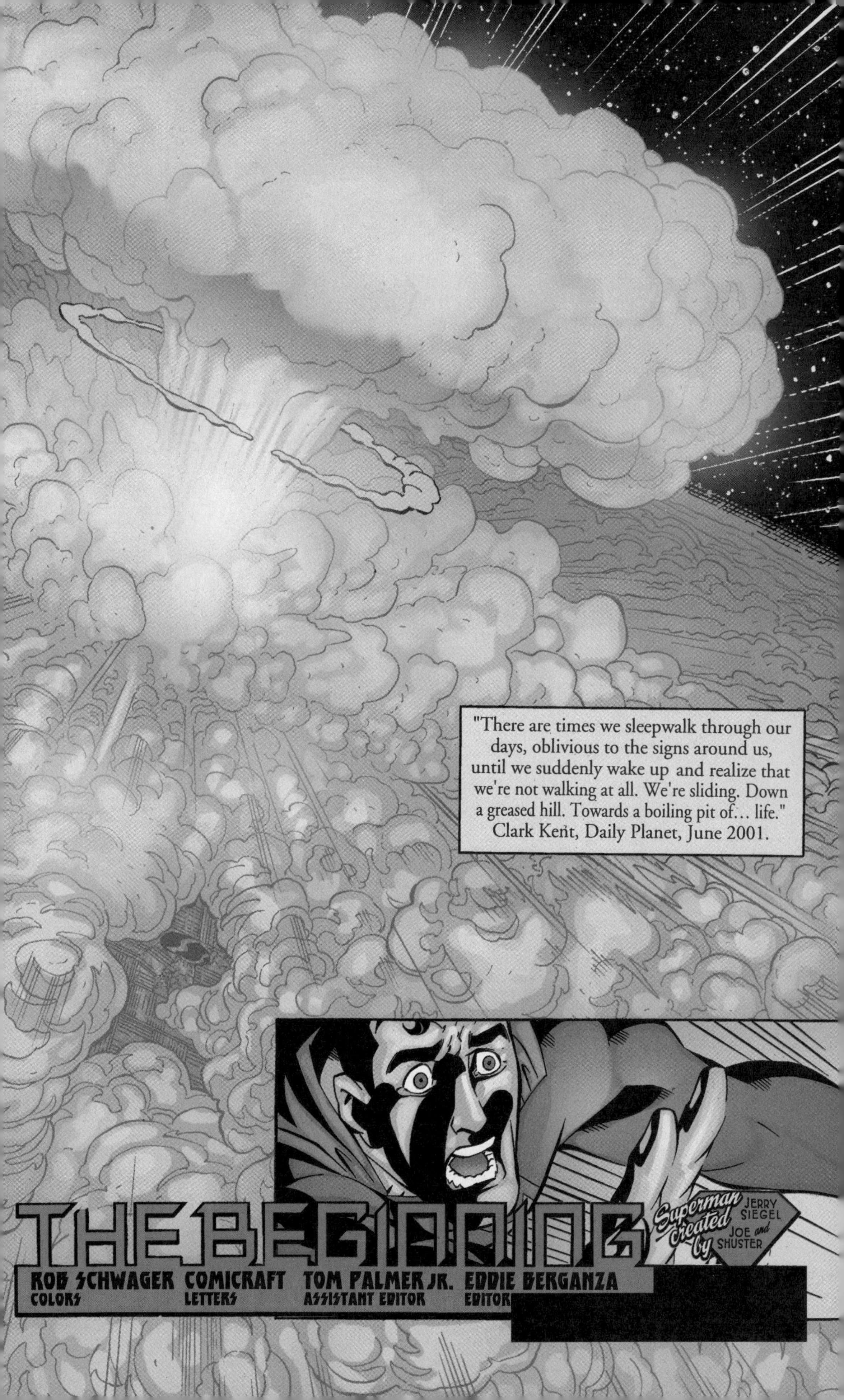
"There are times we sleepwalk through our days, oblivious to the signs around us, until we suddenly wake up and realize that we're not walking at all. We're sliding. Down a greased hill. Towards a boiling pit of... life."
Clark Kent, Daily Planet, June 2001.
THE BEGINNING
Superman created by JERRY SIEGEL and JOE SHUSTER
ROB SCHWAGER COLORS
COMICRAFT LETTERS
TOM PALMER JR. ASSISTANT EDITOR
EDDIE BERGANZA EDITOR
[redacted]

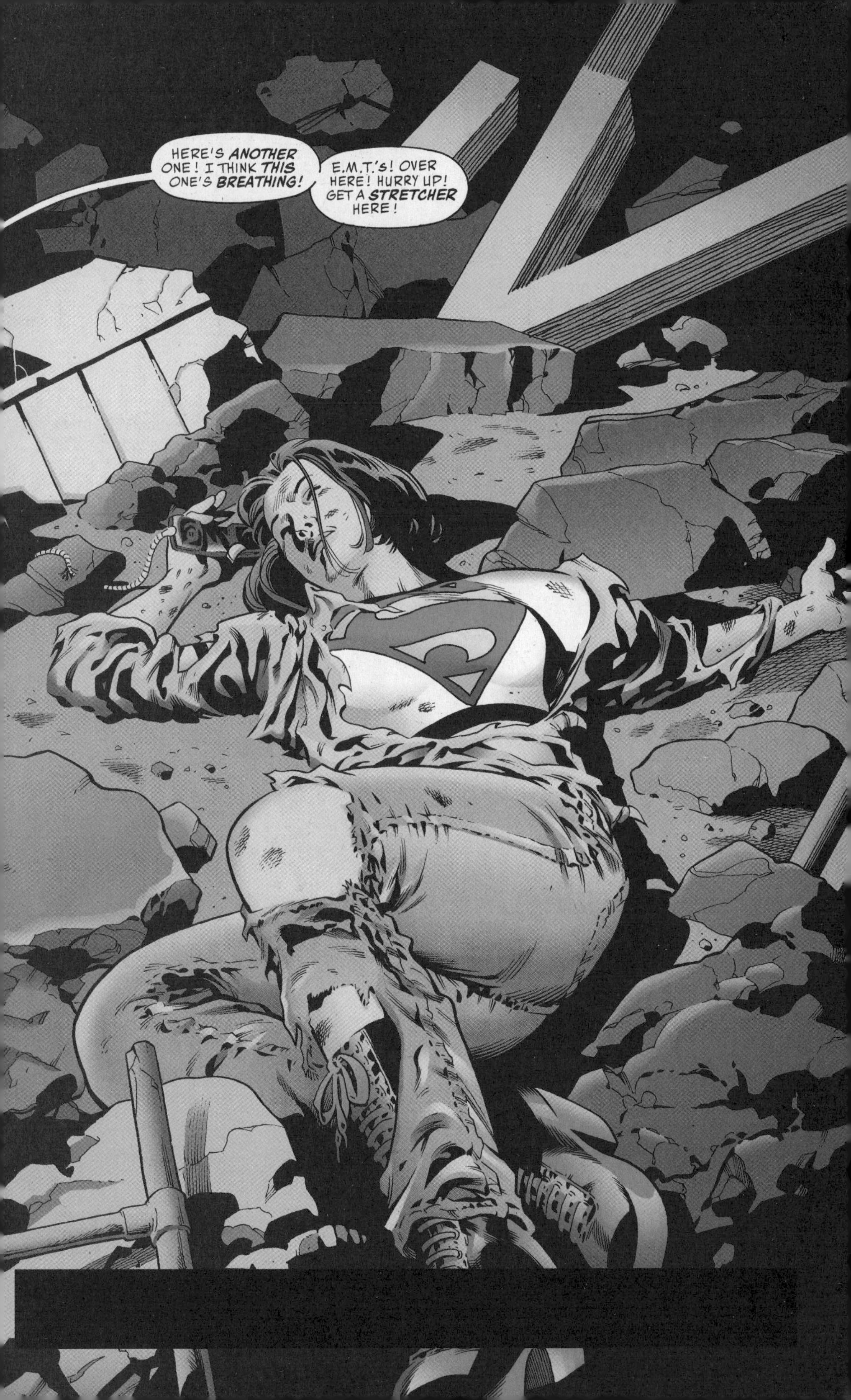
HERE'S ANOTHER ONE! I THINK THIS ONE'S BREATHING!
E.M.T.'s! OVER HERE! HURRY UP! GET A STRETCHER HERE!

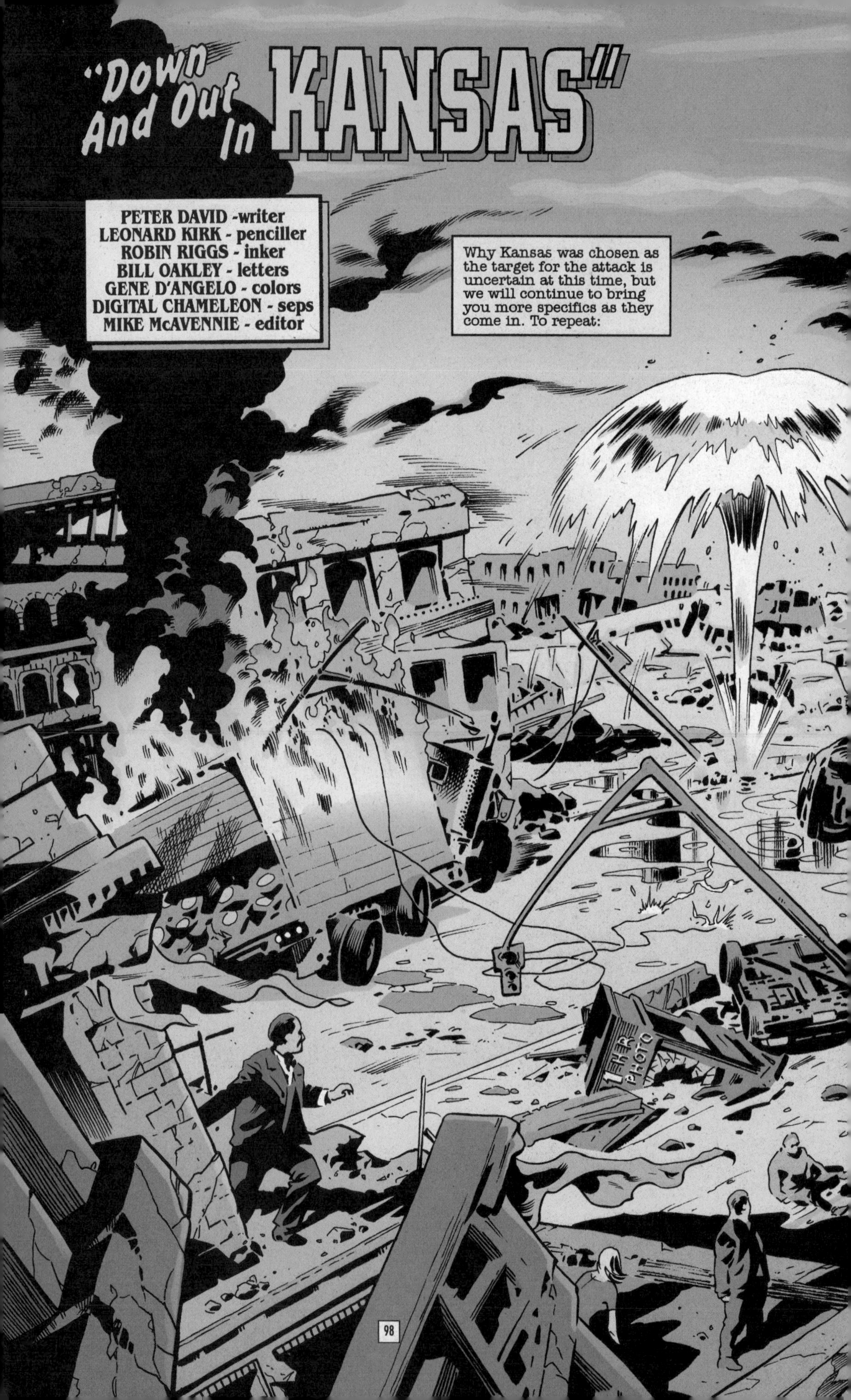
"Down And Out In KANSAS"
PETER DAVID -writer
LEONARD KIRK - penciller
ROBIN RIGGS - inker
BILL OAKLEY - letters
GENE D'ANGELO - colors
DIGITAL CHAMELEON - seps
MIKE McAVENNIE - editor
Why Kansas was chosen as the target for the attack is uncertain at this time, but we will continue to bring you more specifics as they come in. To repeat:
1 HR PHOTO

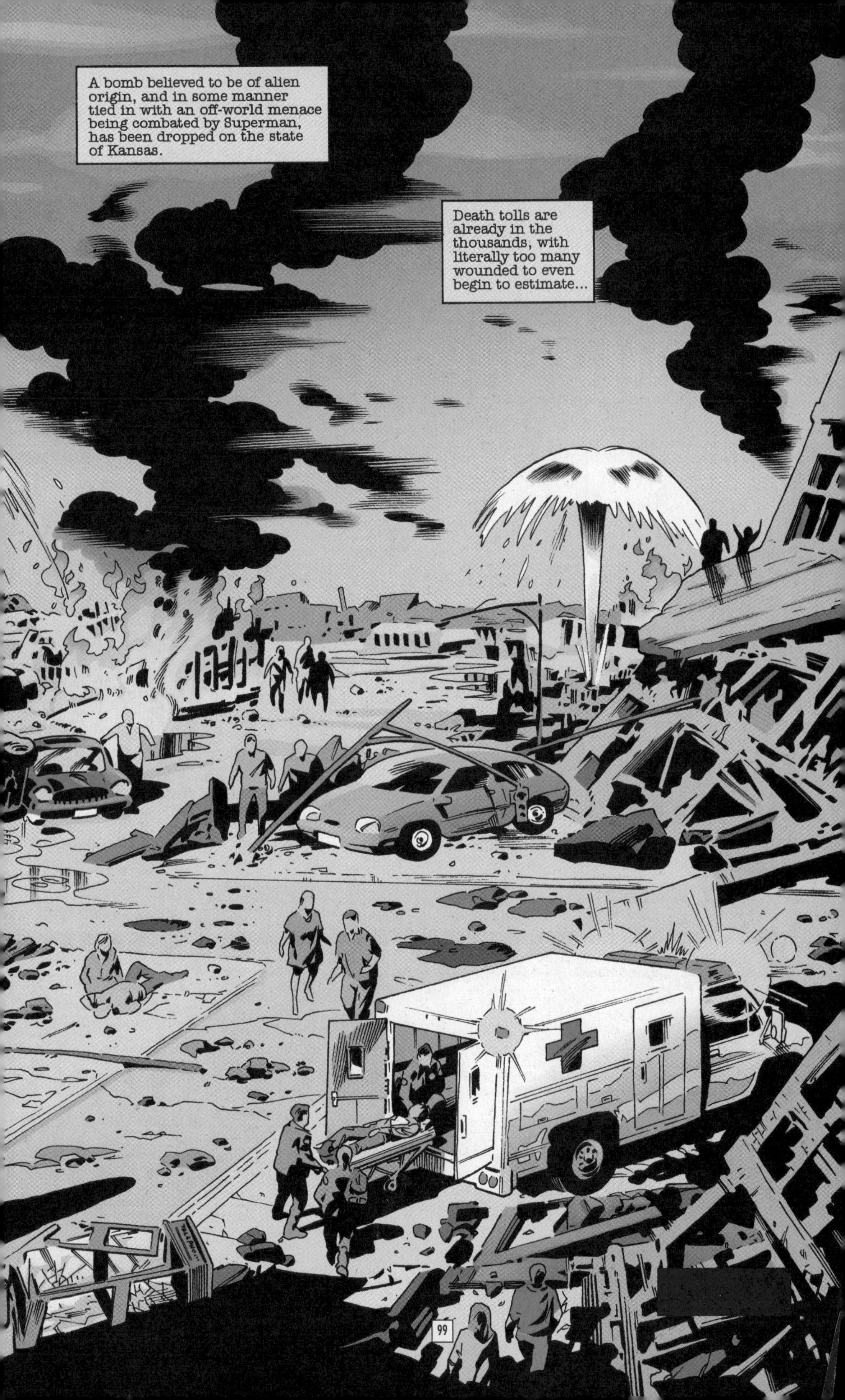
A bomb believed to be of alien origin, and in some manner tied in with an off-world menace being combated by Superman, has been dropped on the state of Kansas.
Death tolls are already in the thousands, with literally too many wounded to even begin to estimate...

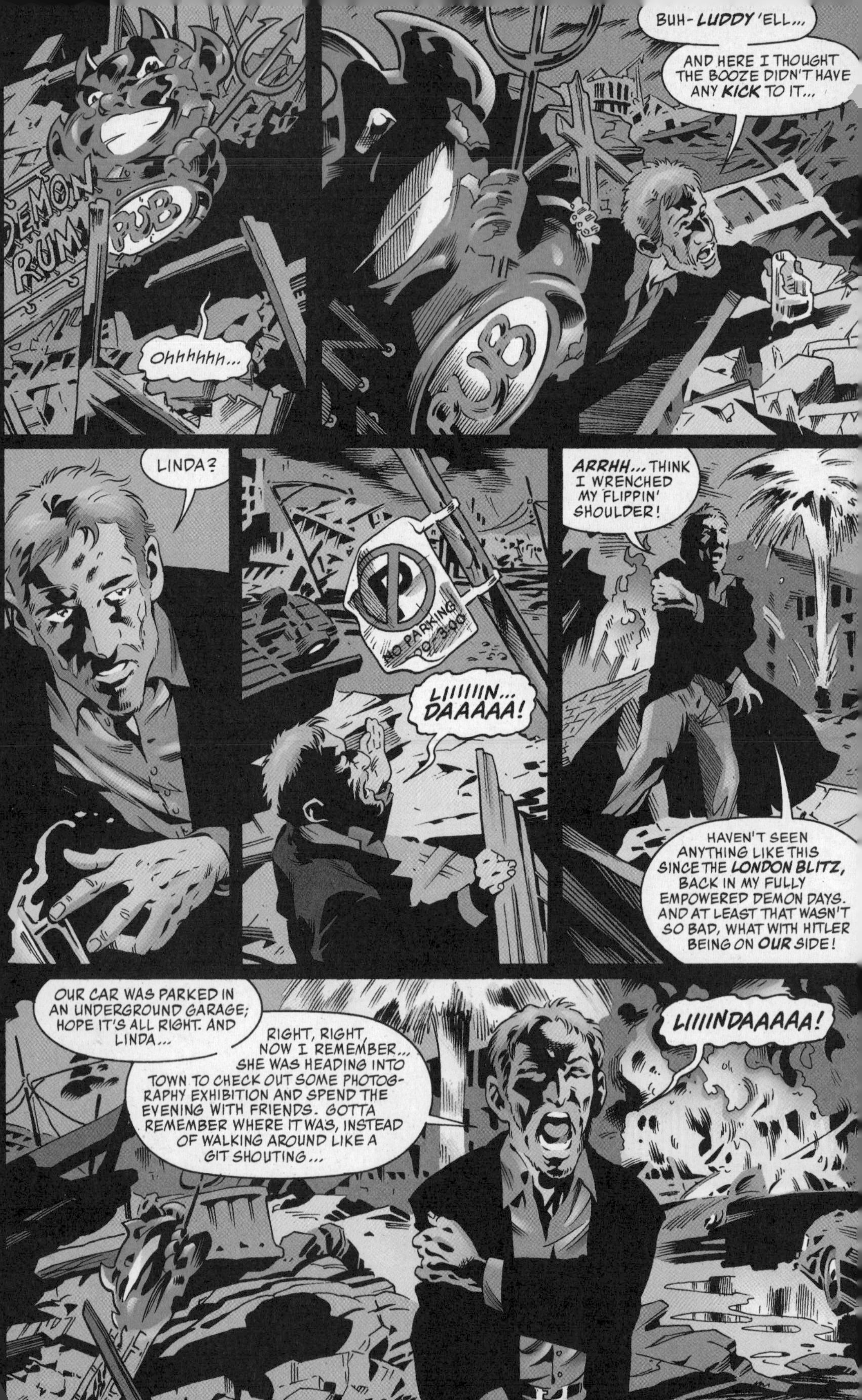

Ohhhhhh...
BUH-LUDDY 'ELL...
AND HERE I THOUGHT THE BOOZE DIDN'T HAVE ANY KICK TO IT...
DEMON RUM PUB
LINDA?
NO PARKING
LIIIIIN... DAAAAA!
ARRHH... THINK I WRENCHED MY 'FLIPPIN' SHOULDER!
HAVEN'T SEEN ANYTHING LIKE THIS SINCE THE LONDON BLITZ, BACK IN MY FULLY EMPOWERED DEMON DAYS. AND AT LEAST THAT WASN'T SO BAD, WHAT WITH HITLER BEING ON OUR SIDE!
OUR CAR WAS PARKED IN AN UNDERGROUND GARAGE; HOPE IT'S ALL RIGHT. AND LINDA...
RIGHT, RIGHT, NOW I REMEMBER... SHE WAS HEADING INTO TOWN TO CHECK OUT SOME PHOTOGRAPHY EXHIBITION AND SPEND THE EVENING WITH FRIENDS. GOTTA REMEMBER WHERE IT WAS, INSTEAD OF WALKING AROUND LIKE A GIT SHOUTING...
LIIIINDAAAAA!

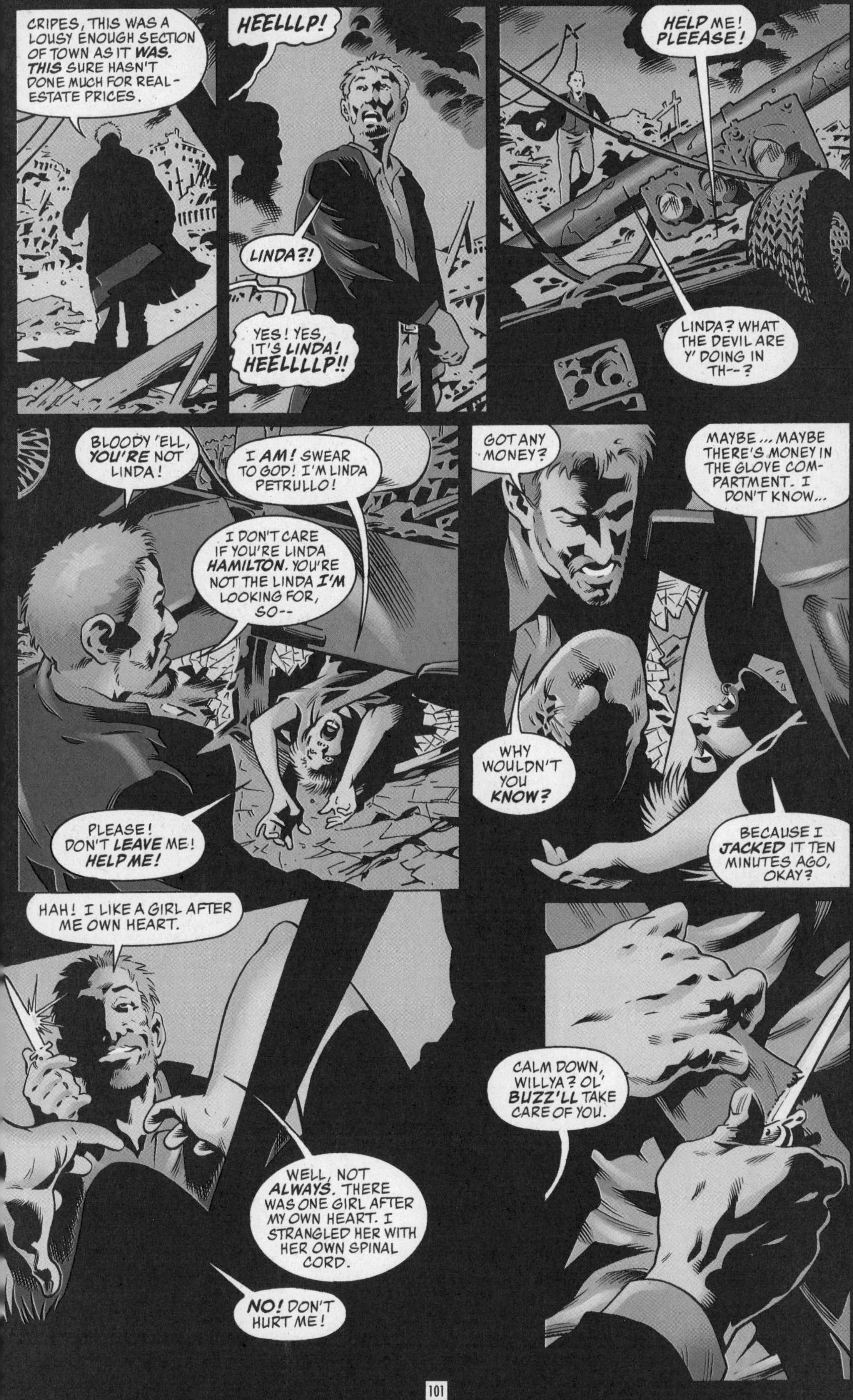

CRIPES, THIS WAS A LOUSY ENOUGH SECTION OF TOWN AS IT WAS. THIS SURE HASN'T DONE MUCH FOR REAL-ESTATE PRICES.
HEELLLP!
LINDA?!
YES! YES, IT'S LINDA! HEELLLLP!!
HELP ME! PLEEASE!
LINDA? WHAT THE DEVIL ARE Y' DOING IN TH--?
BLOODY 'ELL, YOU'RE NOT LINDA!
I AM! SWEAR TO GOD! I'M LINDA PETRULLO!
I DON'T CARE IF YOU'RE LINDA HAMILTON. YOU'RE NOT THE LINDA I'M LOOKING FOR, SO--
PLEASE! DON'T LEAVE ME! HELP ME!
GOT ANY MONEY?
MAYBE... MAYBE THERE'S MONEY IN THE GLOVE COMPARTMENT. I DON'T KNOW...
WHY WOULDN'T YOU KNOW?
BECAUSE I JACKED IT TEN MINUTES AGO, OKAY?
HAH! I LIKE A GIRL AFTER ME OWN HEART.
WELL, NOT ALWAYS. THERE WAS ONE GIRL AFTER MY OWN HEART. I STRANGLED HER WITH HER OWN SPINAL CORD.
NO! DON'T HURT ME!
CALM DOWN, WILLYA? OL' BUZZ'LL TAKE CARE OF YOU.

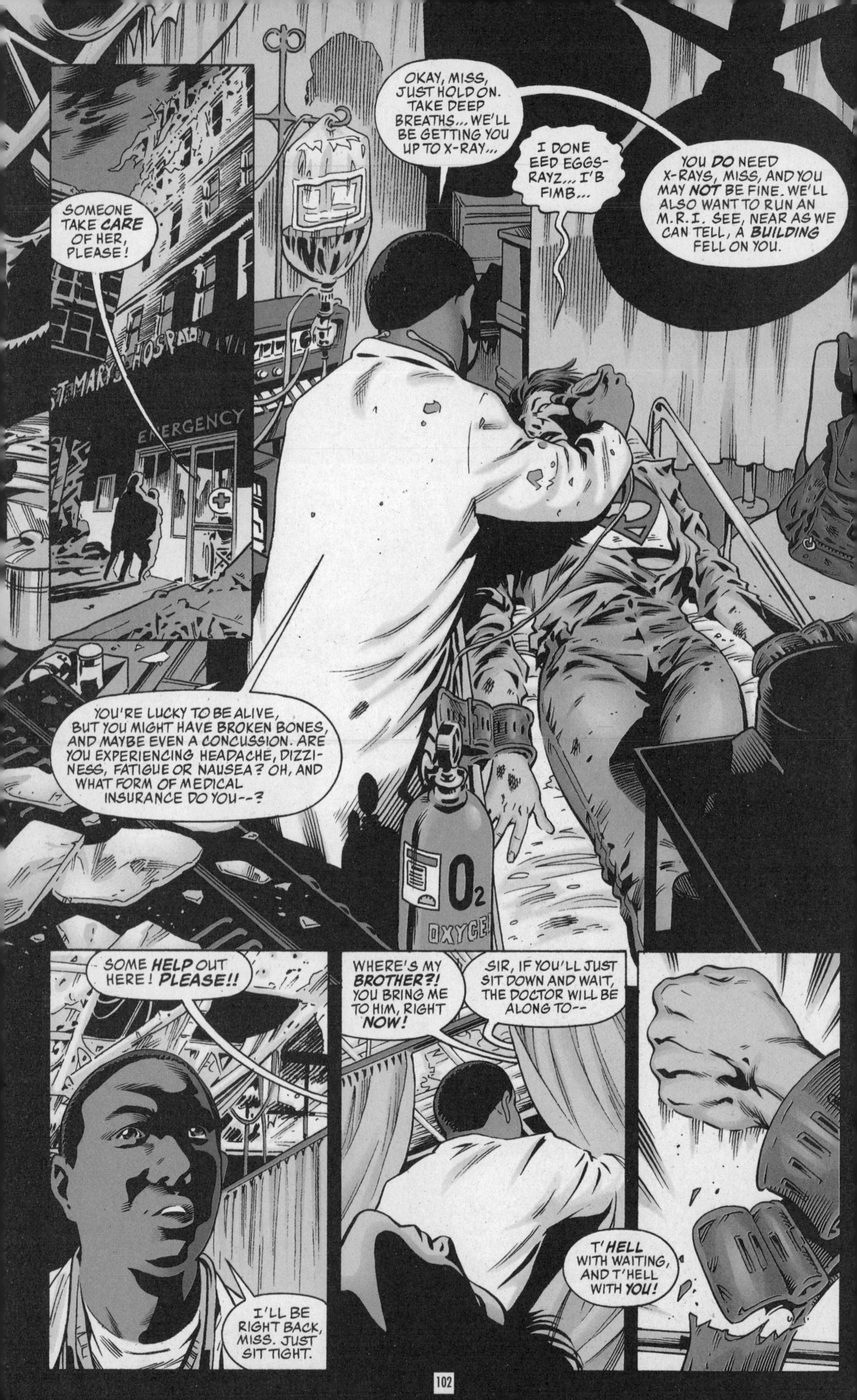
OKAY, MISS, JUST HOLD ON. TAKE DEEP BREATHS... WE'LL BE GETTING YOU UP TO X-RAY...
SOMEONE TAKE CARE OF HER, PLEASE!
ST. MARY'S HOSPITAL
EMERGENCY
I DONE EED EGGS-RAYZ... I'B FIMB...
YOU DO NEED X-RAYS, MISS, AND YOU MAY NOT BE FINE. WE'LL ALSO WANT TO RUN AN M.R.I. SEE, NEAR AS WE CAN TELL, A BUILDING FELL ON YOU.
YOU'RE LUCKY TO BE ALIVE, BUT YOU MIGHT HAVE BROKEN BONES, AND MAYBE EVEN A CONCUSSION. ARE YOU EXPERIENCING HEADACHE, DIZZINESS, FATIGUE OR NAUSEA? OH, AND WHAT FORM OF MEDICAL INSURANCE DO YOU--?
O2
OXYGE
SOME HELP OUT HERE! PLEASE!!
I'LL BE RIGHT BACK, MISS. JUST SIT TIGHT.
WHERE'S MY BROTHER?! YOU BRING ME TO HIM, RIGHT NOW!
SIR, IF YOU'LL JUST SIT DOWN AND WAIT, THE DOCTOR WILL BE ALONG TO--
T'HELL WITH WAITING, AND T'HELL WITH YOU!

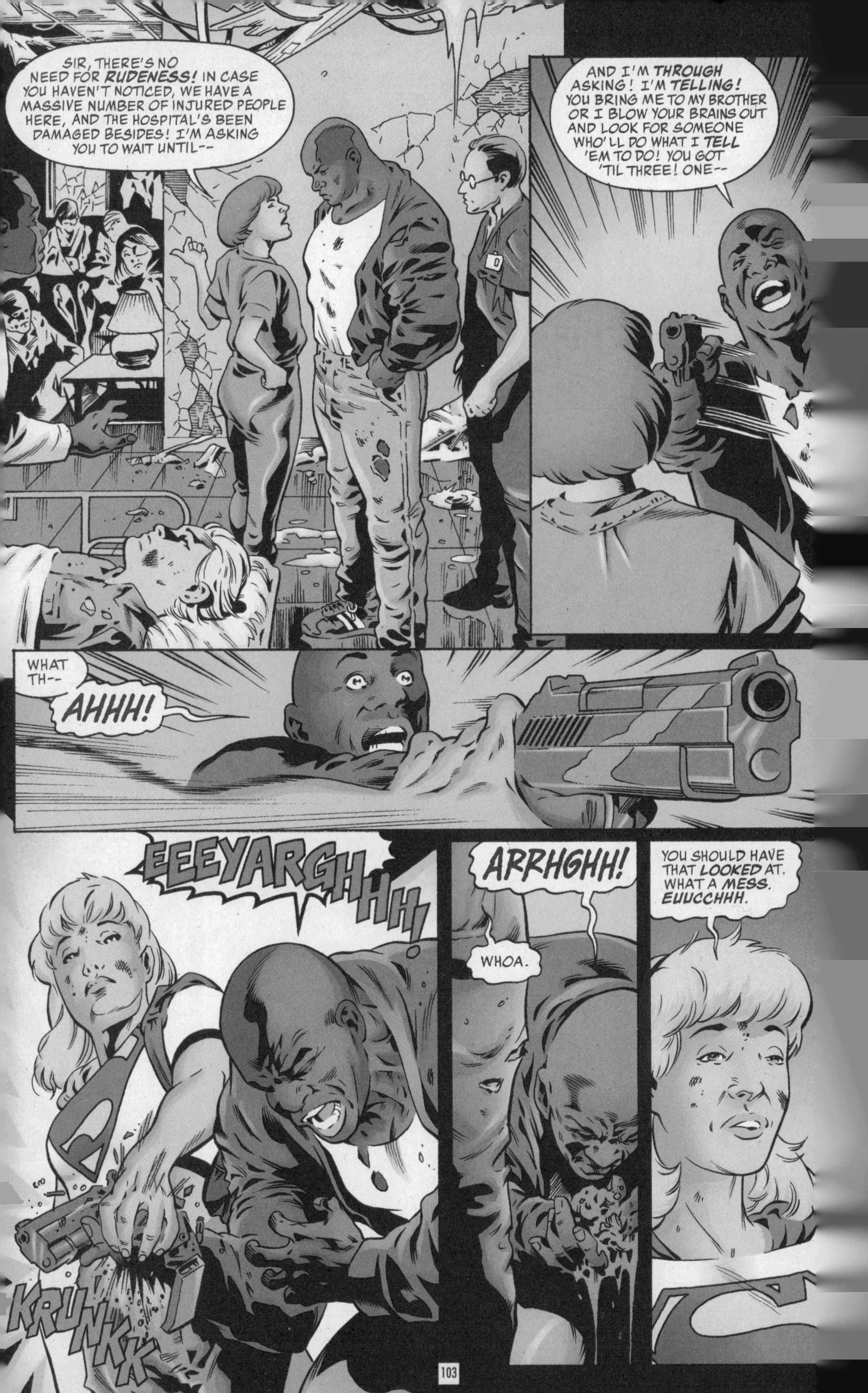
SIR, THERE'S NO NEED FOR RUDENESS! IN CASE YOU HAVEN'T NOTICED, WE HAVE A MASSIVE NUMBER OF INJURED PEOPLE HERE, AND THE HOSPITAL'S BEEN DAMAGED BESIDES! I'M ASKING YOU TO WAIT UNTIL--
AND I'M THROUGH ASKING! I'M TELLING! YOU BRING ME TO MY BROTHER OR I BLOW YOUR BRAINS OUT AND LOOK FOR SOMEONE WHO'LL DO WHAT I TELL 'EM TO DO! YOU GOT 'TIL THREE! ONE--
WHAT TH--
AHHH!
EEEYARGHHHH!
KRUNKKK
ARRHGHH!
WHOA.
YOU SHOULD HAVE THAT LOOKED AT. WHAT A MESS. EUUCCHHH.

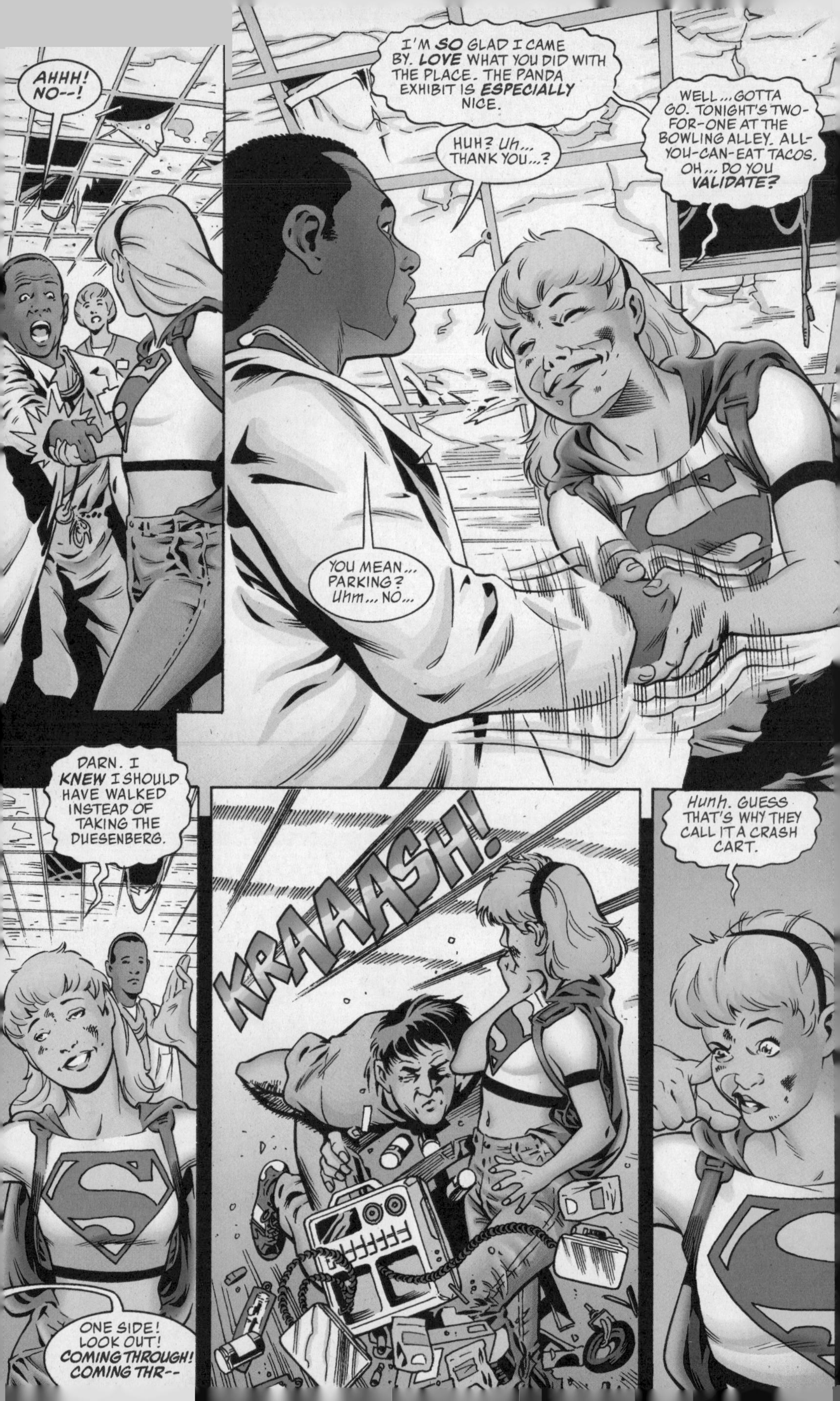
AHHH! NO--!
I'M SO GLAD I CAME BY. LOVE WHAT YOU DID WITH THE PLACE. THE PANDA EXHIBIT IS ESPECIALLY NICE.
HUH? Uh... THANK YOU...?
WELL... GOTTA GO. TONIGHT'S TWO-FOR-ONE AT THE BOWLING ALLEY. ALL-YOU-CAN-EAT TACOS. OH... DO YOU VALIDATE?
YOU MEAN... PARKING? Uhm... NO...
DARN. I KNEW I SHOULD HAVE WALKED INSTEAD OF TAKING THE DUESENBERG.
ONE SIDE! LOOK OUT! COMING THROUGH! COMING THR--
KRAAASH!
Hunh. GUESS THAT'S WHY THEY CALL IT A CRASH CART.

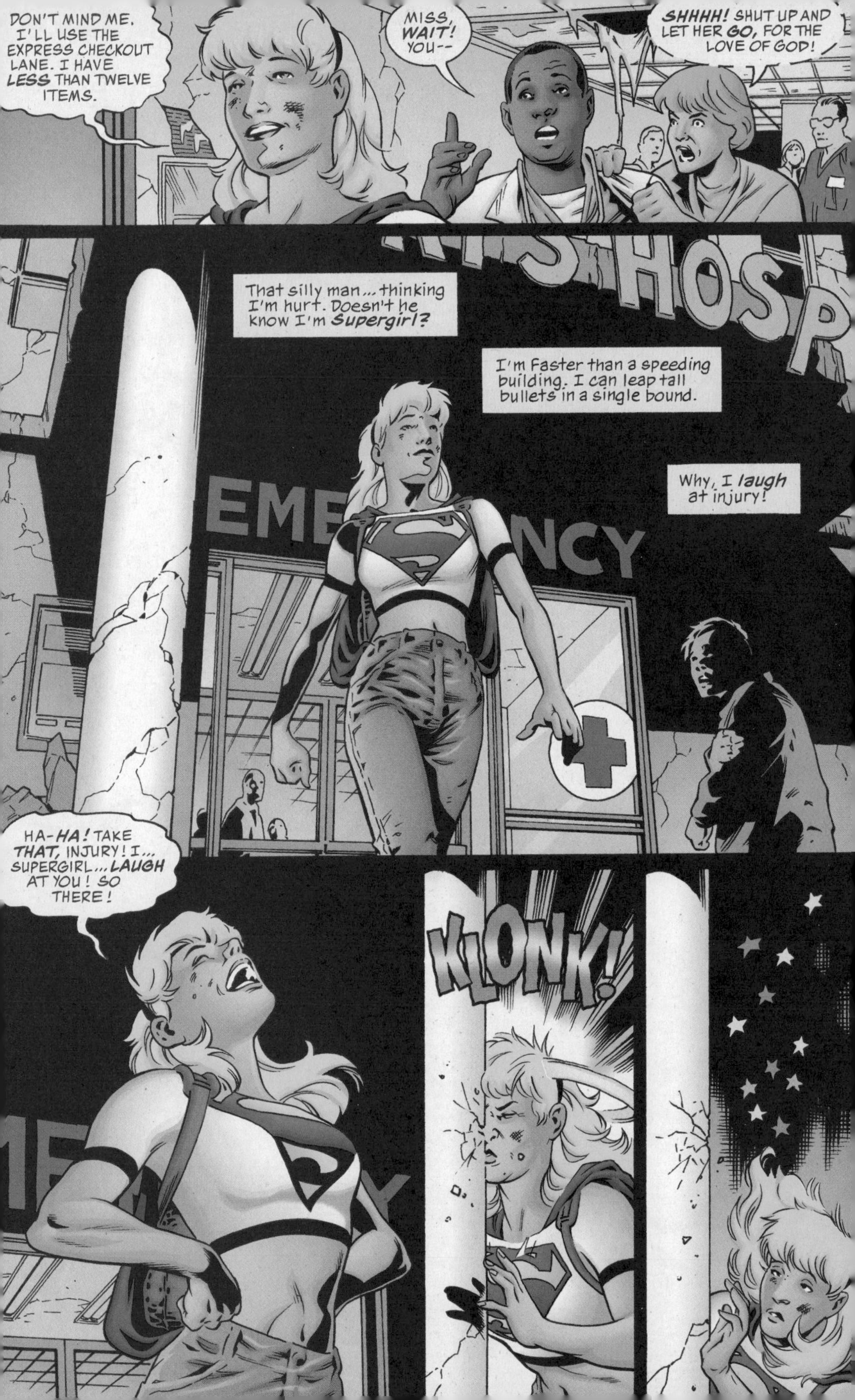
DON'T MIND ME. I'LL USE THE EXPRESS CHECKOUT LANE. I HAVE LESS THAN TWELVE ITEMS.
MISS, WAIT! YOU--
SHHHH! SHUT UP AND LET HER GO, FOR THE LOVE OF GOD!
HOSP
That silly man... thinking I'm hurt. Doesn't he know I'm Supergirl?
I'm Faster than a speeding building. I can leap tall bullets in a single bound.
Why, I laugh at injury!
EME NCY
HA-HA! TAKE THAT, INJURY! I... SUPERGIRL... LAUGH AT YOU! SO THERE!
KLONK!

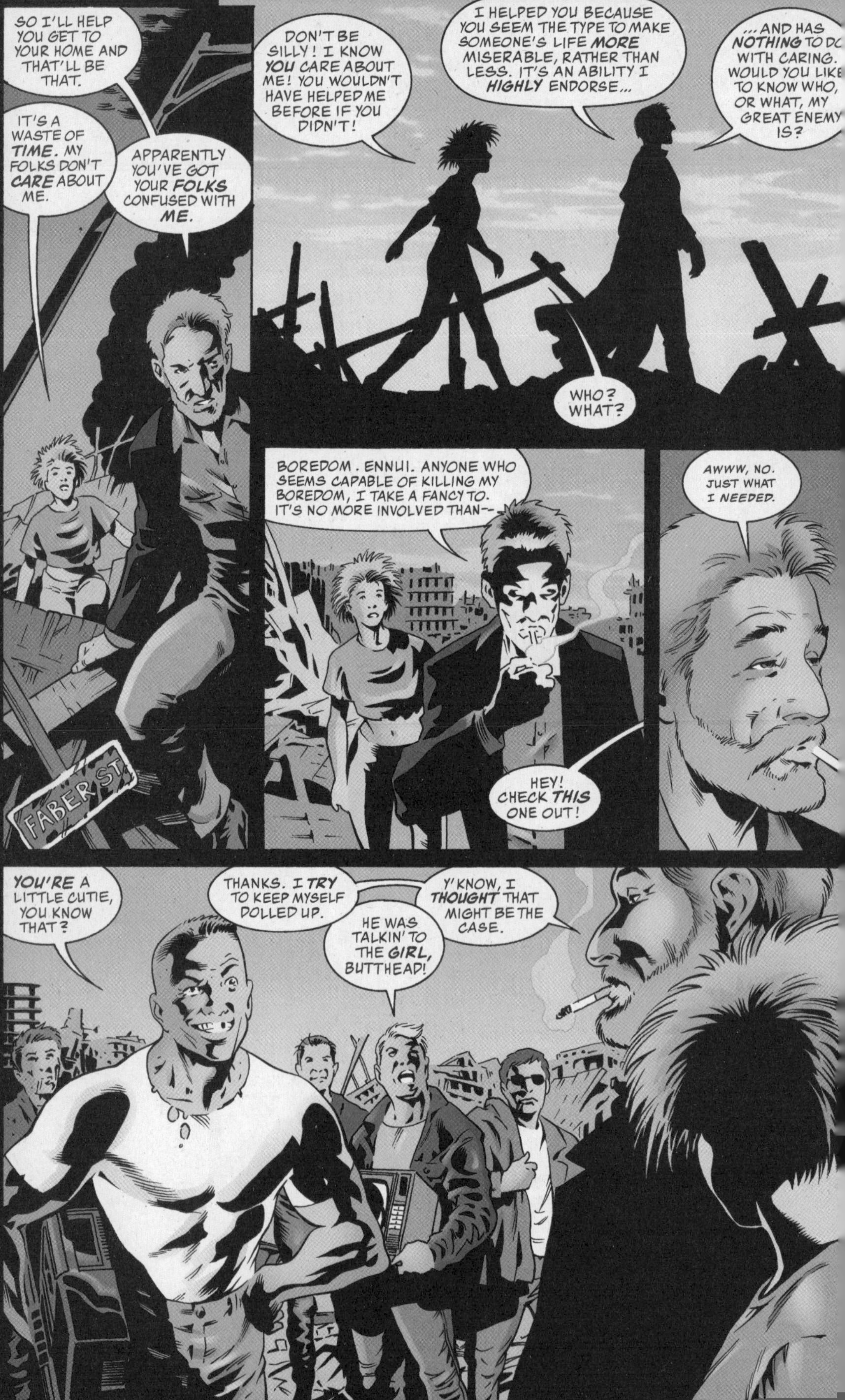
SO I'LL HELP YOU GET TO YOUR HOME AND THAT'LL BE THAT.
IT'S A WASTE OF TIME. MY FOLKS DON'T CARE ABOUT ME.
APPARENTLY YOU'VE GOT YOUR FOLKS CONFUSED WITH ME.
FABER ST.
DON'T BE SILLY! I KNOW YOU CARE ABOUT ME! YOU WOULDN'T HAVE HELPED ME BEFORE IF YOU DIDN'T!
I HELPED YOU BECAUSE YOU SEEM THE TYPE TO MAKE SOMEONE'S LIFE MORE MISERABLE, RATHER THAN LESS. IT'S AN ABILITY I HIGHLY ENDORSE...
...AND HAS NOTHING TO DO WITH CARING. WOULD YOU LIKE TO KNOW WHO, OR WHAT, MY GREAT ENEMY IS?
WHO? WHAT?
BOREDOM. ENNUI. ANYONE WHO SEEMS CAPABLE OF KILLING MY BOREDOM, I TAKE A FANCY TO. IT'S NO MORE INVOLVED THAN--
HEY! CHECK THIS ONE OUT!
AWWW, NO. JUST WHAT I NEEDED.
YOU'RE A LITTLE CUTIE, YOU KNOW THAT?
THANKS. I TRY TO KEEP MYSELF DOLLED UP.
HE WAS TALKIN' TO THE GIRL, BUTTHEAD!
Y'KNOW, I THOUGHT THAT MIGHT BE THE CASE.

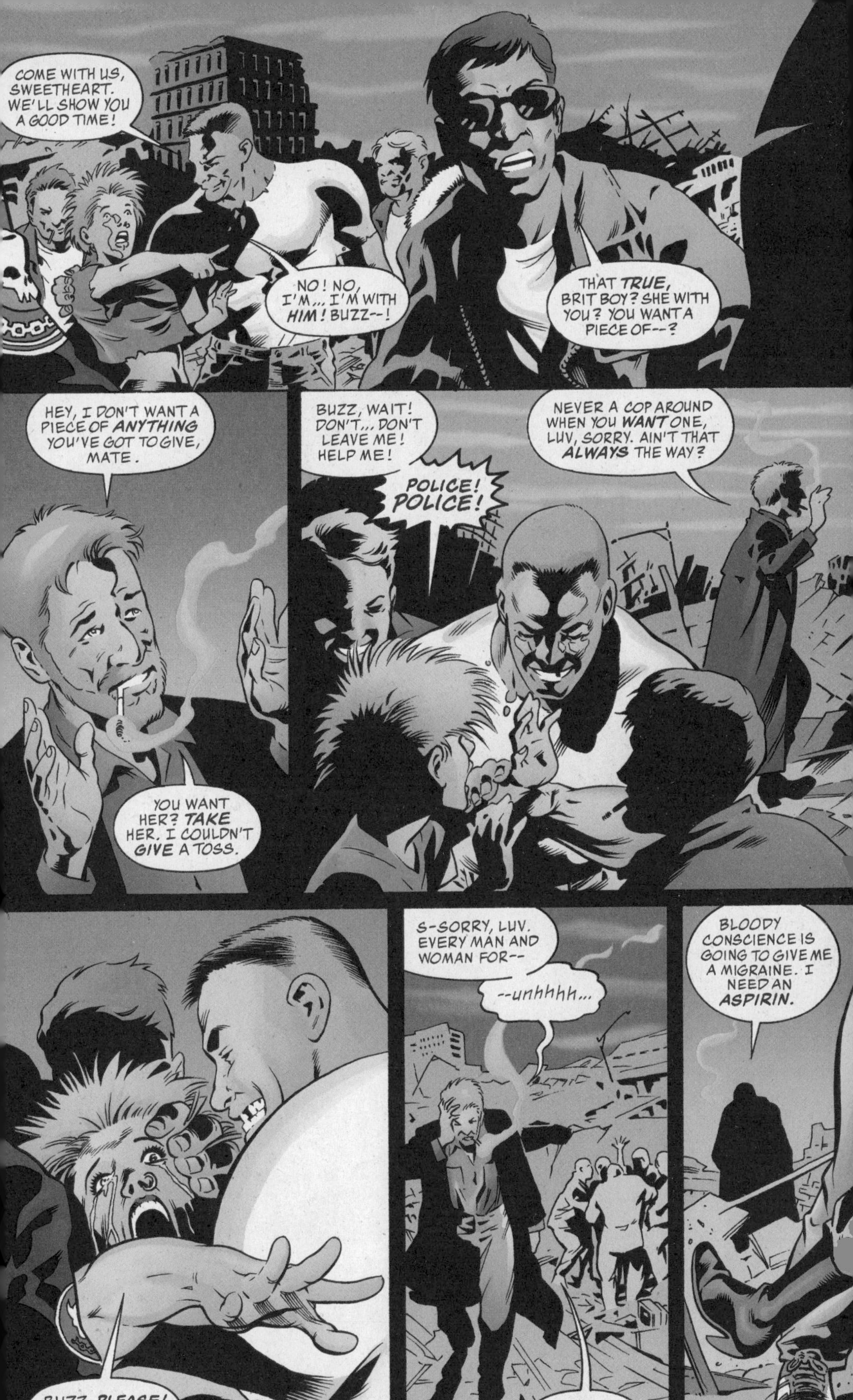
COME WITH US, SWEETHEART. WE'LL SHOW YOU A GOOD TIME!
NO! NO, I'M... I'M WITH HIM! BUZZ--!
THAT TRUE, BRIT BOY? SHE WITH YOU? YOU WANT A PIECE OF--?
HEY, I DON'T WANT A PIECE OF ANYTHING YOU'VE GOT TO GIVE, MATE.
YOU WANT HER? TAKE HER. I COULDN'T GIVE A TOSS.
BUZZ, WAIT! DON'T... DON'T LEAVE ME! HELP ME!
POLICE! POLICE!
NEVER A COP AROUND WHEN YOU WANT ONE, LUV, SORRY. AIN'T THAT ALWAYS THE WAY?
BUZZ, PLEASE! I'M BEGGING YOU! BUZZ--!!
S-SORRY, LUV. EVERY MAN AND WOMAN FOR--
--unhhhh...
...FOR THEMSELVES...
BLOODY CONSCIENCE IS GOING TO GIVE ME A MIGRAINE. I NEED AN ASPIRIN.

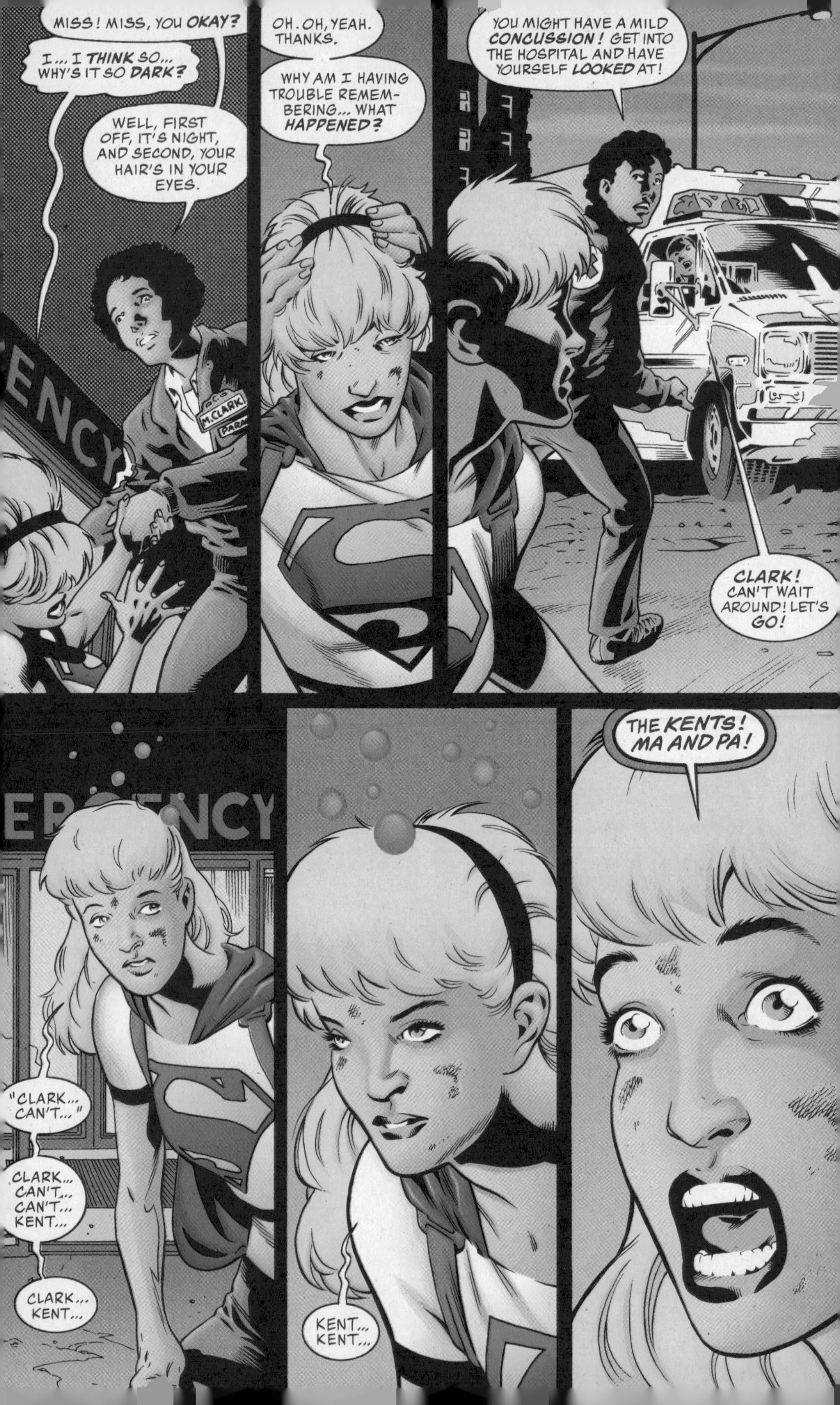
MISS! MISS, YOU OKAY?
I... I THINK SO... WHY'S IT SO DARK?
WELL, FIRST OFF, IT'S NIGHT, AND SECOND, YOUR HAIR'S IN YOUR EYES.
M. CLARK
OH. OH, YEAH. THANKS.
WHY AM I HAVING TROUBLE REMEMBERING... WHAT HAPPENED?
YOU MIGHT HAVE A MILD CONCUSSION! GET INTO THE HOSPITAL AND HAVE YOURSELF LOOKED AT!
CLARK! CAN'T WAIT AROUND! LET'S GO!
"CLARK... CAN'T..."
CLARK... CAN'T... CAN'T... KENT...
CLARK... KENT...
KENT... KENT...
THE KENTS! MA AND PA!

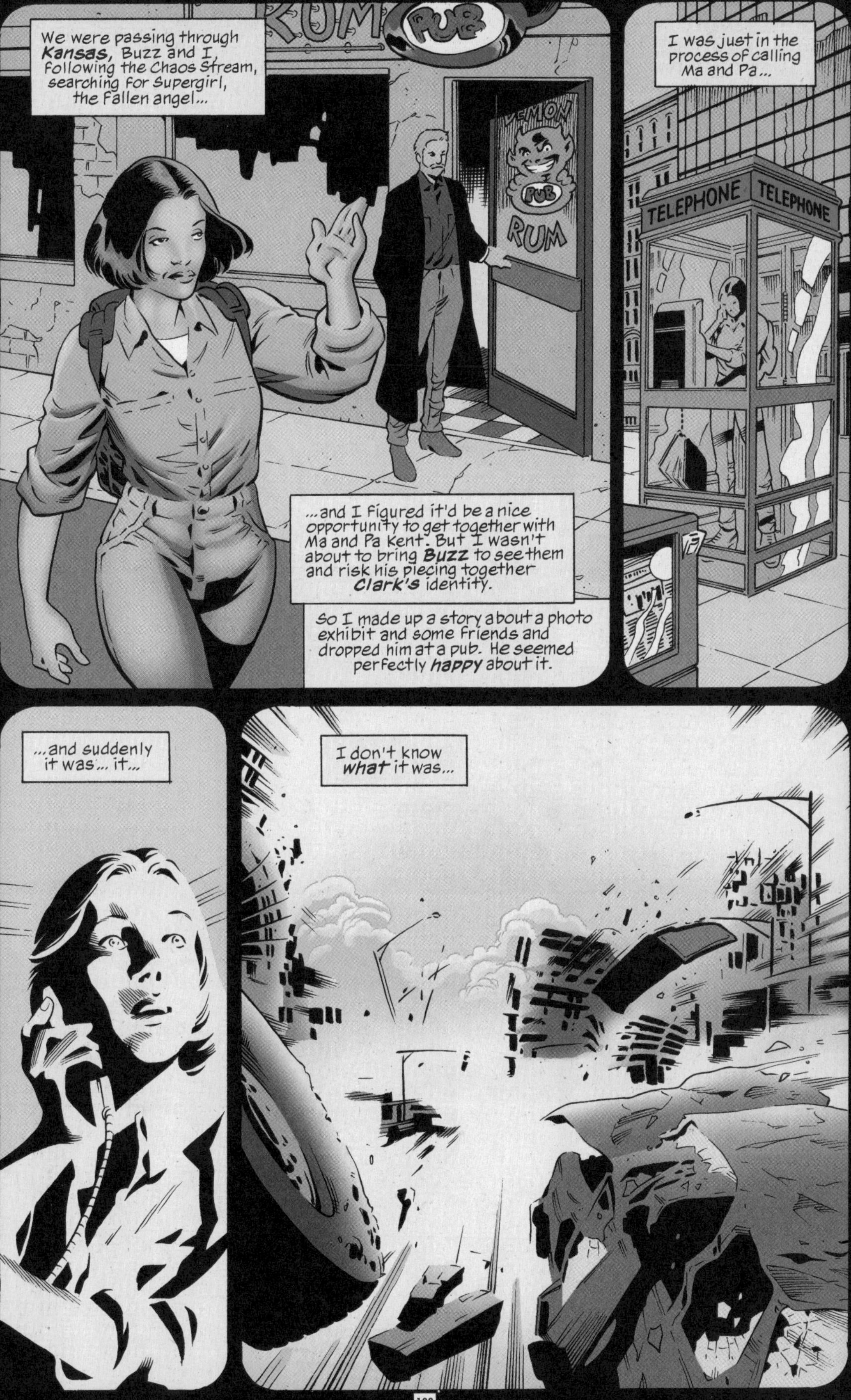

RUM PUB
We were passing through Kansas, Buzz and I, following the Chaos Stream, searching for Supergirl, the fallen angel...
DEMON PUB RUM
...and I figured it'd be a nice opportunity to get together with Ma and Pa Kent. But I wasn't about to bring Buzz to see them and risk his piecing together Clark's identity.
So I made up a story about a photo exhibit and some friends and dropped him at a pub. He seemed perfectly happy about it.
I was just in the process of calling Ma and Pa...
TELEPHONE TELEPHONE
...and suddenly it was... it...
I don't know what it was...

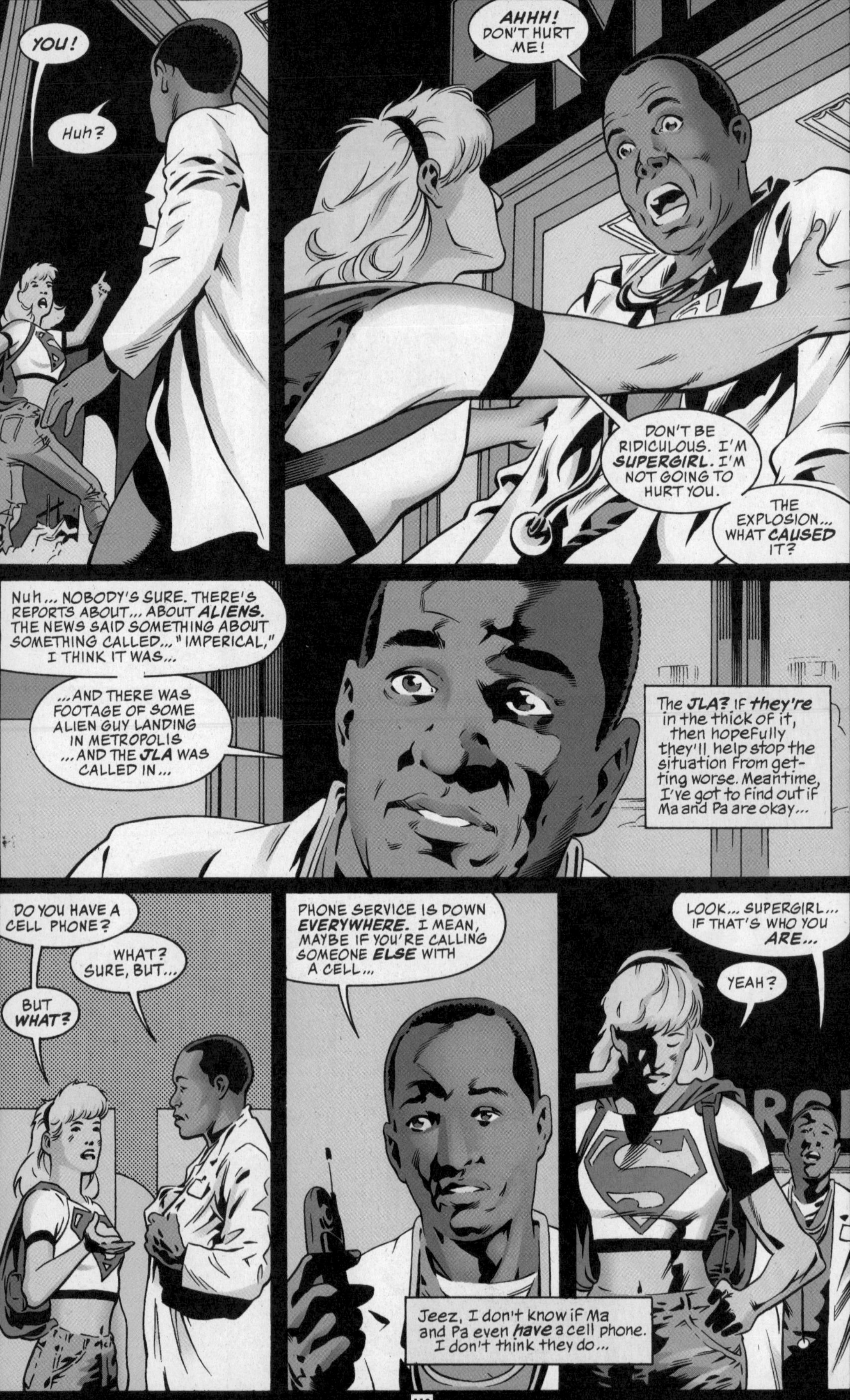
YOU!
Huh?
AHHH! DON'T HURT ME!
DON'T BE RIDICULOUS. I'M SUPERGIRL. I'M NOT GOING TO HURT YOU.
THE EXPLOSION... WHAT CAUSED IT?
Nuh... NOBODY'S SURE. THERE'S REPORTS ABOUT... ABOUT ALIENS. THE NEWS SAID SOMETHING ABOUT SOMETHING CALLED... "IMPERICAL," I THINK IT WAS...
...AND THERE WAS FOOTAGE OF SOME ALIEN GUY LANDING IN METROPOLIS ...AND THE JLA WAS CALLED IN...
The JLA? If they're in the thick of it, then hopefully they'll help stop the situation from getting worse. Meantime, I've got to find out if Ma and Pa are okay...
DO YOU HAVE A CELL PHONE?
WHAT? SURE, BUT...
BUT WHAT?
PHONE SERVICE IS DOWN EVERYWHERE. I MEAN, MAYBE IF YOU'RE CALLING SOMEONE ELSE WITH A CELL...
Jeez, I don't know if Ma and Pa even have a cell phone. I don't think they do...
LOOK... SUPERGIRL... IF THAT'S WHO YOU ARE...
YEAH?

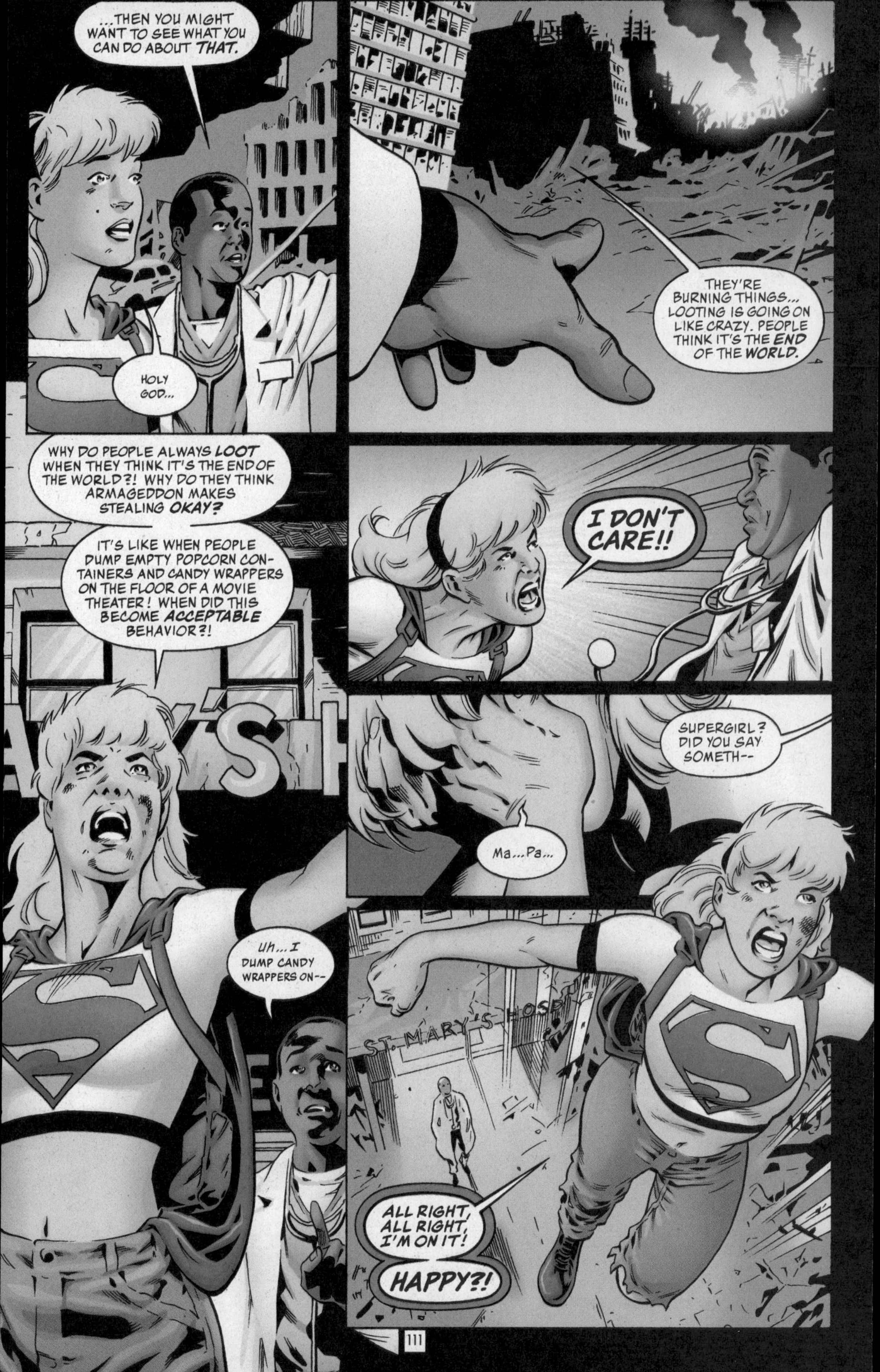
...THEN YOU MIGHT WANT TO SEE WHAT YOU CAN DO ABOUT THAT.
HOLY GOD...
THEY'RE BURNING THINGS... LOOTING IS GOING ON LIKE CRAZY. PEOPLE THINK IT'S THE END OF THE WORLD.
WHY DO PEOPLE ALWAYS LOOT WHEN THEY THINK IT'S THE END OF THE WORLD?! WHY DO THEY THINK ARMAGEDDON MAKES STEALING OKAY?
IT'S LIKE WHEN PEOPLE DUMP EMPTY POPCORN CONTAINERS AND CANDY WRAPPERS ON THE FLOOR OF A MOVIE THEATER! WHEN DID THIS BECOME ACCEPTABLE BEHAVIOR?!
I DON'T CARE!!
SUPERGIRL? DID YOU SAY SOMETH--
Ma...Pa...
Uh... I DUMP CANDY WRAPPERS ON--
ST. MARY'S HOSP
ALL RIGHT, ALL RIGHT, I'M ON IT!
HAPPY?!

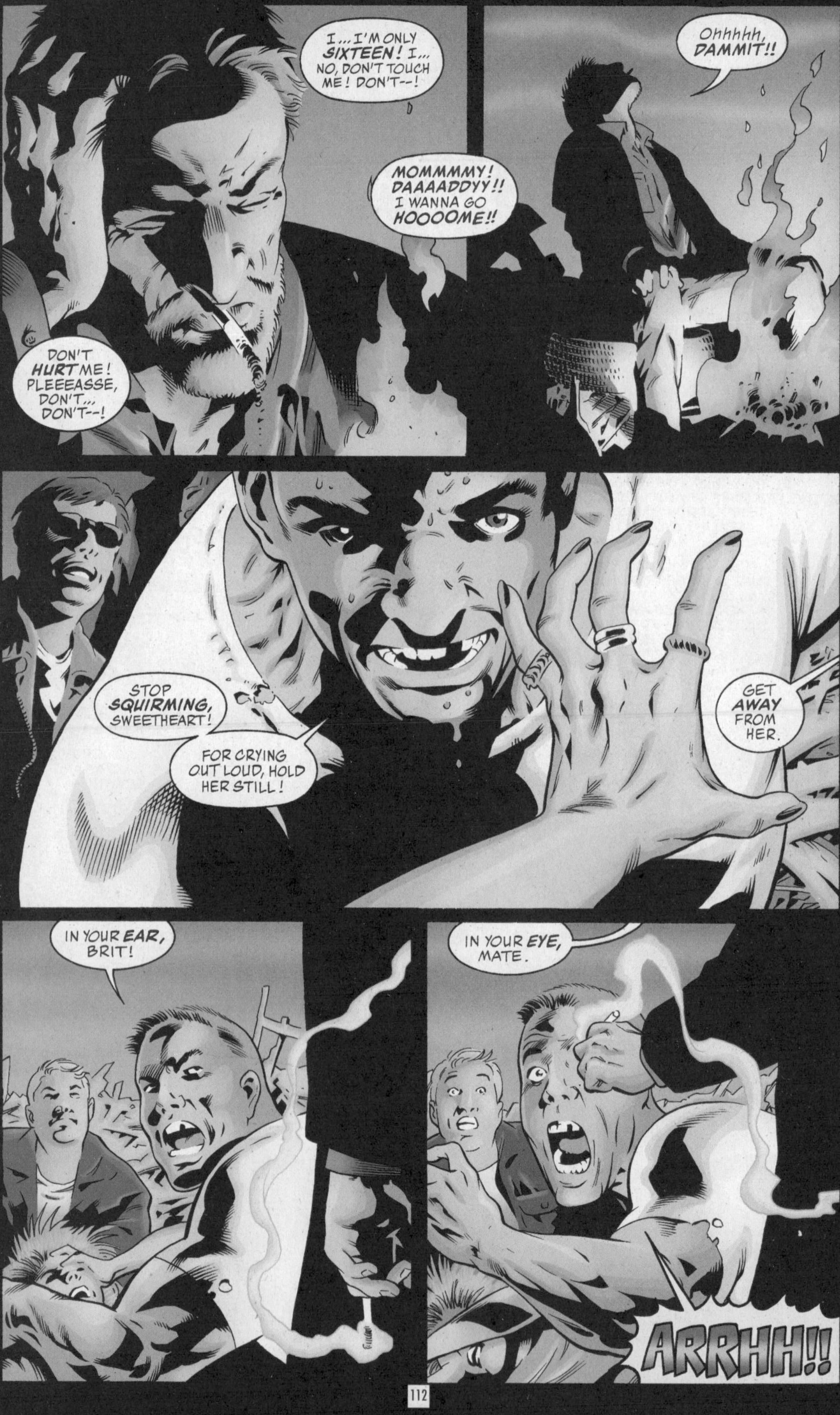

I... I'M ONLY SIXTEEN! I... NO, DON'T TOUCH ME! DON'T--!
MOMMMMY! DAAAADDYY!! I WANNA GO HOOOOME!!
DON'T HURT ME! PLEEEASSE, DON'T... DON'T--!
Ohhhhh, DAMMIT!!
STOP SQUIRMING, SWEETHEART!
FOR CRYING OUT LOUD, HOLD HER STILL!
GET AWAY FROM HER.
IN YOUR EAR, BRIT!
IN YOUR EYE, MATE.
ARRHH!!

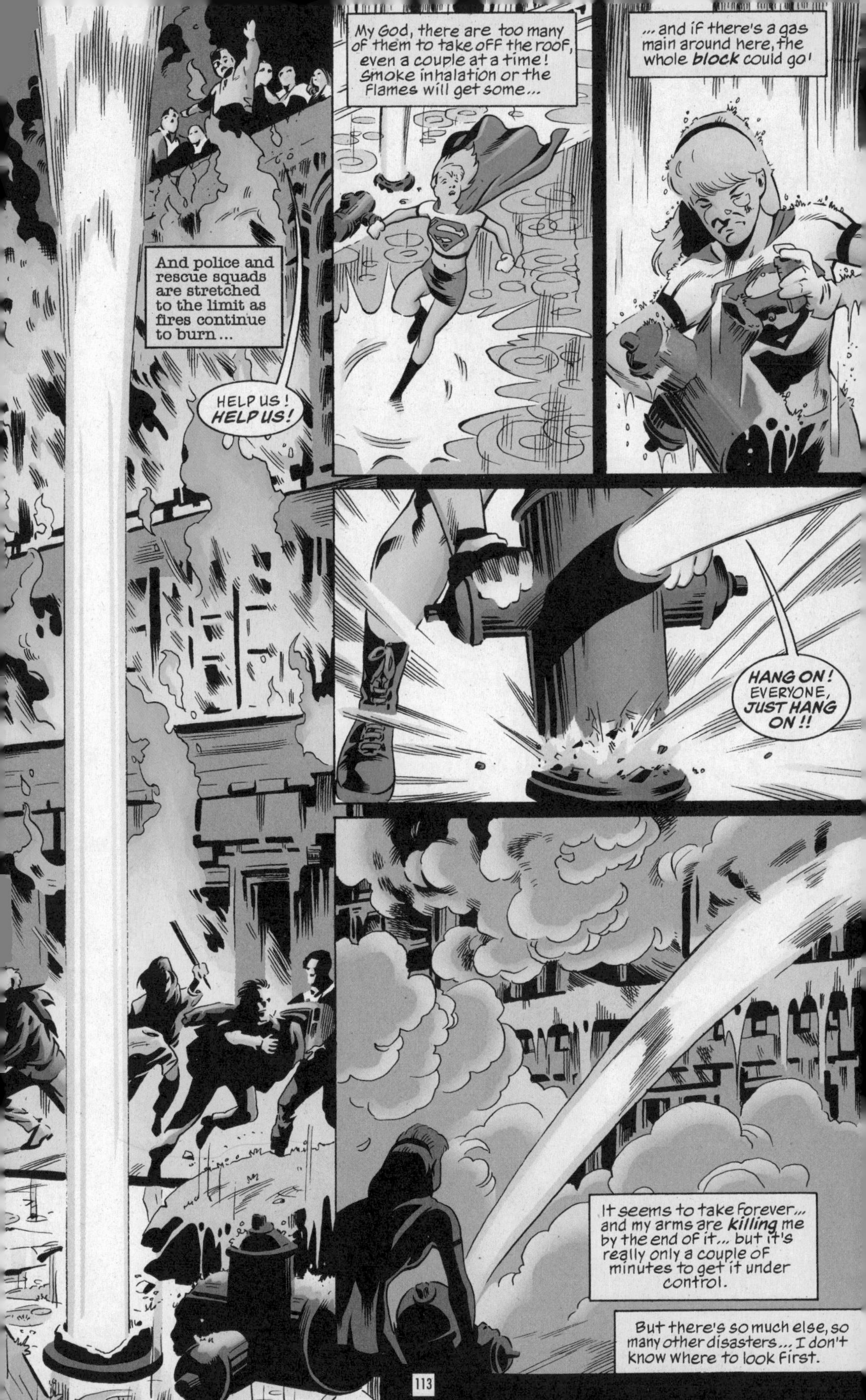
And police and rescue squads are stretched to the limit as fires continue to burn...
HELP US! HELP US!
My God, there are too many of them to take off the roof, even a couple at a time! Smoke inhalation or the Flames will get some...
...and if there's a gas main around here, the whole block could go!
HANG ON! EVERYONE, JUST HANG ON!!
It seems to take forever... and my arms are killing me by the end of it... but it's really only a couple of minutes to get it under control.
But there's so much else, so many other disasters... I don't know where to look first.

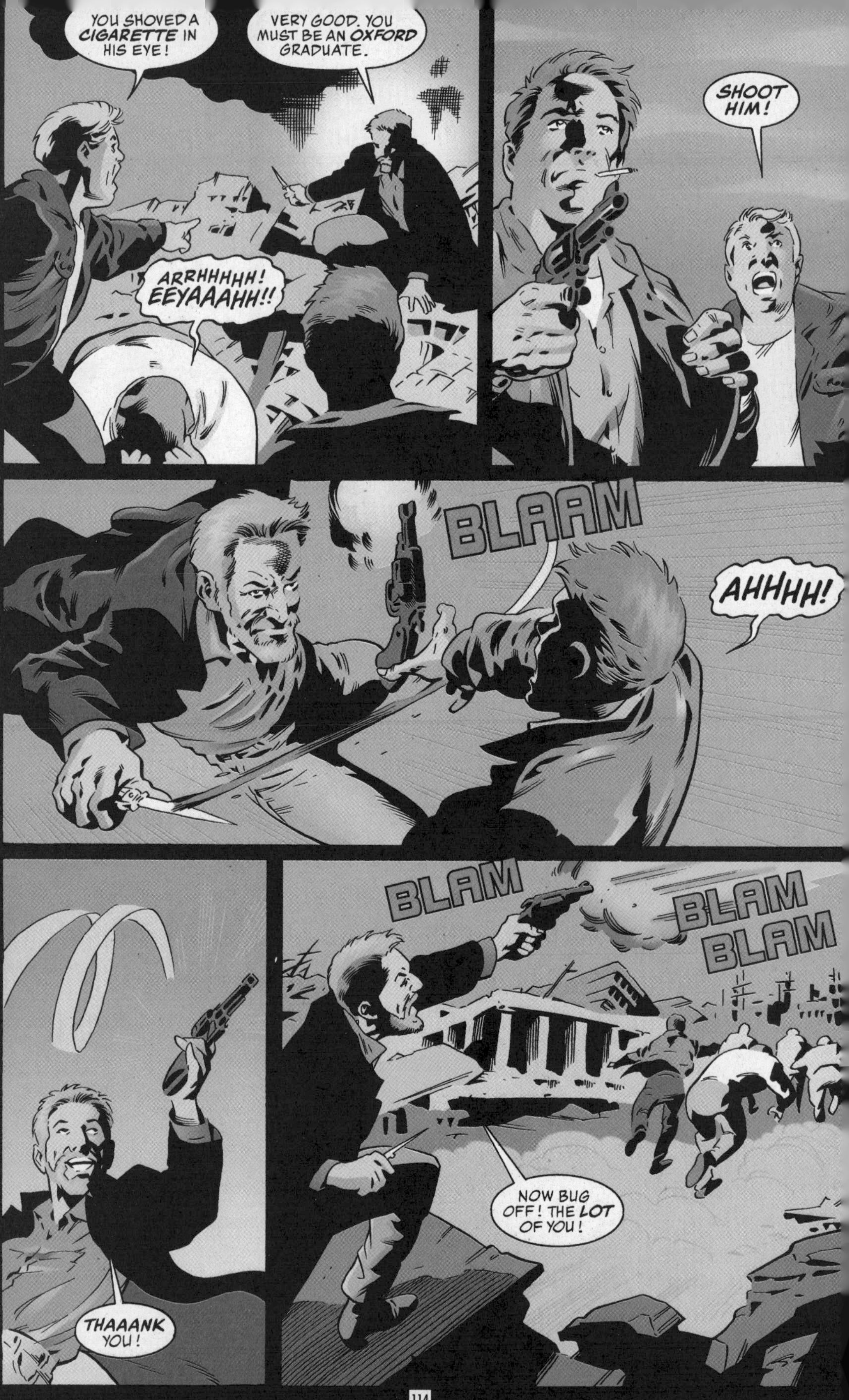

YOU SHOVED A CIGARETTE IN HIS EYE!
VERY GOOD. YOU MUST BE AN OXFORD GRADUATE.
ARRHHHHH! EEYAAAHH!!
SHOOT HIM!
BLAAM
AHHHH!
THAAANK YOU!
BLAM
BLAM
BLAM
NOW BUG OFF! THE LOT OF YOU!

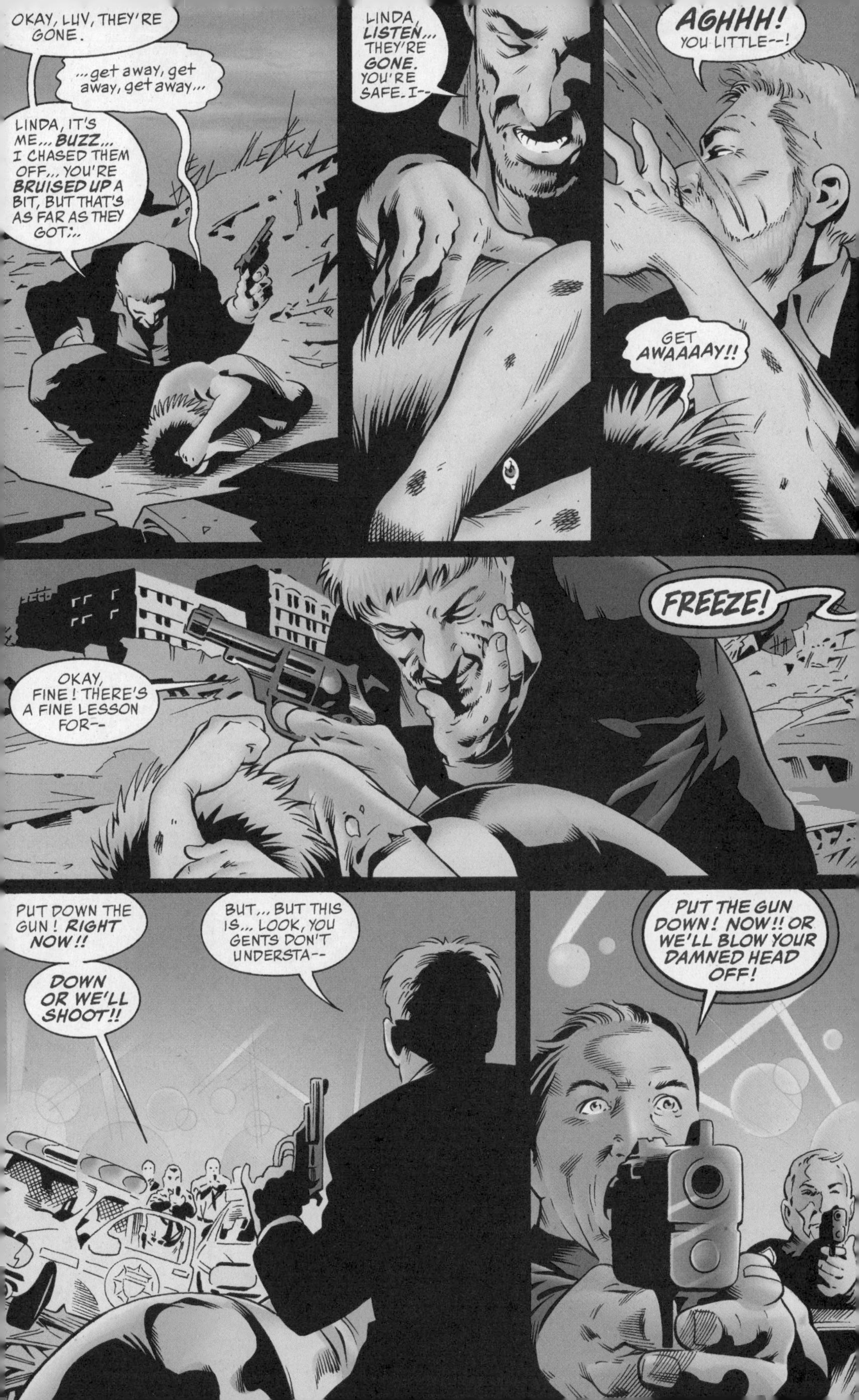
OKAY, LUV, THEY'RE GONE.
...get away, get away, get away...
LINDA, IT'S ME... BUZZ... I CHASED THEM OFF... YOU'RE BRUISED UP A BIT, BUT THAT'S AS FAR AS THEY GOT...
LINDA, LISTEN... THEY'RE GONE. YOU'RE SAFE. I--
AGHHH! YOU LITTLE--!
GET AWAAAAY!!
OKAY, FINE! THERE'S A FINE LESSON FOR--
FREEZE!
PUT DOWN THE GUN! RIGHT NOW!!
DOWN OR WE'LL SHOOT!!
BUT... BUT THIS IS... LOOK, YOU GENTS DON'T UNDERSTA--
PUT THE GUN DOWN! NOW!! OR WE'LL BLOW YOUR DAMNED HEAD OFF!

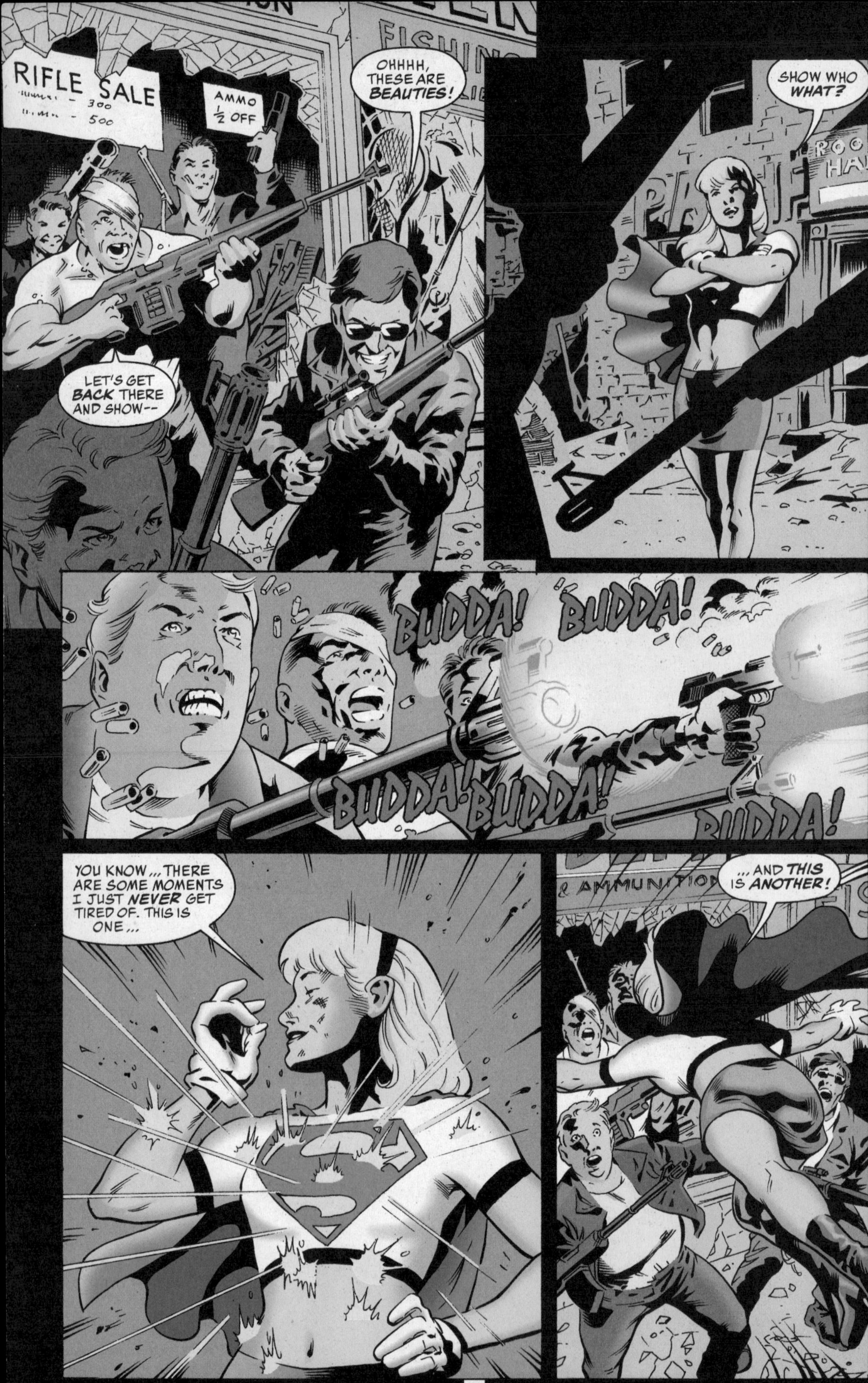
RIFLE SALE
AMMO 1/2 OFF
OHHHH, THESE ARE BEAUTIES!
LET'S GET BACK THERE AND SHOW--
SHOW WHO WHAT?
BUDDA! BUDDA!
BUDDA! BUDDA!
BUDDA!
YOU KNOW... THERE ARE SOME MOMENTS I JUST NEVER GET TIRED OF. THIS IS ONE...
& AMMUNITION
...AND THIS IS ANOTHER!

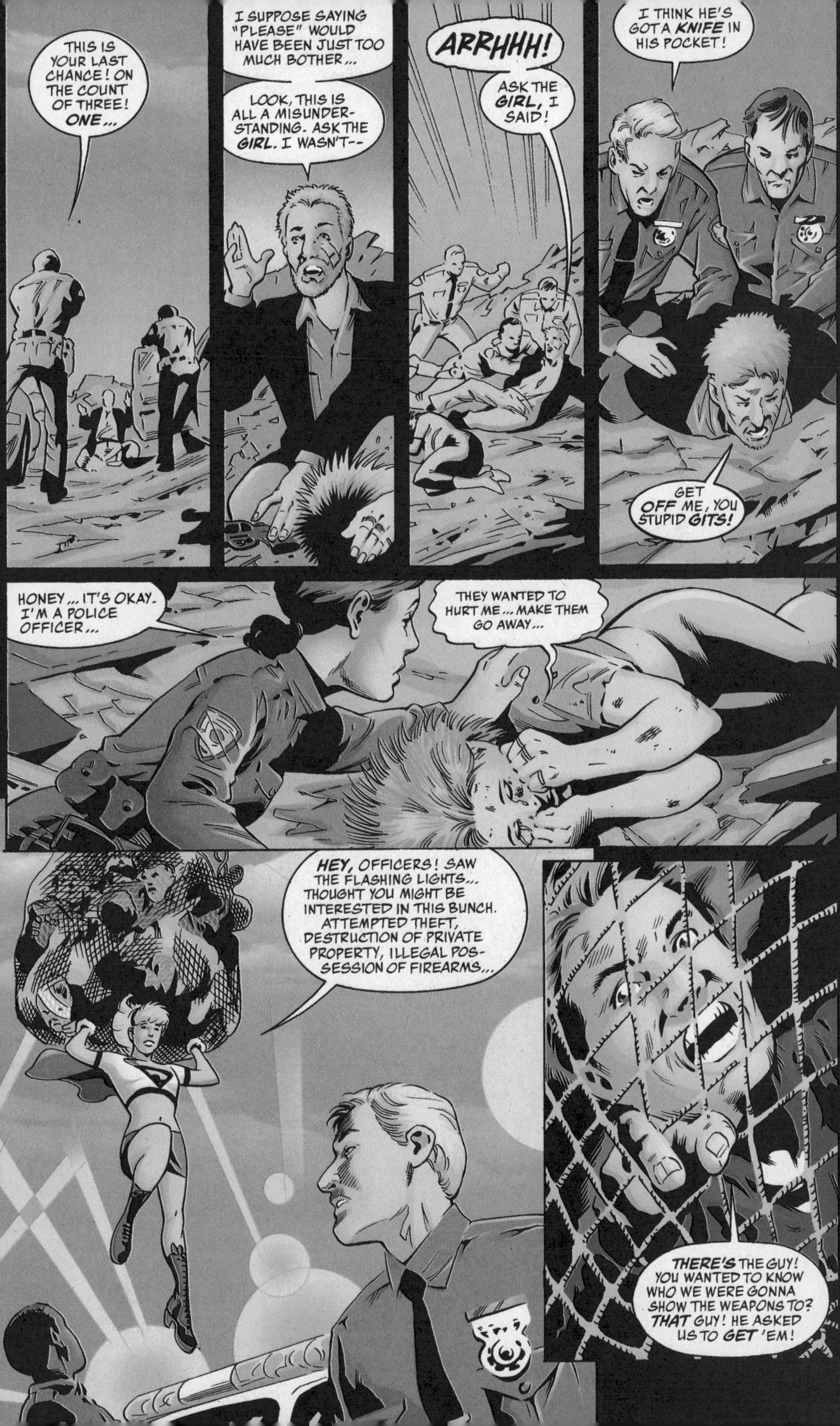
THIS IS YOUR LAST CHANCE! ON THE COUNT OF THREE! ONE...
I SUPPOSE SAYING "PLEASE" WOULD HAVE BEEN JUST TOO MUCH BOTHER...
LOOK, THIS IS ALL A MISUNDER-STANDING. ASK THE GIRL. I WASN'T--
ARRHHH!
ASK THE GIRL, I SAID!
I THINK HE'S GOT A KNIFE IN HIS POCKET!
GET OFF ME, YOU STUPID GITS!
HONEY... IT'S OKAY. I'M A POLICE OFFICER...
THEY WANTED TO HURT ME... MAKE THEM GO AWAY...
HEY, OFFICERS! SAW THE FLASHING LIGHTS... THOUGHT YOU MIGHT BE INTERESTED IN THIS BUNCH. ATTEMPTED THEFT, DESTRUCTION OF PRIVATE PROPERTY, ILLEGAL POS-SESSION OF FIREARMS...
THERE'S THE GUY! YOU WANTED TO KNOW WHO WE WERE GONNA SHOW THE WEAPONS TO? THAT GUY! HE ASKED US TO GET 'EM!

**THERE** YOU ARE! I WAS LOOKIN' ALL OVER FOR--

WHAT THE HELL IS GOING **ON** HERE?

THIS IS **NUTS!** SUPERGIRL, **LISTEN** TO ME! I WAS TRYING TO **HELP** HER! I **SAVED** HER!

C'MON, YOU **KNOW** I CAN'T LIE TO YOU!

THESE GUYS CLAIM HE'S ONE OF THEM...

THIS CREEP AND SOME PALS WERE ATTACKING THIS GIRL, APPARENTLY. WHEN WE SHOWED UP, HE WAS SHOUTING SOMETHING ABOUT TEACHING HER A **LESSON.**

HE HAD A GUN **AND** A KNIFE, AND SHE WAS CLAWING AT HIM TO KEEP HIM AWAY. BRAVE KID... SHE'S IN A STATE OF SHOCK NOW... BARELY COHERENT...

**THESE** GUYS ARE THE ONES I SAVED HER **FROM!** SUPERGIRL, PLEASE...

I...I WAS DOING THE **RIGHT** THING...

OH, YEAH. BECAUSE YOU'D **NEVER** TAKE ADVANTAGE OF A YOUNG WOMAN.

EXCUSE ME. I HAVE **INNOCENT** PEOPLE TO HELP.

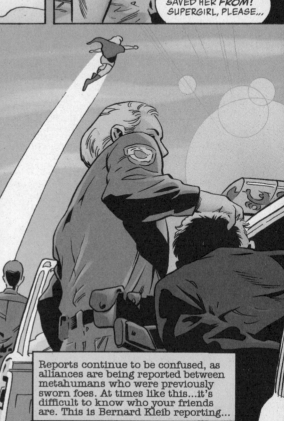

Reports continue to be confused, as alliances are being reported between metahumans who were previously sworn foes. At times like this...it's difficult to know who your friends are. This is Bernard Kleib reporting...

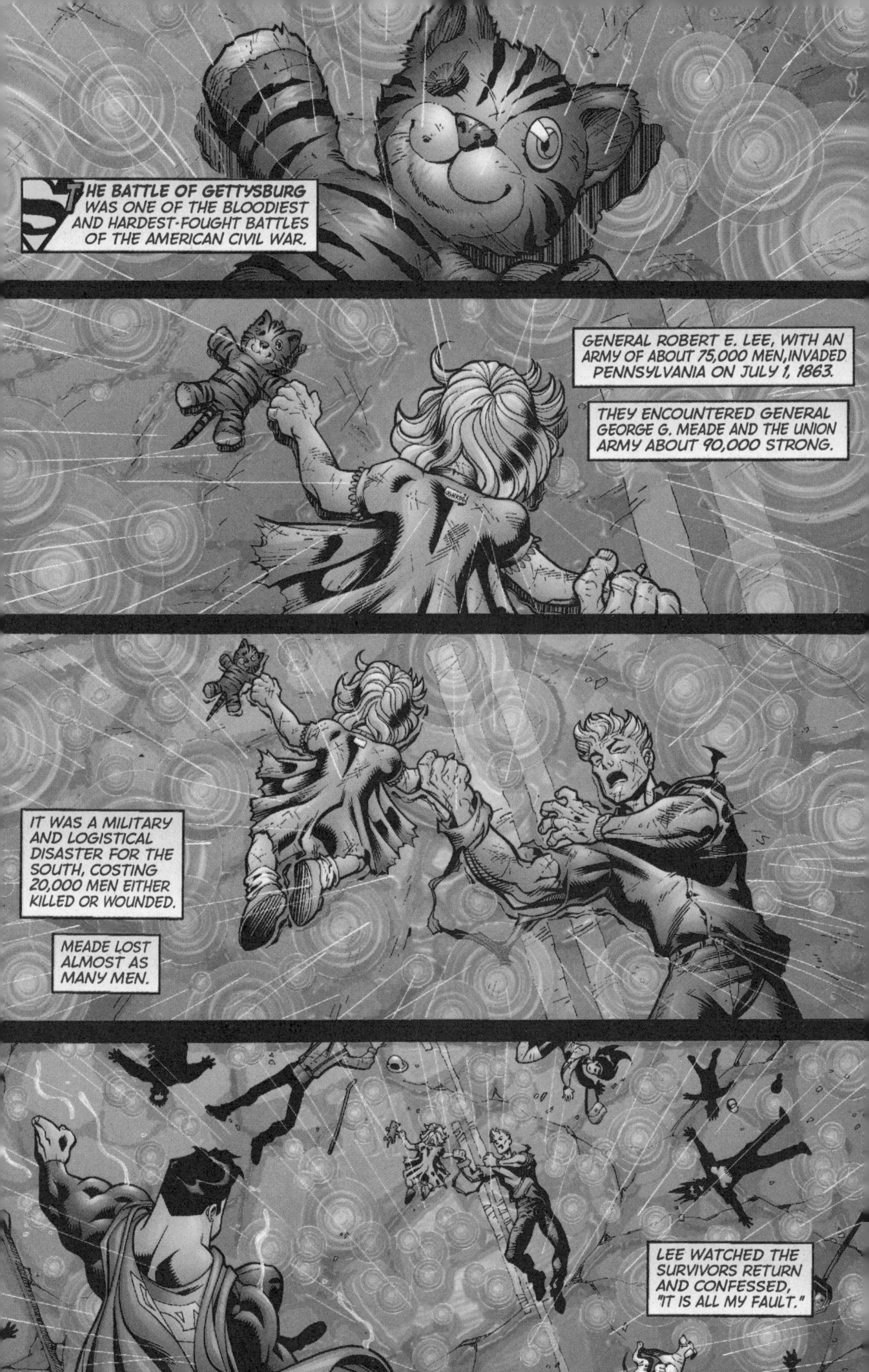
THE BATTLE OF GETTYSBURG WAS ONE OF THE BLOODIEST AND HARDEST-FOUGHT BATTLES OF THE AMERICAN CIVIL WAR.
GENERAL ROBERT E. LEE, WITH AN ARMY OF ABOUT 75,000 MEN, INVADED PENNSYLVANIA ON JULY 1, 1863.
THEY ENCOUNTERED GENERAL GEORGE G. MEADE AND THE UNION ARMY ABOUT 90,000 STRONG.
IT WAS A MILITARY AND LOGISTICAL DISASTER FOR THE SOUTH, COSTING 20,000 MEN EITHER KILLED OR WOUNDED.
MEADE LOST ALMOST AS MANY MEN.
LEE WATCHED THE SURVIVORS RETURN AND CONFESSED, "IT IS ALL MY FAULT."

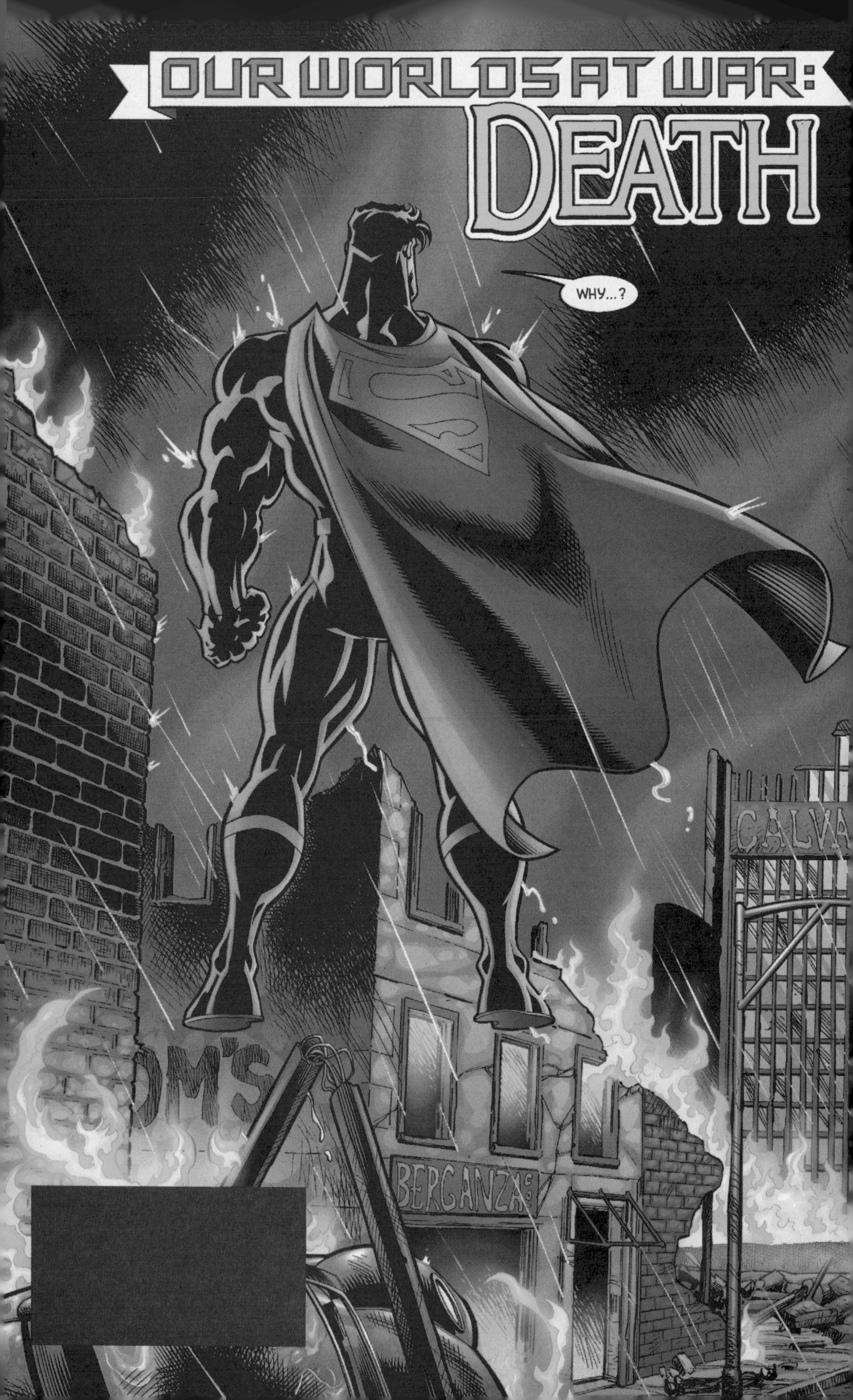
OUR WORLDS AT WAR:
DEATH
WHY...?
CALVA
OM'S
BERGANZA Co
[redacted]

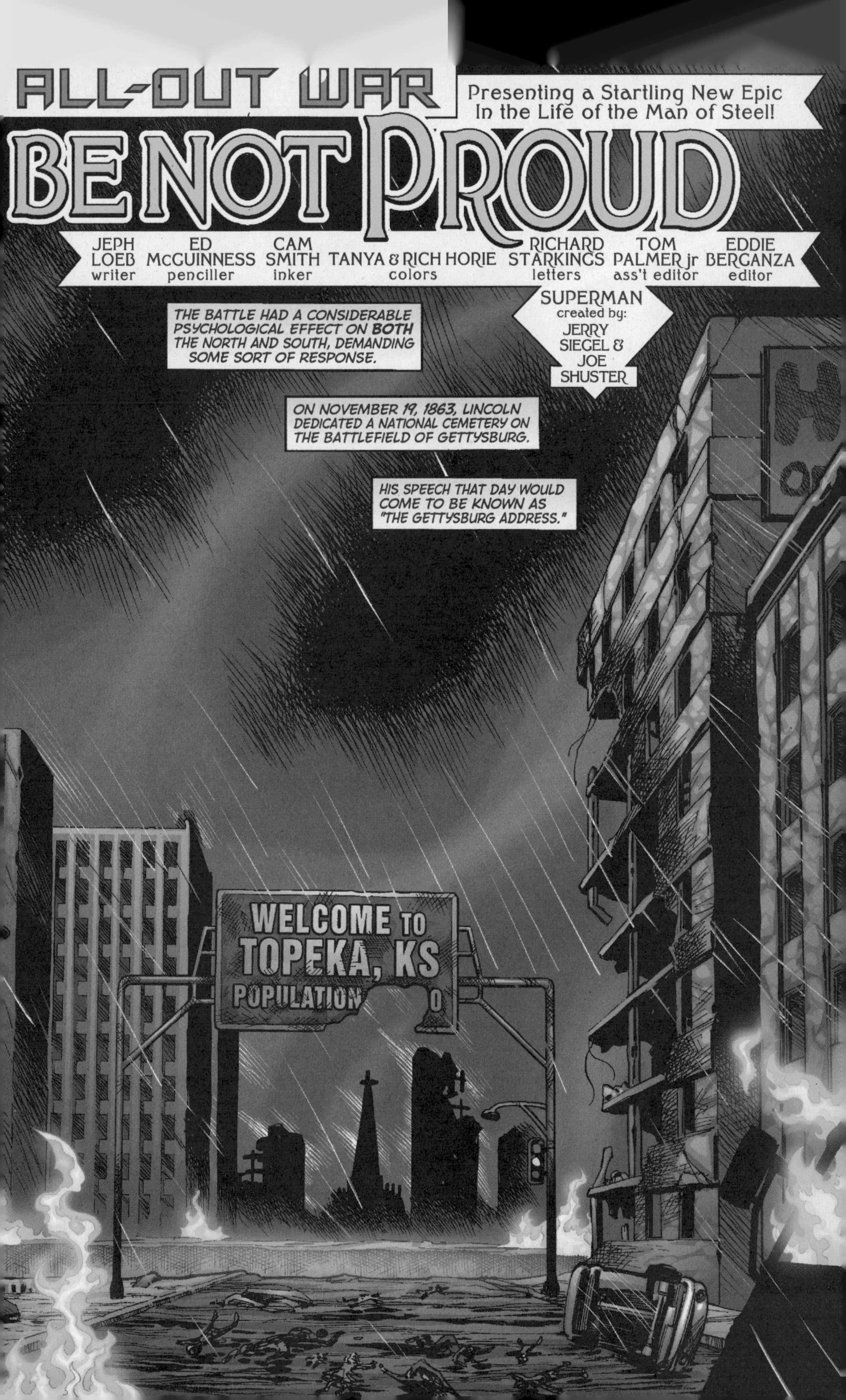

ALL-OUT WAR
Presenting a Startling New Epic In the Life of the Man of Steel!
BE NOT PROUD
JEPH LOEB writer
ED McGUINNESS penciller
CAM SMITH inker
TANYA & RICH HORIE colors
RICHARD STARKINGS letters
TOM PALMER jr ass't editor
EDDIE BERGANZA editor
SUPERMAN created by: JERRY SIEGEL & JOE SHUSTER
THE BATTLE HAD A CONSIDERABLE PSYCHOLOGICAL EFFECT ON BOTH THE NORTH AND SOUTH, DEMANDING SOME SORT OF RESPONSE.
ON NOVEMBER 19, 1863, LINCOLN DEDICATED A NATIONAL CEMETERY ON THE BATTLEFIELD OF GETTYSBURG.
HIS SPEECH THAT DAY WOULD COME TO BE KNOWN AS "THE GETTYSBURG ADDRESS."
WELCOME TO TOPEKA, KS
POPULATION 0

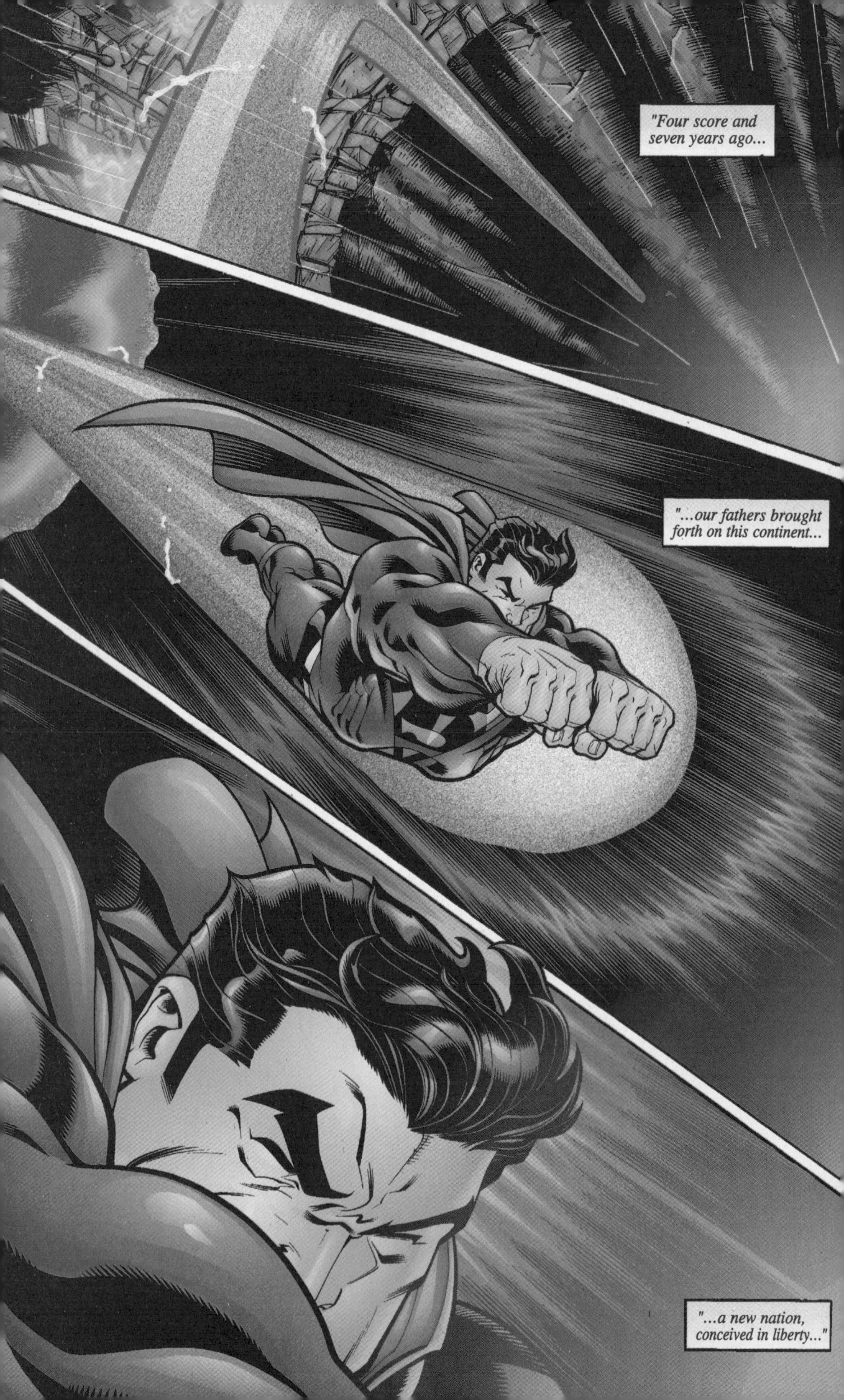
"Four score and seven years ago...
"...our fathers brought forth on this continent...
"...a new nation, conceived in liberty..."

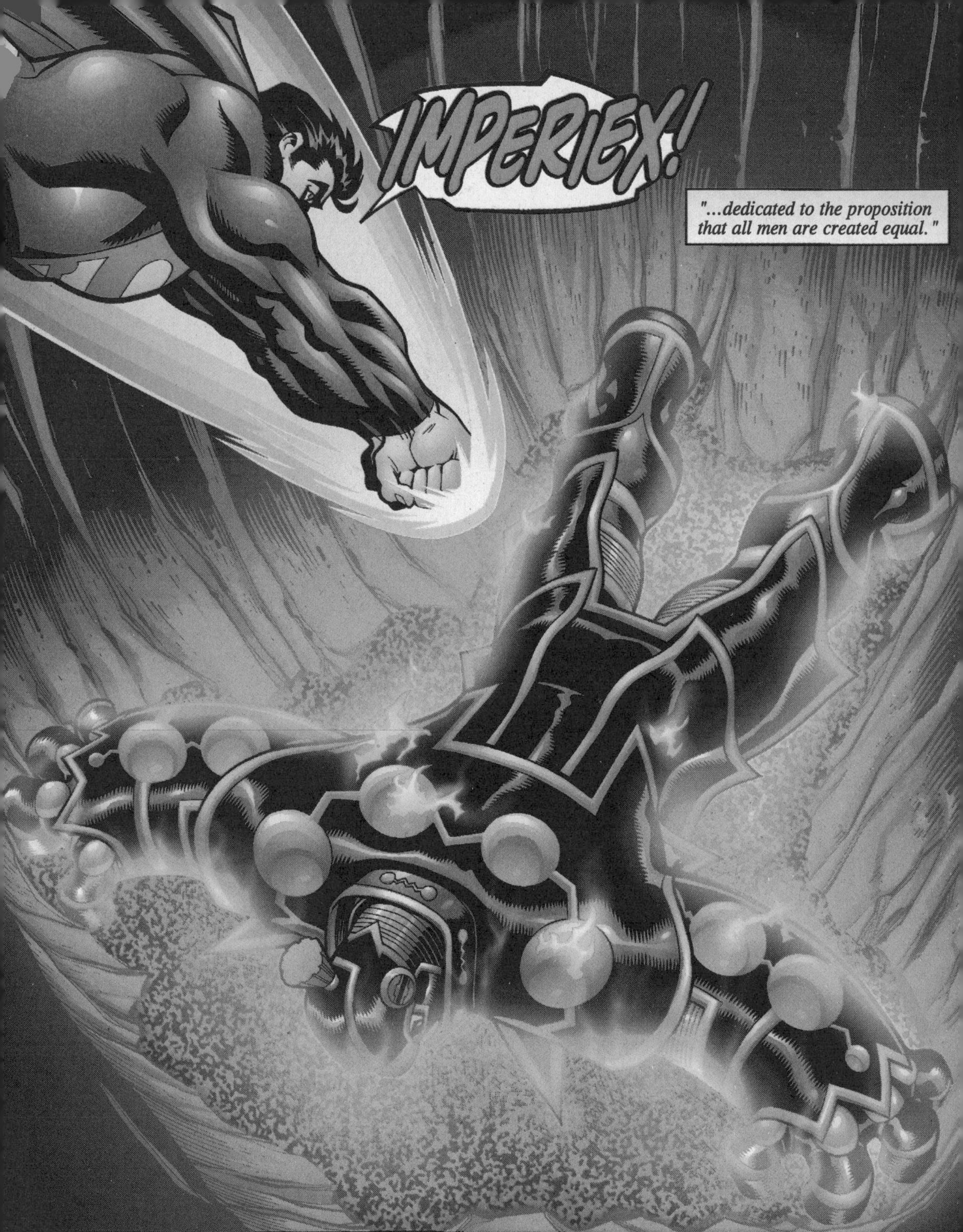
IMPERIEX!
"...dedicated to the proposition that all men are created equal."

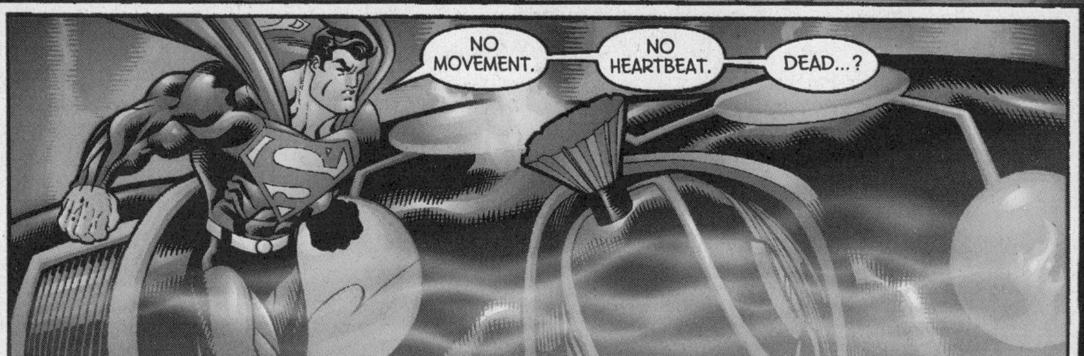
NO MOVEMENT.
NO HEARTBEAT.
DEAD...?

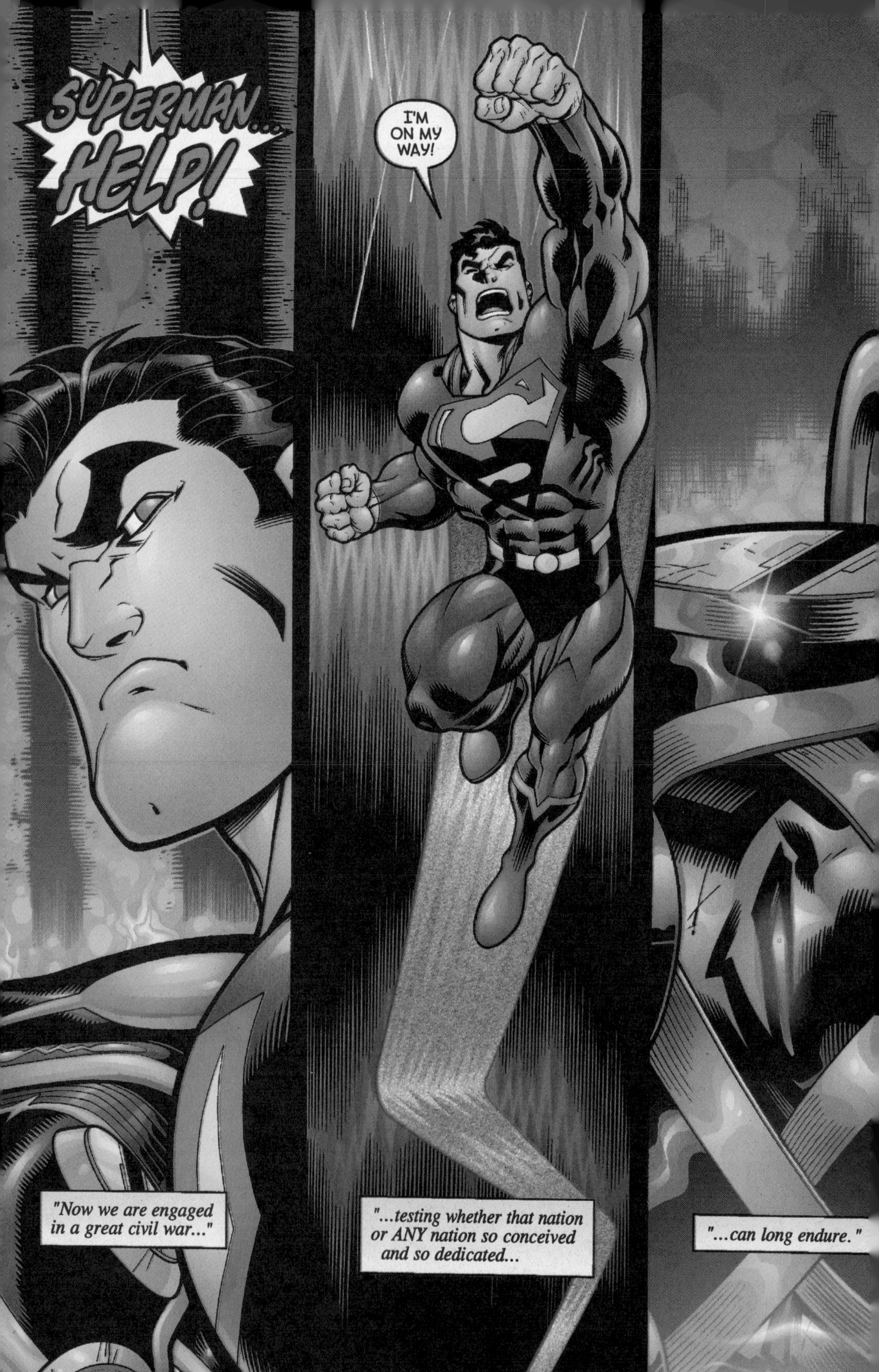
SUPERMAN... HELP!
I'M ON MY WAY!
"Now we are engaged in a great civil war..."
"...testing whether that nation or ANY nation so conceived and so dedicated...
"...can long endure."

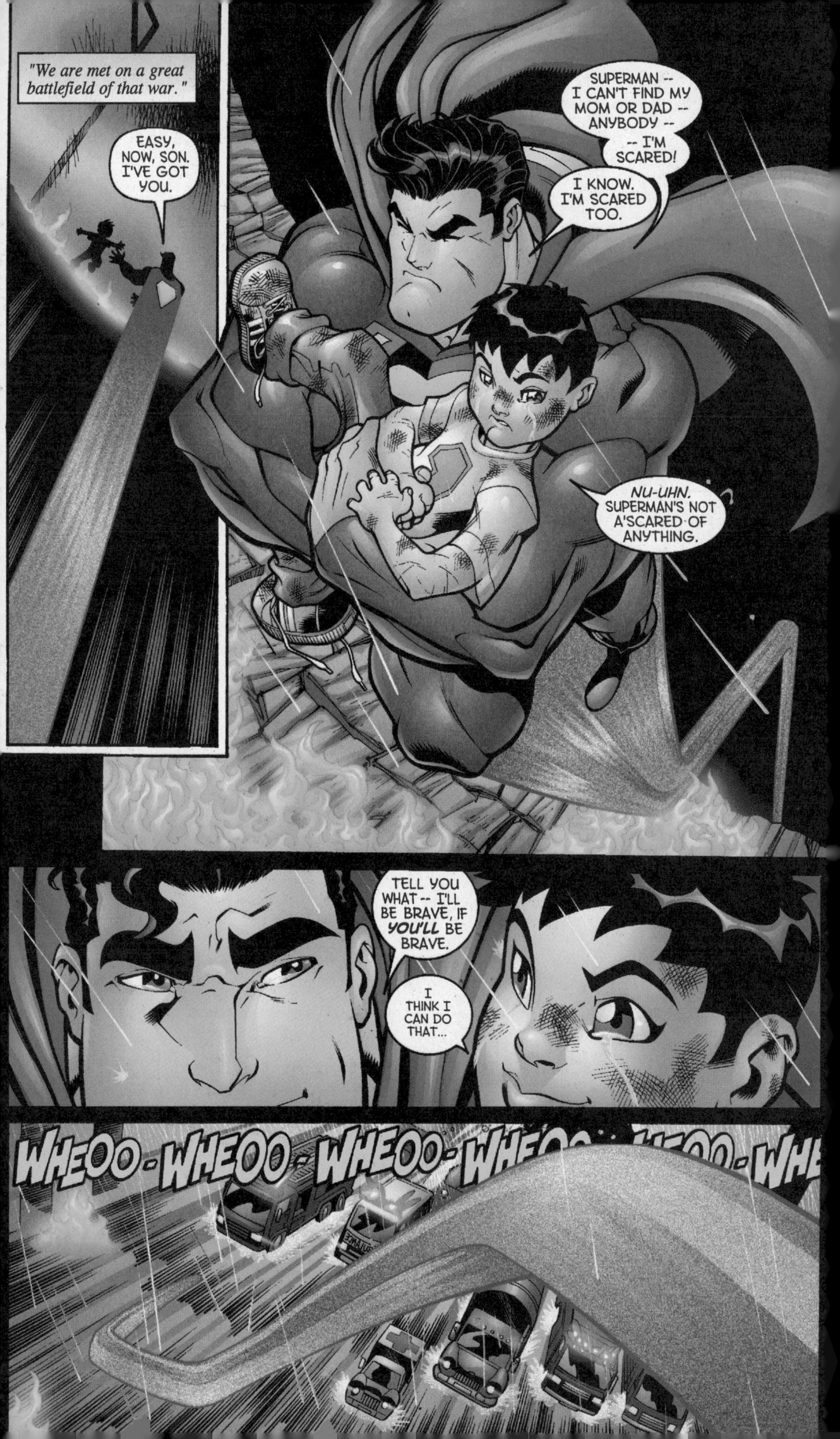
"We are met on a great battlefield of that war."
EASY, NOW, SON. I'VE GOT YOU.
SUPERMAN -- I CAN'T FIND MY MOM OR DAD -- ANYBODY --
-- I'M SCARED!
I KNOW. I'M SCARED TOO.
NU-UHN. SUPERMAN'S NOT A'SCARED OF ANYTHING.
TELL YOU WHAT -- I'LL BE BRAVE, IF YOU'LL BE BRAVE.
I THINK I CAN DO THAT...
WHEOO-WHEOO-WHEOO-WHE

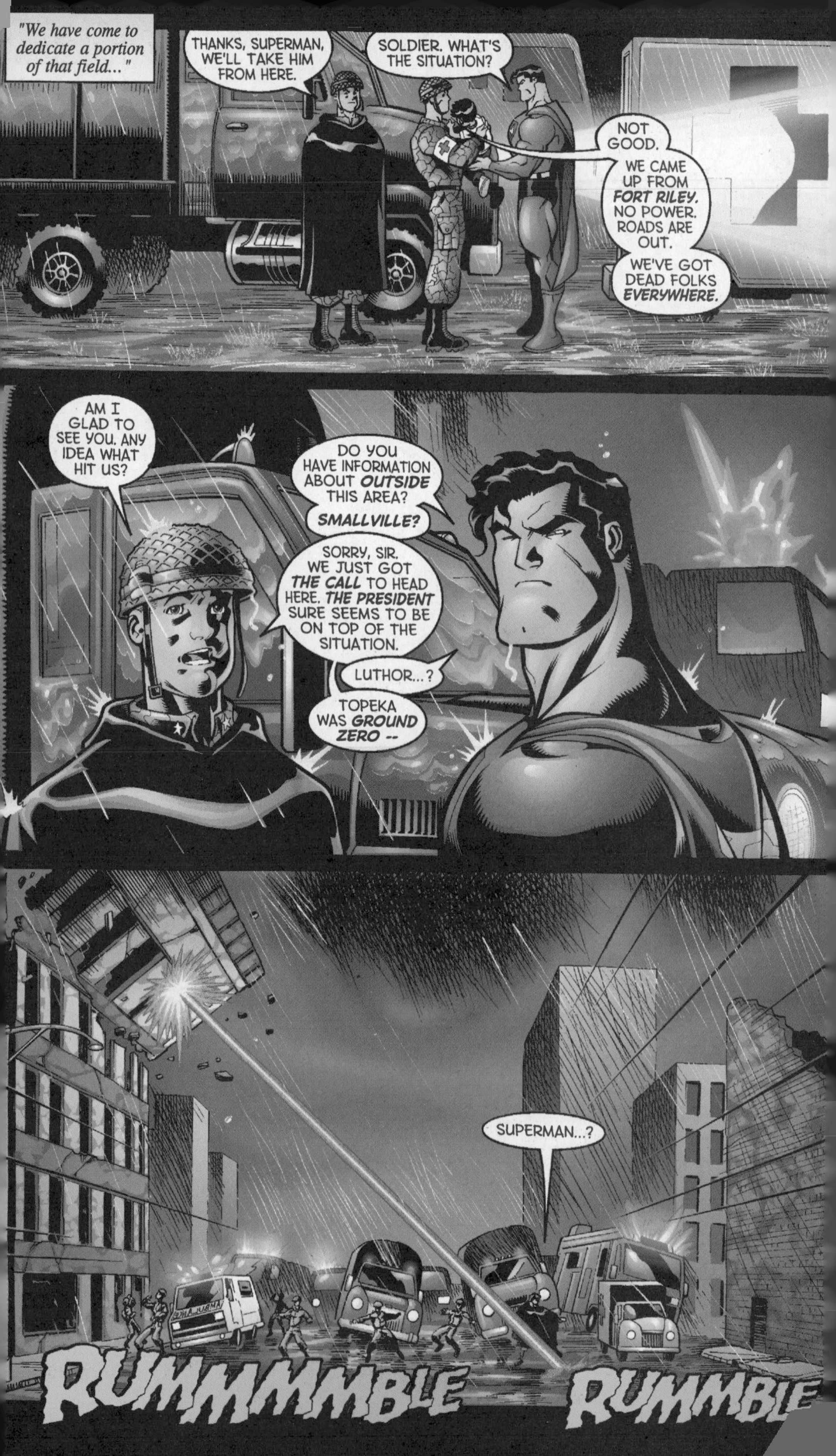
"We have come to dedicate a portion of that field..."
THANKS, SUPERMAN, WE'LL TAKE HIM FROM HERE.
SOLDIER. WHAT'S THE SITUATION?
NOT GOOD.
WE CAME UP FROM FORT RILEY. NO POWER. ROADS ARE OUT.
WE'VE GOT DEAD FOLKS EVERYWHERE.
AM I GLAD TO SEE YOU. ANY IDEA WHAT HIT US?
DO YOU HAVE INFORMATION ABOUT OUTSIDE THIS AREA?
SMALLVILLE?
SORRY, SIR. WE JUST GOT THE CALL TO HEAD HERE. THE PRESIDENT SURE SEEMS TO BE ON TOP OF THE SITUATION.
LUTHOR...?
TOPEKA WAS GROUND ZERO --
SUPERMAN...?
RUMMMMBLE
RUMMBLE

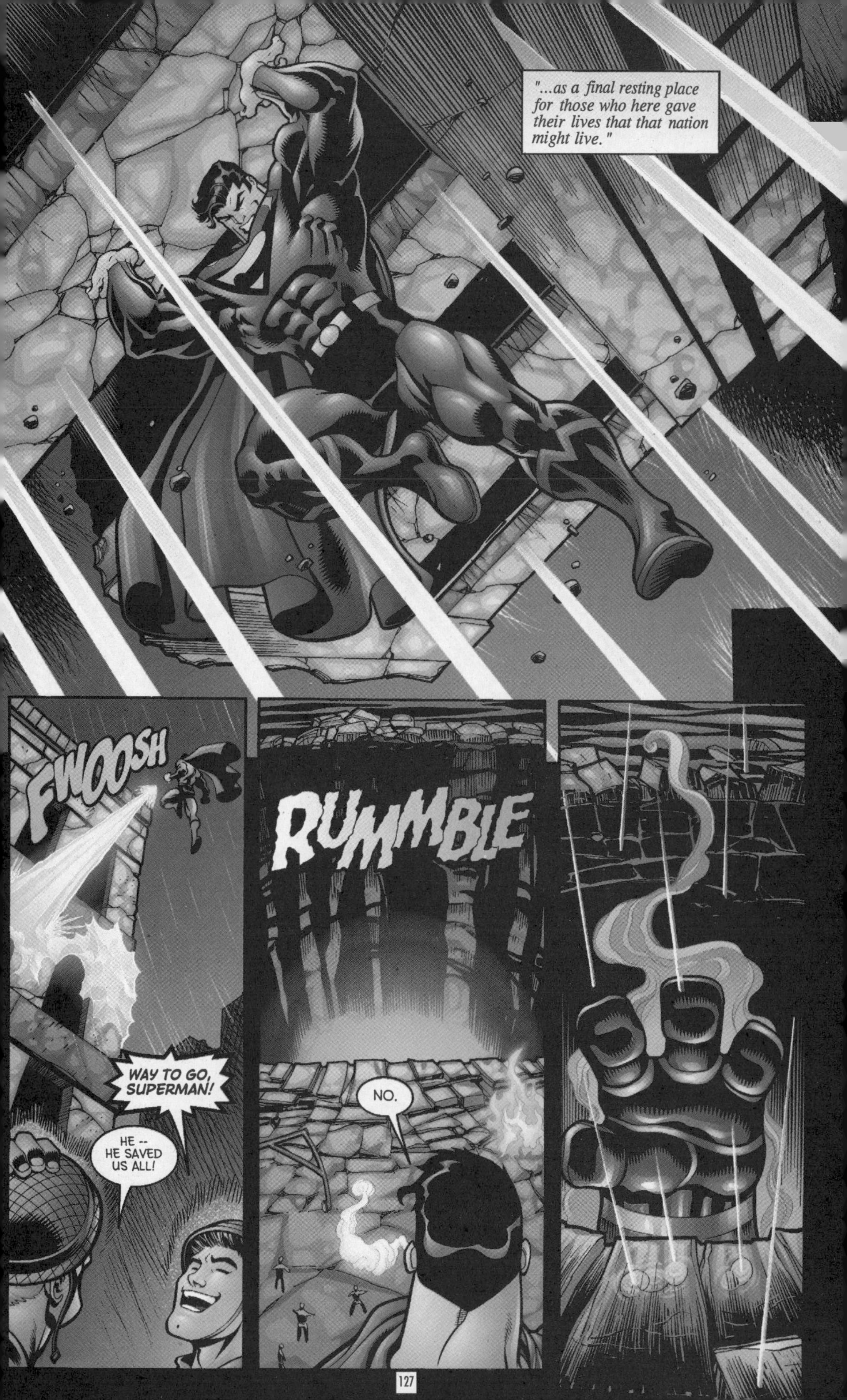
"...as a final resting place for those who here gave their lives that that nation might live."
FWOOSH
WAY TO GO, SUPERMAN!
HE -- HE SAVED US ALL!
RUMMBLE
NO.

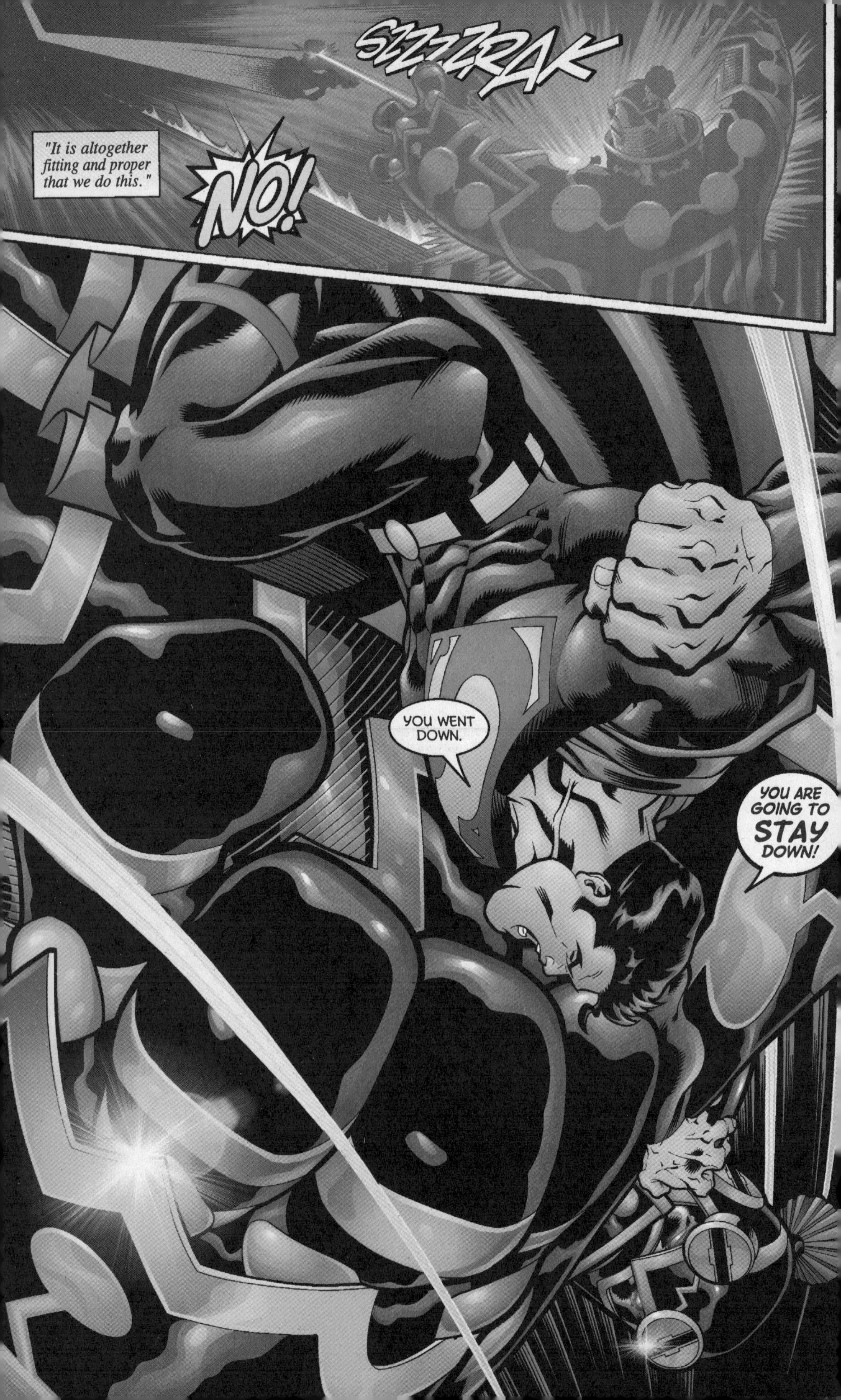
SIZZZRAK
"It is altogether fitting and proper that we do this."
NO!
YOU WENT DOWN.
YOU ARE GOING TO STAY DOWN!

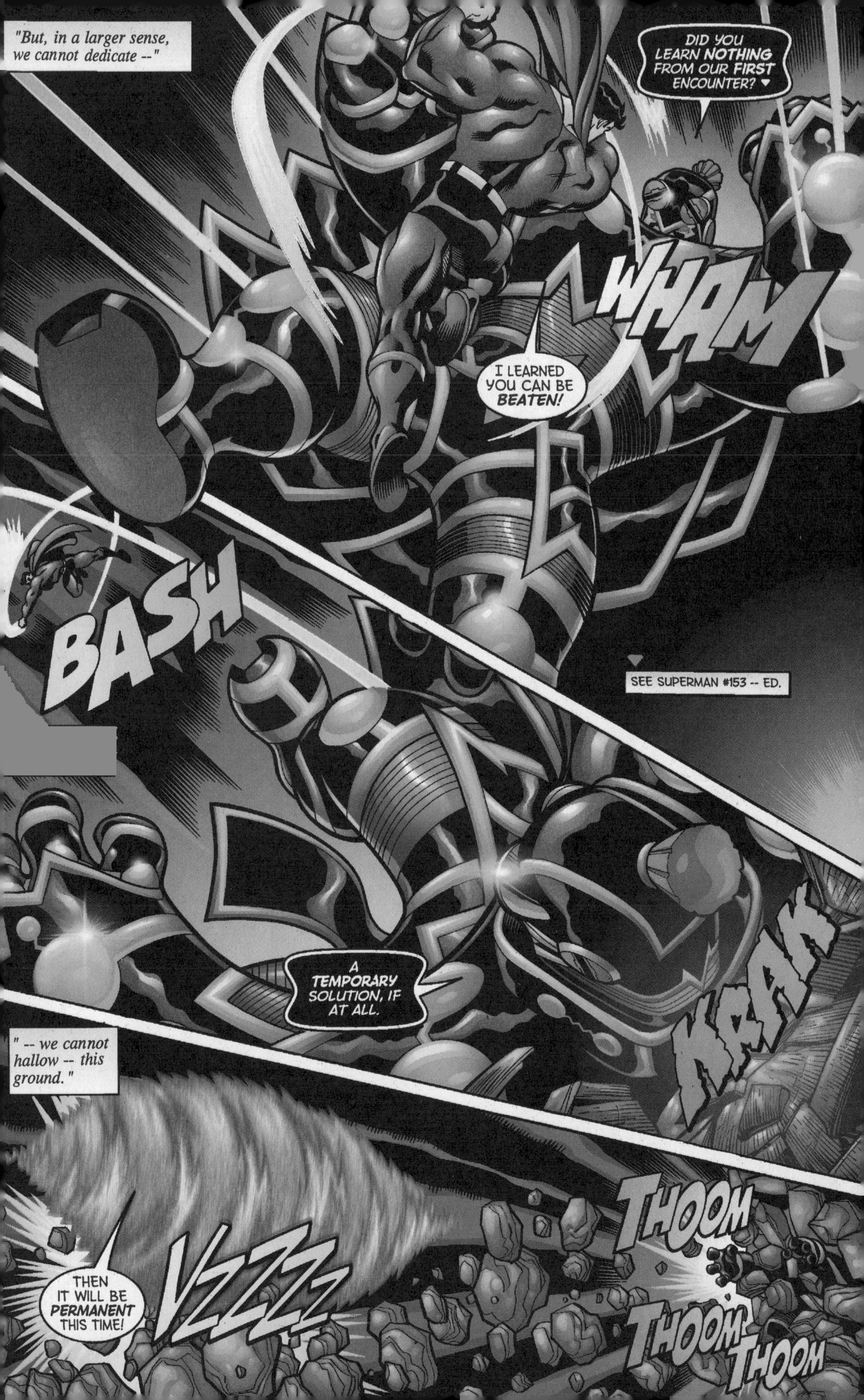
"But, in a larger sense, we cannot dedicate --"
DID YOU LEARN NOTHING FROM OUR FIRST ENCOUNTER?
WHAM
I LEARNED YOU CAN BE BEATEN!
BASH
SEE SUPERMAN #153 -- ED.
A TEMPORARY SOLUTION, IF AT ALL.
KRAK
" -- we cannot hallow -- this ground."
THEN IT WILL BE PERMANENT THIS TIME!
VZZZZ
THOOM
THOOM THOOM THOOM

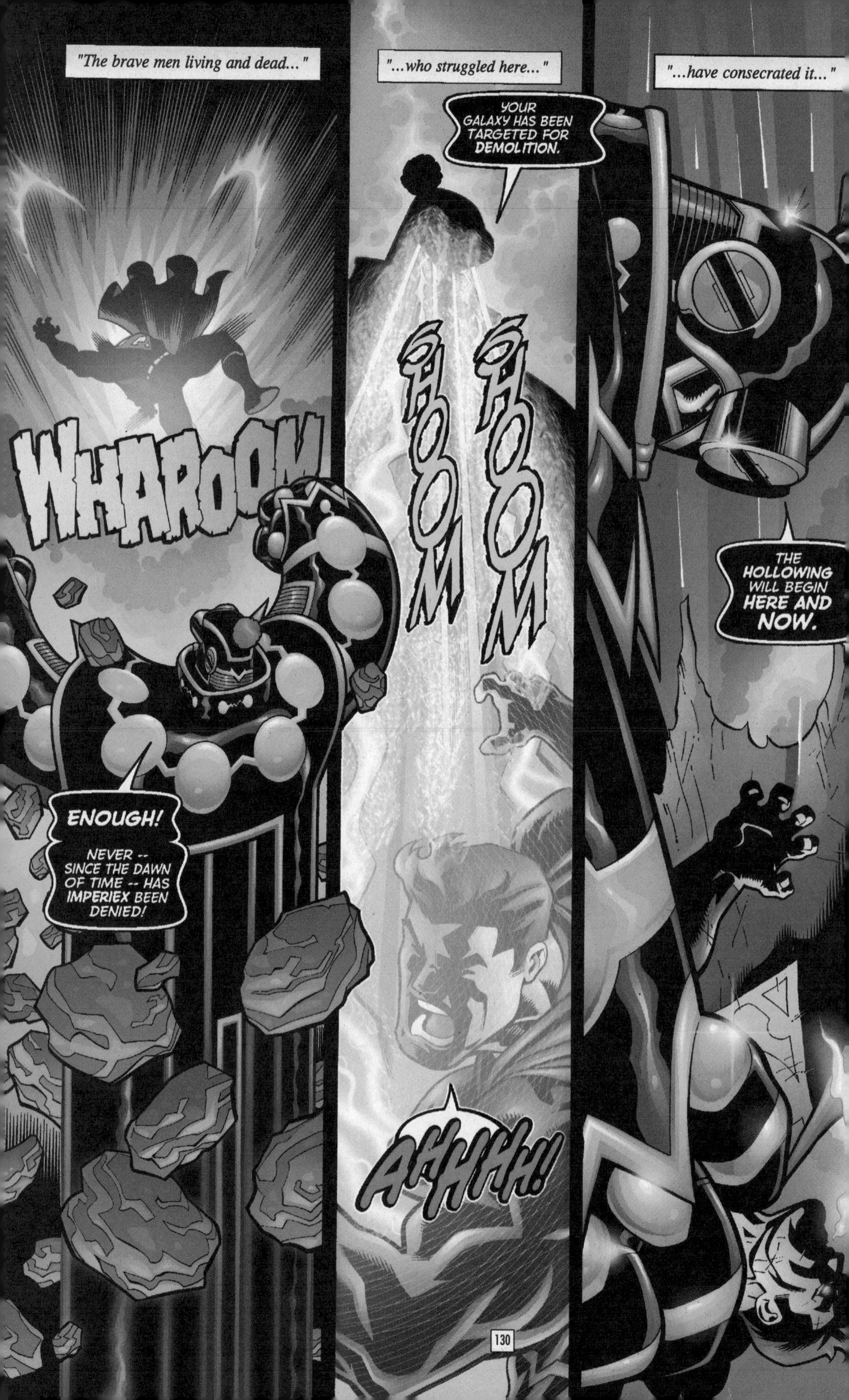
"The brave men living and dead..."
WHAROOM
ENOUGH!
NEVER -- SINCE THE DAWN OF TIME -- HAS IMPERIEX BEEN DENIED!
"...who struggled here..."
YOUR GALAXY HAS BEEN TARGETED FOR DEMOLITION.
SHOOOM
SHOOOM
AHHHHH!
"...have consecrated it..."
THE HOLLOWING WILL BEGIN HERE AND NOW.

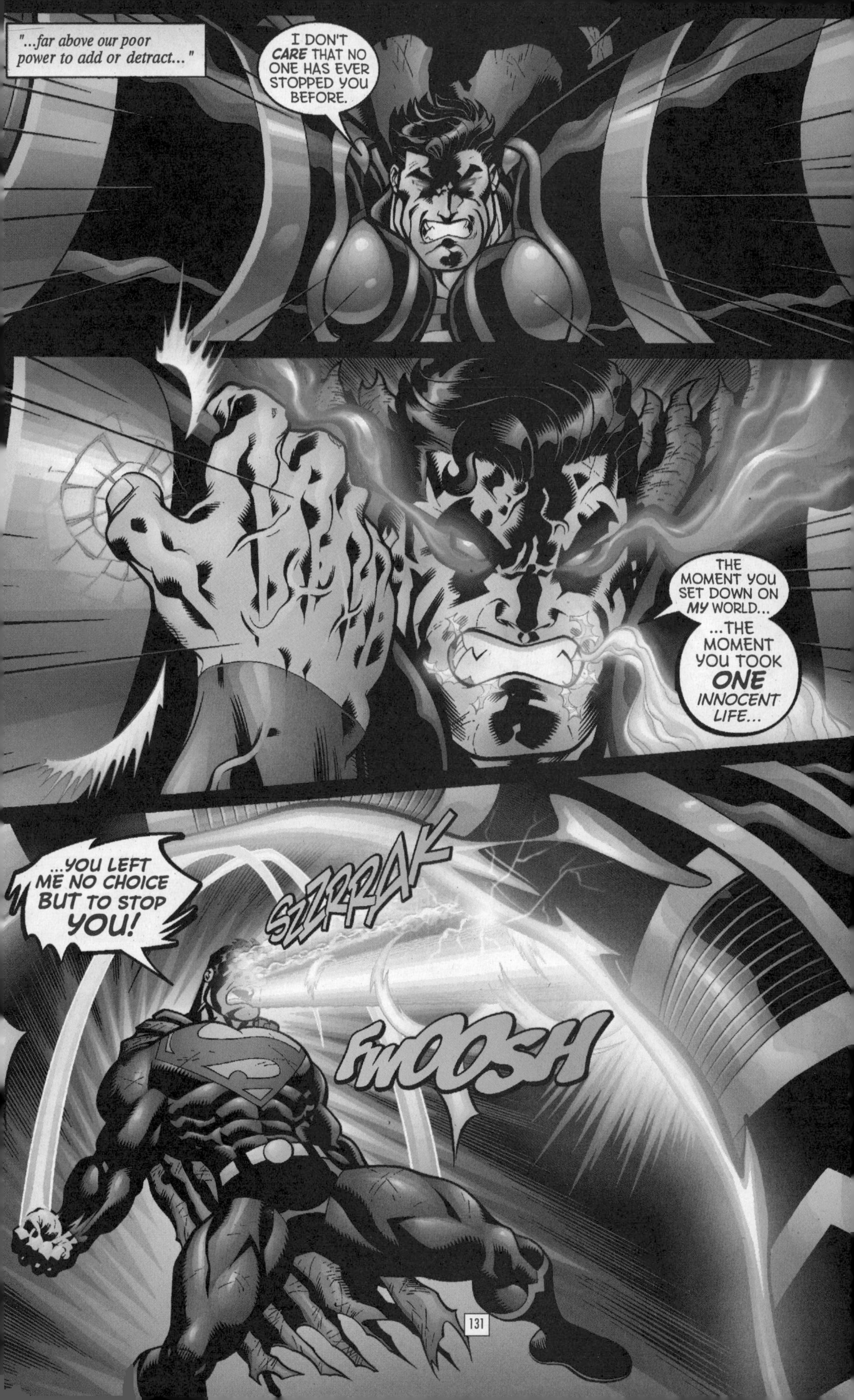
"...far above our poor power to add or detract..."
I DON'T CARE THAT NO ONE HAS EVER STOPPED YOU BEFORE.
THE MOMENT YOU SET DOWN ON MY WORLD...
...THE MOMENT YOU TOOK ONE INNOCENT LIFE...
...YOU LEFT ME NO CHOICE BUT TO STOP YOU!
SZZRRAK
FWOOSH

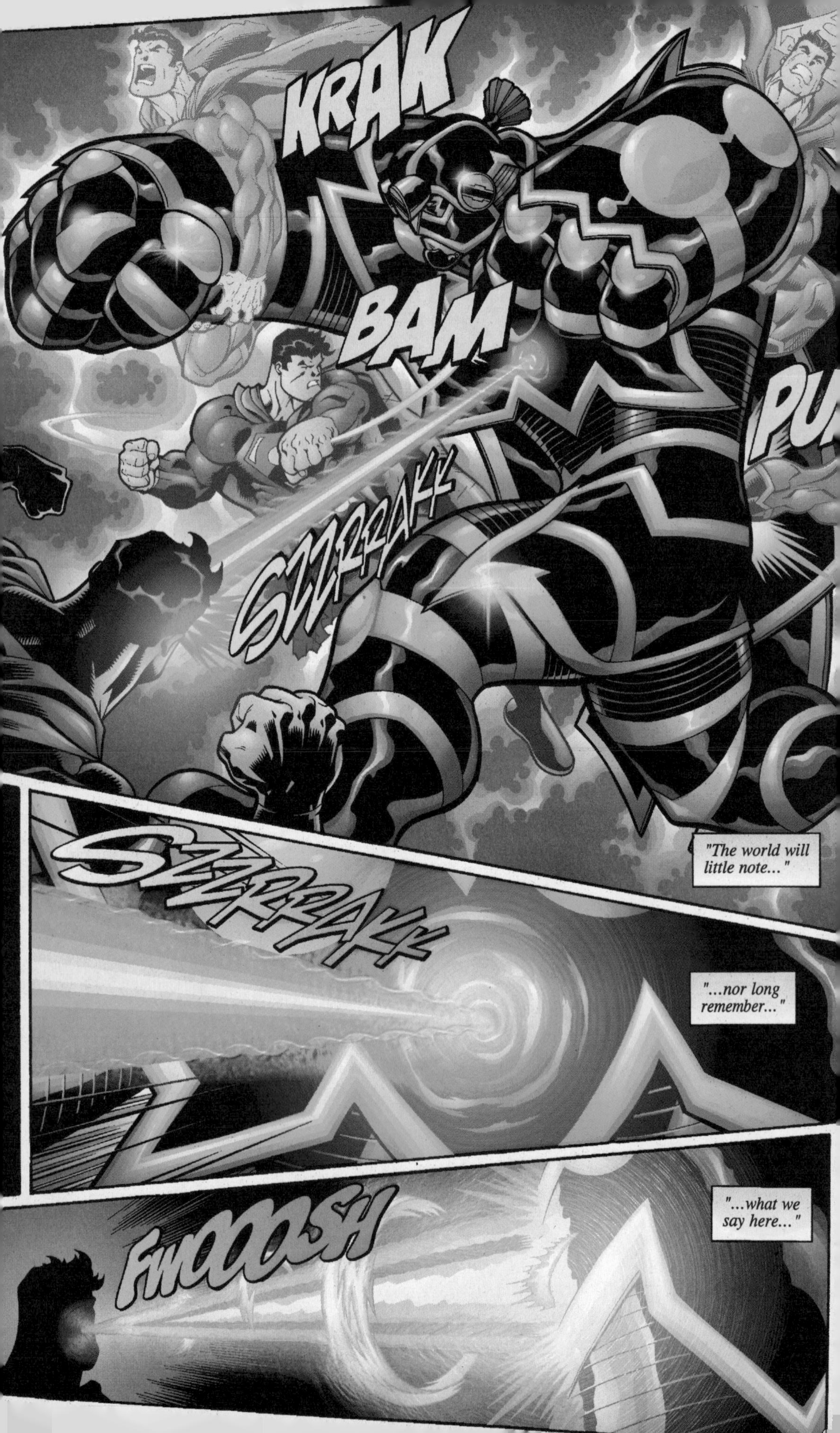

KRAK
BAM
SZZRRAKK
"The world will little note..."
SZZRRAKK
"...nor long remember..."
FWOOOSH
"...what we say here..."

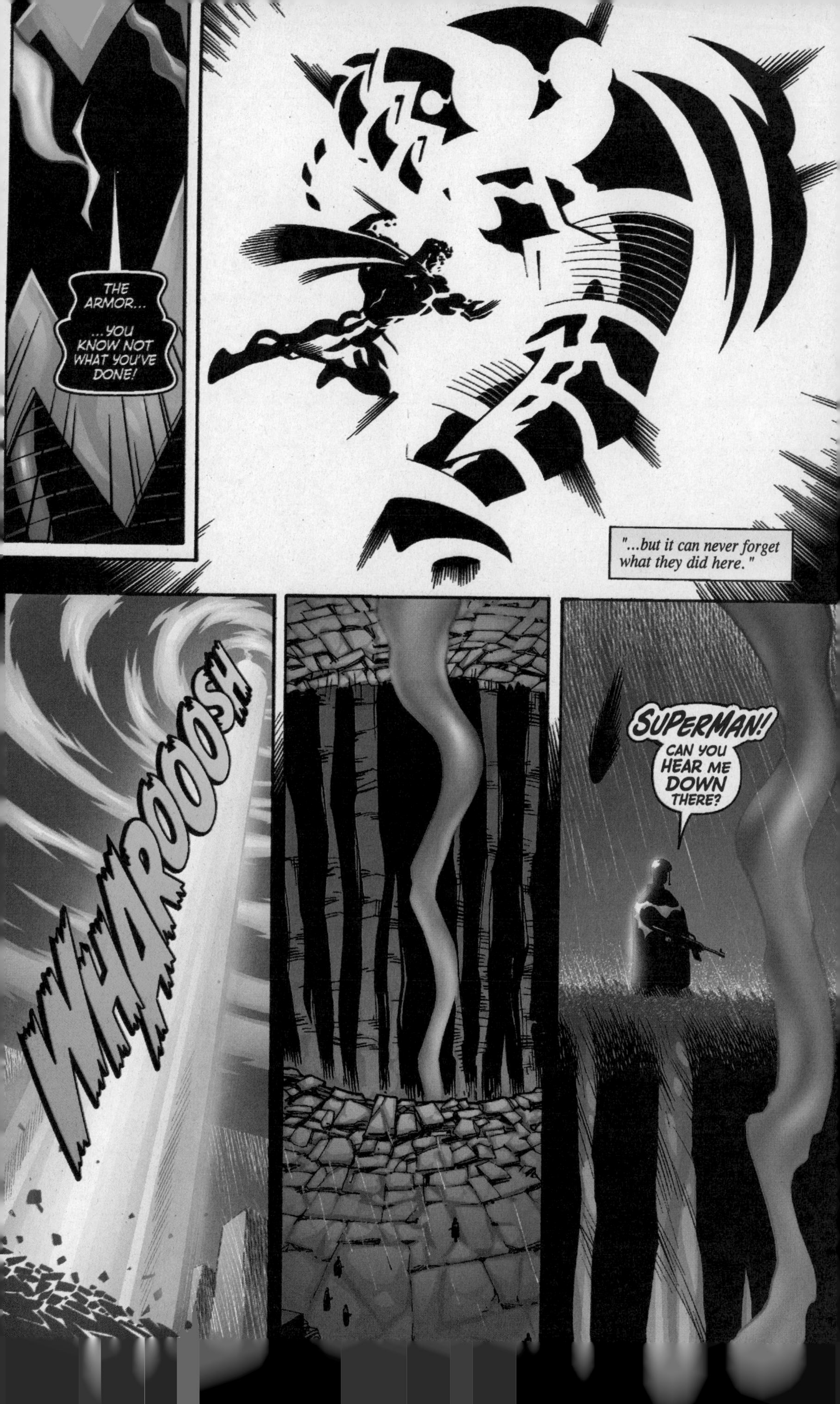
THE ARMOR...
...YOU KNOW NOT WHAT YOU'VE DONE!
"...but it can never forget what they did here."
WHAROOOSH
SUPERMAN! CAN YOU HEAR ME DOWN THERE?

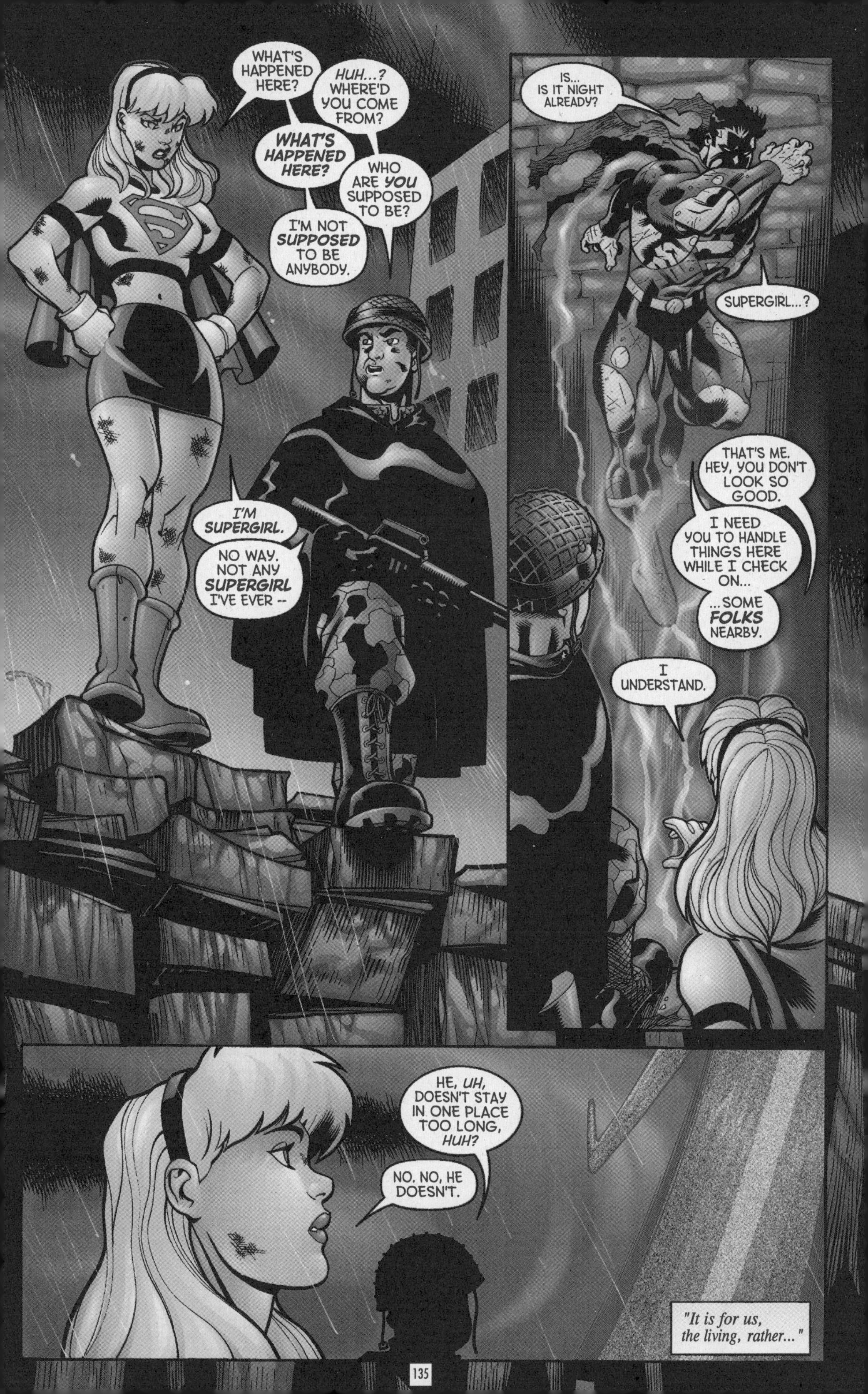
WHAT'S HAPPENED HERE?
HUH...? WHERE'D YOU COME FROM?
WHAT'S HAPPENED HERE?
WHO ARE YOU SUPPOSED TO BE?
I'M NOT SUPPOSED TO BE ANYBODY.
I'M SUPERGIRL.
NO WAY. NOT ANY SUPERGIRL I'VE EVER --
IS... IS IT NIGHT ALREADY?
SUPERGIRL...?
THAT'S ME. HEY, YOU DON'T LOOK SO GOOD.
I NEED YOU TO HANDLE THINGS HERE WHILE I CHECK ON...
...SOME FOLKS NEARBY.
I UNDERSTAND.
HE, UH, DOESN'T STAY IN ONE PLACE TOO LONG, HUH?
NO. NO, HE DOESN'T.
"It is for us, the living, rather..."

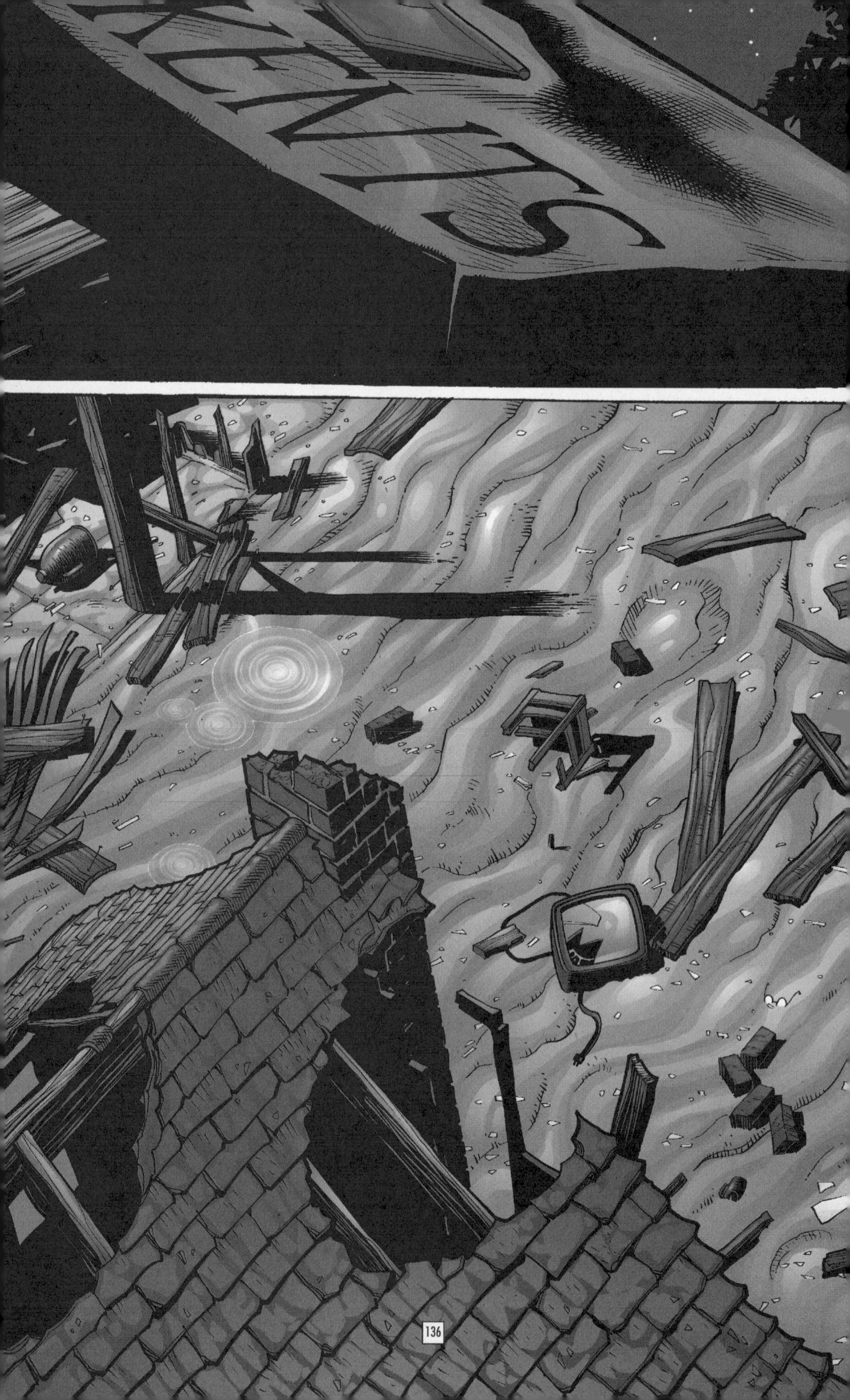
KENTS

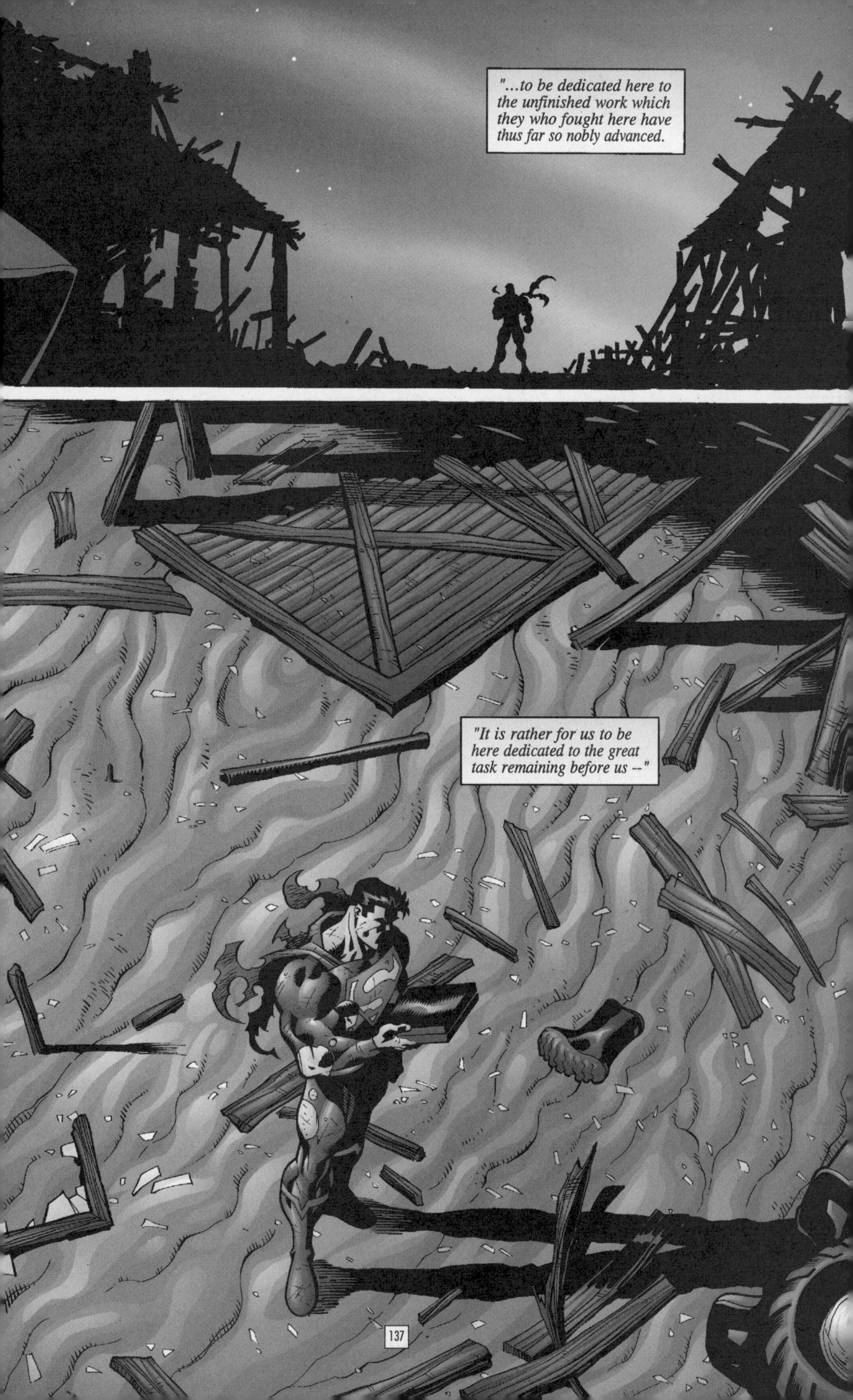
"...to be dedicated here to the unfinished work which they who fought here have thus far so nobly advanced.
"It is rather for us to be here dedicated to the great task remaining before us --"

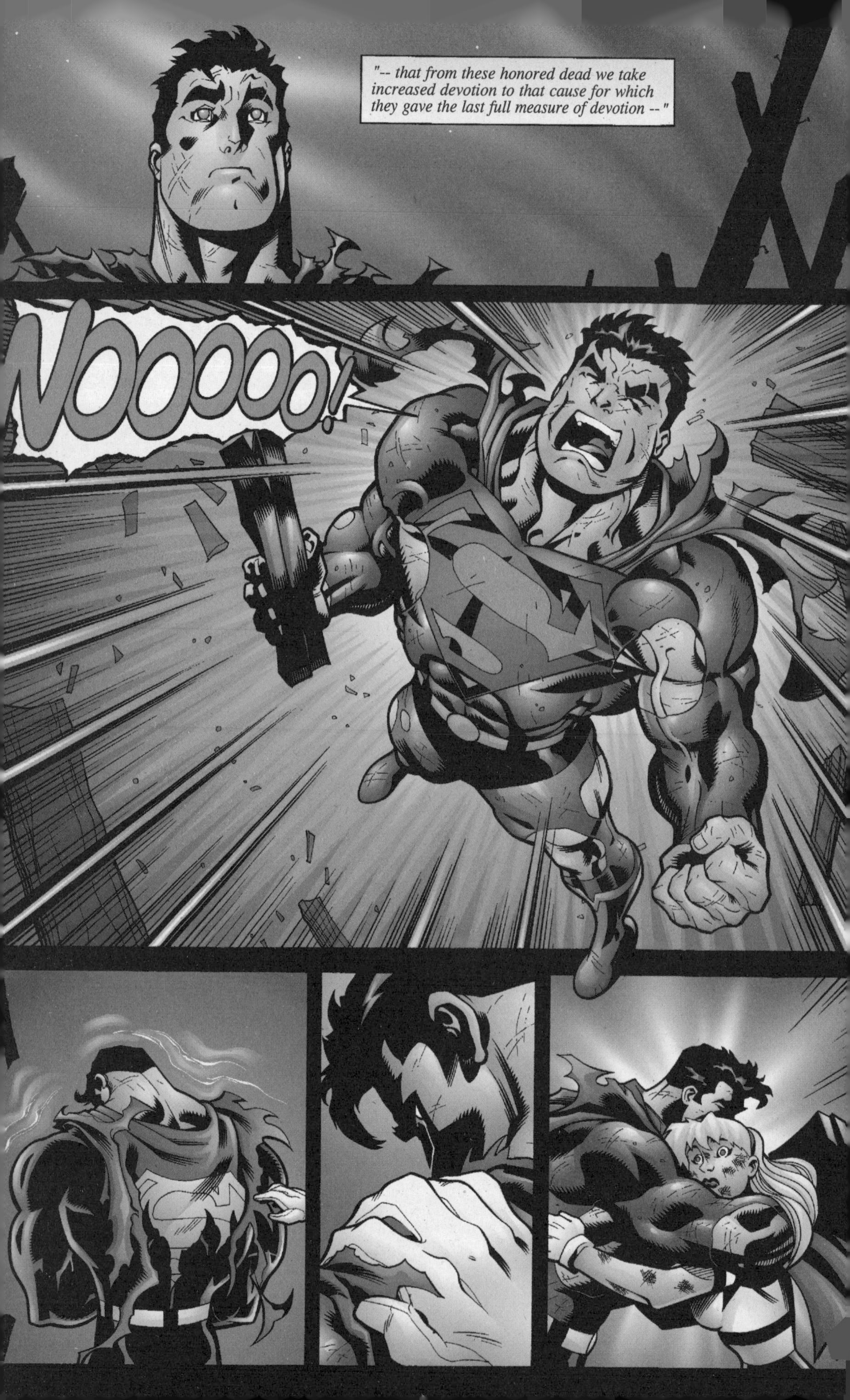
"-- that from these honored dead we take increased devotion to that cause for which they gave the last full measure of devotion -- "
NOOOOO!

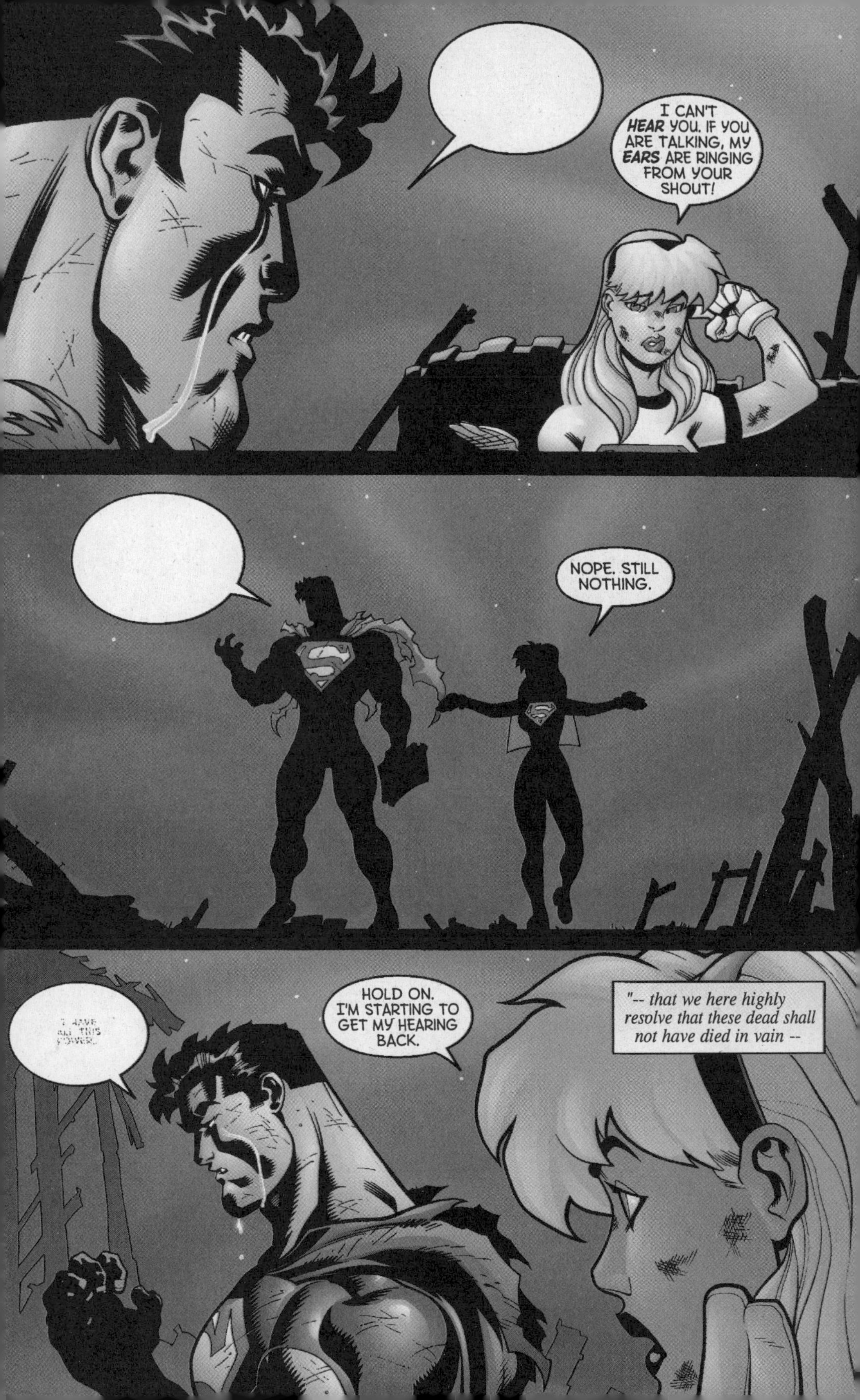
I CAN'T HEAR YOU. IF YOU ARE TALKING, MY EARS ARE RINGING FROM YOUR SHOUT!
NOPE. STILL NOTHING.
HOLD ON. I'M STARTING TO GET MY HEARING BACK.
"-- that we here highly resolve that these dead shall not have died in vain --

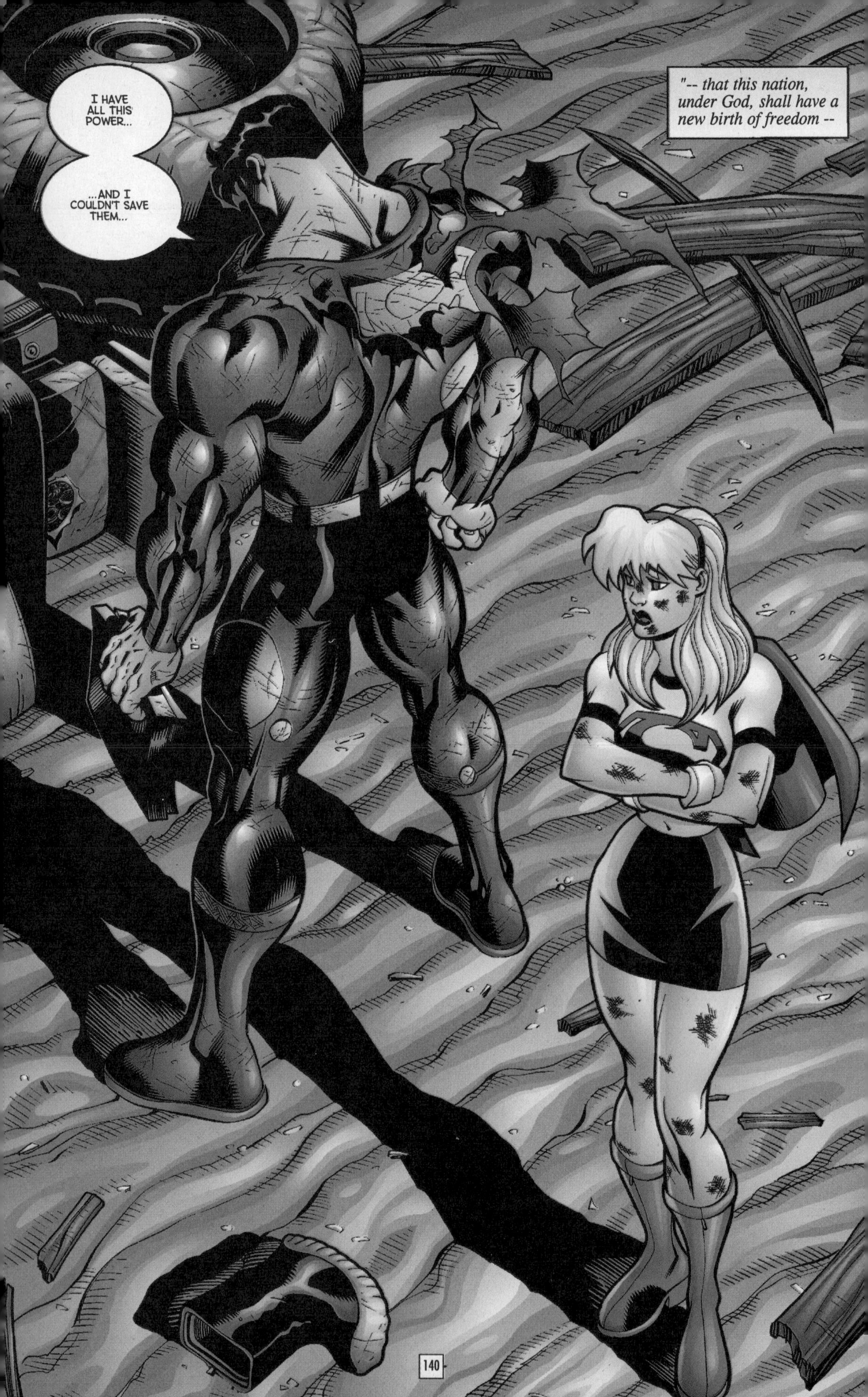
I HAVE ALL THIS POWER...
...AND I COULDN'T SAVE THEM...
"-- that this nation, under God, shall have a new birth of freedom --

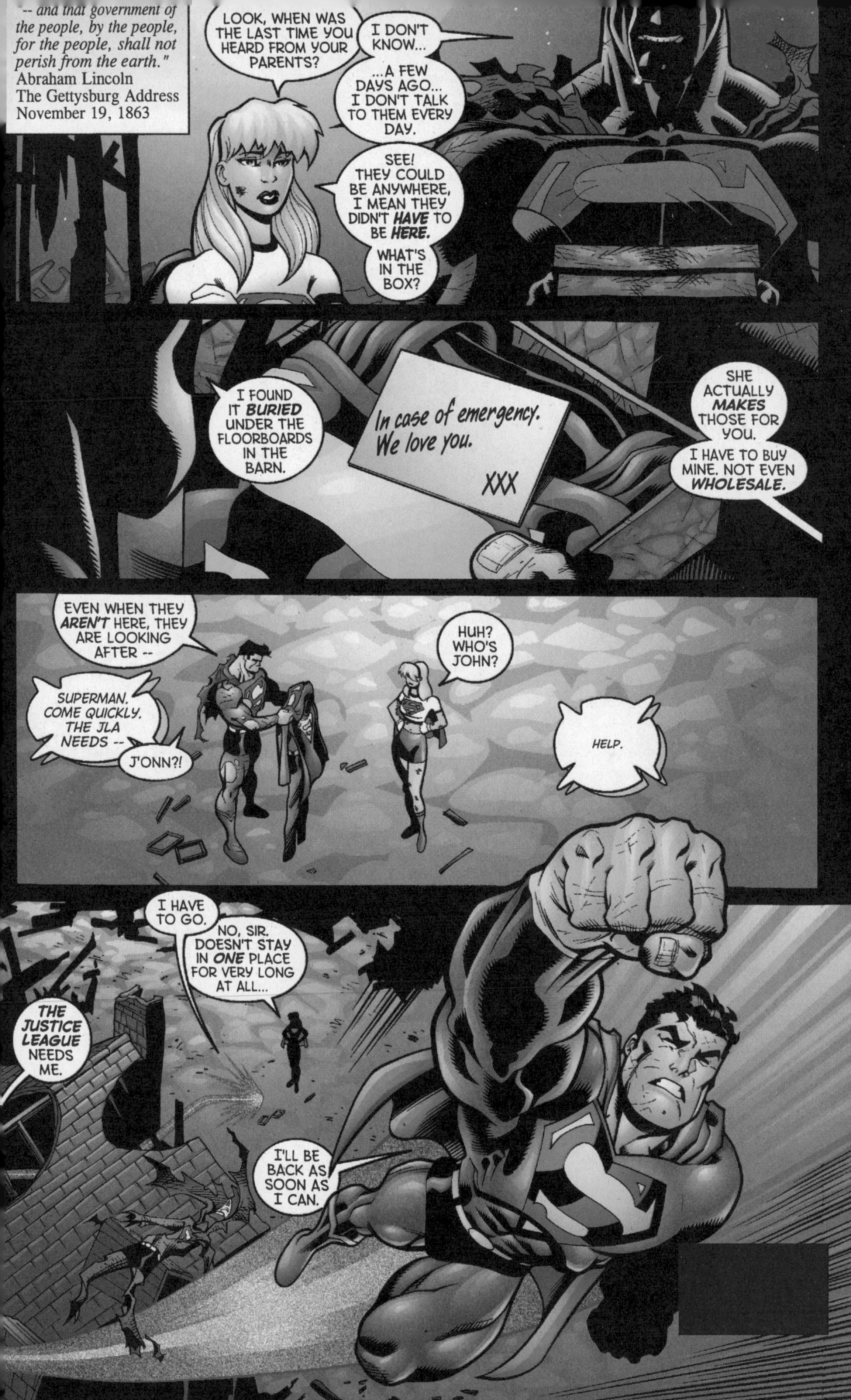

"-- and that government of the people, by the people, for the people, shall not perish from the earth." Abraham Lincoln The Gettysburg Address November 19, 1863
LOOK, WHEN WAS THE LAST TIME YOU HEARD FROM YOUR PARENTS?
I DON'T KNOW...
...A FEW DAYS AGO... I DON'T TALK TO THEM EVERY DAY.
SEE! THEY COULD BE ANYWHERE, I MEAN THEY DIDN'T HAVE TO BE HERE.
WHAT'S IN THE BOX?
I FOUND IT BURIED UNDER THE FLOORBOARDS IN THE BARN.
In case of emergency. We love you.
XXX
SHE ACTUALLY MAKES THOSE FOR YOU.
I HAVE TO BUY MINE. NOT EVEN WHOLESALE.
EVEN WHEN THEY AREN'T HERE, THEY ARE LOOKING AFTER --
SUPERMAN. COME QUICKLY. THE JLA NEEDS --
J'ONN?!
HUH? WHO'S JOHN?
HELP.
I HAVE TO GO.
NO, SIR. DOESN'T STAY IN ONE PLACE FOR VERY LONG AT ALL...
THE JUSTICE LEAGUE NEEDS ME.
I'LL BE BACK AS SOON AS I CAN.
[redacted]

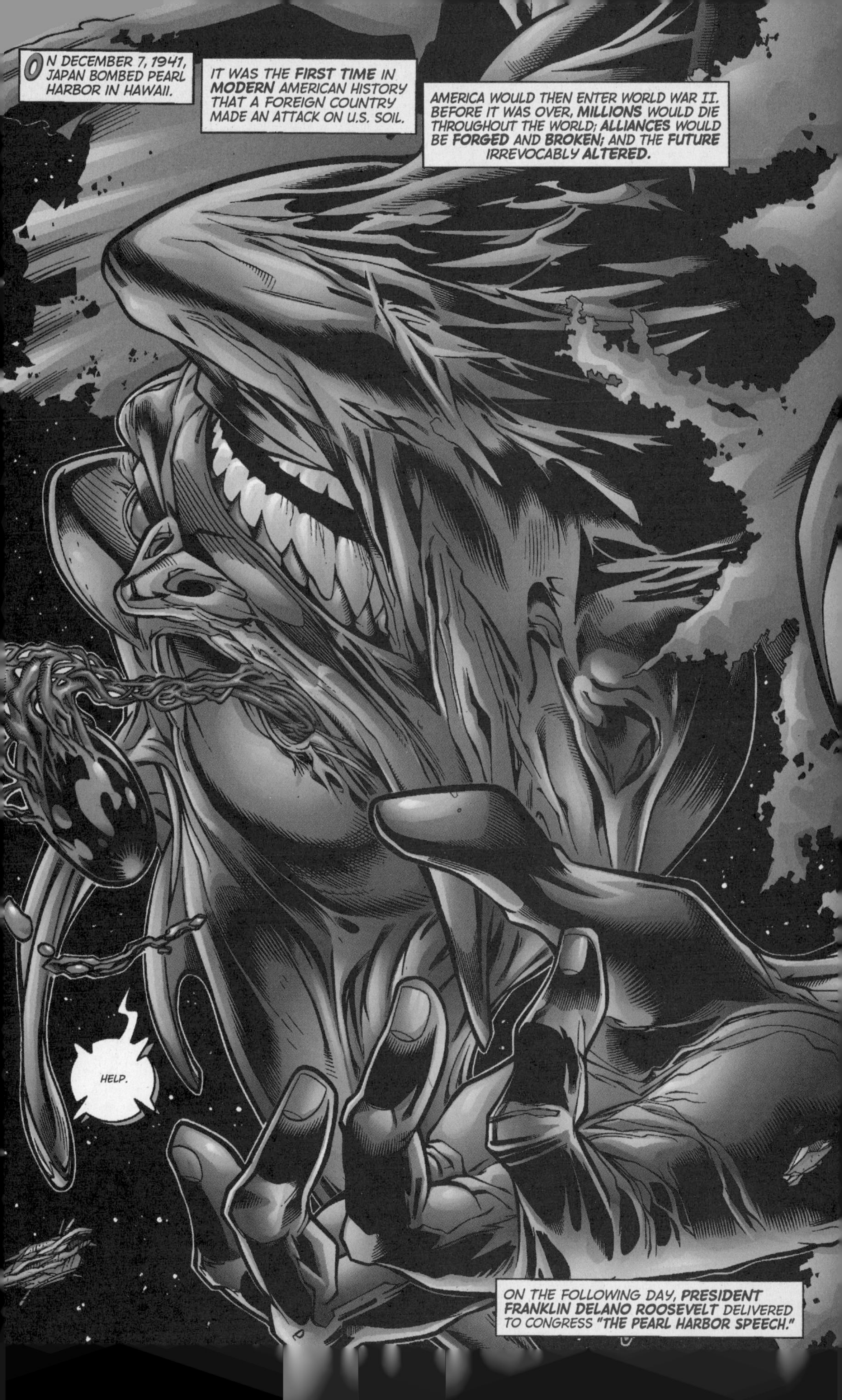
ON DECEMBER 7, 1941, JAPAN BOMBED PEARL HARBOR IN HAWAII.
IT WAS THE FIRST TIME IN MODERN AMERICAN HISTORY THAT A FOREIGN COUNTRY MADE AN ATTACK ON U.S. SOIL.
AMERICA WOULD THEN ENTER WORLD WAR II. BEFORE IT WAS OVER, MILLIONS WOULD DIE THROUGHOUT THE WORLD; ALLIANCES WOULD BE FORGED AND BROKEN; AND THE FUTURE IRREVOCABLY ALTERED.
HELP.
ON THE FOLLOWING DAY, PRESIDENT FRANKLIN DELANO ROOSEVELT DELIVERED TO CONGRESS "THE PEARL HARBOR SPEECH."

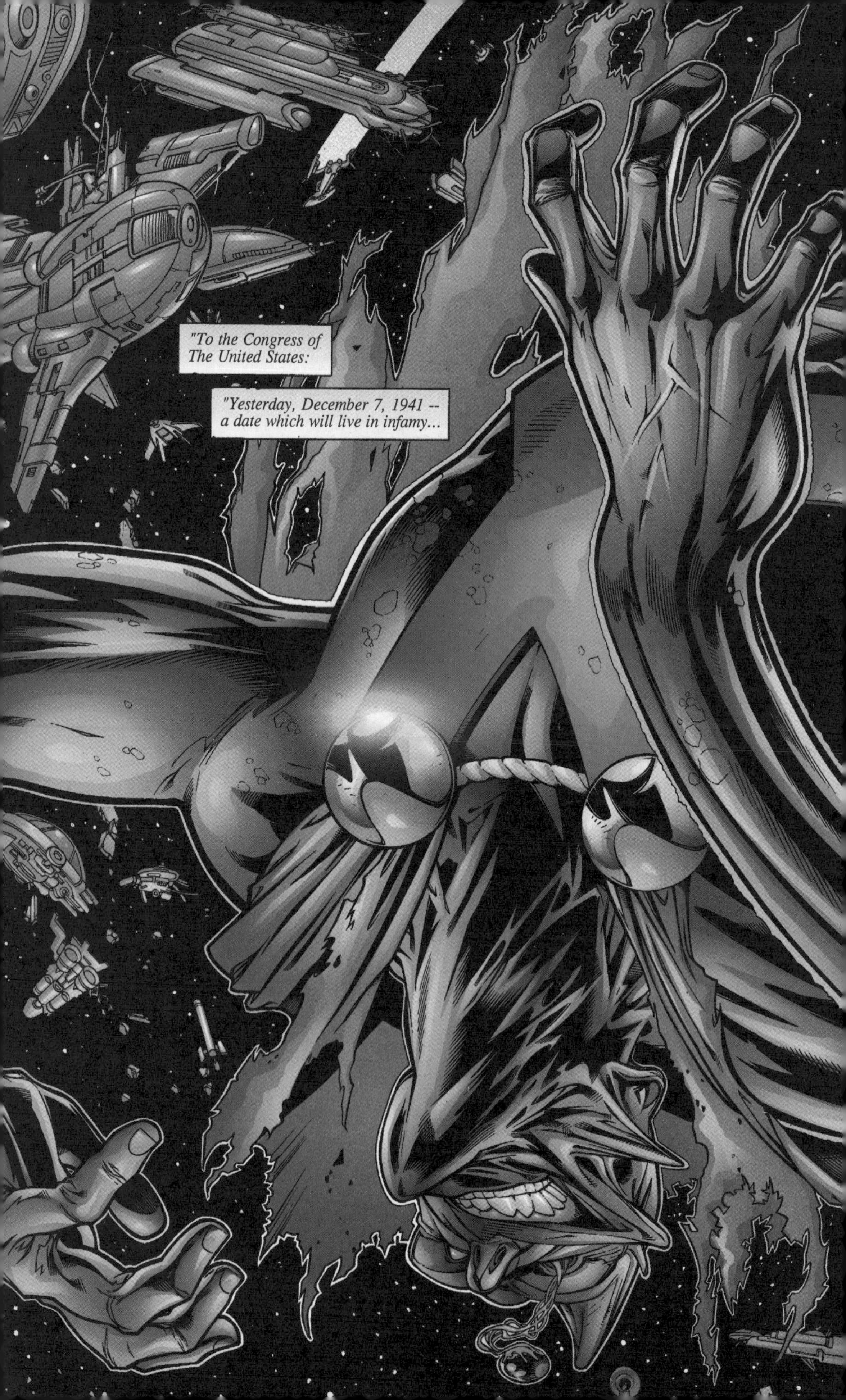
"To the Congress of
The United States:
"Yesterday, December 7, 1941 --
a date which will live in infamy...

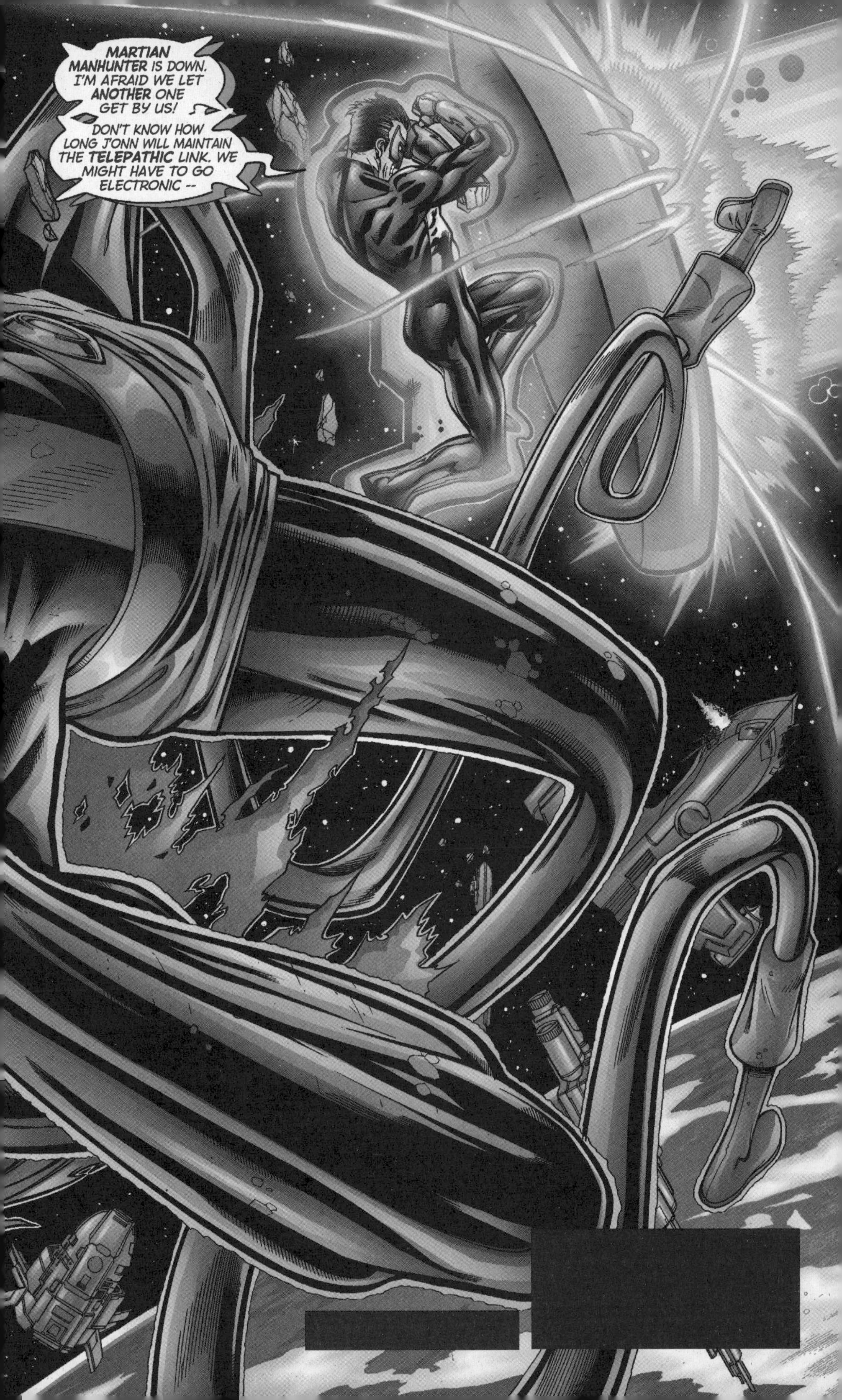

MARTIAN MANHUNTER IS DOWN. I'M AFRAID WE LET ANOTHER ONE GET BY US!
DON'T KNOW HOW LONG J'ONN WILL MAINTAIN THE TELEPATHIC LINK. WE MIGHT HAVE TO GO ELECTRONIC --
[redacted]

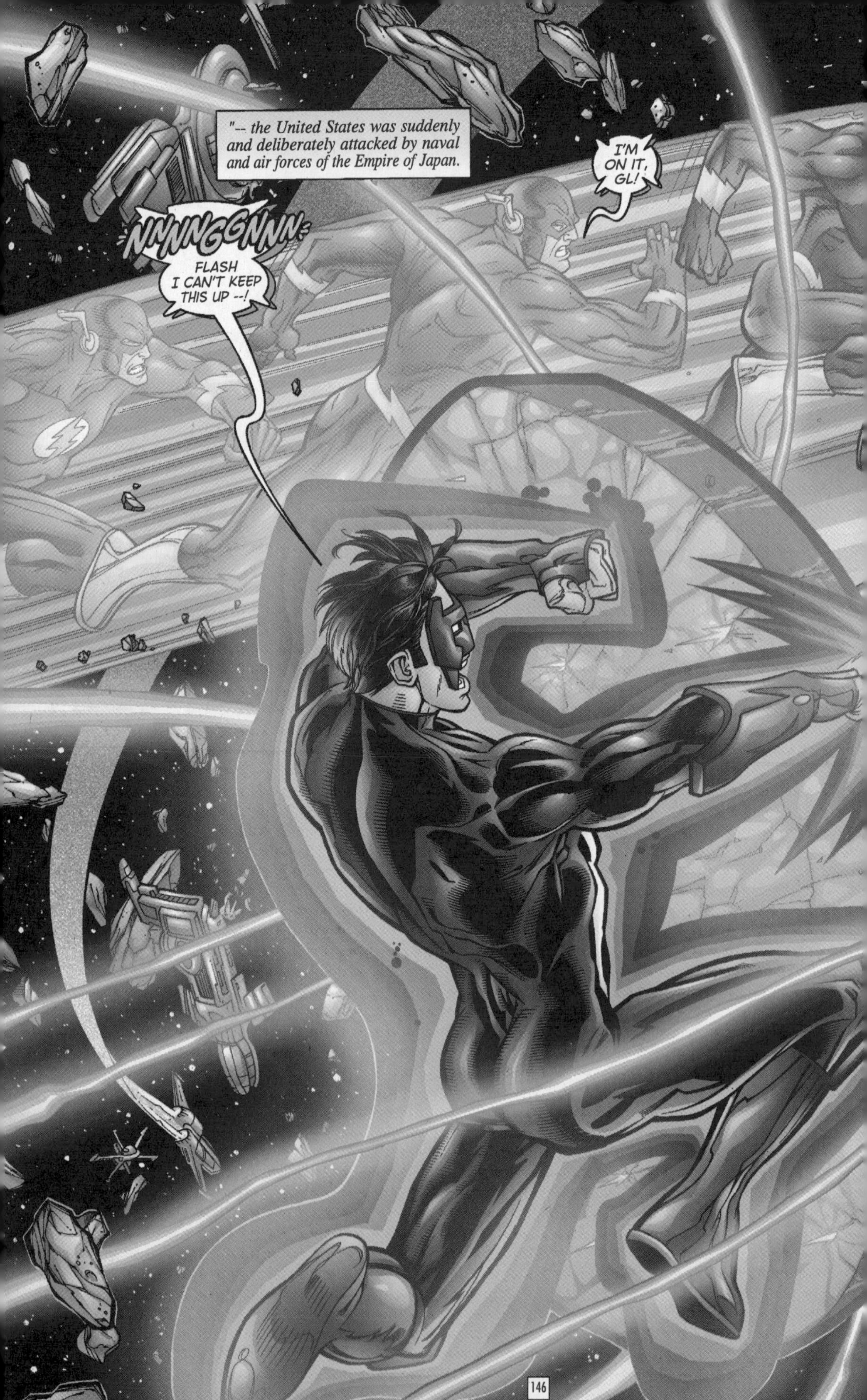
"-- the United States was suddenly and deliberately attacked by naval and air forces of the Empire of Japan.
I'M ON IT, GL!
NNNNGGNNN
FLASH I CAN'T KEEP THIS UP --!

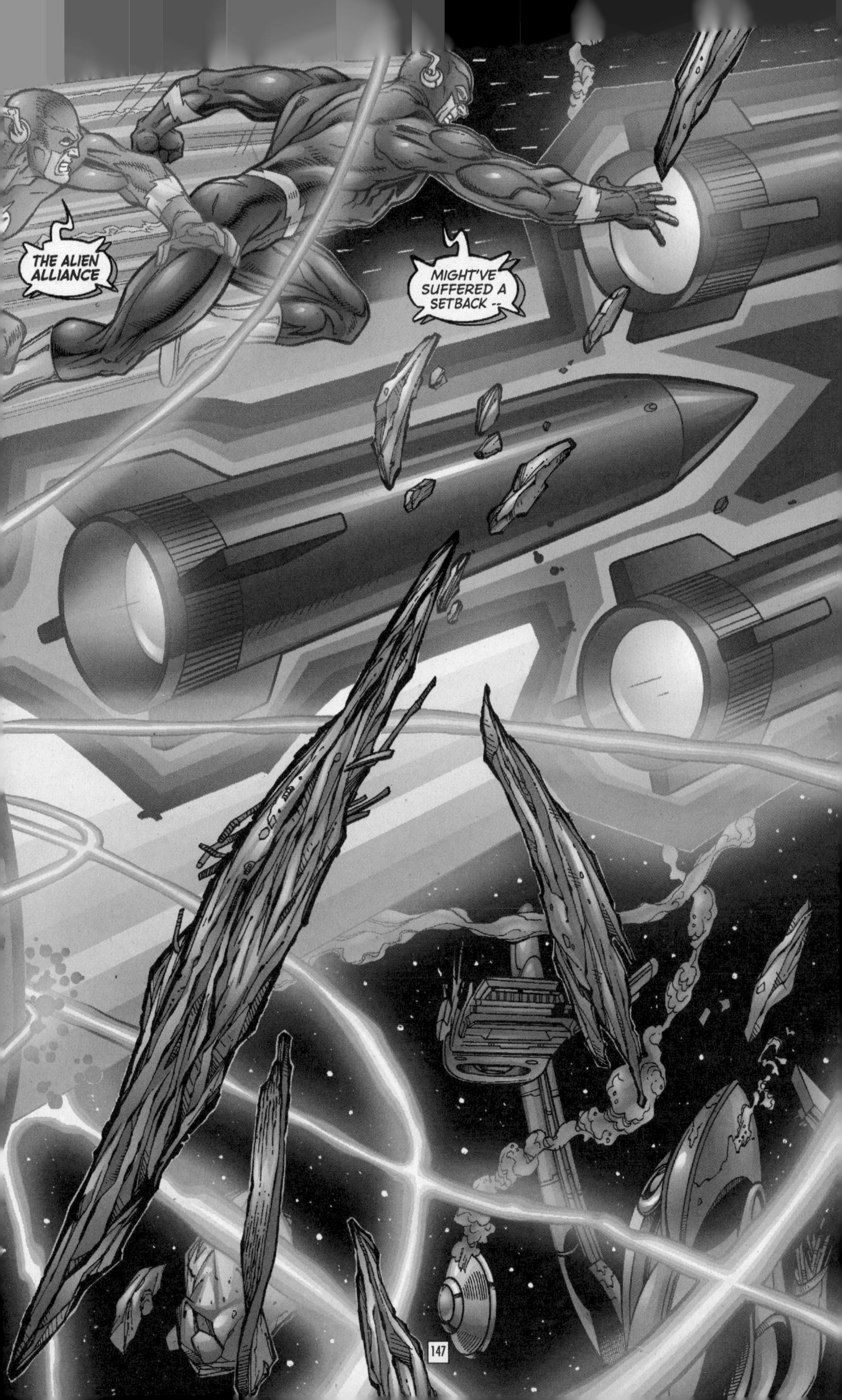

THE ALIEN ALLIANCE
MIGHT'VE SUFFERED A SETBACK --

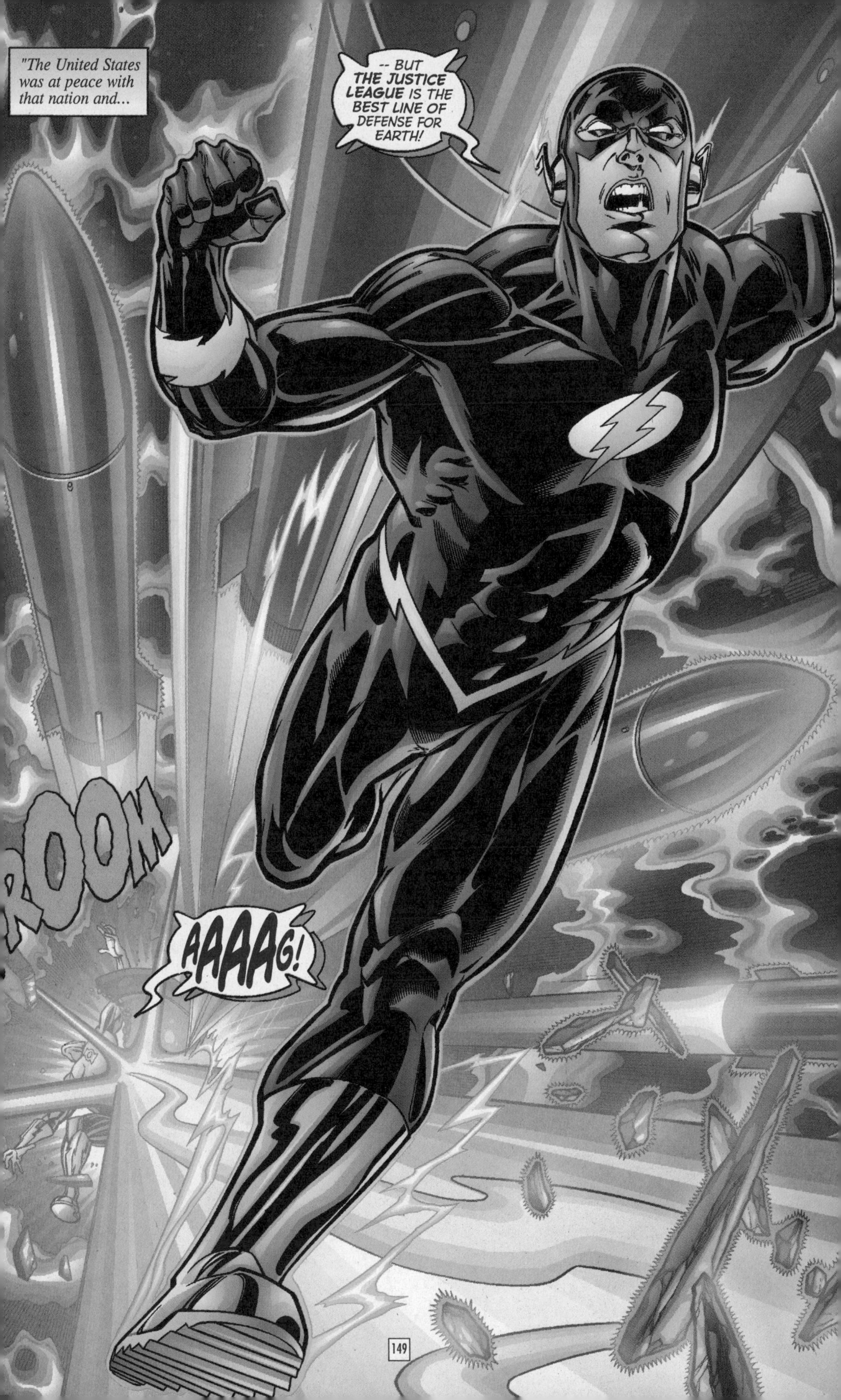
"The United States was at peace with that nation and...
-- BUT THE JUSTICE LEAGUE IS THE BEST LINE OF DEFENSE FOR EARTH!
ROOM
AAAAG!

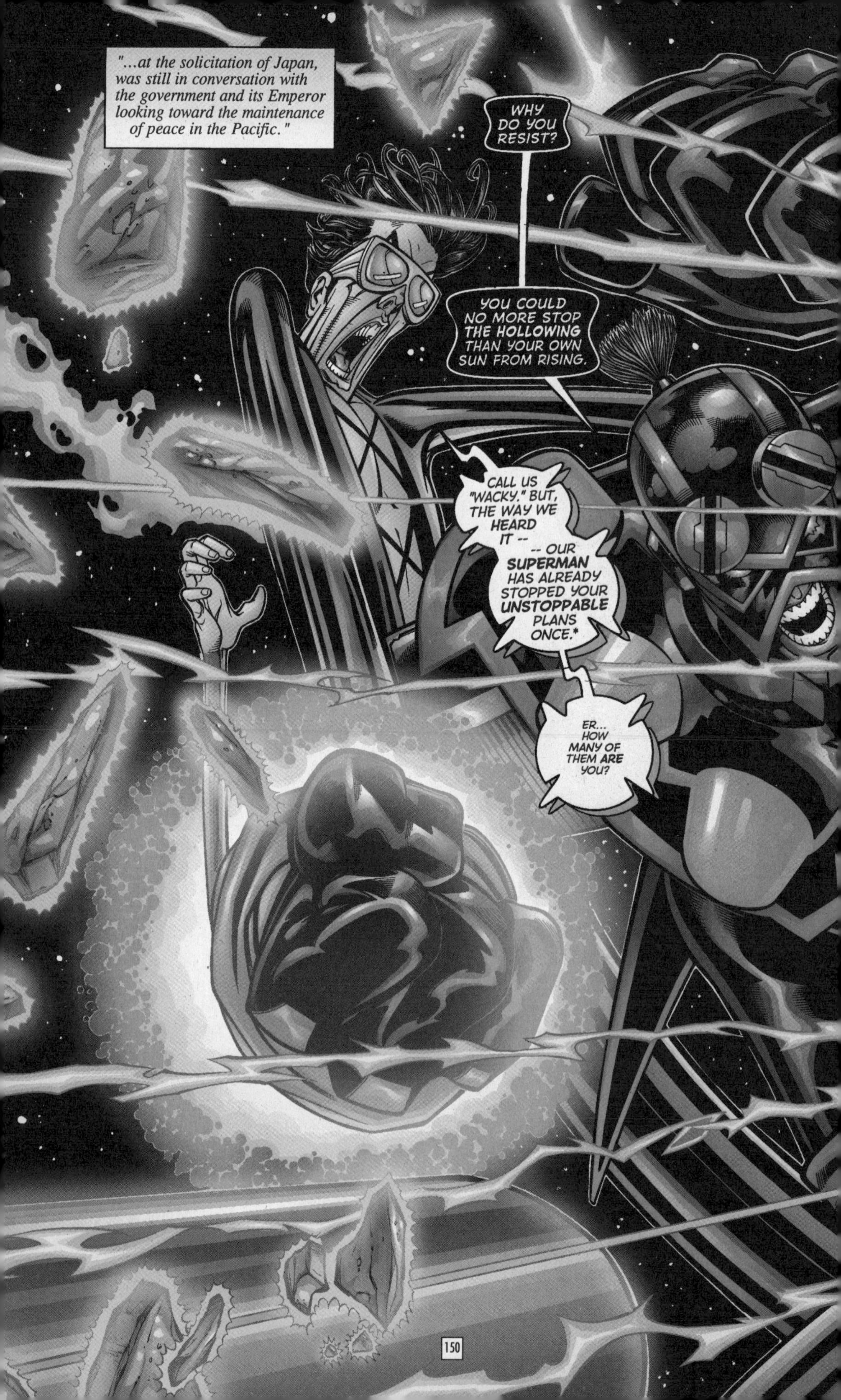

"...at the solicitation of Japan, was still in conversation with the government and its Emperor looking toward the maintenance of peace in the Pacific."
WHY DO YOU RESIST?
YOU COULD NO MORE STOP THE HOLLOWING THAN YOUR OWN SUN FROM RISING.
CALL US "WACKY," BUT, THE WAY WE HEARD IT --
-- OUR SUPERMAN HAS ALREADY STOPPED YOUR UNSTOPPABLE PLANS ONCE.*
ER... HOW MANY OF THEM ARE YOU?

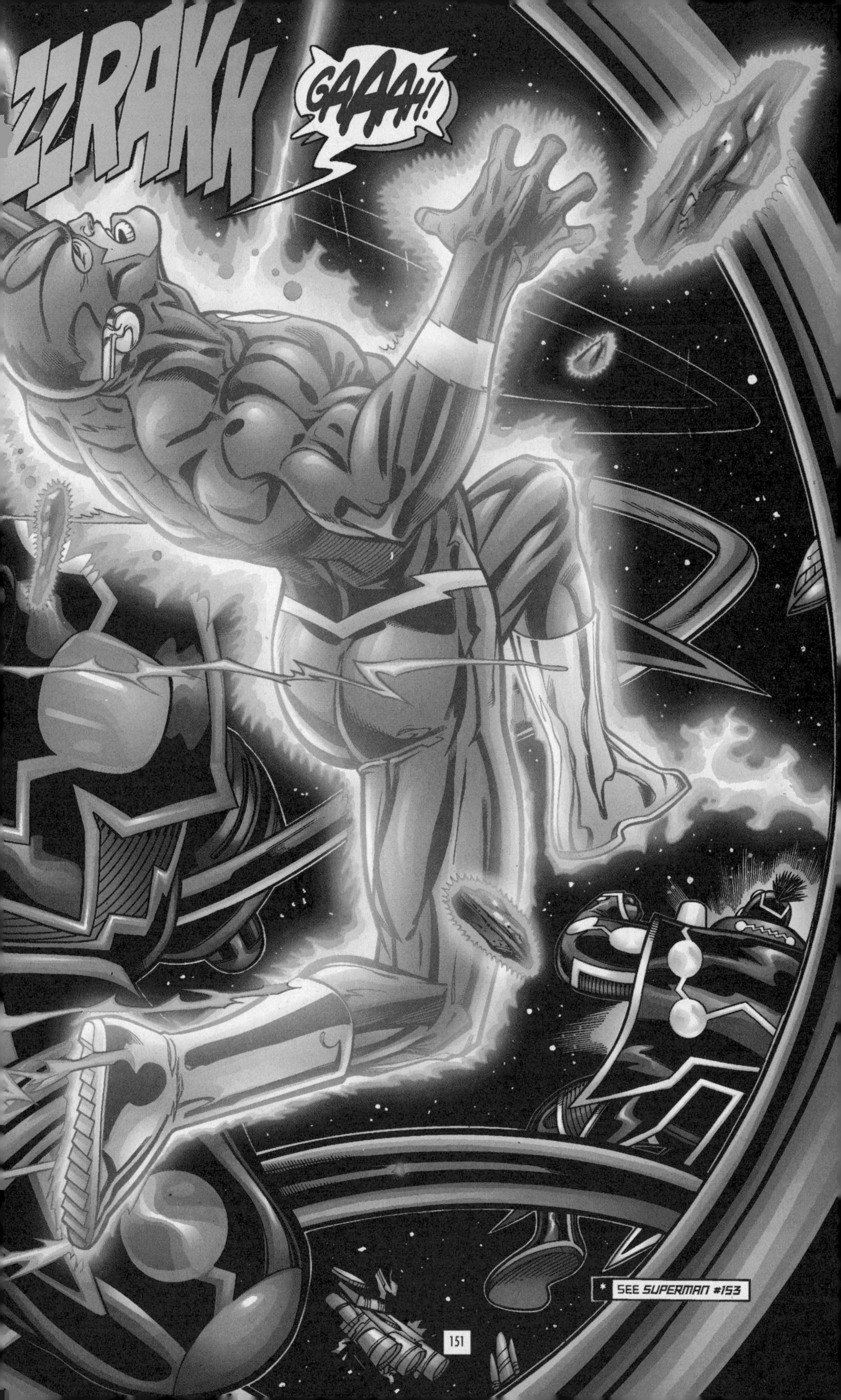
ZZRAKK
GAAAH!!
* SEE SUPERMAN #153

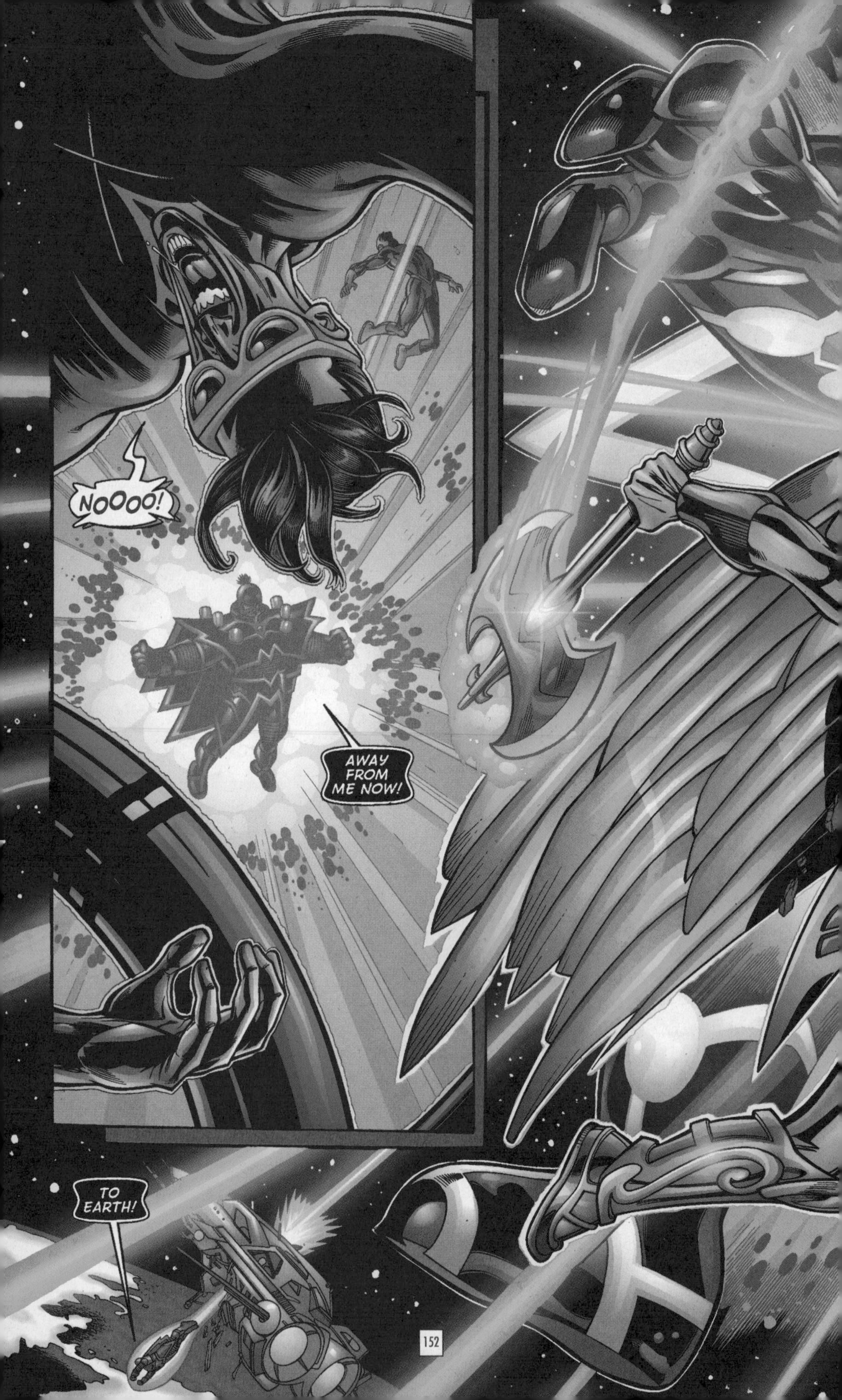
NOOOO!
AWAY FROM ME NOW!
TO EARTH!

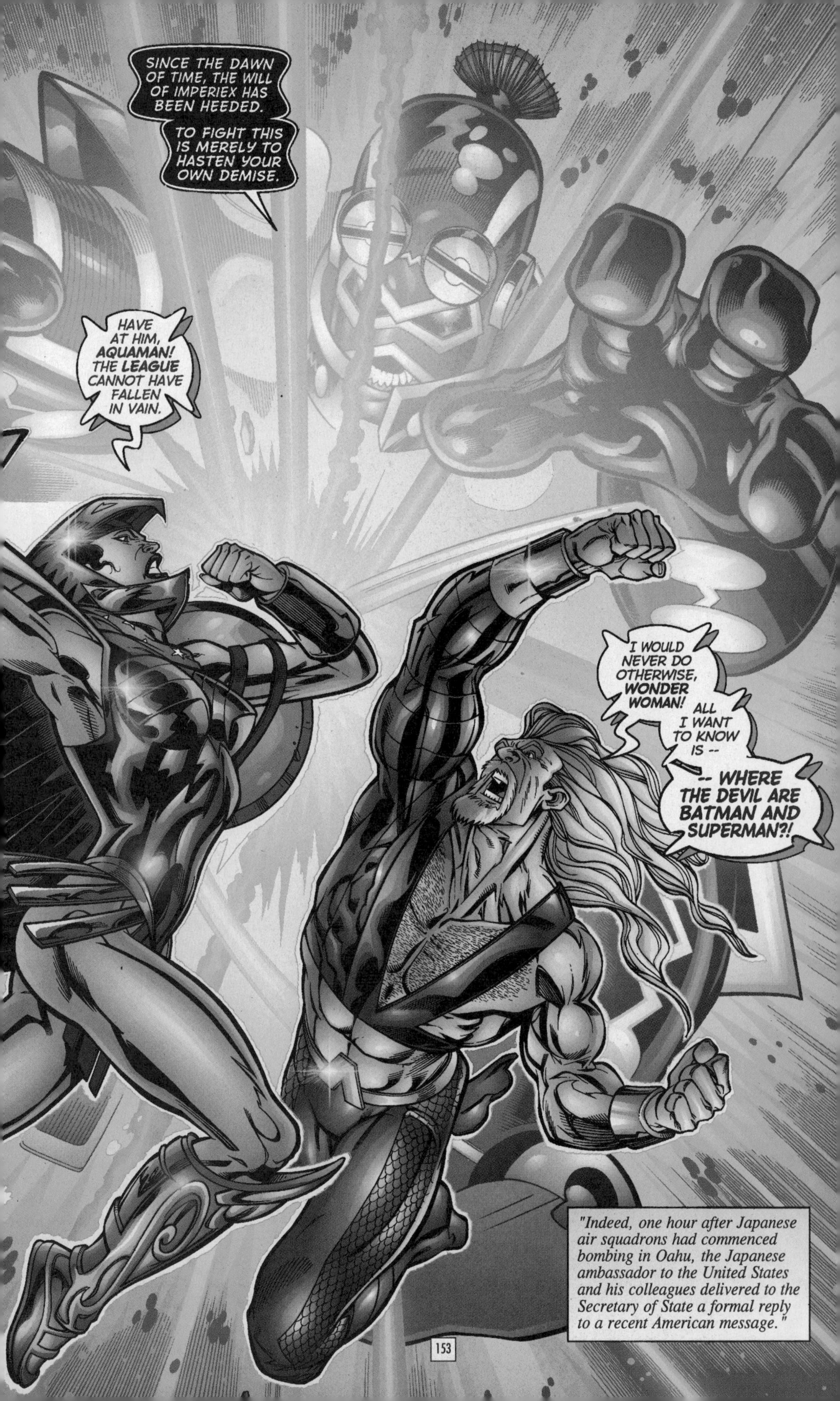
SINCE THE DAWN OF TIME, THE WILL OF IMPERIEX HAS BEEN HEEDED.
TO FIGHT THIS IS MERELY TO HASTEN YOUR OWN DEMISE.
HAVE AT HIM, AQUAMAN! THE LEAGUE CANNOT HAVE FALLEN IN VAIN.
I WOULD NEVER DO OTHERWISE, WONDER WOMAN! ALL I WANT TO KNOW IS --
-- WHERE THE DEVIL ARE BATMAN AND SUPERMAN?!
"Indeed, one hour after Japanese air squadrons had commenced bombing in Oahu, the Japanese ambassador to the United States and his colleagues delivered to the Secretary of State a formal reply to a recent American message."

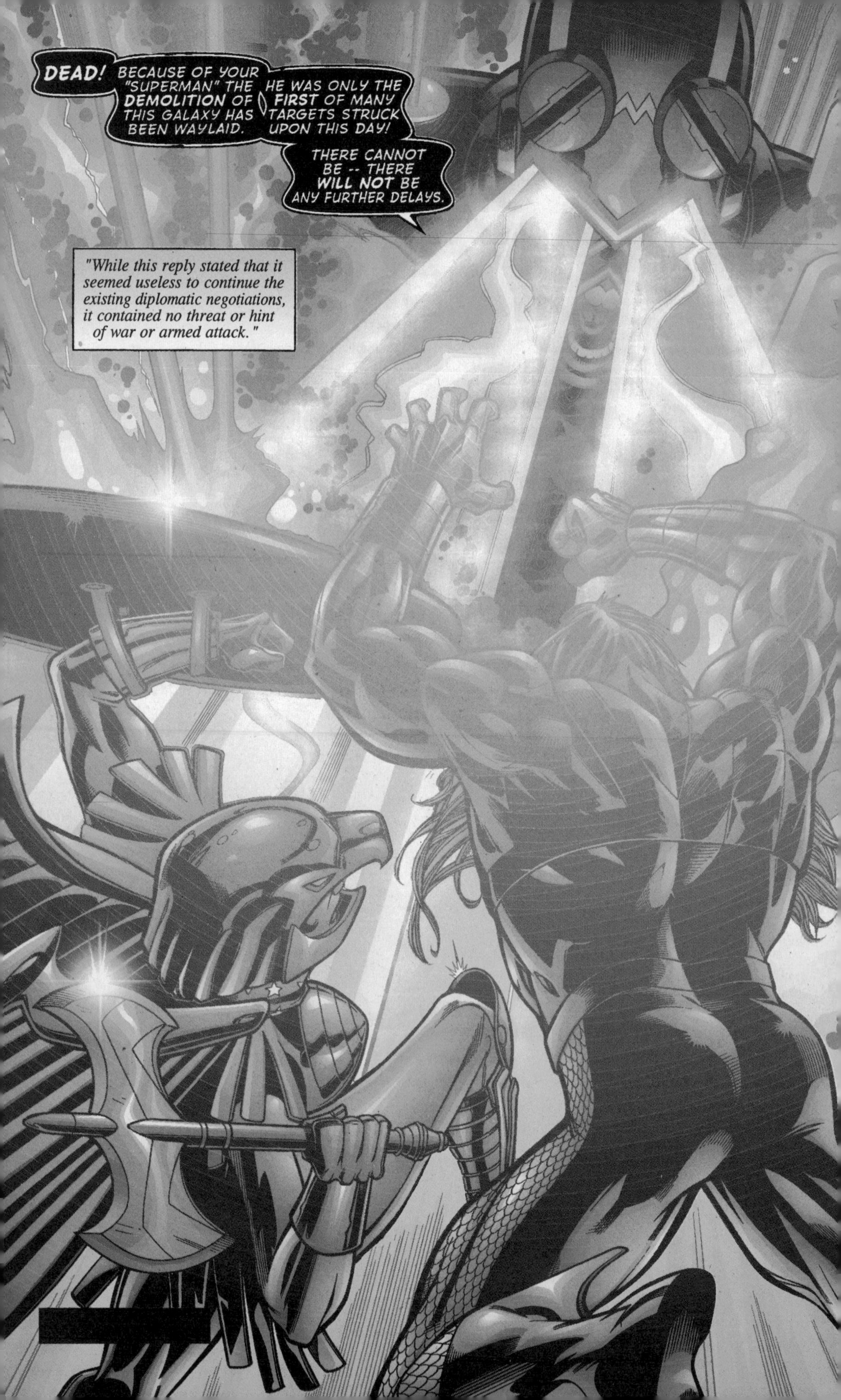
DEAD!
BECAUSE OF YOUR "SUPERMAN" THE DEMOLITION OF THIS GALAXY HAS BEEN WAYLAID.
HE WAS ONLY THE FIRST OF MANY TARGETS STRUCK UPON THIS DAY!
THERE CANNOT BE -- THERE WILL NOT BE ANY FURTHER DELAYS.
"While this reply stated that it seemed useless to continue the existing diplomatic negotiations, it contained no threat or hint of war or armed attack."

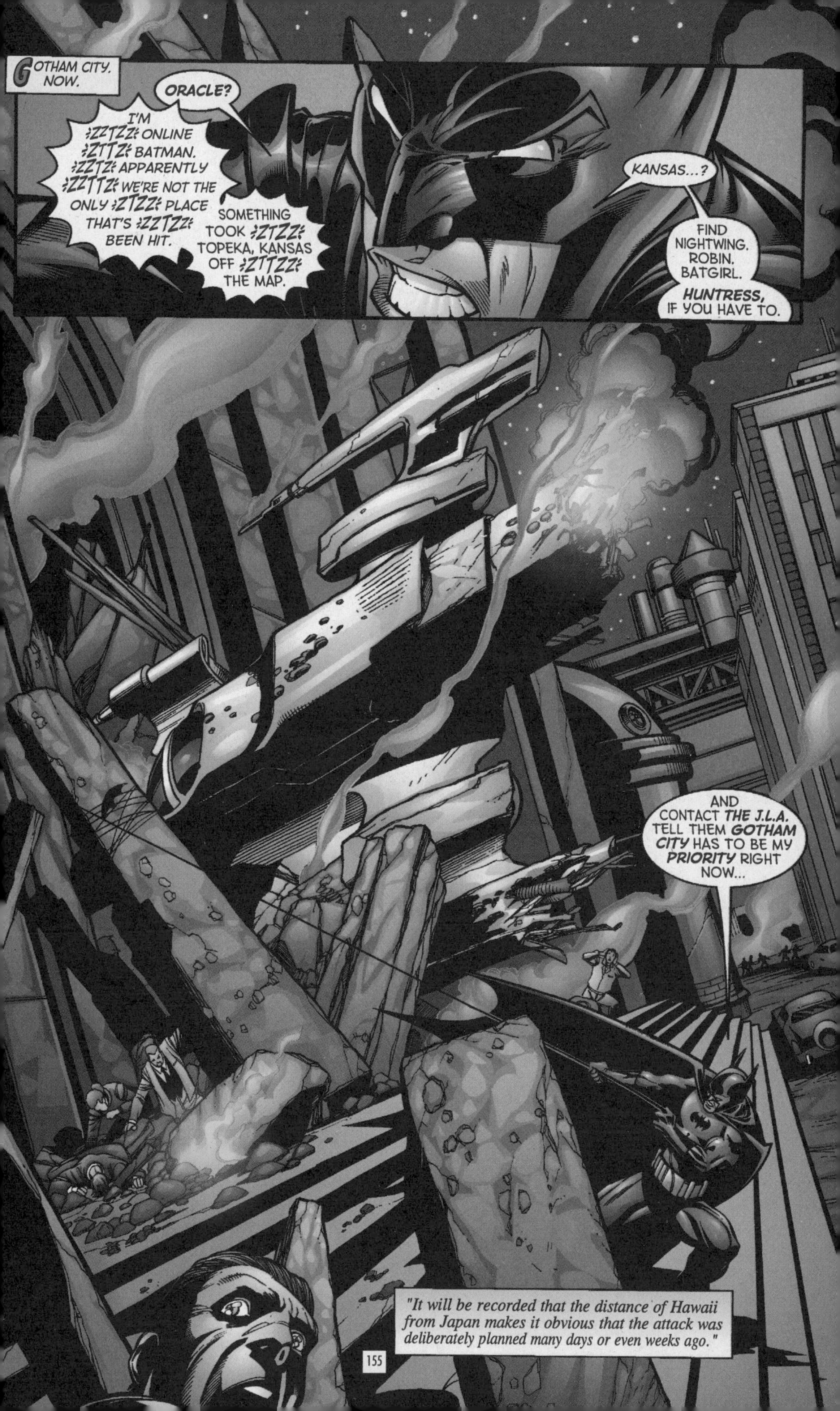

GOTHAM CITY. NOW.
ORACLE?
I'M ZZTZZ ONLINE ZTTZ BATMAN. ZZTZ APPARENTLY ZZTTZ WE'RE NOT THE ONLY ZTZZ PLACE THAT'S ZZTZZ BEEN HIT.
SOMETHING TOOK ZTZZ TOPEKA, KANSAS OFF ZTTZZ THE MAP.
KANSAS...?
FIND NIGHTWING. ROBIN. BATGIRL.
HUNTRESS, IF YOU HAVE TO.
AND CONTACT THE J.L.A. TELL THEM GOTHAM CITY HAS TO BE MY PRIORITY RIGHT NOW...
"It will be recorded that the distance of Hawaii from Japan makes it obvious that the attack was deliberately planned many days or even weeks ago."

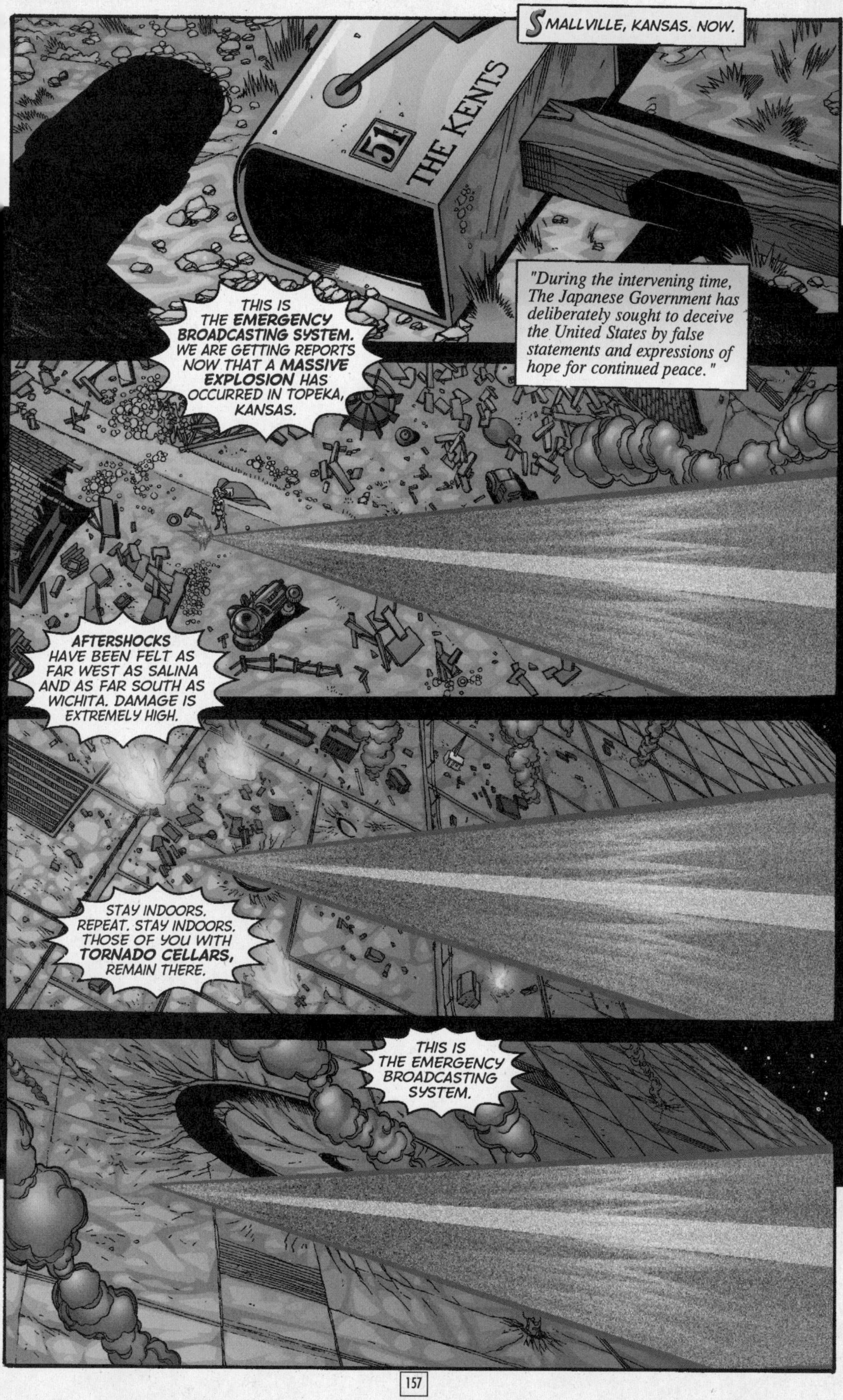
SMALLVILLE, KANSAS. NOW.
51
THE KENTS
"During the intervening time, The Japanese Government has deliberately sought to deceive the United States by false statements and expressions of hope for continued peace."
THIS IS THE EMERGENCY BROADCASTING SYSTEM. WE ARE GETTING REPORTS NOW THAT A MASSIVE EXPLOSION HAS OCCURRED IN TOPEKA, KANSAS.
AFTERSHOCKS HAVE BEEN FELT AS FAR WEST AS SALINA AND AS FAR SOUTH AS WICHITA. DAMAGE IS EXTREMELY HIGH.
STAY INDOORS. REPEAT. STAY INDOORS. THOSE OF YOU WITH TORNADO CELLARS, REMAIN THERE.
THIS IS THE EMERGENCY BROADCASTING SYSTEM.

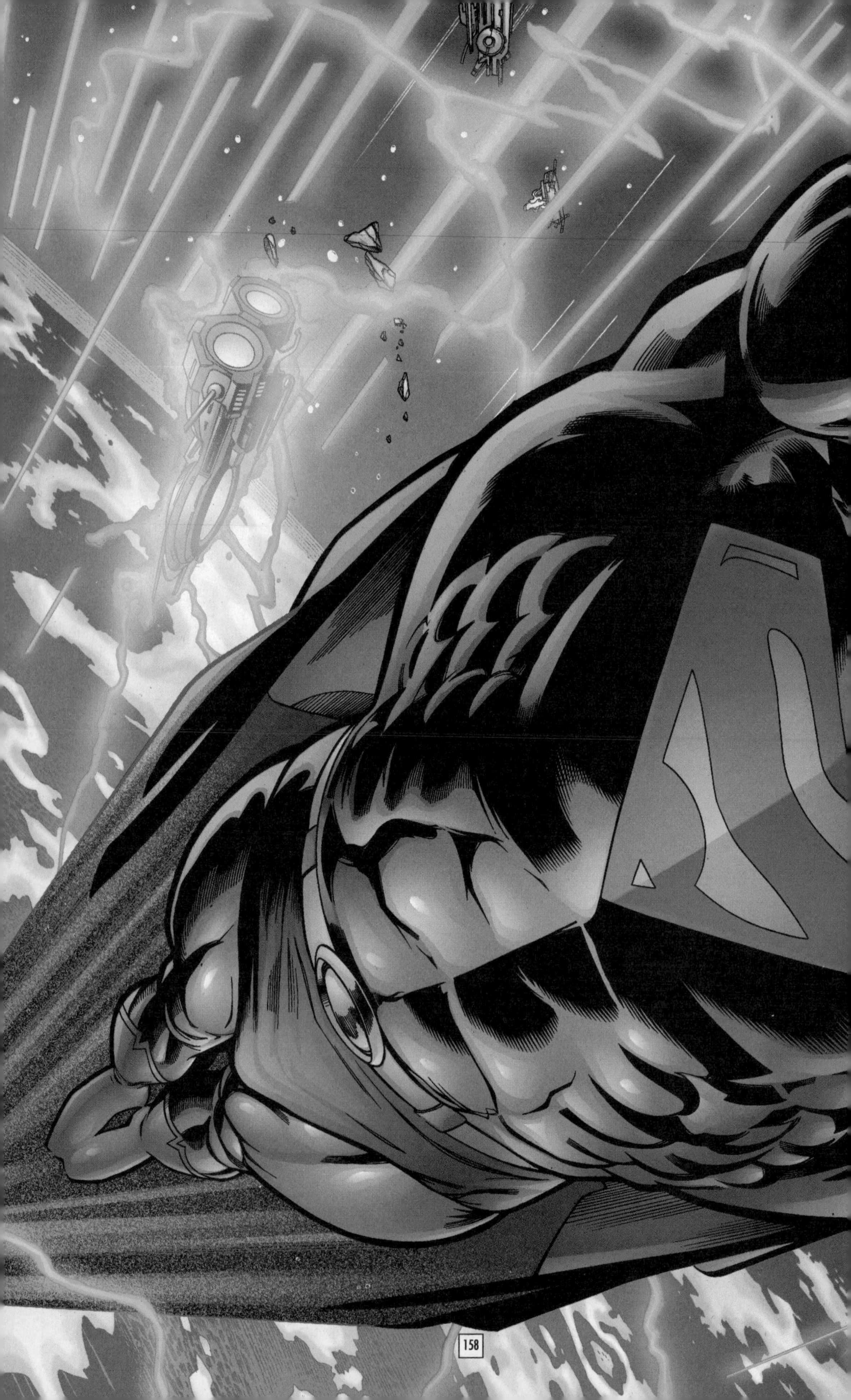

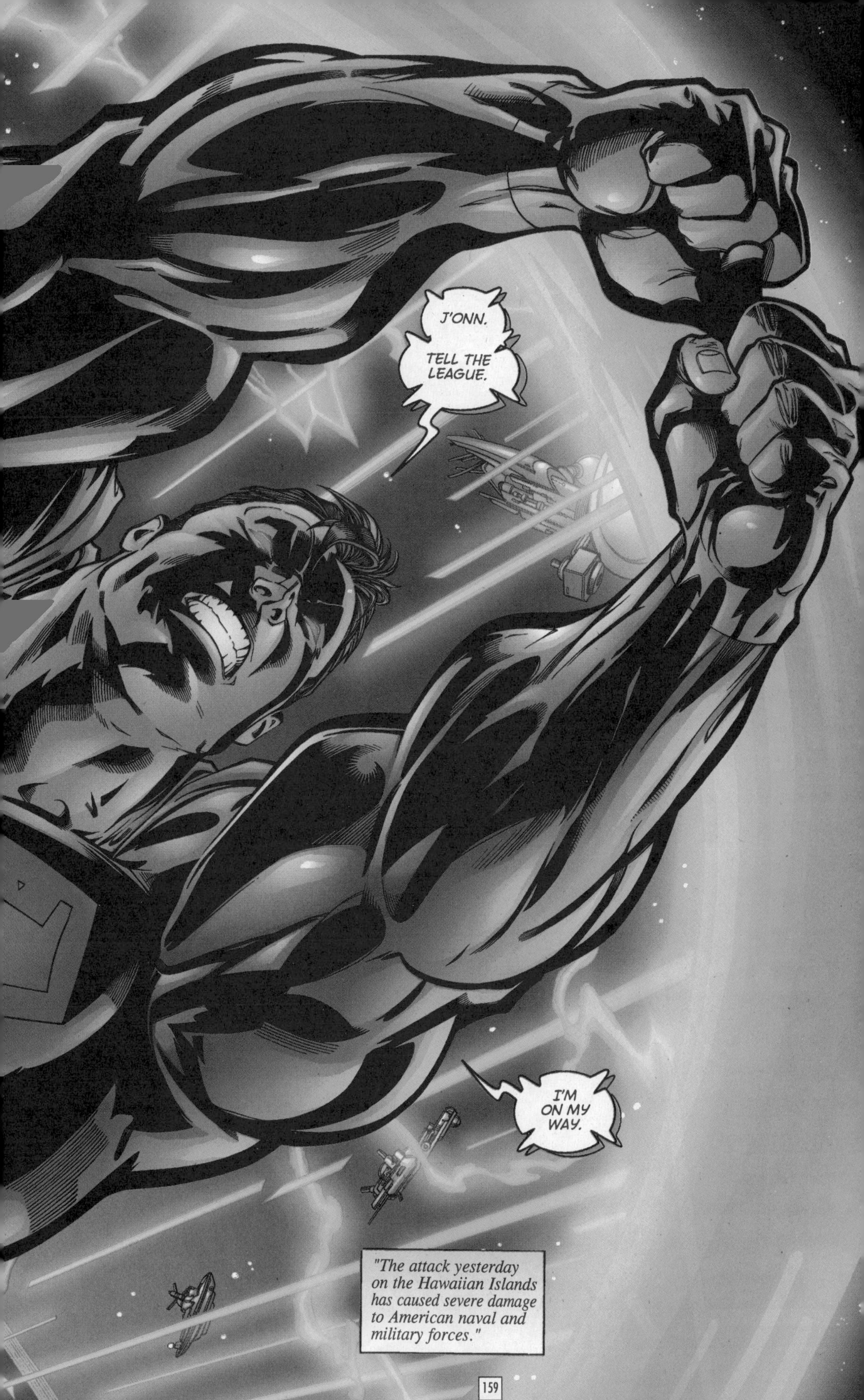
J'ONN.
TELL THE LEAGUE.
I'M ON MY WAY.
"The attack yesterday on the Hawaiian Islands has caused severe damage to American naval and military forces."

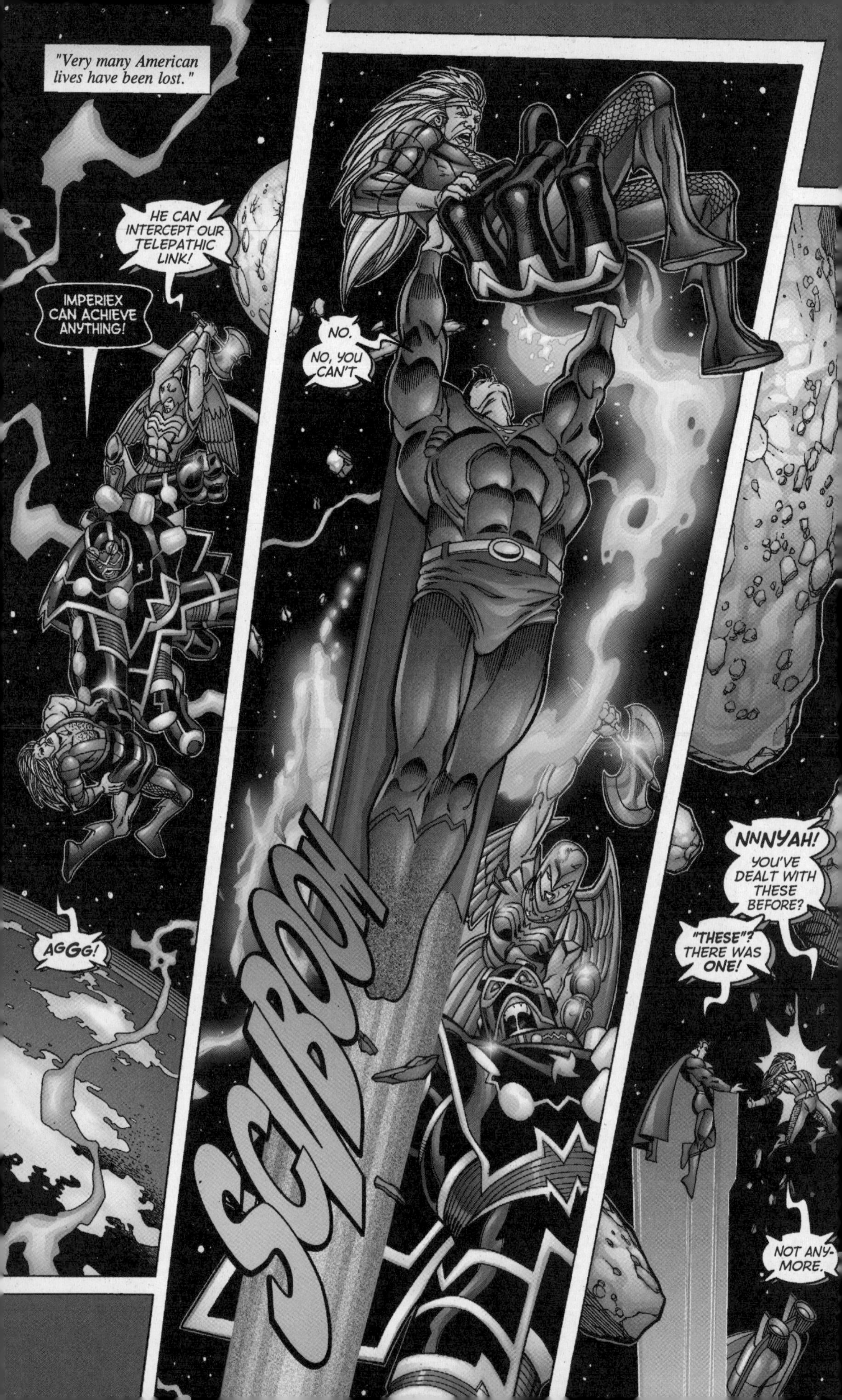
"Very many American lives have been lost."
HE CAN INTERCEPT OUR TELEPATHIC LINK!
IMPERIEX CAN ACHIEVE ANYTHING!
AGGG!
NO.
NO, YOU CAN'T.
SCHBOOM
NNNYAH!
YOU'VE DEALT WITH THESE BEFORE?
"THESE"? THERE WAS ONE!
NOT ANY-MORE.

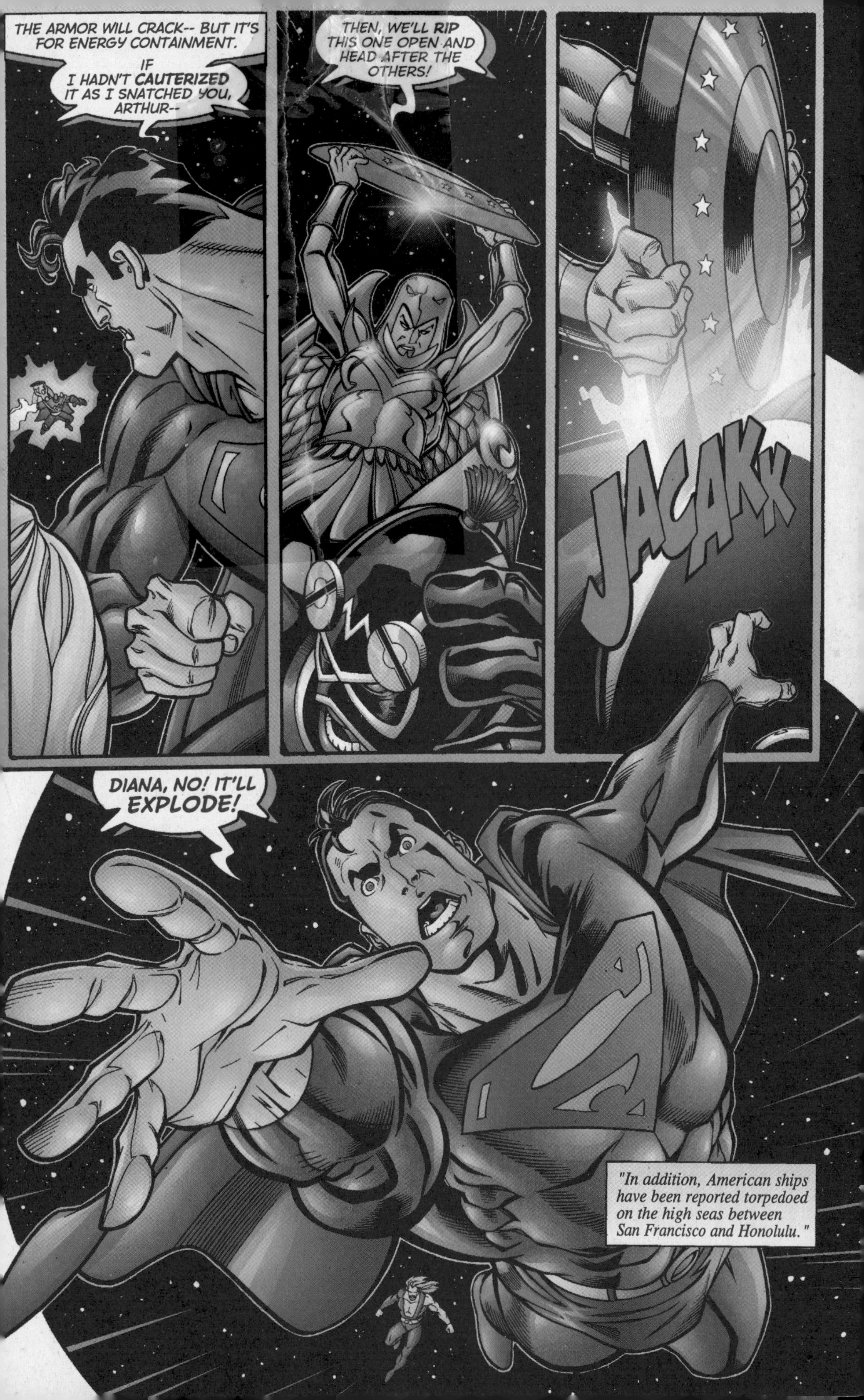
THE ARMOR WILL CRACK-- BUT IT'S FOR ENERGY CONTAINMENT.
IF I HADN'T CAUTERIZED IT AS I SNATCHED YOU, ARTHUR--
THEN, WE'LL RIP THIS ONE OPEN AND HEAD AFTER THE OTHERS!
JACAKK
DIANA, NO! IT'LL EXPLODE!
"In addition, American ships have been reported torpedoed on the high seas between San Francisco and Honolulu."

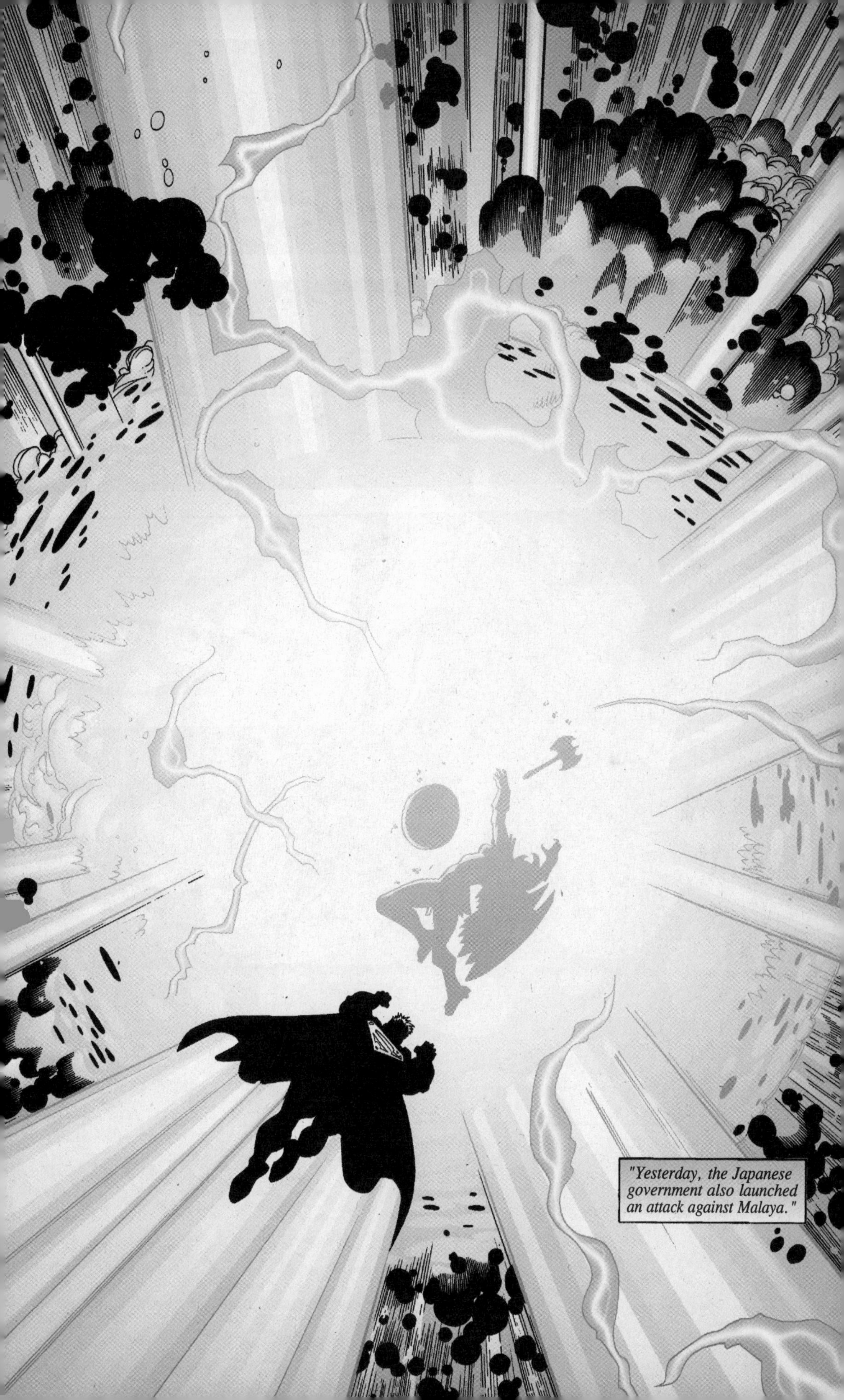
"Yesterday, the Japanese government also launched an attack against Malaya."

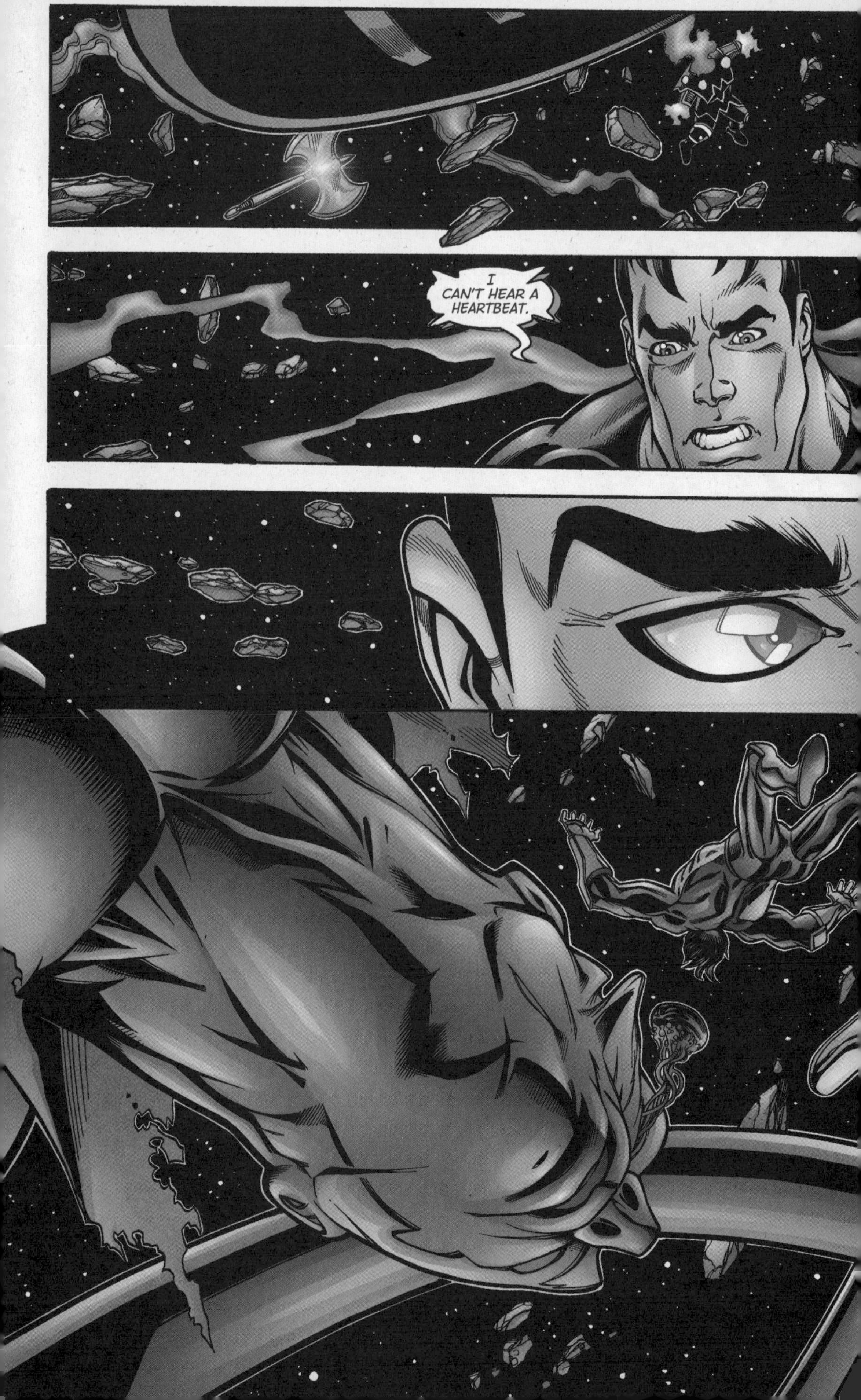
I CAN'T HEAR A HEARTBEAT.

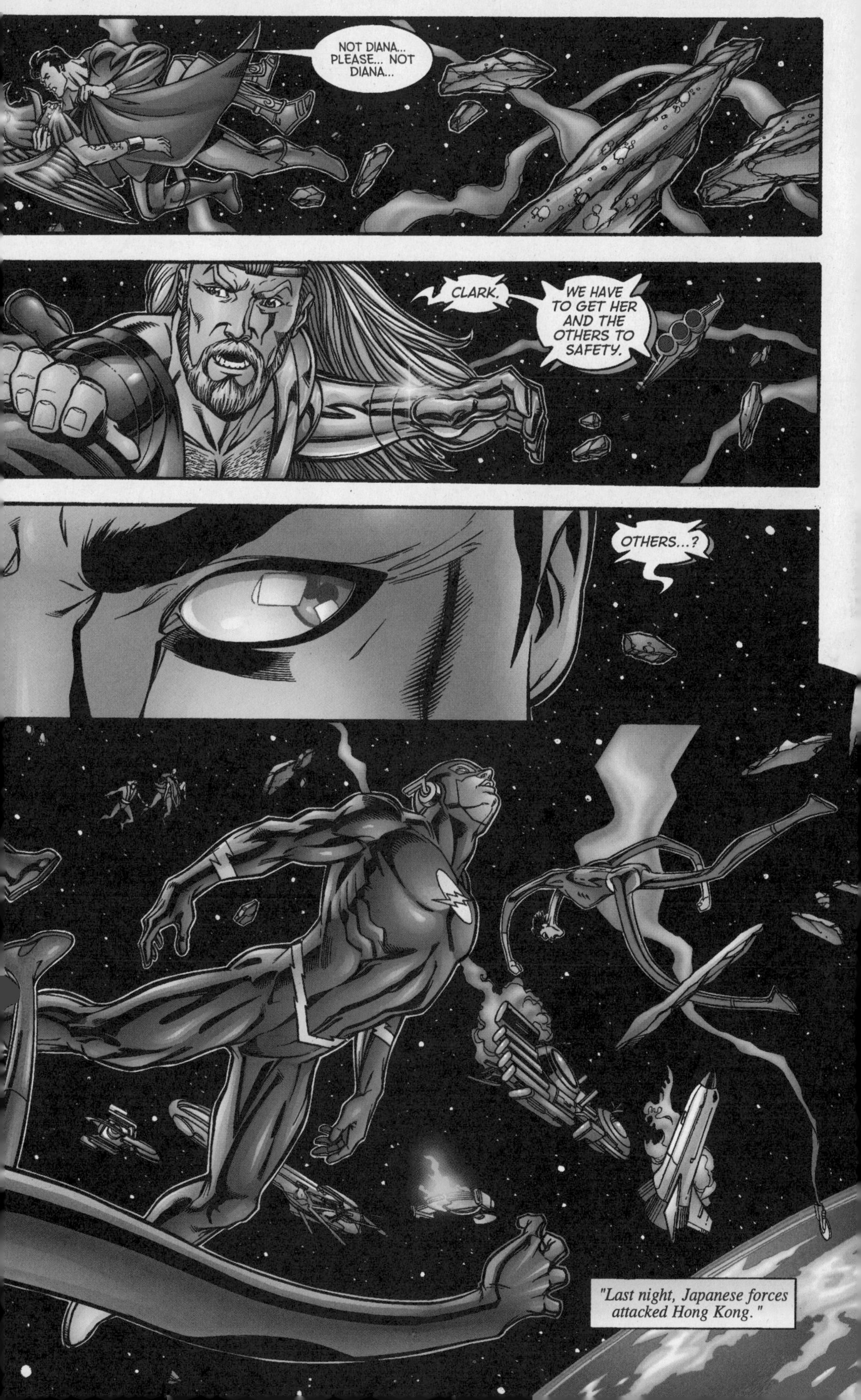
NOT DIANA... PLEASE... NOT DIANA...
CLARK.
WE HAVE TO GET HER AND THE OTHERS TO SAFETY.
OTHERS...?
"Last night, Japanese forces attacked Hong Kong."

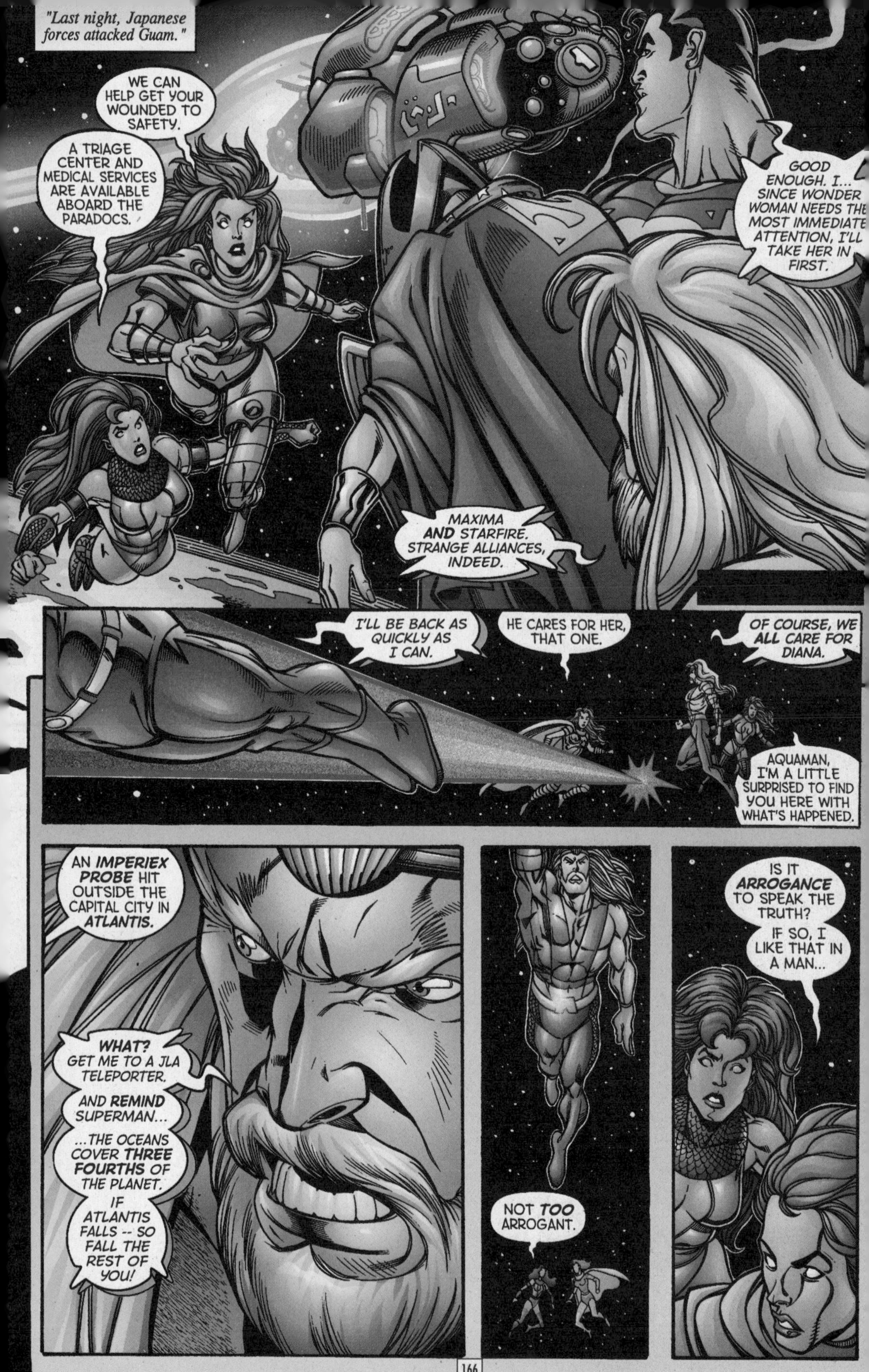
"Last night, Japanese forces attacked Guam."
WE CAN HELP GET YOUR WOUNDED TO SAFETY.
A TRIAGE CENTER AND MEDICAL SERVICES ARE AVAILABLE ABOARD THE PARADOCS.
GOOD ENOUGH. I... SINCE WONDER WOMAN NEEDS THE MOST IMMEDIATE ATTENTION, I'LL TAKE HER IN FIRST.
MAXIMA AND STARFIRE. STRANGE ALLIANCES, INDEED.
I'LL BE BACK AS QUICKLY AS I CAN.
HE CARES FOR HER, THAT ONE.
OF COURSE, WE ALL CARE FOR DIANA.
AQUAMAN, I'M A LITTLE SURPRISED TO FIND YOU HERE WITH WHAT'S HAPPENED.
AN IMPERIEX PROBE HIT OUTSIDE THE CAPITAL CITY IN ATLANTIS.
WHAT? GET ME TO A JLA TELEPORTER.
AND REMIND SUPERMAN...
...THE OCEANS COVER THREE FOURTHS OF THE PLANET.
IF ATLANTIS FALLS -- SO FALL THE REST OF YOU!
NOT TOO ARROGANT.
IS IT ARROGANCE TO SPEAK THE TRUTH?
IF SO, I LIKE THAT IN A MAN...

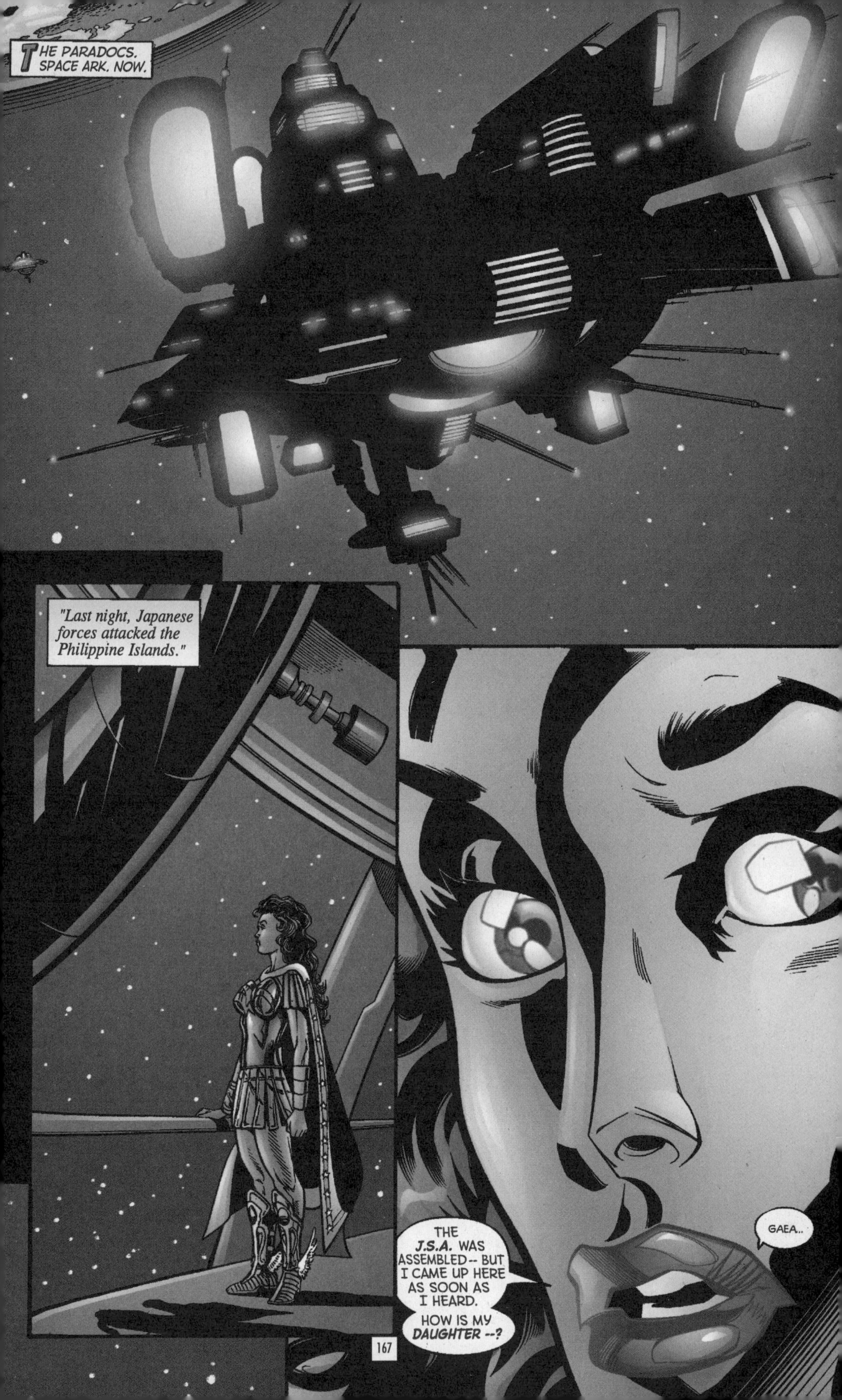
THE PARADOCS. SPACE ARK. NOW.
"Last night, Japanese forces attacked the Philippine Islands."
THE J.S.A. WAS ASSEMBLED-- BUT I CAME UP HERE AS SOON AS I HEARD.
HOW IS MY DAUGHTER --?
GAEA..

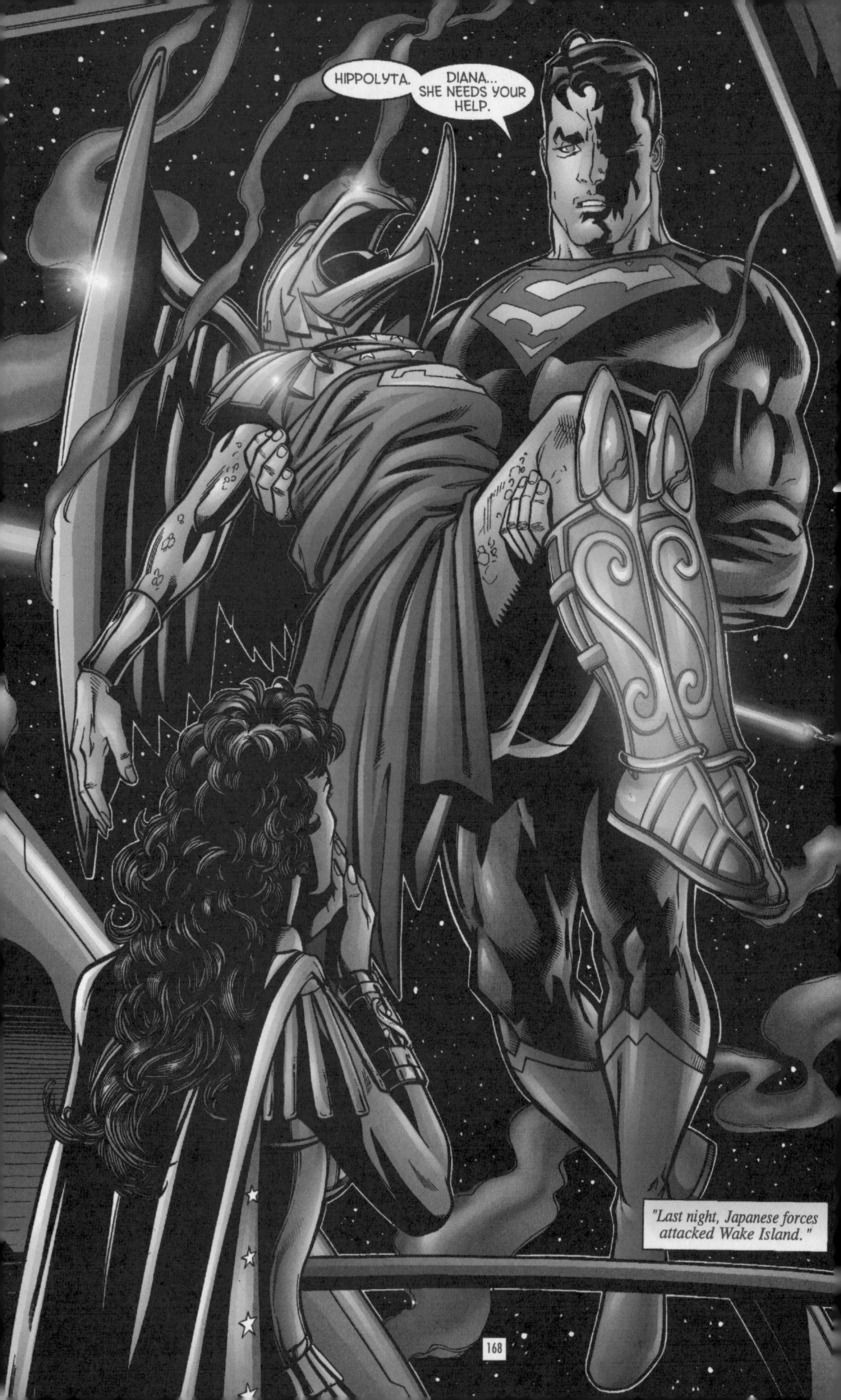
HIPPOLYTA.
DIANA... SHE NEEDS YOUR HELP.
"Last night, Japanese forces attacked Wake Island."

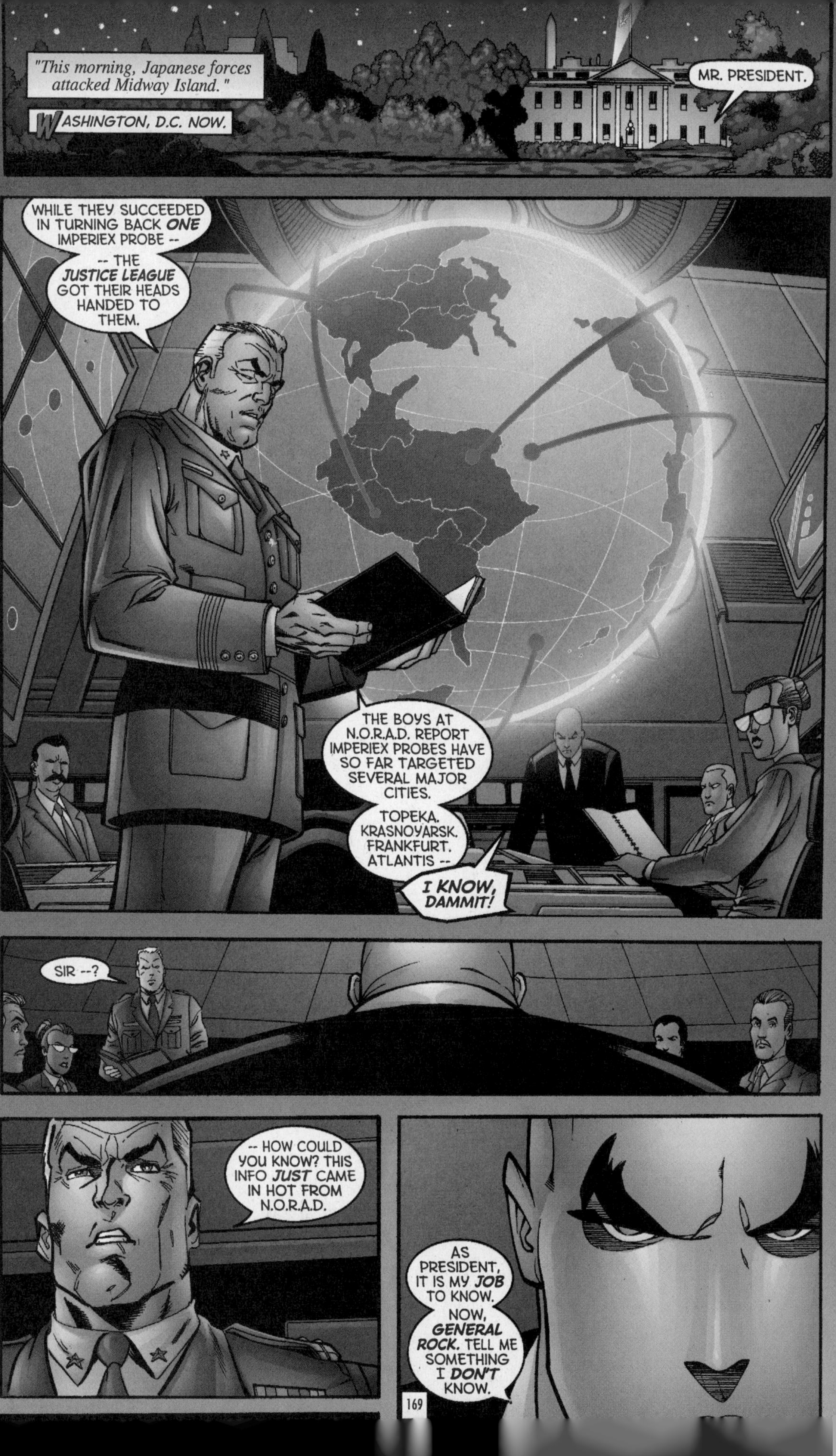
"This morning, Japanese forces attacked Midway Island."
WASHINGTON, D.C. NOW.
MR. PRESIDENT.
WHILE THEY SUCCEEDED IN TURNING BACK ONE IMPERIEX PROBE --
-- THE JUSTICE LEAGUE GOT THEIR HEADS HANDED TO THEM.
THE BOYS AT N.O.R.A.D. REPORT IMPERIEX PROBES HAVE SO FAR TARGETED SEVERAL MAJOR CITIES.
TOPEKA. KRASNOYARSK. FRANKFURT. ATLANTIS --
I KNOW, DAMMIT!
SIR --?
-- HOW COULD YOU KNOW? THIS INFO JUST CAME IN HOT FROM N.O.R.A.D.
AS PRESIDENT, IT IS MY JOB TO KNOW.
NOW, GENERAL ROCK. TELL ME SOMETHING I DON'T KNOW.

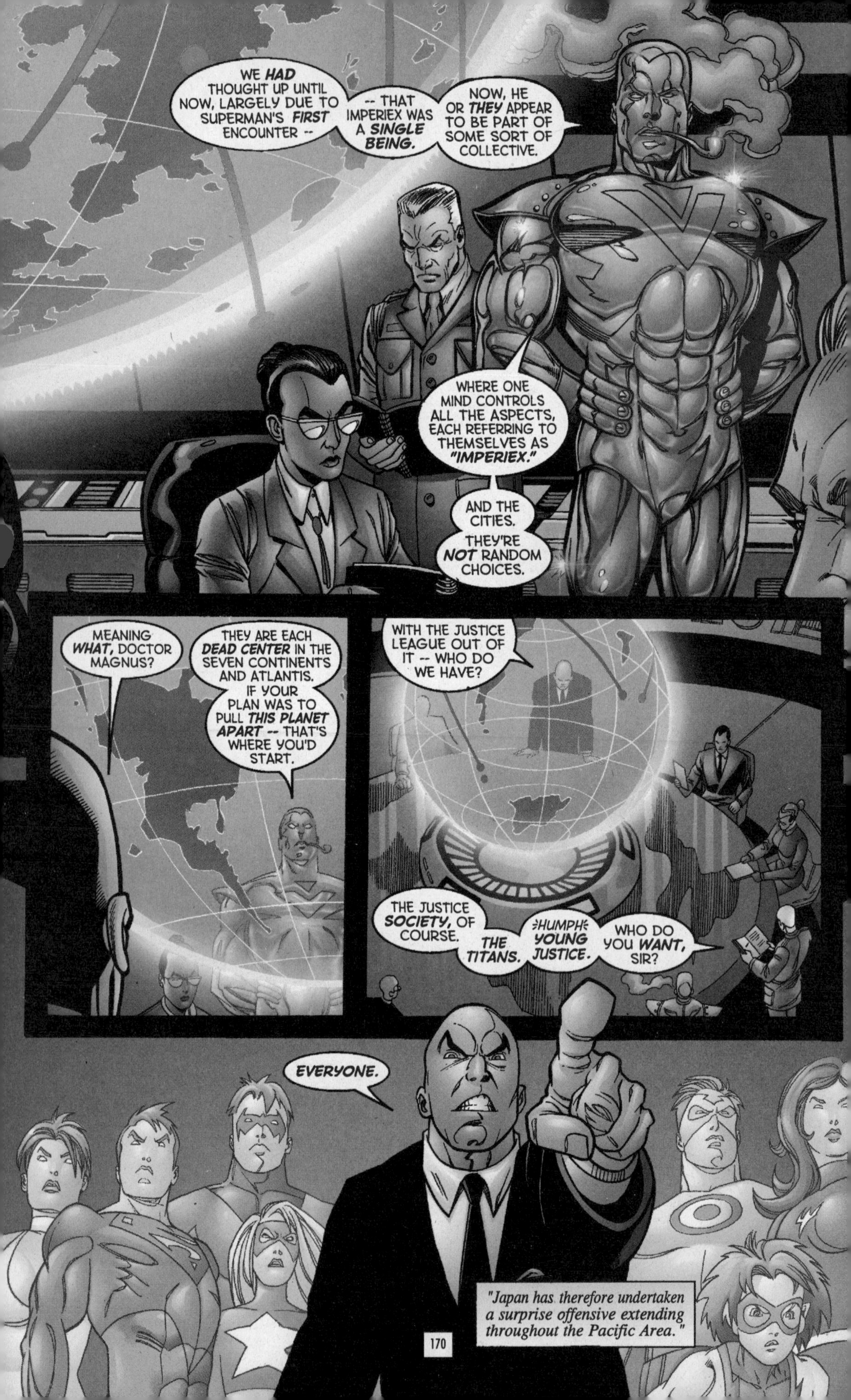
WE HAD THOUGHT UP UNTIL NOW, LARGELY DUE TO SUPERMAN'S FIRST ENCOUNTER --
-- THAT IMPERIEX WAS A SINGLE BEING.
NOW, HE OR THEY APPEAR TO BE PART OF SOME SORT OF COLLECTIVE.
WHERE ONE MIND CONTROLS ALL THE ASPECTS, EACH REFERRING TO THEMSELVES AS "IMPERIEX."
AND THE CITIES.
THEY'RE NOT RANDOM CHOICES.
MEANING WHAT, DOCTOR MAGNUS?
THEY ARE EACH DEAD CENTER IN THE SEVEN CONTINENTS AND ATLANTIS.
IF YOUR PLAN WAS TO PULL THIS PLANET APART -- THAT'S WHERE YOU'D START.
WITH THE JUSTICE LEAGUE OUT OF IT -- WHO DO WE HAVE?
THE JUSTICE SOCIETY, OF COURSE.
THE TITANS.
HUMPH YOUNG JUSTICE.
WHO DO YOU WANT, SIR?
EVERYONE.
"Japan has therefore undertaken a surprise offensive extending throughout the Pacific Area."

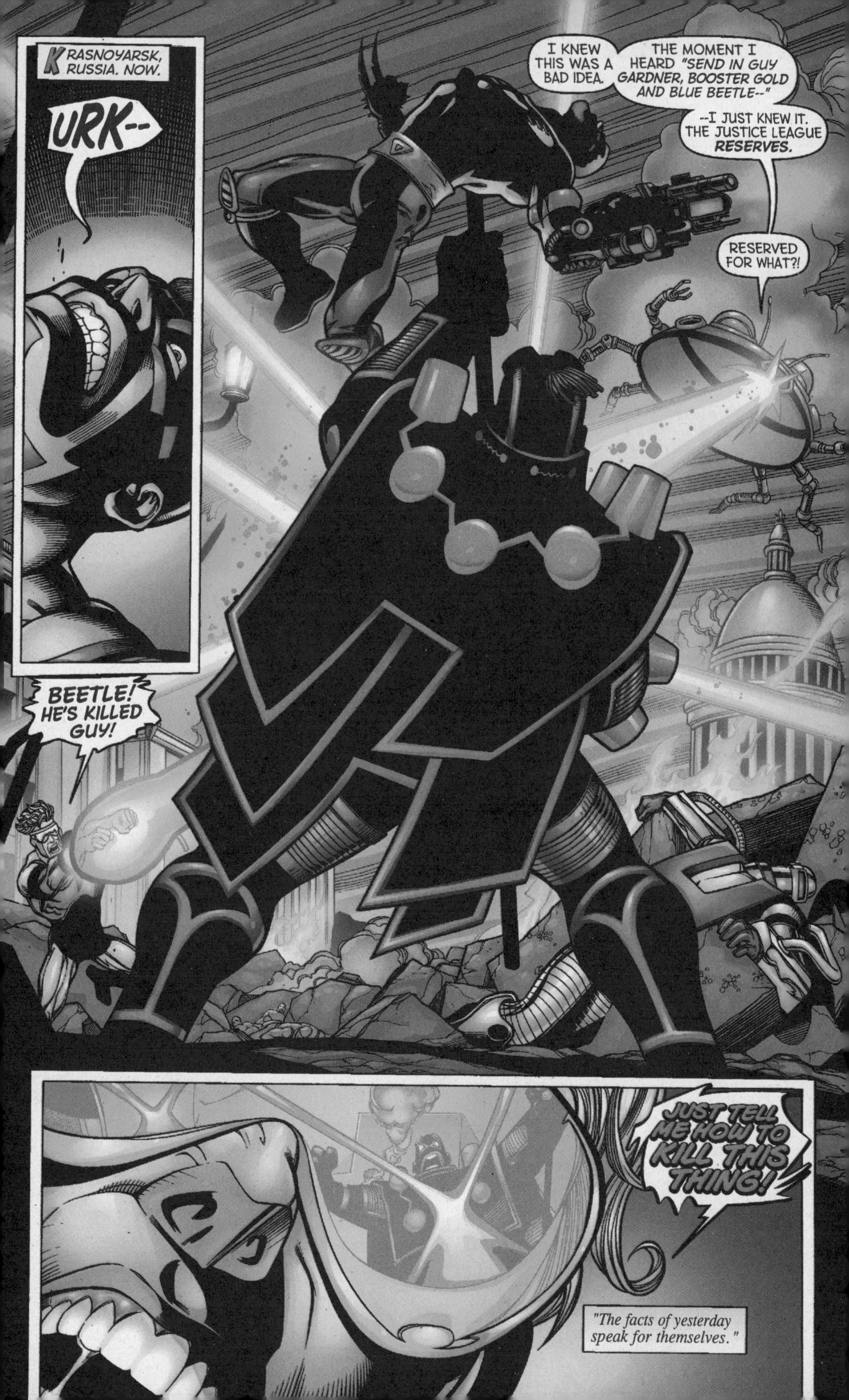
KRASNOYARSK, RUSSIA. NOW.
URK--
I KNEW THIS WAS A BAD IDEA.
THE MOMENT I HEARD "SEND IN GUY GARDNER, BOOSTER GOLD AND BLUE BEETLE--"
--I JUST KNEW IT. THE JUSTICE LEAGUE RESERVES.
RESERVED FOR WHAT?!
BEETLE! HE'S KILLED GUY!
JUST TELL ME HOW TO KILL THIS THING!
"The facts of yesterday speak for themselves."

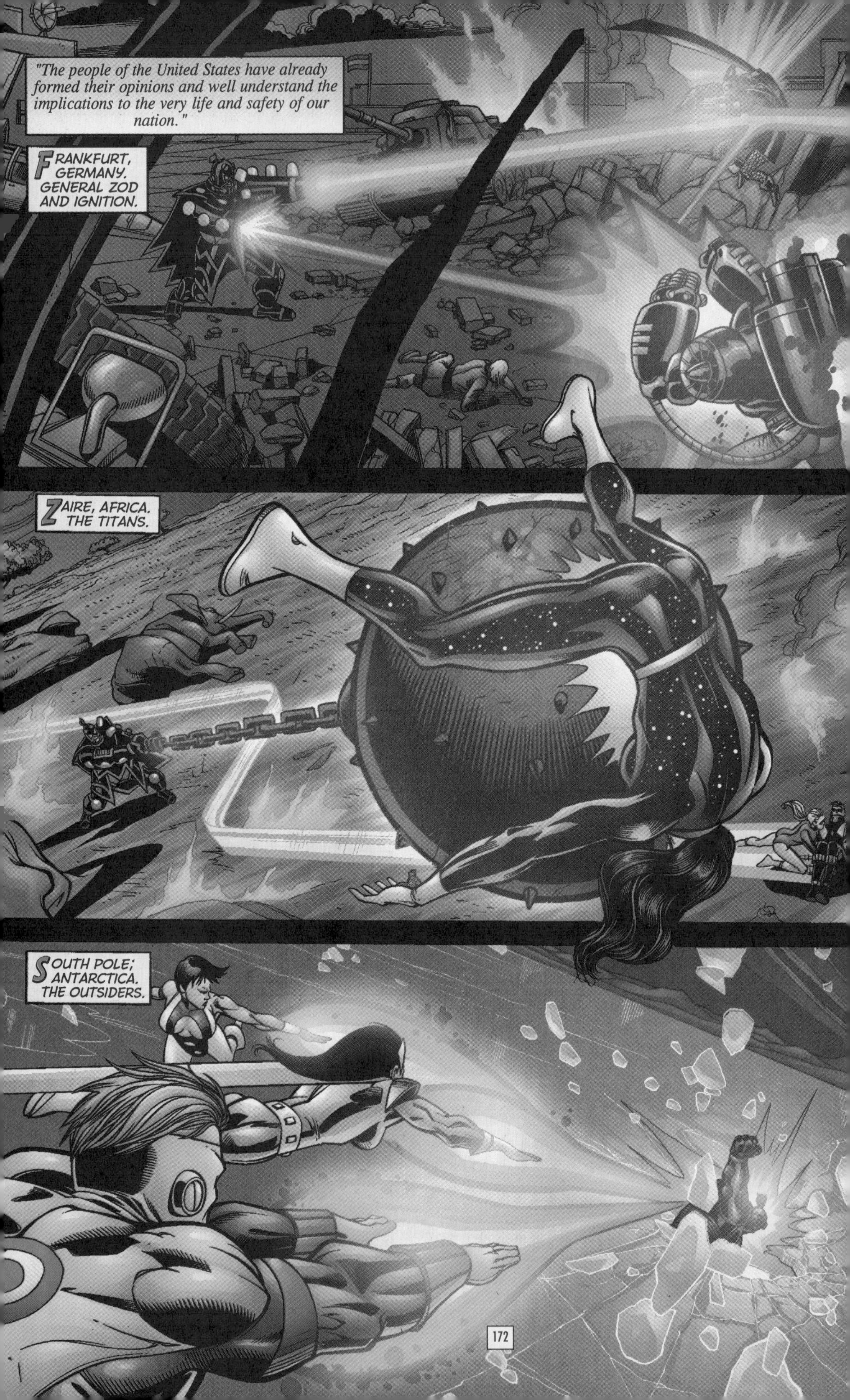
"The people of the United States have already formed their opinions and well understand the implications to the very life and safety of our nation."
FRANKFURT, GERMANY. GENERAL ZOD AND IGNITION.
ZAIRE, AFRICA. THE TITANS.
SOUTH POLE; ANTARCTICA. THE OUTSIDERS.

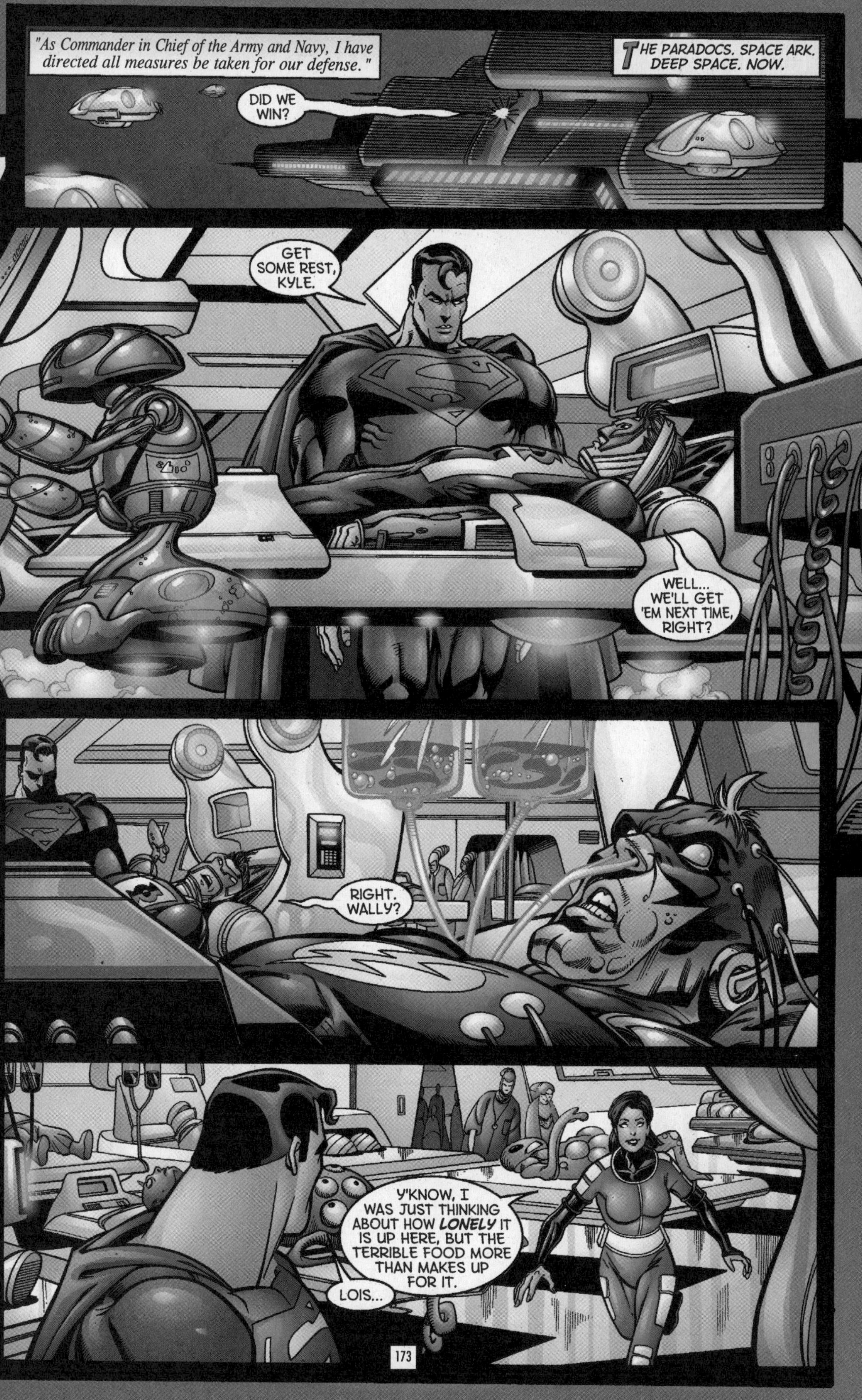
"As Commander in Chief of the Army and Navy, I have directed all measures be taken for our defense."
THE PARADOCS. SPACE ARK. DEEP SPACE. NOW.
DID WE WIN?
GET SOME REST, KYLE.
WELL... WE'LL GET 'EM NEXT TIME, RIGHT?
RIGHT. WALLY?
Y'KNOW, I WAS JUST THINKING ABOUT HOW LONELY IT IS UP HERE, BUT THE TERRIBLE FOOD MORE THAN MAKES UP FOR IT.
LOIS...

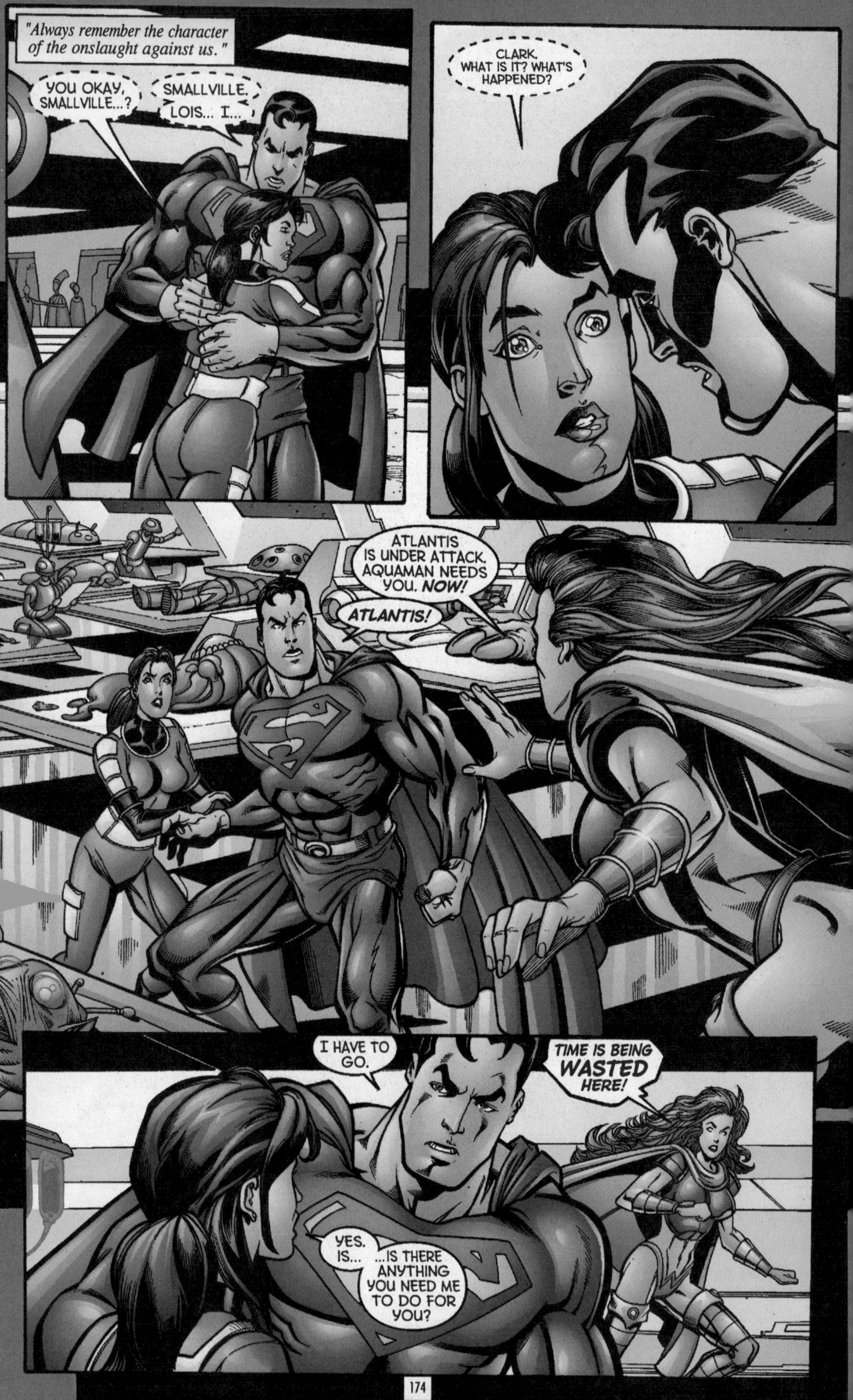
"Always remember the character of the onslaught against us."
YOU OKAY, SMALLVILLE...?
SMALLVILLE. LOIS... I...
CLARK. WHAT IS IT? WHAT'S HAPPENED?
ATLANTIS IS UNDER ATTACK. AQUAMAN NEEDS YOU. *NOW!*
*ATLANTIS!*
I HAVE TO GO.
TIME IS BEING **WASTED** HERE!
YES. IS... ...IS THERE ANYTHING YOU NEED ME TO DO FOR YOU?

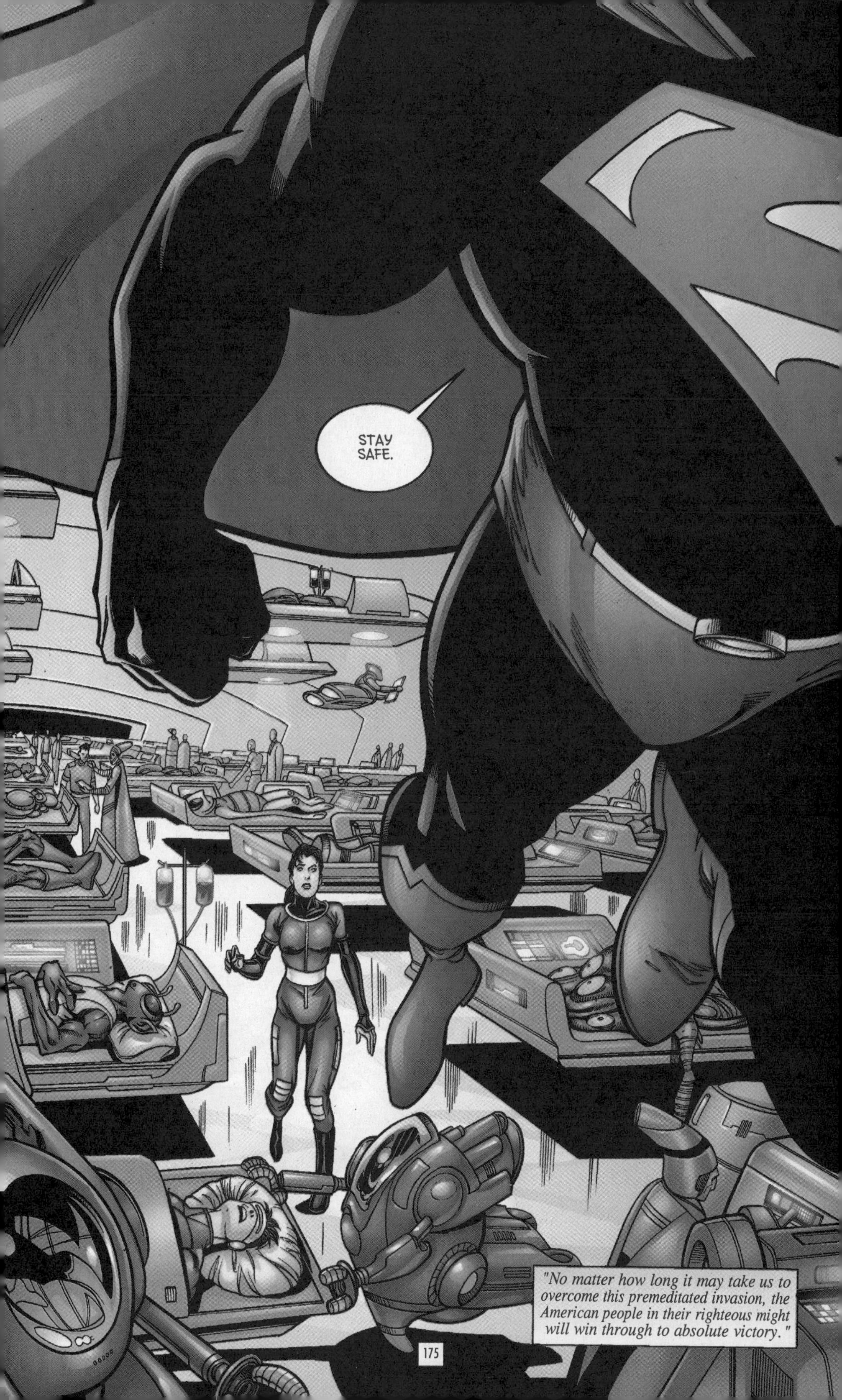
STAY SAFE.
"No matter how long it may take us to overcome this premeditated invasion, the American people in their righteous might will win through to absolute victory."

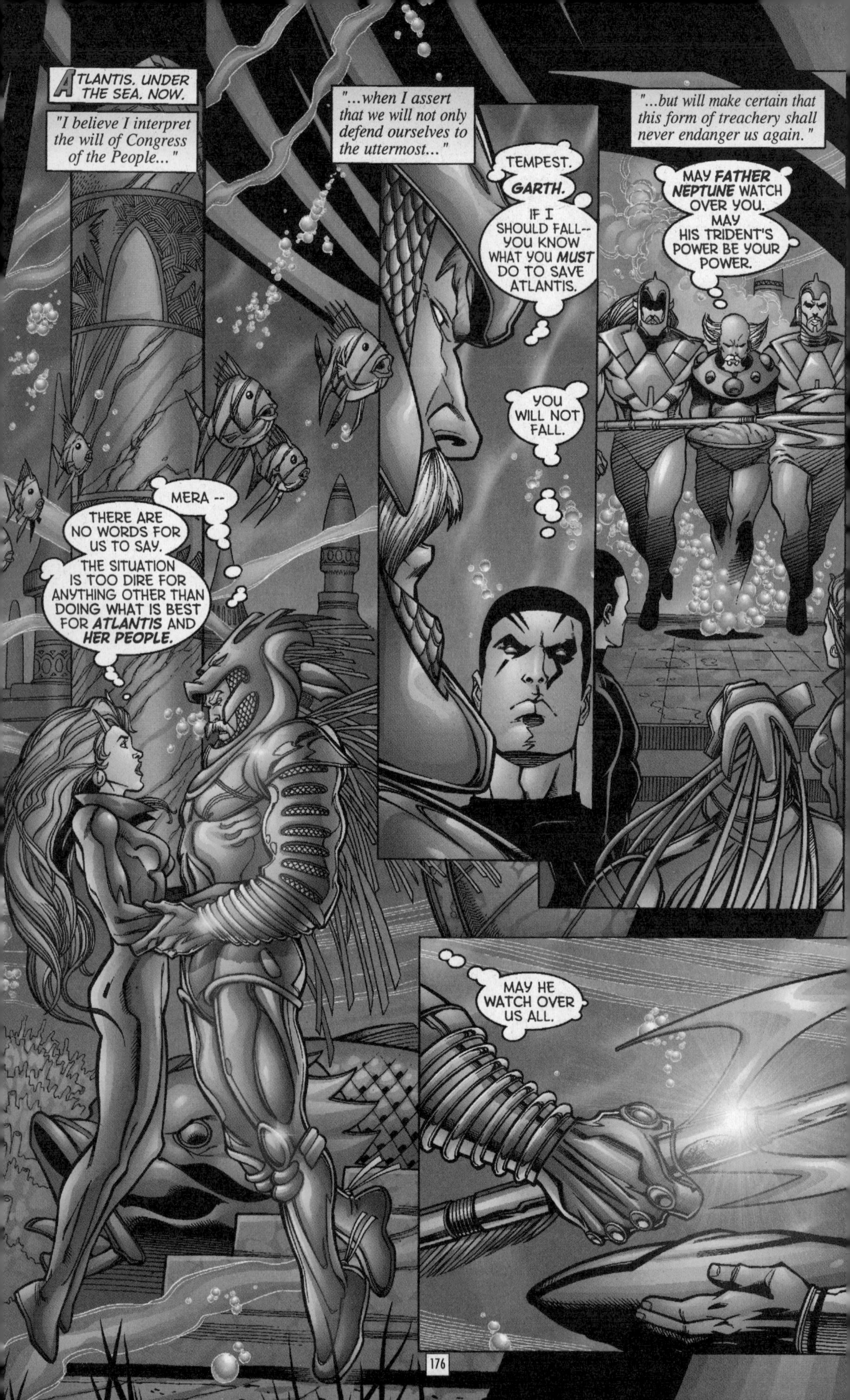
ATLANTIS. UNDER THE SEA. NOW.
"I believe I interpret the will of Congress of the People..."
"...when I assert that we will not only defend ourselves to the uttermost..."
"...but will make certain that this form of treachery shall never endanger us again."
TEMPEST. GARTH.
IF I SHOULD FALL-- YOU KNOW WHAT YOU MUST DO TO SAVE ATLANTIS.
MAY FATHER NEPTUNE WATCH OVER YOU. MAY HIS TRIDENT'S POWER BE YOUR POWER.
YOU WILL NOT FALL.
MERA --
THERE ARE NO WORDS FOR US TO SAY. THE SITUATION IS TOO DIRE FOR ANYTHING OTHER THAN DOING WHAT IS BEST FOR ATLANTIS AND HER PEOPLE.
MAY HE WATCH OVER US ALL.

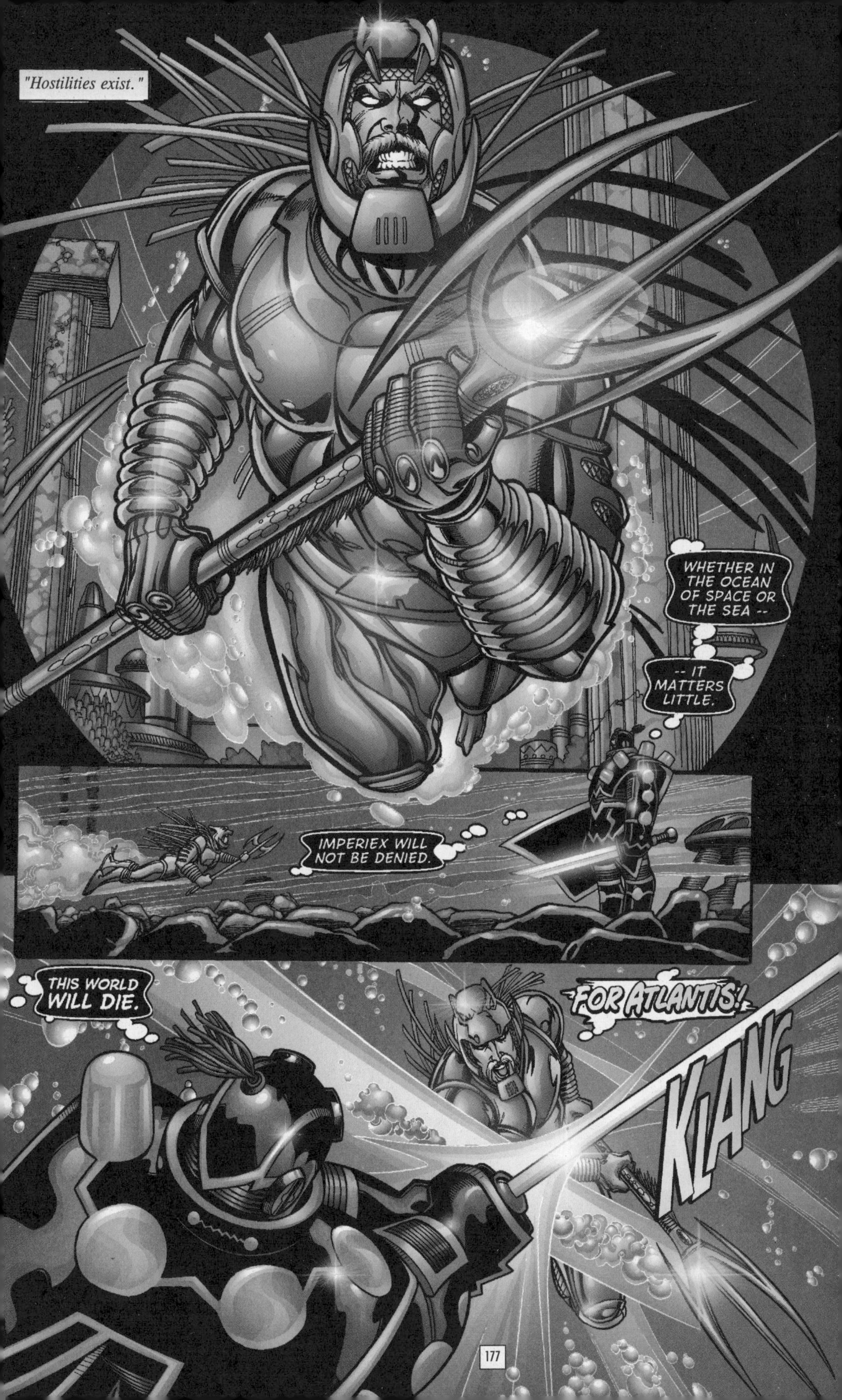
"Hostilities exist."
WHETHER IN THE OCEAN OF SPACE OR THE SEA --
-- IT MATTERS LITTLE.
IMPERIEX WILL NOT BE DENIED.
THIS WORLD WILL DIE.
FOR ATLANTIS!
KLANG

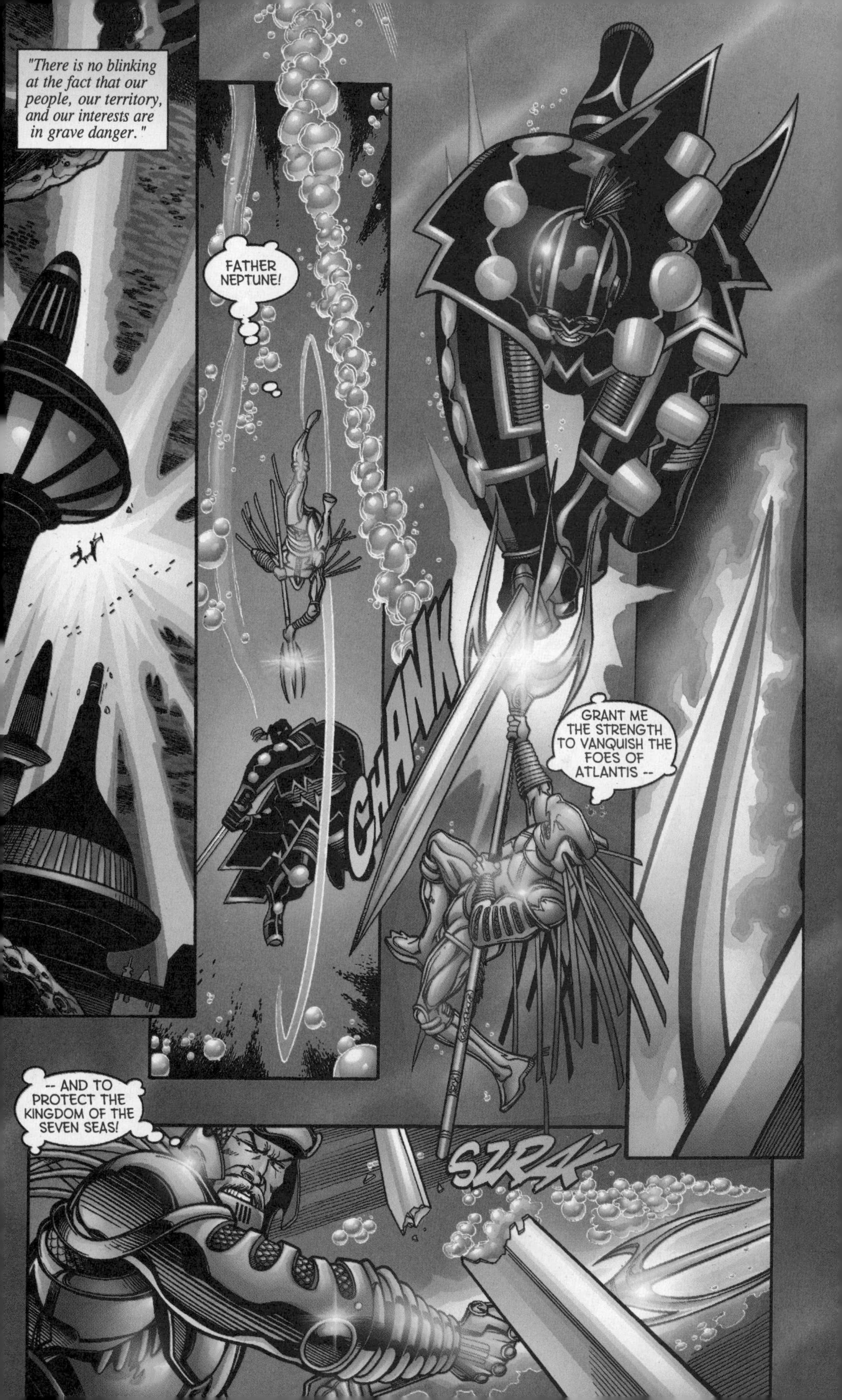
"There is no blinking at the fact that our people, our territory, and our interests are in grave danger."
FATHER NEPTUNE!
CHANK
GRANT ME THE STRENGTH TO VANQUISH THE FOES OF ATLANTIS --
-- AND TO PROTECT THE KINGDOM OF THE SEVEN SEAS!
SZRAK

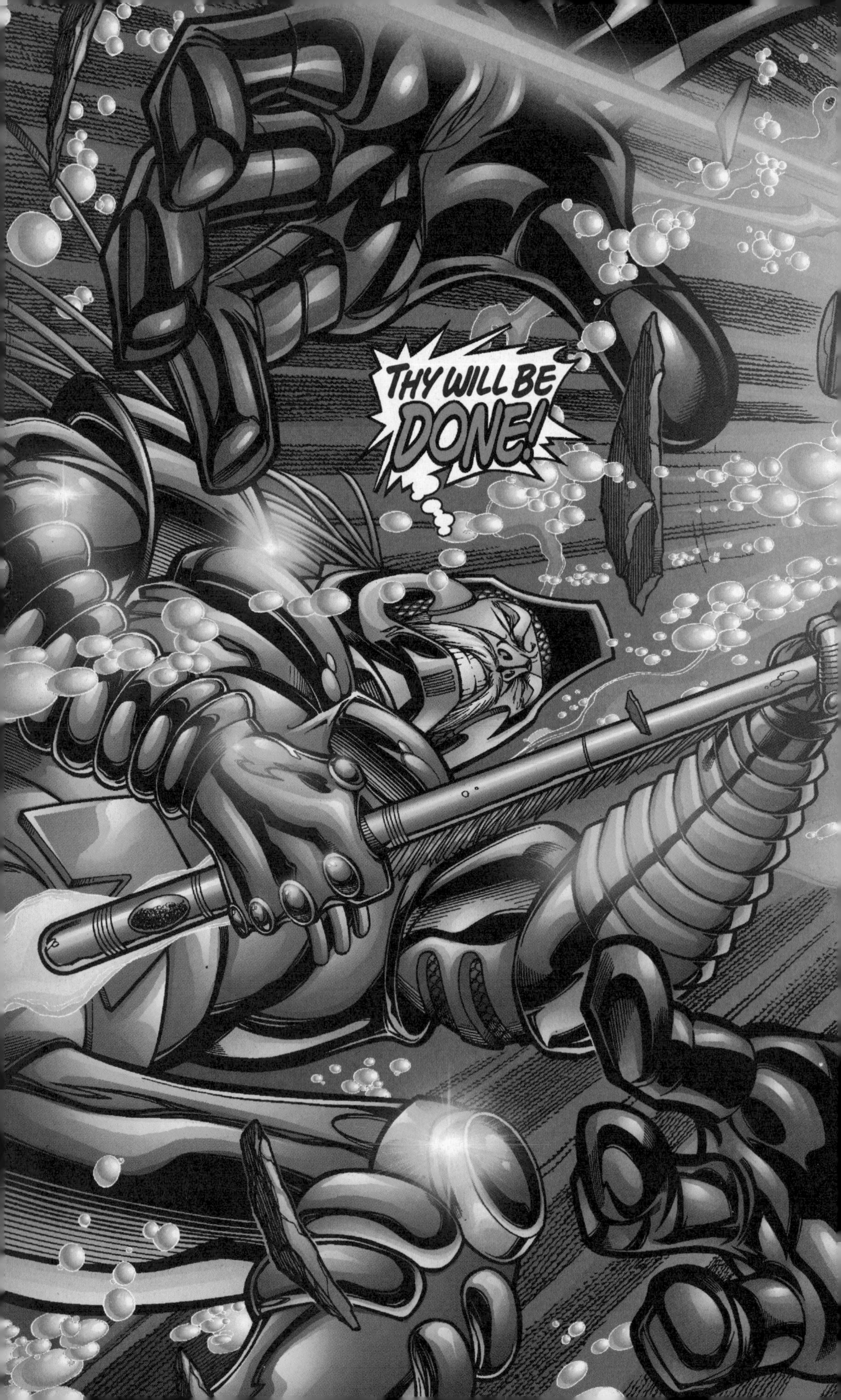
THY WILL BE DONE!

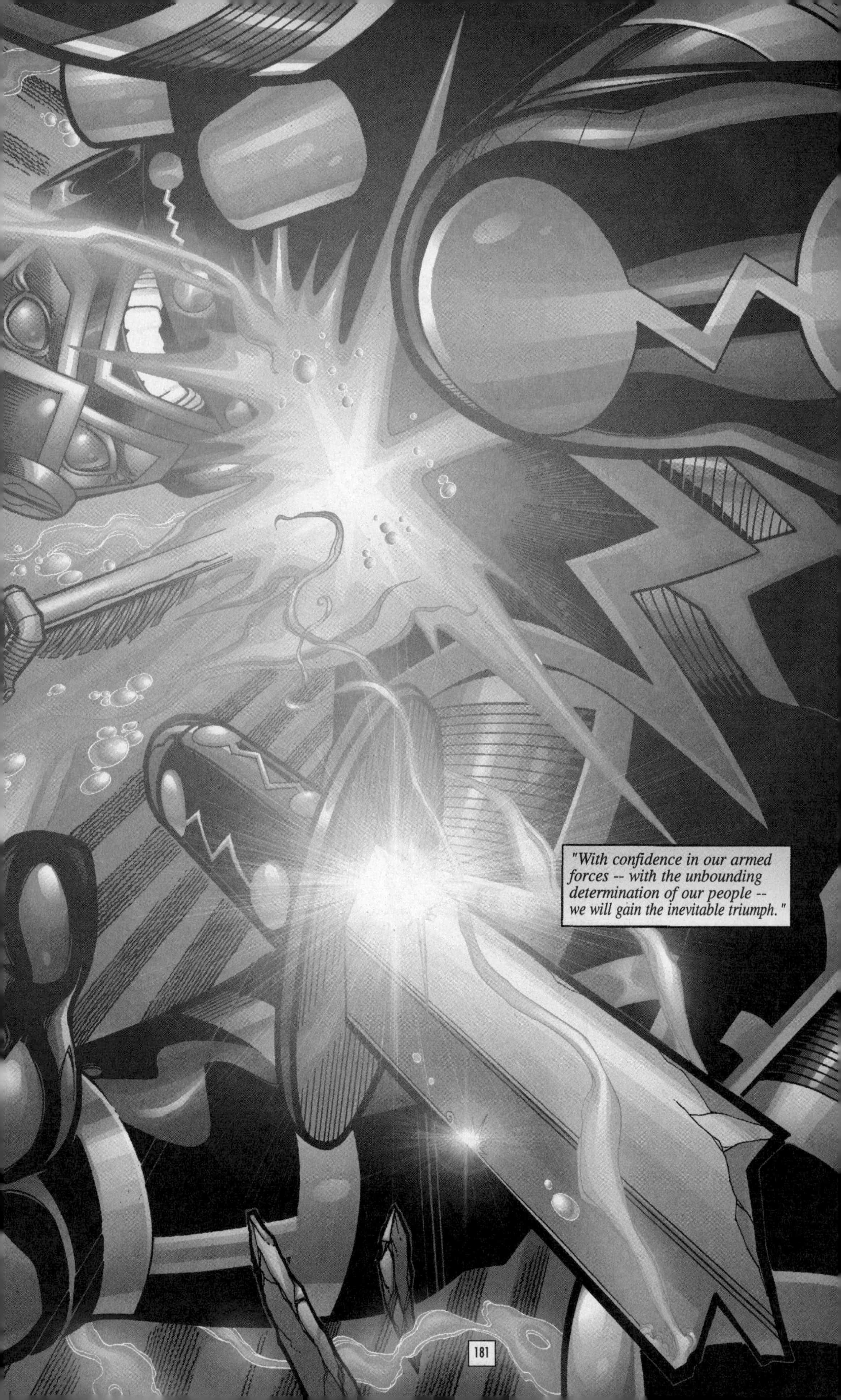
"With confidence in our armed forces -- with the unbounding determination of our people -- we will gain the inevitable triumph."

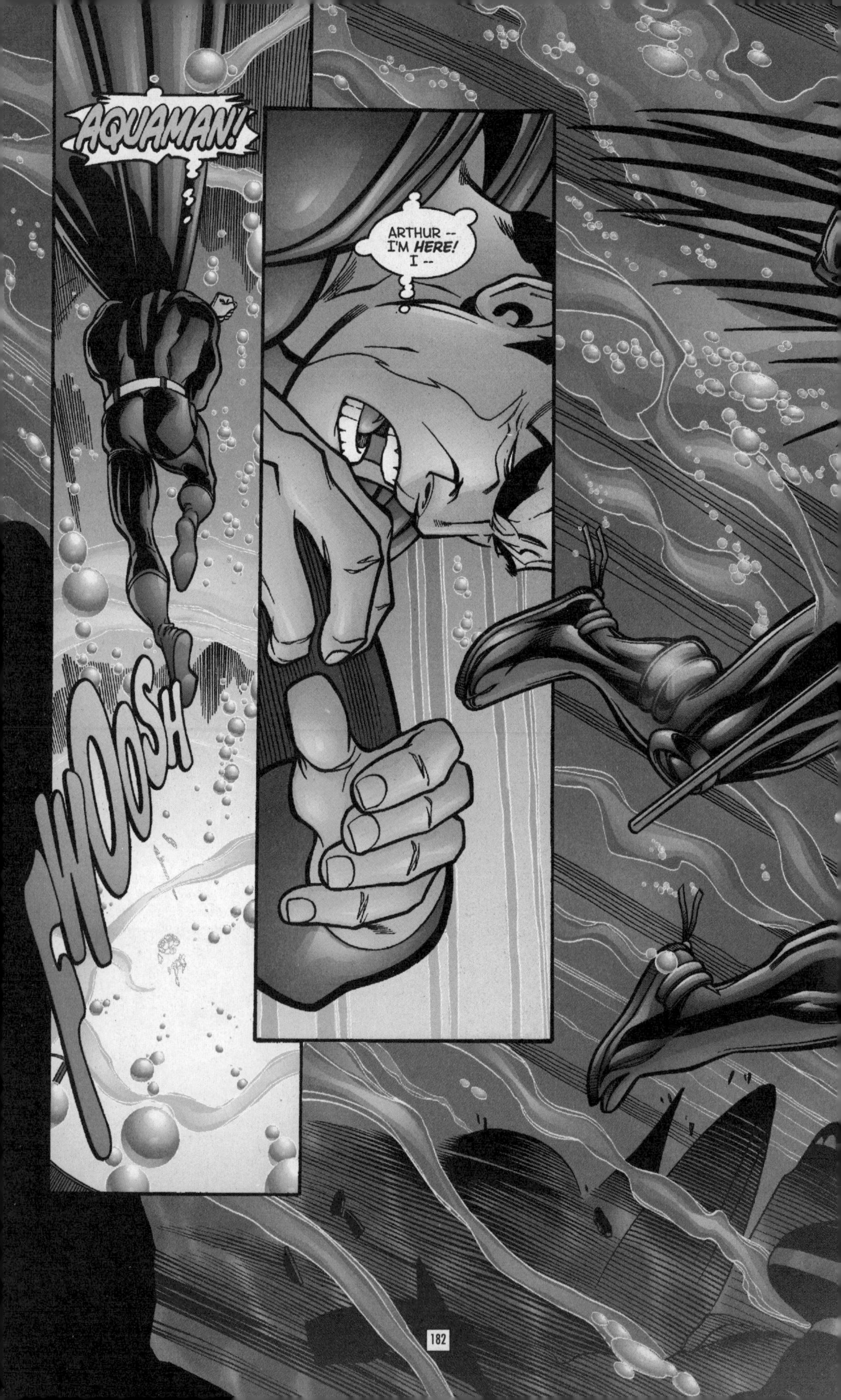

AQUAMAN!
ARTHUR -- I'M HERE! I --
WHOOSH

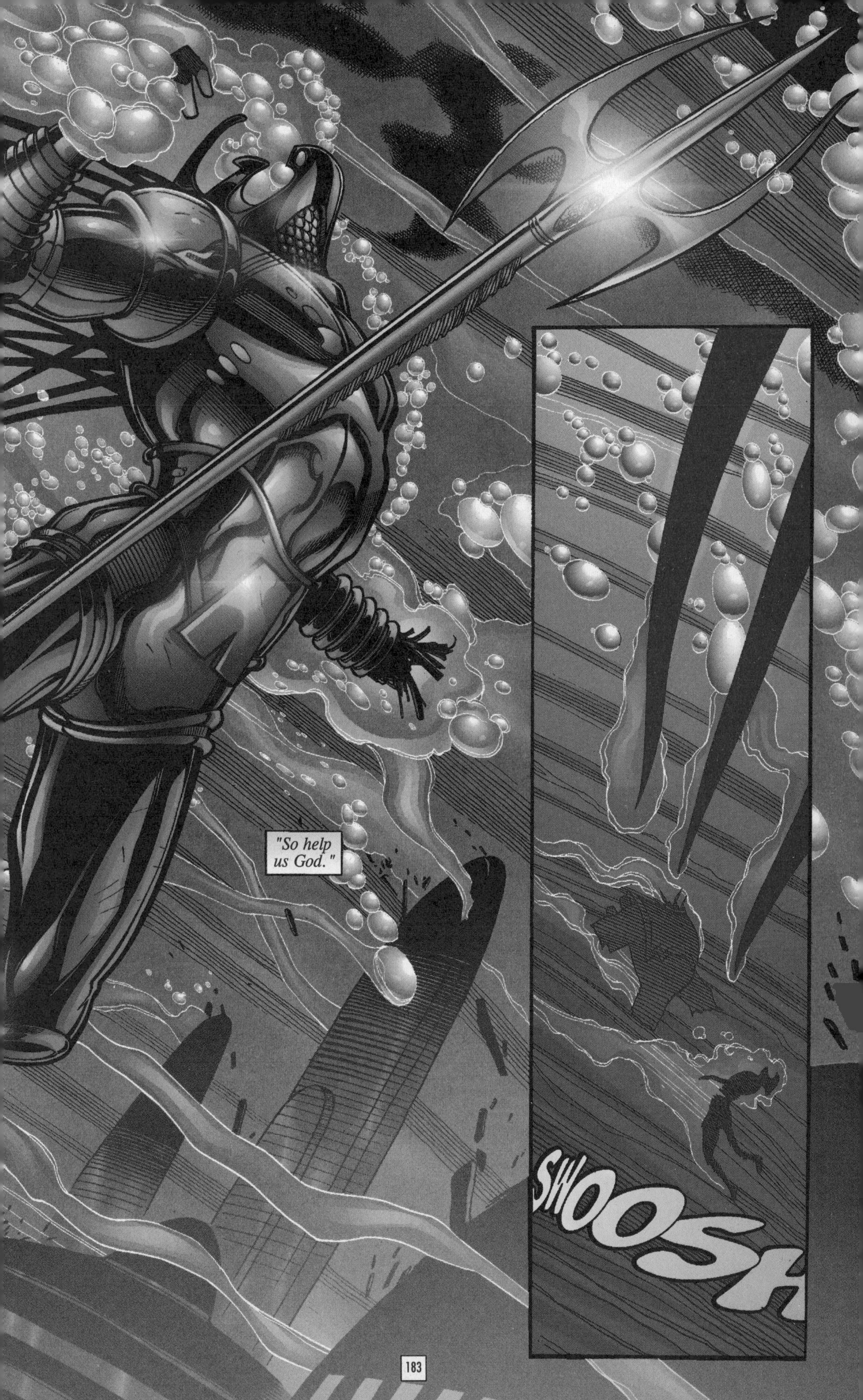

"So help us God."
SWOOSH

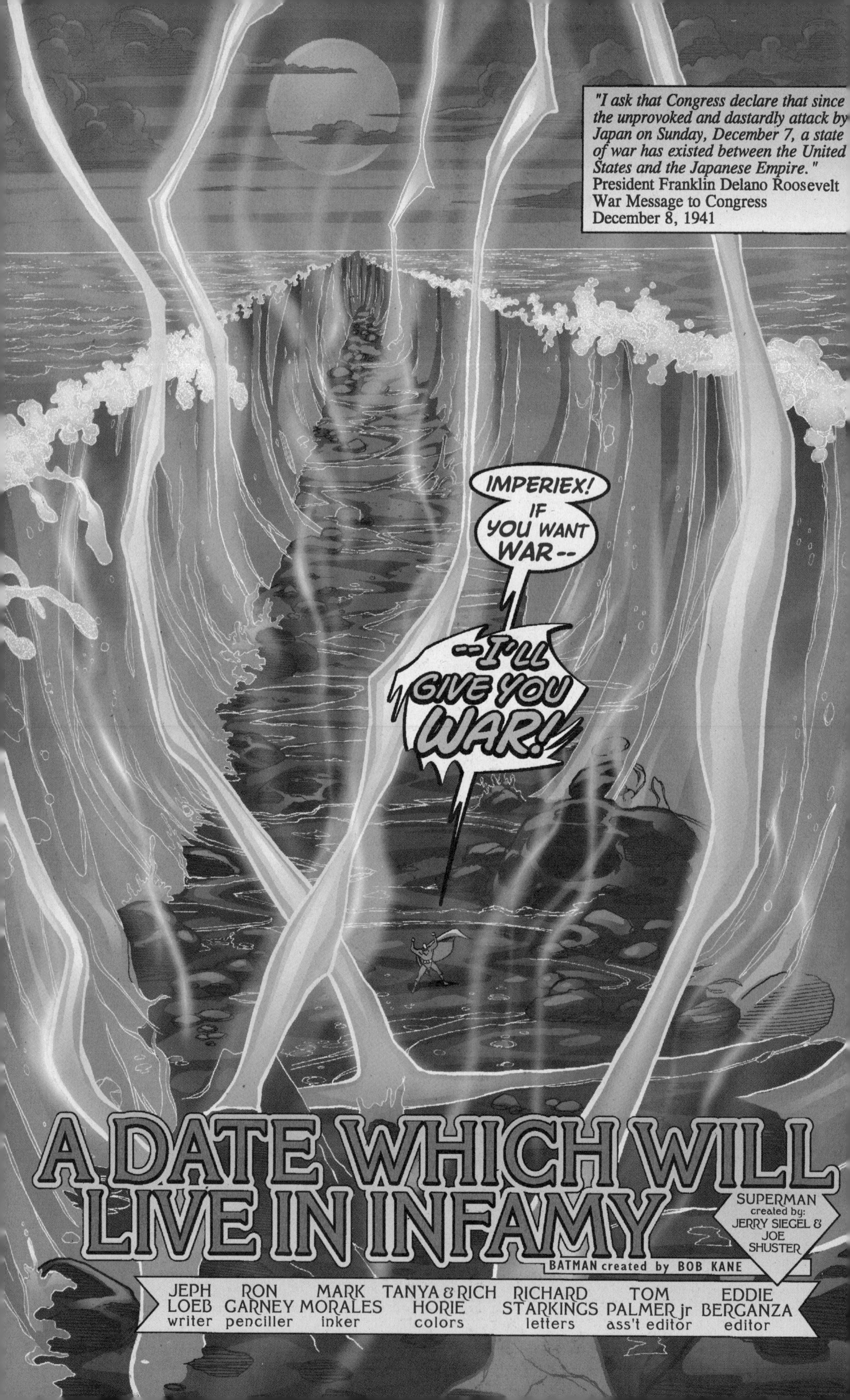
"I ask that Congress declare that since the unprovoked and dastardly attack by Japan on Sunday, December 7, a state of war has existed between the United States and the Japanese Empire." President Franklin Delano Roosevelt War Message to Congress December 8, 1941
IMPERIEX! IF YOU WANT WAR --
-- I'LL GIVE YOU WAR!
A DATE WHICH WILL LIVE IN INFAMY
SUPERMAN created by: JERRY SIEGEL & JOE SHUSTER
BATMAN created by BOB KANE
JEPH LOEB writer
RON GARNEY penciller
MARK MORALES inker
TANYA & RICH HORIE colors
RICHARD STARKINGS letters
TOM PALMER jr ass't editor
EDDIE BERGANZA editor

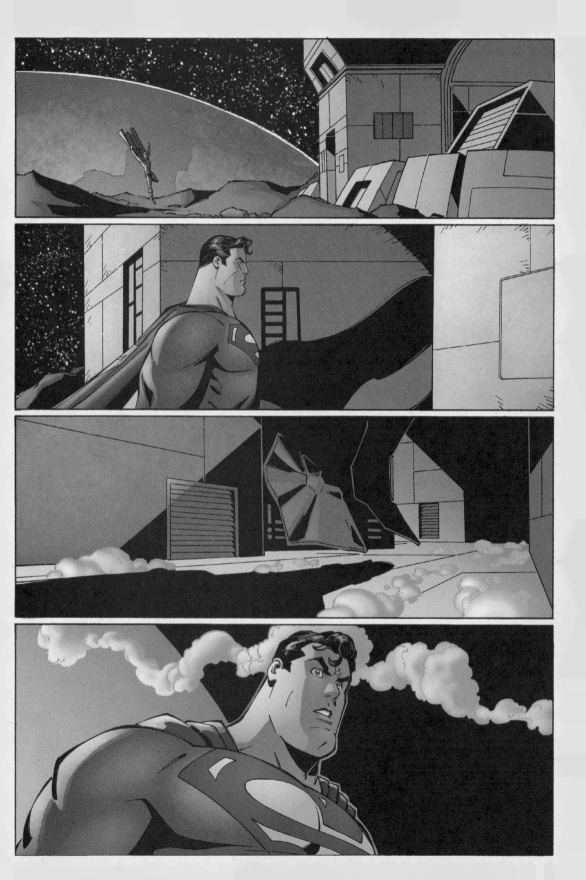

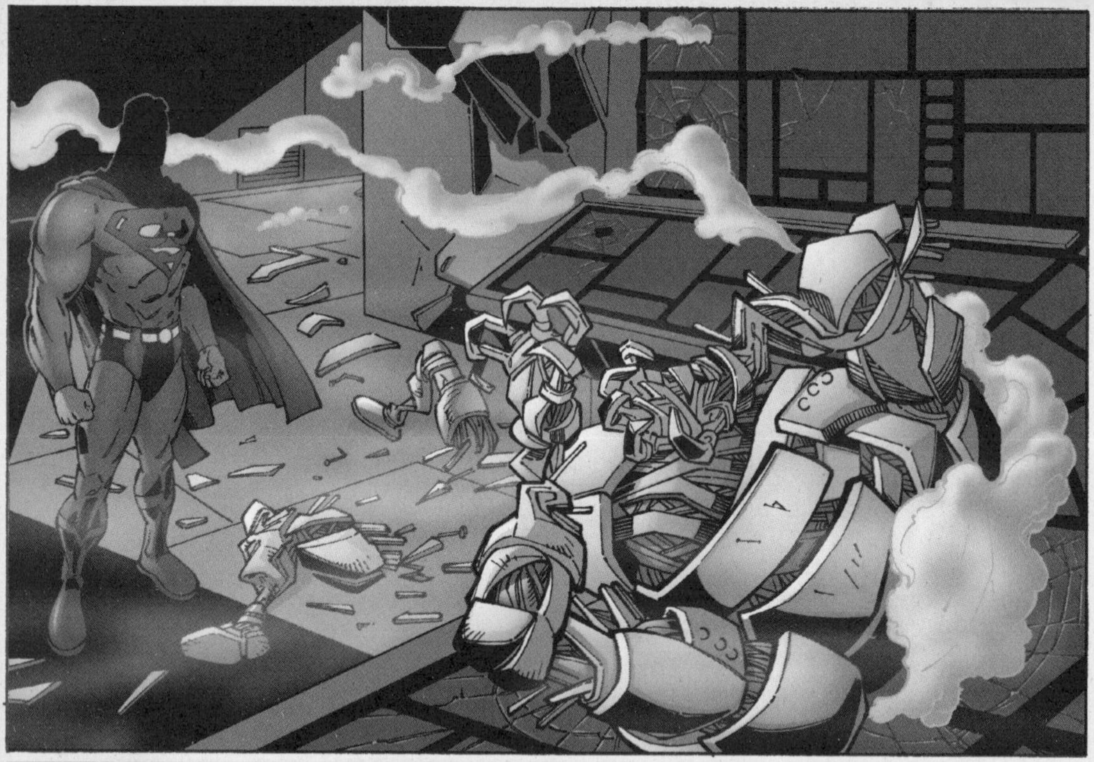

# THE DOOMSDAY PROTOCOL

CASEY - WIERINGO - STUCKER - OAKLEY - WILDSTORM - PALMER JR. - BERGANZA

SUPERMAN CREATED BY JERRY SIEGEL & JOE SHUSTER

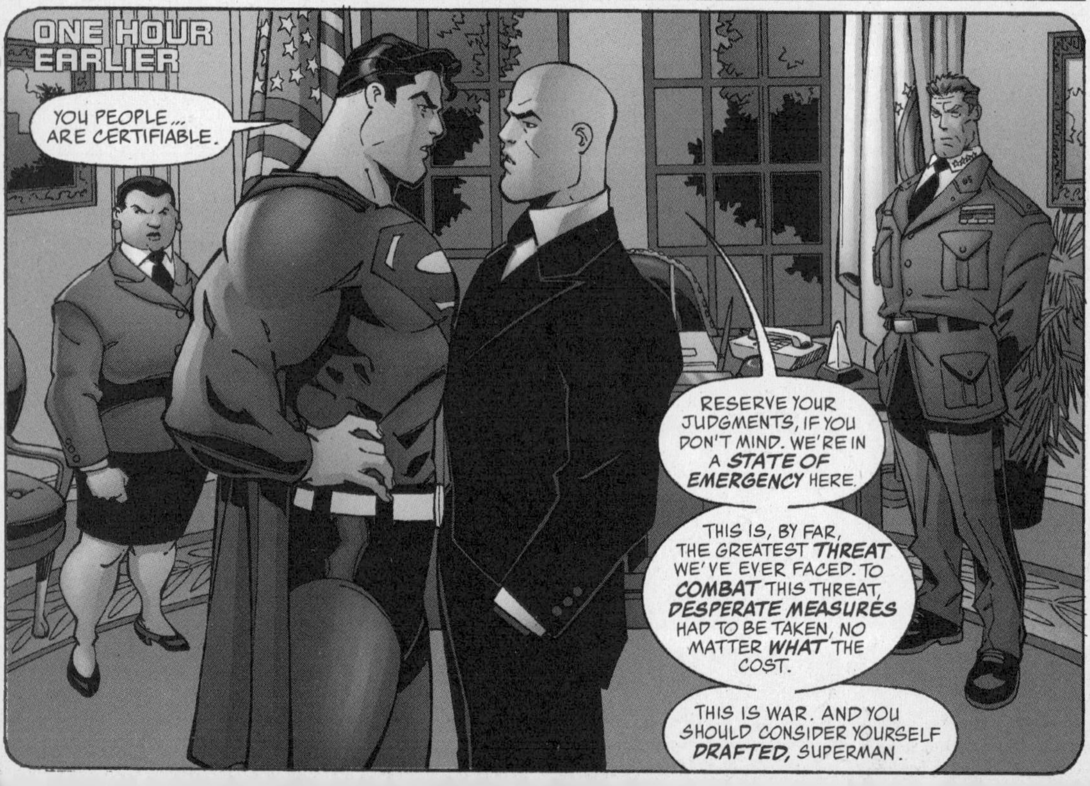
ONE HOUR EARLIER
YOU PEOPLE... ARE CERTIFIABLE.
RESERVE YOUR JUDGMENTS, IF YOU DON'T MIND. WE'RE IN A STATE OF EMERGENCY HERE.
THIS IS, BY FAR, THE GREATEST THREAT WE'VE EVER FACED. TO COMBAT THIS THREAT, DESPERATE MEASURES HAD TO BE TAKEN, NO MATTER WHAT THE COST.
THIS IS WAR. AND YOU SHOULD CONSIDER YOURSELF DRAFTED, SUPERMAN.

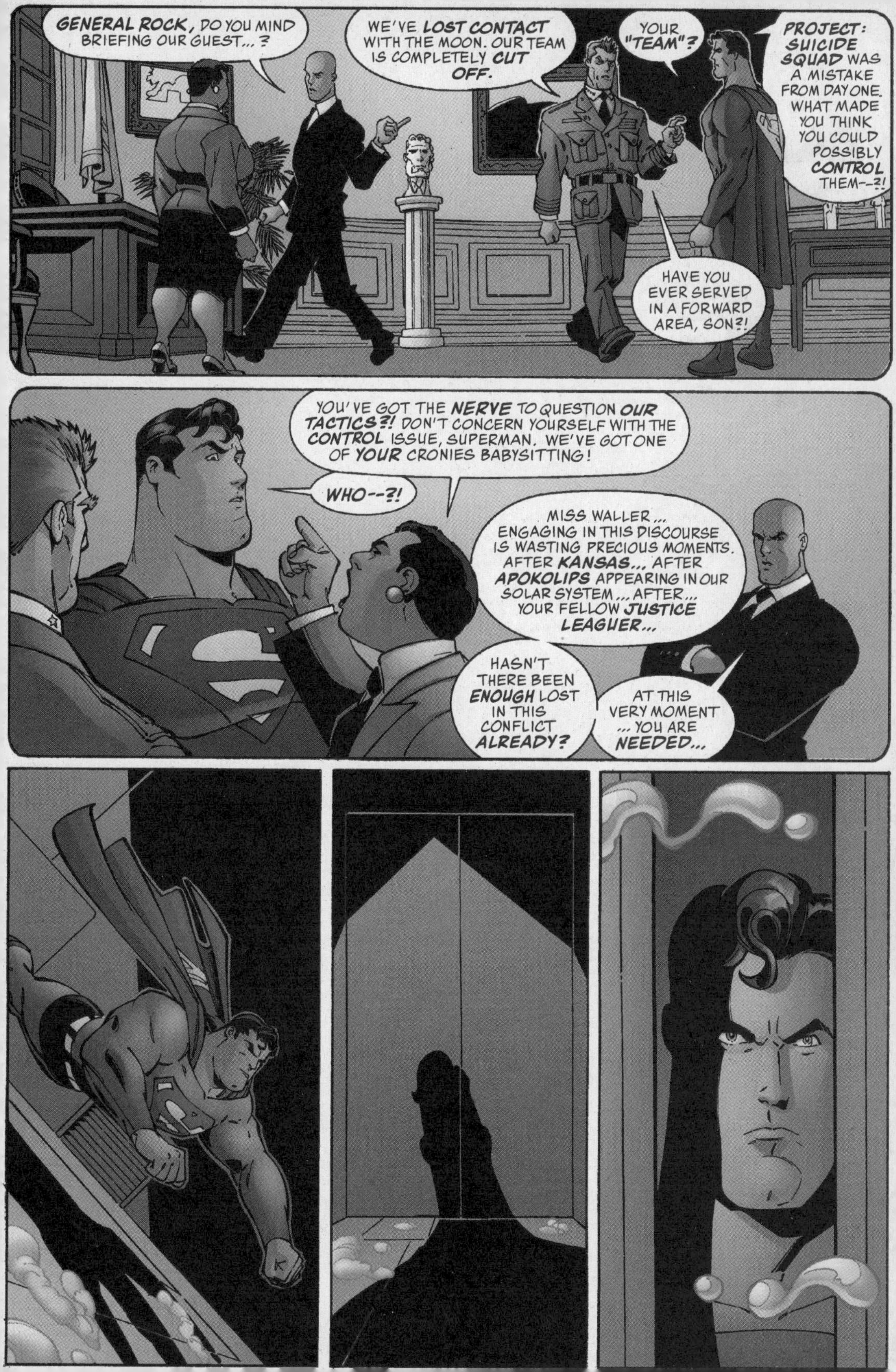
GENERAL ROCK, DO YOU MIND BRIEFING OUR GUEST...?
WE'VE LOST CONTACT WITH THE MOON. OUR TEAM IS COMPLETELY CUT OFF.
YOUR "TEAM"?
PROJECT: SUICIDE SQUAD WAS A MISTAKE FROM DAY ONE. WHAT MADE YOU THINK YOU COULD POSSIBLY CONTROL THEM--?!
HAVE YOU EVER SERVED IN A FORWARD AREA, SON?!
YOU'VE GOT THE NERVE TO QUESTION OUR TACTICS?! DON'T CONCERN YOURSELF WITH THE CONTROL ISSUE, SUPERMAN. WE'VE GOT ONE OF YOUR CRONIES BABYSITTING!
WHO--?!
MISS WALLER... ENGAGING IN THIS DISCOURSE IS WASTING PRECIOUS MOMENTS. AFTER KANSAS... AFTER APOKOLIPS APPEARING IN OUR SOLAR SYSTEM... AFTER... YOUR FELLOW JUSTICE LEAGUER...
HASN'T THERE BEEN ENOUGH LOST IN THIS CONFLICT ALREADY?
AT THIS VERY MOMENT ... YOU ARE NEEDED...

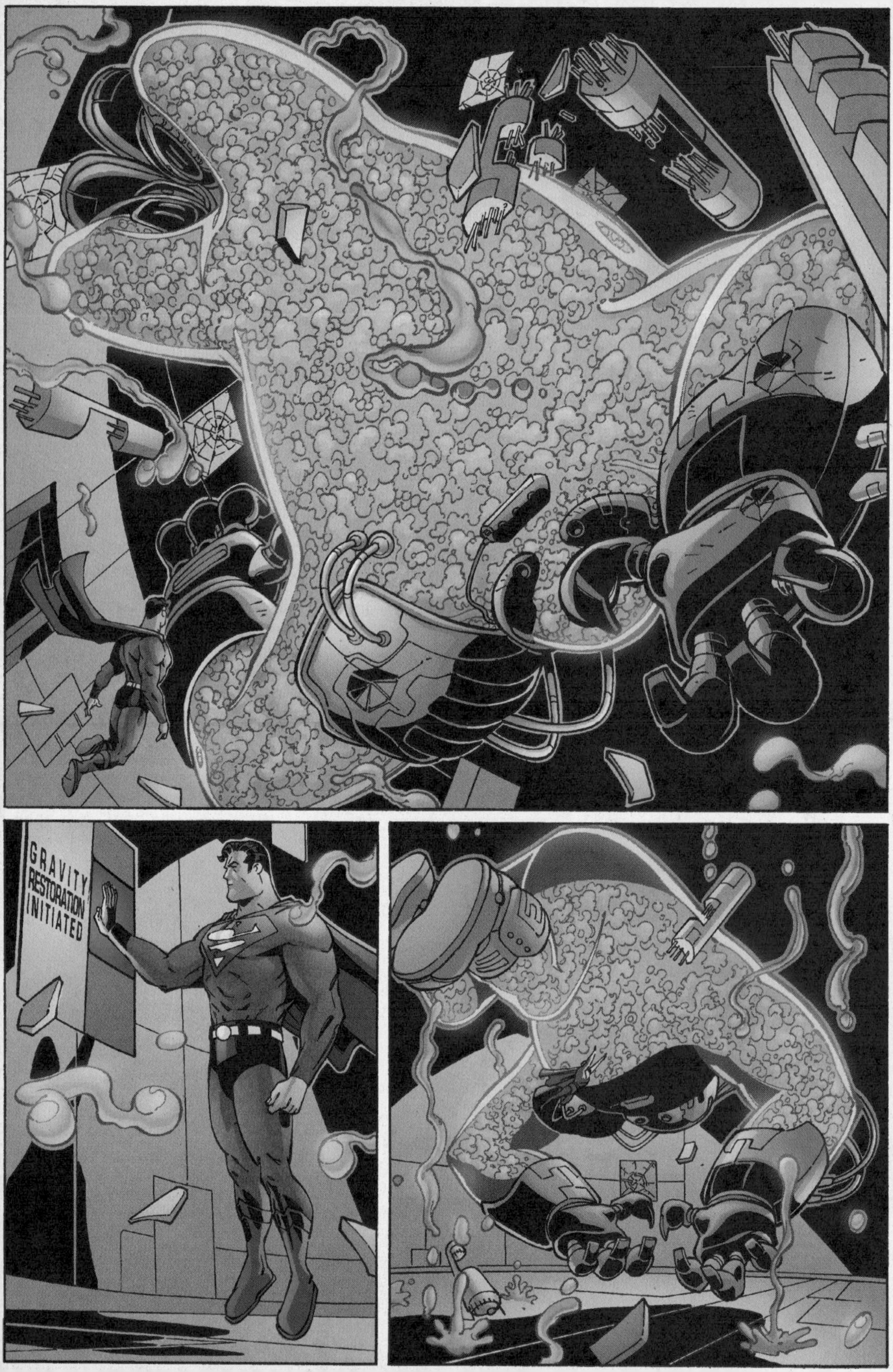
GRAVITY RESTORATION INITIATED

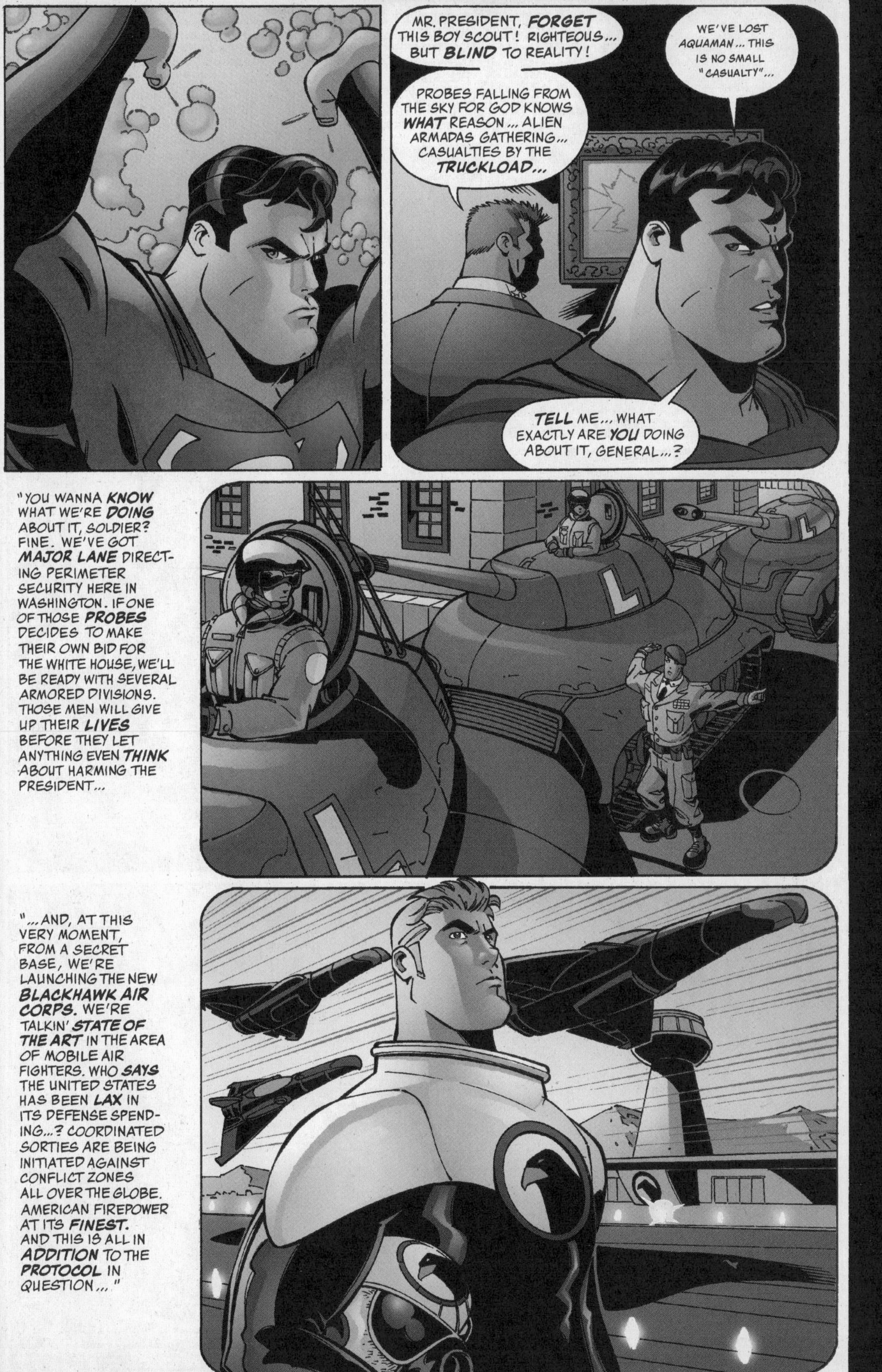
MR. PRESIDENT, FORGET THIS BOY SCOUT! RIGHTEOUS... BUT BLIND TO REALITY!
PROBES FALLING FROM THE SKY FOR GOD KNOWS WHAT REASON... ALIEN ARMADAS GATHERING... CASUALTIES BY THE TRUCKLOAD...
WE'VE LOST AQUAMAN... THIS IS NO SMALL "CASUALTY"...
TELL ME... WHAT EXACTLY ARE YOU DOING ABOUT IT, GENERAL...?
"YOU WANNA KNOW WHAT WE'RE DOING ABOUT IT, SOLDIER? FINE. WE'VE GOT MAJOR LANE DIRECTING PERIMETER SECURITY HERE IN WASHINGTON. IF ONE OF THOSE PROBES DECIDES TO MAKE THEIR OWN BID FOR THE WHITE HOUSE, WE'LL BE READY WITH SEVERAL ARMORED DIVISIONS. THOSE MEN WILL GIVE UP THEIR LIVES BEFORE THEY LET ANYTHING EVEN THINK ABOUT HARMING THE PRESIDENT...
"...AND, AT THIS VERY MOMENT, FROM A SECRET BASE, WE'RE LAUNCHING THE NEW BLACKHAWK AIR CORPS. WE'RE TALKIN' STATE OF THE ART IN THE AREA OF MOBILE AIR FIGHTERS. WHO SAYS THE UNITED STATES HAS BEEN LAX IN ITS DEFENSE SPENDING...? COORDINATED SORTIES ARE BEING INITIATED AGAINST CONFLICT ZONES ALL OVER THE GLOBE. AMERICAN FIREPOWER AT ITS FINEST. AND THIS IS ALL IN ADDITION TO THE PROTOCOL IN QUESTION..."

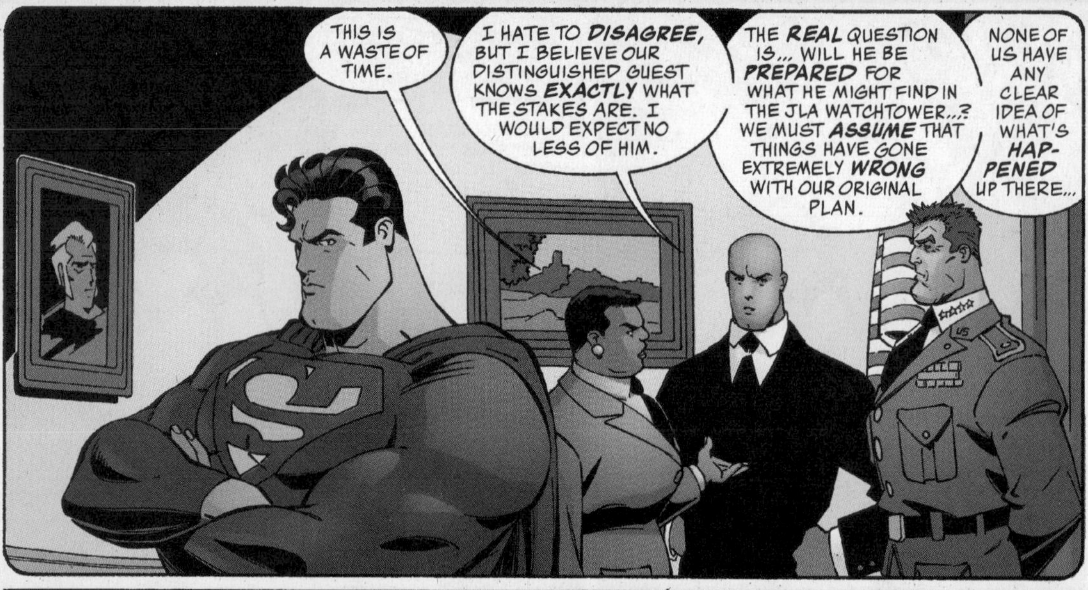
THIS IS A WASTE OF TIME.
I HATE TO DISAGREE, BUT I BELIEVE OUR DISTINGUISHED GUEST KNOWS EXACTLY WHAT THE STAKES ARE. I WOULD EXPECT NO LESS OF HIM.
THE REAL QUESTION IS... WILL HE BE PREPARED FOR WHAT HE MIGHT FIND IN THE JLA WATCHTOWER...? WE MUST ASSUME THAT THINGS HAVE GONE EXTREMELY WRONG WITH OUR ORIGINAL PLAN.
NONE OF US HAVE ANY CLEAR IDEA OF WHAT'S HAPPENED UP THERE...

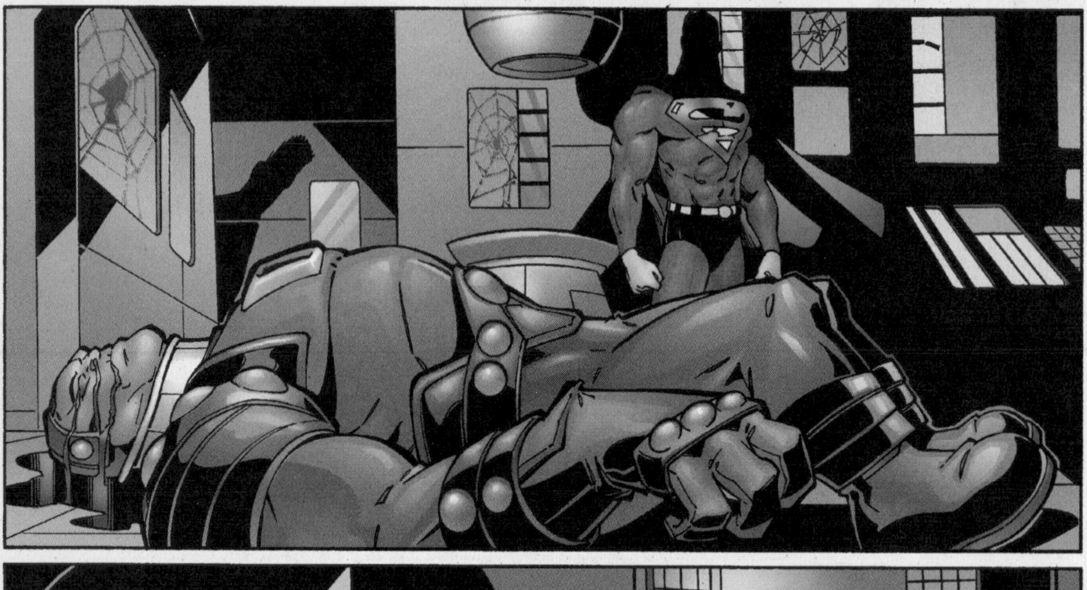

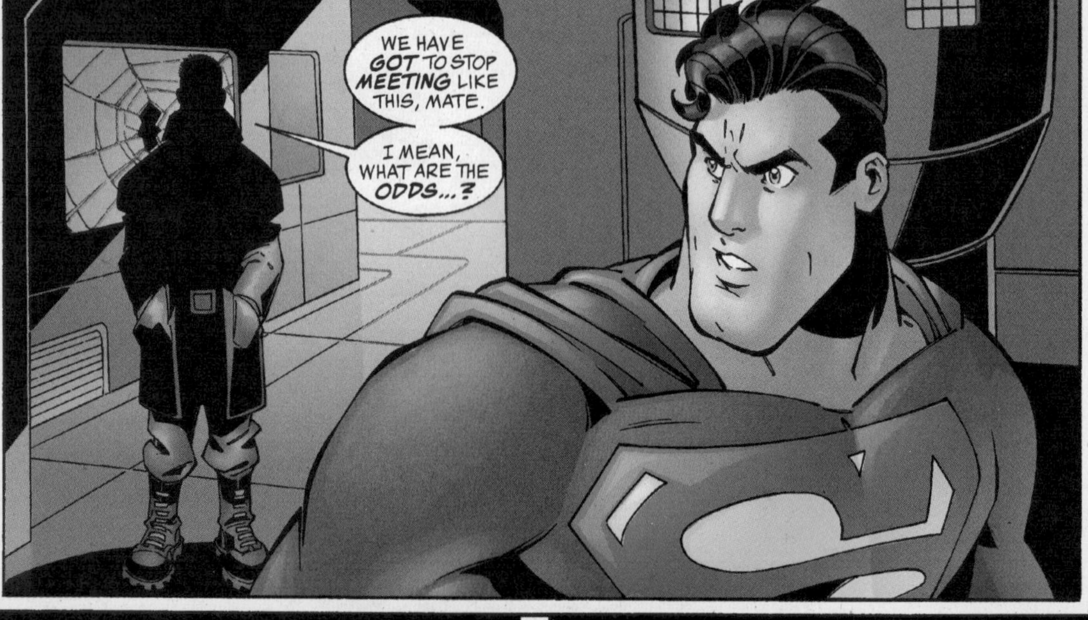
WE HAVE GOT TO STOP MEETING LIKE THIS, MATE.
I MEAN, WHAT ARE THE ODDS...?

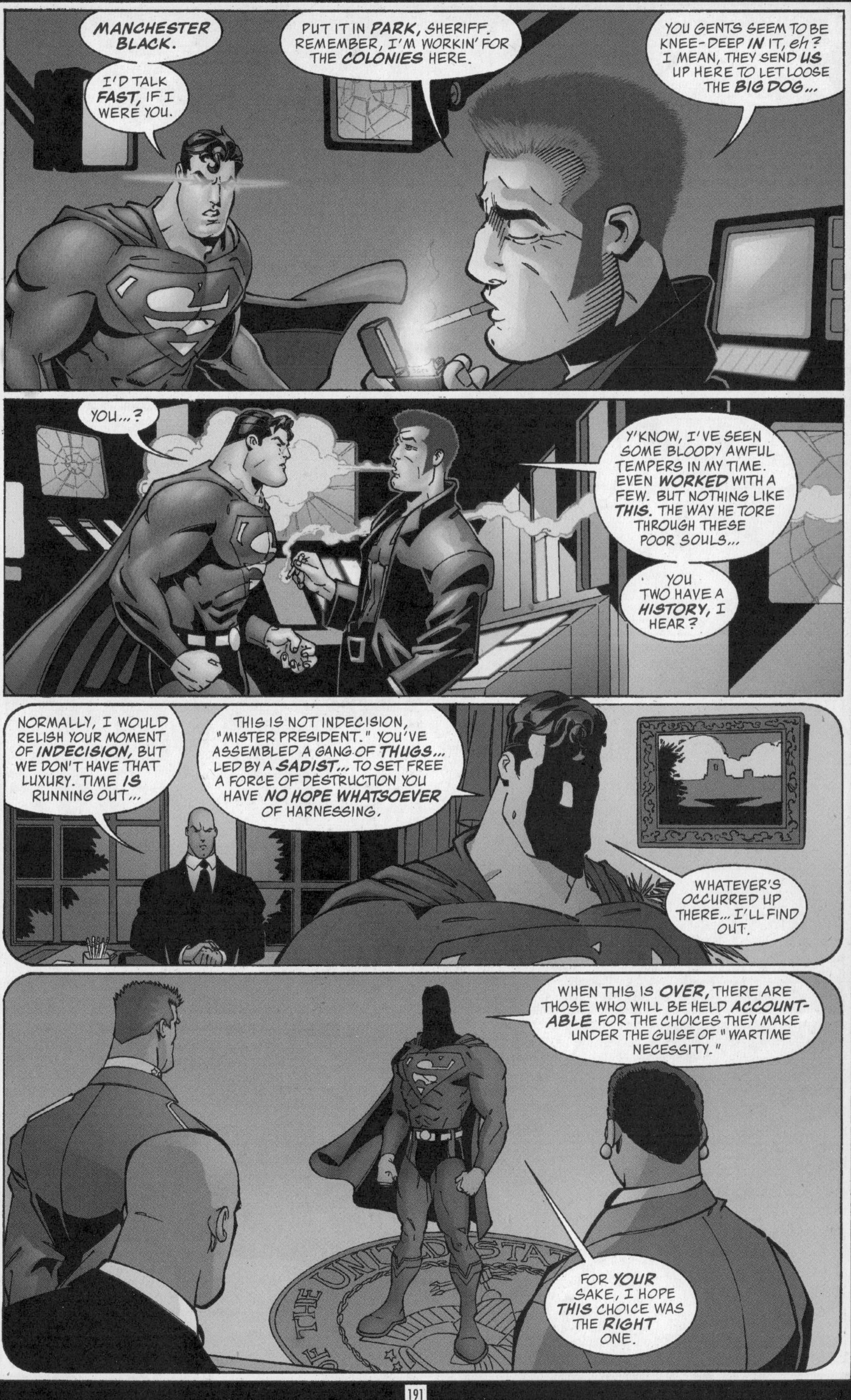
MANCHESTER BLACK.
I'D TALK FAST, IF I WERE YOU.
PUT IT IN PARK, SHERIFF. REMEMBER, I'M WORKIN' FOR THE COLONIES HERE.
YOU GENTS SEEM TO BE KNEE-DEEP IN IT, eh? I MEAN, THEY SEND US UP HERE TO LET LOOSE THE BIG DOG...
YOU...?
Y'KNOW, I'VE SEEN SOME BLOODY AWFUL TEMPERS IN MY TIME. EVEN WORKED WITH A FEW. BUT NOTHING LIKE THIS. THE WAY HE TORE THROUGH THESE POOR SOULS...
YOU TWO HAVE A HISTORY, I HEAR?
NORMALLY, I WOULD RELISH YOUR MOMENT OF INDECISION, BUT WE DON'T HAVE THAT LUXURY. TIME IS RUNNING OUT...
THIS IS NOT INDECISION, "MISTER PRESIDENT." YOU'VE ASSEMBLED A GANG OF THUGS... LED BY A SADIST... TO SET FREE A FORCE OF DESTRUCTION YOU HAVE NO HOPE WHATSOEVER OF HARNESSING.
WHATEVER'S OCCURRED UP THERE... I'LL FIND OUT.
WHEN THIS IS OVER, THERE ARE THOSE WHO WILL BE HELD ACCOUNTABLE FOR THE CHOICES THEY MAKE UNDER THE GUISE OF "WARTIME NECESSITY."
FOR YOUR SAKE, I HOPE THIS CHOICE WAS THE RIGHT ONE.

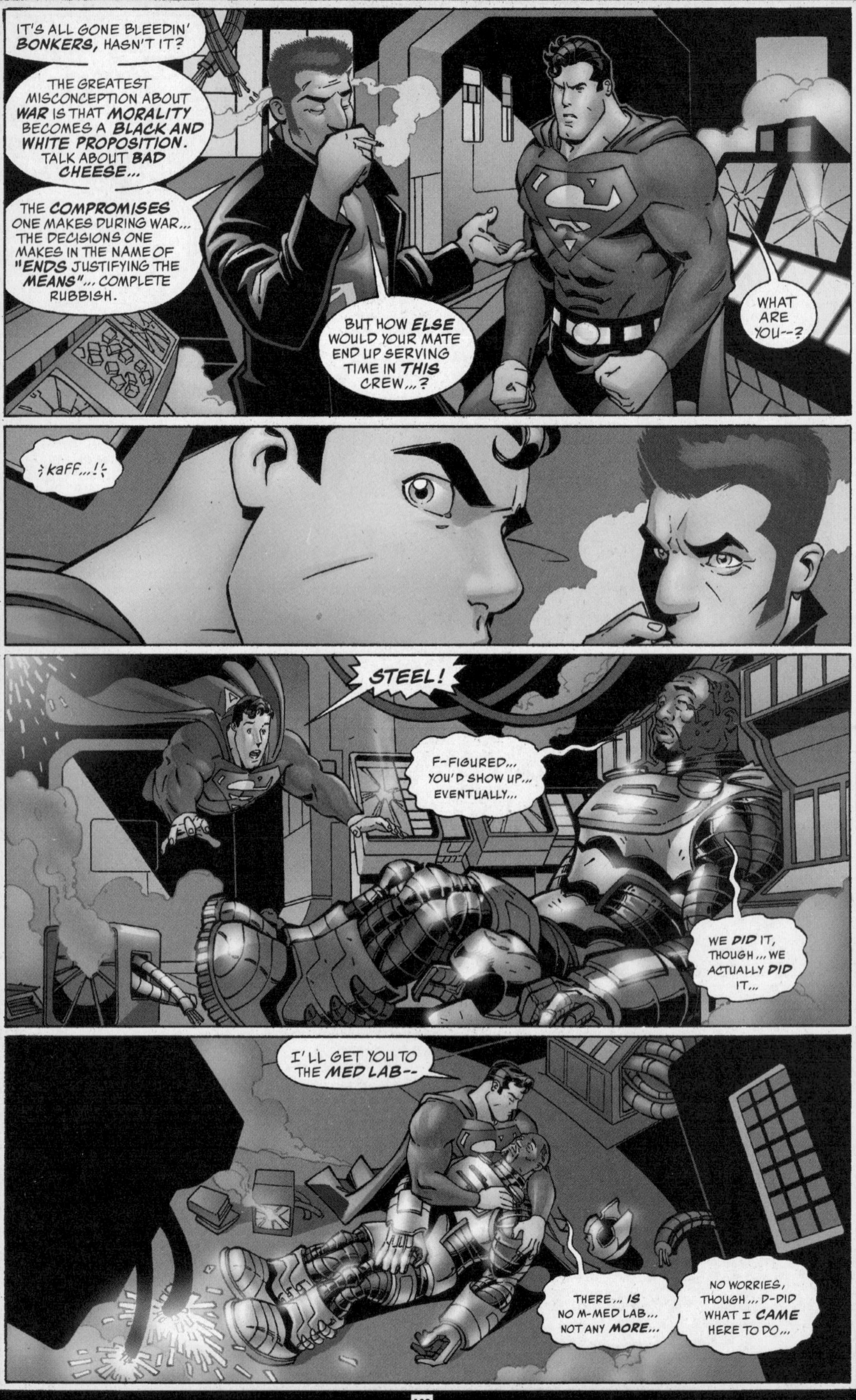
IT'S ALL GONE BLEEDIN' BONKERS, HASN'T IT?
THE GREATEST MISCONCEPTION ABOUT WAR IS THAT MORALITY BECOMES A BLACK AND WHITE PROPOSITION. TALK ABOUT BAD CHEESE...
THE COMPROMISES ONE MAKES DURING WAR... THE DECISIONS ONE MAKES IN THE NAME OF "ENDS JUSTIFYING THE MEANS"... COMPLETE RUBBISH.
BUT HOW ELSE WOULD YOUR MATE END UP SERVING TIME IN THIS CREW...?
WHAT ARE YOU--?
kaff...!
STEEL!
F-FIGURED... YOU'D SHOW UP... EVENTUALLY...
WE DID IT, THOUGH... WE ACTUALLY DID IT...
I'LL GET YOU TO THE MED LAB--
THERE... IS NO M-MED LAB... NOT ANY MORE...
NO WORRIES, THOUGH... D-DID WHAT I CAME HERE TO DO...

GOOD LUCK WITH THE BEASTIE...
BLACK--!
LET HIM GO...
...HE'S... COMPLETELY INCONSEQUENTIAL TO WHAT'S HAPPENING HERE...
I'D NEVER... SEEN IT IN ACTION BEFORE. ONCE FREED... IT WAS... PRIMAL... BRUTAL... NOW I UNDERSTAND HOW IT COULD'VE DONE... WHAT IT DID... TO YOU...
NOW... FORGET ABOUT ME. I'VE DONE MY JOB. YOURS IS JUST BEGINNING. YOU NEED TO... WATCH HIM...
MAKE SURE... HE DOES WHAT HE WAS FREED TO DO...
--SIGNAL COMING IN ON A WEAK EMERGENCY CHANNEL. GO AHEAD.
KKKK NOT SURE HOW LONG BACKUP SYSTEMS WILL LAST HERE... KKK YOU NEED TO SEND A TEAM UP HERE NOW. YOUR "INVESTMENT," MANCHESTER BLACK, BURNED UP THE TELEPORTER CIRCUITRY ON HIS WAY OUT... KKKK
KKK --NEEDS IMMEDIATE MEDICAL ATTENTION-- KKK --I'M ON MY WAY TO THE ARMADA PERIMETER KKK
SUPERMAN OUT.

He'd fought a war once **before.** In the streets of Metropolis. It was a war he ultimately **lost** as he succumbed to the sheer **brutality** of his opponent... and for the first time, he felt the cold hand of **death** gripped around his heart. And in that moment, he did not resist. He did not deny its pull. His opponent had become... his **killer.**

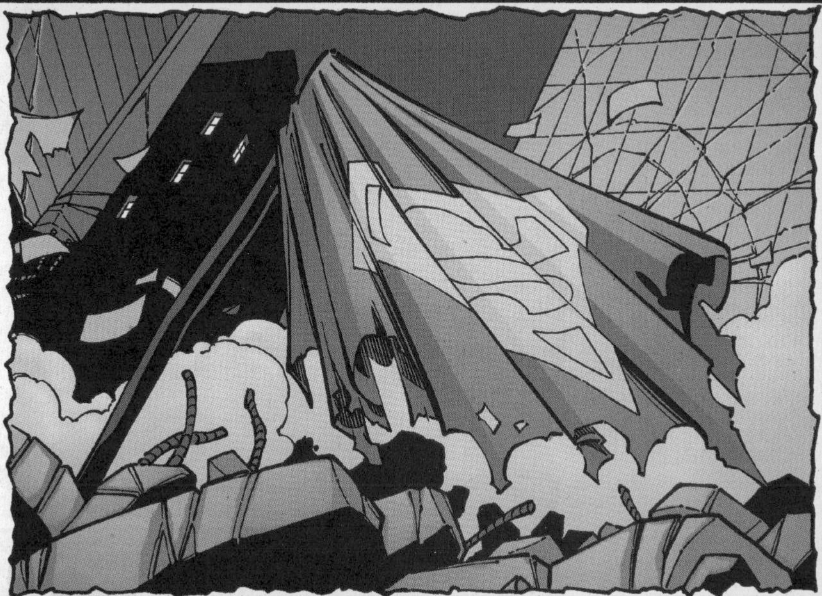

But he had **returned** from nothingness. Death could not keep him from those he loved. Now war has found him once again... and on a scale he had rarely even had **nightmares** about. Facing not only **death,** but the complete and total **end of everything.** Here, in the outer reaches of the solar system, he was **witnessing** it firsthand. This war had already claimed **lives.** An **alien armada** fought till their last breath.

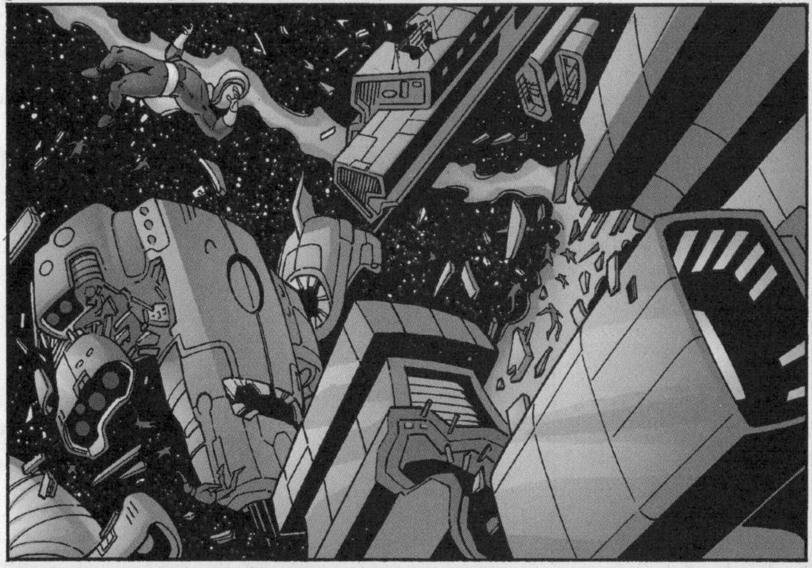

So many choices made, just in the past few days, that have **tested** his own moral compass. So many decisions he wonders if he'll live to **regret.** So many already **fallen,** so many already **lost,** and the greatest battles have yet to be **fought.** He tries not to **think** too much about it, as more **immediate** concerns weigh on his mind. And violent **memories** prey upon his judgment...

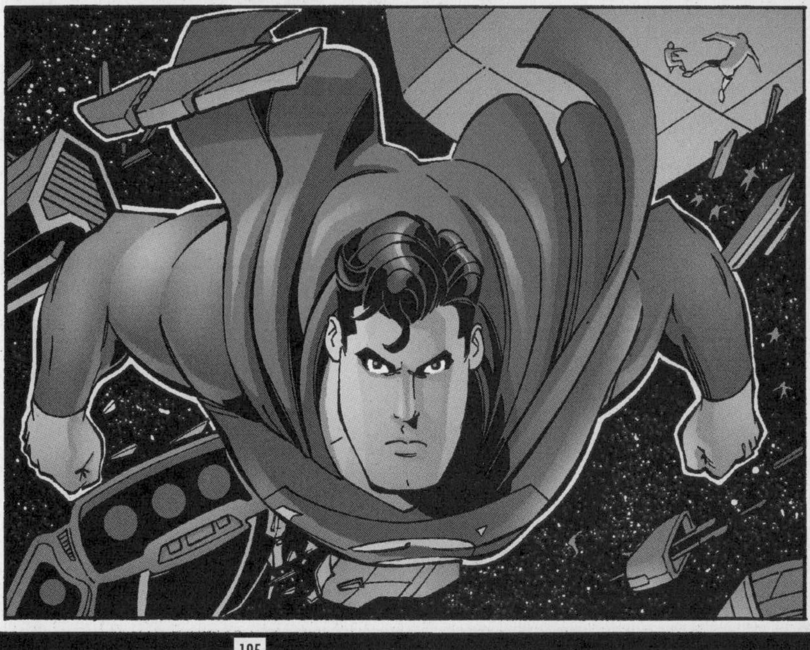

**He** had certainly felt **PAIN** before, but never like **THIS**. The memory of each and every blow rings like bells within his brain. The **TASTE** of his own **BLOOD**. The stink of unstoppable **RAGE** raining down calcified **FURY** upon his head. Truth be told... a small part of him had actually **WELCOMED** the peaceful embrace of death. He saw it as the only true **ESCAPE** from what he still feared was an **INESCAPABLE** truth...

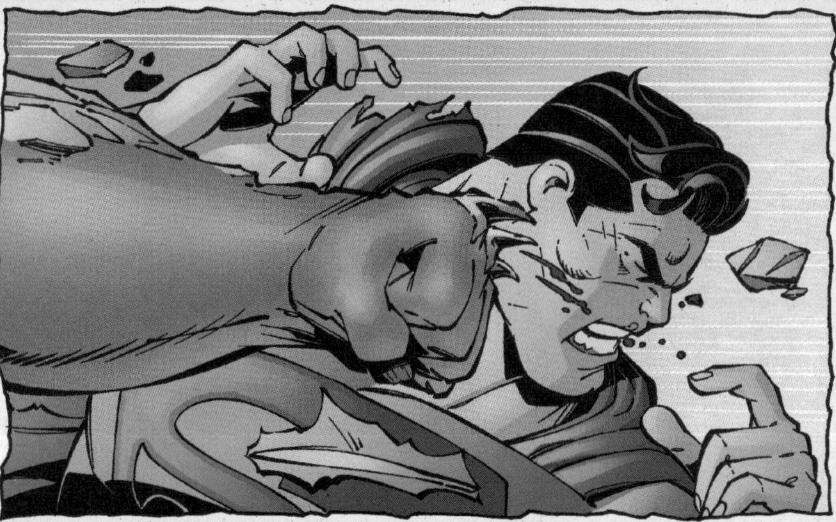

...This was a true **ANOMALY** in the universe. This was a being of such immeasurable **POWER** that its **NAME**, in any translation--be it a recognizable or wholly alien tongue--struck unholy terror into the hearts of those who heard it. No **MERCY** involved. No **CRACKS** in the veneer of indestructibility. It had never had an **EARTHLY** name until **RECENTLY**, earning it rightly with the **MURDER** of the greatest hero of the age. It was a name that parents frightened their children with. It was a name that had become **MYTH**.

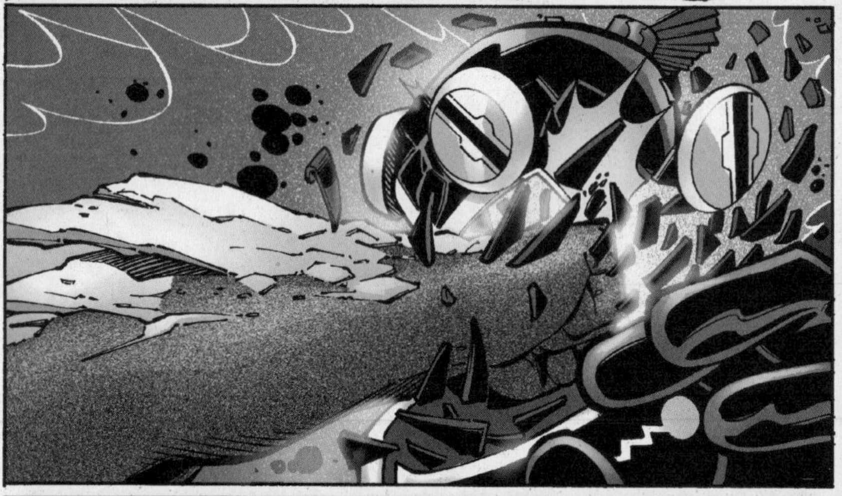

**DOOMSDAY.**

The creature that had **KILLED SUPERMAN**. And now it lived **AGAIN**. He could engage it once again. Every fiber in his body screamed out to **DESTROY** this... engine of pure destruction. He could **MAKE** that choice right **NOW**. And who would **BLAME** him? But, with the **UNIVERSE** held hostage... only **ONE** choice was clear. Another **COMPROMISE**. Another decision he feared he would live to **REGRET**...

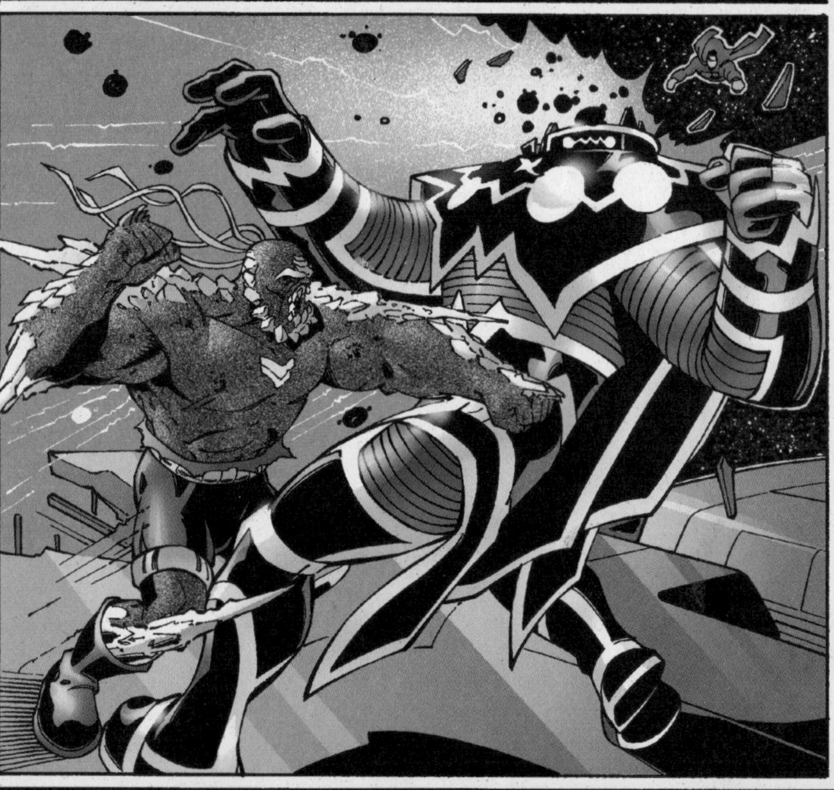

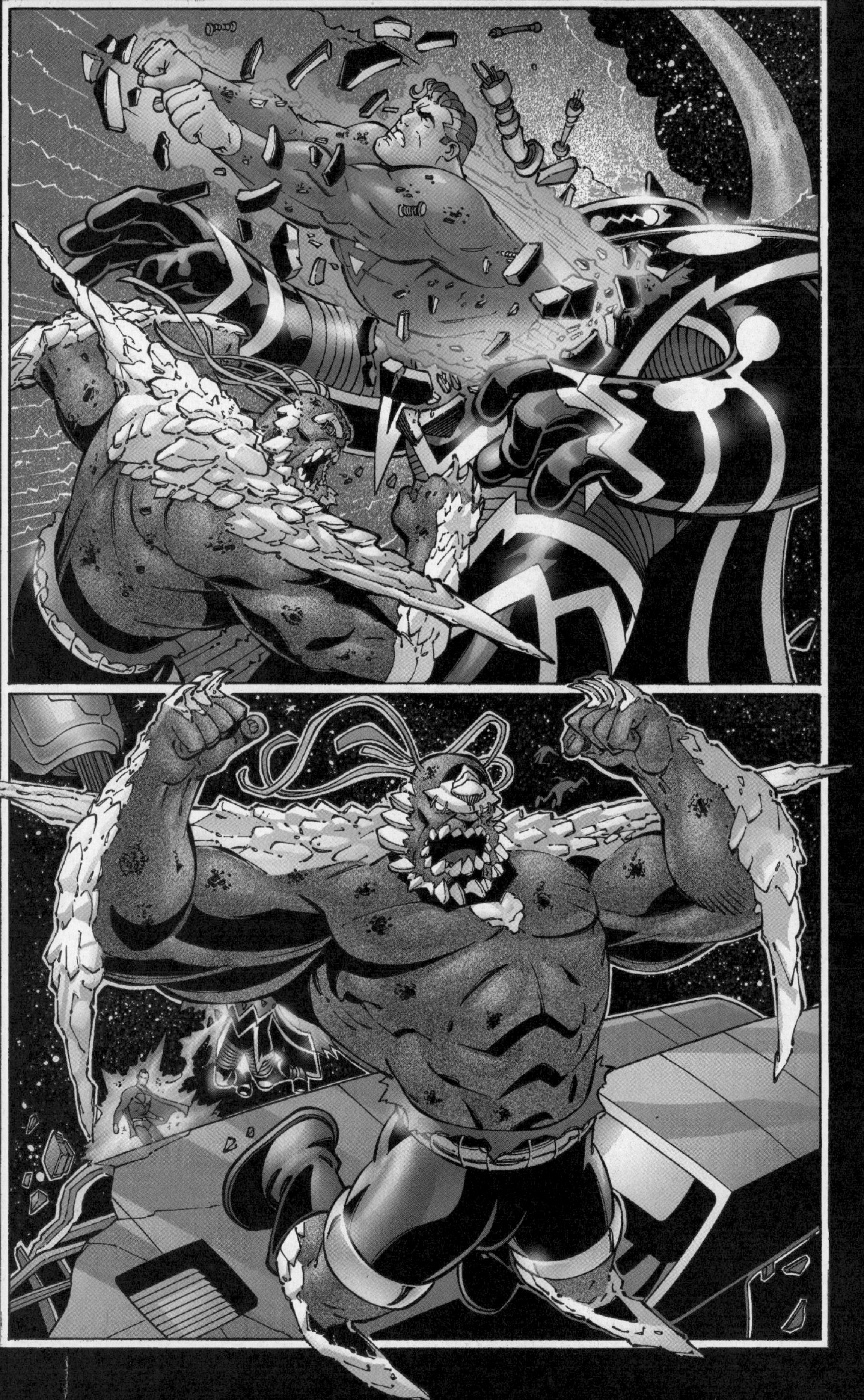

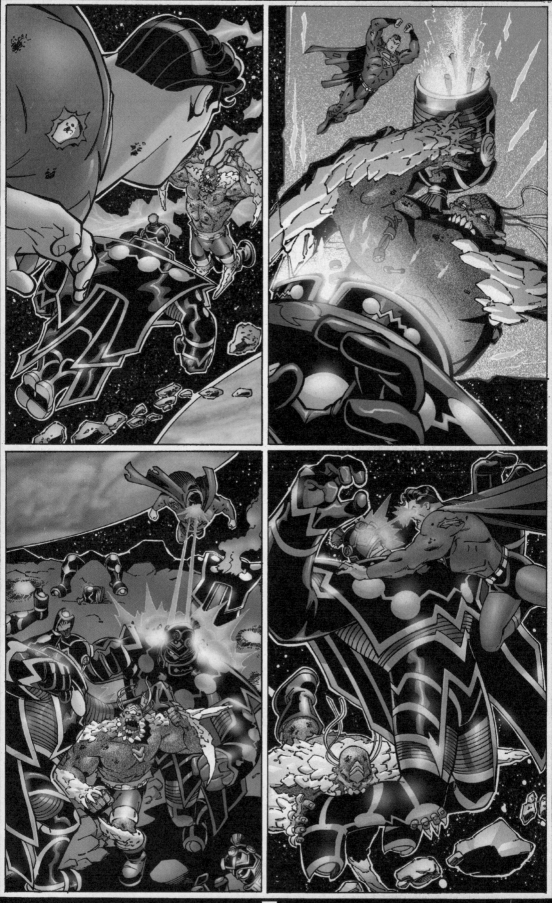

IT HAS BECOME **PRIMAL.** IT HAS BECOME SECOND NATURE. **TIME** HAS LOST ALL MEANING, HERE IN THE DEPTHS OF SPACE. HOW LONG HAVE THEY BEEN MAKING THIS TREK? HOURS? DAYS? HE HAS **NO IDEA.** NOR DOES HE **CARE,** AS THIS **ALLIANCE** WITH ONE OF HIS DEADLIEST ADVERSARIES HAS PUT HIM AT WAR WITH HIS OWN **CONSCIENCE.** THIS BEING A WAR HE CANNOT AFFORD TO **FIGHT** AT THE MOMENT, HE HAS PUT THOSE THOUGHTS ASIDE, **NUMBING HIMSELF** INTO THE NECESSARY STATE OF **VIOLENCE.** THE DESTRUCTION OF SO MANY **PROBES** HAS DEMONSTRATED AN **IMPORTANT LESSON** TO HIM ... THAT, IN WAR, **EMOTION** CAN HINDER THE ULTIMATE GOAL ... TO **WIN.**

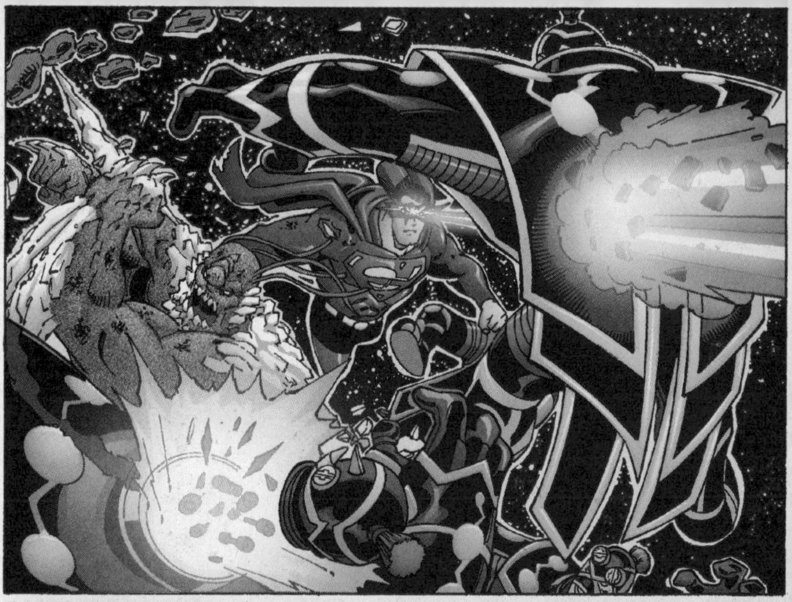

AS HIS "PARTNER" IS TRULY DESTRUCTION **PERSONIFIED,** SO HAS **HE** BECOME. AND FROM THAT TRANSFORMATION... **SUCCESS.** FAR AWAY FROM THE HUMANITY HE HOLDS IN SUCH HIGH MEASURE, WHERE THE PROBES SEEMED FAR MORE **DEADLY,** HE HAS **CUT LOOSE.** SUBSEQUENTLY, THE PROBES HAVE OFFERED LITTLE RESISTANCE. HE CAN'T HELP BUT THINK ... IF ONLY HE'D COME TO THIS CONCLUSION ON **EARTH,** HOW MANY MIGHT'VE BEEN **SAVED...?** IS THIS HOW MEN LIKE **LUTHOR** CAN WALK BETWEEN THE RAINDROPS...? BY CULTIVATING THEIR INHERENT **RUTHLESSNESS...** THEIR **LACK OF CONSCIENCE...?**

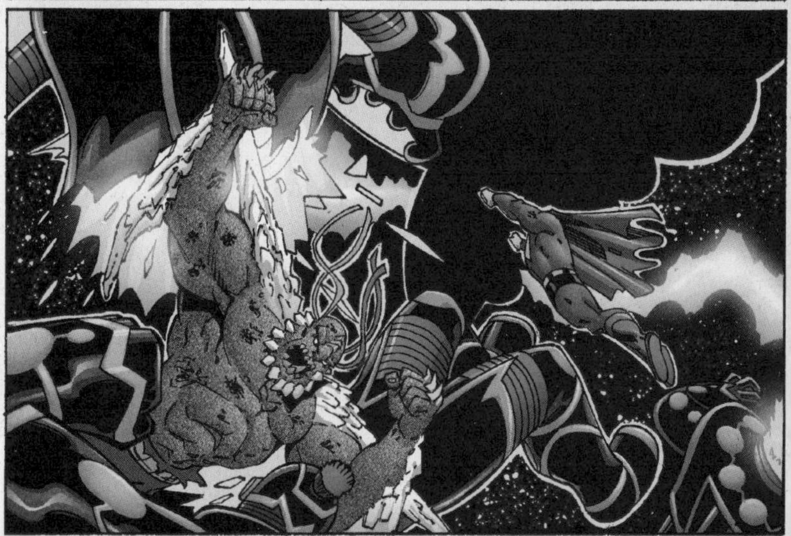

SO HE PLOWS **AHEAD,** CONFIDENT IN HIS POWERS. CONFIDENT IN HIS MINDSET AND HIS DECISIONS. READY TO STARE INTO THE ABYSS WITHOUT BLINKING. FOR A MOMENT, HE THINKS OF **LOIS.** HE THINKS OF HIS **PARENTS.** BUT ONLY FOR A MOMENT. SUCH THOUGHTS ARE **DANGEROUS.** HE **KNOWS** THAT NOW. HE IS READY TO FACE THE **TRUE** THREAT OF THIS CONFLICT... THE TRUE **ENEMY...**

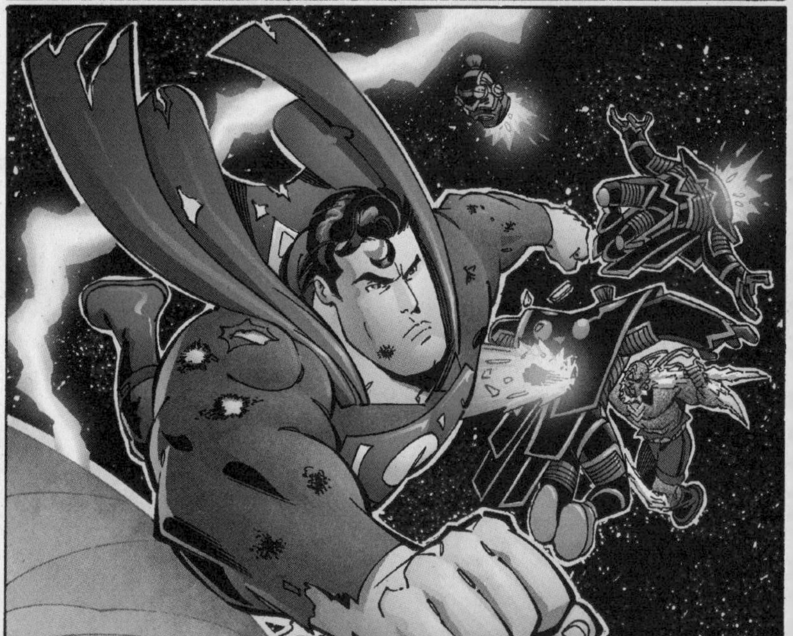

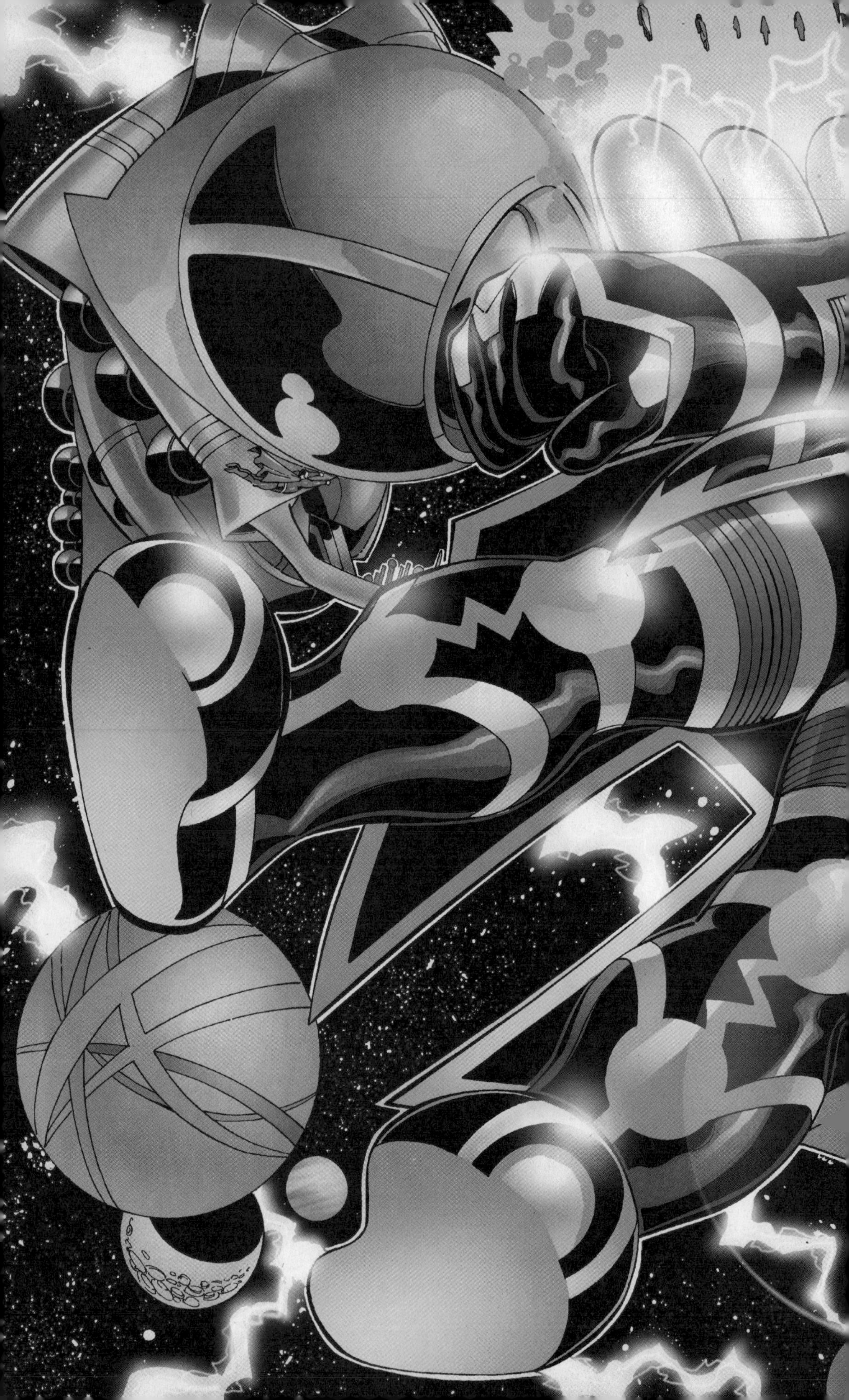

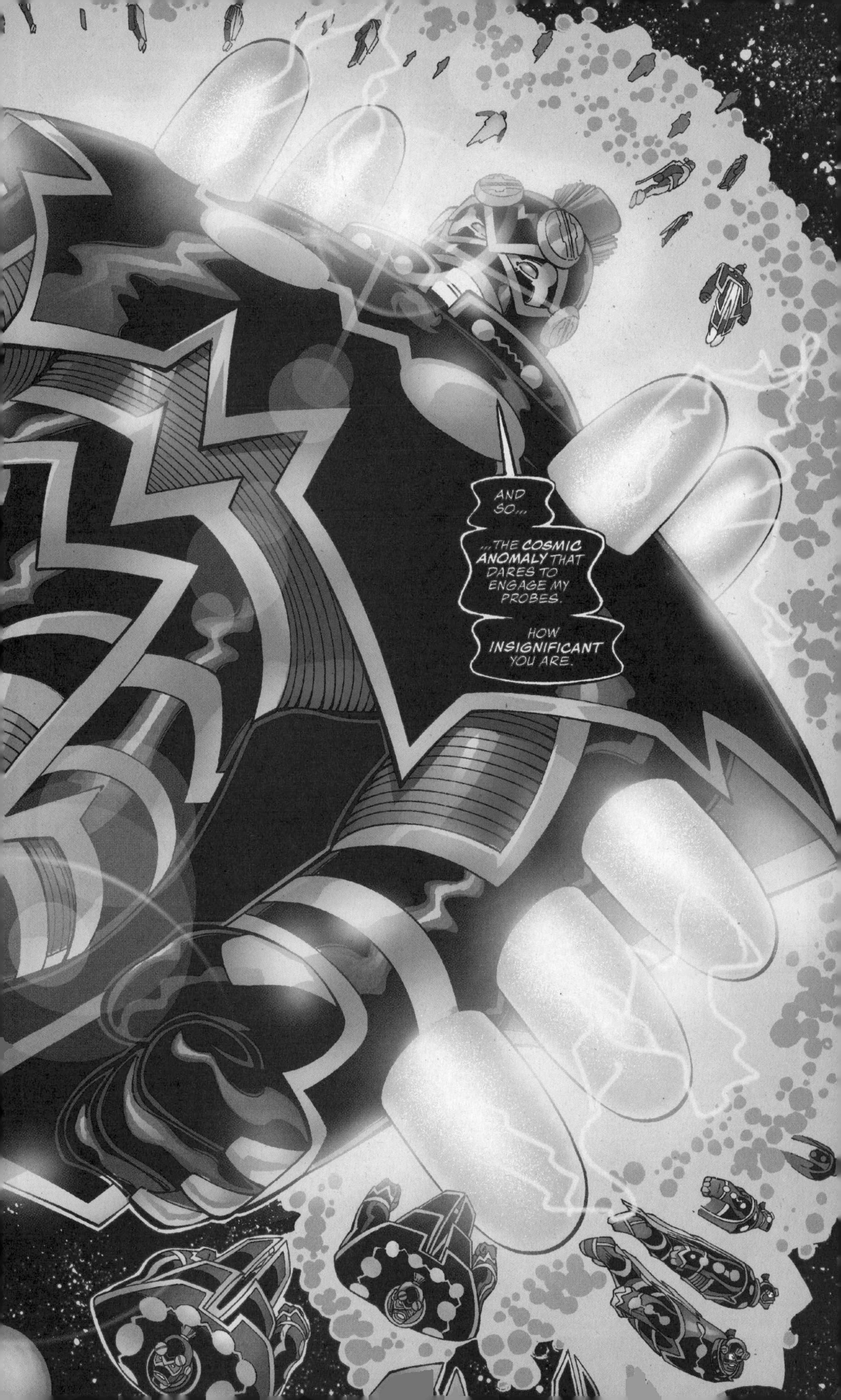
AND SO...
...THE COSMIC ANOMALY THAT DARES TO ENGAGE MY PROBES.
HOW INSIGNIFICANT YOU ARE.

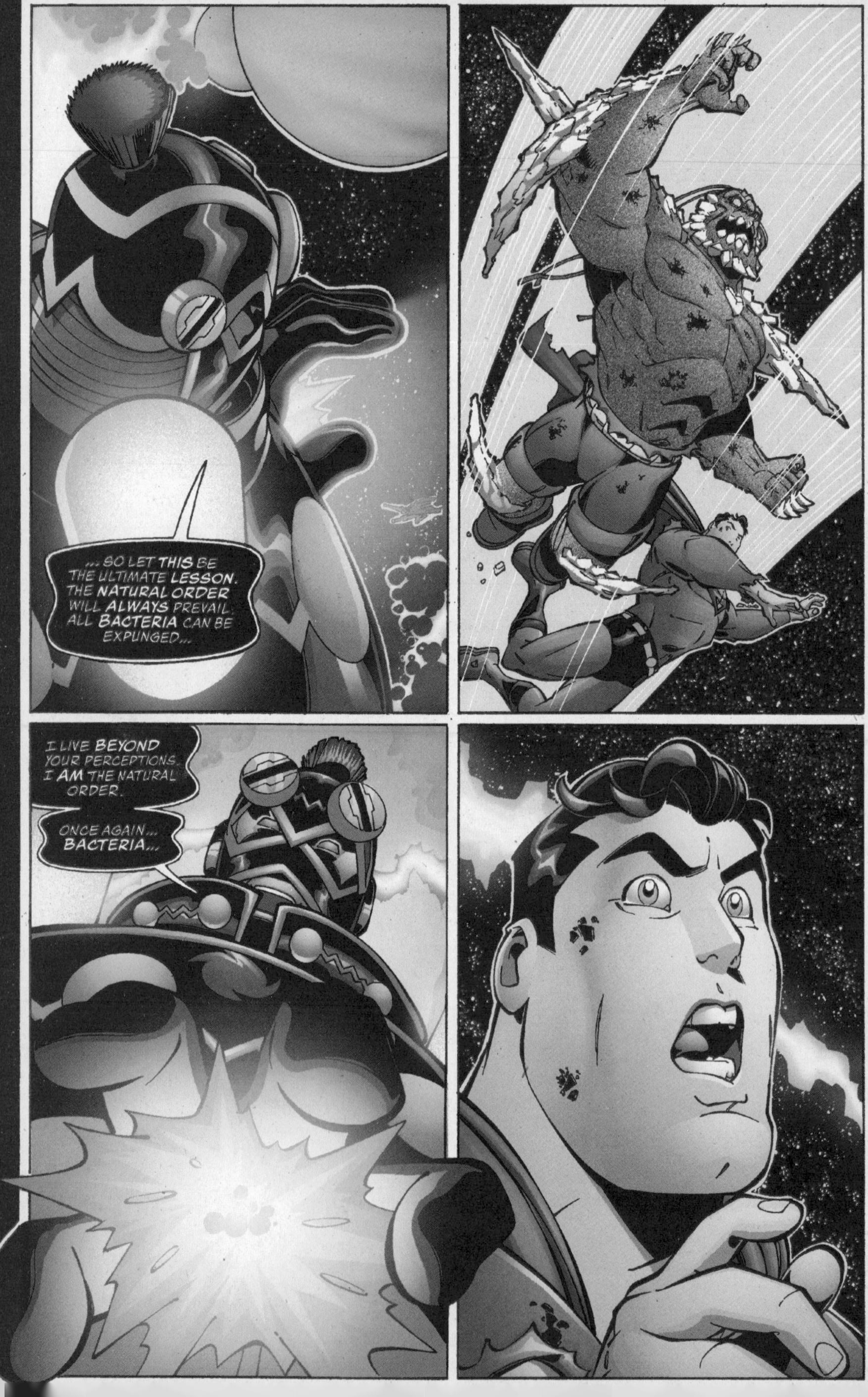
...SO LET THIS BE THE ULTIMATE LESSON. THE NATURAL ORDER WILL ALWAYS PREVAIL. ALL BACTERIA CAN BE EXPUNGED...
I LIVE BEYOND YOUR PERCEPTIONS. I AM THE NATURAL ORDER.
ONCE AGAIN... BACTERIA...

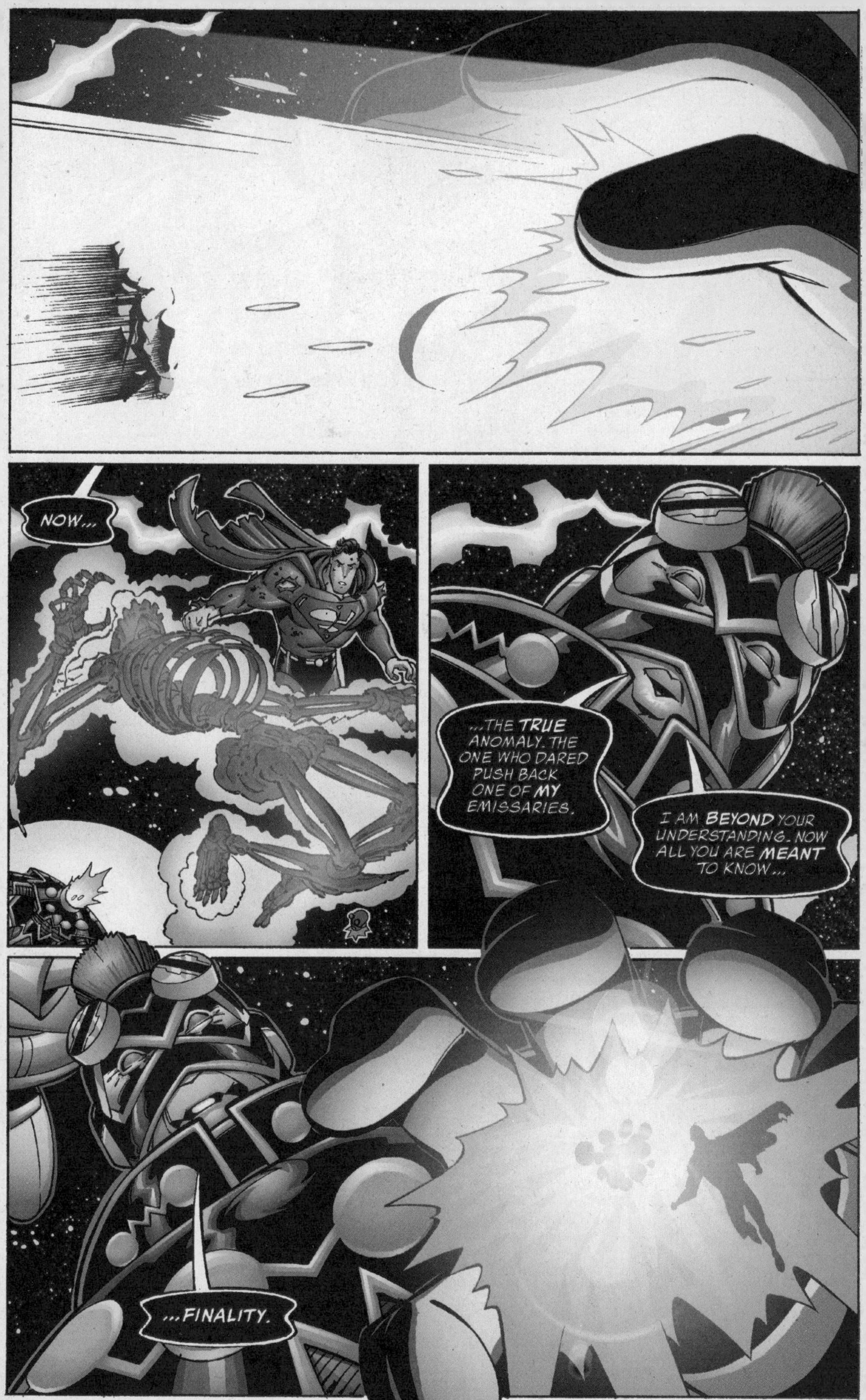
NOW...
...THE TRUE ANOMALY. THE ONE WHO DARED PUSH BACK ONE OF MY EMISSARIES.
I AM BEYOND YOUR UNDERSTANDING. NOW ALL YOU ARE MEANT TO KNOW...
...FINALITY.

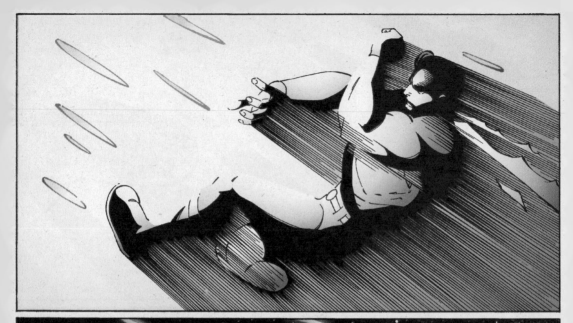

VERY WELL.

THE DESTINY OF **IMPERIEX** IS WRITTEN IN THE STARS. LET NATURE PROCEED.

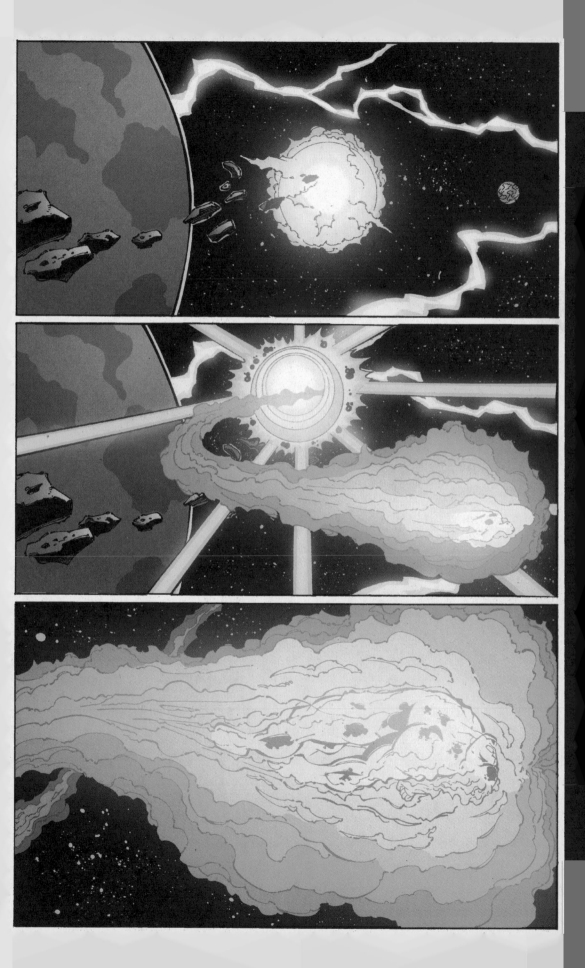

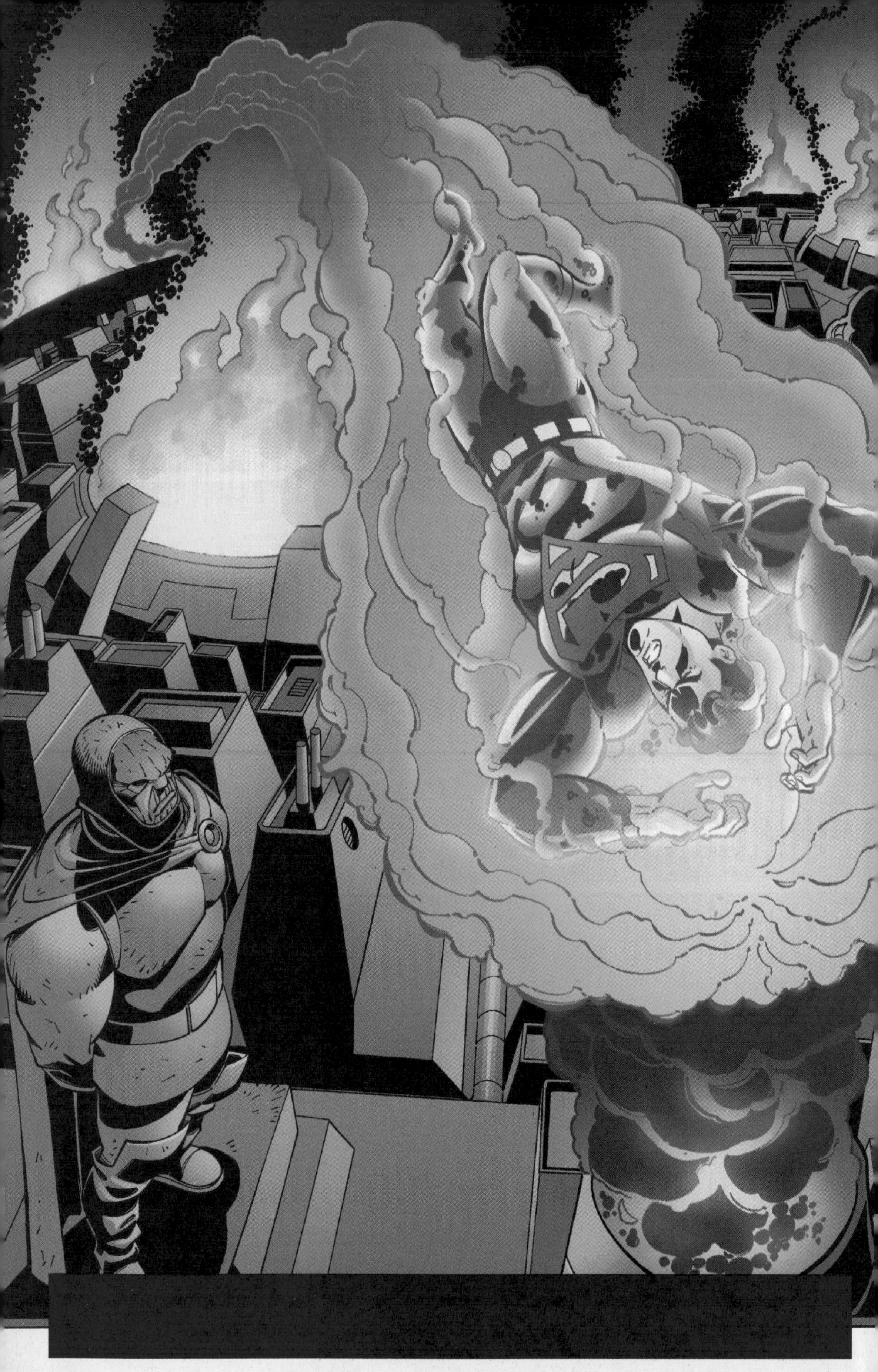

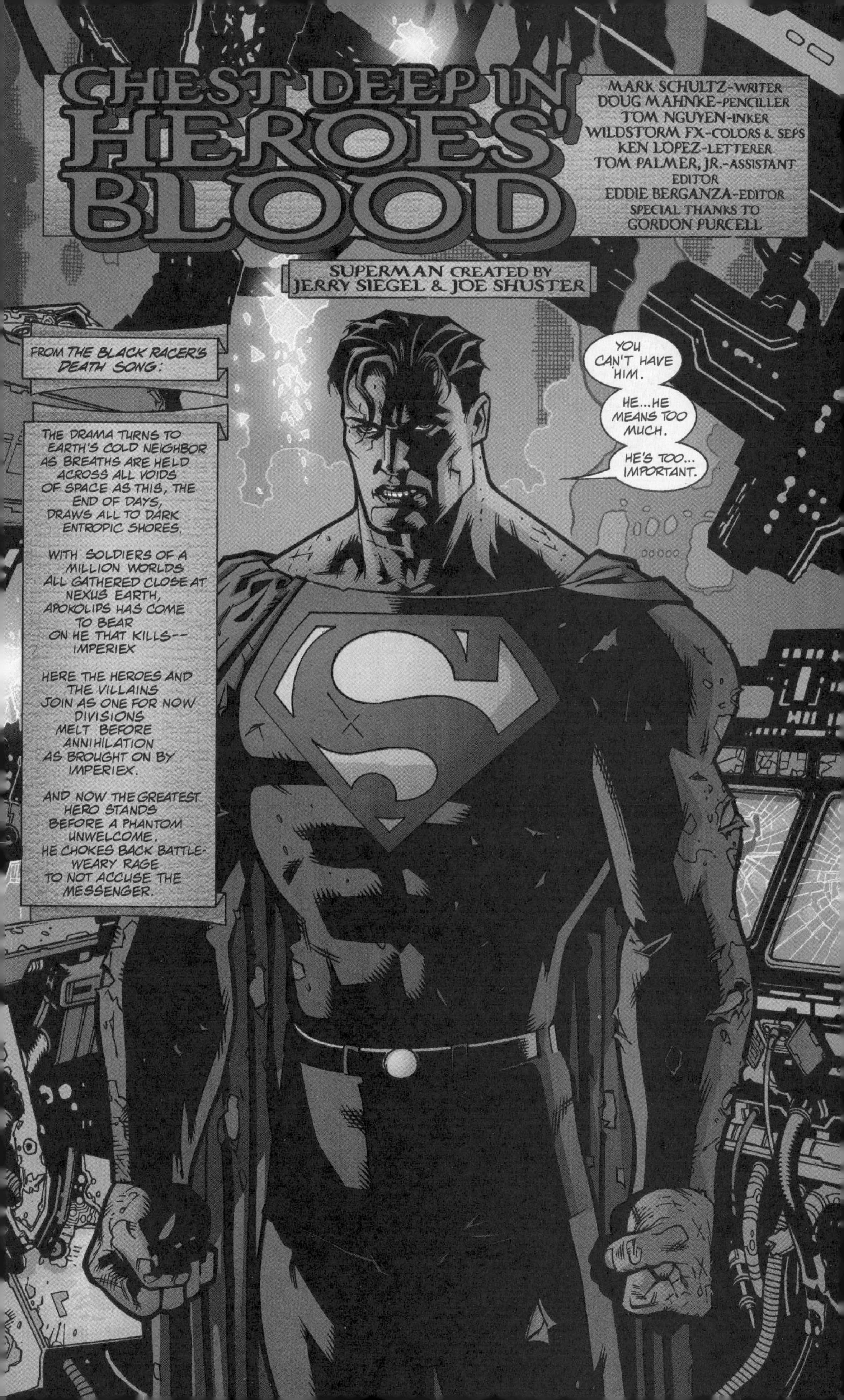
CHEST DEEP IN HEROES' BLOOD
MARK SCHULTZ-WRITER
DOUG MAHNKE-PENCILLER
TOM NGUYEN-INKER
WILDSTORM FX-COLORS & SEPS
KEN LOPEZ-LETTERER
TOM PALMER, JR.-ASSISTANT EDITOR
EDDIE BERGANZA-EDITOR
SPECIAL THANKS TO GORDON PURCELL
SUPERMAN CREATED BY JERRY SIEGEL & JOE SHUSTER
FROM THE BLACK RACER'S DEATH SONG:
THE DRAMA TURNS TO EARTH'S COLD NEIGHBOR AS BREATHS ARE HELD ACROSS ALL VOIDS OF SPACE AS THIS, THE END OF DAYS, DRAWS ALL TO DARK ENTROPIC SHORES.
WITH SOLDIERS OF A MILLION WORLDS ALL GATHERED CLOSE AT NEXUS EARTH, APOKOLIPS HAS COME TO BEAR ON HE THAT KILLS--IMPERIEX
HERE THE HEROES AND THE VILLAINS JOIN AS ONE FOR NOW DIVISIONS MELT BEFORE ANNIHILATION AS BROUGHT ON BY IMPERIEX.
AND NOW THE GREATEST HERO STANDS BEFORE A PHANTOM UNWELCOME. HE CHOKES BACK BATTLE-WEARY RAGE TO NOT ACCUSE THE MESSENGER.
YOU CAN'T HAVE HIM.
HE...HE MEANS TOO MUCH.
HE'S TOO... IMPORTANT.

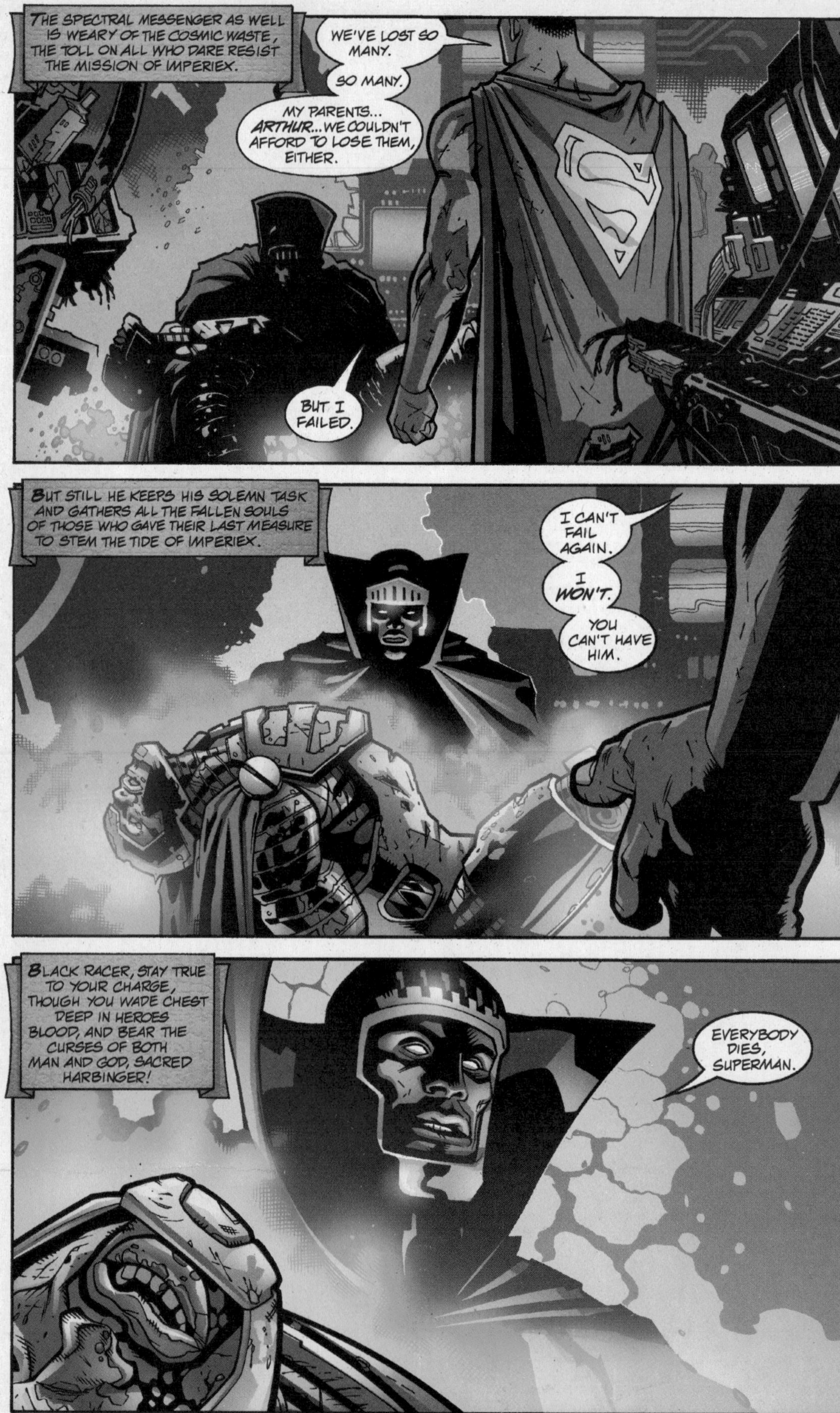
THE SPECTRAL MESSENGER AS WELL IS WEARY OF THE COSMIC WASTE, THE TOLL ON ALL WHO DARE RESIST THE MISSION OF IMPERIEX.
WE'VE LOST SO MANY.
SO MANY.
MY PARENTS... ARTHUR... WE COULDN'T AFFORD TO LOSE THEM, EITHER.
BUT I FAILED.
BUT STILL HE KEEPS HIS SOLEMN TASK AND GATHERS ALL THE FALLEN SOULS OF THOSE WHO GAVE THEIR LAST MEASURE TO STEM THE TIDE OF IMPERIEX.
I CAN'T FAIL AGAIN.
I WON'T.
YOU CAN'T HAVE HIM.
BLACK RACER, STAY TRUE TO YOUR CHARGE, THOUGH YOU WADE CHEST DEEP IN HEROES BLOOD, AND BEAR THE CURSES OF BOTH MAN AND GOD, SACRED HARBINGER!
EVERYBODY DIES, SUPERMAN.

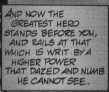

AND NOW THE GREATEST HERO STANDS BEFORE YOU, AND RAILS AT THAT WHICH IS WRIT BY A HIGHER POWER THAT DAZED AND NUMB HE CANNOT SEE.

DON'T. I'M WARNING YOU...

THIS IS *TOO* MUCH.

NO MORTAL BEING IS SO PERFECT TO ACCEPT ANNIHILATION COMPLETE, BUT FIRST MADE MANIFEST BY HEROES' LIFELINES, ONE BY ONE.

I MUST. YOU KNOW THIS IS A GREAT HONOR.

NOT EVERYONE DIES A WARRIOR TO BE PERSONALLY ESCORTED INTO ETERNITY BY THE BLACK RACER.

NEITHER YOU, BLACK-EST OF RACERS, NOR THE SUPERMAN OPPOSED CAN FOREVER BEAR UNBROKEN...

I KNOW. BUT *THIS* TIME...

...I CAN'T LET YOU.

...THE WEIGHT OF ALL WHO'VE GONE BEFORE.

DO NOT BE FOOLISH, SUPERMAN. YOU CANNOT FIGHT...

# BARRRROOOM

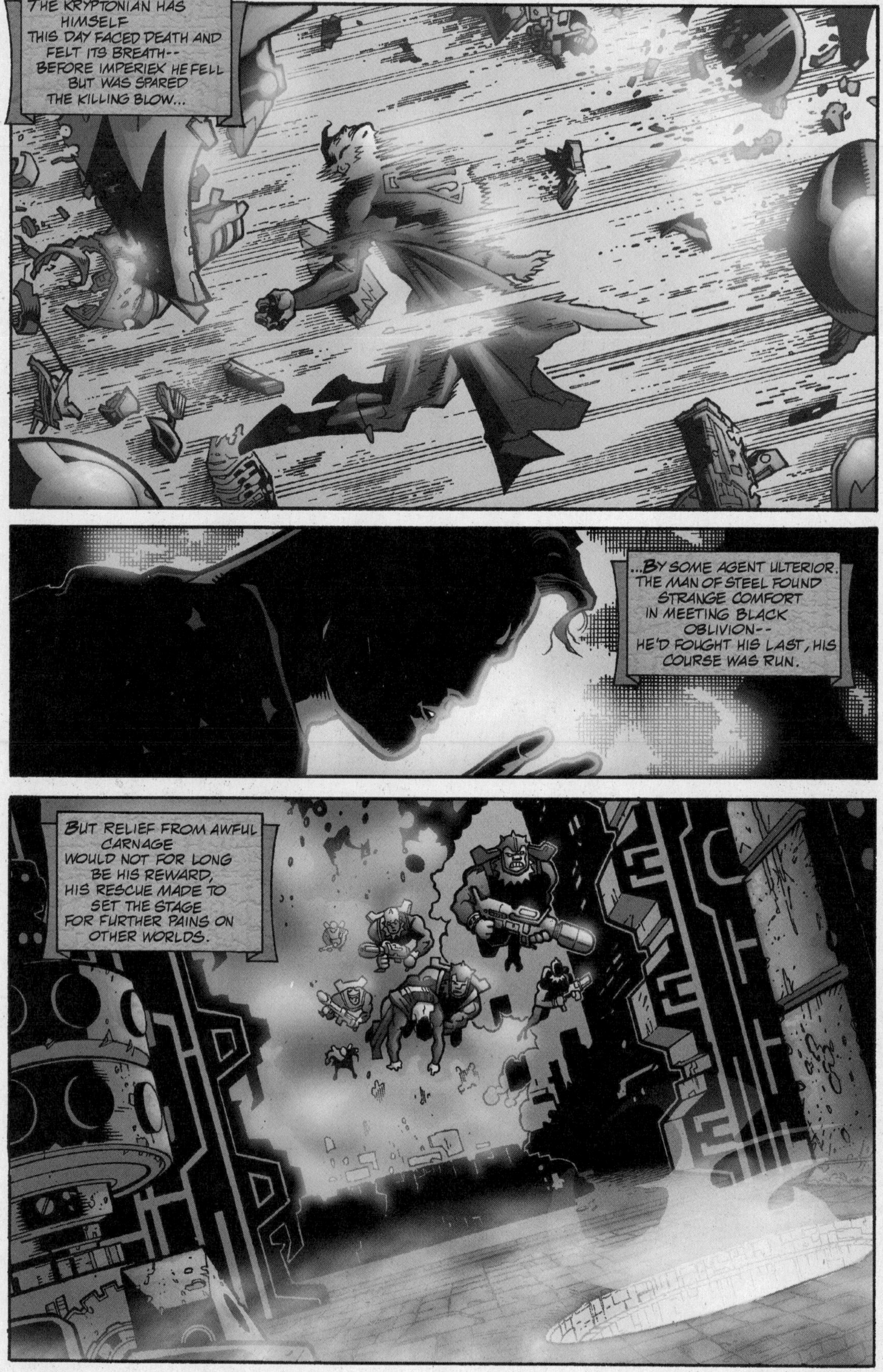
THE KRYPTONIAN HAS HIMSELF THIS DAY FACED DEATH AND FELT ITS BREATH-- BEFORE IMPERIEX HE FELL BUT WAS SPARED THE KILLING BLOW...
...BY SOME AGENT ULTERIOR. THE MAN OF STEEL FOUND STRANGE COMFORT IN MEETING BLACK OBLIVION-- HE'D FOUGHT HIS LAST, HIS COURSE WAS RUN.
BUT RELIEF FROM AWFUL CARNAGE WOULD NOT FOR LONG BE HIS REWARD, HIS RESCUE MADE TO SET THE STAGE FOR FURTHER PAINS ON OTHER WORLDS.

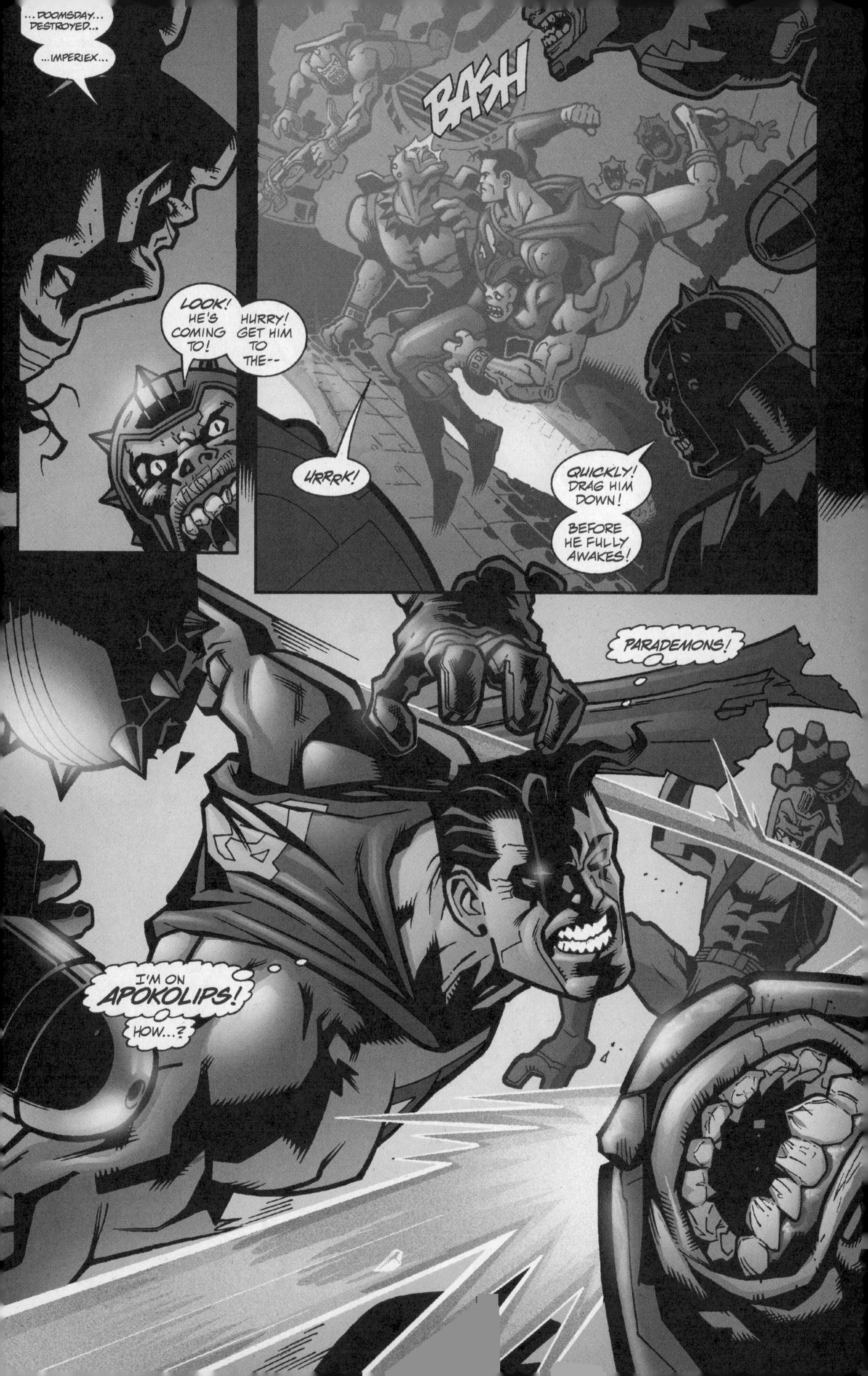
...DOOMSDAY... DESTROYED...
...IMPERIEX...
BASH
LOOK! HE'S COMING TO!
HURRY! GET HIM TO THE--
URRRK!
QUICKLY! DRAG HIM DOWN!
BEFORE HE FULLY AWAKES!
PARADEMONS!
I'M ON APOKOLIPS!
HOW...?

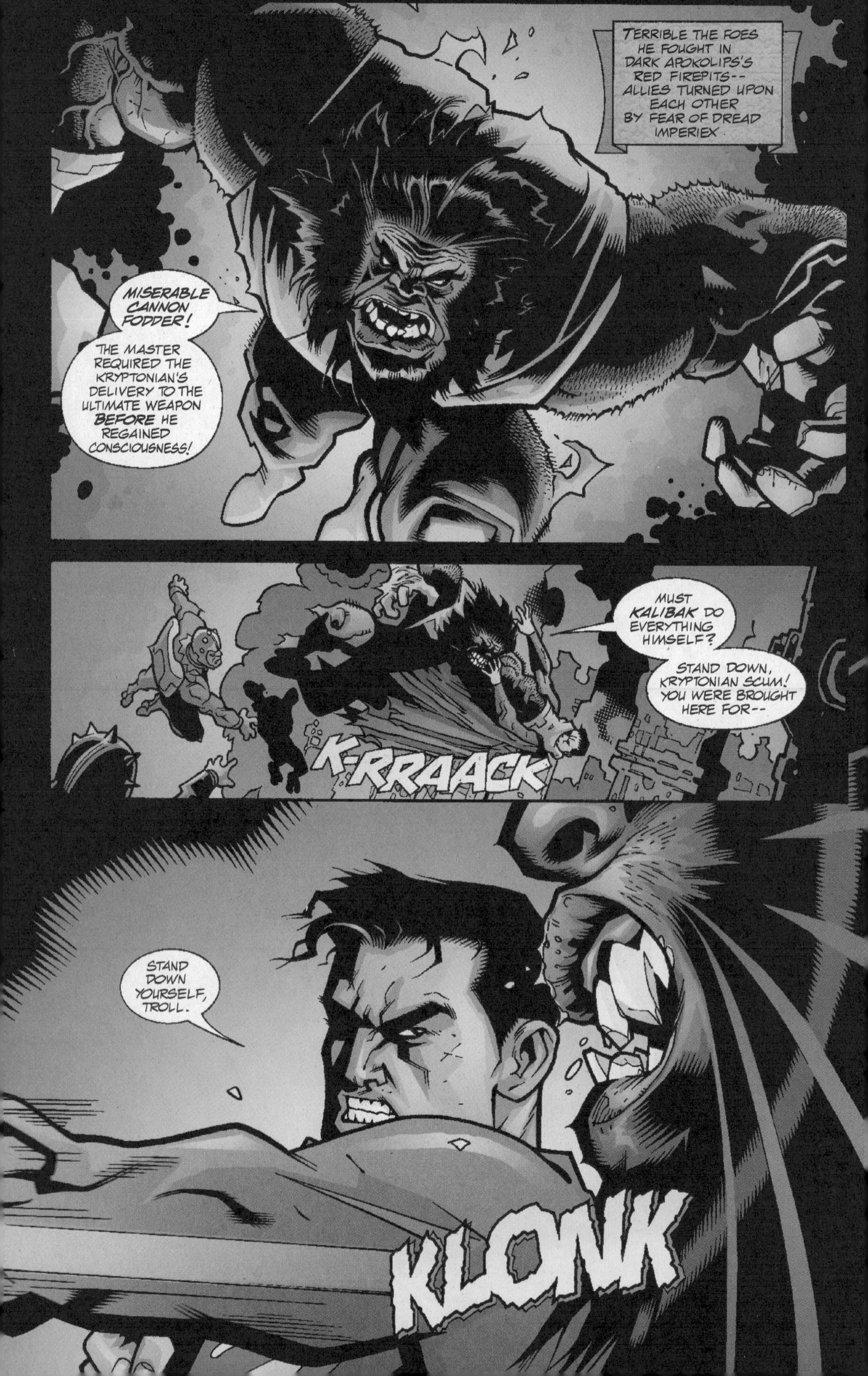

TERRIBLE THE FOES HE FOUGHT IN DARK APOKOLIPS'S RED FIREPITS-- ALLIES TURNED UPON EACH OTHER BY FEAR OF DREAD IMPERIEX
MISERABLE CANNON FODDER!
THE MASTER REQUIRED THE KRYPTONIAN'S DELIVERY TO THE ULTIMATE WEAPON BEFORE HE REGAINED CONSCIOUSNESS!
MUST KALIBAK DO EVERYTHING HIMSELF?
STAND DOWN, KRYPTONIAN SCUM! YOU WERE BROUGHT HERE FOR--
K-RRAACK
STAND DOWN YOURSELF, TROLL.
KLONK

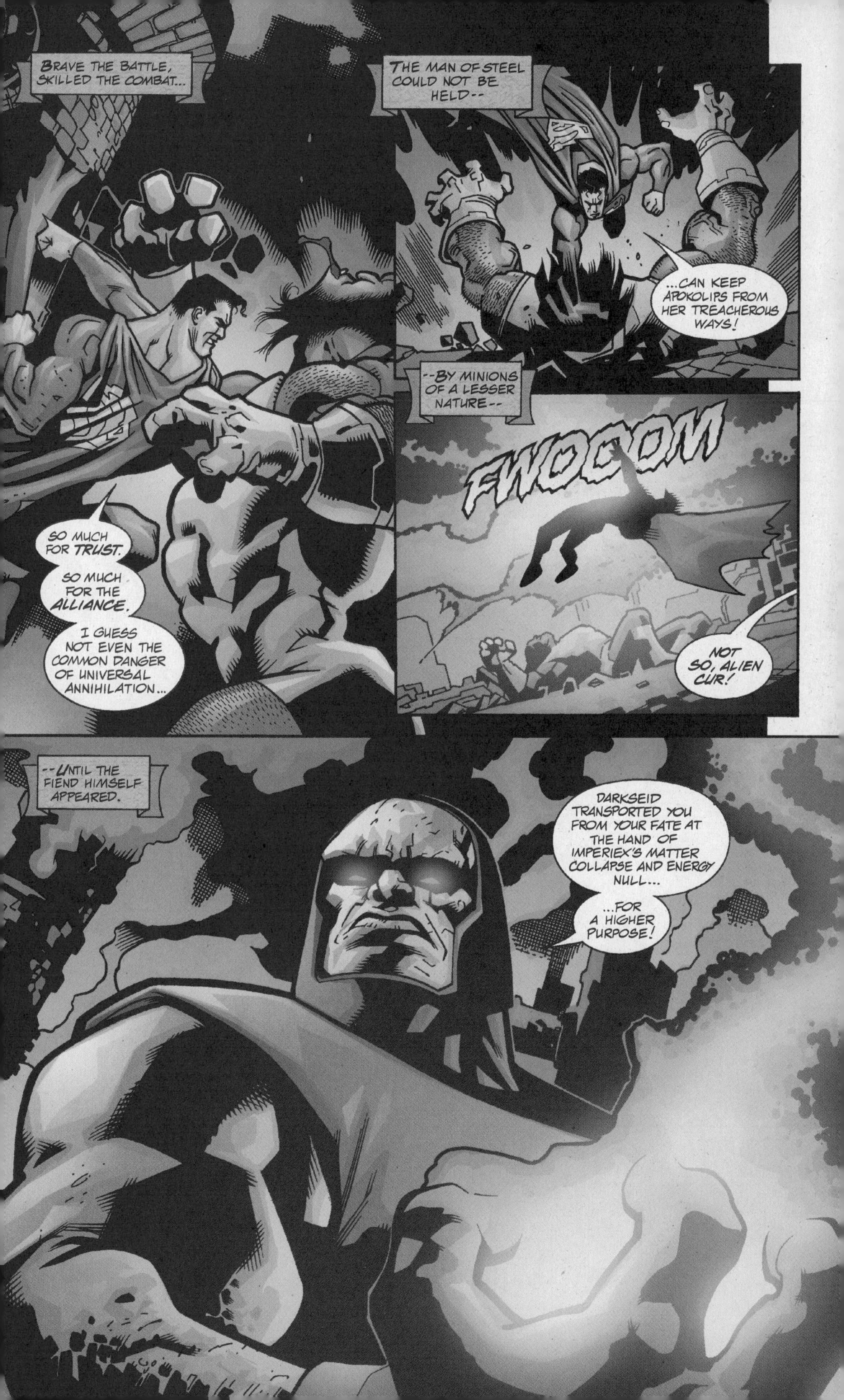
BRAVE THE BATTLE, SKILLED THE COMBAT...
SO MUCH FOR TRUST.
SO MUCH FOR THE ALLIANCE.
I GUESS NOT EVEN THE COMMON DANGER OF UNIVERSAL ANNIHILATION...
THE MAN OF STEEL COULD NOT BE HELD--
...CAN KEEP APOKOLIPS FROM HER TREACHEROUS WAYS!
--BY MINIONS OF A LESSER NATURE--
FWOOOM
NOT SO, ALIEN CUR!
--UNTIL THE FIEND HIMSELF APPEARED.
DARKSEID TRANSPORTED YOU FROM YOUR FATE AT THE HAND OF IMPERIEX'S MATTER COLLAPSE AND ENERGY NULL...
...FOR A HIGHER PURPOSE!

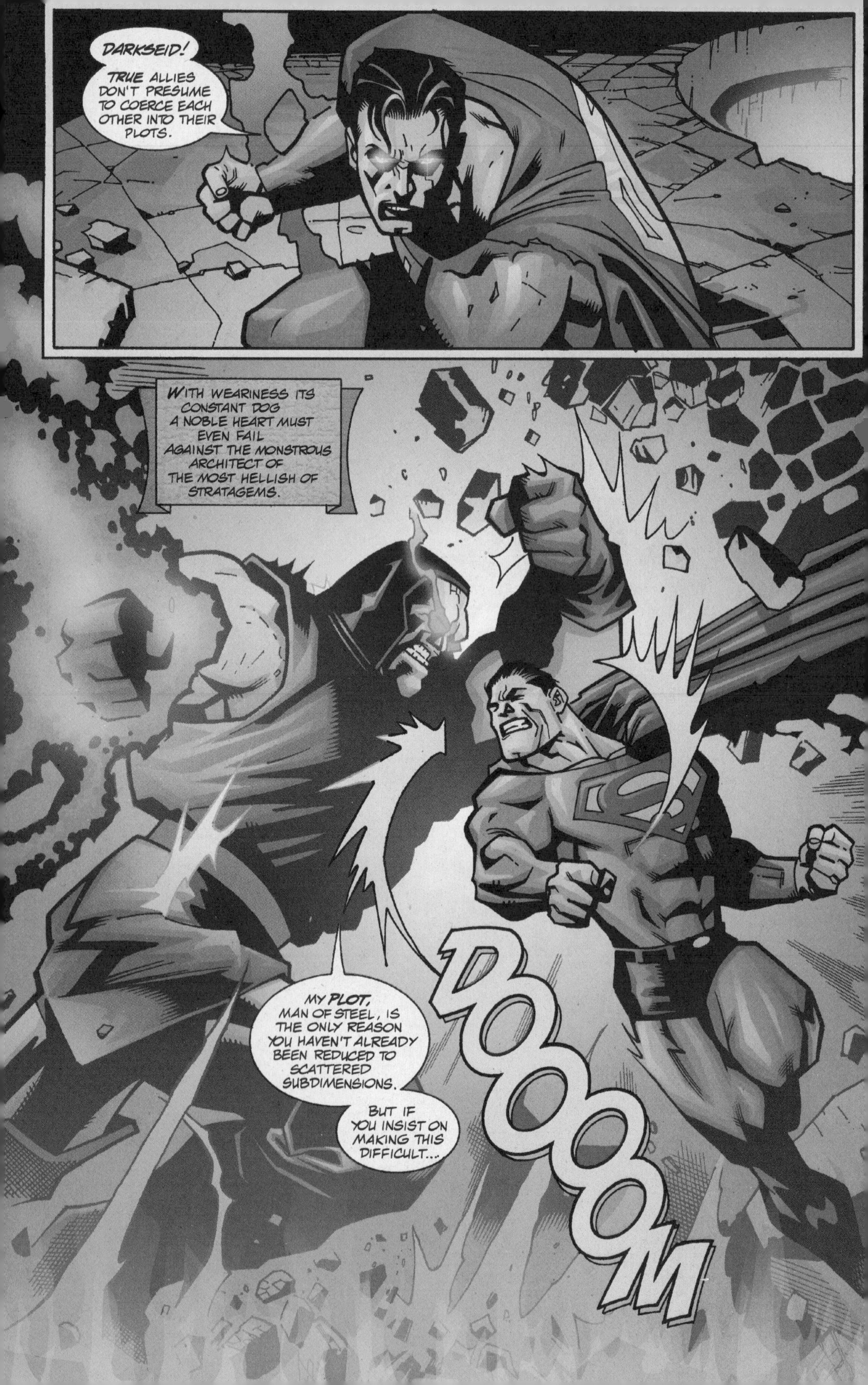
DARKSEID!
TRUE ALLIES DON'T PRESUME TO COERCE EACH OTHER INTO THEIR PLOTS.
WITH WEARINESS ITS CONSTANT DOG A NOBLE HEART MUST EVEN FAIL AGAINST THE MONSTROUS ARCHITECT OF THE MOST HELLISH OF STRATAGEMS.
MY PLOT, MAN OF STEEL, IS THE ONLY REASON YOU HAVEN'T ALREADY BEEN REDUCED TO SCATTERED SUBDIMENSIONS.
BUT IF YOU INSIST ON MAKING THIS DIFFICULT...
DOOOOOM

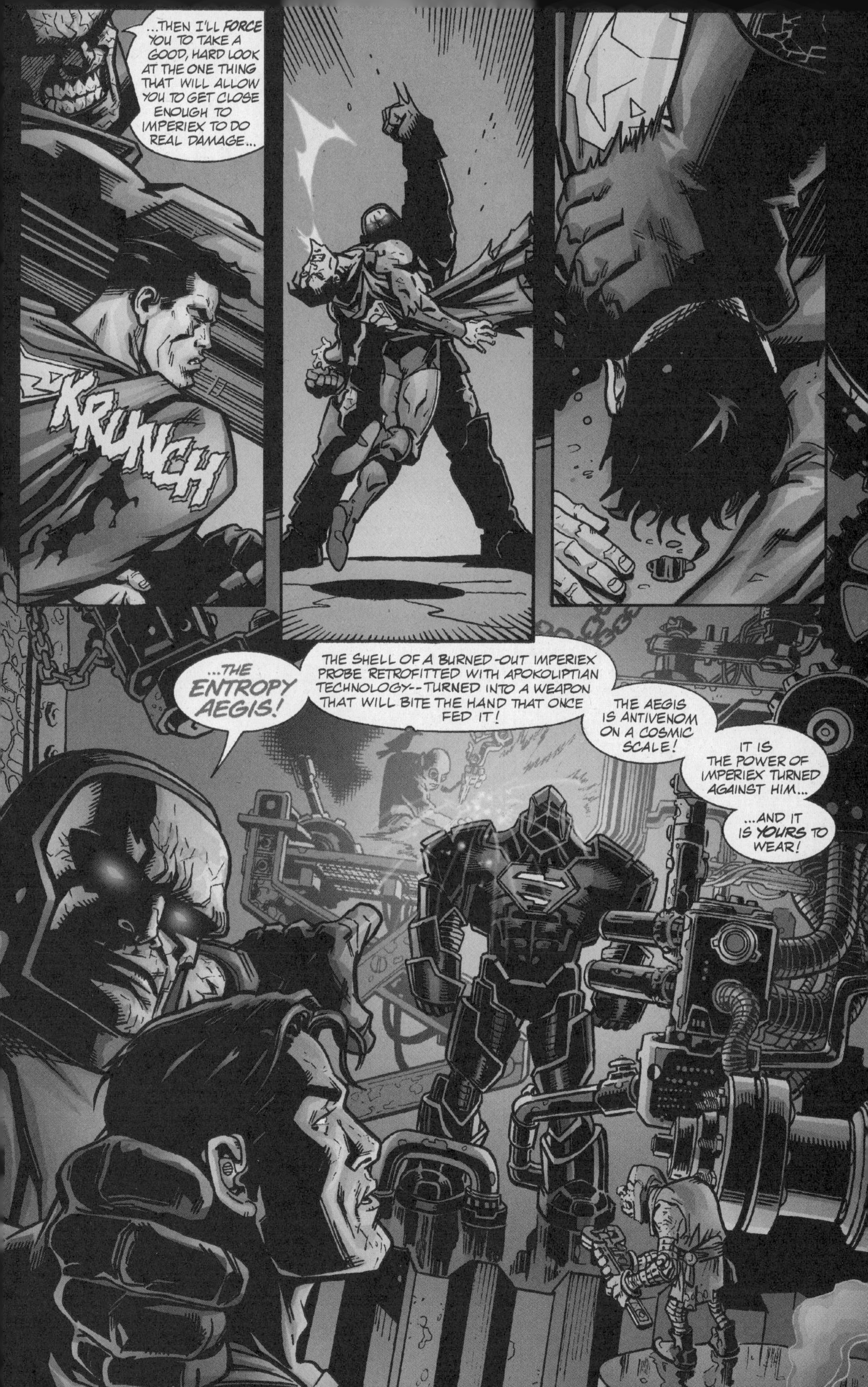
...THEN I'LL FORCE YOU TO TAKE A GOOD, HARD LOOK AT THE ONE THING THAT WILL ALLOW YOU TO GET CLOSE ENOUGH TO IMPERIEX TO DO REAL DAMAGE...
KRUNCH
...THE ENTROPY AEGIS!
THE SHELL OF A BURNED-OUT IMPERIEX PROBE RETROFITTED WITH APOKOLIPTIAN TECHNOLOGY--TURNED INTO A WEAPON THAT WILL BITE THE HAND THAT ONCE FED IT!
THE AEGIS IS ANTIVENOM ON A COSMIC SCALE!
IT IS THE POWER OF IMPERIEX TURNED AGAINST HIM...
...AND IT IS YOURS TO WEAR!

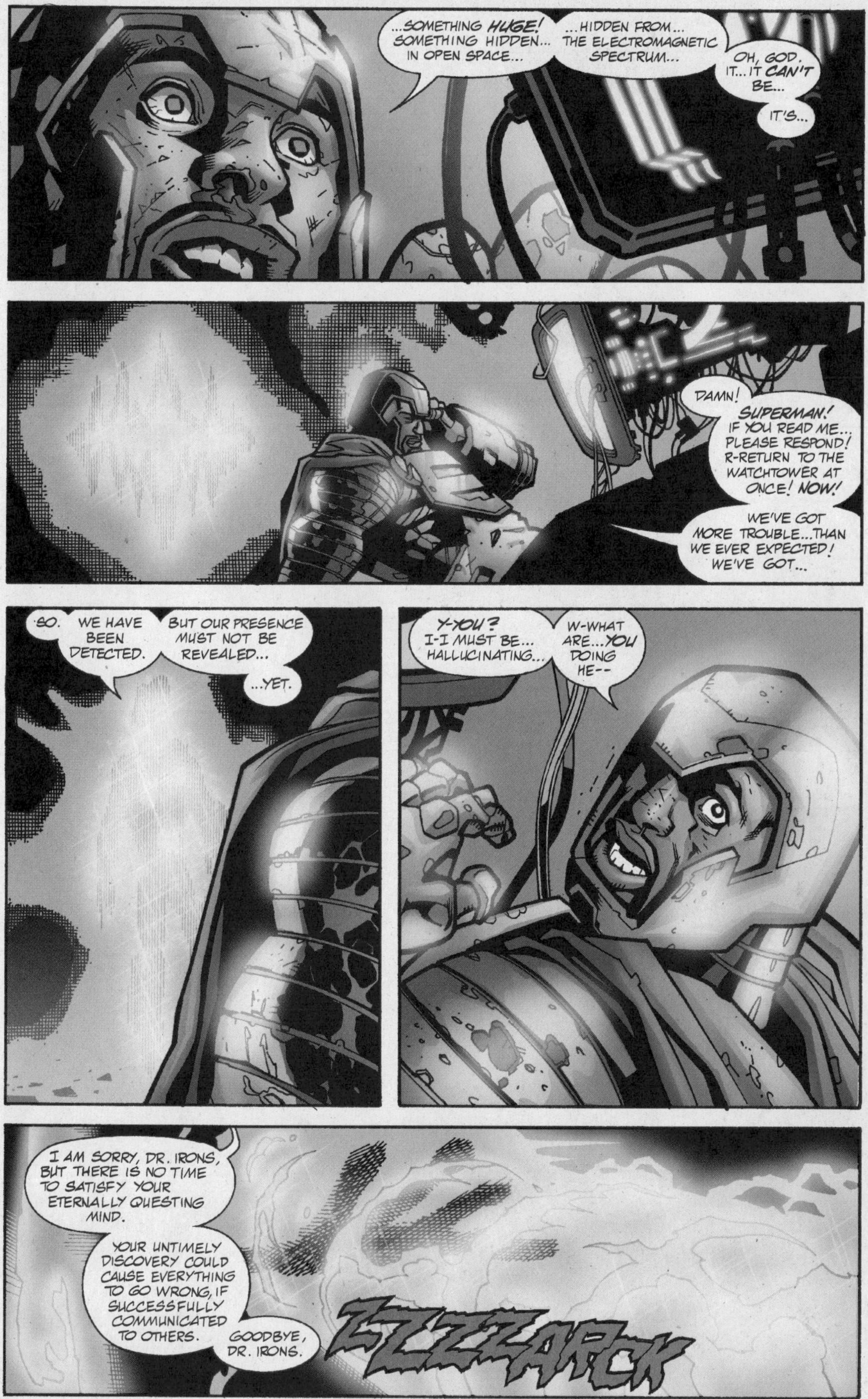
...SOMETHING HUGE! SOMETHING HIDDEN... IN OPEN SPACE...
...HIDDEN FROM... THE ELECTROMAGNETIC SPECTRUM...
OH, GOD. IT... IT CAN'T BE...
IT'S...
DAMN!
SUPERMAN! IF YOU READ ME... PLEASE RESPOND! R-RETURN TO THE WATCHTOWER AT ONCE! NOW!
WE'VE GOT MORE TROUBLE...THAN WE EVER EXPECTED! WE'VE GOT...
SO. WE HAVE BEEN DETECTED.
BUT OUR PRESENCE MUST NOT BE REVEALED...
...YET.
Y-YOU? I-I MUST BE... HALLUCINATING...
W-WHAT ARE...YOU DOING HE--
I AM SORRY, DR. IRONS, BUT THERE IS NO TIME TO SATISFY YOUR ETERNALLY QUESTING MIND.
YOUR UNTIMELY DISCOVERY COULD CAUSE EVERYTHING TO GO WRONG, IF SUCCESSFULLY COMMUNICATED TO OTHERS.
GOODBYE, DR. IRONS.
ZZZZARCK

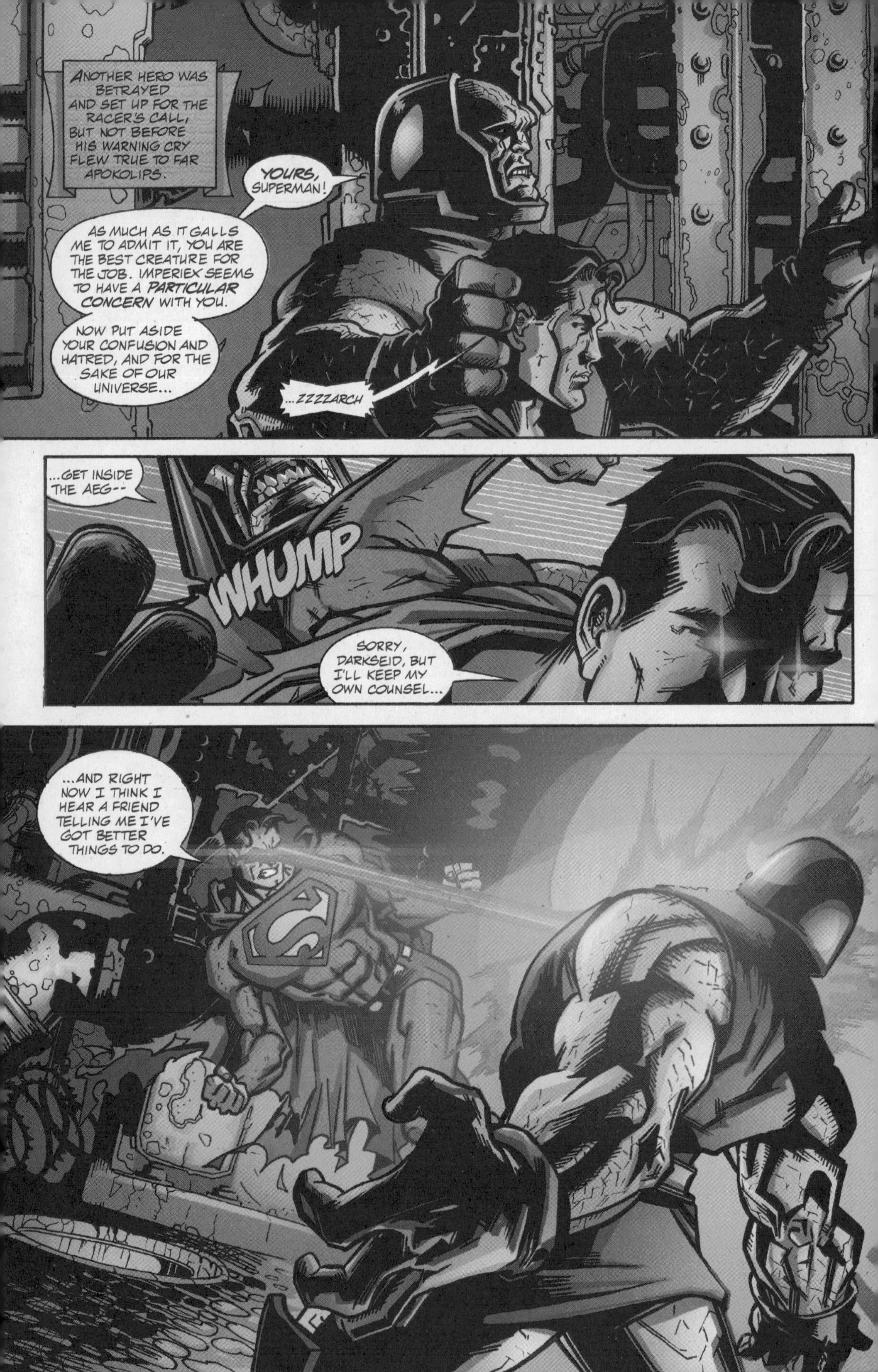

ANOTHER HERO WAS BETRAYED AND SET UP FOR THE RACER'S CALL, BUT NOT BEFORE HIS WARNING CRY FLEW TRUE TO FAR APOKOLIPS.
YOURS, SUPERMAN!
AS MUCH AS IT GALLS ME TO ADMIT IT, YOU ARE THE BEST CREATURE FOR THE JOB. IMPERIEX SEEMS TO HAVE A PARTICULAR CONCERN WITH YOU.
NOW PUT ASIDE YOUR CONFUSION AND HATRED, AND FOR THE SAKE OF OUR UNIVERSE...
...ZZZZARCH
...GET INSIDE THE AEG--
WHUMP
SORRY, DARKSEID, BUT I'LL KEEP MY OWN COUNSEL...
...AND RIGHT NOW I THINK I HEAR A FRIEND TELLING ME I'VE GOT BETTER THINGS TO DO.

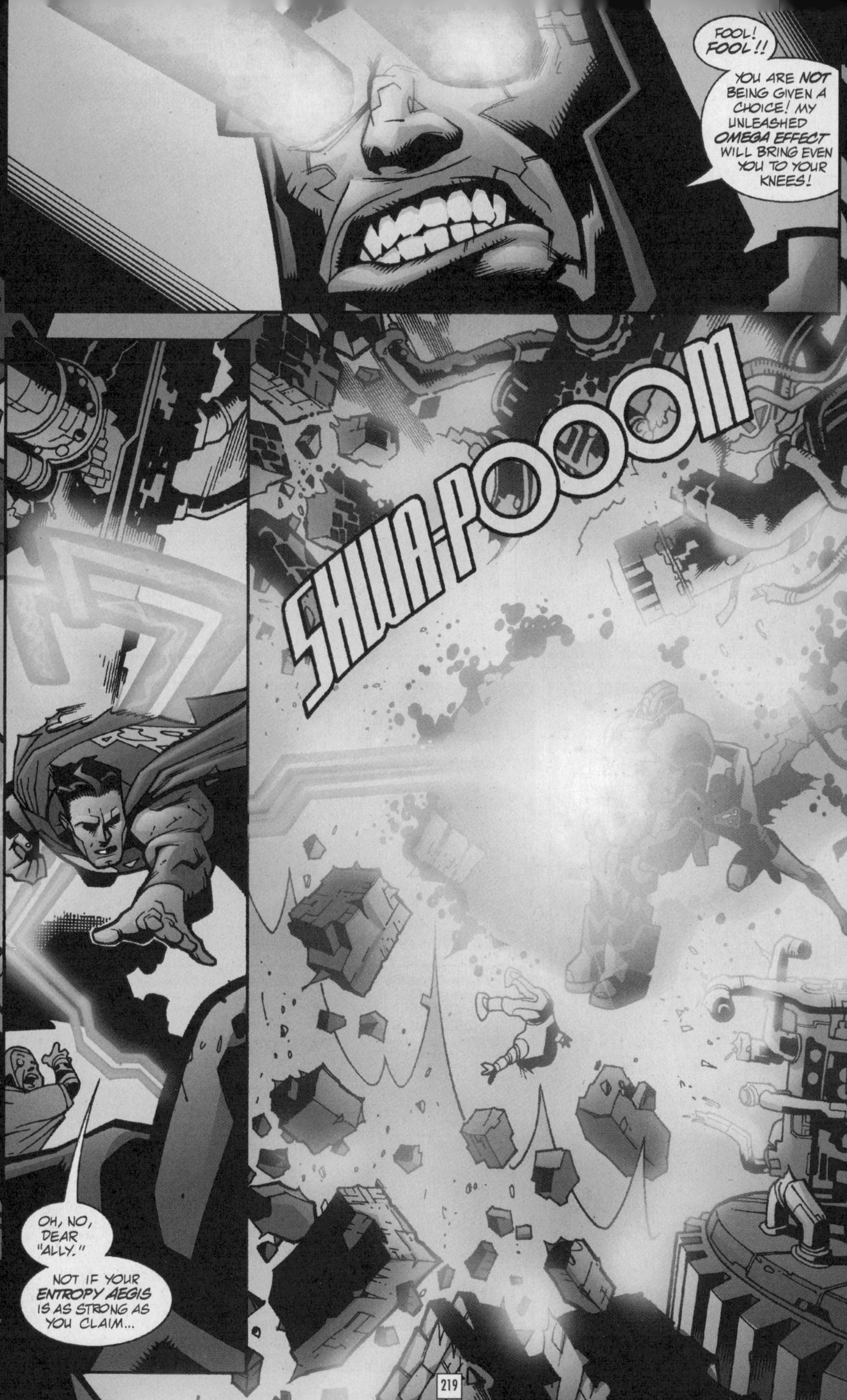
FOOL! FOOL!!
YOU ARE NOT BEING GIVEN A CHOICE! MY UNLEASHED OMEGA EFFECT WILL BRING EVEN YOU TO YOUR KNEES!
SHWA-POOOOM
OH, NO, DEAR "ALLY."
NOT IF YOUR ENTROPY AEGIS IS AS STRONG AS YOU CLAIM...

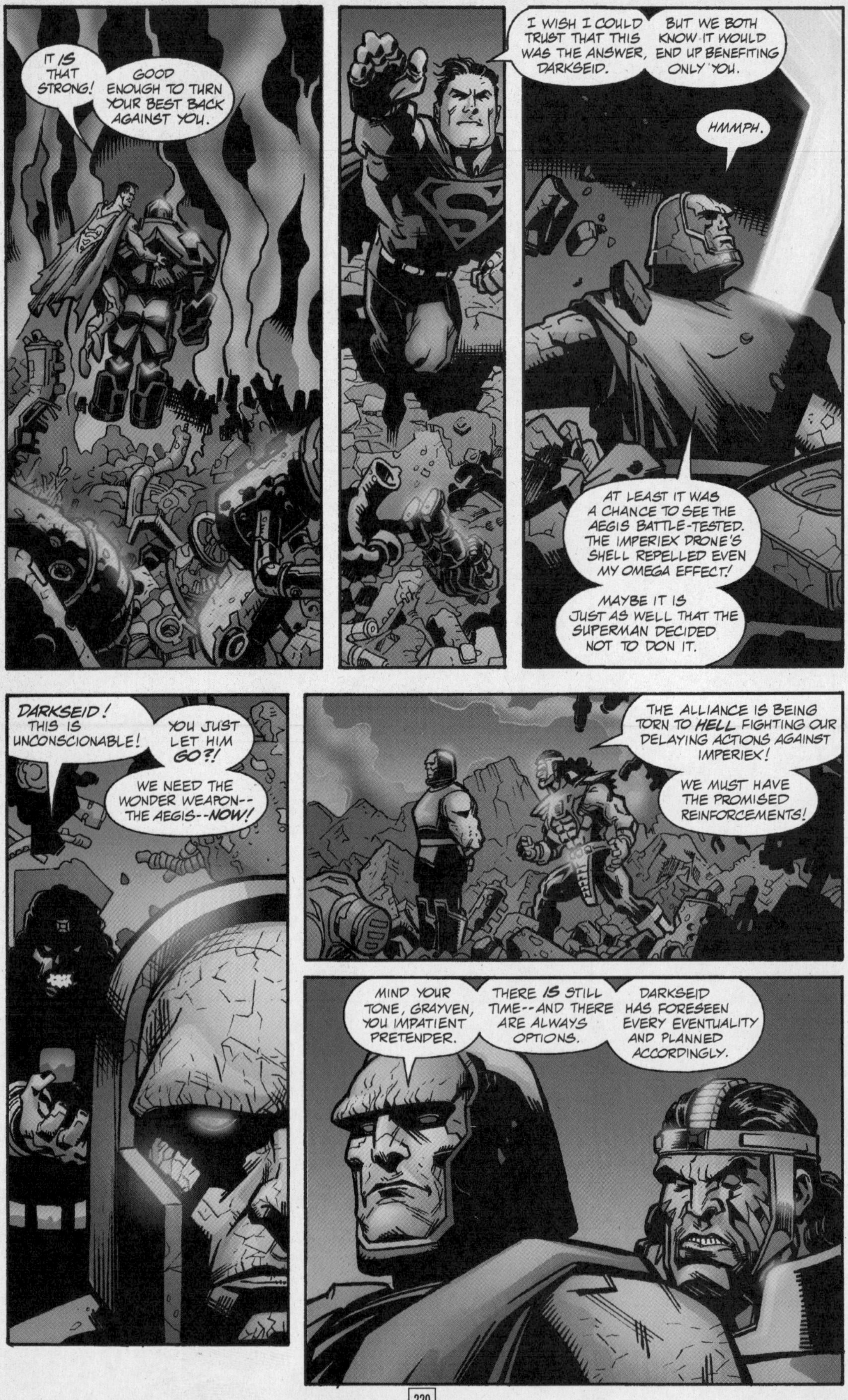
IT IS THAT STRONG!
GOOD ENOUGH TO TURN YOUR BEST BACK AGAINST YOU.
I WISH I COULD TRUST THAT THIS WAS THE ANSWER, DARKSEID.
BUT WE BOTH KNOW IT WOULD END UP BENEFITING ONLY YOU.
HMMPH.
AT LEAST IT WAS A CHANCE TO SEE THE AEGIS BATTLE-TESTED. THE IMPERIEX DRONE'S SHELL REPELLED EVEN MY OMEGA EFFECT!
MAYBE IT IS JUST AS WELL THAT THE SUPERMAN DECIDED NOT TO DON IT.
DARKSEID! THIS IS UNCONSCIONABLE!
YOU JUST LET HIM GO?!
WE NEED THE WONDER WEAPON--THE AEGIS--NOW!
THE ALLIANCE IS BEING TORN TO HELL FIGHTING OUR DELAYING ACTIONS AGAINST IMPERIEX!
WE MUST HAVE THE PROMISED REINFORCEMENTS!
MIND YOUR TONE, GRAYVEN, YOU IMPATIENT PRETENDER.
THERE IS STILL TIME--AND THERE ARE ALWAYS OPTIONS.
DARKSEID HAS FORESEEN EVERY EVENTUALITY AND PLANNED ACCORDINGLY.

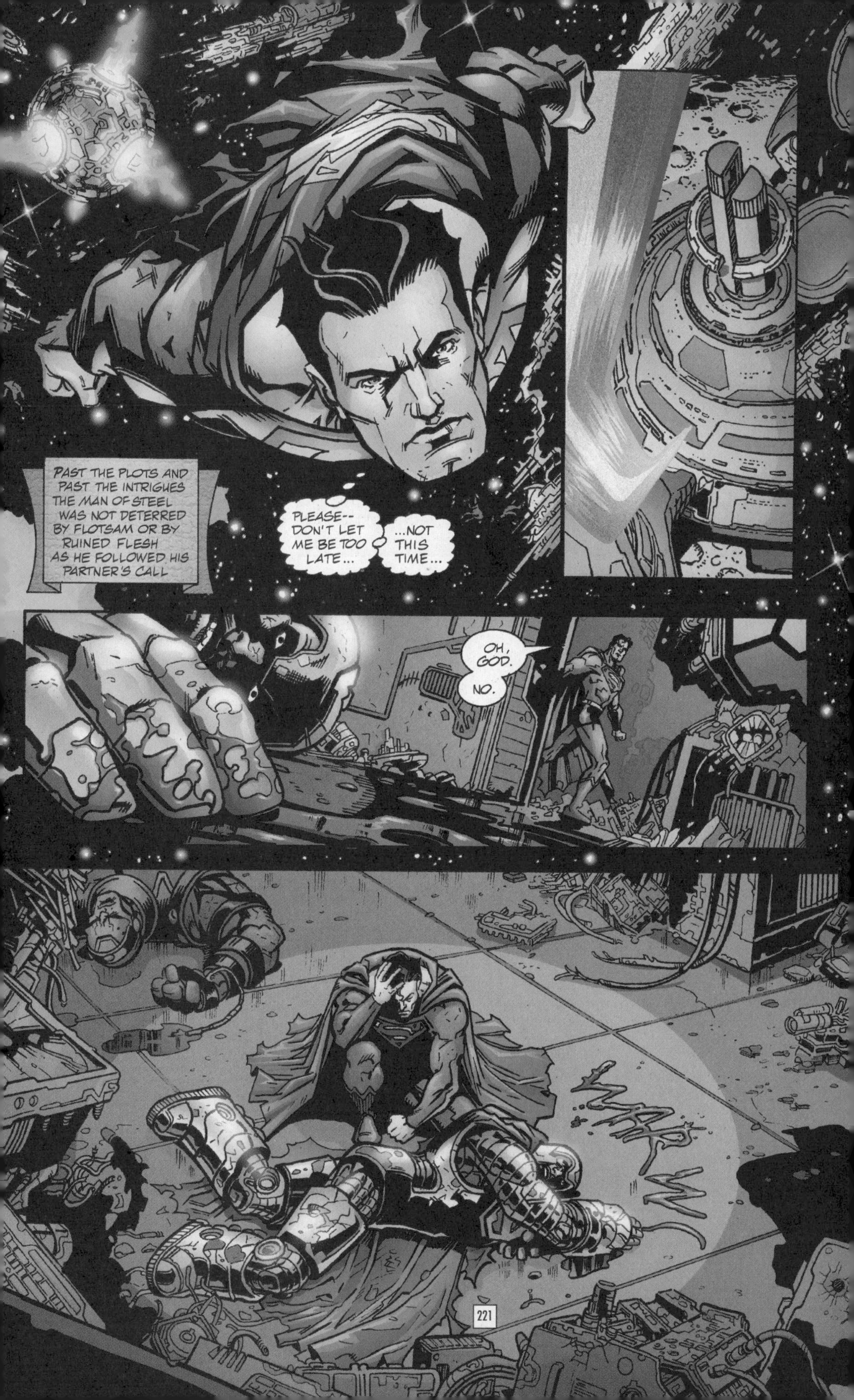
PAST THE PLOTS AND PAST THE INTRIGUES THE MAN OF STEEL WAS NOT DETERRED BY FLOTSAM OR BY RUINED FLESH AS HE FOLLOWED HIS PARTNER'S CALL
PLEASE-- DON'T LET ME BE TOO LATE...
...NOT THIS TIME...
OH, GOD.
NO.

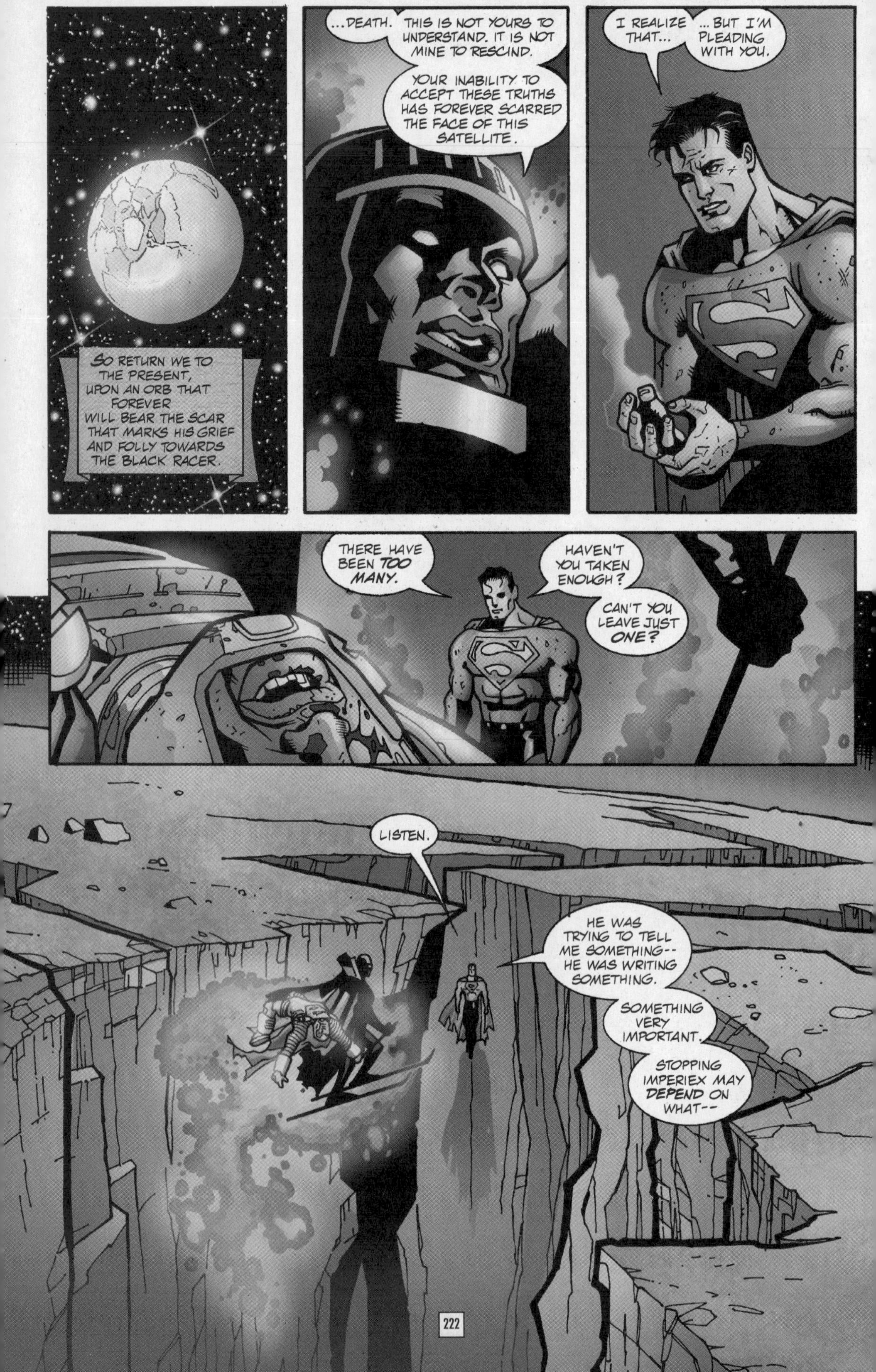

SO RETURN WE TO THE PRESENT, UPON AN ORB THAT FOREVER WILL BEAR THE SCAR THAT MARKS HIS GRIEF AND FOLLY TOWARDS THE BLACK RACER.
...DEATH.
THIS IS NOT YOURS TO UNDERSTAND. IT IS NOT MINE TO RESCIND.
YOUR INABILITY TO ACCEPT THESE TRUTHS HAS FOREVER SCARRED THE FACE OF THIS SATELLITE.
I REALIZE THAT...
...BUT I'M PLEADING WITH YOU.
THERE HAVE BEEN TOO MANY.
HAVEN'T YOU TAKEN ENOUGH?
CAN'T YOU LEAVE JUST ONE?
LISTEN.
HE WAS TRYING TO TELL ME SOMETHING-- HE WAS WRITING SOMETHING.
SOMETHING VERY IMPORTANT.
STOPPING IMPERIEX MAY DEPEND ON WHAT--

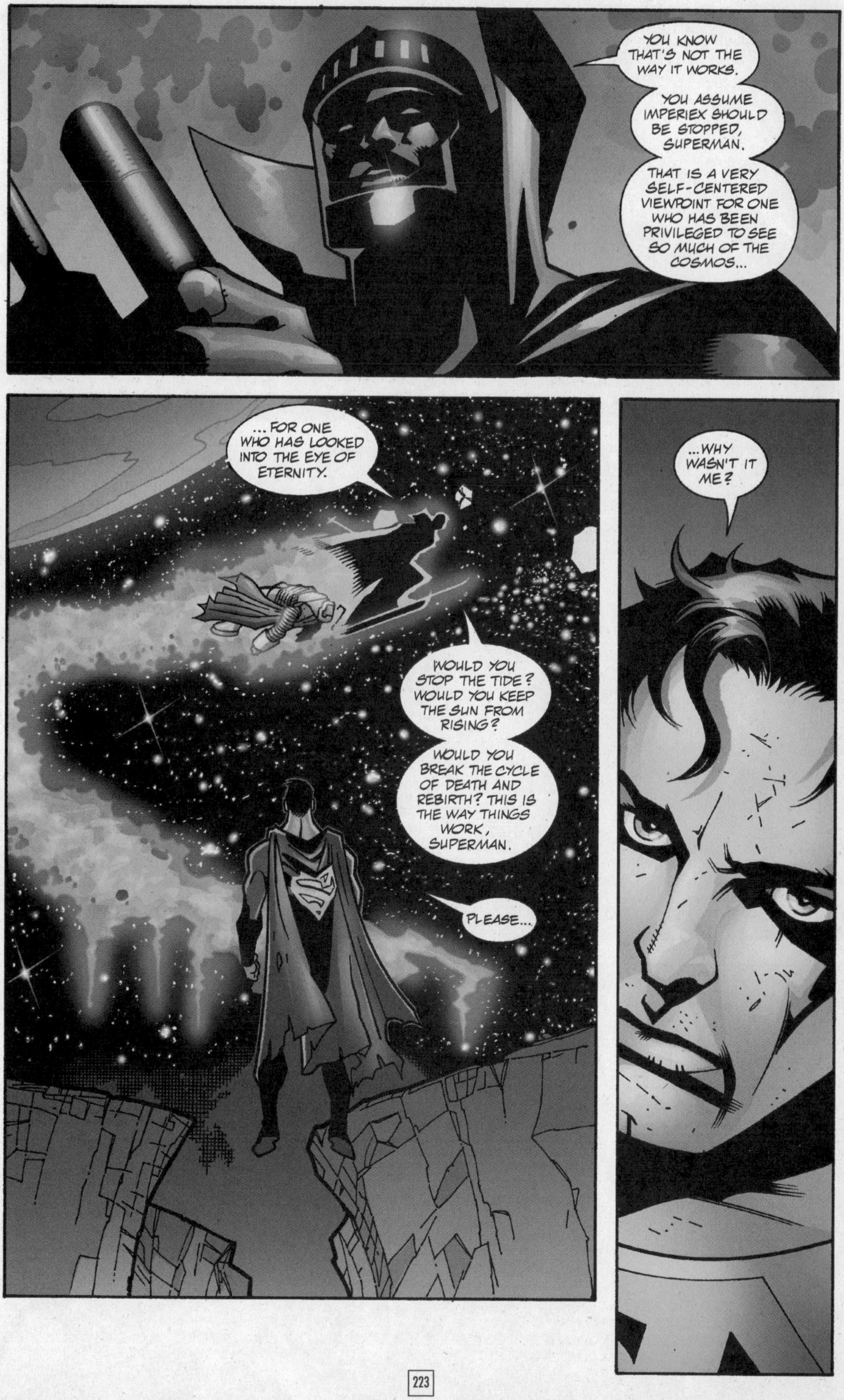
YOU KNOW THAT'S NOT THE WAY IT WORKS.
YOU ASSUME IMPERIEX SHOULD BE STOPPED, SUPERMAN.
THAT IS A VERY SELF-CENTERED VIEWPOINT FOR ONE WHO HAS BEEN PRIVILEGED TO SEE SO MUCH OF THE COSMOS...
... FOR ONE WHO HAS LOOKED INTO THE EYE OF ETERNITY.
WOULD YOU STOP THE TIDE? WOULD YOU KEEP THE SUN FROM RISING?
WOULD YOU BREAK THE CYCLE OF DEATH AND REBIRTH? THIS IS THE WAY THINGS WORK, SUPERMAN.
PLEASE...
...WHY WASN'T IT ME?

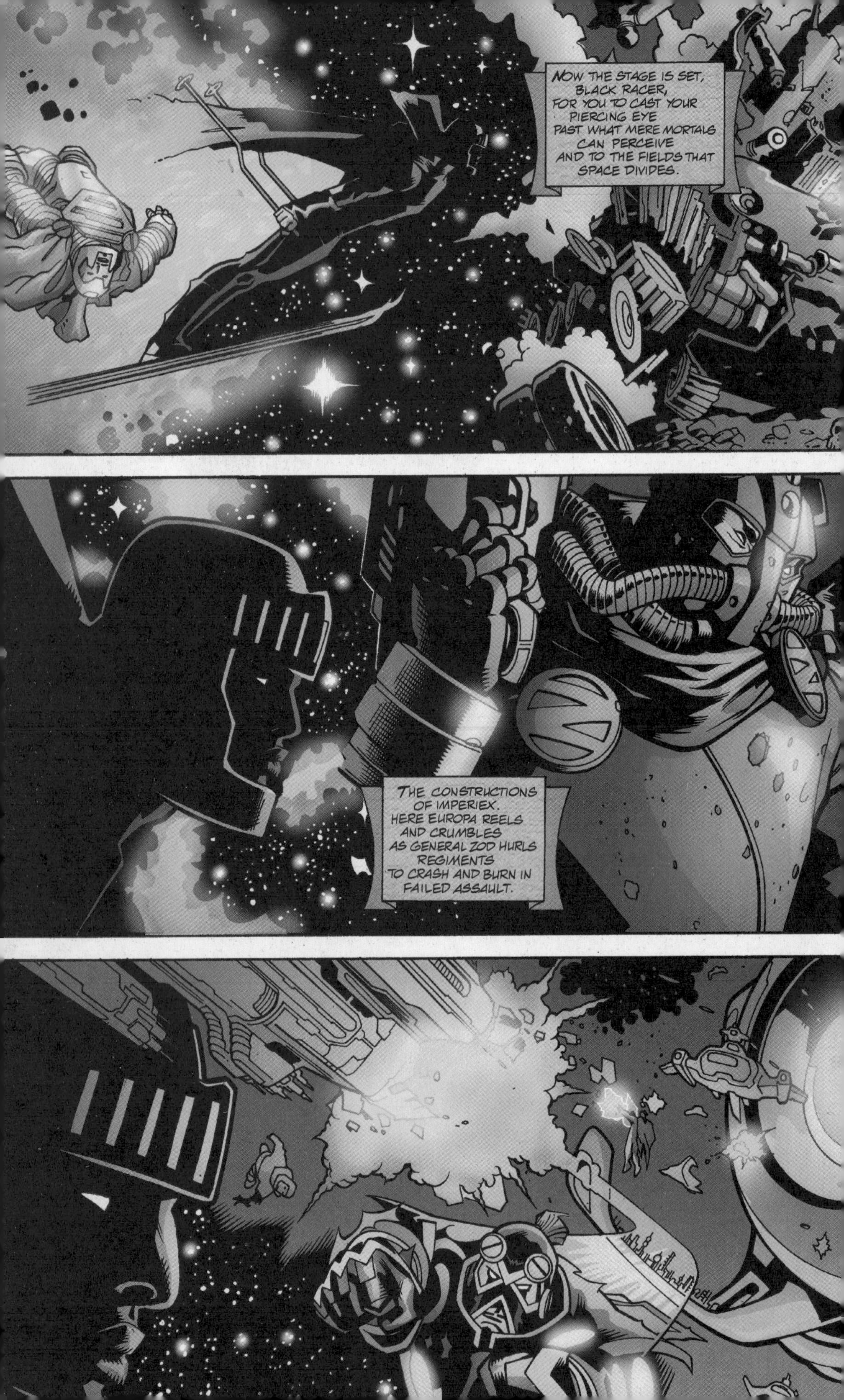
NOW THE STAGE IS SET, BLACK RACER, FOR YOU TO CAST YOUR PIERCING EYE PAST WHAT MERE MORTALS CAN PERCEIVE AND TO THE FIELDS THAT SPACE DIVIDES.
THE CONSTRUCTIONS OF IMPERIEX. HERE EUROPA REELS AND CRUMBLES AS GENERAL ZOD HURLS REGIMENTS TO CRASH AND BURN IN FAILED ASSAULT.

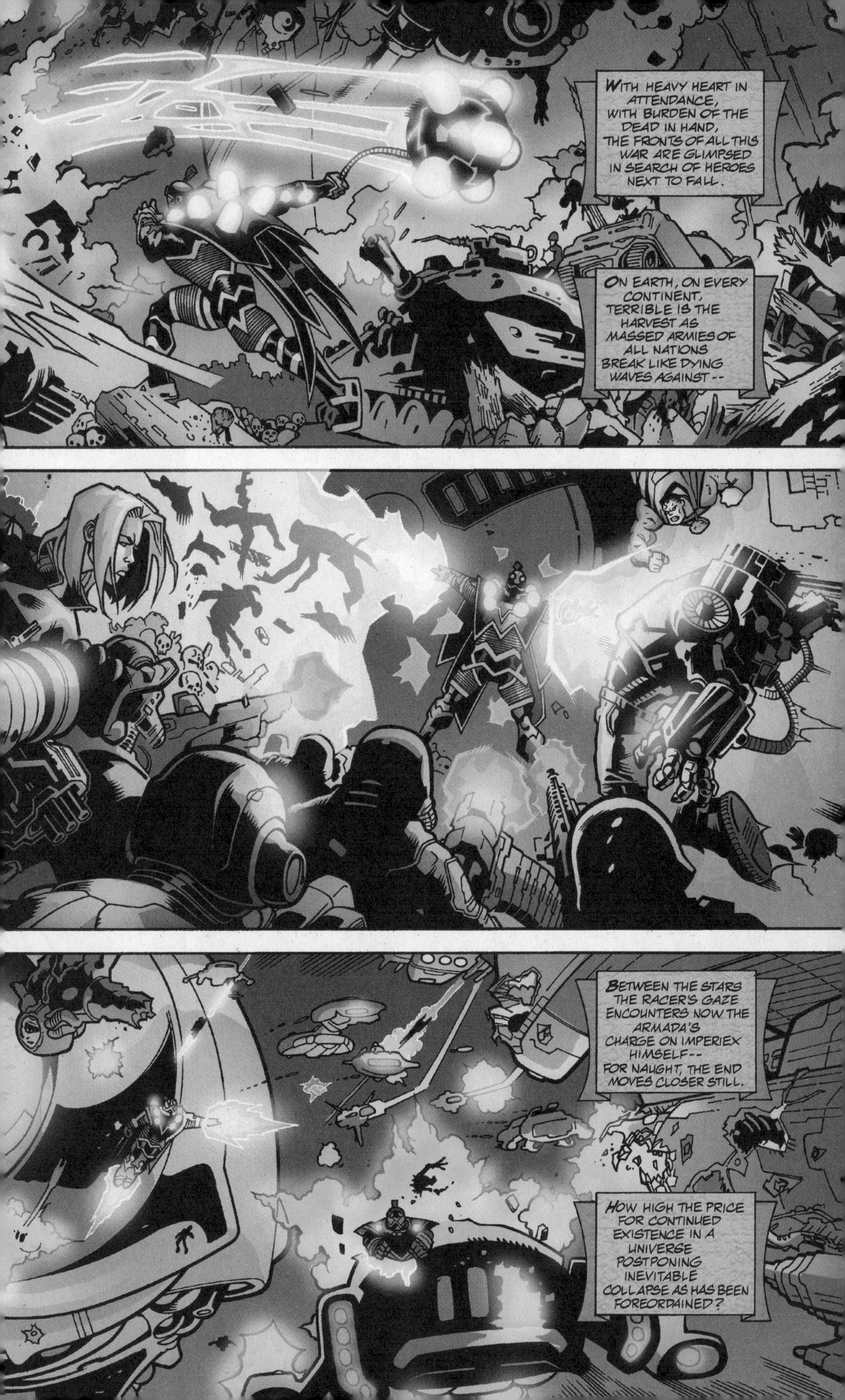
WITH HEAVY HEART IN ATTENDANCE, WITH BURDEN OF THE DEAD IN HAND, THE FRONTS OF ALL THIS WAR ARE GLIMPSED IN SEARCH OF HEROES NEXT TO FALL.
ON EARTH, ON EVERY CONTINENT, TERRIBLE IS THE HARVEST AS MASSED ARMIES OF ALL NATIONS BREAK LIKE DYING WAVES AGAINST --
BETWEEN THE STARS THE RACER'S GAZE ENCOUNTERS NOW THE ARMADA'S CHARGE ON IMPERIEX HIMSELF-- FOR NAUGHT, THE END MOVES CLOSER STILL.
HOW HIGH THE PRICE FOR CONTINUED EXISTENCE IN A UNIVERSE POSTPONING INEVITABLE COLLAPSE AS HAS BEEN FOREORDAINED?

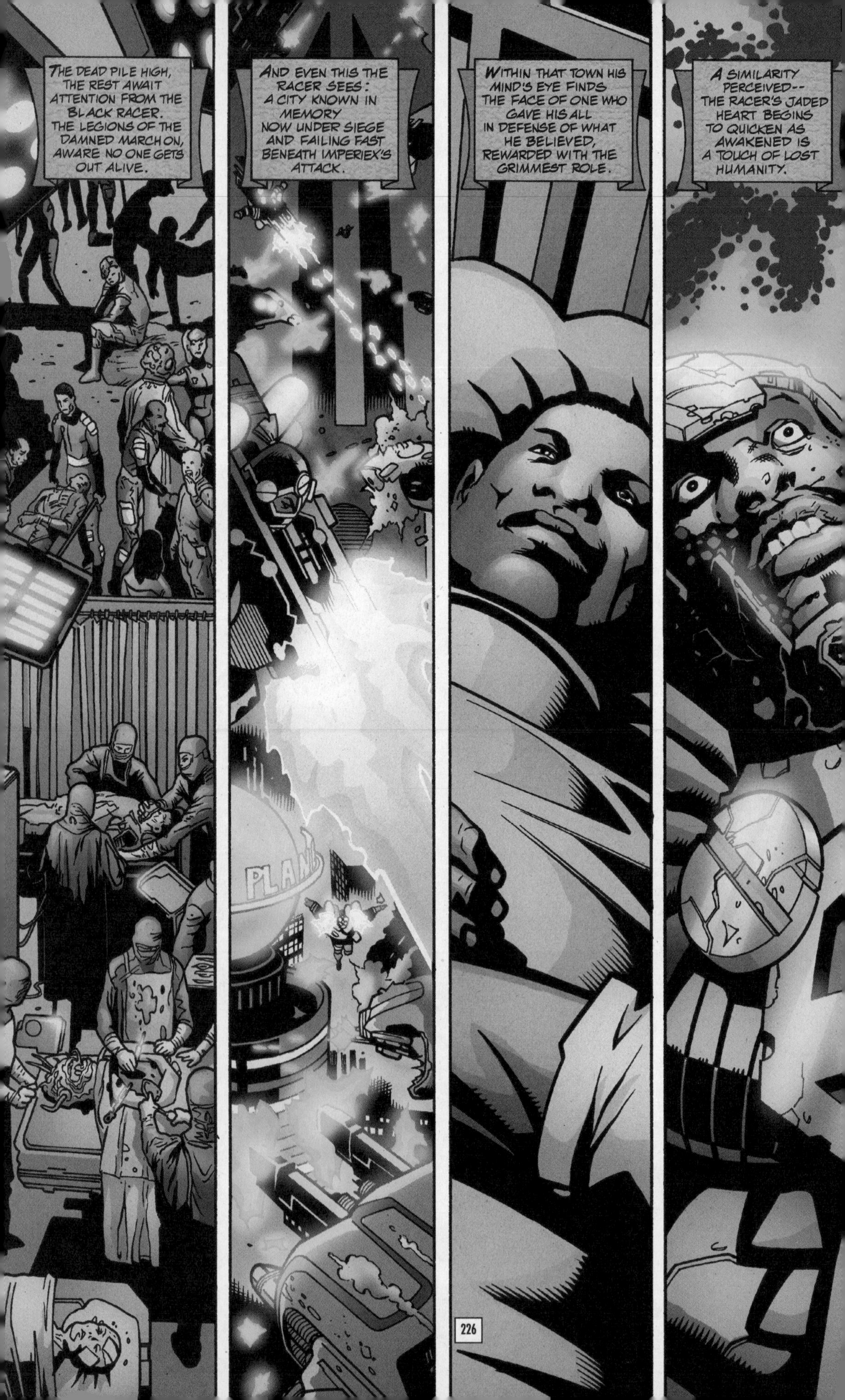
THE DEAD PILE HIGH, THE REST AWAIT ATTENTION FROM THE BLACK RACER. THE LEGIONS OF THE DAMNED MARCH ON, AWARE NO ONE GETS OUT ALIVE.
AND EVEN THIS THE RACER SEES: A CITY KNOWN IN MEMORY NOW UNDER SIEGE AND FAILING FAST BENEATH IMPERIEX'S ATTACK.
PLAN
WITHIN THAT TOWN HIS MIND'S EYE FINDS THE FACE OF ONE WHO GAVE HIS ALL IN DEFENSE OF WHAT HE BELIEVED, REWARDED WITH THE GRIMMEST ROLE.
A SIMILARITY PERCEIVED-- THE RACER'S JADED HEART BEGINS TO QUICKEN AS AWAKENED IS A TOUCH OF LOST HUMANITY.

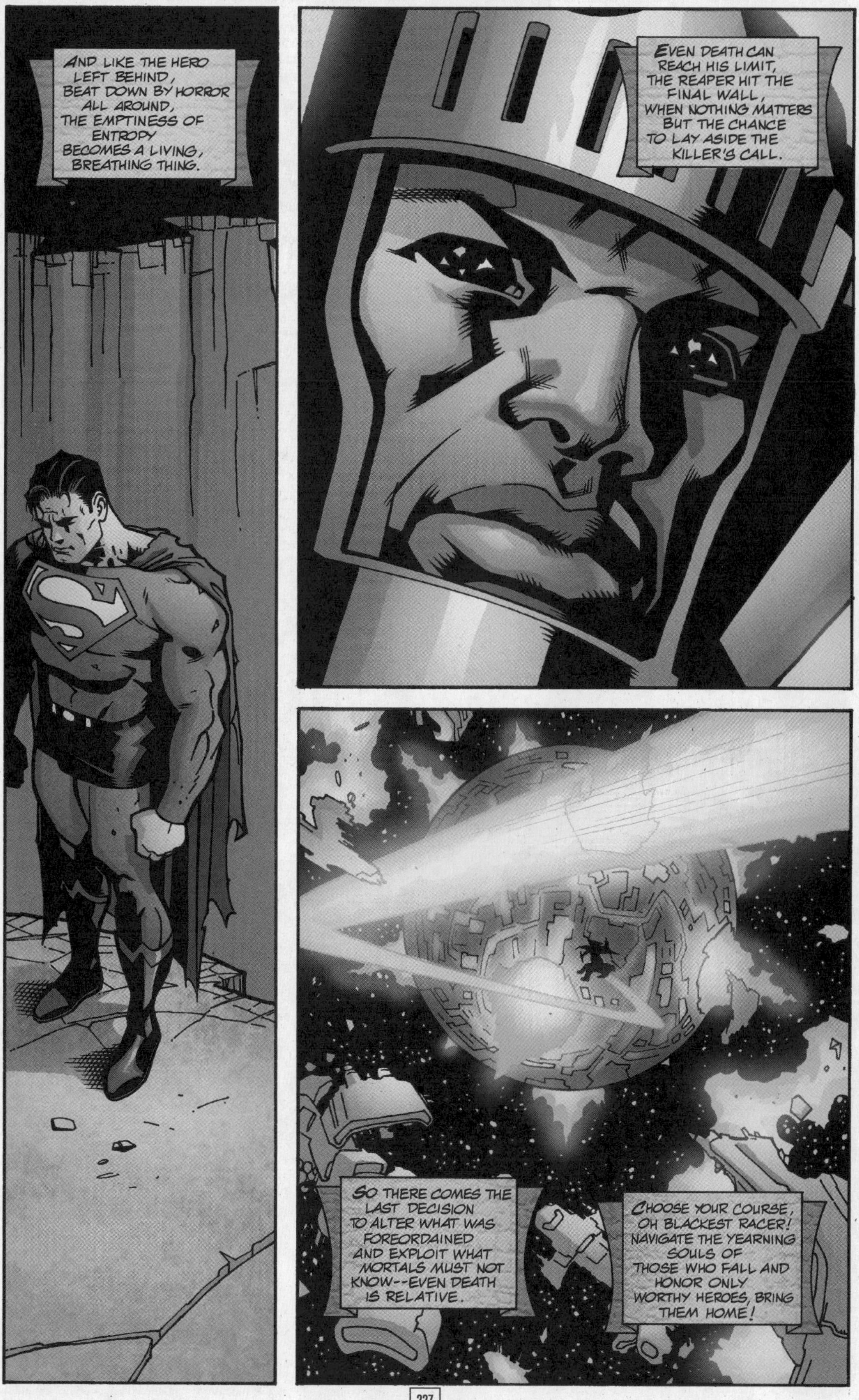
AND LIKE THE HERO LEFT BEHIND, BEAT DOWN BY HORROR ALL AROUND, THE EMPTINESS OF ENTROPY BECOMES A LIVING, BREATHING THING.
EVEN DEATH CAN REACH HIS LIMIT, THE REAPER HIT THE FINAL WALL, WHEN NOTHING MATTERS BUT THE CHANCE TO LAY ASIDE THE KILLER'S CALL.
SO THERE COMES THE LAST DECISION TO ALTER WHAT WAS FOREORDAINED AND EXPLOIT WHAT MORTALS MUST NOT KNOW--EVEN DEATH IS RELATIVE.
CHOOSE YOUR COURSE, OH BLACKEST RACER! NAVIGATE THE YEARNING SOULS OF THOSE WHO FALL AND HONOR ONLY WORTHY HEROES, BRING THEM HOME!

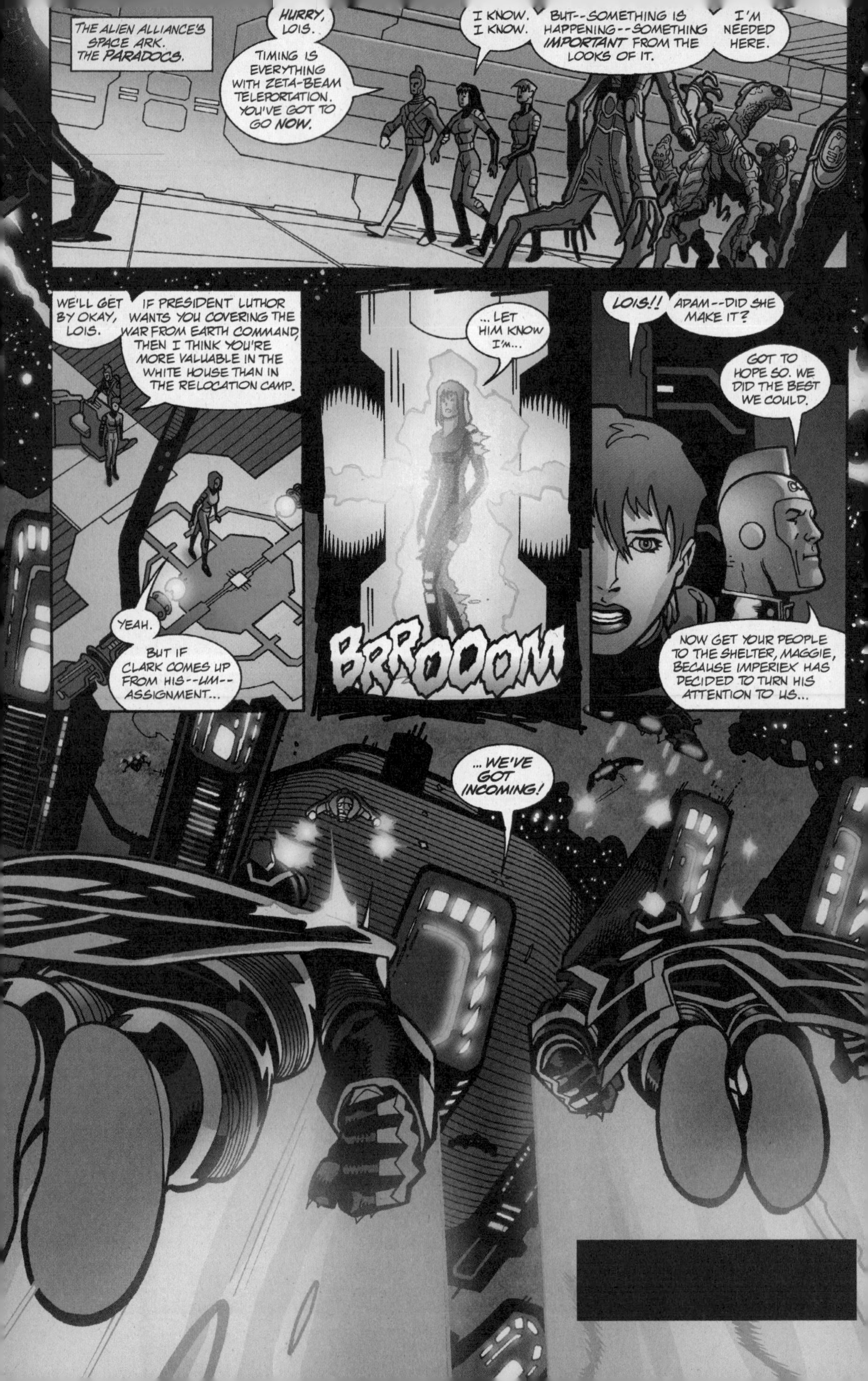
THE ALIEN ALLIANCE'S SPACE ARK. THE PARADOCS.
HURRY, LOIS.
TIMING IS EVERYTHING WITH ZETA-BEAM TELEPORTATION. YOU'VE GOT TO GO NOW.
I KNOW. I KNOW.
BUT--SOMETHING IS HAPPENING--SOMETHING IMPORTANT FROM THE LOOKS OF IT.
I'M NEEDED HERE.
WE'LL GET BY OKAY, LOIS.
IF PRESIDENT LUTHOR WANTS YOU COVERING THE WAR FROM EARTH COMMAND, THEN I THINK YOU'RE MORE VALUABLE IN THE WHITE HOUSE THAN IN THE RELOCATION CAMP.
YEAH.
BUT IF CLARK COMES UP FROM HIS--UM--ASSIGNMENT...
...LET HIM KNOW I'M...
BRROOOM
LOIS!!
ADAM--DID SHE MAKE IT?
GOT TO HOPE SO. WE DID THE BEST WE COULD.
NOW GET YOUR PEOPLE TO THE SHELTER, MAGGIE, BECAUSE IMPERIEX HAS DECIDED TO TURN HIS ATTENTION TO US...
...WE'VE GOT INCOMING!
[redacted]

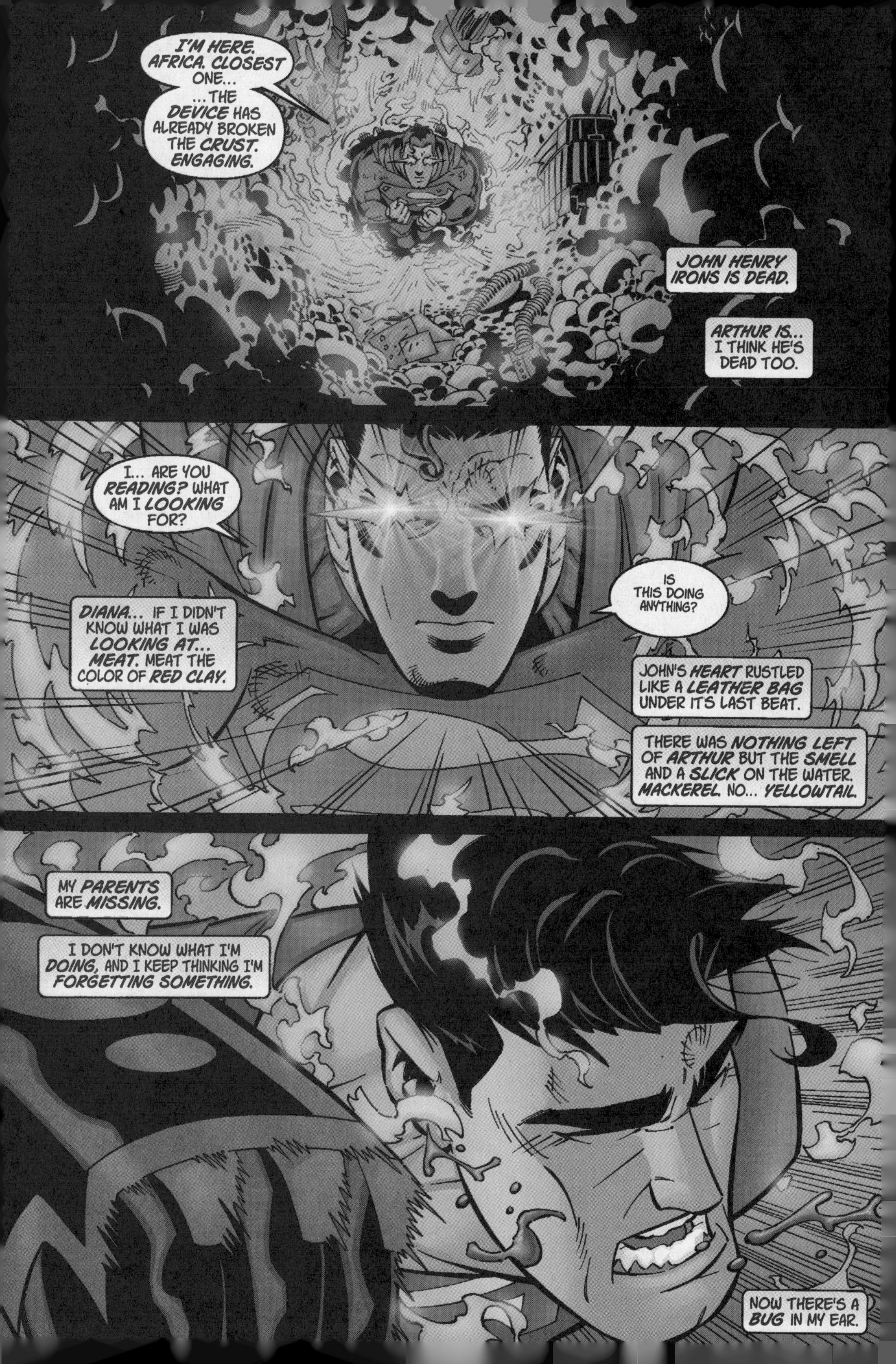
I'M HERE. AFRICA. CLOSEST ONE... ...THE DEVICE HAS ALREADY BROKEN THE CRUST. ENGAGING.
JOHN HENRY IRONS IS DEAD.
ARTHUR IS... I THINK HE'S DEAD TOO.
I... ARE YOU READING? WHAT AM I LOOKING FOR?
IS THIS DOING ANYTHING?
DIANA... IF I DIDN'T KNOW WHAT I WAS LOOKING AT... MEAT. MEAT THE COLOR OF RED CLAY.
JOHN'S HEART RUSTLED LIKE A LEATHER BAG UNDER ITS LAST BEAT.
THERE WAS NOTHING LEFT OF ARTHUR BUT THE SMELL AND A SLICK ON THE WATER. MACKEREL. NO... YELLOWTAIL.
MY PARENTS ARE MISSING.
I DON'T KNOW WHAT I'M DOING, AND I KEEP THINKING I'M FORGETTING SOMETHING.
NOW THERE'S A BUG IN MY EAR.

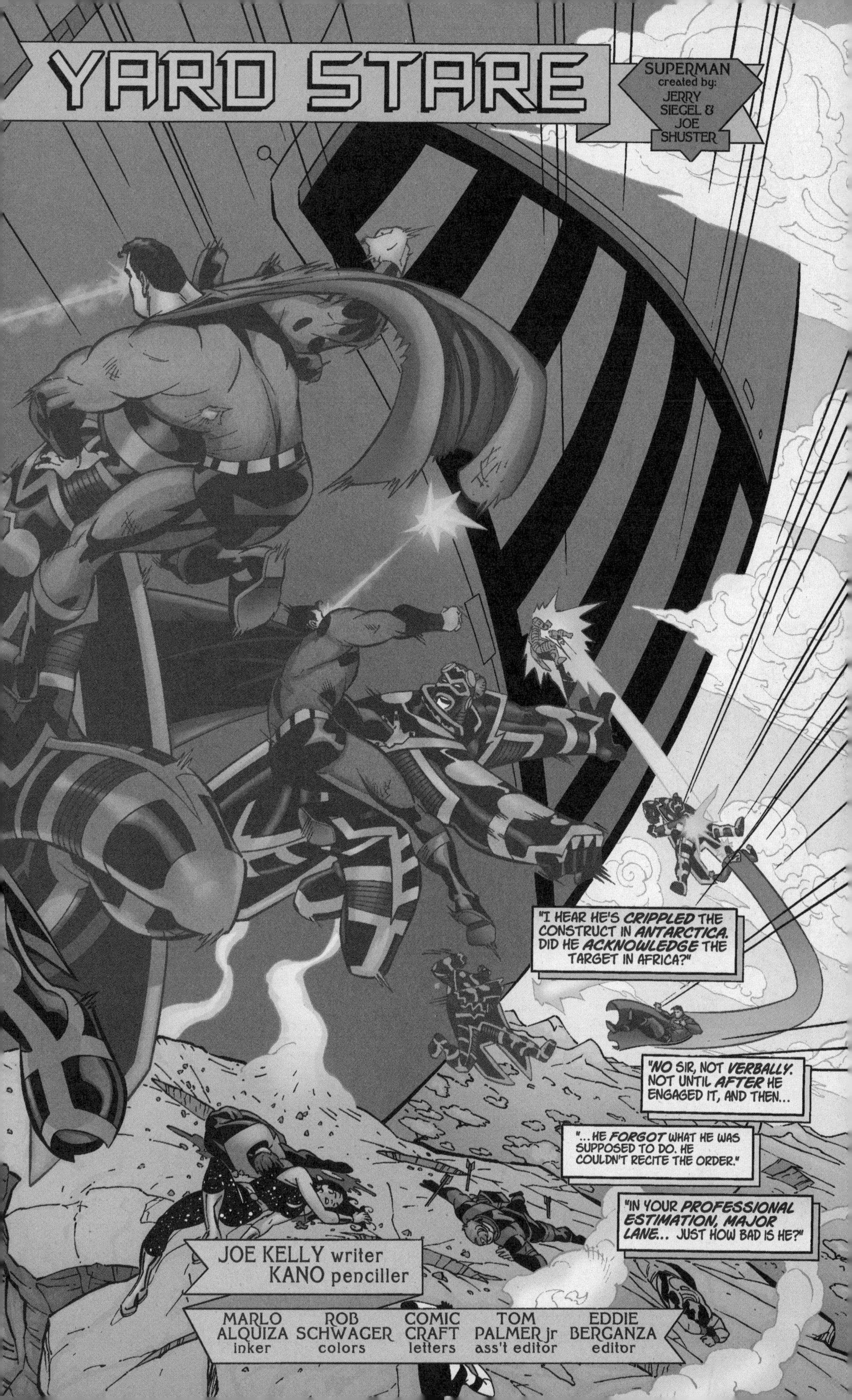
YARD STARE
SUPERMAN created by: JERRY SIEGEL & JOE SHUSTER
"I HEAR HE'S CRIPPLED THE CONSTRUCT IN ANTARCTICA. DID HE ACKNOWLEDGE THE TARGET IN AFRICA?"
"NO SIR, NOT VERBALLY. NOT UNTIL AFTER HE ENGAGED IT, AND THEN...
"...HE FORGOT WHAT HE WAS SUPPOSED TO DO. HE COULDN'T RECITE THE ORDER."
"IN YOUR PROFESSIONAL ESTIMATION, MAJOR LANE... JUST HOW BAD IS HE?"
JOE KELLY writer
KANO penciller
MARLO ALQUIZA inker
ROB SCHWAGER colors
COMIC CRAFT letters
TOM PALMER jr ass't editor
EDDIE BERGANZA editor

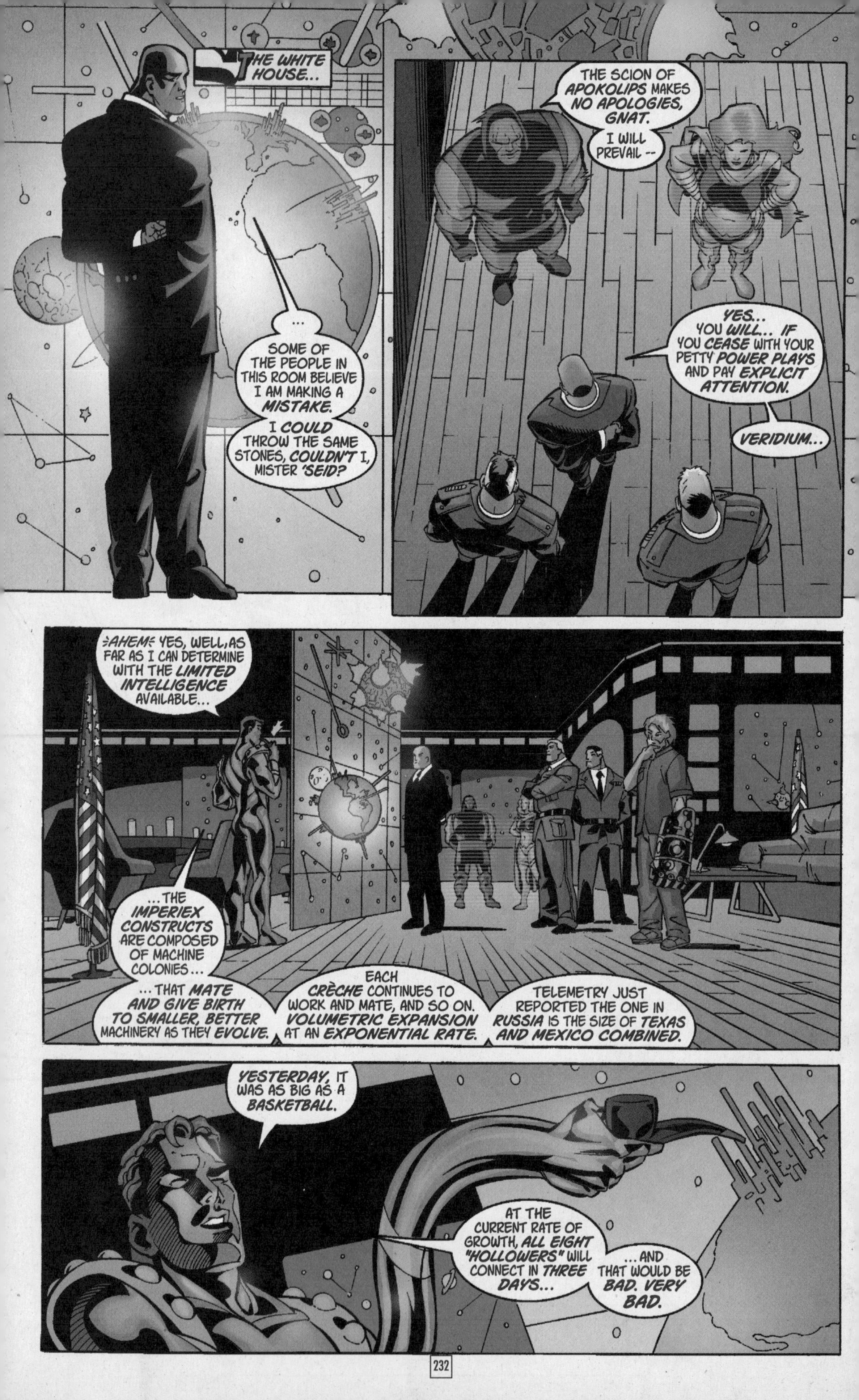
THE WHITE HOUSE...
...
SOME OF THE PEOPLE IN THIS ROOM BELIEVE I AM MAKING A MISTAKE.
I COULD THROW THE SAME STONES, COULDN'T I, MISTER 'SEID?
THE SCION OF APOKOLIPS MAKES NO APOLOGIES, GNAT.
I WILL PREVAIL --
YES... YOU WILL... IF YOU CEASE WITH YOUR PETTY POWER PLAYS AND PAY EXPLICIT ATTENTION.
VERIDIUM...
≠AHEM≠ YES, WELL, AS FAR AS I CAN DETERMINE WITH THE LIMITED INTELLIGENCE AVAILABLE...
...THE IMPERIEX CONSTRUCTS ARE COMPOSED OF MACHINE COLONIES...
...THAT MATE AND GIVE BIRTH TO SMALLER, BETTER MACHINERY AS THEY EVOLVE.
EACH CRÈCHE CONTINUES TO WORK AND MATE, AND SO ON. VOLUMETRIC EXPANSION AT AN EXPONENTIAL RATE.
TELEMETRY JUST REPORTED THE ONE IN RUSSIA IS THE SIZE OF TEXAS AND MEXICO COMBINED.
YESTERDAY, IT WAS AS BIG AS A BASKETBALL.
AT THE CURRENT RATE OF GROWTH, ALL EIGHT "HOLLOWERS" WILL CONNECT IN THREE DAYS...
...AND THAT WOULD BE BAD. VERY BAD.

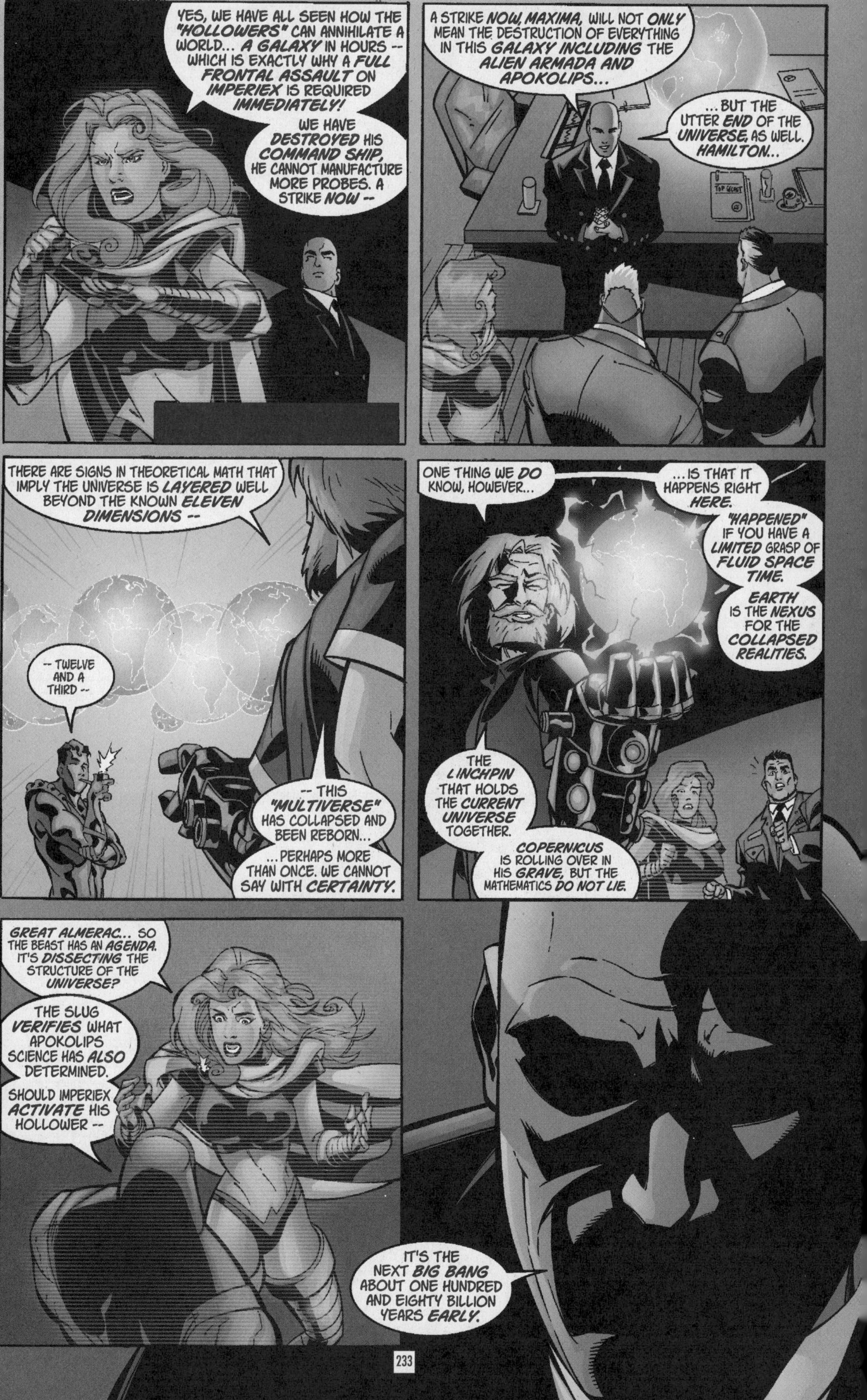
YES, WE HAVE ALL SEEN HOW THE "HOLLOWERS" CAN ANNIHILATE A WORLD... A GALAXY IN HOURS -- WHICH IS EXACTLY WHY A FULL FRONTAL ASSAULT ON IMPERIEX IS REQUIRED IMMEDIATELY!
WE HAVE DESTROYED HIS COMMAND SHIP, HE CANNOT MANUFACTURE MORE PROBES. A STRIKE NOW --
A STRIKE NOW, MAXIMA, WILL NOT ONLY MEAN THE DESTRUCTION OF EVERYTHING IN THIS GALAXY INCLUDING THE ALIEN ARMADA AND APOKOLIPS...
... BUT THE UTTER END OF THE UNIVERSE, AS WELL. HAMILTON...
TOP SECRET
THERE ARE SIGNS IN THEORETICAL MATH THAT IMPLY THE UNIVERSE IS LAYERED WELL BEYOND THE KNOWN ELEVEN DIMENSIONS --
-- TWELVE AND A THIRD --
-- THIS "MULTIVERSE" HAS COLLAPSED AND BEEN REBORN...
... PERHAPS MORE THAN ONCE. WE CANNOT SAY WITH CERTAINTY.
ONE THING WE DO KNOW, HOWEVER...
... IS THAT IT HAPPENS RIGHT HERE.
"HAPPENED" IF YOU HAVE A LIMITED GRASP OF FLUID SPACE TIME.
EARTH IS THE NEXUS FOR THE COLLAPSED REALITIES.
THE LINCHPIN THAT HOLDS THE CURRENT UNIVERSE TOGETHER.
COPERNICUS IS ROLLING OVER IN HIS GRAVE, BUT THE MATHEMATICS DO NOT LIE.
GREAT ALMERAC... SO THE BEAST HAS AN AGENDA. IT'S DISSECTING THE STRUCTURE OF THE UNIVERSE?
THE SLUG VERIFIES WHAT APOKOLIPS SCIENCE HAS ALSO DETERMINED.
SHOULD IMPERIEX ACTIVATE HIS HOLLOWER --
IT'S THE NEXT BIG BANG ABOUT ONE HUNDRED AND EIGHTY BILLION YEARS EARLY.

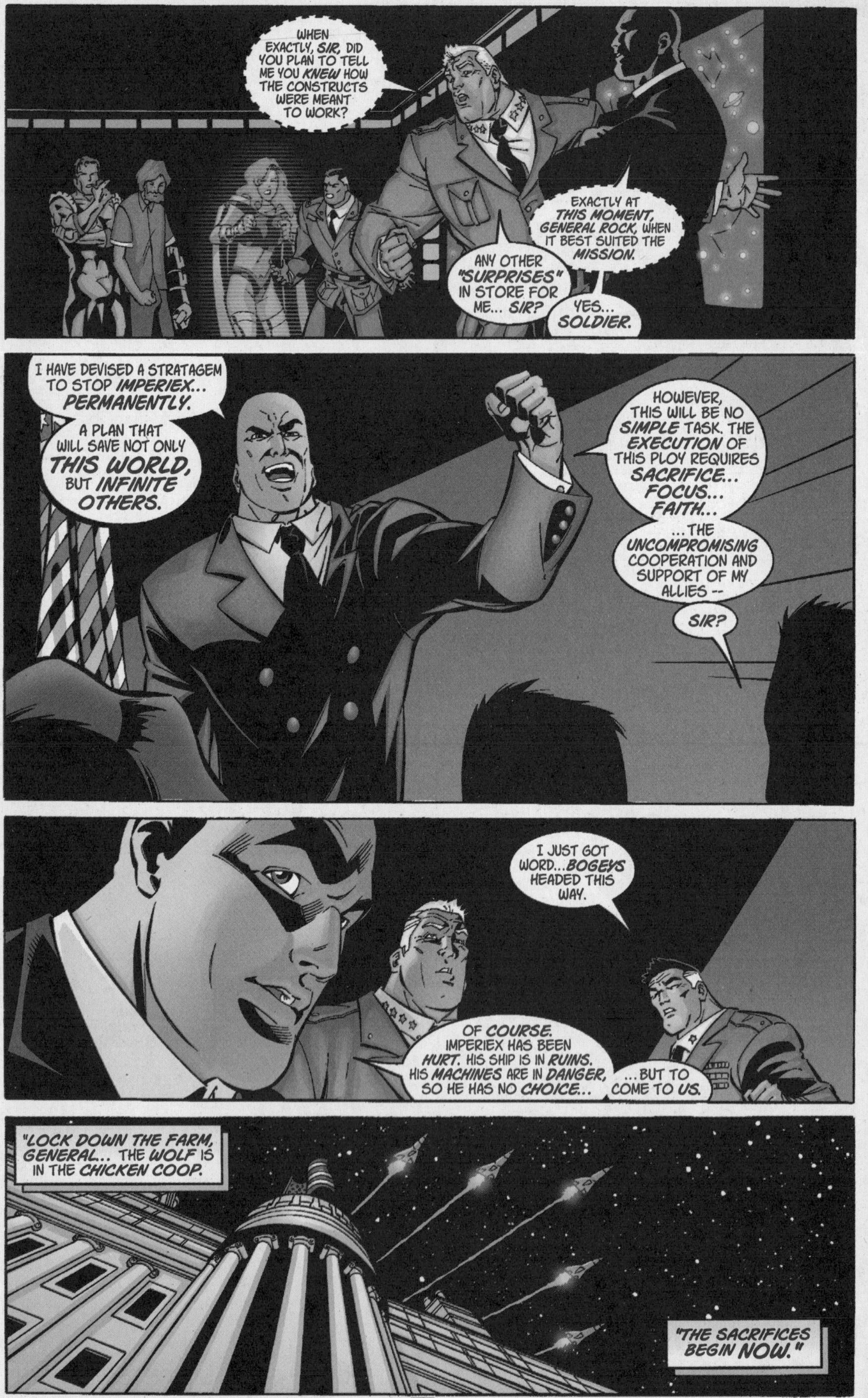
WHEN EXACTLY, SIR, DID YOU PLAN TO TELL ME YOU KNEW HOW THE CONSTRUCTS WERE MEANT TO WORK?
EXACTLY AT THIS MOMENT, GENERAL ROCK, WHEN IT BEST SUITED THE MISSION.
ANY OTHER "SURPRISES" IN STORE FOR ME... SIR?
YES... SOLDIER.
I HAVE DEVISED A STRATAGEM TO STOP IMPERIEX... PERMANENTLY.
A PLAN THAT WILL SAVE NOT ONLY THIS WORLD, BUT INFINITE OTHERS.
HOWEVER, THIS WILL BE NO SIMPLE TASK. THE EXECUTION OF THIS PLOY REQUIRES SACRIFICE... FOCUS... FAITH...
...THE UNCOMPROMISING COOPERATION AND SUPPORT OF MY ALLIES --
SIR?
I JUST GOT WORD...BOGEYS HEADED THIS WAY.
OF COURSE. IMPERIEX HAS BEEN HURT. HIS SHIP IS IN RUINS. HIS MACHINES ARE IN DANGER, SO HE HAS NO CHOICE...
...BUT TO COME TO US.
"LOCK DOWN THE FARM, GENERAL... THE WOLF IS IN THE CHICKEN COOP.
"THE SACRIFICES BEGIN NOW."

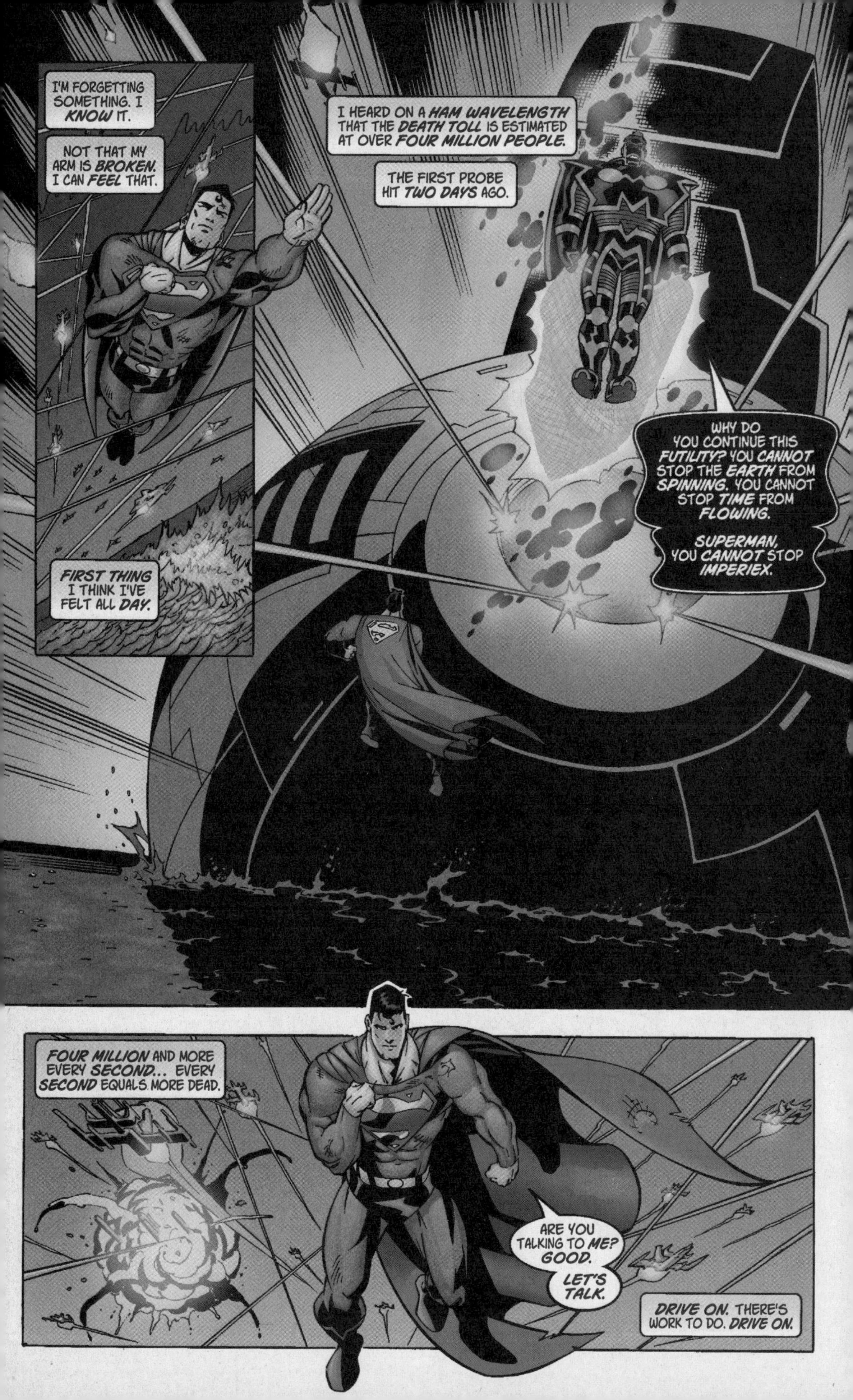

I'M FORGETTING SOMETHING. I KNOW IT.
NOT THAT MY ARM IS BROKEN. I CAN FEEL THAT.
FIRST THING I THINK I'VE FELT ALL DAY.
I HEARD ON A HAM WAVELENGTH THAT THE DEATH TOLL IS ESTIMATED AT OVER FOUR MILLION PEOPLE.
THE FIRST PROBE HIT TWO DAYS AGO.
WHY DO YOU CONTINUE THIS FUTILITY? YOU CANNOT STOP THE EARTH FROM SPINNING. YOU CANNOT STOP TIME FROM FLOWING.
SUPERMAN, YOU CANNOT STOP IMPERIEX.
FOUR MILLION AND MORE EVERY SECOND... EVERY SECOND EQUALS MORE DEAD.
ARE YOU TALKING TO ME? GOOD.
LET'S TALK.
DRIVE ON. THERE'S WORK TO DO. DRIVE ON.

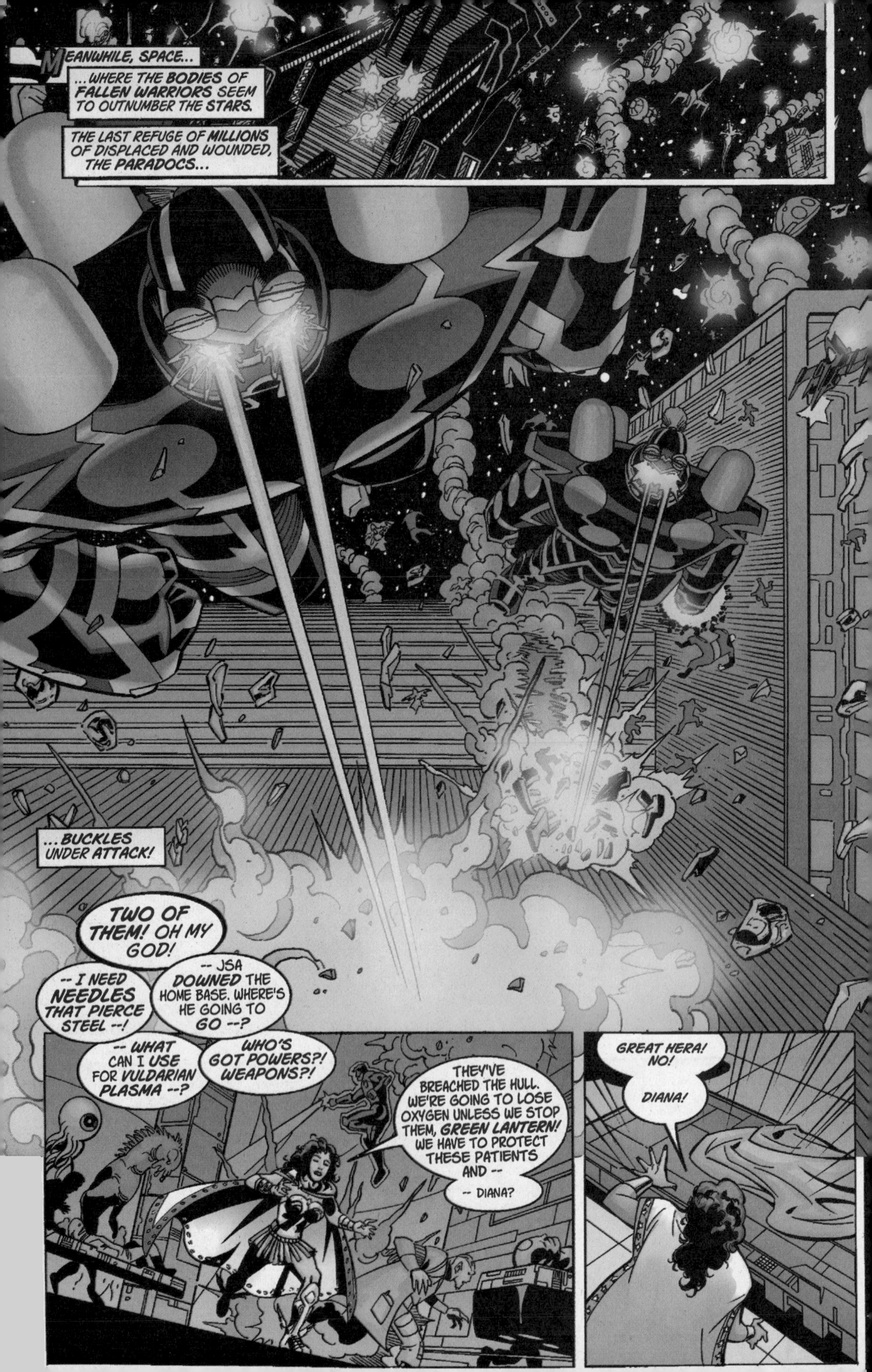

MEANWHILE, SPACE...
...WHERE THE BODIES OF FALLEN WARRIORS SEEM TO OUTNUMBER THE STARS.
THE LAST REFUGE OF MILLIONS OF DISPLACED AND WOUNDED, THE PARADOCS...
...BUCKLES UNDER ATTACK!
TWO OF THEM! OH MY GOD!
-- I NEED NEEDLES THAT PIERCE STEEL --!
-- JSA DOWNED THE HOME BASE. WHERE'S HE GOING TO GO --?
-- WHAT CAN I USE FOR VULDARIAN PLASMA --?
WHO'S GOT POWERS?! WEAPONS?!
THEY'VE BREACHED THE HULL. WE'RE GOING TO LOSE OXYGEN UNLESS WE STOP THEM, GREEN LANTERN! WE HAVE TO PROTECT THESE PATIENTS AND --
-- DIANA?
GREAT HERA! NO!
DIANA!

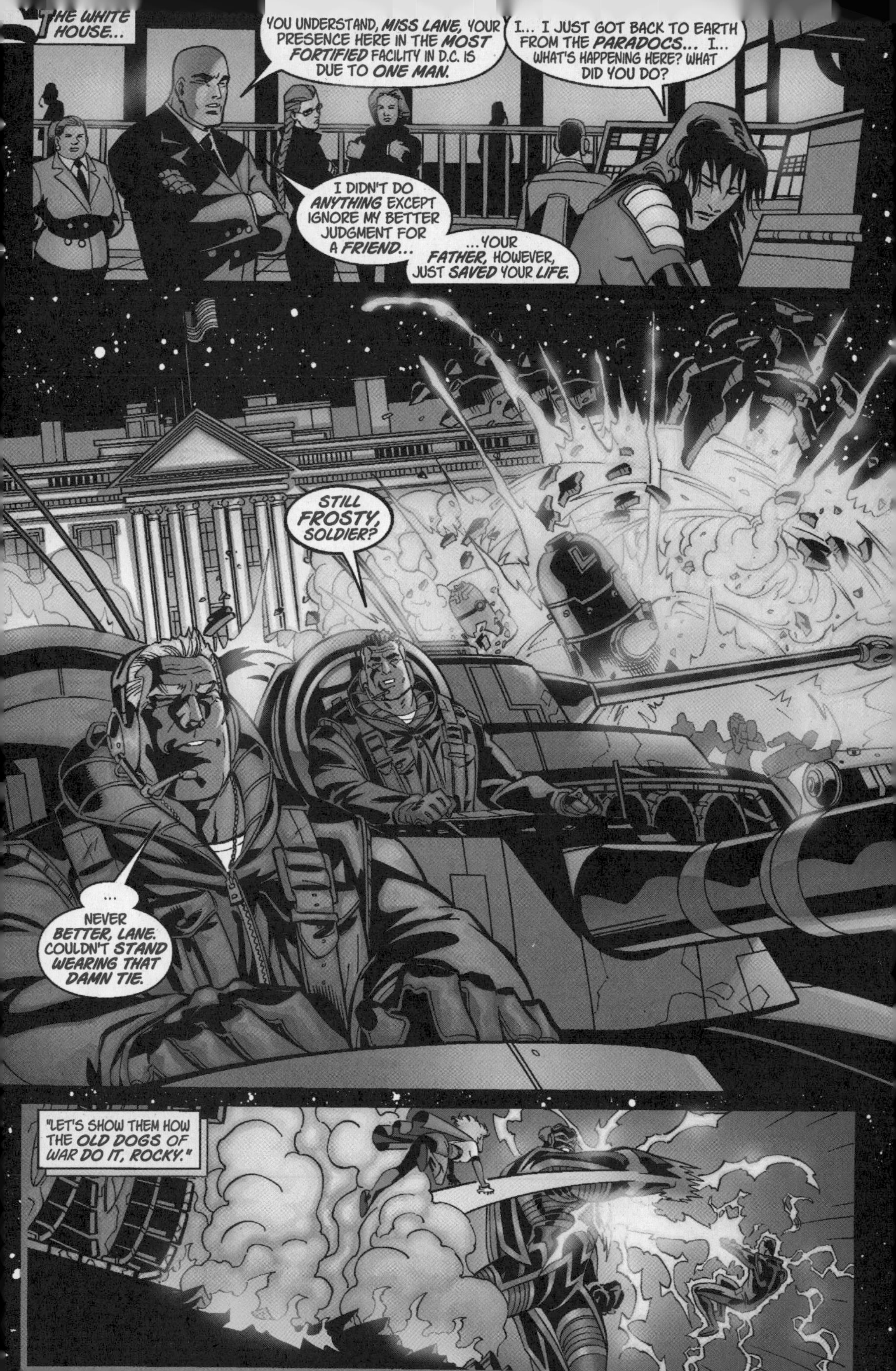
THE WHITE HOUSE...
YOU UNDERSTAND, MISS LANE, YOUR PRESENCE HERE IN THE MOST FORTIFIED FACILITY IN D.C. IS DUE TO ONE MAN.
I... I JUST GOT BACK TO EARTH FROM THE PARADOCS... I... WHAT'S HAPPENING HERE? WHAT DID YOU DO?
I DIDN'T DO ANYTHING EXCEPT IGNORE MY BETTER JUDGMENT FOR A FRIEND...
...YOUR FATHER, HOWEVER, JUST SAVED YOUR LIFE.
STILL FROSTY, SOLDIER?
... NEVER BETTER, LANE. COULDN'T STAND WEARING THAT DAMN TIE.
"LET'S SHOW THEM HOW THE OLD DOGS OF WAR DO IT, ROCKY."

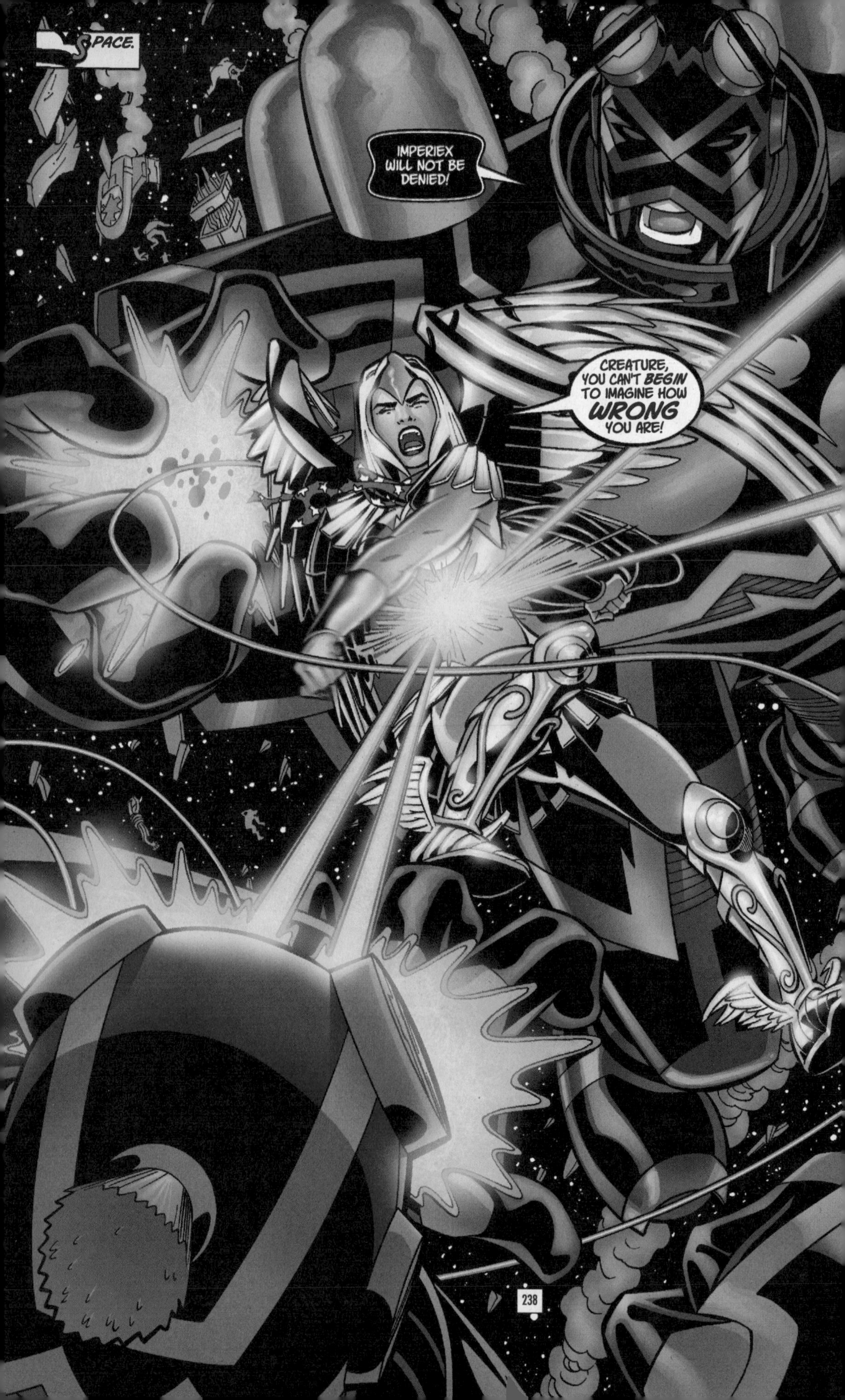
SPACE.
IMPERIEX WILL NOT BE DENIED!
CREATURE, YOU CAN'T BEGIN TO IMAGINE HOW WRONG YOU ARE!

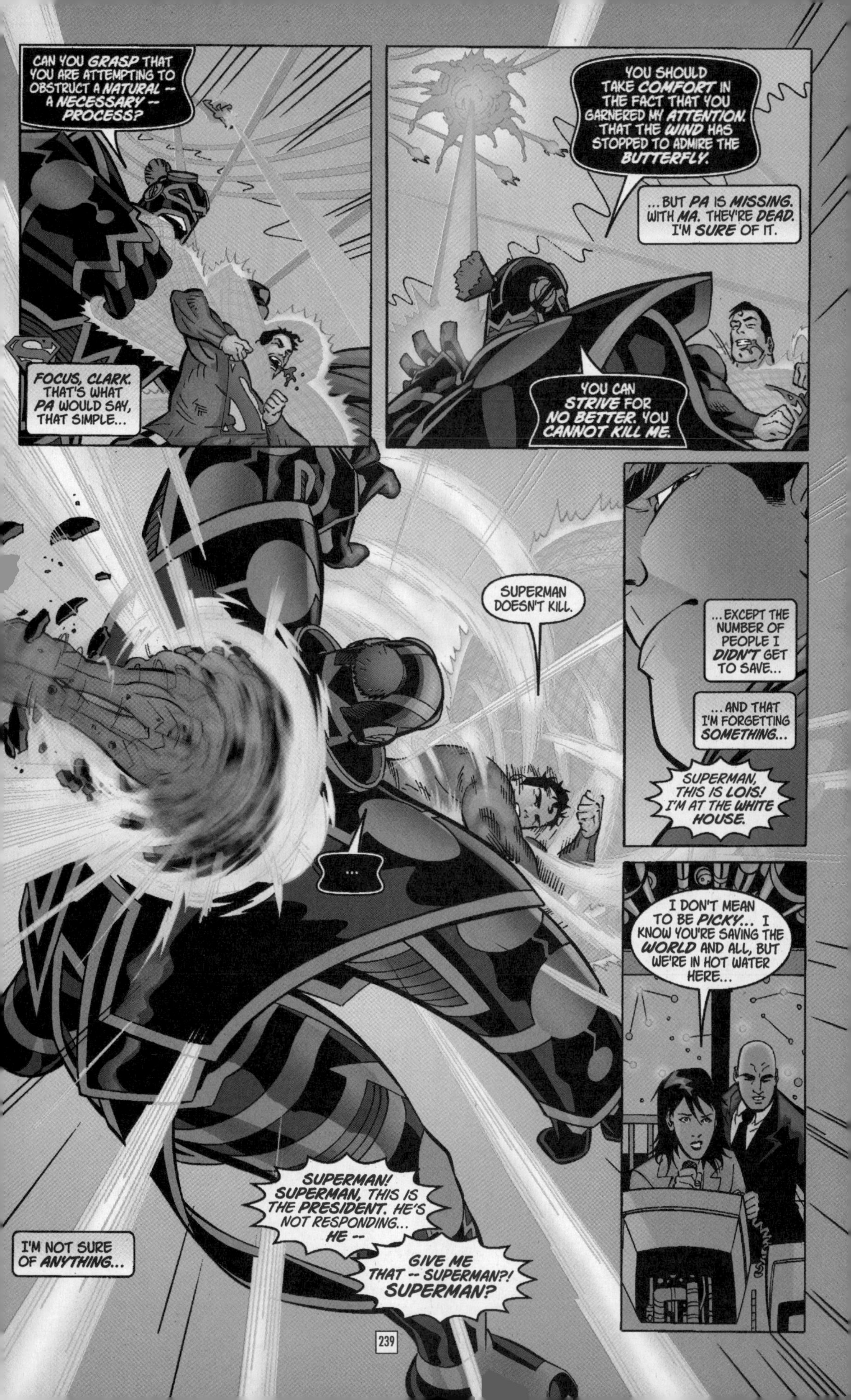
CAN YOU GRASP THAT YOU ARE ATTEMPTING TO OBSTRUCT A NATURAL -- A NECESSARY -- PROCESS?
FOCUS, CLARK. THAT'S WHAT PA WOULD SAY, THAT SIMPLE...
YOU SHOULD TAKE COMFORT IN THE FACT THAT YOU GARNERED MY ATTENTION. THAT THE WIND HAS STOPPED TO ADMIRE THE BUTTERFLY.
...BUT PA IS MISSING. WITH MA. THEY'RE DEAD. I'M SURE OF IT.
YOU CAN STRIVE FOR NO BETTER. YOU CANNOT KILL ME.
SUPERMAN DOESN'T KILL.
...
...EXCEPT THE NUMBER OF PEOPLE I DIDN'T GET TO SAVE...
...AND THAT I'M FORGETTING SOMETHING...
SUPERMAN, THIS IS LOIS! I'M AT THE WHITE HOUSE.
I DON'T MEAN TO BE PICKY... I KNOW YOU'RE SAVING THE WORLD AND ALL, BUT WE'RE IN HOT WATER HERE...
SUPERMAN! SUPERMAN, THIS IS THE PRESIDENT. HE'S NOT RESPONDING... HE --
GIVE ME THAT -- SUPERMAN?! SUPERMAN?
I'M NOT SURE OF ANYTHING...

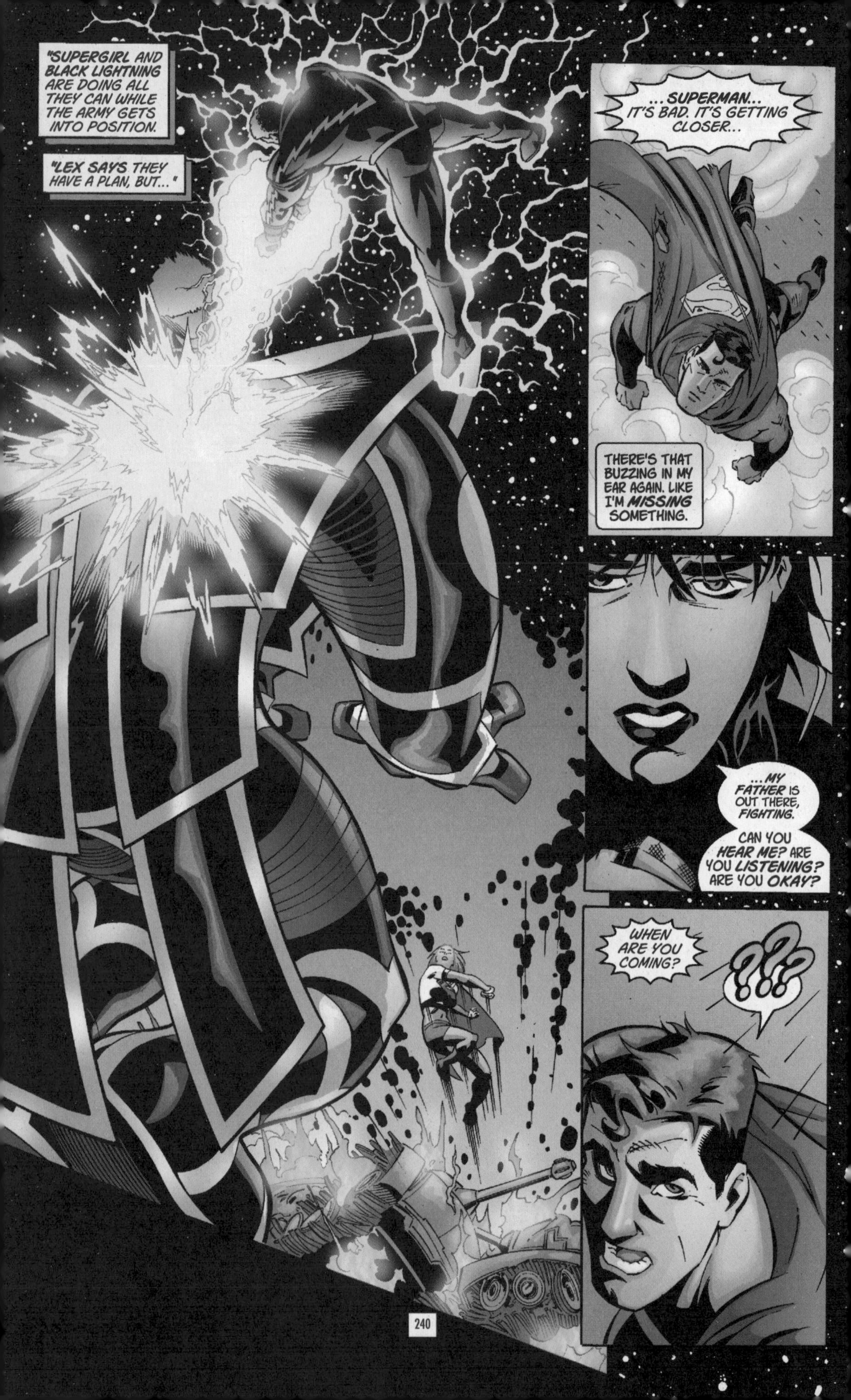
"SUPERGIRL AND BLACK LIGHTNING ARE DOING ALL THEY CAN WHILE THE ARMY GETS INTO POSITION.
"LEX SAYS THEY HAVE A PLAN, BUT..."
...SUPERMAN... IT'S BAD. IT'S GETTING CLOSER...
THERE'S THAT BUZZING IN MY EAR AGAIN. LIKE I'M MISSING SOMETHING.
...MY FATHER IS OUT THERE, FIGHTING.
CAN YOU HEAR ME? ARE YOU LISTENING? ARE YOU OKAY?
WHEN ARE YOU COMING?
???

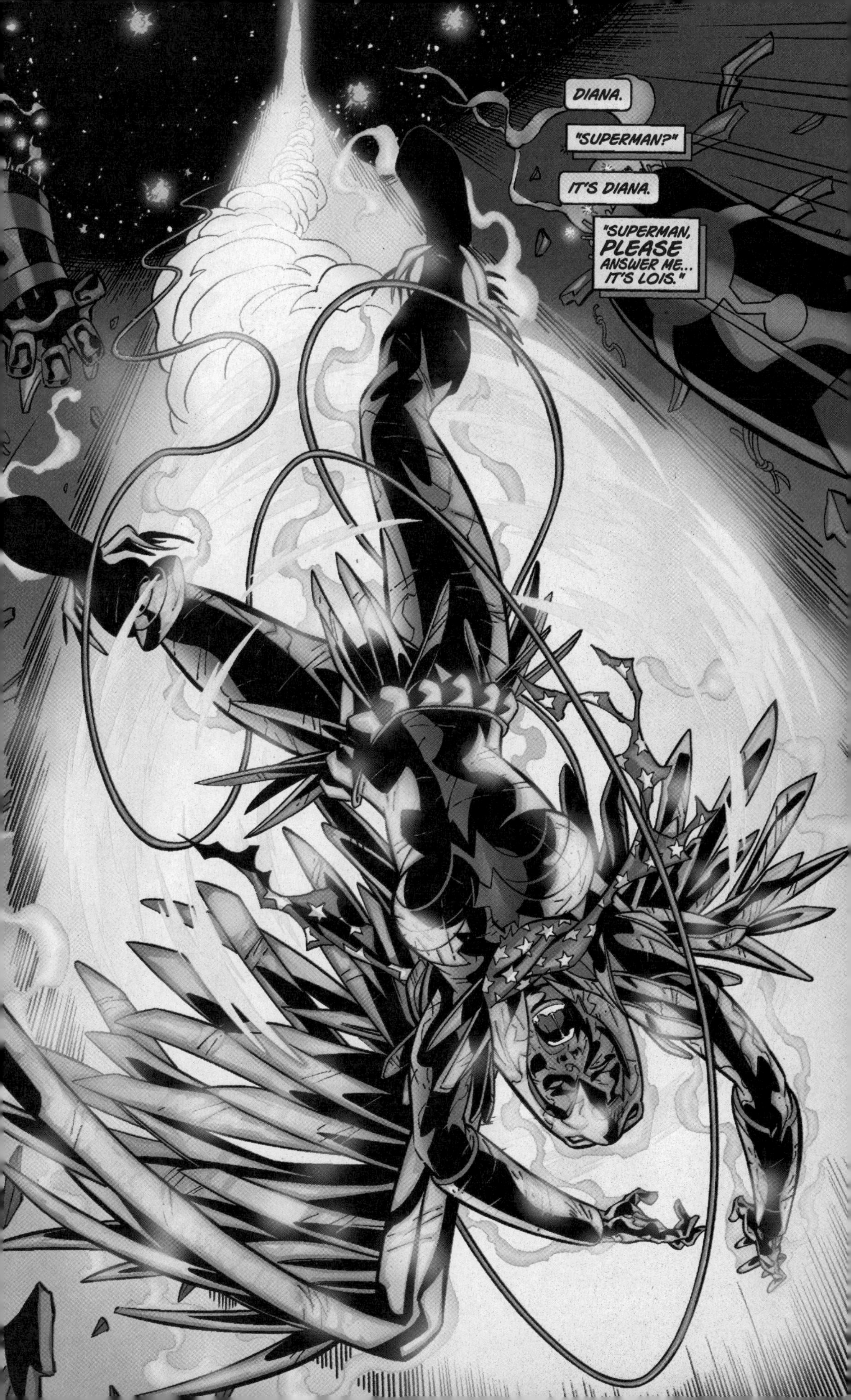
DIANA.
"SUPERMAN?"
IT'S DIANA.
"SUPERMAN, PLEASE ANSWER ME... IT'S LOIS."

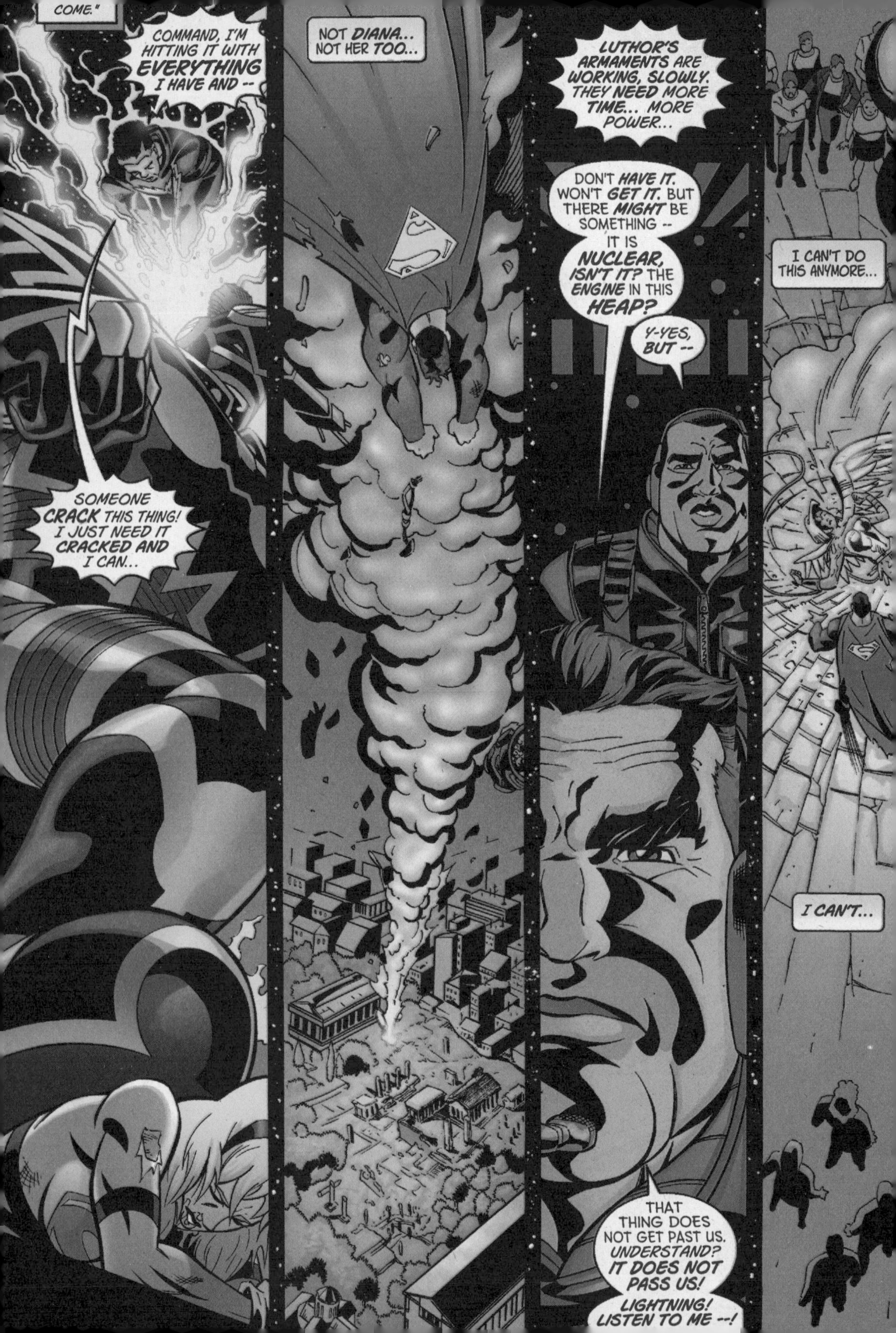
COME."
COMMAND, I'M HITTING IT WITH EVERYTHING I HAVE AND --
SOMEONE CRACK THIS THING! I JUST NEED IT CRACKED AND I CAN...
NOT DIANA... NOT HER TOO...
LUTHOR'S ARMAMENTS ARE WORKING, SLOWLY. THEY NEED MORE TIME... MORE POWER...
DON'T HAVE IT. WON'T GET IT. BUT THERE MIGHT BE SOMETHING -- IT IS NUCLEAR, ISN'T IT? THE ENGINE IN THIS HEAP?
Y-YES, BUT --
THAT THING DOES NOT GET PAST US. UNDERSTAND? IT DOES NOT PASS US!
LIGHTNING! LISTEN TO ME --!
I CAN'T DO THIS ANYMORE...
I CAN'T...

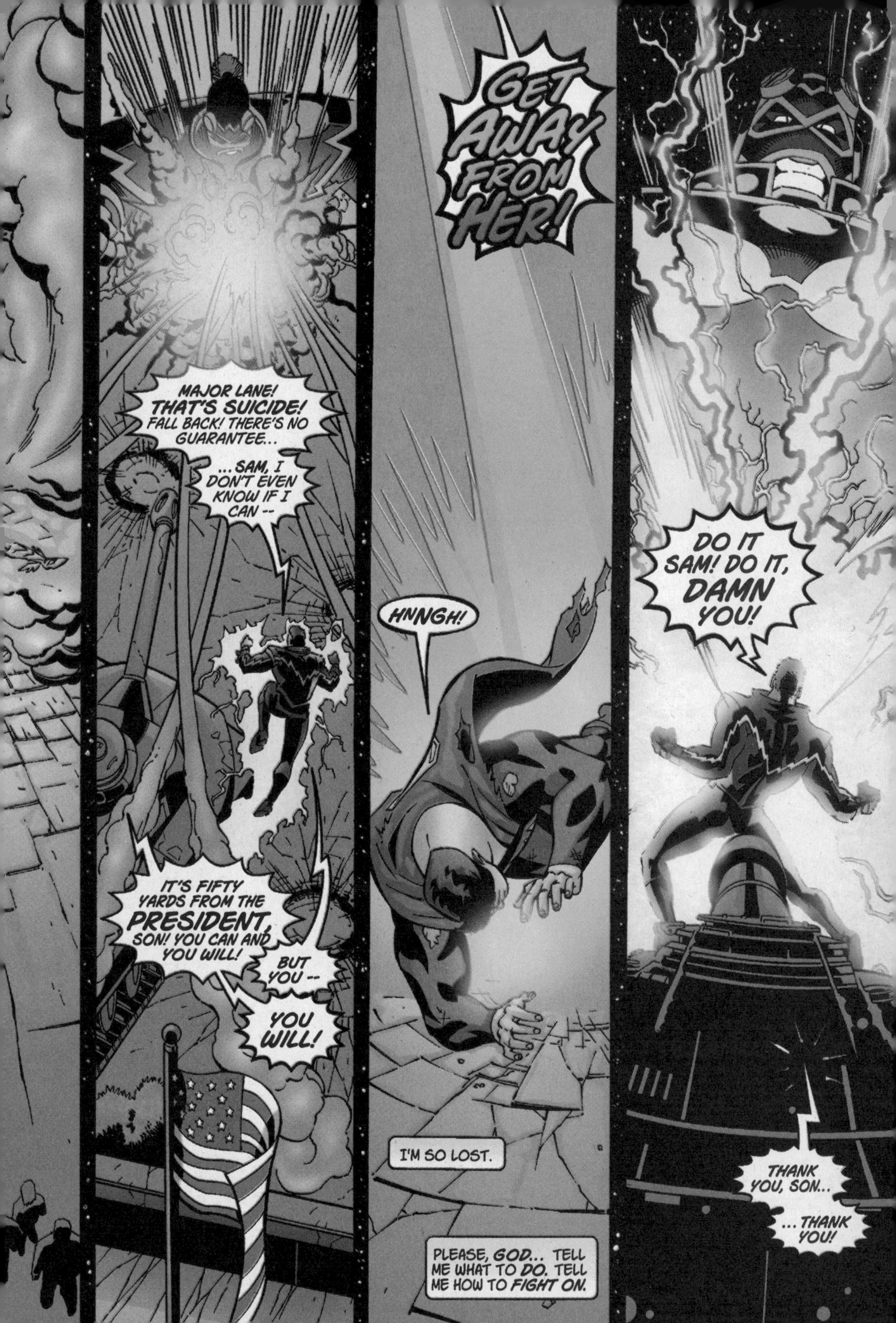
MAJOR LANE! THAT'S SUICIDE! FALL BACK! THERE'S NO GUARANTEE...
... SAM, I DON'T EVEN KNOW IF I CAN --
IT'S FIFTY YARDS FROM THE PRESIDENT, SON! YOU CAN AND YOU WILL!
BUT YOU --
YOU WILL!
GET AWAY FROM HER!
HNNGH!
I'M SO LOST.
PLEASE, GOD... TELL ME WHAT TO DO. TELL ME HOW TO FIGHT ON.
DO IT SAM! DO IT, DAMN YOU!
THANK YOU, SON...
... THANK YOU!

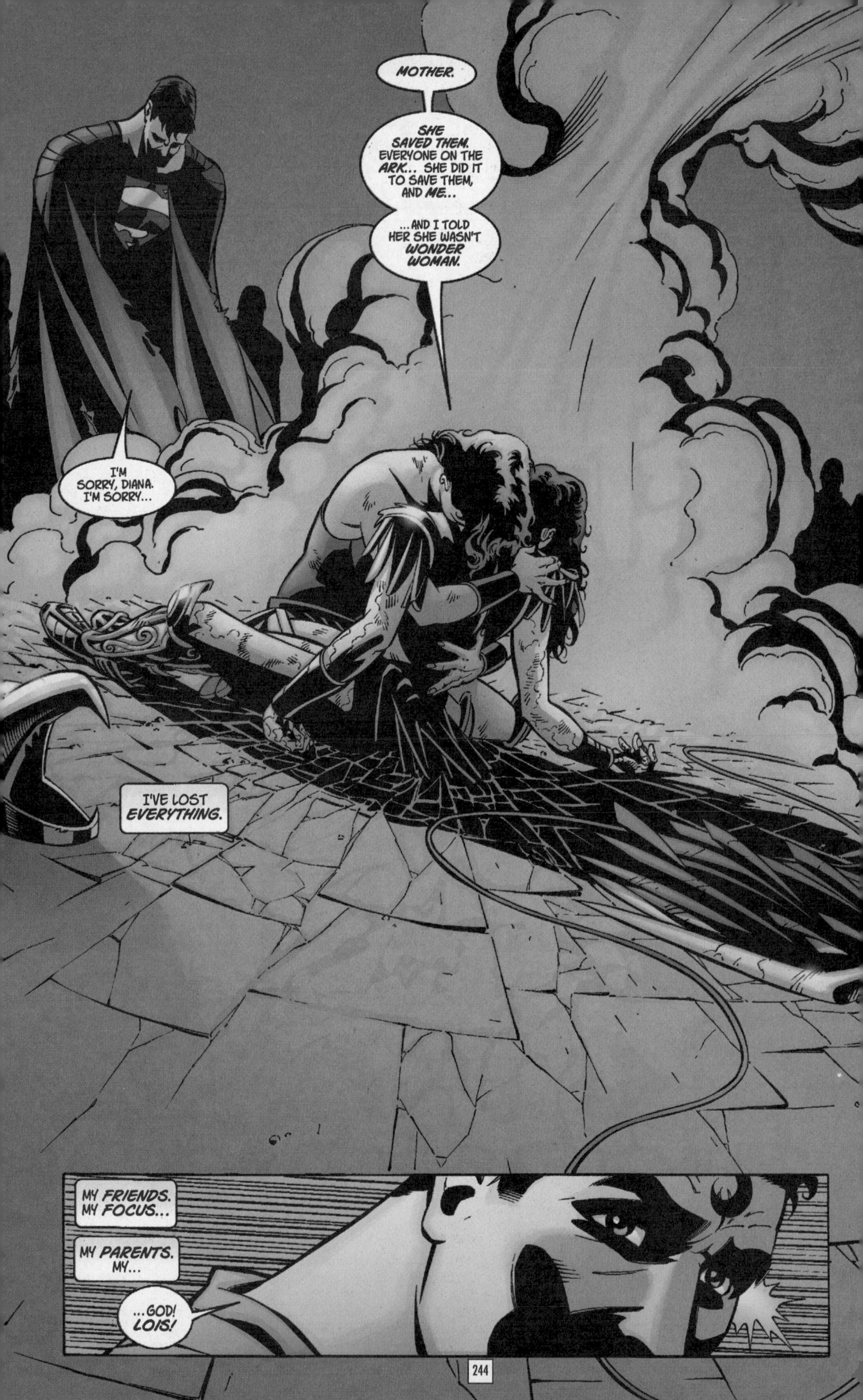
MOTHER.
SHE SAVED THEM. EVERYONE ON THE ARK... SHE DID IT TO SAVE THEM, AND ME...
...AND I TOLD HER SHE WASN'T WONDER WOMAN.
I'M SORRY, DIANA. I'M SORRY...
I'VE LOST EVERYTHING.
MY FRIENDS. MY FOCUS...
MY PARENTS. MY...
...GOD! LOIS!

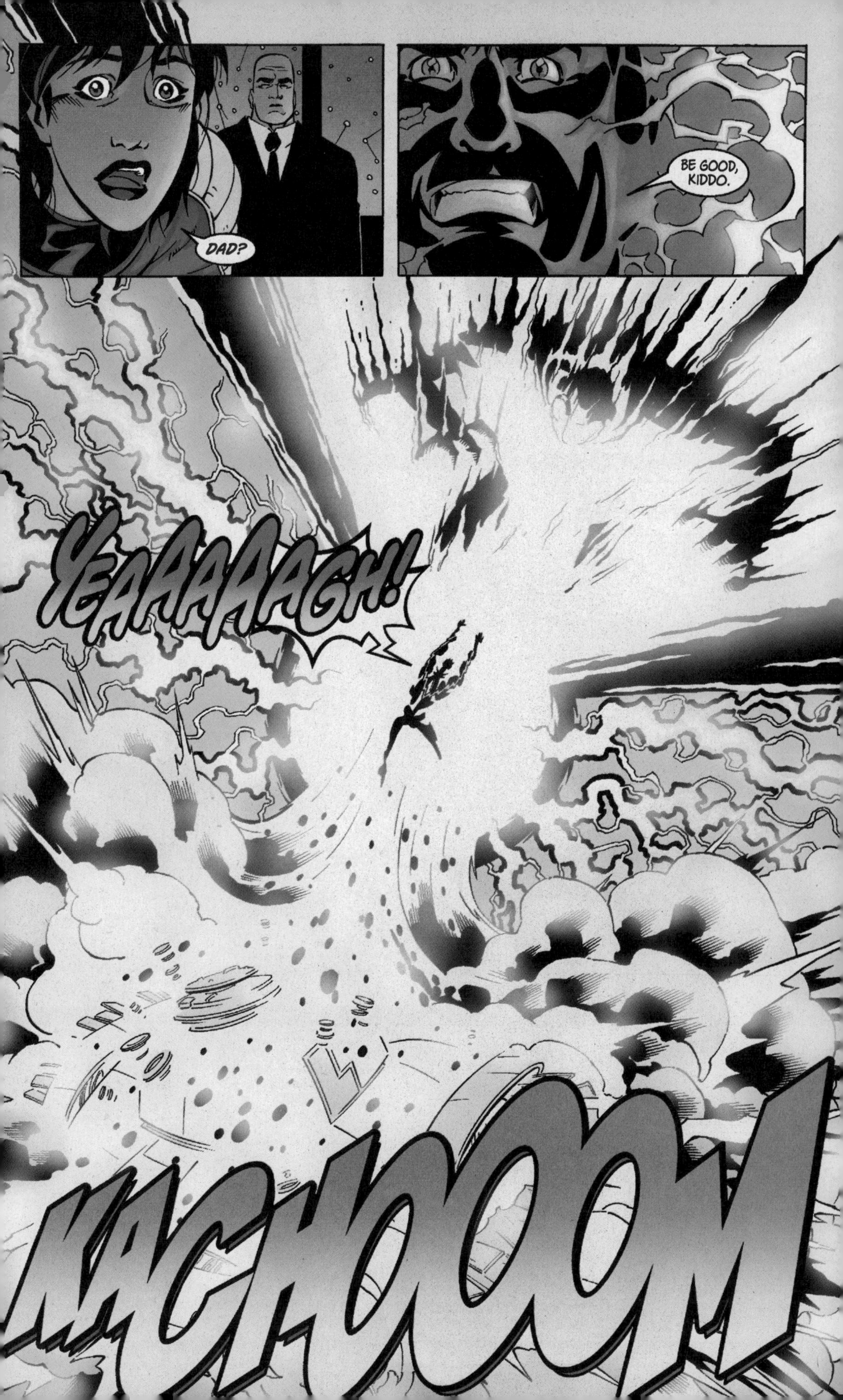
DAD?
BE GOOD, KIDDO.
YEAAAAAGH!
KACHOOOM

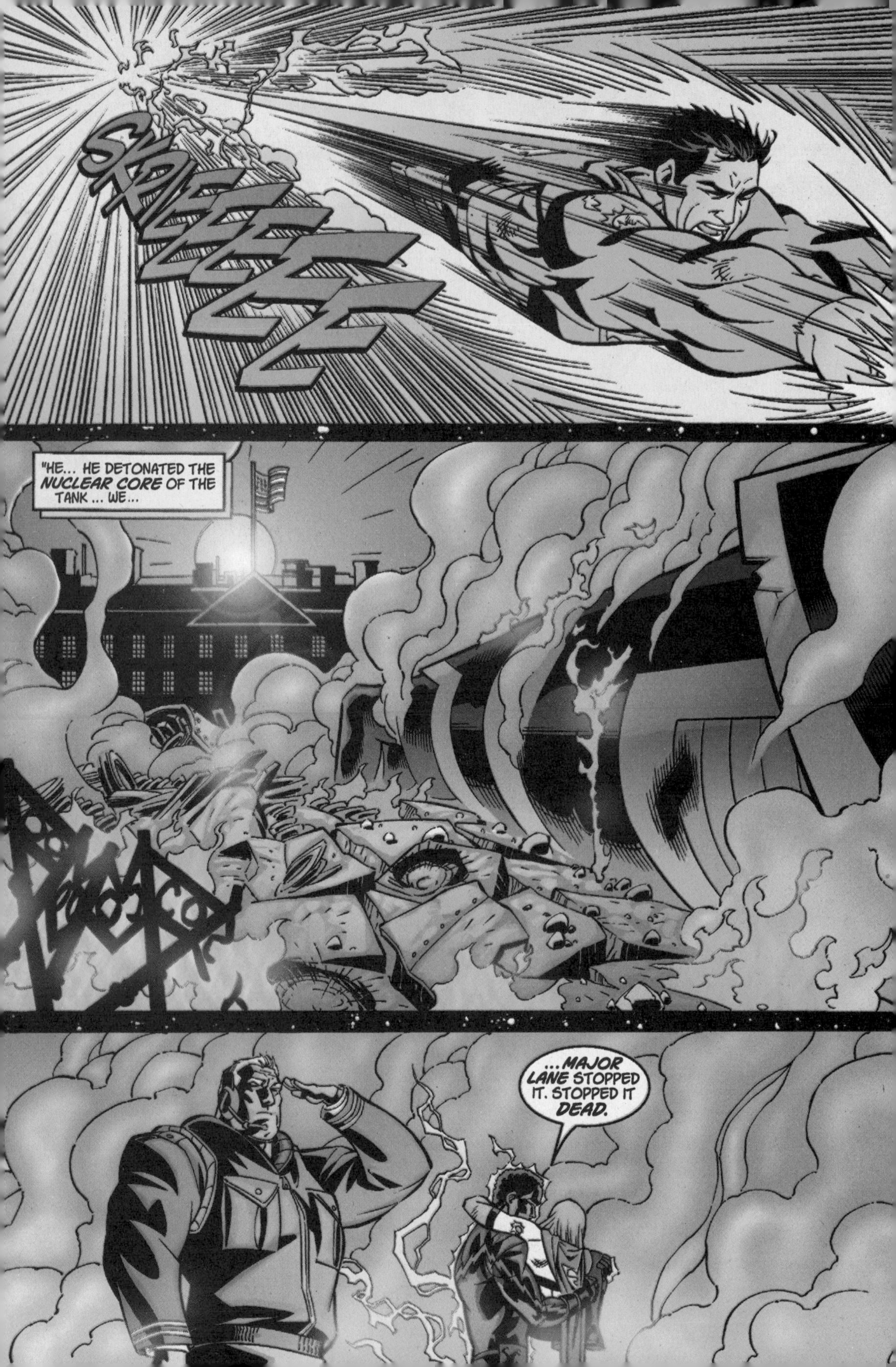
"HE... HE DETONATED THE NUCLEAR CORE OF THE TANK ... WE...
...MAJOR LANE STOPPED IT. STOPPED IT DEAD.

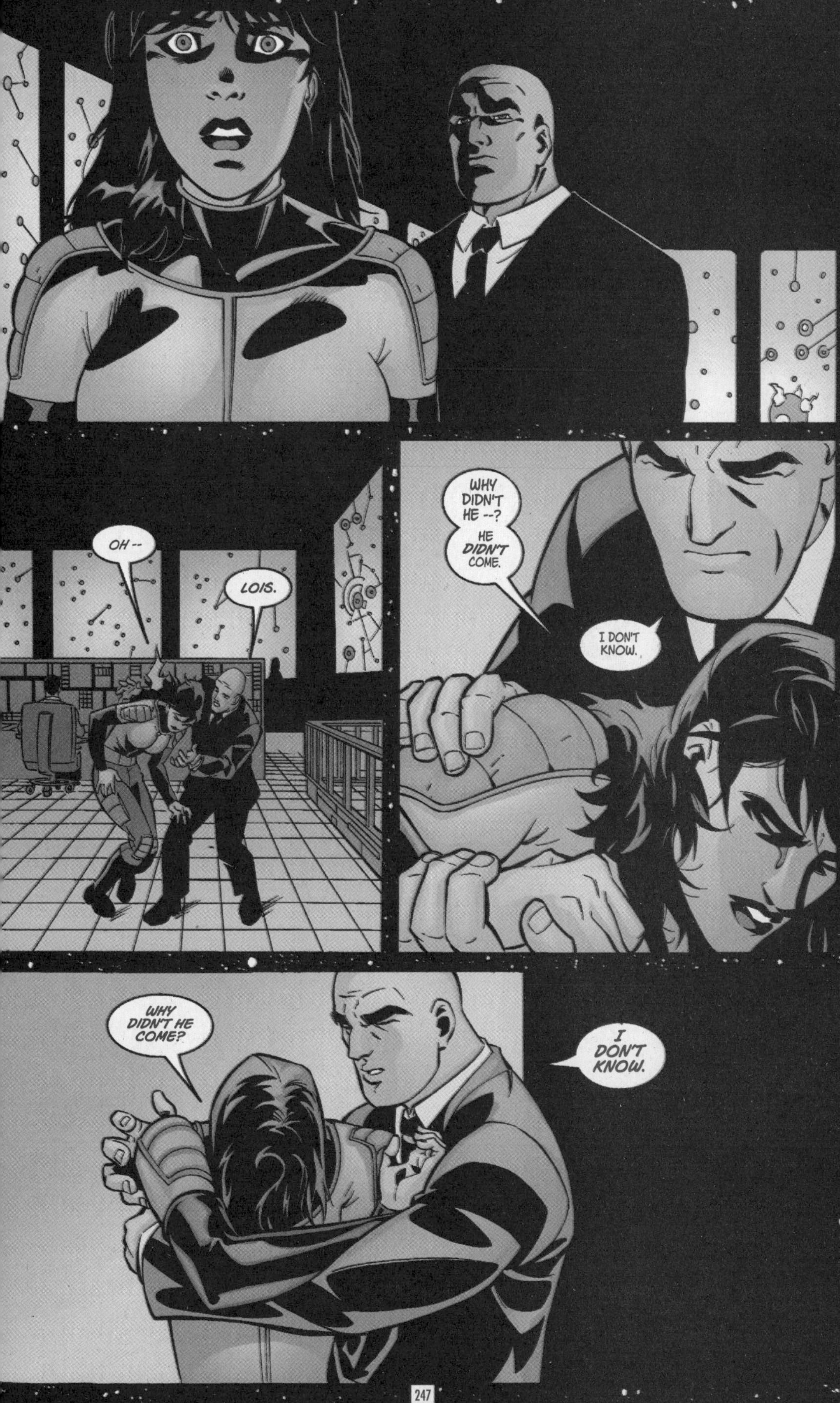
OH --
LOIS.
WHY DIDN'T HE --?
HE DIDN'T COME.
I DON'T KNOW.
WHY DIDN'T HE COME?
I DON'T KNOW.

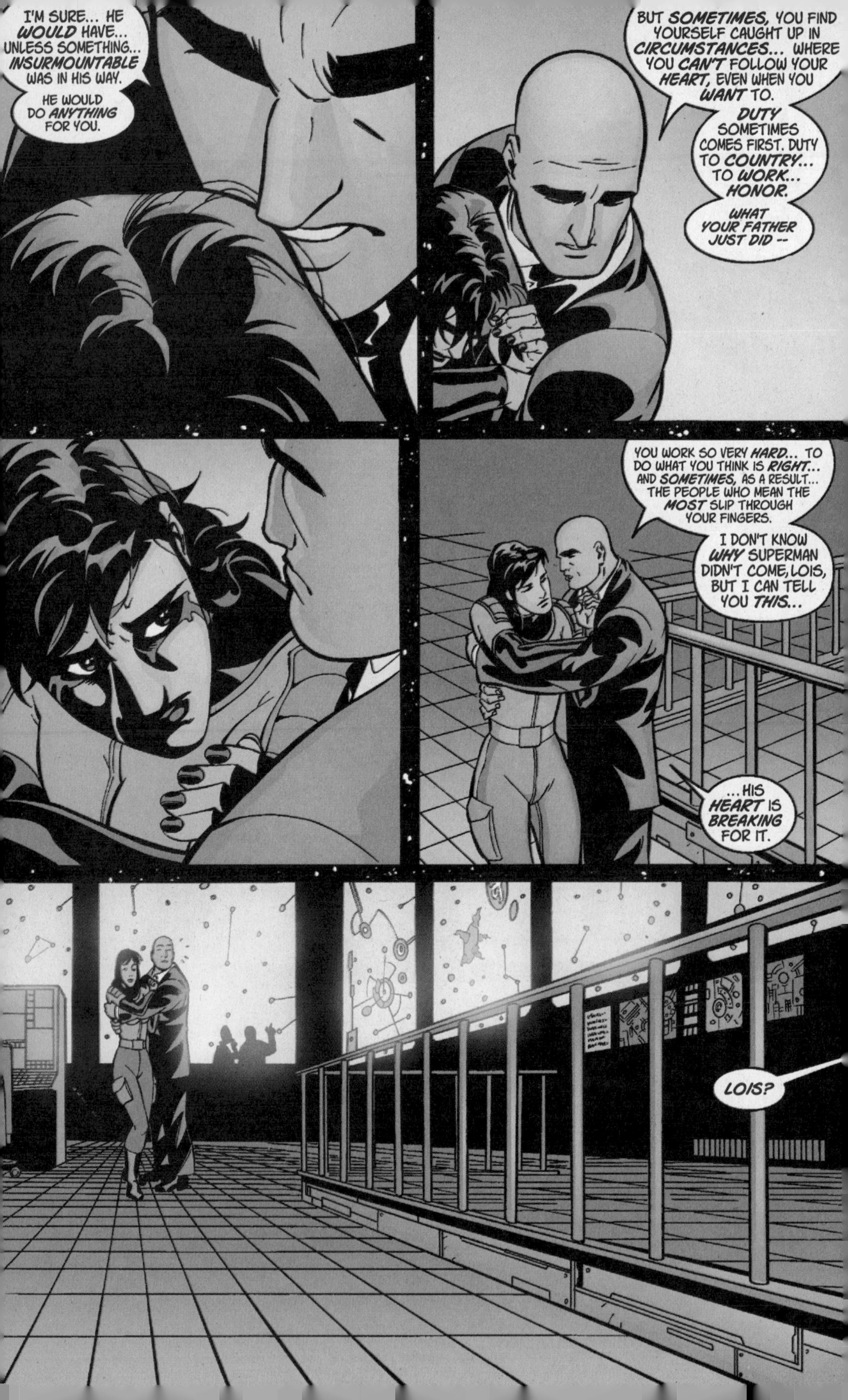
I'M SURE... HE WOULD HAVE... UNLESS SOMETHING... INSURMOUNTABLE WAS IN HIS WAY.
HE WOULD DO ANYTHING FOR YOU.
BUT SOMETIMES, YOU FIND YOURSELF CAUGHT UP IN CIRCUMSTANCES... WHERE YOU CAN'T FOLLOW YOUR HEART, EVEN WHEN YOU WANT TO.
DUTY SOMETIMES COMES FIRST. DUTY TO COUNTRY... TO WORK... HONOR.
WHAT YOUR FATHER JUST DID --
YOU WORK SO VERY HARD... TO DO WHAT YOU THINK IS RIGHT... AND SOMETIMES, AS A RESULT... THE PEOPLE WHO MEAN THE MOST SLIP THROUGH YOUR FINGERS.
I DON'T KNOW WHY SUPERMAN DIDN'T COME, LOIS, BUT I CAN TELL YOU THIS...
...HIS HEART IS BREAKING FOR IT.
LOIS?

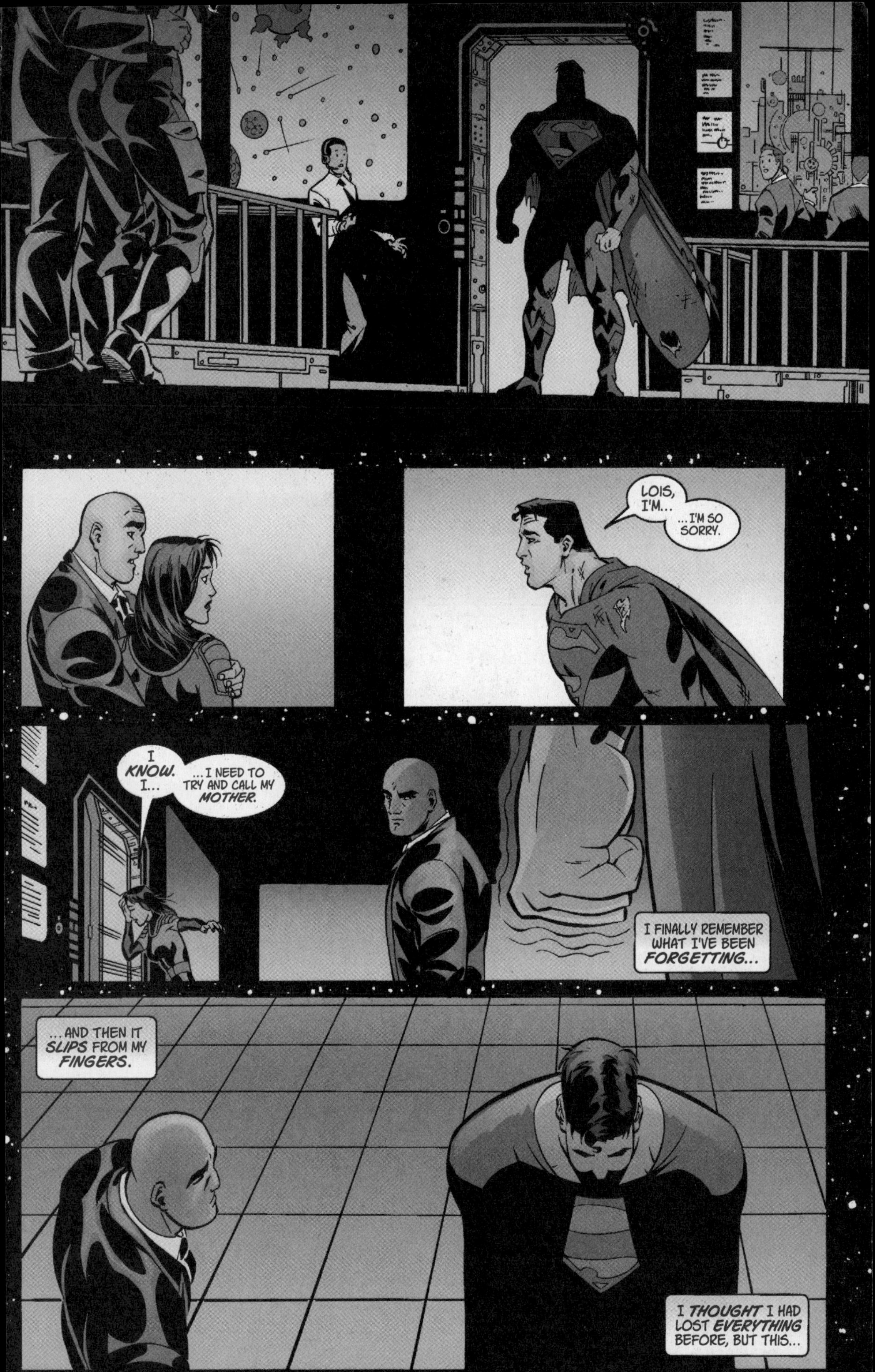
LOIS, I'M...
...I'M SO SORRY.
I KNOW. I...
...I NEED TO TRY AND CALL MY MOTHER.
I FINALLY REMEMBER WHAT I'VE BEEN FORGETTING...
...AND THEN IT SLIPS FROM MY FINGERS.
I THOUGHT I HAD LOST EVERYTHING BEFORE, BUT THIS...

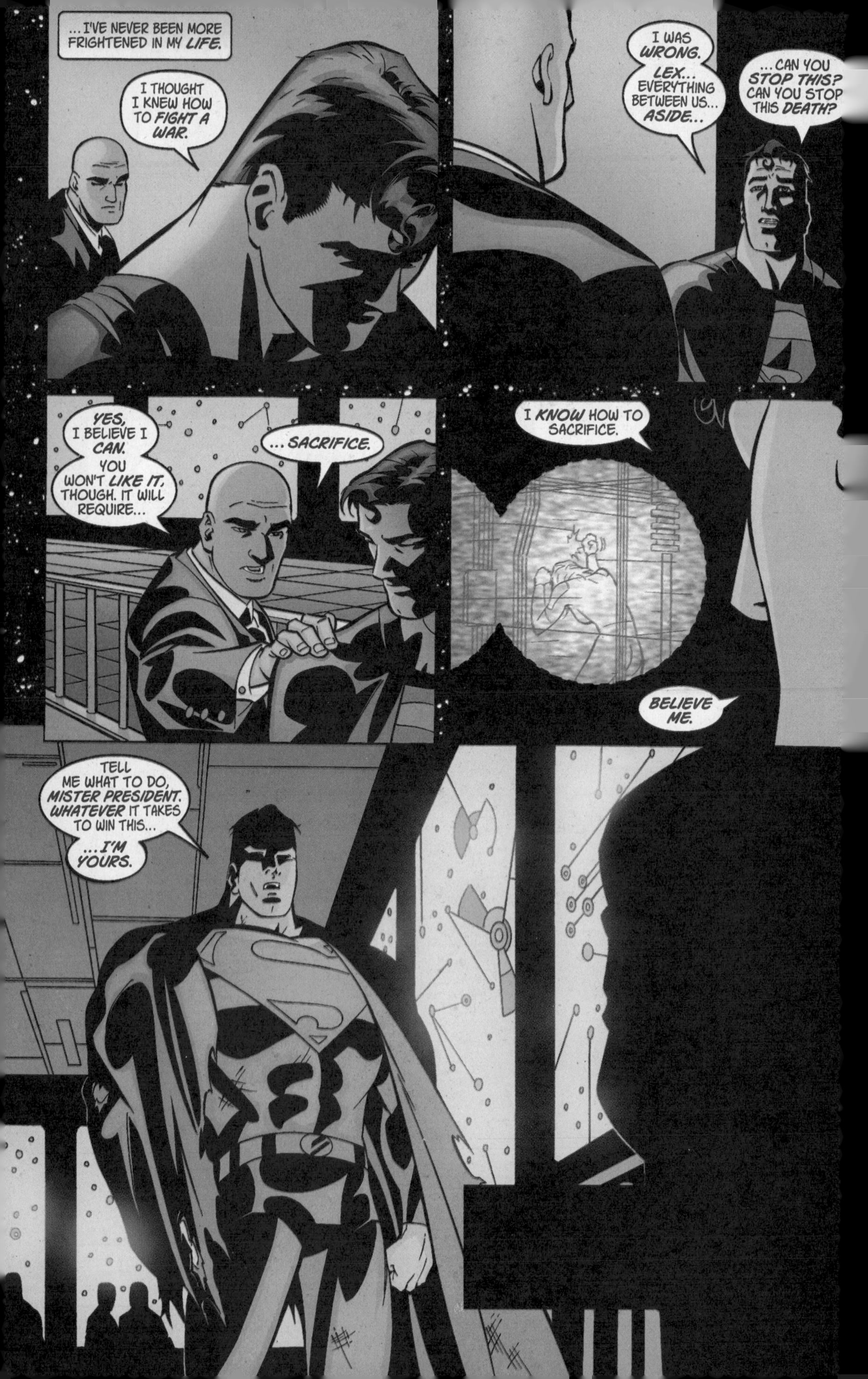
...I'VE NEVER BEEN MORE FRIGHTENED IN MY LIFE.
I THOUGHT I KNEW HOW TO FIGHT A WAR.
I WAS WRONG. LEX... EVERYTHING BETWEEN US... ASIDE...
...CAN YOU STOP THIS? CAN YOU STOP THIS DEATH?
YES, I BELIEVE I CAN. YOU WON'T LIKE IT, THOUGH. IT WILL REQUIRE...
...SACRIFICE.
I KNOW HOW TO SACRIFICE.
BELIEVE ME.
TELL ME WHAT TO DO, MISTER PRESIDENT. WHATEVER IT TAKES TO WIN THIS...
...I'M YOURS.

COVER
GALLERY

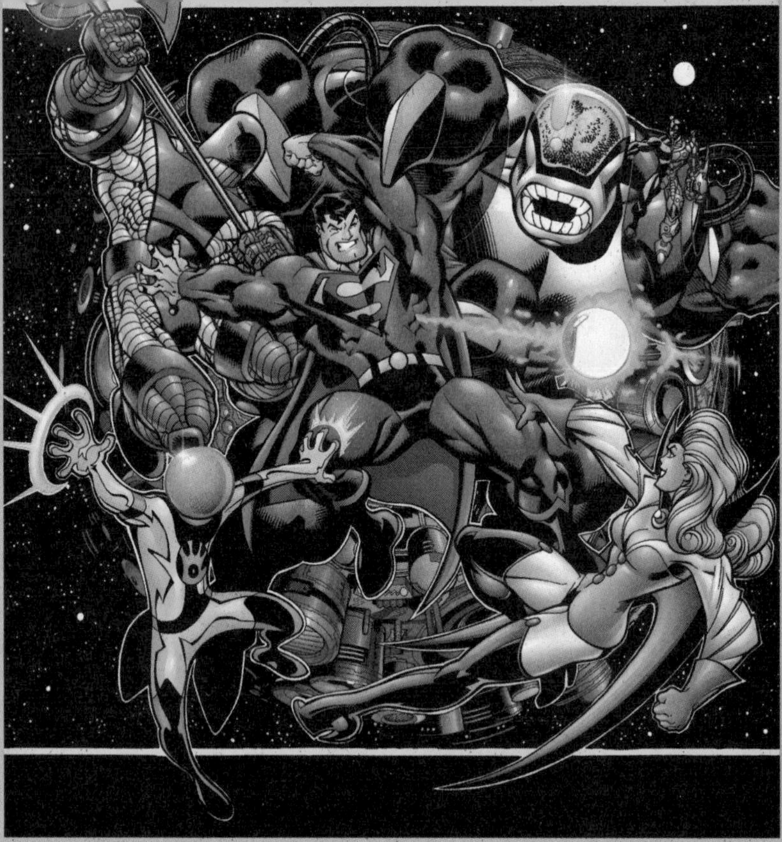

ED McGUINNESS AND CAM SMITH

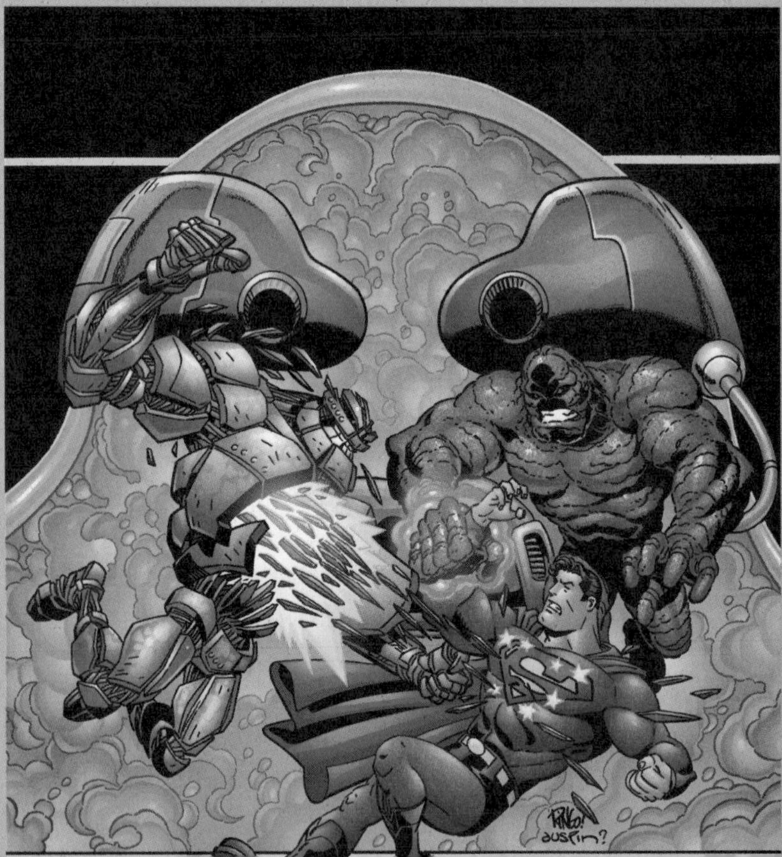
RINGO!
austin?

WIERINGO AND TERRY AUSTIN

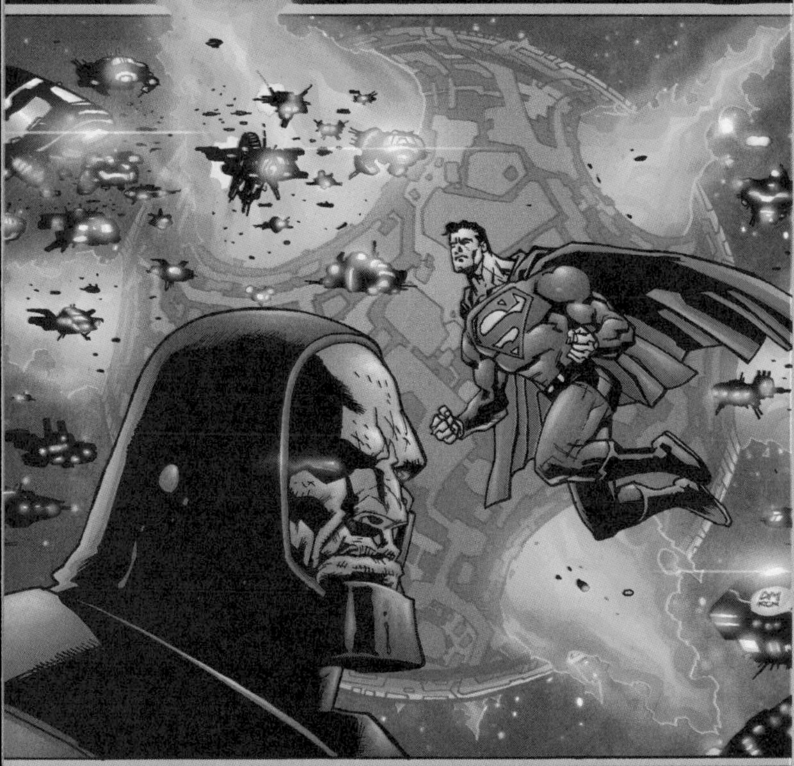

DOUG MAHNKE AND TOM NGUYEN

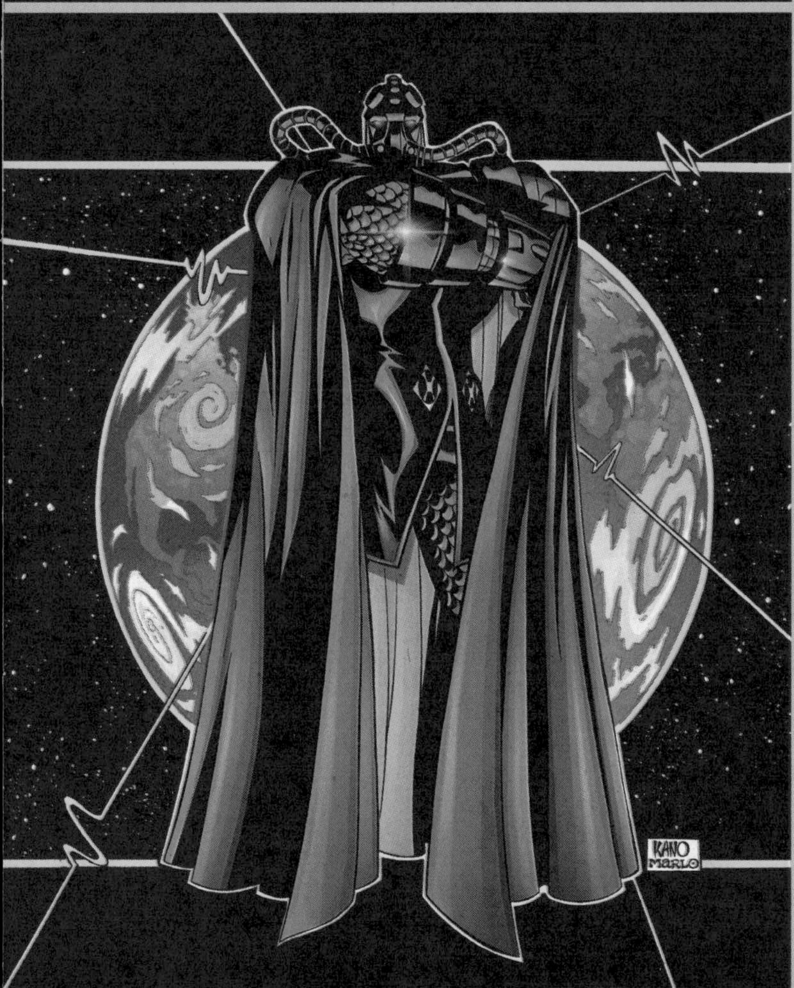
KANO
MARLO

KANO AND MARLO ALQUIZA

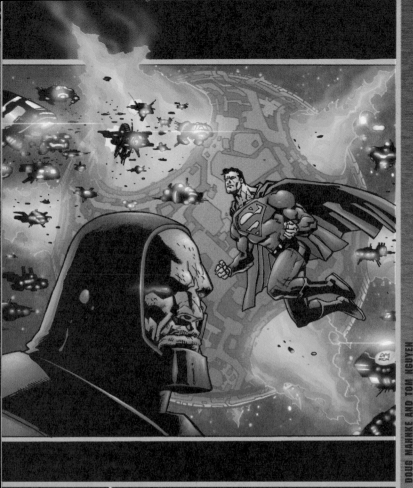

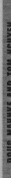

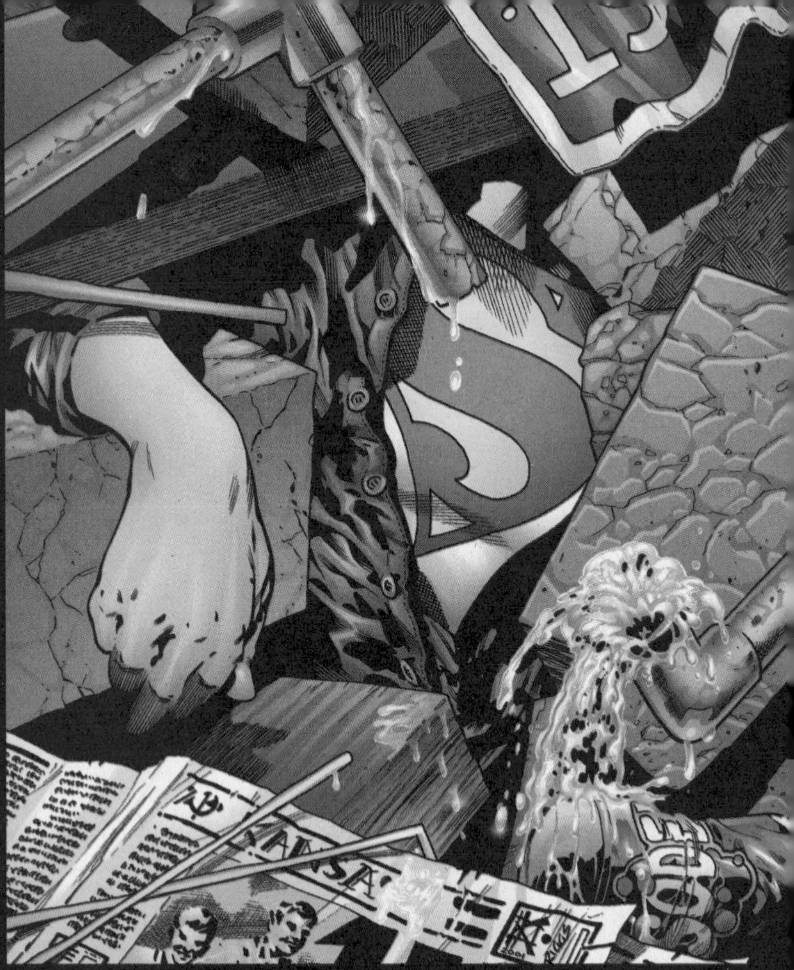

LEONARD KIRK AND ROBIN RIGGS

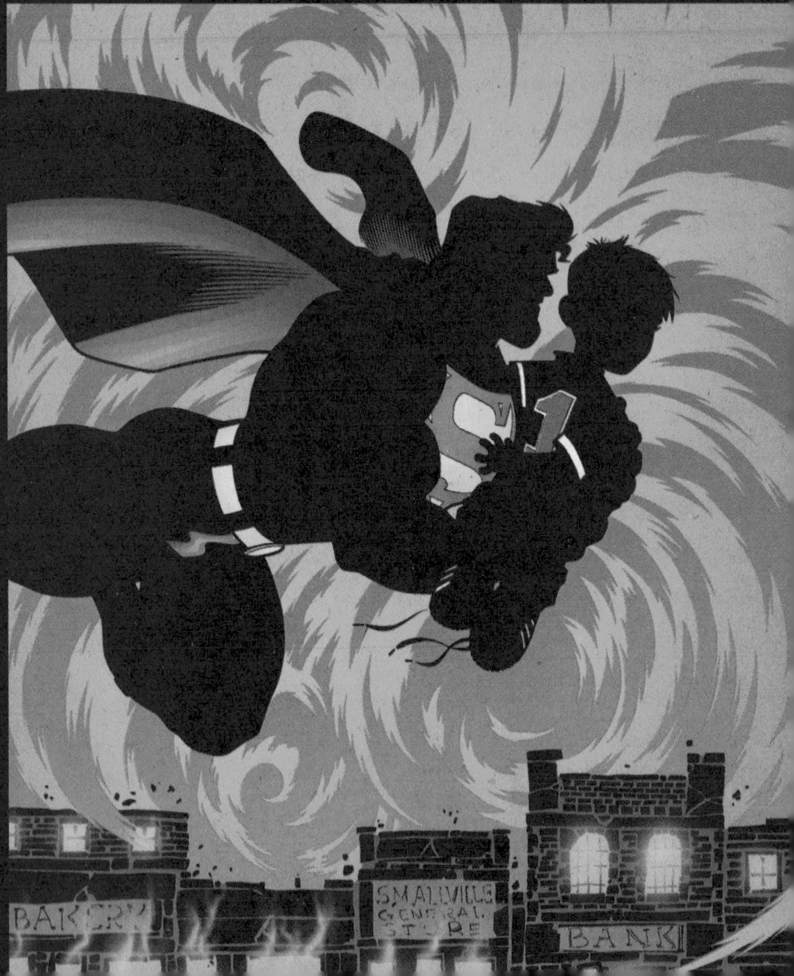
BAKERY
SMALLVILLE GENERAL STORE
BANK

ED McGUINNESS AND CAM SMITH

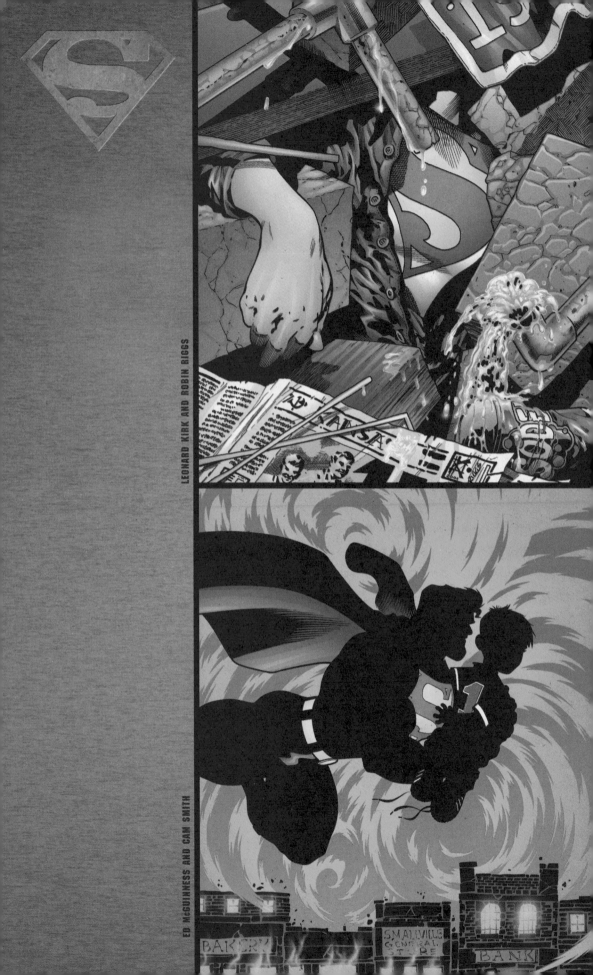

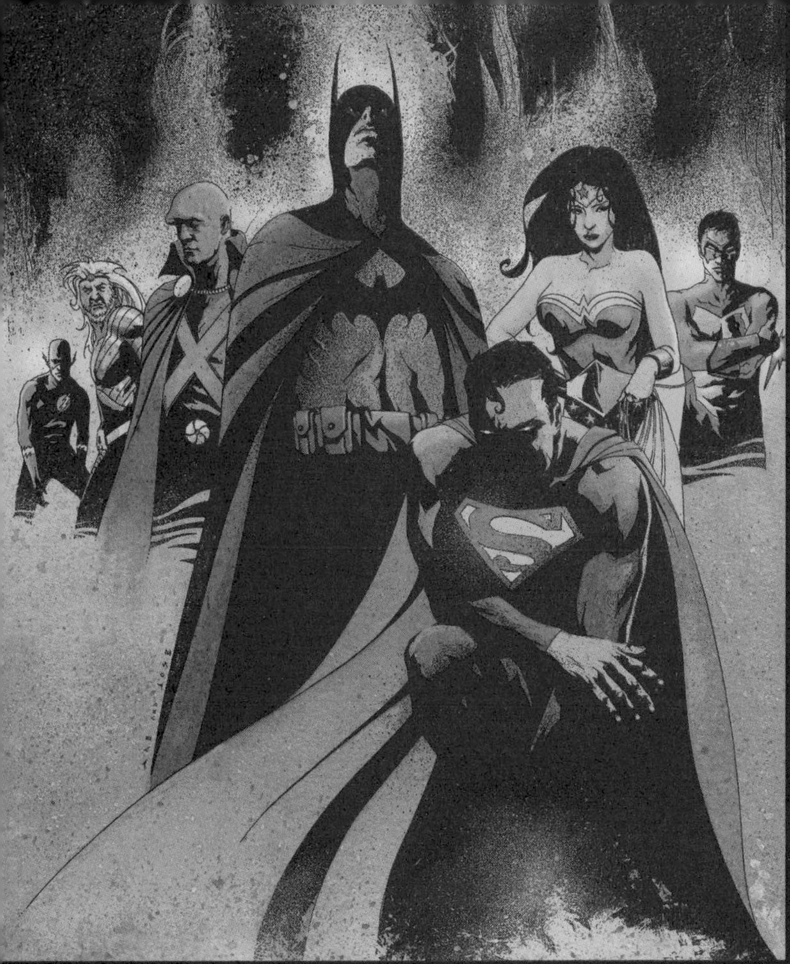

JAE LEE

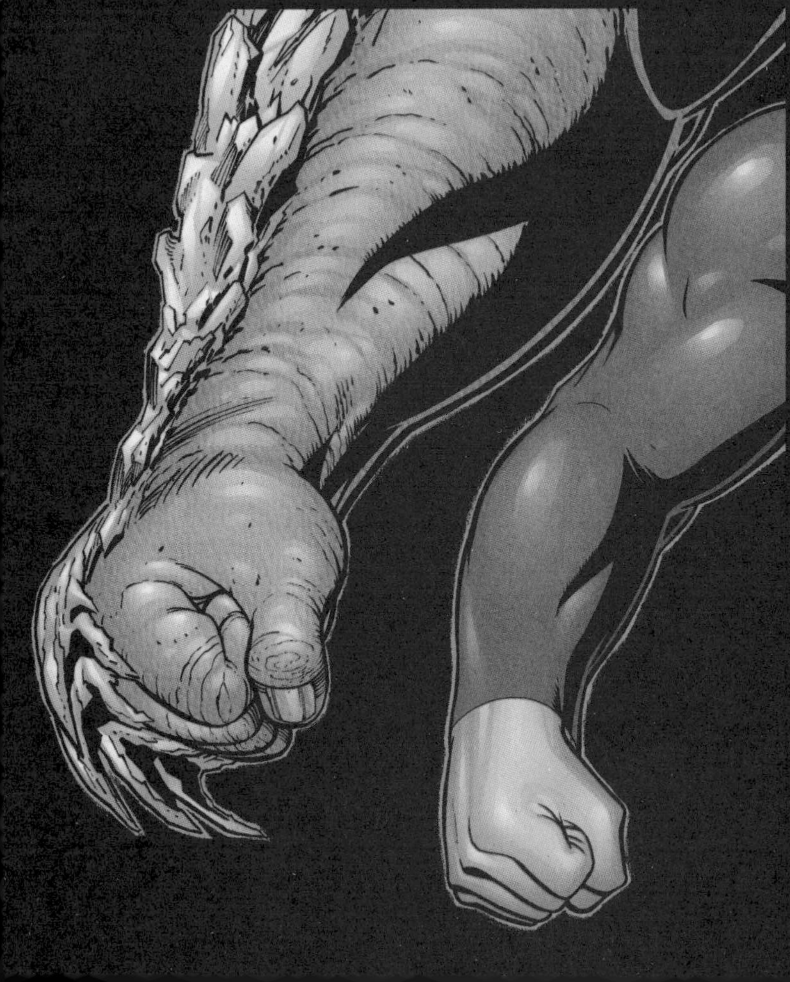

MIKE WIERINGO AND JOSÉ MARZÁN, JR.

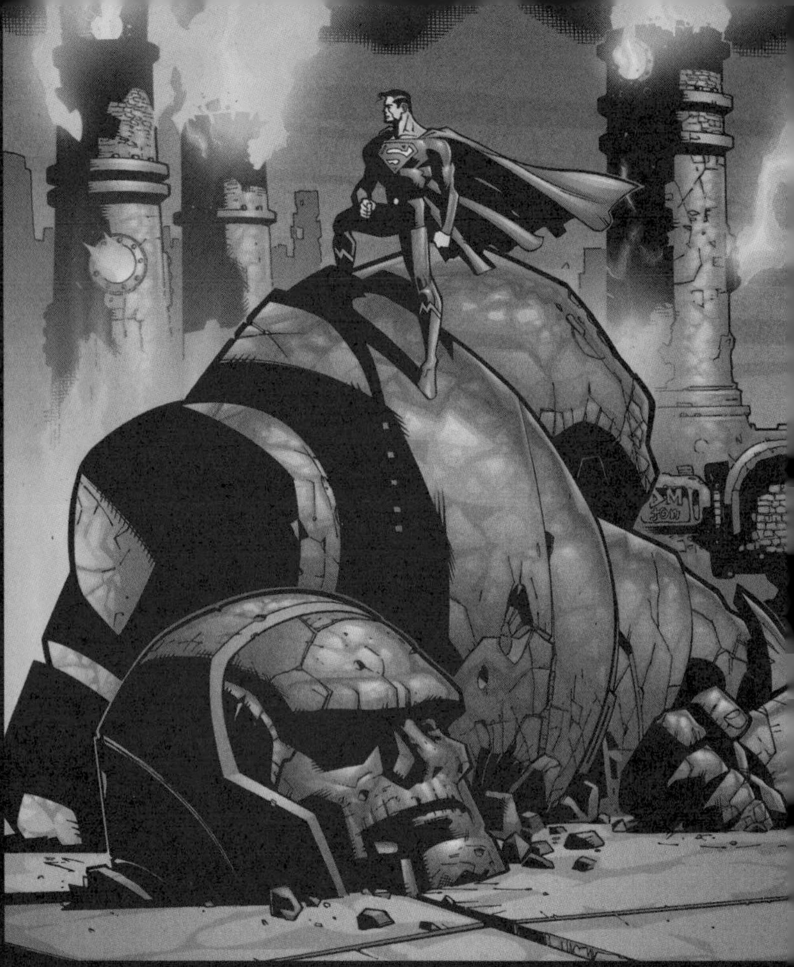

DOUG MAHNKE AND TOM NGUYEN

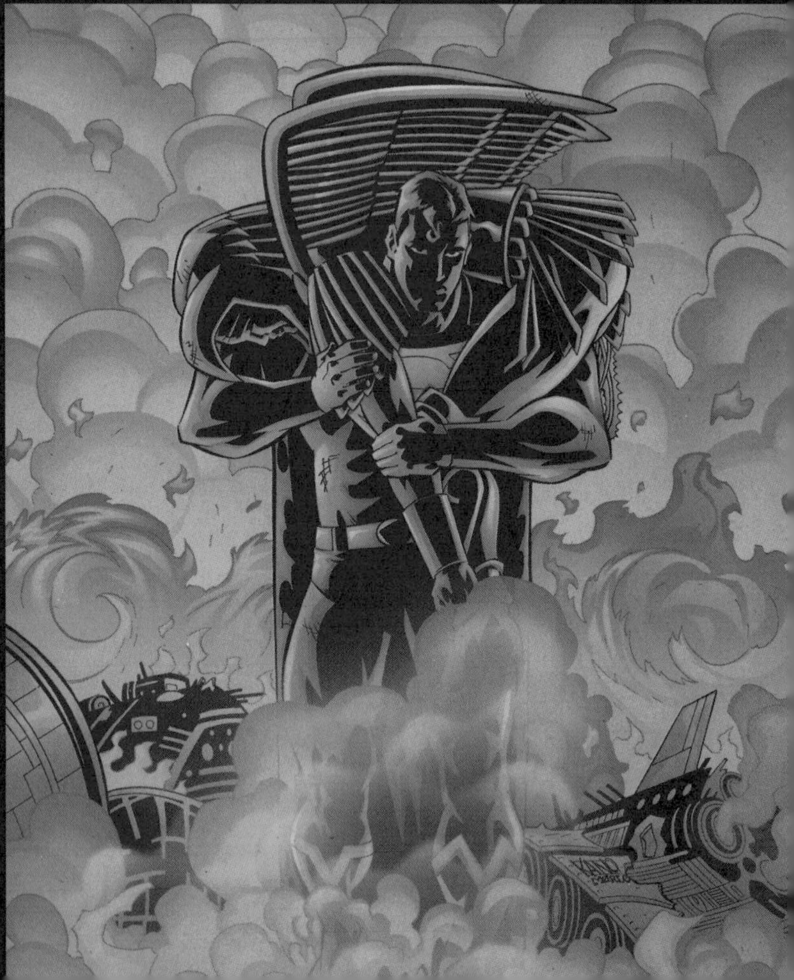

KANO AND MARLO ALQUIZA

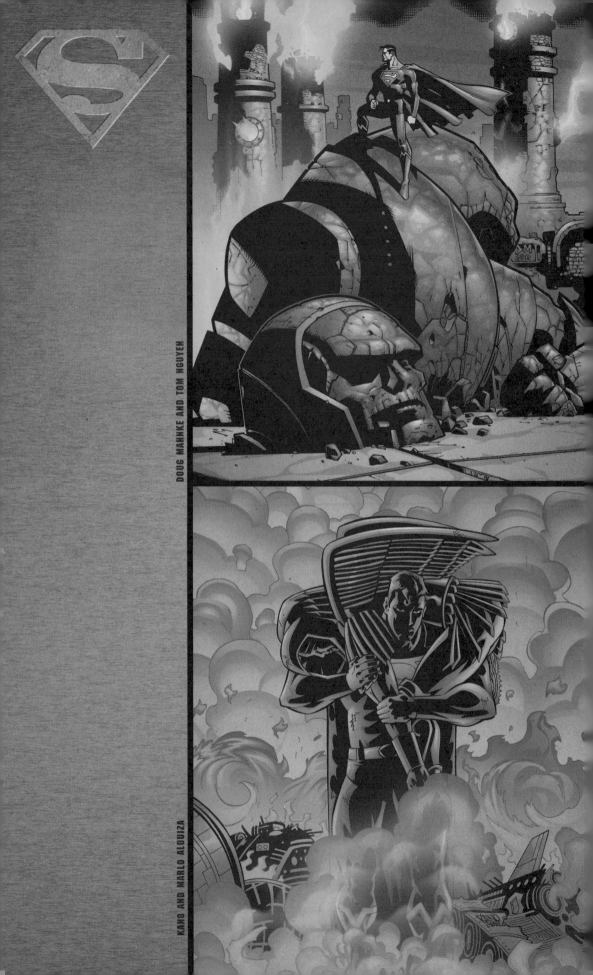

# THE ART OF WAR

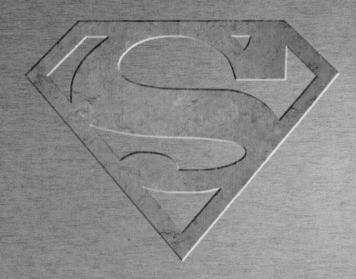

# IMPERIEX

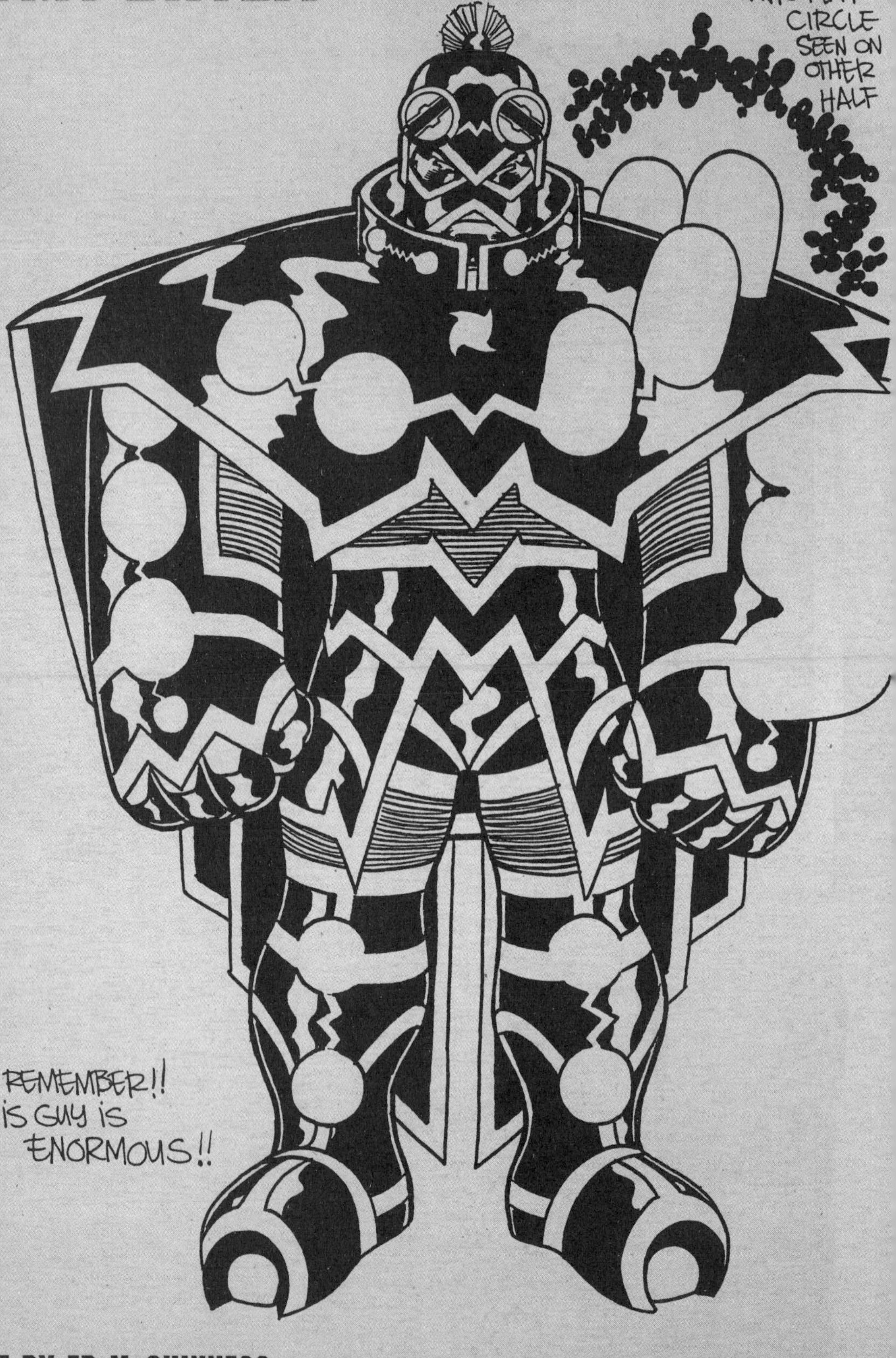


**ART BY ED McGUINNESS**

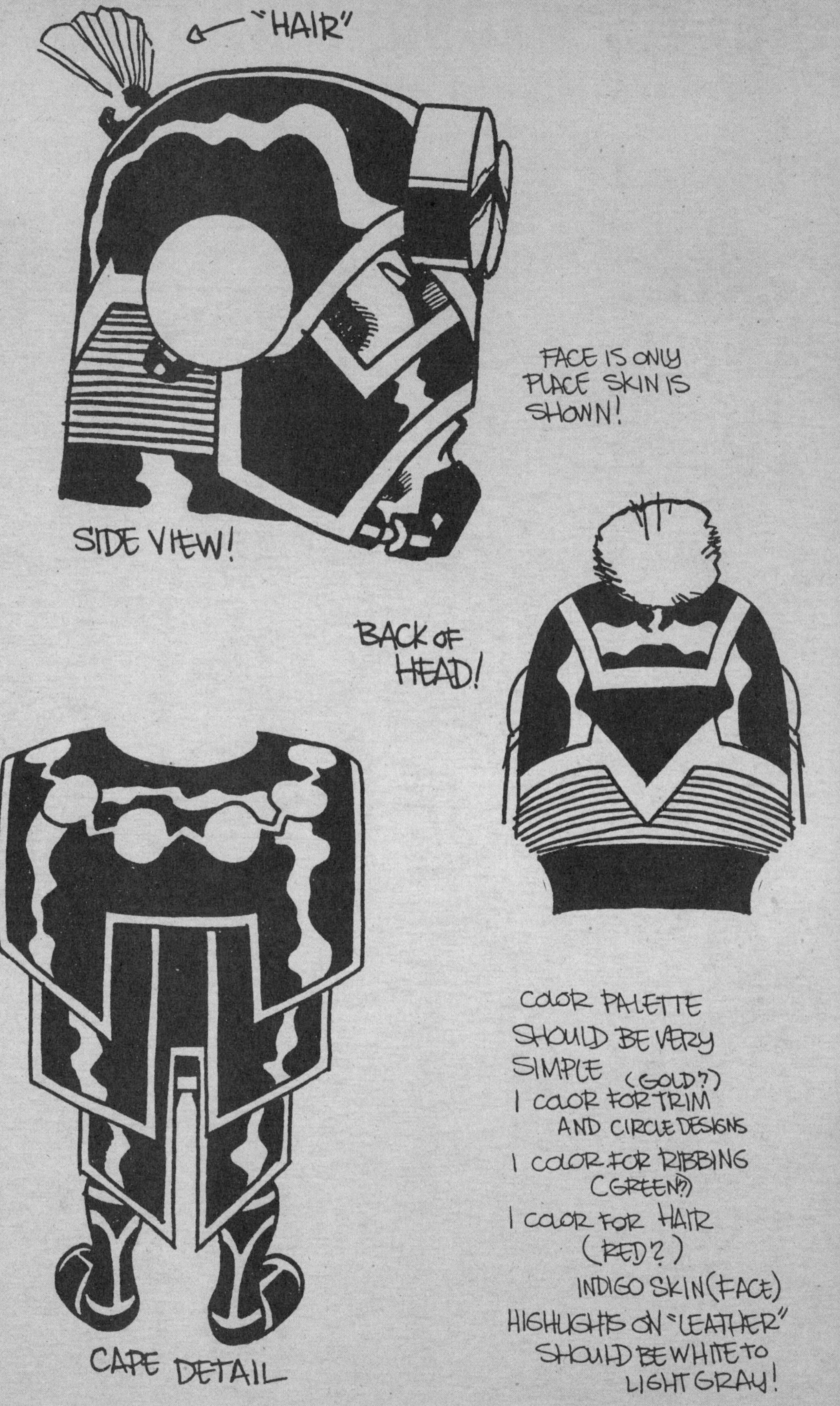
"HAIR"
SIDE VIEW!
FACE IS ONLY PLACE SKIN IS SHOWN!
BACK OF HEAD!
CAPE DETAIL
COLOR PALETTE SHOULD BE VERY SIMPLE
(GOLD?) 1 COLOR FOR TRIM AND CIRCLE DESIGNS
1 COLOR FOR RIBBING (GREEN?)
1 COLOR FOR HAIR (RED?)
INDIGO SKIN (FACE)
HIGHLIGHTS ON "LEATHER" SHOULD BE WHITE TO LIGHT GRAY!

# EARTH'S MECHANICAL ARMY

The BATTALION is a fully armed giant robot. It holds 12 infantrymen. Smaller versions of these robots — all the result of B13 tech — are employed to guard LexCorp.

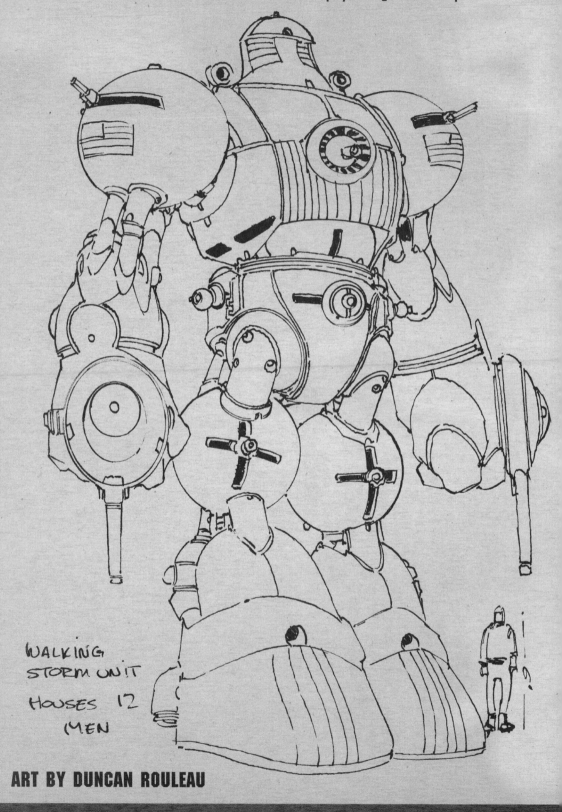

WALKING
STORM UNIT
HOUSES 12
MEN

## ART BY DUNCAN ROULEAU

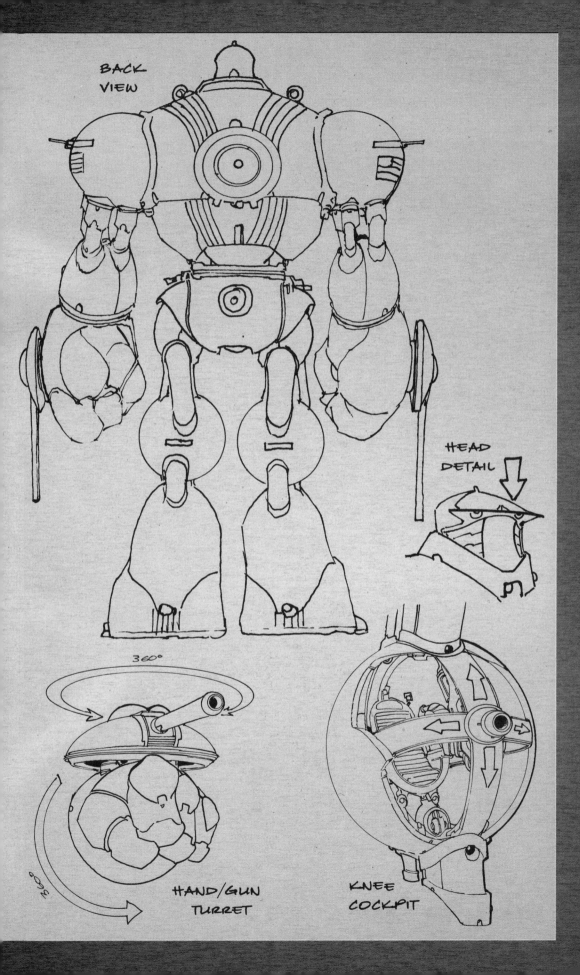

BACK VIEW

HEAD DETAIL

360°

HAND/GUN TURRET

KNEE COCKPIT

# LEXCORP'S FLYING TANKS

Any rumors of Flying Saucers in recent months could have been due to early field tests of LexCorp's FLYING TANKS. With its speed and maneuverability while hovering — as well as a turret that spins 360 degrees — this land vehicle is light-years ahead of any conventional armored tank. These tanks were being readied in preparation for the Pokolistan crisis.

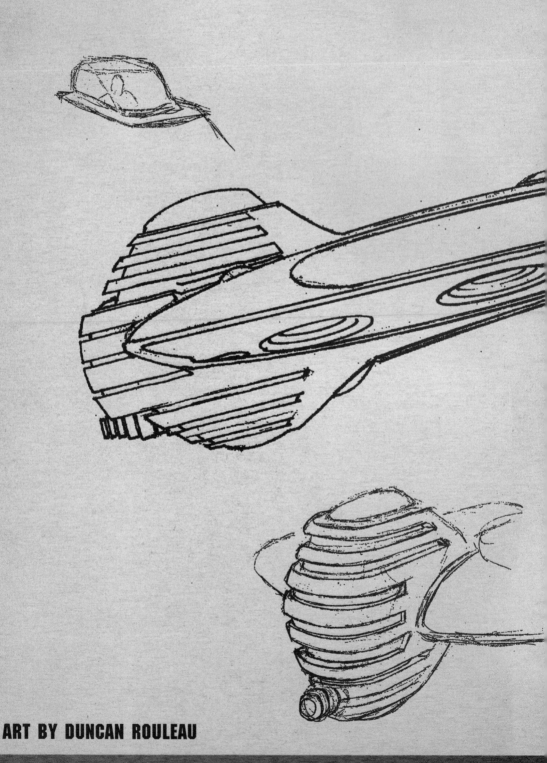

**ART BY DUNCAN ROULEAU**

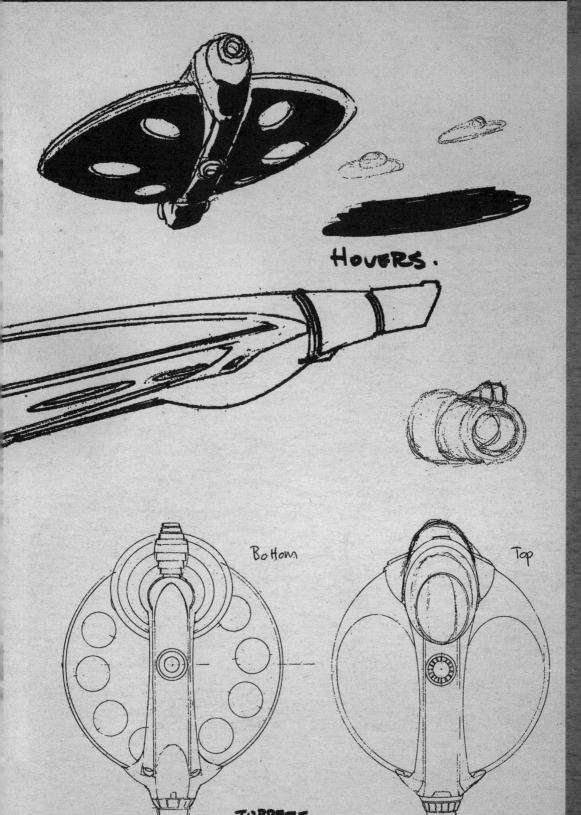

HOVERS.

Bottom

Top

TURRETS
SPIN
360°

# SUPERMAN

## THE NEVER-ENDING BATTLE CONTINUES IN THESE BOOKS FROM DC COMICS:

### FOR READERS OF ALL AGES

**SUPERMAN: ADVENTURES OF THE MAN OF STEEL**
P. Dini/S. McCloud/R. Burchett/
B. Blevins

**SUPERMAN: PEACE ON EARTH**
Paul Dini/Alex Ross

**BATMAN & SUPERMAN ADVENTURES: WORLD'S FINEST**
Paul Dini/Joe Staton/Terry Beatty

### GRAPHIC NOVELS

**SON OF SUPERMAN**
H. Chaykin/D. Tischman/
J.H. Williams III/M. Gray

**SUPERMAN: END OF THE CENTURY**
Stuart Immonen/José Marzán Jr.

### COLLECTIONS

**THE KENTS**
J. Ostrander/T. Truman/
T. Mandrake/M. Bair

**THE DEATH OF SUPERMAN**
Trilogy
**THE DEATH OF SUPERMAN**
**WORLD WITHOUT A SUPERMAN**
**THE RETURN OF SUPERMAN**
Various writers and artists

**SUPERMAN: THE MAN OF STEEL**
John Byrne/Dick Giordano

**SUPERMAN/DOOMSDAY: HUNTER/PREY**
Dan Jurgens/Brett Breeding

**SUPERMAN: THE DARK SIDE**
J.F. Moore/Kieron Dwyer/
Hilary Barta

**SUPERMAN: THE DEATH OF CLARK KENT**
Various writers and artists

**SUPERMAN: THE DOOMSDAY WARS**
Dan Jurgens/Norm Rapmund

**SUPERMAN: EXILE**
Various writers and artists

**SUPERMAN FOR ALL SEASONS**
Jeph Loeb/Tim Sale

**SUPERMAN: KRISIS OF THE KRIMSON KRYPTONITE**
Various writers and artists

**SUPERMAN: PANIC IN THE SKY**
Various writers and artists

**SUPERMAN TRANSFORMED!**
Various writers and artists

**SUPERMAN: THE TRIAL OF SUPERMAN**
Various writers and artists

**SUPERMAN: THE WEDDING AND BEYOND**
Various writers and artists

**SUPERMAN: THEY SAVED LUTHOR'S BRAIN**
R. Stern/J. Byrne/B. McLeod/
J. Guice/K. Dwyer/various

**SUPERMAN VS. THE REVENGE SQUAD**
Various writers and artists

**SUPERMAN: WHATEVER HAPPENED TO THE MAN OF TOMORROW?**
A. Moore/C. Swan/G. Pérez/
K. Schaffenberger

**SUPERMAN: THE DAILIES**
Jerry Siegel/Joe Shuster

**SUPERMAN: THE SUNDAY CLASSICS**
Jerry Siegel/Joe Shuster

**SUPERMAN IN THE SIXTIES**
Various writers and artists

**THE GREATEST SUPERMAN STORIES EVER TOLD**
Various writers and artists

**LOIS & CLARK: THE NEW ADVENTURES OF SUPERMAN**
Various writers and artists

**STEEL: THE FORGING OF A HERO**
Various writers and artists

**SUPERGIRL**
P. David/G. Frank/T. Dodson/
C. Smith/K. Story
**KINGDOM COME**
Mark Waid/Alex Ross

**LEGENDS OF THE WORLD'S FINEST**
Walter Simonson/Dan Brereton

**SUPERMAN/BATMAN: ALTERNATE HISTORIES**
Various writers and artists

### ARCHIVE EDITIONS

**SUPERMAN ARCHIVES Vol. 1**
(SUPERMAN 1-4)
**SUPERMAN ARCHIVES Vol. 2**
(SUPERMAN 5-8)
**SUPERMAN ARCHIVES Vol. 3**
(SUPERMAN 9-12)
**SUPERMAN ARCHIVES Vol. 4**
(SUPERMAN 13-16)
**SUPERMAN ARCHIVES Vol. 5**
(SUPERMAN 17-20)
All by Jerry Siegel/Joe Shuster

**SUPERMAN: THE ACTION COMICS ARCHIVES Vol. 1**
(ACTION COMICS 1, 7-20)
**SUPERMAN: THE ACTION COMICS ARCHIVES Vol. 2**
(ACTION COMICS 21-36)
All by Jerry Siegel/Joe Shuster

**WORLD'S FINEST COMICS ARCHIVES Vol. 1**
(SUPERMAN 76,
WORLD'S FINEST 71-85)
B. Finger/E. Hamilton/C. Swan/
**WORLD'S FINEST COMICS ARCHIVES Vol. 2**
(WORLD'S FINEST 86-101)
B. Finger/D. Sprang/various

TO FIND MORE COLLECTED EDITIONS AND MONTHLY COMIC BOOKS FROM DC COMICS,
CALL 1-888-COMIC BOOK FOR THE NEAREST COMICS SHOP
OR GO TO YOUR LOCAL BOOK STORE.

Visit us at www.dccomics.com